FROMMER'S

COMPREHENSIVE TRAVEL GUIDE

SOUTH PACIFIC '92-'93

by Bill Goodwin

PRENTICE HALL TRAVEL

NEW YORK • LONDON • TORONTO • SYDNEY • TOKYO • SINGAPORE

FROMMER BOOKS

Published by Prentice Hall General Reference
A division of Simon & Schuster Inc.
15 Columbus Circle
New York, NY 10023

ISBN 0-13-327248-6
ISSN 1044-2367

Design by Robert Bull Design
Maps by Geografix Inc.

Manufactured in the United States of America

FROMMER'S SOUTH PACIFIC '92–'93
Editor-in-Chief: Marilyn Wood
Senior Editors: Judith de Rubini, Amit Shah
Editors: Alice Fellows, Paige Hughes, Theodore Stavrou
Assistant Editors: Peter Katucki, Lisa Renaud
Contributing Editor: Sara Hinsey
Managing Editor: Leanne Coupe

CONTENTS

4 TAHITI 84

5 MOOREA, BORA BORA & OTHER ISLANDS 121

6 RAROTONGA & THE COOK ISLANDS 164

7 GETTING TO KNOW THE SAMOAS 210

8 WESTERN SAMOA 225

SPECIAL FEATURES

9 AMERICAN SAMOA 253

SPECIAL FEATURES

10 TONGA 270

SPECIAL FEATURES

11 GETTING TO KNOW FIJI 311

12 NADI & THE CORAL COAST 341

13 SUVA 373

14 LEVUKA, SAVUSAVU & TAVEUNI 392

15 VANUATU 410

SPECIAL FEATURES

16 NEW CALEDONIA 440

SPECIAL FEATURES

17 SOLOMON ISLANDS 476

SPECIAL FEATURES

APPENDIX 504

INDEX 506

LIST OF MAPS

To my Father,
with love
and thanks for an interesting life.

ACKNOWLEDGMENTS

I wish to thank the many individuals and organizations who helped make this book possible.

As usual, the staffs of the South Pacific tourist information offices were friendly and helpful. I am particularly grateful to Patrick Picard-Robson and Maeva Salmon in French Polynesia; Chris Wong and Dorice Reid in the Cook Islands; Vensel Margraff and Shaddow Fau in Western Samoa; Emma Randall in American Samoa; Isimeli Bainimara and Allyson Makutu in Fiji; Jean-Michel Foutrein, Sylvie Coquelet and Jean-Jacques Ajapuhnya in New Caledonia; and Wilson Maelaua and Jack Barley in Solomon Islands.

My deep personal thanks go to Nancy Monseaux, Max Parrish, and Suzanne Davis, whose generosity made this book possible; to my sister, Jean Goodwin Marlowe, who has consistently given much-needed moral support; to Bill and Donna Wilder, who introduced me to the South Pacific and let me use their home beside the Moorea lagoon; and to Hérald Adams and Dick Beaulieu, who have been of enormous help in French Polynesia and Fiji. Everyone should have friends like these.

The format used in this edition required an extraordinary amount of work on the part of my editors at Prentice Hall Travel, especially by Sara Hinsey and Lisa Renaud, who saved me untold hours by putting it all on diskettes, and by Amit Shah, who kept the heat on without being obnoxious about it. Thanks.

INVITATION TO THE READERS

In researching this book, I have come across many wonderful establishments, the best of which I have included here. I am sure that many of you will also come across appealing hotels, inns, restaurants, guesthouses, shops, and attractions. Please don't keep them to yourself. Share your experiences, especially if you want to comment on places that have been included in this edition that have changed for the worse. You can address your letters to:

Bill Goodwin
Frommer's South Pacific '92–'93
c/o Prentice Hall Travel
15 Columbus Circle
New York, NY 10023

A DISCLAIMER

Readers are advised that prices fluctuate in the course of time and travel information changes under the impact of the varied and volatile factors that affect the travel industry. Neither the author nor the publisher can be held responsible for the experiences of readers while traveling. Readers are invited to write to the publisher with ideas, comments, and suggestions for future editions.

SAFETY ADVISORY

Whenever you're traveling in an unfamiliar city or country, stay alert. Be aware of your immediate surroundings. Wear a moneybelt and keep a close eye on your possessions. Be particularly careful with cameras, purses, and wallets, all favorite targets of thieves and pickpockets.

CHAPTER 1

GETTING TO KNOW THE SOUTH PACIFIC

The very names of the South Pacific islands—names like Tahiti, Bora Bora, Fiji, Tonga, Rarotonga, Samoa—have conjured up images of an earthly paradise ever since European explorers first came back with reports of their tropical splendor and uninhibited people more than two centuries ago. The images have been embellished by such literary giants as Herman Melville, Robert Louis Stevenson, W. Somerset Maugham, Jack London, and James A. Michener, and brought to the silver screen by the likes of Clark Gable and Mel Gibson.

Today, the South Pacific still lives up to its fabled reputation and is a modern traveler's delight. It has more than luxurious resorts set on palm-draped beaches beside blue lagoons. There are many of those, but you'll also find rafting adventures down white-water rivers, long hikes through steep mountain valleys (where the inhabitants still wear grass skirts or penis sheaths), sailing excursions to uninhabited islands, diving on magnificent coral reefs, a look into the flaming bowels of the earth from the lip of a rumbling volcano, strolls through some of World War II's bloodiest battlefields, and deserted beaches for getting away from what we conceited Westerners call "civilization."

Above all, there are the Pacific Islanders. In their way, they are some of the most civilized folks to be found anywhere. Certainly they are the nicest. If the beauty of their islands doesn't charm you, then their highly infectious smiles surely will.

1. INTRODUCING THE ISLANDS

Despite the popular image of beautiful island women seducing Fletcher Christian and the crew of HMS *Bounty* into history's most famous mutiny, there is no "typical" South Pacific people or island. The region is divided into two great areas, Polynesia and Melanesia, each with its own distinct geography, peoples, history, and cultures. There is vast diversity even within Polynesia and Melanesia, especially in the latter. French Polynesia, the Cook Islands, Tonga, Western Samoa, and American Samoa are in Polynesia. Vanuatu, New Caledonia, and Solomon Islands are in Melanesia. Fiji sits on the border; while its indigenous peoples appear more Melanesian than Polynesian,

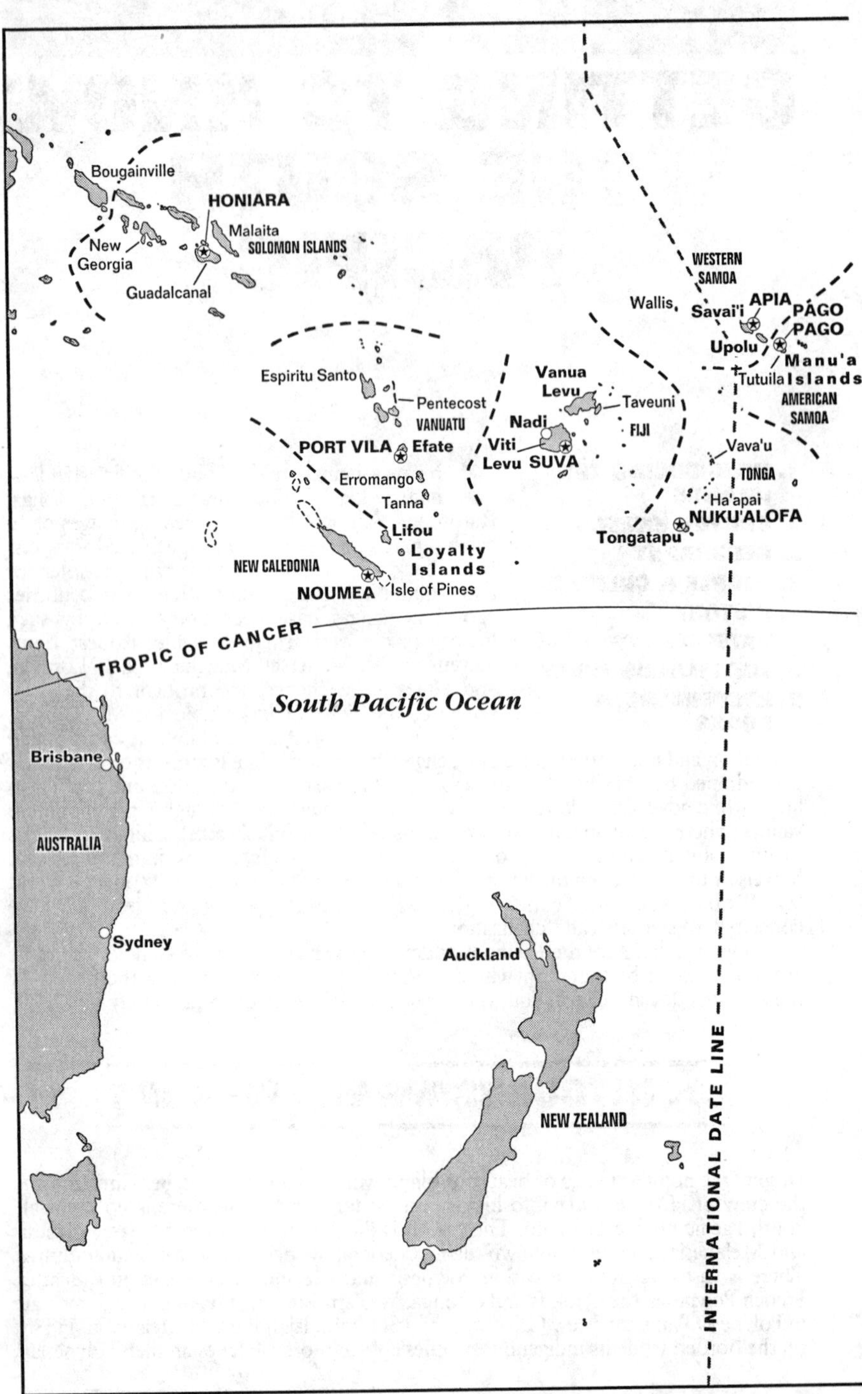

Bougainville
HONIARA
Malaita
New
Georgia
SOLOMON ISLANDS
Guadalcanal
WESTERN
SAMOA
Wallis
Savai'i
APIA
PAGO
PAGO
Upolu
Manu'a
Islands
Tutuila
AMERICAN
SAMOA
Espiritu Santo
Pentecost
VANUATU
Vanua
Levu
Taveuni
Nadi
FIJI
PORT VILA
Efate
Viti
Levu
SUVA
Vava'u
TONGA
Erromango
Tanna
Ha'apai
NUKU'ALOFA
Lifou
Tongatapu
Loyalty
Islands
NEW CALEDONIA
NOUMEA
Isle of Pines
TROPIC OF CANCER
South Pacific Ocean
Brisbane
AUSTRALIA
Sydney
Auckland
NEW ZEALAND
INTERNATIONAL DATE LINE

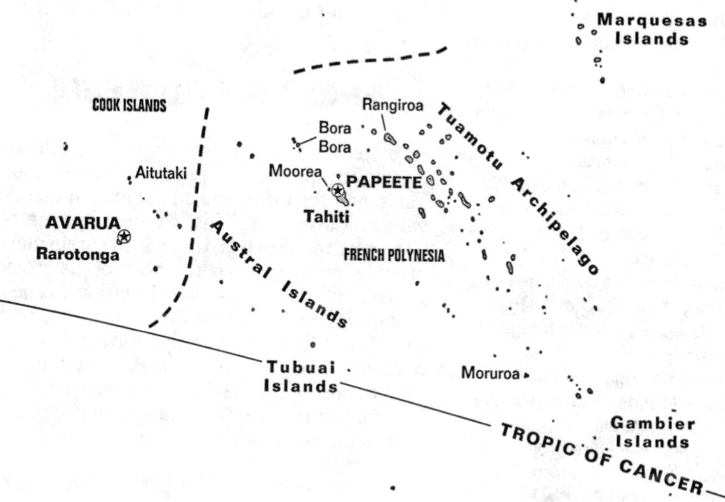

South Pacific Ocean
Pukapuka
Marquesas Islands
COOK ISLANDS
Rangiroa
Tuamotu Archipelago
Bora Bora
Aitutaki
Moorea
PAPEETE
Tahiti
AVARUA
Rarotonga
Austral Islands
FRENCH POLYNESIA
Tubuai Islands
Moruroa
Gambier Islands
TROPIC OF CANCER
Pitcairn
N
0
500 km
310 mi

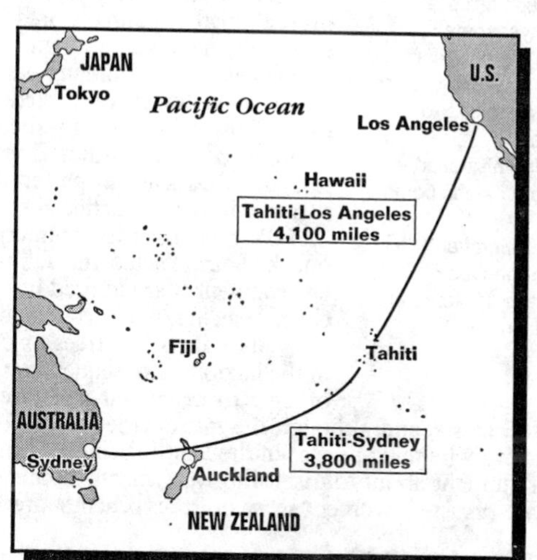

JAPAN
Tokyo
Pacific Ocean
U.S.
Los Angeles
Hawaii
Tahiti-Los Angeles
4,100 miles
Fiji
Tahiti
AUSTRALIA
Tahiti-Sydney
3,800 miles
Sydney
Auckland
NEW ZEALAND

DID YOU KNOW . . . ?

- The countries covered in this book occupy a total area larger than the United States, but they have less dry land than half of Florida.
- When you reach a point some 1,650 miles east of the Marquesas Islands, you are as far away from land as you can get.
- Except for Antarctica, Polynesia was the last part of the earth to be settled by humans.
- Melanesia's six million people speak nearly 25% of all the world's languages.
- Thanks to European diseases and emigration, Polynesia's population of some 1.1 million is about the same as when Captain Cook explored the islands in the 1770s.
- Twice as many Samoans reside in the United States as live in American Samoa.
- Rather than have a commoner in the family, King Taufa'ahau Tupou of Tonga annulled the marriage of his niece.
- There are no dogs on Aitutaki in the Cook Islands; legend says the people ate them all.
- Toads reportedly were brought to American Samoa to control the mosquito population; now both mosquitoes and toads are pests.
- In pre-European days, some islanders practiced cannibalism, infanticide, strangling widows, and using live humans as rollers to launch new canoes.
- Most fundamentalist missionaries working in the South Pacific come from the U.S.
- The total cost of a funeral and related activities in the Cook Islands often exceeds 10 years of annual per capita income.

their culture is a mix of the two. Adding to the diversity are numerous Asians, East Indians, and Europeans who now live alongside the Polynesians and Melanesians who were there first.

Let's make a quick tour to see what each island country or territory contributes to the smörgåsbord. Like Capt. James Cook, the great British explorer who discovered much of the South Pacific during the late 18th century, we will travel from east to west for no other reason than that's the way the trade winds blow. This arrangement does not mean that I favor one island over another. I like them all.

FRENCH POLYNESIA

If there were a "major league" of islands based on spectacular physical beauty, then Tahiti and the other French Polynesian islands would dominate it. This is especially true of **Moorea** and **Bora Bora,** which surely must provide Hollywood with most of its stock footage of glorious tropical settings. Their mountains seem to leap out of lagoons, and those on Moorea serrate the horizon like the back of some primordial dinosaur resting on the sea just 12 miles (20km) west of Tahiti. The sunsets over those shark's-teeth ridges are deservedly some of the most photographed in the world.

As the name states, this part of Polynesia is French, and the Gallic joie de vivre is a mere overlay on the Tahitians' laid-back life-style, one of the most storied—and studied—in all of Polynesia. The Tahitians' easygoing attitude about most things captivated Europeans of the 1770s, who saw in them the perfect example of Jean-Jacques Rousseau's "noble savage," who lived in perfect harmony with nature without the artificial social restraints.

Like their islander counterparts throughout the South Pacific, the Tahitians lived in an environment that required little in the way of clothes, shelter, or effort to gather food, which grew abundantly on trees or could be found in the lagoons. Consequently, they had plenty of time to make war and love. That general attitude about life still exists, and although the missionaries of the 1800s had their impact, it was not as overwhelming here as in the South Pacific's "Bible Belt" farther west. Tahitians aren't uptight about tourists who wear shorts around town; still, the majority of the bare-breasted women seen on the beaches are Europeans or Australians.

Wherever the French go, good food and wine are sure to follow, and Tahiti is no exception. The restaurants are outstanding—not just French, but Italian, Chinese,

IMPRESSIONS

In the South Seas the Creator seems to have laid himself out to show what He can do . . .

—Rupert Brooke, 1914

I would get up in the morning, put on my pareu, brew my coffee and suddenly reflect that by rights I should be in a pair of long trousers, jangling a bunch of keys ready to open the store. I had escaped!

—Tom Neale, 1966

---

and Vietnamese. Eating out is a pure joy tempered only by the price of a meal, which like everything else in French Polynesia is relatively expensive.

Papeete, the capital, is a busy little city (pop. 95,000 or so) overrun by cars, trucks, and motor scooters. A building boom has drastically changed its face over the past 15 years, and the town has lost much of its old charm. So I will say from the outset and repeat later on: To find Polynesia, put your sights on Moorea, Bora Bora, and Tahiti's other companion islands.

THE COOK ISLANDS

About 500 miles west of French Polynesia lie the Cook Islands, deservedly one of the most popular South Pacific destinations in recent years. Tiny **Rarotonga,** the principal island and the capital, is a miniature Tahiti in terms of its mountains, beaches, and reefs. **Aitutaki,** about 150 miles north of Rarotonga, bears the same relationship to Bora Bora. Unlike Papeete, however, its main town, **Avarua** (pop. 4,500), is a quiet little backwater, a picturesque village out of a W. Somerset Maugham short story. The Cook Islanders are very much like the Tahitians, sharing with them a life-style, many of the old Polynesian legends and gods, and about 60% of their native language.

Despite the similarities, several differences between the Cook Islands and French Polynesia work to the advantage of English-speaking, value-conscious travelers. One is that since the Cooks were a New Zealand territory from 1901 until 1965 and still are associated with New Zealand, most Cook Islanders are fluent in English. And they still use the New Zealand dollar as their primary currency, which means that for anyone spending American money, these islands will be a good value as long as the Kiwi dollar remains valued significantly less than its U.S. counterpart, as it has been in recent years. And since the Cooks' prime tourist market is New Zealand, most accommodation units are reasonably priced and, in the tradition of Kiwi motels, come with full kitchens.

IMPRESSIONS

I have often been mildly amused when I think that the great American novel was not written about New England or Chicago. It was written about a white whale in the South Pacific.

—James A. Michener, 1951

Travel writers—and travel agents—may continue to popularize the Pacific as a place of great sensuality, but my impression of those islands is of churches and cholesterol, of Christianity and canned corned beef, of tubby evangelists Bible-thumping to an almost deafening degree.

—Paul Theroux, 1991

THE SAMOAS

The heart of Polynesia, independent **Western Samoa** is like a cultural museum, especially when compared to its much smaller cousin, **American Samoa.** The peoples of the two Samoas are related by family and tradition if not politics. While traditional Samoan culture still exists in the American islands, it is preserved to a remarkable degree in Western Samoa, relatively unchanged by modern materialism. Traditional Samoan villages with their turtle-shaped houses rest peacefully along the coasts of the two main Western Samoan islands. There are good hotels in **Apia,** the picturesque capital, from which to fan out and meet the friendly Samoans and sample their truly remarkable and undeveloped beaches, one of which was the setting for the Gary Cooper movie *Return to Paradise.*

The dramatic beauty of Moorea and Bora Bora in French Polynesia is rivaled, if not exceeded, by that of **Tutuila,** the main island in American Samoa. The mountains drop straight down into fabled **Pago Pago,** the finest harbor in the South Pacific and the main reason America has had a presence there since 1890. This presence has resulted in a blend of cultures—the Samoan emphasis on extended families and communal ownership of property, especially land, and the American emphasis on business and progress. The result of the latter is that Pago Pago harbor is dominated—and polluted—by two large tuna canneries. The road around it is often clogged with vehicles as American Samoans rush to and fro past supermarkets, shopping centers, and fast-food establishments (no McDonald's or similar franchises, however).

Despite its economic development and Pago Pago's growing role as a regional transportation and shipping center, tourism plays a minor role in American Samoa. There is only one hotel, which is in serious need of repair, and restaurants other than fast-food outlets are few.

TONGA

South of Samoa lies Tonga, Polynesia's only surviving kingdom and its only country never controlled by a European power. From his Victorian palace in **Nuku'alofa,** King Taufa'ahau Tupou IV—all 300-plus pounds of him—rules over a nobility that carries European titles but is in reality a pure Polynesian system of high chiefs. Despite considerable grumbling among his commoner subjects in recent years, he and the nobles control the government and all the land, of which they are obligated to give 8¼ acres to every adult Tongan male.

When the king isn't making decisions, riding his bicycle, rowing his boat, or flying around from island to island wearing a motorbike helmet and ski goggles, he will probably be in church; Tonga is the heart of the South Pacific "Bible Belt." While things are slow on Sunday in most island countries, they stop completely in Tonga—everything, that is, except picnics at Tonga's beautiful beaches.

While the relatively flat topography of **Tongatapu,** the main island, offers little in the way of dramatic scenic beauty, **Vava'u** in the north offers long and narrow fjords and a plethora of small, deserted islands. **Neiafu,** the only town on Vava'u, is a throwback to the old days of traders and beachcombers.

FIJI

Fiji is visited by more people of every income bracket than any other place in the South Pacific. Accordingly, its tourism industry is the most developed and varied in the area. There are luxury resorts costing more than $600 per couple a night and small hostels where a bunk goes for $5. In between are a variety of fine establishments, affordable for all. Fiji also has many inexpensive restaurants that offer excellent value.

Fiji's fabulous beaches, gorgeous mountains, intriguing outer islands, colorful coral reefs, and some of the South Pacific's top scuba-diving and cruise operations

IMPRESSIONS

A low ribbon of reef and sand encircling a lagoon, an atoll is the very soul of Pacific romance.

—John Dyson, 1982

---

make it a don't-miss destination. And because its international airport at **Nadi** is a major regional hub, Fiji is a prime place to begin or end a trip to the South Pacific.

Although known for its rainy climate, Fiji's cosmopolitan capital city, **Suva,** gives a glimpse of the colonial era when Great Britain ruled the 300-plus islands of the archipelago. Suva's citizenry reflects Fiji's fascinating mix of peoples. About half the nation's population is made up of friendly, easygoing Fijians. The other half is mostly industrious East Indians whose ancestors came to work the sugarcane plantations—which make Fiji one of the richest South Pacific countries—and stayed to form a class of intellectuals and merchants. This stark contrast in cultures has resulted in political strains, but it also makes Fiji an interesting place to get into a conversation.

VANUATU

Known as the New Hebrides until it became independent in 1980, Vanuatu is a blend of the new and the ancient. The lovely main town, **Port Vila,** has an air of sophistication developed in pre-independence days when the New Hebrides had a joint government of Great Britain and France known as a "Condominium." The arrangement was commonly referred to as a "Pandemonium" government because of the difficulty the joint administration had in making decisions. The French presence has left a legacy: Cosmopolitan shops line the winding main street and gourmet restaurants overlook a glistening harbor. Port Vila's hotels run the gamut from small, intimate family-run establishments to large international resorts.

Though undeveloped, the outer islands are great attractions for adventurous travelers. **Tanna** has fire-spitting Yasur, the world's most accessible active volcano, and a village whose residents decided not to adopt Western ways but to continue living in the style of their ancestors, complete with grass skirts and penis sheaths. Other villagers on Tanna belong to a unique "cargo cult" that worships a mysterious American named John Frum. **Espíritu Santo** has the ruins of a huge American naval base that supported the bloody World War II Battle of Guadalcanal in Solomon Islands and was the primary setting for James A. Michener's *Tales of the South Pacific.* And **Pentecost** has its ritual "land dives" during which village men climb high towers made of tree limbs, make a few confessions about the status of their love lives, and dive off head first—vines tied to their ankles stop them just short of smashing their skulls on the ground.

NEW CALEDONIA

Another French South Pacific territory, New Caledonia is a blend of French and Melanesian cultures. An active Melanesian independence movement pitting the

---

IMPRESSIONS

All the time our visits to the islands have been more like dreams than realities: the people, the life, the beachcombers, the old stories and songs I have picked up, so interesting; the climate, the scenery, and (in some places) the women, so beautiful.

—Robert Louis Stevenson, 1889

indigenous peoples against the French settlers resulted in unrest and unfortunate bloodshed from 1984 until 1988, when both sides agreed to a 10-year truce. Under the peace accords, a referendum is scheduled for 1998 to decide whether New Caledonia will remain French or become an independent country.

In the meantime, the territory has settled down and visitors now venture outside the capital, **Nouméa,** a busy, misplaced bit of the French Riviera in the South Pacific. Nouméa has two long, curving beaches right in town (both featuring excellent hotels), sophisticated shops carrying luxury French goods, and so many restaurants it would take a month to sample them all. Outside of Nouméa, the remainder of the 240-mile-long main island and all of those lying offshore are dominated by the Melanesians rather than the French. Visitors are welcomed on **Lifou** in the **Loyalty Islands** and on the enchanting **Isle of Pines.** Although neither Lifou nor the Isle of Pines has first-class accommodations, both have incredibly beautiful beaches.

SOLOMON ISLANDS

For the generation that fought World War II, the name **Guadalcanal** conjures up an image not of paradise but of hell. The bloody, 6-month-long battle fought here in 1942 and 1943 effectively stopped the Japanese advance across the South Pacific toward New Caledonia and Australia. Before then there was no town on Guadalcanal; today, Solomon Islands' capital, **Honiara,** sits where the Americans put Quonset huts and built a harbor after the battle was won, and it still has a dusty, Wild West feel.

The main attractions on Guadalcanal are battle sites and war relics scattered here and there. In the mid-1980s, New Zealand and Australian bomb squads had to clear the land for an extension of Henderson Field, which was started by the Japanese in 1942. The strip was captured and completed by the U.S. Marines, and fought over and bombed for 6 months. There is also excellent scuba diving in the crystal-clear waters over the many ships and planes sunk or ditched throughout the islands, including "Iron Bottom Sound" between Guadalcanal and Savo islands, where the Japanese and American navies and air forces suffered huge losses.

There are other potential destinations in Solomon Islands, most of them examples of undeveloped Melanesia. **Munda** and **Gizo** in the Western Province, where a young U.S. Navy lieutenant named John F. Kennedy was stranded when his PT boat was shot out from under him during World War II, have simple but comfortable hotels. Picnics to "Kennedy Island" are popular outings from Gizo.

2. GEOGRAPHY

This book covers a great variety of islands scattered across a vast area of the South Pacific below the equator. Some of them barely break the surface of the sea; others soar into the clouds. Some are tiny pinpoints on a map, while others are clearly visible on photographs of the Pacific taken from weather satellites orbiting thousands of miles above the earth.

THE FORMATION OF THE ISLANDS

According to geological theories, the South Pacific islands were created by "plate tectonics." In simple terms, they were formed when sections of the earth's crust slowly moved over "hot spots" in the molten core below, or ran into each other.

Most of the Pacific Ocean sits on the aptly named Pacific Plate, which creeps ever so slowly northwest. As cracks in the Pacific Plate pass over hot spots in the core, molten lava escapes through the plate. Over millions of years, the resulting volcanoes

IMPRESSIONS

Missionaries, traders, and broken white folk living on the bounty of the natives, are to be found in almost every isle and hamlet . . .
—ROBERT LOUIS STEVENSON, 1889

build great seamounts that eventually break the surface of the sea and form islands in mid-ocean. Most of the islands in Polynesia are the tops of volcanoes that rose from the sea in this fashion. Most are round.

Many mid-ocean islands still have soaring mountains. Others have sunk back into the sea, leaving only a thin necklace of coral atolls around lagoons to mark their original boundaries. In some cases, the atolls have once again been lifted to form flat islands that seem to sit on the sea like plates. Still others, partially sunken islands, have the remnants of mountains sticking up in their lagoons.

Another plate-tectonics phenomenon has created islands in the southwestern Pacific. The Indo-Australian Plate, upon which Australia sits, runs into the Pacific Plate along a line that snakes its way from New Zealand north through Tonga and Fiji, then west to New Caledonia and northwest through Vanuatu, Solomon Islands, and on into Papua New Guinea. Most of these islands were created when the edge of one plate lifted up over the other—by as much as a foot every 100 years in some places.

Unlike the mid-ocean volcanic islands, which tend to be round, the "uplift" islands of New Caledonia, Vanuatu, and Solomon Islands tend to be long and narrow. They also have considerable ongoing volcanic activity, caused by the friction generated along great faults. There are so many volcanoes all along the edge of the Pacific Plate that the entire rim of this great ocean is known as "The Ring of Fire."

The overlapping of plates not only causes great uplifts of land, but it is also responsible for long, narrow depressions on the bottom of the sea. One of these, the Tonga Trench, parallels the islands of Tonga and is one of the deepest parts of the Pacific Ocean.

FLORA & FAUNA

Most species of plants and animals native to the South Pacific originated in Southeast Asia and worked their way eastward across the Pacific, by natural distribution or in the company of humans. The farther east one goes, however, the more the number of native species diminishes. Very few local plants or animals came from the Americas, the one notable exception being the sweet potato, believed to have been brought back by early Polynesians who may have voyaged in their canoes as far as South America.

PLANTS

In addition to the west-to-east difference in distribution, there is a difference in flora based on island geology: High, mountainous islands have a greater variety of plants than do the atolls or raised atolls. The interiors of high islands are covered with ferns, native bush, or grass throughout the South Pacific.

Typical tropical plants—coconut palms, breadfruit, taro, paper mulberry, pepper (kava), and bananas—were brought to the isolated mid-ocean islands by ancient settlers primarily because of their usefulness as food or fiber. Accordingly, they are generally found in the inhabited areas of the islands and not so often in the bush.

With a few exceptions—the white gardenia known as the *tiare Tahiti* is the best known—tropical flowers also worked their way east in the company of humans. Bougainvillea, hibiscus, allamanda, poinsettia, poinciana (the flame tree), croton, frangipani (plumeria), ixora, canna, and water lilies all give colorful testament to the islanders' love for flowers of every hue in the rainbow. The aroma of the white, yellow, or pink frangipani in the Polynesian leis and headbands is so sweet it's used as perfume in many island countries.

ANIMALS

The only mammals native to South Pacific islands are the fruit bat, or "flying fox," and some species of insect-eating bats. Dogs, chickens, pigs, rats, and mice were introduced by early settlers. Crocodiles are found in Vanuatu and Solomon Islands, but there are few land snakes or other reptiles elsewhere in the islands. The notable exceptions are geckos and skinks, those little lizards that seem to be everywhere. Don't go berserk when one of them walks upside-down across the ceiling of your bungalow. They are harmless and actually perform a valuable service by snaring and swallowing mosquitoes.

BIRDS

The number and variety of species of bird life diminish progressively as you go eastward—Tahiti in the east has significantly fewer native land birds than the islands to the west.

Most land birds live in the bush away from settlements and the accompanying cats, dogs, and rats that might have an appetite for them or their eggs. For this reason the birds most likely to be seen are terns, boobies, herons, petrels, and noddies. Of the birds that are not indigenous, the Indian mynah is the most numerous. Brought to the South Pacific early in this century to control insects, the mynah quickly became a noisy nuisance in its own right. The squawks and cackles of these gregarious black birds with white trim are one of nature's alarm clocks throughout the islands.

THE SEA

The tropical South Pacific Ocean virtually teems with sea life, from colorful reef fish to the horrific Great White sharks featured in *Jaws,* from the paua clams that make tasty chowders in the Cook Islands to the deep-sea tuna that keep the canneries going at Pago Pago.

CORAL REEFS

The great reefs in the South Pacific were built by more than 600 species of coral, more than 10 times the number found in the Caribbean. Billions of tiny coral polyps build their own skeletons on top of those left by their ancestors, until they reach the level of low tide. Then they grow outward, extending the edge of the reef. The old skeletons are white, while the living polyps present a rainbow of colors; they grow best and are most colorful in the clear, salty water on the outer edge or in channels, where the tides and waves wash fresh seawater along and across the reef. A reef can grow as much as 2 inches a year in ideal conditions. Unfortunately, pollution, rising seawater temperature, and a proliferation of crown-of-thorns starfish have greatly hampered reef growth—and beauty—in many parts of the South Pacific.

Many visitors are disappointed after arriving in the South Pacific to find relatively few beaches where the surf pounds the sand. The coral reefs are responsible. Although the islands have thousands of powdery beaches, the surf usually slams against the reef far offshore and not on the beaches. For the most part, be content to step right into one of those huge bathtubs known as lagoons.

A Few Warnings

Corals belong to a family of stinging creatures and can be painful to the skin. Even the old white skeletons can cause nasty coral cuts that can become infected almost overnight. Wash and apply a good antiseptic or antibacterial ointment to all coral cuts and scrapes as soon as possible.

Since coral cannot grow in fresh water, the flow of rivers and streams into the lagoon creates narrow channels, known as passes, through the reef. Currents can be very strong in the passes, and most drownings occur when a victim is caught in the swift flow and carried out to sea. Unless you are an accomplished snorkeler, **stay away from the passes** and in the protected, shallow water of the inner lagoons. Always **seek local advice** before snorkeling or swimming in a lagoon away from the hotel beaches. Most of the diving operators listed in this book teach scuba courses and conduct snorkeling tours. If you don't know what you're doing, go with them.

Don't deface the reef. Many South Pacific countries have laws protecting their reefs, so think twice about breaking off a gorgeous chunk of coral to take home as a souvenir. You could land in the slammer.

SEA LIFE

The lagoons are like gigantic aquariums filled with numerous tropical fish and other marine life. Nearly every main South Pacific town has a bookshop with pamphlets containing photographs and describing these creatures—buy one so you'll recognize what's swimming on the other side of your face mask.

Most South Pacific countries restrict the use of spearguns, so ask before you go in search of the catch of your life. As noted in Chapter 2, sea turtles are on the list of endangered species, and the importation of their shells is prohibited by many countries, including the United States.

By and large, the South Pacific's marine creatures are harmless to humans, but here are a few to avoid.

Warnings

There are some islands in the western South Pacific where **sharks** are present in considerable numbers. For the most part, however, the danger presented by sharks is exaggerated. During the course of an average year there will be about 50 shark attacks on humans worldwide, and the people-eaters generally stay in the deep waters beyond the reefs and only occasionally wander in looking for a meal. Reef sharks, which live in lagoons, are usually well fed and have little interest in humans other than curiosity. Nevertheless, don't take chances. Caution is always wise.

Sharks are attracted to bright objects such as watches and knives, so be careful what you wear in the water. Seek local advice before swimming off a strange beach, especially one where no one else is swimming. Don't swim in areas where sewage or edible wastes are dumped, and never swim alone if you have any suspicion that sharks might be present. If you do see a shark, don't panic. Splashing in the water or urinating will only encourage them. Calmly retreat and get out of the water as quickly as you can without creating a disturbance.

Those round things on the rocks and reefs that look like pin cushions are **sea urchins,** whose spikes can be more painful than needles. If you get stuck with one, soak the area in hot water, vinegar, or urine for about 15 minutes. That will stop the pain. The spike itself is made of calcium. If you can't find a member of your hotel staff to pull it out, it will dissolve and disappear in about 2 weeks on its own.

The sting inflicted by **jellyfish** can hurt like the devil but seldom is life-threatening. Adolph's Meat Tenderizer is a great antidote, but you're as likely to find it in the South Pacific as you are to be stung. Otherwise, use rubbing alcohol to swab the affected areas, not water or any petroleum-based compound.

The **stone fish** is so named because it looks like a piece of stone or coral as it lies buried in the sand on the lagoon bottom with only its back and 13 venomous spikes sticking out. Its venom both decomposes the blood and intoxicates the nervous system of its victims, causing paralysis and even death. You'll know by the intense pain if you're stuck. Serum is available, so get to a hospital at once.

Sea snakes, cone shells, crown-of-thorns starfish, moray eels, lion fish, and demon stingers can all be painful, if not deadly. The last thing these creatures want is to tangle with a human, so keep your hands to yourself.

3. PEOPLE & CULTURE

Surely Capt. Samuel Wallis and his scurvy-ridden crew in the HMS *Dolphin* could hardly believe their eyes that June day in 1767 when an army of large brown-skinned men paddled more than 500 canoes across the lagoon at Matavai Bay, many of them loaded with pigs, chickens, coconuts, fruit, and young women, nude to the waist, "who played a great many droll and wanton tricks" on the Englishmen who had just discovered Tahiti.

Where had the "wanton" natives of this remote island come from? How had these people, who lived a late Stone Age existence, crossed the vast Pacific long before Europeans had the courage to sail out of sight of land on the Atlantic? Those questions baffled the early European explorers of the South Pacific, and they continue to intrigue scientists and scholars to this day.

Thor Heyerdahl may have drifted in a raft named *Kon Tiki* from South America to French Polynesia in 1947 to prove his theory that the Polynesians came from the Americas, but it is generally accepted today that they and other native South Pacific islanders had their origins in Southeast Asia many thousands of years ago.

No one is sure because none of the South Pacific cultures had a written language until the missionaries arrived in the early 19th century. In addition, much early settlement may have occurred during the last Ice Age, when so much water was frozen in the polar ice caps that the level of the sea was considerably lower than it is today. The earliest South Pacific islanders more than likely lived along the coasts, so their ancient dwellings and any anthropological artifacts they may have contained are now covered by hundreds of feet of seawater and coral.

THE EARLIEST SETTLERS

Based on archeological discoveries and linguistic studies, the generally accepted view today is that a race of early humans, Australoids, migrated from Southeast Asia to Papua New Guinea and Australia during the Ice Age, when those areas were joined as one landmass. The oceans were so much lower that the Australoids would have had to cross over stretches of water no more than 30 to 50 miles wide during their migration down through what is now the island nation of Indonesia.

The Australian Aborigines and many of the Highland tribes of Papua New Guinea are believed to be descendants of these first arrivals. Some experts believe that the Australoids also moved west as well as east from Asia, and that many modern-day Africans are also their descendants.

Between 5,000 and 10,000 years ago another group, the Papuans, arrived from Southeast Asia, settled along the coasts, and either absorbed the Australoids or drove them into more remote regions. The languages spoken by the Papuans were completely different from those of the Australoids.

AUSTRONESIANS

Several thousands of years later the Papuans in turn were pushed inland and out into the more eastern South Pacific islands by the arrival—again from Southeast Asia—of a lighter-skinned race known as Austronesians. Although there was considerable intermarrying between the two races, many descendants of the Papuans who live on Bougainville in Papua New Guinea and in the western Solomon Islands are some of the darkest-skinned people on earth, and to this day they speak languages that are different from those brought by the Austronesians.

The Austronesian family of languages, whose origins have been traced by linguists to present-day Taiwan, are spoken from Madagascar off the coast of Africa through Indonesia, Malaysia, the Philippines, parts of Vietnam, and across the South Pacific as far as Easter Island off the coast of South America. No other group of ancient languages spread to so much of the earth's surface. On the other hand, the languages spoken in most of New Guinea, much of Solomon Islands, and by all the Australian Aborigines are unrelated to those of the Austronesians and may date back to the Papuans or even to the first Australoid settlers more than 30,000 years ago.

The most tangible remains of the early Austronesians are remnants of pottery, the first shards of which were found during the 1970s in Lapita, a New Caledonian village. Lapita pottery, which probably originated in the Bismarck Archipelago in Papua New

IMPRESSIONS

Now the cunning lay in this, that the Polynesians have rules of hospitality that have all the force of laws; an etiquette of absolute rigidity made it necessary for the people of the village not only to give lodging to the strangers, but to provide them with food and drink for as long as they wished to stay.

—W. SOMERSET MAUGHAM, 1921

Guinea, spread as far east as Tonga. Throughout the area it was decorated with geometric designs similar to those used today on tapa cloth (see "What to Buy" in Chapter 2). For more than 1,000 years it was the only type of pottery in the South Pacific. Apparently, however, the Lapita culture died out some 2,500 years ago, and the Polynesians who moved east stopped using pottery altogether by A.D. 1000.

MELANESIANS

The islands settled by the Papuans and Austronesians are known collectively today as Melanesia, which includes Papua New Guinea, Solomon Islands, Vanuatu, New Caledonia, and Fiji. The name Melanesia was derived from the Greek words *melas,* which means black, and *nesos,* which means islands. The Melanesians in general have negroid features—brown-to-black skin, flat or hooked noses, full lips, and wiry hair—but the interbreeding among the successive waves of migrants resulted in many subgroups with varying physical characteristics.

In addition to the differences in physical features, the dispersal of earlier settlers into the remote hinterlands caused a huge variety of cultures and languages to develop. For example, the native peoples on Bougainville in Papua New Guinea and nearby New Georgia, Choiseul, and the Shortlands in Solomon Islands primarily have dark skin and speak Papuan languages. There is a transition population on the next island to the east, Santa Isabel, where a Papuan language is spoken on the west end and an Austronesian tongue on the east. The next island to the east, Santa Cruz, has a lighter-skinned population that speaks languages belonging only to the Austronesian family.

A DIVERSITY OF CULTURES

Throughout Melanesia, as is the case in each of these islands, the cultures and languages change from the coast to the interior and virtually from one valley to the next. As each tribe was pushed inland by the next wave of immigrants, it became isolated and developed a culture and a language that were quite distinct from those of its neighbors. Tanna Island in Vanuatu has five distinct languages. The tribes often waged war with their neighbors, whose language they could not understand. To a large extent they have overcome this problem today by using Pidgin English as a common language in Vanuatu and the Solomons.

IMPRESSIONS

Everyone is welcome in Polynesia, though after a period of time the stranger is encouraged to move on—go "off-island," in the Pacific phrase.

—PAUL THEROUX, 1991

I wish I could tell you about the South Pacific. The way it actually was. The endless ocean. The infinite specks of coral we call islands. Coconut palms nodding gracefully toward the ocean. Reefs upon which waves broke into spray, the inner lagoons, lovely beyond description.

—JAMES A. MICHENER, 1947

Unlike the Polynesians to the east, most of whom live near the sea and take at least part of their food from the lagoons, Melanesians tend to dwell inland and rely on small gardens to provide their staples, such as tapioca and yams. Pigs are abundant but are kept primarily for their tusks and as items of wealth rather than as food, although they may be slaughtered by the score for ceremonial feasts.

Pigs and other items are often used by men to buy their way up the social ladder, for the leaders in Melanesia are usually chosen by village councils rather than by heredity. Women, on the other hand, are considered in most tribes to be little more than chattel. A man often pays a hefty "bride price" in pigs, pigs' tusks, produce, or shell money for a new wife, only to send her to sleep with the hogs he has left after paying for her. Women even breast-feed the piglets in some remote areas.

MELANESIAN RELIGION & "CUSTOM"

Before the missionaries' arrival, religion in Melanesia tended to be strongly animist. Nearly everything had a spirit, which elaborate masks and other objects invoked during dances and ceremonies. Ancestors were believed to remain in this world rather than journey on to a heaven or hell, and skulls of the deceased—thought to be the resting place of the human spirit—were kept in some communities. So strong were some local religions that the first missionaries were quickly dispatched with clubs and eaten—cannibalism and even head-hunting were common throughout Melanesia, usually in connection with religious or social rites. Despite the widespread and often politically powerful influence of Christianity today, the old religions—if not cannibalism and head-hunting—live on in many of the tribes.

So does "custom," by which the Melanesians mean their traditional ways of life. Throughout Melanesia there is a determined effort, especially in rural areas, to preserve the old traditions in the face of growing Western influences. This means that on many islands visitors can see Melanesian life-styles virtually unchanged for hundreds of years, complete with thatch houses and grass skirts.

POLYNESIANS

Those "wanton" young women encountered by Captain Wallis and his crew in Tahiti were not Melanesians but Polynesians, the second great ethnic group of the South Pacific.

Unlike the Austronesians, the Polynesians' ancestors did not stop in Fiji on their migration from Southeast Asia but pushed on to colonize a vast triangle of the Pacific that extends from Hawaii in the north to Easter Island in the southeast and New Zealand in the southwest, and includes Tonga, the Samoas, the Cook Islands, and French Polynesia. Archeologists now believe that they settled in Samoa, the so-called cradle of Polynesian culture, more than 3,000 years ago and then slowly fanned out to the Marquesas Islands in northeastern French Polynesia and from there to Hawaii, Tahiti, Easter Island, the Cooks, and New Zealand.

Some experts theorize that the Polynesians belong to a distinct ethnic group whose ancestors came into the South Pacific along the Melanesian islands but moved east when they found them already inhabited by the earlier Australoid, Papuan, and Austronesian settlers. Other scholars believe, however, that the Polynesians are an intermediate race, perhaps an admixture of Melanesians and Micronesians to the north who developed their own culture in the isolation of the remote South Pacific islands.

Either way, Polynesians are significantly different from the Melanesians to the west. Most have copper skin and black hair that is straight or wavy rather than frizzy. They are taller and generally much heavier in build than the Melanesians. Despite their large size, Polynesians tend to be quite graceful and athletic. Many of them have left their marks as professional football and rugby players in the United States, Australia, and New Zealand.

The languages spoken throughout Polynesia belong to the Austronesian family and are similar from one major island group to another. Cook Islanders, for example, say that they can understand about 60% of Tahitian without ever having heard it before. Tongans and Samoans say they can get the gist of each others' conversations. For example, the word for "house" is *fale* in Tongan and Samoan, *fare* in Tahitian, *'are* in Cook Islands Maori, *hale* in Hawaiian, and *vale* in Fijian.

The Polynesians were extraordinary mariners and navigators. They built large, double-hulled canoes capable of carrying hundreds of people, animals, and plants, and they sailed thousands of miles across the Pacific long before Columbus dared cross the Atlantic. They navigated by the stars, the wind, the clouds, the shape of the waves, and the flight pattern of birds—a remarkable achievement for a people who on land used no metal tools and gave up the use of pottery of any kind thousands of years ago.

POLYNESIAN SOCIETY

Like the Melanesians, the Polynesians frequently fought wars among their tribes, though generally the Polynesian wars were not so bloody and not so often followed by a cannibalistic orgy at the expense of the losers.

Unlike the Melanesians, they developed highly structured societies, and to this day they place great emphasis on hereditary bloodline when choosing leaders. Most members of the modern Western Samoan parliament, for example, must hold the inherited title of *matai.* Strong and sometimes despotic chiefdoms developed on many islands, and Tonga and Samoa were once ruled by a single powerful chief. The present king of Tonga carries on the tradition of central leaders who were so powerful in the 1700s that they conquered much of Fiji and brought to the Melanesians there many Polynesian customs, including their tradition of hereditary chiefs. Just to make sure, the victorious Tongans made the conquered Fijian chiefs take Tongan wives, and Tongan blood flows today in the veins of many Fijian chiefs, who are known, as they are in Polynesia, by the title *tui.*

In some places, such as Tahiti, the Polynesians developed a rigid class system of chiefs, priests, nobility, commoners, and slaves. Their societies emphasized elaborate ceremonies, and even today ceremonies featuring kava—a slightly narcotic drink—play an important role in Samoa. Everyday life was governed by a system based on *tabu,* a rigid list of things a person could and could not do depending on his or her status in life. Tabu and similar words (*tapu, tambu*) are used throughout the South Pacific to mean "do not enter," and it has found its way into English as "taboo."

Western principles of ownership have made their inroads, but by and large everything in Polynesia—especially land—is owned communally by the family. In effect, the Polynesian system is pure communism at the family level. If your brother has just harvested a crop of taro, and you're hungry, then some of that taro belongs to you. The same principle applies to a can of corned beef sitting on a shelf in a grocery store, which partially explains why Polynesian-owned grocery shops often teeter on the edge of bankruptcy.

When coupled with the warm climate, fertile soil, and lagoons stocked with fish, this system of sharing has kept Polynesia relatively prosperous. There is little abject poverty, and while many of the islanders would be considered poor by Western standards, no one goes hungry and no one sleeps without a roof over his or her head. Most of the thatch roofs in Polynesia today are actually bungalows at the resort hotels; nearly everyone else sleeps under tin.

It's little wonder, then, that visitors are greeted throughout Polynesia by friendly,

---

IMPRESSIONS

From the moment the boat slid into the glassy water near shore it had seemed that all my plugs had been pulled.

—John Dyson, 1982

IMPRESSIONS

The South Pacific is memorable because when you are in the islands you simply cannot ignore nature. You cannot avoid looking up at the stars, large as apples on a new tree. You cannot deafen your ear to the thunder of the surf. The bright sands, the screaming birds, and the wild winds are always with you.

—JAMES A. MICHENER, 1951

peaceful, and extraordinarily courteous people who are unhurried by the cares of the more modern world. The service they render at the hotels may reflect their slow pace, but after all, why are you going to the South Pacific? Your drink will get there in the due course of "island time," so sit back, relax, and make an effort to meet your marvelous hosts.

POLYNESIAN RELIGIONS

At the risk of over simplification, the Polynesians believed in a supreme spirit who ruled over a plethora of lesser deities who, in turn, governed the sun, fire, volcanoes, the sea, war, and fertility. *Tikis* were carved of stone or wood to give each god a home (but not a permanent residence) during religious ceremonies, and great stone *marae* were built as temples and meeting places for the chiefs. Sacrifices—sometimes human—would be offered to the gods, and cannibalism was not unknown in Polynesia, though it was not as widely practiced there as it was in Melanesia.

SEX & THE SINGLE POLYNESIAN

The puritanical Christian missionaries who arrived in the early 19th century were successful in convincing the islanders that they should clothe their hitherto nearly naked bodies. The Polynesians, however, were less willing to give up their old sexual mores, which bore no resemblance whatsoever to the teachings of the missionaries. Sex to the early Polynesians was as much a part of life as any other daily activity, and they uninhibitedly engaged in it with a variety of partners from adolescence until marriage. Even today there exists a somewhat laissez-faire attitude toward premarital sex.

Every child, whether born in wedlock or not, is accepted immediately into one of the extended families that are the bedrock of Polynesian society. Mothers, fathers, grandparents, aunts, uncles, cousins of every degree—all are part of the close-knit Polynesian family. Relationships sometimes are so blurred that every adult woman within a mile—even its mother—can be known as a child's "auntie."

Further, male transvestism, homosexuality, and bisexuality are a fact of life in French Polynesia, the Samoas, Tonga, and, to a lesser extent, in Fiji. In those societies young boys are often reared as girls by families with a shortage of female offspring. Some of these youths grow up to be heterosexual; others become homosexual or bisexual and, often appearing publicly in women's attire, actively seek out the company of tourists. In some cases male transvestites are commonly taken as sexual partners by otherwise heterosexual men. In Tahitian, these males are known as *mahus;* in Samoan, *fa'afafines;* in Tongan, *fakaleitis.*

Although illegal, both male and female prostitution is common in some of the larger towns, such as Papeete and Suva. See "Health & Insurance" in Chapter 2 for information about acquired immune deficiency syndrome (AIDS) in the South Pacific.

4. HISTORY

Melanesians and Polynesians had been living on their islands for thousands of years before Europeans had the foggiest notion that the Pacific Ocean existed. And even after Vasco Nuñez de Balboa cut across the Isthmus of Panama and discovered this largest of oceans in 1513, more than 250 years went by before Europeans paid much attention to the islands that lay upon it.

In the meantime, the Pacific was the domain of a few Spanish and Portuguese explorers. Their goal, beginning with Ferdinand Magellan's monumental voyage around Cape Horn and across the Pacific in 1521, was to find a route from Europe (and later from Peru) to the rich Spice Islands, now Indonesia and the Philippines. Magellan stumbled upon few Pacific islands, and none below the equator. The route he pioneered took subsequent Spanish voyagers north of the South Pacific islands, although Álvaro de Mendaña did discover some of the Solomon, Cook, and Marquesas islands during voyages in 1568 and 1595, respectively, and another Spaniard, Pedro Fernández de Quirós, happened upon some of the Tuamotu, Cook, and New Hebrides (now Vanuatu) islands in 1606.

The Dutch took a turn in 1642, when the governor-general of Batavia in the Dutch East Indies (now Jakarta, Indonesia) sent Abel Tasman on a historic voyage into the Pacific, this one from the west rather than from the east on the usual route around the bottom of South America. During the next year, Tasman discovered and explored much of Australia, New Zealand, Tonga, and Fiji. The Dutch did nothing to exploit his discoveries, nor did they follow up on those of Jacob Roggeveen, who found Easter Island and Samoa 80 years later in 1722.

TERRA AUSTRALIS INCOGNITA

A theory came into vogue in Europe during the latter half of the 18th century that an unknown southern land—a *terra australis incognita*—lay somewhere in the southern hemisphere. It had to exist, the theory went, for otherwise the unbalanced earth would wobble off into space. King George III of Great Britain—the same King George against whom the American Revolution was fought—took great interest in the idea and launched a series of voyages to find the unknown southern continent and claim it for the Crown.

In 1764, he sent Capt. John Byron—the poet's grandfather—on a voyage in HMS *Dolphin.* Byron followed a northerly course across the Pacific, happened upon Tokelau, and went on around the world in a fast 2 years without doing much searching for the mysterious continent. Not discouraged, King George immediately put Capt. Samuel Wallis in command of the *Dolphin* and sent it out again. Wallis had no better luck discovering the unknown continent, but it was on this trip in 1767 that he stumbled upon and claimed Tahiti.

DATELINE

- **30,000 B.C.** Australoid peoples settle in southwest Pacific.
- **7000–3500 B.C.** Papuans arrive from Southeast Asia.
- **3000–1000 B.C.** Austronesians arrive from Asia, push eastward.
- **1000 B.C.** Polynesians migrate eastward to Samoa and Tonga.
- **1513** Balboa discovers the Pacific Ocean.
- **1521** Magellan crosses the Pacific.
- **1568** Mendaña discovers the Marquesas and some of Cooks and Solomon Islands.
- **1595** Mendaña fails to colonize Solomons; dies there.
- **1606** De Quirós discovers islands in the Tuamotus, Cooks and the New Hebrides (Vanuatu).
- **1642** Abel Tasman explores western Pacific, finds Tonga and Fiji.
- **1722** Roggeveen happens upon Easter Island and Samoa.
- **1764** Byron fails to find *terra australis incognita.*
- **1767** Wallis discovers Tahiti; Carteret finds Solomons.
- **1768** Bougainville also discovers Tahiti.
- **1769–71** Captain Cook observes

(continues)

VENUS DISCOVERED

Less than a year later, the French explorer Louis Antoine de Bougainville also arrived in Tahiti. Although anchoring at a different part of the island, he was given the same rousing reception that had greeted Wallis—hundreds of canoes bearing fruit, pigs, chickens, and bare-breasted young women. Bougainville noted in his journal that one young Tahitian woman came aboard and "carelessly dropped the cloth which covered her and appeared to the eyes of all beholders much as Venus showed herself to the Phrygian shepherd—having indeed the form of that goddess." He promptly named his discovery New Cythère—the Island of Love. The Tahiti Tourist Promotion Board has been unable to come up with anything better.

The Tahitians didn't tell Bougainville that Wallis had already been there, so he claimed Tahiti for France and departed 10 days after he arrived, taking with him a young Tahitian named Ahutoru, who became a sensation in France. He was seen by many as living proof of Rousseau's theory that man was at his best a "noble savage."

Bougainville sailed west from Tahiti, discovered several islands in Samoa, and explored the Solomon Islands, of which Bougainville—now part of Papua New Guinea—still bears his name. So does the brightly flowering tropical shrub known as bougainvillea. He was the first Frenchman to circumnavigate the globe and was treated to a rousing reception when he returned home in 1769.

CAPT. JAMES COOK

In 1768, shortly after Wallis had returned to England, the Lords of the Admiralty picked a lieutenant from the junior ranks, gave him command of a converted collier, and sent him to Tahiti. His mission was to observe the transit of the real Venus—the planet, that is—across the sun, an astronomical event that would not occur again until 1874 but which, if measured from widely separated points on the globe, would enable scientists for the first time to accurately gauge the distance between the earth and the sun and thereby determine longitude on the earth's surface. A second and highly secret mission was to sail on from Tahiti and to find the still-unknown southern continent. The young lieutenant who was entrusted with these missions was to become the most famous of all South Pacific explorers: Capt. James Cook.

Like Rousseau and Bougainville, Cook was a product of the Age of Enlightenment. Not only a master navigator, he was a mathematician, astronomer, and practical physician who was the first captain of any ship to prevent scurvy among his crewmen, initially with sauerkraut and later with fresh fruits and vegetables. He was ideally suited in skills, temperament, and powers of observation for this first of three great voyages of discovery he was to undertake.

On that first trip Cook took with him Joseph Banks, a young botanist who would later become president of the Royal Botanical Society; Daniel Solander, a prominent

DATELINE

transit of Venus from Tahiti, explores South Pacific.

- **1772–74** On second voyage, Cook finds New Caledonia, Norfolk Island, more of the Cook Islands and Fiji.
- **1778–79** Cook explores northwest America, dies in Hawaii.
- **1787** La Pérouse disappears during voyage of discovery.
- **1789** Fletcher Christian leads mutiny on the *Bounty*.
- **1797** First missionaries arrive, at Tahiti.
- **1800–10** Whalers, merchants, and sandalwood traders flock to islands, bring guns and whisky.
- **1808** Last *Bounty* mutineer discovered on Pitcairn.
- **1820–50** *Bêche-de-mer* trade flourishes; Western-style towns founded in Tahiti, Samoa, Tonga, Fiji, Vanuatu.
- **1839** Rev. John Williams killed and eaten on Erromango.
- **1842** France annexes Tahiti; Herman Melville arrives in Papeete the same day.
- **1865** First Chinese brought to Ta-

(continues)

Swedish naturalist; and Charles Green, the assistant Astronomer Royal. Later he would take along William Hodges, whose paintings of the South Pacific islands were to England in the 18th century what television pictures of the planets are to the world today.

Arriving in Tahiti in 1769, Cook and his party observed the transit of Venus from a sandy peninsula on the north shore that he appropriately named Point Venus. The measurements proved to be somewhat less than useful, but the observations of Tahiti, made during a stay of 6 months, were of immense importance in understanding the "noble savages" who lived there.

Cook then sailed southeast to carry out the second part of his mission. He discovered the Society Islands northwest of Tahiti, the Australs to the south, and then fully explored the coasts of New Zealand and eastern Australia, neither of which had been visited by Europeans since Tasman's voyage in 1642. After nearly sinking his ship on the Great Barrier Reef, he left the South Pacific through the strait between Australia and Papua New Guinea, which he named for his converted collier, the *Endeavor*. He returned to London in 1771.

COOK'S OTHER VOYAGES

Nine months later, Cook was dispatched again to find the unknown southern continent, this time with two ships, the *Resolution* and the *Adventure*. During this voyage of 3 years, he visited Tonga and discovered some of what now are Fiji and the Cook Islands, Niue, New Caledonia, and Norfolk Island. He became the first man to sail below the Antarctic Circle, and although failing to sight Antarctica, he laid to rest the theory that a large landmass lay in the tropical South Pacific.

Cook's mission during a third voyage, in 1778–79, was to find a northwest passage between the Atlantic and the Pacific. He visited Tahiti for a third time and then headed north. A few weeks later, he discovered the Hawaiian Islands and ventured on to North America, where he explored the northwest coast until he was turned back by ice in the Bering Strait. With winter coming on, he returned to Hawaii. There, on February 14, 1779, during a petty skirmish with the Hawaiians on the Big Island, Capt. James Cook was killed. He was 51 years old.

With the exception of the Hawaiians who smashed his skull, Captain Cook was revered throughout the Pacific. He came not for gold and plunder but for knowledge and understanding. Although he claimed many of the islands for Britain, he once said that he hoped they never would be colonized. He often was firm with the islanders, but he always treated them fairly and respected their traditions. His commanding presence and the respect showed him by his crews caused the Polynesian chiefs to look upon him as one of their own. Today you will find a Cook's Bay, a Cooktown, a Cook Strait, any number of Captain Cook's landing places, and an entire island nation named for this giant of an explorer who filled in the charts of the South Pacific.

DATELINE

hiti to harvest cotton.

- **1874** Britain accepts Fiji as a colony.
- **1879** First Indians brought to Fiji.
- **1884** International date line established.
- **1888** Foiling France, Britain declares protectorate over the Cook Islands.
- **1889** Unrest in Western Samoa; hurricane destroys U.S., British, and German warships at Apia. Robert Louis Stevenson settles in Apia.
- **1890** Germany takes Western Samoa, U.S. gets Eastern Samoa, Britain claims protectorate over Tonga.
- **1891** Paul Gauguin arrives in Tahiti.
- **1893** Britain claims protectorate over Solomon Islands.
- **1894** Robert Louis Stevenson dies in Samoa.
- **1901** Paul Gauguin dies in French Polynesia.
- **1906** Britain and France jointly claim the New Hebrides.
- **1915** During World War I, German Admiral von Spee shells Papeete.
- **1917** Count von Luckner captured in Fiji after his

(continues)

MUTINY ON THE BOUNTY

One of Captain Cook's navigators would become even more famous when he later inspired a mutiny that became part of the lore of the South Pacific: Capt. William Bligh.

Based on reports of Cook and others, a group of West Indian planters and merchants asked King George III to bring breadfruit, which they saw as a cheap source of food for their slaves, from Tahiti to Jamaica. In 1787 William Bligh was put in command of HMS *Bounty* and sent to do just that. Bligh carefully selected his officers, one of whom was a former shipmate named Fletcher Christian.

After failing to round Cape Horn, Bligh turned the *Bounty* around and sailed to Tahiti by way of South Africa and Australia. This made him late arriving, and he had to wait for several months for the season when breadfruit could be transplanted. During this time the crew frolicked ashore and enjoyed all the pleasures of Tahiti. Finally, with 1,015 breadfruit plantings loaded, Bligh sailed the *Bounty* west, discovering Aitutaki in the present-day Cook Islands before arriving in Tonga. For whatever reason—Bligh's harshness as a skipper and the lures of the Tahitian women are blamed equally—at dawn on April 28, 1789, Fletcher Christian and part of the crew overpowered Bligh and set him, 18 of his loyal officers and crewmen, a compass, a cask of water, and a few provisions adrift in a longboat. The breadfruit plantings were thrown into the sea.

The mutinous crew turned the *Bounty* around and sailed back to Tahiti, where they put ashore 25 other crew members who were loyal to Bligh. They knew they couldn't stay there, for surely Tahiti would be the first place the Royal Navy looked when it came hunting for them, so most of the mutineers moved on. The *Bounty* presumably visited Rarotonga in the Cook Islands, and the mutineers actually remained for a while on Tubuai until violence erupted with the native inhabitants there. They returned to Tahiti, and then Christian and eight other mutineers, accompanied by their Tahitian wives and six Tahitian men, sailed away for the last time.

Meantime, Captain Bligh and his crew of 17 (one was killed when they put ashore briefly in Tonga) managed to sail the *Bounty*'s longboat through Fiji, the Great Barrier Reef, and on to Timor in the Dutch East Indies—a journey of more than 3,600 miles that stands as one of the epic open-boat voyages of all time. From there they hitched a ride back to England, whereupon the Royal Navy immediately dispatched HMS *Pandora* to the South Seas to search out and bring back the mutineers.

The *Pandora* proceeded to Tahiti and rounded up all members of the *Bounty*'s crew left there. The mutineers were placed in close-fitting irons and crammed into a small, stifling deckhouse that was quickly nicknamed "Pandora's Box." After a fruitless search through the islands to the west, the *Pandora* sailed toward home. While trying to find the entrance to the Torres Strait, she struck a reef and sank the next day. Four of the 14 mutineers drowned. The others, along with the ship's captain and crew, sailed in four boats the rest of the way to Timor, from where they were taken back to England. The 10 mutineers were tried

DATELINE

German raider runs aground in the Cook Islands.

- **1933** Charles Nordhoff and James Norman Hall publish *Munity on the Bounty*, a best-seller.
- **1935** *Mutiny on the Bounty* starring Clark Gable and Charles Laughton is a smash box-office hit.
- **1941** Japanese bomb Pearl Harbor in Hawaii, begin advance into the South Pacific.
- **1942–44** Allied forces strike Guadalcanal in Solomon Islands, use other islands as bases for attacks on Japanese.
- **1947** James A. Michener's *Tales of the South Pacific* is published; gives rise to musical and movie *South Pacific*.
- **1959–60** International airports open at Tahiti and Fiji.
- **1960** MGM remakes *Mutiny on the Bounty* starring Marlon Brando.
- **1962** Western Samoa becomes independent.
- **1965** Cook Islands gain local autonomy in association with New Zealand.
- **1966** France explodes first nuclear bomb in Tuamotus.
- **1970** Fiji gains independence from

(continues)

by a court-martial. Four were acquitted, three others were convicted but pardoned, and three were hanged. Peter Heywood, one of those pardoned by the king, wrote the first Tahitian dictionary while waiting in prison to be tried.

Captain Bligh returned to Tahiti a few years later in another ship, collected another load of breadfruit, and took it to Jamaica. The slaves there wouldn't eat it, however, so the entire venture went for naught. Bligh later became governor of the penal colony of New South Wales in Australia.

In February 1808, more than 18 years after the mutiny, the *Topaz,* an American whaling ship operating far to the southeast of Tahiti, happened upon a rocky island that had been discovered but inaccurately plotted in 1767. The captain was astonished when some half-caste teenagers rowed out and greeted him not in Tahitian but in perfect English. He had found the last of the mutineers. All but one of them apparently had been killed during fights or by disease over the intervening years. Their Tahitian wives and children survived, however, and to this day their descendants live on this lonely island named Pitcairn.

The mutineers had burned and sunk the *Bounty* after they landed on Pitcairn, but its rudder has been recovered and now is on display at the Fiji Museum in Suva.

If all this sounds familiar, it's because you may have seen Clark Gable, Charles Laughton, Marlon Brando, or Mel Gibson in one of three movies based on the mutiny.

DATELINE

Britain.

- **1978** Solomon Islands becomes independent.
- **1980** The New Hebrides become Vanuatu.
- **1985** Treaty of Rarotonga declares South Pacific to be a nuclear-free zone.
- **1987** Fiji's military overthrows elected government.
- **1988** New Caledonia peace accords signed.
- **1990** Pres. George Bush and island leaders meet at summit conference.

WHALERS, TRADERS & BEACHBUMS

The American ship that found the mutineers' retreat at Pitcairn in 1808 was one of many whalers that came into the South Pacific after Cook and others put the area on the map. They roamed the seas looking for their giant prey, and their ruffian crews made dens of iniquity of many ports of call—Lahaina and Honolulu in Hawaii, Papeete and Nuku Hiva in Polynesia, Levuka in Fiji. Many crewmen jumped ship and lived on the islands, some of them even casting their lots—and their guns—with rival chiefs during tribal wars. With their assistance, some chiefs were able to extend their domain over entire islands or groups of islands.

One such deserter, who jumped ship in the Marquesas Islands and later went to Tahiti in the early 1840s, was Herman Melville. He returned to New England and wrote two books, *Typee* and *Omoo,* about his South Pacific exploits. They were the start of his literary career.

Along with the whalers came traders. Some of them sailed from island to island in search of sandalwood, pearls, shells, and the sea slugs known as *bêche-de-mer,* which they would trade for beads, cloth, whisky, and guns and then sell at high prices in China. Others established stores and became the catalysts for Western-style trading towns. The merchants brought more guns and alcohol to people who had never used them before. They also put pressure on local leaders to coin money, which introduced a cash economy where none had existed before. The effects of these two elements—alcohol and money—on the easygoing, communal traditions of the Pacific islanders were far-reaching.

Diseases brought by the Europeans and Americans were even more devastating. The Polynesians had little if any resistance to such Western ailments as measles, influenza, tuberculosis, pneumonia, typhoid fever, and venereal disease. Within a few years, epidemics had swept through many islands, killing the majority of their inhabitants. Captain Cook had estimated the population of Tahiti at some 200,000 when he first went there in 1769. It had dropped to fewer than 8,000 some 40 years later.

THE MISSIONARIES

The reports of the islands by Cook and Bougainville may have brought word of noble savages living in paradise to some people in Europe; to others, they heralded heathens to be rescued from hell. So while guns, alcohol, and diseases were destroying the islanders' bodies, a stream of missionaries arrived on the scene to save their souls.

The "opening" of the South Pacific coincided with a fundamentalist religious revival in England, and it wasn't long before the London Missionary Society (LMS) was on the scene in Tahiti. Its first missionaries, who arrived in the LMS ship *Duff* in 1797, were the first Protestant missionaries to leave England for a foreign country. The LMS chose Tahiti because there "the difficulties were least."

With its belief in a supreme being, Christianity—albeit puritanical—was easy for the Polynesians to accept, and they converted in vast numbers at the urging of missionaries who flooded the islands. The missionaries demanded that all tikis, which they saw as idols, be destroyed, the lasting result being that most Polynesian tikis carved for the tourist souvenir trade today resemble those of New Zealand, where the Anglican missionaries were less demanding than their fundamentalist counterparts in the islands. They also insisted that the heathen marae be torn down. Many have been restored, however, and can be visited in the islands today.

Roman Catholic missionaries made less puritanical progress in Tahiti after the French took over there in the early 1840s, but for the most part the South Pacific was the domain of the Protestants. The LMS extended its influence west through the Cook Islands and the Samoas, and the Wesleyans had luck in Tonga. Of the Non-French Polynesian islands, only New Zealand did not become a bastion of puritanism. Today, thanks to those early missionaries, most sidewalks still are rolled up on Sunday throughout the islands.

Melanesia was a different story. The old religions, with their beliefs in many spirits and the worship of ancestors, died hard. So did cannibalism in many places. When John Williams, the LMS missionary who built ships, discovered islands, and spread the word from Tahiti west, tried to land on Erromango in the New Hebrides (now Vanuatu) in November 1839, he was promptly beaten to death. His corpse was stripped and hauled off into the bush. There is no evidence to confirm the story, but it is widely believed that the Erromangans made a meal of him.

Christianity finally caught on in Melanesia in the late 19th century and early 20th century, and today it's firmly established in Westernized areas. Walter Lini, the prime minister of Vanuatu, is an Anglican minister, and the clergy carry significant political power in Solomon Islands. However, there are still many Melanesian islands where the people have been reluctant to accept Christianity—or for that matter any Western ways other than T-shirts and shower sandals.

LATER MIGRATIONS

Perhaps one reason the Melanesians were suspicious of Europeans was the widespread practice of "blackbirding," or slave trading, that sprang up to satisfy the need for cheap labor on the cotton, sugar, and copra plantations that were established throughout the islands and in Australia's Queensland colony during the mid-1800s. Notorious slave traders, such as the infamous Bully Hayes, went into the islands and brought back thousands of Melanesian men to work the plantations. Erromanga was one of the hardest hit, and it has been the slowest to accept Western customs. The only remote benefit of "blackbirding" was that it spread Pidgin English throughout the area. For the first time, Melanesians had a lingua franca through which to communicate across their multitude of linguistic barriers.

There is an old story about a South Pacific planter who offered an islander a job on his copra plantation. Copra is dried coconut meat, from which oil is pressed for use in soaps, cosmetics, and other products; extraction of the meat requires hours of back-breaking labor for very low wages.

"Let me get this straight," said the islander, who was sitting against a palm beside the lagoon. A pile of fruit from the nearby trees rested beside him on one side, a line of freshly caught fish on the other. "You want me to break my back for you for 30 years, after which you will pay me a pension so I can spend the rest of my life leaning against this palm, eating my fruit, and fishing in the lagoon. I may be uncivilized, but I am not stupid."

The planters in Tahiti already knew that the Polynesians felt this way about the necessity of Western-style employment, and the Melanesians brought by the "blackbirders" to work Tahiti's only cotton plantation proved no more enthusiastic. Accordingly, Chinese indentured laborers were brought to Tahiti in the 1860s. When the plantation failed, some of them stayed and became farmers and merchants. Their descendants now form the merchant class of French Polynesia.

The same thing happened in Fiji, where large sugar plantations were developed in the late 1800s. In the absence of a willing local labor force, workers were imported from India. Again, many stayed behind, and today almost half of Fiji's more than 700,000 citizens and the overwhelming majority of its merchants and business leaders are of Indian descent.

Other workers, especially Tonkinese from French Indochina (now Vietnam), were later imported to New Caledonia after nickel was discovered there, and to the New Hebrides to work the large plantations founded by French settlers. Most of these were later repatriated, but there remain a significant number of Vietnamese in New Caldeonia and Vanuatu. Bloody Mary, James A. Michener's infamous character in *Tales of the South Pacific,* was a Tonkinese.

COLONIALISM

Although Captain Cook laid claim to many islands, with the exceptions of much larger Australia and New Zealand, Britain was reluctant to take on such far-flung colonies. Accordingly, colonialism was not a significant factor in the South Pacific islands until the late 19th century. The one exception was France's declaring a protectorate over Tahiti in 1842.

That changed, however, when imperial Germany came to the scene and colonized the northern half of New Guinea and the western islands of Samoa. Britain then took over the southern half of New Guinea (which was known as Papua) and all of Fiji and Solomon Islands, entered into a joint condominium government with France over the New Hebrides, and agreed to protect the Kingdom of Tonga from takeover by another foreign power. France moved into New Caledonia, and the United States stepped into the eastern Samoan islands, which became known as American Samoa. The Cook Islands were claimed by Britain but almost immediately were included within the boundaries of newly independent New Zealand. Within a period of 30 years, every South Pacific island group except Tonga became a colony.

Germany was stripped of its colonies after World War I, with Australia taking over in New Guinea and New Zealand gaining Western Samoa. Otherwise, the colonial structure remained the same politically until the 1960s.

Economically, the islands came under the sphere of Australia and, to a somewhat lesser extent, New Zealand. Large Australian companies, such as Burns Philp and Carpenters, built up trading and shipping empires based on the exchange of retail goods for copra and other local produce, and Australian and New Zealand banks came to dominate finance in most islands outside the French and American territories.

WORLD WARS I & II

Thousands of Pacific islanders went off to fight with their colonial rulers during World War I. With two exceptions, however, the islands themselves escaped action.

In the first, a small German naval force under Admiral von Spee sped across the Pacific during 1915, sinking Allied merchant ships and shelling the town of Papeete.

Two years later, the colorful Count von Luckner brought his German raider *Seeadler* (Sea Eagle), a converted American windjammer, into the Pacific to hunt for merchant prey. In need of water after 3 months's prowling, which netted only three small sailing vessels, von Luckner put into Mopelia atoll in the remote northern Cook

Islands. While there, a sudden tidal wave swept the *Seeadler* on the reef, tearing out its bottom. Outfitting one of the ship's launches, von Luckner and five heavily armed crewmen set out for Rarotonga to steal another ship. He could have captured the town of Avarua but steered away when he saw a ship in port (in reality it was a wreck sitting upright on the reef). He then headed for Fiji, where he landed on Wakaya. When an alert Fijian constable became suspicious, the colonial authorities sent one armed policeman and five unarmed constables in a small cattle trading boat to investigate. Thinking they faced a superior force, von Luckner unwittingly surrendered.

The South Pacific suddenly emerged from its backwater status and leaped onto the front pages during World War II. Within weeks after the Japanese bombed Pearl Harbor and launched the Pacific war in December 1941, they began a drive toward Australia and New Zealand. The avenue they chose ran through New Guinea and Solomon Islands. They advanced quickly to Rabaul on New Britain, where they set up a major command base, and on to the north shore of New Guinea; from there they drove over the Owen Stanley Range toward Port Moresby, the capital of what is today Papua New Guinea but which then was a trust territory administered by Australia. The Australians fought them every inch of the way in a battle that seesawed back and forth along the Kokoda Trail. The Japanese came within sight of Port Moresby, but that was all.

They also sent an invasion force by sea around the eastern end of Papua New Guinea toward Port Moresby. The Allies intercepted them on May 8, 1942. The ensuing Battle of the Coral Sea was the first engagement between naval forces in which none of the ships ever came within sight of the enemy: The entire battle was fought in the air between the respective naval air forces. When the smoke cleared, both sides had suffered tremendous damage to their ships and the battle essentially was a draw. The Japanese, however, gave up their invasion plans and were never able to repair the damage done to their air forces.

Turning eastward, the Japanese captured Solomon Islands and in July 1942 began constructing an airfield on Guadalcanal, which would put them within bombing range of U.S. bases being built in the New Hebrides. The U.S. Marines invaded Guadalcanal and nearby Tulagi on August 8, and one bloody jungle skirmish and sea battle after another took place during the next 6 months. By February 1943, Guadalcanal was entirely in U.S. hands. The Japanese advance in the southwestern Pacific had been stopped, and the stage was soon set for the counteroffensive that inched its way northward along "The Slot" through the Solomons and reached Bougainville as the war ended.

Although the South Pacific fighting took place only in Papua New Guinea and Solomon Islands, many other islands played significant supporting roles. The main Allied command base was at Nouméa in New Caledonia. Major forward bases were built on Santo and at Port Vila in the New Hebrides prior to the Guadalcanal campaign, and Guadalcanal itself was turned into a small city after the battle there was won.

Airstrips and training bases were built all over the South Pacific. Out-of-the-way islands like Bora Bora and Aitutaki became refueling stops on transpacific flights, and the Samoas and Fiji were invaded by thousands of U.S. Marines and GIs preparing for the fighting farther west and north. Entire communities with modern infrastructures were built in weeks, only to be abandoned almost overnight when the war ended.

Never before had the South Pacific been exposed to so many people from overseas, and the effect on the islanders was profound. The profusion of new things that arrived on their islands, and the wages paid them for working on the Allied bases, brought a wave of Western influence. In some places, especially in Melanesia, the experience was so overwhelming that some local people started "cargo cults" and began worshiping Americans or the airplanes with which they brought mana from heaven. Many of their islands for the first time had air links to the outside world (many of the airfields built during the war are still in use today).

Another legacy was left behind when the soldiers, sailors, and marines went home: thousands of half-caste children.

5. THE ISLANDS TODAY

The travel posters with idyllic scenes of beaches and palm trees notwithstanding, the South Pacific today is much more than a tourist's heaven. Its small nations and territories have many of the same problems faced by developing countries everywhere, but they are also fortunate in many respects. The climate and the soil on most islands are generous, and with a communal family system intact in most places, hunger and homelessness are virtually nonexistent. Some of the islands, especially in Melanesia, hold vast mineral wealth that is just beginning to be discovered and exploited.

Perhaps the greatest resource of the South Pacific is the islanders themselves. They have a strong sense of tradition, and although they face difficulties, they are making major efforts to keep the best of the old while emerging into the modern, developed world.

I have found that most Pacific islanders are innately friendly and hospitable. They also are reserved and shy around strangers, of whom they have seen many. What seems like disinterest on their part will quickly melt if you smile. They usually will reward your cheerful greeting with an enormous grin.

In other words, your ticket to paradise is a smile.

GOVERNMENTS

Colonialism began to crumble in the South Pacific when New Zealand granted independence to Western Samoa in 1962 and 3 years later gave complete local autonomy to the Cook Islands. Fiji became independent of Great Britain in 1970, Britain left Solomon Islands in 1978, and in 1980 Britain and France gave up their condominium government in the New Hebrides, which became the independent Republic of Vanuatu.

Except Fiji, which as we went to press was working on a new constitution, all of these young nations have governments based on the Westminster parliamentary system, with wrinkles tailored to fit the traditions of their citizenries. Almost everywhere there is a council of chiefs or village "head men" to advise the modern-style governments on custom and tradition. Local governments are very strong in Melanesia, where there has always been a tradition of making decisions by consensus at the village level. In Polynesia and Fiji, where powerful chiefs often ruled by heredity, the national governments tend to be more centralized, and strong individuals (not to be confused with despots) have been at the helm of many of them. Assuming Fiji develops a republican legislature, national governments are democratic to one extent or another, and elections in the small countries, where everyone seems to know everyone else, often are hard-fought and sometimes bitter. Usually the victors take office and the vanquished keep on grouching until the polls open again. The bloodless military coup of May 1987 in Fiji, which overthrew that country's first Indian-dominated government, was a shock to observers, since it was so diametrically opposed to this democratic tradition.

Of the old colonial powers, only the United States and France remain. American Samoans have shown great reluctance to push for independence for several reasons, the major of them being that they are eligible for U.S. passports and most U.S. federal-aid programs. This means that the U.S. government supplies more than half of their own government's expenditures. The infrastructure in American Samoa—from

IMPRESSIONS

Sentimentalists who moan against natives improving their diet with refrigerators and can openers—"Why, they live on Chinese bread, Australian beef and American pork and beans"—could complain with equal logic that dear old ladies in Boston no longer dip tallow candles because they prefer electricity.

—JAMES A. MICHENER, 1951

schools to roads—is relatively advanced for this reason. A big government payroll and the busy tuna canneries at Pago Pago have given the American Samoans a standard of living that is matched in the South Pacific only in the French territories. Except for the amount of federal assistance, which is determined in Washington, they have almost complete say over their domestic affairs.

The role of France in New Caledonia and French Polynesia is another matter.

THE NUCLEAR-FREE MOVEMENT

The biggest regional issue in the 1990s is one left over from the 1980s: the question of nuclear arms and power. A nuclear-free movement swept the region, and the heads of the independent governments, including those of New Zealand and Australia, met in Rarotonga in 1985 and drafted a treaty calling for the South Pacific to become a nuclear-free zone.

The movement has directed some of its efforts at keeping nuclear-powered or nuclear-armed warships out of South Pacific ports, but at least an equal effort has been aimed at France. Since 1966, France has tested its nuclear weapons—first in the air, now underground—in the Tuamotu Archipelago some 700 miles southeast of Tahiti. These tests are a continuing sore point for the nearby nations. The issue came to the world's attention in 1985, when French secret agents sank the *Rainbow Warrior,* flagship of the protest group Greenpeace, in Auckland, New Zealand. Greenpeace was preparing the *Rainbow Warrior* for a protest voyage to Moruroa when the French agents struck.

Another Greenpeace target in the early 1990s has been U.S. plans to destroy its stockpile of chemical weapons at Johnston Atoll south of Hawaii. In order to help defuse that issue, Pres. George Bush met in Honolulu in 1990 with the heads of government of most Pacific island states. The first such summit conference of its kind, it demonstrated a growing awareness on the part of the U.S. government of the needs and concerns of the islanders.

LAND RIGHTS & ENVIRONMENT

To compound France's problems, throughout the 1980s many in the Melanesian minority in New Caledonia clamored for independence for their nickel-rich islands. Violence erupted, but in 1988 both sides agreed to a 10-year hiatus during which they will work together to achieve a solution. When I was there recently, peace had returned to the territory, and a building boom was in progress in Nouméa.

Even in Tahiti, a vocal minority has been promoting total local autonomy, if not complete independence, from France. Although not directly related to the independence sentiments, a riot that destroyed part of Papeete in 1987 sprang from a labor dispute between Tahitian and French dockworkers. (You may find that older Tahitians warm to you when they discover that you are not French.)

Underlying these independence movements and many other political issues in the South Pacific is the fundamental question of land rights. Simply stated, there just isn't much land in the islands, and the indigenous peoples want to keep it for themselves and to maintain their customary ownership of it. Vanuatu abolished freehold property when it became independent in 1980 and returned all land to its customary owners. The prospect of Indians rewriting the laws that protect Fijian land rights prompted most Fijians to strongly support the Pro-Fijian coups. Violence broke out on the Papua New Guinea island of Bougainville, adjacent to Solomon Islands, during 1989 because the customary landowners wanted a bigger share of the profits from the island's huge copper mine.

Just as they are protective of their land, the islanders also are concerned about the surrounding ocean. The Pacific island states have been staunch opponents of drift-net fishing, which they see not only as killing porpoises and other sea life unnecessarily but as stripping them of a vital, if not their only, significant resource. Many islanders also are very active in promoting environmental efforts to reduce pollution of the oceans. Also, the greenhouse effect is of no little concern since an increase in world temperatures could raise the level of the sea by melting the polar ice caps; with much of their land barely above water as it is, this result could be disastrous for many low-lying islands.

THE PACIFIC WAY

In addition to the regional issues, there are local problems to be solved. Fiji still must adopt a constitution and hold elections, probably in mid-1992. New Caledonia has much work to do prior to its independence referendum in 1998. French Polynesia has its own independence movement and a huge territorial debt which must be addressed. More and more Tongans are campaigning for increased accountability if not outright democracy, from their king and his government. Western Samoa confronts serious economic problems.

Although they once were fierce warriors and even today excel on the rugby field, violence has not been the islanders' preferred choice of problem solving, especially since the coming of Christianity. Instead, they lean to discussion, compromise, and consensus, often during all-night kava-drinking sessions. It's a method they call "The Pacific Way." My recent travels through the region have revealed that by and large, The Pacific Way is working. As a result, the South Pacific overall is a peaceful and thoroughly enchanting place to visit.

6. RECOMMENDED BOOKS

Rather than list the hundreds of books about the South Pacific, I have picked some of the best that are likely to be readily available in the United States and Canada, either in bookstores or at your local library. Many other tomes, especially scholarly works, have been published in Australia, New Zealand, and the islands themselves (notably by the University of the South Pacific in Suva, Fiji, and by Vava'u Press in Tonga). Libraries in those countries may have much wider South Pacific selections than do their counterparts in North America.

A number of out-of-print island classics have been reissued in paperback by Mutual Publishing Company, a small Hawaii firm. If your bookseller doesn't stock them, Mutual's address is 2055 North King Street, Honolulu, HI 96819 (tel. 808/924-7732). In some cases, I give a book's original publisher and date of publication followed by the recent Mutual edition and its date.

I have divided my recommended books into five categories: general, history and politics, people and cultures, travel, and fiction.

GENERAL

The National Geographic Society's *The Isles of the South Pacific,* by Maurice Shadbolt and Olaf Ruhen (1971) is somewhat out-of-date but still has lovely color photographs. The writing is in the National Geo's usual style. *Island Realm* by Ian Todd (Angus & Robertson, 1974) is another dated but still colorful coffee-table book with a short description of each island group. *Living Corals* by Douglas Faulkner and Richard Chesher (Clarkson N. Potter, 1979) shows in living color what you will see underwater.

For reference purposes, *The South Pacific: An Introduction* by Ron Crocombe (University of the South Pacific, 1989) provides a wealth of political and economic data, as does *Pacific Islands Yearbook* (John Carter, editor; Pacific Publications, 1989); both are published in Sydney, Australia.

If you have time to read only one South Pacific book, *The Lure of Tahiti* (Mutual, 1986) should be it. Editor A. Grove Day includes 18 short stories, excerpts, and essays; there is a little here from all the great fiction writers mentioned below, plus selections from Captains Cook, Bougainville, and Bligh. Although it deals only with the famous Island of Love, this book will give you in one read an understanding of the lure not just of Tahiti but of the entire South Pacific.

HISTORY & POLITICS

Although several of the early English and French explorers published accounts of their exploits, *The Journals of Captain James Cook* stand out as the most exhaustive and evenhanded. Edited by J. C. Beaglehole, they were published in three volumes (one for each voyage) by Cambridge University in 1955, 1961, and 1967. The 3,000-plus pages make fascinating if somewhat heavy-duty reading. A. Grenfell Price edited many of Cook's key passages and provides short transitional explanations in *The Explorations of Captain James Cook in the Pacific* (Dover, 1971). Lynne Withey gives a readable, modern-prose account in *Voyages of Discovery: Captain Cook and the Exploration of the Pacific* (Morrow, 1987).

The explorers' visits and their consequences are the subject of Alan Moorehead's *The Fatal Impact: The Invasion of the South Pacific, 1767-1840*. About half this book, which is loaded with original sketches and paintings of the time, is devoted to what happened to Tahiti and the Tahitians; the rest, to Australia and the Antarctic.

Three other very readable books trace Tahiti's postdiscovery history. *Tahiti: Island of Love* by Robert Langdon (Pacific Publications, 1979) takes the island's story up to 1977. *Tahiti: A Paradise Lost* by David Howarth (Penquin, 1985) more thoroughly covers the same early ground as Langdon but stops with France's taking possession in 1842. Edward Dodd's *The Rape of Tahiti* (Dodd, Mead, 1983) covers the island from prehistory to 1900. Sympathetic to the Tahitians, the late Mr. Dodd is at his best when recounting Queen Pomare's woes at the time of France's acquisition of her realm.

No history of the South Pacific would be complete without an examination of the Europeans who found their way there and left their mark, especially in letters. *Mad About Islands* by A. Grove Day (Mutual, 1987) follows the island exploits of literary figures Herman Melville, Robert Louis Stevenson, Jack London, and W. Somerset Maugham. Also included are Charles Nordhoff and James Norman Hall, coauthors of the so-called "Bounty Trilogy" and other works about the islands (see "Fiction," below). *In Search of Paradise* by Paul L. Briand (Mutual, 1987) recounts the Nordhoff and Hall story in detail. *A Dream of Islands* by Gavan Dawes (Norton, 1980) tells of the missionary John Williams as well as of Melville, Stevenson, and painter Paul Gauguin.

The great South Pacific battles of World War II are examined by historian Samuel Elliott Morrison in his *The Two-Ocean War* (Little, Brown, 1961; Ballantine, 1972).

For descriptions of the islands during the 1950s, see Eugene Burdick's *The Blue of Capricorn* (Houghton Mifflin, 1961; Mutual, 1986). Better known as coauthor of *The Ugly American,* Burdick includes several short stories among his essays. In *Tales from Paradise* (BBC Publications, 1986), June Knox-Mawer tells charming yarns of the final years of British rule in Fiji and the Solomons, as seen by a colonial official's wife.

Former *New York Times* reporter Robert Turnbull traveled the islands in the 1970s and reported his findings in *Tin Roofs and Palm Trees* (University of Washington Press, 1977). Scott L. Malcolmson did the same in the late 1980s; his somewhat opinionated views of the political situations in Fiji, New Caledonia, and French Polynesia are in *Tuturani: A Political Journey in the Pacific Islands* (Poseidon, 1990).

For a political document, order a copy of *Problems in Paradise: United States Interests in the South Pacific* (U.S. House of Representatives, 1990) from the U.S. Government Printing Office in Washington, D.C. It's an excellent—even readable—report by a special congressional delegation that toured the islands for 12 days in 1989.

PEOPLES & CULTURES

Peter Bellwood's *The Polynesians: Prehistory of an Island People* (Thames & Hudson, 1987) is valuable both for its examination of the Polynesians' history before the coming of Europeans and its explanation of the various island cultures that existed at that time. The book contains sketches of island life by the early explorers and photographs of ancient handcrafts that have been unearthed or preserved.

To find out how the islanders managed to sail great distances over open ocean without modern navigation tools, check out Prof. David Lewis's *We, the Navigators* (University of Hawaii, 1972).

Many scholarly treatises have been written about the Polynesian and Melanesian ways of life, particularly under the sponsorship of the University of the South Pacific in Fiji, the University of Hawaii, and the Bernice P. Bishop Museum in Honolulu. The most interesting and readable accounts, however, are by persons who lived among the islanders and then wrote about it.

In the most famous, *Coming of Age in Samoa* (1928), Margaret Mead tells of her year studying promiscuous adolescent girls in the Manu'a islands of American Samoa. The book created quite a stir when it was published in a more modest time than the present. Mrs. Mead's interpretation of Samoan sex customs were taken to task by New Zealander Derek Freeman in *Margaret Mead and Samoa: The Making and Unmaking of an Anthropological Myth* (1983).

Bengt Danielsson, a Swedish anthropologist who has lived in Tahiti since arriving there on Thor Heyerdahl's *Kon Tiki* raft in 1947, paints a much broader picture of Polynesian sexuality in *Love in the South Seas* (Mutual, 1986). He finds that some of the old ways have gone, others are still hanging on.

Heyerdahl tells his tale and explains his theory of Polynesian migration (since debunked) in *Kon Tiki* (Rand McNally, 1950; translated by F. K. Lyon). In 1936, Heyerdahl and wife, Liv, lived for a year in the Marquesas. The resulting book, *Fatu-Hiva: Back to Nature* (Doubleday, 1975), provides an in-depth look at Marquesan life at the time.

Lastly, two American writers give unscholarly but thoroughly entertaining accounts of Polynesian island life. Robert Dean Frisbie spent several years as a trader in the Cook Islands and tells about it in his charming *The Book of Puka-Puka* (1928; Mutual, 1986). The other, Robert Lee Eskridge, spent a year on Mangareva in French Polynesia; his charming book is appropriately titled *Manga Reva* (Bobbs-Merrill, 1931; Mutual, 1986).

TRAVEL

Although he lived in Western Samoa for several years, Robert Louis Stevenson wrote very little fiction about the South Pacific. He was, however, a prolific author of articles and letters about his travels and events leading up to Germany's acquisition of the islands in 1890. *In the South Seas* (1901) is the major collection of his essays and letters. *Island Landfalls* (Cannongate, 1987) is a recent compilation which also includes three Stevenson short stories with South Seas settings: "The Bottle Imp," "The Isle of Voices," and "The Beach at Falesà."

Jack London sailed the islands extensively in his yacht, *Snark*, and wrote about it in *Cruise of the Snark* (1911). London and his wife sold the boat in Solomon Islands after they both became too ill to continue what was to be an around-the-world voyage.

Sir David Attenborough, who later produced the popular television series "Life on Earth," traveled to Papua New Guinea, Vanuatu, Fiji, and Tonga in the late 1950s in order to film, among other things, the Pentecost land divers and Tongan Queen Salote's royal kava ceremony. Sir David informingly tells of his trips in *Journeys to the Past* (Penguin, 1983).

John Dyson rode interisland trading boats throughout the South Pacific and wrote about the experiences in *The South Seas Dream* (Little, Brown, 1982). It's an entertaining and fairly recent account of the islands and their more colorful inhabitants. Although I mentioned it under the "History and Politics" category above, Scott Malcolmson's *Tuturani: A Political Journal in the Pacific Islands* (Poseidon, 1990) in many respects also qualifies as a travel book.

Few travel books dedicated to particular island countries are readily available outside the South Pacific. One of the best is Ronald Wright's enjoyable *On Fiji Islands* (Penguin, 1986). It's packed with insights about the character of the Fijians and Indians.

I mention in the chapters that follow the best language phrasebooks available in each island country. If you want to get a head start on Fijian, Tongan, Samoan, Tahitian, and pidgin, try to find a copy of Prof. Charles Hamblin's *Languages of Asia and the Pacific: A Traveler's Phrasebook* (Angus & Robertson, 1984). Words in each language are listed side by side.

FICTION

Starting with Herman Melville's *Typee* (1846) and *Omoo* (1847)—semifictional accounts of his adventures in the Marquesas and Tahiti, respectively—the South Pacific has spawned a wealth of fiction. Although it does not tell of the islands, much of Melville's classic *Moby Dick* (1851) takes place in the South Pacific Ocean.

After Melville came Julien Viaud, a French naval officer who fell in love with a Tahitian woman during a short sojourn in Tahiti. Writing under the pen name Pierre Loti, his *The Marriage of Loti* (1880; KPI, 1986) is a classic tale of lost love between a Polynesian and a European.

In addition to his nonfiction *Cruise of the Snark,* Jack London produced many short stories which were collected in *South Sea Tales* (1911; Mutual, 1985) and *A Son of the Sun* (1912; reprinted as *Captain David Grieff* by Mutual, 1985). The yarns in the former are set primarily in the Solomons near the end of those islands' headhunter days. In the latter, London created Capt. David Grieff, an interisland schooner skipper who was later to feature in the television series, "Adventures in Paradise."

W. Somerset Maugham's *The Moon and Sixpence* (1919) is a fictional account of the life of Paul Gauguin. Maugham changed the name to Charles Strickland and made the painter English instead of French. (Gauguin's own novel, *Noa Noa,* was published in English in 1928, long after his death.) Maugham also produced a volume of South Pacific short stories, *The Trembling of a Leaf* (1921; Mutual, 1985). The most famous is "Rain," the tragic story of prostitute Sadie Thompson and the fundamentalist missionary she led astray in American Samoa. Maugham's "The Fall of Edward Bernard" is my personal favorite; it's the story of a Chicagoan who forsakes love and fortune back home for "beauty, truth, and goodness" in Tahiti.

Next on the scene were the aforementioned Charles Nordhoff and James Norman Hall (more about them in Chapters 3 and 4). Together they wrote the most famous of all South Pacific novels, *Mutiny on the Bounty* (1932). They immediately followed that enormous success with two other novels: *Men Against the Sea* (1934), based on Bligh's epic longboat voyage after the mutiny; and *Pitcairn's Island* (1935), about the mutineers' sorry demise on their remote hideaway.

Nordhoff and Hall later wrote *The Hurricane* (1936), a novel which has been made into two movies of the same title; the latest version (1977) starred Mia Farrow. Hall alone wrote *The Forgotten One* (Mutual, 1986), a collection of short stories and essays.

The second most famous South Pacific novel appeared just after World War II: James A. Michener's *Tales of the South Pacific* (MacMillan, 1947). A U.S. Navy historian, Michener spent much of the war on Espíritu Santo in the New Hebrides (now Vanuatu), which is the setting for most of the book. Rodgers and Hammerstein turned the novel into *South Pacific,* one of the most successful Broadway plays ever, and a blockbuster movie of the same name.

Michener toured the islands a few years later and wrote *Return to Paradise* (Random House, 1951), a collection of essays and short stories. The essays are particularly valuable since they describe the islands as they were after World War II but before large numbers of tourists began to arrive via jet aircraft; in other words, near the end of the region's backwater, beachcomber days. His piece on Fiji accurately predicts the Fijian-Indian problems that have plagued that country.

CHAPTER 2

PLANNING A TRIP TO THE SOUTH PACIFIC

Since the South Pacific can hold some surprises, wise planning is essential to get the most out of your time and money spent in this vast and varied modern paradise.

This book covers nine small countries, each of them different, each with its own set of details. They all have their own sources of information, entry requirements, currencies, governments, Customs, laws, internal transportation, styles of accommodation, and food. This chapter tells you how to plan a trip to the South Pacific islands in general. It augments, but is not a substitute for, the information contained in the individual chapters that follow.

1. INFORMATION, ENTRY REQUIREMENTS & MONEY

SOURCES OF INFORMATION

For general information about the South Pacific, contact the **Pacific Asia Travel Association (PATA),** 1 Montgomery Street, West Tower, Suite 1750, San Francisco, CA 94104 (tel. 415/986-4646). PATA's South Pacific Regional Office, 80 William Street, Suite 203, Level 2, Woolloomooloo, NSW 2011, Australia (tel. 02/332-3599), directly handles the island countries.

The U.S. Department of State maintains a 24-hour **Travel Advisory** (tel. 202/647-5225) to keep you abreast of political or other problems throughout the world.

See the "Information, Entry Requirements & Money" sections in the individual chapters for the address of each country's tourist information office.

ENTRY REQUIREMENTS

All South Pacific countries require new arrivals to have a **passport** that will be valid for the duration of the visit, an onward or round-trip airline ticket, and sufficient funds to pay for their stay. Your passport should be valid for 6 months beyond the date you expect to return home. Since some immigration departments don't look kindly upon young backpackers, credit cards may not be enough to meet the "sufficient funds" requirement in all countries. If you fit this category of traveler, carry sufficient traveler's checks.

Except for Australians entering the French territories, advance **visas** generally are not required for stays of 30 days or less (France no longer requires New Zealanders to have visas before arriving in Tahiti and New Caledonia). Extensions of up to 3 months usually are granted to visitors who still have their round-trip tickets and enough money—and who behave themselves.

If you fall in love with (or in) the South Pacific and start thinking about emigrating there, think some more. It's not impossible, but these small countries make it very difficult for Westerners to live there on a permanent basis. Write to each country's immigration department for its stringent regulations. Foreign ownership of land is equally restricted—not impossible, but difficult.

Valid home country **driver's licenses** are recognized throughout the South Pacific; however, you will need to present yours in the Cook Islands and Tonga in order to get a local license. No new test will be administered; it's just a way for these two countries to raise a little revenue. I have never found an international driver's license to be useful.

MONEY

CURRENCIES

American Samoa uses U.S. dollars. In the Cook Islands, local and New Zealand dollars circulate side by side. French Polynesia and New Caledonia both use the French Pacific franc, the value of which is pegged directly to the regular French franc. Otherwise, each South Pacific country has its own currency. The local Cook Islands money and the currencies of Western Samoa, Tonga, Vanuatu, and Solomon Islands are virtually worthless outside those countries; you may also have difficulty changing French Pacific francs once you leave Tahiti or Nouméa. See the specific chapters for details.

U.S., Australian, and New Zealand dollars are accepted widely in the islands, and the local banks will change most other major currencies. Accordingly, don't bother changing Australian, New Zealand, Canadian, British, German, French, Swiss, or any other major currency before leaving home.

TRAVELER'S CHECKS

Banks in all the main towns and most major hotels, resorts, restaurants, and car-rental firms accept American Express, Thomas Cook, VISA, Bank of America, Citicorp, and MasterCard traveler's checks. You won't necessarily be able to cash them on many outer islands with limited, if any, banking facilities. American Express traveler's checks are handy in New Caledonia, where the company's local representative will cash them without charging the hefty fee extracted by the local banks.

CREDIT CARDS

In general, most hotels, car-rental companies, and many restaurants and large shops accept **American Express, VISA,** and **MasterCard,** with **Diners Club** present but not as widespread. In Solomon Islands, only American Express and MasterCard are accepted. Always ask first, and when you're away from the main towns, don't count on putting anything on plastic.

Holders of VISA and MasterCard can get cash advances at Westpac Bank and ANZ Bank. Between them, these two Australian corporations have offices in every South Pacific country except Tonga and the Samoas. The American Express agents in Tahiti, Fiji, and New Caledonia will cash card members' personal checks.

WHAT WILL IT COST?

There is a common misconception that the South Pacific is a terribly expensive place to visit. Granted, it costs a fair sum to cross the thousands of miles of ocean to get there from North America or Europe, but basically this reputation is a bum rap. Although some resorts in French Polynesia and Fiji can set a couple back more than $500 a day (much more in a few cases), and a beer in some Tahitian or New Caledonian nightclubs can run as much as $10, cost-conscious travelers can get excellent value throughout the islands.

The South Pacific has a wide range of hotels and restaurants; accordingly, how much you spend a day depends both on where you go and on the standard of living you desire. The chapters that follow contain precise prices for each country and territory. As you will see, prices vary substantially from island to island. If cost is a factor, compare this information before deciding which islands to visit.

A note for backpackers: The South Pacific is more expensive than, say, Southeast Asia. On the other hand, most island countries now have hostels, campgrounds, and hotels with dormitories where a bunk or tent site can be had most places for $5 to $10 (in French Polynesia the price jumps to about $15). Some of these establishments tend to go up and down in cleanliness and friendliness. On the other hand, there aren't many of them (they are numerous in Fiji, less so elsewhere). Once you get on this narrow "trail" through the islands and start talking to your fellow backpackers, you will quickly find out which places are in, which are out.

Prices in this book are given in local currency with the U.S. dollar equivalent in parentheses, based on the rate of exchange at the time of writing. **The $ sign used alone denotes U.S. dollars.**

The **price ranges** for restaurants include the costs of appetizers and main courses. As a general rule, doubling the cost of a main course will yield the price of a full meal.

Inflation is as much a fact of life in the South Pacific as it is anywhere else, if not more so. The island countries import much of what is consumed by the local tourist industry and all of their petroleum, so the price of everything depends largely on both the exchange value of the local currency and the price of crude oil. While the prices you find may vary from those given in this book, the price ranges should remain intact. If a hotel or restaurant is in the expensive range today, have no fear but that it will be there tomorrow.

2. WHEN TO GO — CLIMATE, HOLIDAYS & EVENTS

CLIMATE

The South Pacific islands covered in this book lie within the tropics. Compared to the pronounced winters and summers of the temperate zones, there is little variation from one island group to the next: They are warm and humid all year. Local residents, however, recognize two distinct seasons, which may bear on when you choose to visit.

A somewhat cooler and more comfortable **dry season** occurs during the austral winter from May through October. The winter trade wind blows fairly steadily from the southeast during these months, bringing generally fine tropical weather throughout the area. Rain usually is limited to brief showers. Daytime high temperatures reach the delightful upper 70s to low 80s in French Polynesia, Samoa, Fiji, Vanuatu, and Solomon Islands, with early morning lows in the high 60s. Although there can be warmer periods, high temperatures usually stay in the high 60s or low 70s in Rarotonga, Tonga, and New Caledonia, which are farther away from the equator. Breezy wintertime nights can feel downright chilly in those islands.

November through April—the southern hemisphere's summer—is the warmer and more humid **wet season.** Daytime highs climb into the upper 80s throughout the islands, with nighttime lows about 70°F. Low-pressure troughs and tropical depressions can bring several days of rain at a time, but usually it falls during heavy showers followed by periods of very intense sunshine. This also is the hurricane season (they are known as "cyclones" in this part of the world). The big storms form east of Solomon Islands and usually roar off to the southeast toward Fiji and Tonga. They can be devastating and should never be taken lightly, but generally they move fast enough that their major effect on visitors is a day or two of heavy rain and wind. If you're caught in one, the hotels are experts on knowing what to do to ensure your safety.

Bear in mind that the higher the altitude, the lower the temperature. If you're going up in the mountains, be prepared for much cooler weather.

HOLIDAYS

The busiest tourist season in the South Pacific is the austral winter months of July and August. That's when Australians and New Zealanders head for the islands to escape the cold back home. It's also when residents of Tahiti and New Caledonia head off to their own outer islands in keeping with the traditional July-August holiday break in France.

There also are busy mini-seasons at school holiday time in Australia and New Zealand. These periods vary from one Australian state to another, but in general they are from the end of March through the middle of April, during 2 weeks in late May, 2 more weeks at the beginning of July, 2 more in the middle of September, and from mid-December until mid-January.

With a few exceptions, South Pacific hoteliers do not raise their rates during any of the busy periods.

Australians and New Zealanders normally stay at home on Christmas Day, so the week before Christmas is a good time to get a hotel reservation in the South Pacific. On the other hand, airline seats can be hard to come by, since thousands of islanders who live overseas fly home for the holidays.

SPECIAL EVENTS

The chapters of this book list each country's festivals and special events, which can change the entire nature of a visit to the South Pacific. The annual *Heiva I Tahiti* (or *Tiruai*) in French Polynesia, the King's Birthday in Tonga, and the week of Constitution Day in Rarotonga are just three examples, and every country has at least one such major celebration. These are the best times to see traditional dancing, arts, and sporting events. Be sure to make your reservations well in advance, however, for hotel rooms can be in short supply.

3. HEALTH & INSURANCE

HEALTH

Hospitals and clinics are widespread in the South Pacific, but the quality varies a great deal from place to place. You can get a broken bone set and a coral scrape tended, but treating more serious ailments likely will be beyond the capability of the local hospital. The only American-trained doctors regularly working in the South Pacific are at the Lyndon B. Johnson Tropical Medical Center in American Samoa, which also has one of the best pharmacies in the region.

Pharmacies are numerous, but their products likely will be from New Zealand,

Australia, or Europe and thus unfamiliar to most Americans and Canadians. Take an adequate supply of any prescription medications you may need, and carry them in your hand luggage. Ask your pharmacist for the generic names—not the brand names—of your medications, and keep these with your passport.

With the exception of malaria in Vanuatu and Solomon Islands, the South Pacific poses no major health problem for most travelers, and malaria usually can be prevented by prophylactic medication (see below). If you have a chronic condition, however, you should check with your doctor before visiting the islands.

Although seldom treated, **tap water** in most main towns is safe to drink (Apia and Honiara being notable exceptions). Many travelers suffer from a mild diarrhea often caused by eating too much fresh fruit, not necessarily by the water.

Among minor illnesses, the islands have the common cold and occasional outbreaks of influenza and conjunctivitus ("pinkeye"). I've had pinkeye twice during my recent visits; Sulfair (sulfacetamide sodium), a prescription eyedrop made in the United States, cleared it up in a few days.

Cuts, scratches, and all open sores should be treated promptly in the tropics. I always carry a tube of antibacterial ointment and a package of adhesive bandages such as Band-Aids.

Special precautions should be taken if you are traveling with children. See "Tips for the Disabled, Seniors, Singles & Families," below.

Vaccinations

The only shot required to enter the South Pacific countries is for yellow fever, and then only if you're coming from an infected area of South America or Africa. It's a good idea, however, to have your tetanus, typhoid fever, polio, and diphtheria vaccinations up-to-date.

MALARIA

Malaria is present in Vanuatu and Solomon Islands. It is caused by a blood parasite borne by mosquitoes. The early symptoms often mimic influenza or the common cold—aches, pains, a high temperature. Then comes a deep, shivering chill lasting from ½ hour to 2 hours, followed by a very high temperature and, often, vomiting and delirium. After 4 to 5 hours the patient begins to sweat profusely and the temperature falls. Similar attacks continue to occur at intervals of 2 to 3 days. Malaria is serious, and should be treated immediately.

Since strains of chloroquine-resistant malaria are present in both countries, the U.S. Public Health Service's Centers for Disease Control (CDC) in Atlanta, Georgia, recommend that you take Lariam (the trade name for mefloquine) on a regular basis if you plan to visit those countries. The pills are taken before you leave home, during your visit, and for 6 weeks afterward.

CDC also recommends that you take along a drug named Fansidar (pyrimethamine/sulfadoxine) just in case you come down with malaria while taking Lariam. Fansidar has been known to have lethal side effects, especially among people who are allergic to sulfa drugs, so use it only if you can't get medical attention right away.

Don't forget that children should take antimalarial medication, too.

Both Larium and Fansidar require a doctor's prescription, so consult your personal physician well in advance of leaving home.

DENGUE FEVER

The South Pacific islands also see occasional outbreaks of dengue fever, a mosquito-borne viral disease that in its early stages can be confused with malaria, influenza, or even the common cold. It usually starts with the sudden onset of high fever, excruciating frontal headache, and muscle and joint pain so severe that dengue also is known as "breakbone fever." Many victims also suffer nausea, vomiting, and anorexia, and most get a bruiselike rash which can spread from torso to arms, legs, and face. The symptoms usually go away within 7 to 10 days, but complete recovery can take several weeks or even months.

There is no vaccine to prevent dengue fever, and treatment is strictly for the symptoms, with heavy emphasis on drinking lots of fluids and replenishing vitamins. Aspirin is not recommended as a treatment for the aches and pains; take another form of painkiller.

Fortunately dengue is seldom fatal in adults, but you should take extra precautions to keep children from being bitten by mosquitoes.

If you develop a fever after returning home, be sure to tell your doctor that you recently were in a malaria or dengue area.

Insect Repellents

The best way to avoid both malaria and dengue fever is to avoid mosquitoes. Always wear long sleeves, trousers, shoes, socks, and a good insect repellent from dusk onward in Vanuatu and Solomon Islands. Insect repellent is available in the South Pacific shops, but I always take a good brand. The most effective skin repellents contain "deet" (N, N-diethyltoluamide).

Aerosol sprays containing a pesticide known as permethrin work to repel mosquitoes when applied to clothing. They are sold primarily in lawn and garden shops. Permanone Tick Repellent is one popular brand.

Remember that repellents can be removed by absorption, evaporation, rain, sweating, swimming, or wiping; they must be reapplied periodically.

I also keep a "mosquito coil" burning in my nonair-conditioned rooms at night. They are known in many places by the brand names "Fish" and "Rabbit" (I have found the Fish brand to work best). You can buy them in shops throughout the islands.

There is an active program throughout the South Pacific to prevent the spread of harmful insects, so local officials come aboard most arriving international flights and spray the cabin before anyone is allowed to disembark. The insecticide has been approved by the World Health Organization and is harmless to humans.

AIDS

As pointed out elsewhere in this book, sexual mores in the South Pacific are often quite different from those in Western countries. Sexual relations before marriage—heterosexual, homosexual, and bisexual—are more or less accepted behavior. Further, both male and female prostitution is common in the larger towns, such as Papeete and Suva. Because of these more relaxed sexual mores, and because the acquired immune deficiency syndrome (AIDS) virus has been detected in some of the South Pacific Islands, visitors are advised to exercise at least the same, if not greater, caution in choosing their sexual partners, and in practicing "safe sex," as they would at home.

INSURANCE

Many travelers buy insurance policies providing health and accident, trip cancellation, and lost-luggage protection. The coverage you need will depend on the extent of protection contained in your existing policies. Read them over carefully before purchasing additional insurance.

Some credit-card companies insure their customers against travel accidents if the tickets were purchased with their cards.

Many health insurance companies and health maintenance organizations provide coverage for illness or accidents overseas, but you may have to pay the foreign provider upfront and file for a reimbursement when you get home. You will need adequate receipts, so remember to collect them at the time of treatment. Some traveler's health insurance policies will pay the local provider directly, saving you this hassle.

Since many medical facilities in the South Pacific are not up to Western standards, consider a traveler's health policy providing evacuation to a major medical center in case of serious trouble. The costs can be enormous if you have to be evacuated by air ambulance.

Trip-cancellation insurance covers your loss if you have made nonrefundable deposits, bought airline tickets that provide no or partial refunds, or if you have paid for a charter flight and for some good reason can't make it. Ask if the policy also covers losses resulting from a company going bankrupt.

Lost-luggage insurance covers your loss over and above the limited amounts for which the airlines are responsible, and some policies provide instant payment so you can replace your missing items on the spot.

Your travel agent should know of a company that offers traveler's insurance. Here are some American companies:

Travel Assistance International, 1133 15th St. NW, Suite 400, Washington, DC 20005 (tel. 202/347-2025, or toll free 800/821-2828).

Travel Guard International, 1145 Clark St., Stevens Point, WI 54481-2980 (tel. 715/345-0505, or toll free 800/634-0644 in Wisconsin, 800/782-5151 in rest of U.S.).

Access America, 600 Third Ave., New York, NY 10016 (tel. 212/490-5345, or toll free 800/284-8300).

Health Care Abroad, 243 Church St., Vienna, VA 22180 (tel. 703/281-9500, or toll free 800/237-6615).

4. WHAT TO PACK

CLOTHING

People dress in so many different ways today that I am not about to tell anyone exactly what to take to the South Pacific. In general, the tropical weather and a lack of Laundromats dictate lightweight, easy-care clothing, which usually means cotton-polyester blends. I have a strong personal preference for all-cotton, especially in places where, or months when, the weather is hot and humid, even though it means paying a commercial laundry to keep them looking good. Most hotels have same-day laundry service; nevertheless, I take four sets of clothes.

Long sleeves—even sweaters—come in handy during the winter evenings (June through August) in the more southerly islands and at all times of the year if you're going into the mountains. I have found a lightweight nylon windbreaker to be useful on these occasions.

Evening dress almost everywhere calls for slacks and a tropical "aloha" shirt for men and either a dress or blouse with skirt or slacks for women. Not even the South Pacific's two gambling casinos, in Vanuatu and New Caledonia, require men to wear coats and ties. In other words, you won't need a large wardrobe.

Take along comfortable walking shoes (preferably canvas so they will dry fast), a pair of old tennis or running shoes (as a spare and for exploring the reefs), a pair of sandals, and a hat or visor to protect you from the midday sun. By the way, in the islands the words flip-flops, thongs, zories, jandals, slaps, beachcombers, and even "shoes" all refer to the rubber soles held on the feet by straps between two toes on each foot; they are worn almost everywhere in the islands and are what I mean by "sandals."

Topless sunbathing may be in vogue among the European women in French Polynesia and New Caledonia, but one of the first things the missionaries did in the early 19th century was to convince the South Pacific islanders that nakedness definitely is not next to godliness. This is especially true in the South Pacific "Bible Belt" countries of Tonga, Western Samoa, and American Samoa. In Tonga it is unlawful for men to appear shirtless in public (except at beaches where tourists gather), so you can imagine what they would do to a bare-breasted woman. There and in both Samoas you will see people swimming in what amounts to a full set of clothes.

My rule of thumb is to dress modestly when away from the beach or swimming pool. Demure sundresses are in order throughout the islands; skimpy halter tops are not. Shorts of reasonable length are acceptable on both men and women in the more visited areas of French Polynesia, the Cook Islands, Vanuatu, New Caledonia, and Solomon Islands. Wrap a sarong around your bikini bottoms elsewhere.

OTHER ITEMS

Remember, the tropical sun is always intense, even on seemingly overcast days, so act accordingly to avoid being burned. **Sunscreen** is not uniformly available in the islands—it's expensive where it is—so take a supply with you. **Sunglasses** are a must. I always pack a **folding umbrella;** your bottom parts will dry quickly enough, and it's much cooler than a raincoat.

Color-print **film** is available in all countries, and on some islands (especially Fiji and Vanuatu) is actually less expensive than in the United States. Color-slide film, however, is not readily available, so carry some with you. Most countries' duty-free allowance is 10 rolls.

Toiletries are available in all the main towns, usually in the super-economy size. You won't find any of those convenient trial-size bottles. Take a supply of any special brands—dandruff shampoo leaps to mind—with you. Don't forget your **prescription medications,** a few **Band-Aids,** a small tube of **antibacterial ointment,** and **insect repellent.**

I have found an inflatable **neck cushion** to be invaluable during long, overnight flights.

Eyeglasses are not easily replaced or repaired in most South Pacific countries, so bring spares.

Last but not least, put a **washcloth** in your bag.

READERS RECOMMEND

"We found Aqua Socks to be an invaluable addition to our luggage. They're great for walking on reefs, rocky beaches, snorkeling when not wearing fins, etc. They're available at athletic shoe stores and water sports shops. Another item we made very good use of was a lightweight nylon 'day' bag or pack for beach towel, camera, sun lotion, repellent, etc. Along with insect repellent should go a tube of anti-histamine lotion for the places you missed with the repellent. Ahhh, what relief!"—Maureen Ovregaard, Salem, Ore.

PACKING TIPS

Occasionally the carriers will leave luggage rather than passengers behind in order to meet the weight requirements of their aircraft. That means you could be separated from your bags. Accordingly, pack your carry-on bag as if you were making a weekend trip; that is, include a change of clothes, toiletries, and any items, such as prescription medications, that you cannot live without. Be sure to include a hat, sunglasses, and sunscreen lotion.

BAGGAGE ALLOWANCES

On international flights except to or from the United States and U.S. territories (such as American Samoa), a "weight system" applies. First- and business-class passengers are limited to 30kg (66 lb.) of checked baggage; economy-class passengers, to 20kg (44 lb.).

A "piece system" applies to all flights to or from the United States and U.S. territories. All passengers are limited to two checked bags without regard to weight but with size limitations: when added together, the three dimensions (length, height, depth) of any one first- or business-class bag must not exceed 158cm (62 in.) in length. Economy-class passengers may check two bags whose total measurements do not exceed 270cm (106 in.), with the larger of the two not more than 158cm (62 in.).

If you fly Los Angeles–Papeete-Fiji-Honolulu–Los Angeles, the piece system applies only on the Los Angeles-Papeete, Fiji-Honolulu, and Honolulu–Los Angeles segments. The weight system applies to Papeete-Rarotonga and Rarotonga-Fiji. In other words, pack according to the weight restrictions.

In addition, all international passengers are permitted to carry on board one bag with total measurements not exceeding 115cm (45 in.).

Once you get to the South Pacific, you may find yourself hopping from island to island on one of the smaller domestic air carriers. Depending on the size of aircraft used, the baggage allowance on these carriers may be 10kg (22 lb.) instead of the larger weights permitted on international flights. Check with the individual airlines to avoid showing up at the check-in counter with too much luggage. Most hotels in the main towns have storage facilities where you can safely leave your extra bags during your side trips.

5. TIPS FOR THE DISABLED, SENIORS, SINGLES & FAMILIES

FOR THE DISABLED

Unfortunately the same sensibilities that have led to ramps, handles, accessible toilets, automatic opening doors, telephones at convenient heights, and other helpful aids in Western countries have not made serious inroads in the islands. Nouméa in New Caledonia is the only town with such facilities as wheelchair ramps at the major intersections.

There may be a cultural reason why the South Pacific lags behind in this respect: Usually shy anyway, the islanders traditionally have felt ashamed when something was "wrong" with them and were dreadfully afraid of being made fun of because of it. Even today, many islanders will stay home from work rather than have anyone know they have anything as simple as pinkeye. This may explain the lack of political support in most island countries to provide programs and facilities for the disabled.

That's not to say that some hoteliers haven't taken it upon themselves to provide rooms specially equipped for the disabled. Such improvements are ongoing; I have pointed out a few of them in this book, but inquire when making a reservation if such rooms are available.

The airlines make special arrangements for disabled persons. Be sure to tell them of your needs when you make your reservation.

FOR SENIOR CITIZENS

Just as children are cared for communally in the South Pacific family systems, so are senior citizens. In fact, most islanders live with their extended families from birth to death. Consequently, most of the local governments do not go out of their way to provide programs and other benefits for persons of retirement age. In other words, you won't find many senior citizen discounts. Children get them; you don't.

You might, however, be able to take advantage of special group tours put together by senior citizens' organizations, which can mean big savings on airfares, hotels, and meals. Check with the **American Association of Retired Persons (AARP),** 1909 K Street NW, Washington, DC 20049 (tel. 202/872-4700). **Elderhostel,** Suite 400, 80 Boylston Street, Boston, MA 02116 (tel. 617/426-7788) has fun, low-priced overseas courses for seniors; one to Australia and New Zealand recently included stopovers in the islands.

FOR SINGLES

Having traveled alone through the South Pacific for more years than I care to admit, I can tell you it's a great place to be unattached. After all, this is the land of smiles and genuine warmness to strangers. The attitude soon infects visitors: All I've ever had to do to meet my fellow travelers is wander into a hotel bar, order a beer, and ask the persons next to me where they are from and what they have done in Fiji, Tahiti, etc.

The islands have four playgrounds especially suited to singles. Three are **Club Méditerranées:** two in French Polynesia (one on Moorea, the other on Bora Bora); another is in Nouméa, New Caledonia. The fourth establishment is rocking **Beachcomber Island Resort** in Fiji. See Chapters 5, 12, and 16 for details.

FOR WOMEN TRAVELING ALONE

The South Pacific islands are relatively safe for women traveling alone; however, certain facts of island life should not go unobserved, as sexist as they may seem by Western standards.

No woman, single or married, should wander alone on deserted beaches; in the old days, this was an invitation to head into the bushes, and it could be taken to mean the same today.

Unfortunately, a few island men have decided recently that having sex with a foreign woman—especially a white foreign woman—is for some reason a special feather in their caps. The occasional result: rape. This is not a widespread occurrence, but you should keep it in mind when accepting an offer to have a few beers outside a bar, or to be given a late-night lift back to your hotel or hostel. Any man who seems friendly and harmless when sober can become surly and dangerous when intoxicated, and island men are no exception. Don't let the charm of warm nights and smiling faces lull you into any less caution than you would exercise at home.

As pointed out in Chapter 1, in some Melanesian countries women are considered to be little more than chattel. Although the role of Melanesian women is changing in some places, for the time being women should not visit native villages without at least one male companion.

FOR FAMILIES

While infants and young children are adored by the islanders, childhood does not last as long in the South Pacific as it does in our Western societies. As soon as they are capable, children are put to work, first caring for their younger siblings and cousins and helping out with household chores, later tending the village gardens. It's only as teenagers, and then only if they leave their villages for town, that they know unemployment in the Western sense. Accordingly, few towns and villages have children's facilities, such as playgrounds, outside school property.

With their love of children, the islanders are very good at baby-sitting; however, make sure that you get one who speaks English. The hotels can take care of this for you.

Disposable diapers, cotton swabs (known as Buds, not Q-Tips), and baby food are sold in many main-town stores, but you should take along a supply of such items as children's aspirin, a thermometer, adhesive bandages, any special medications, and such. If your children are very small, perhaps you should discuss your travel plans with your family doctor. Frankly, I would not take young children to Vanuatu and Solomon Islands where malaria is a threat; if you do take them there, remember that children require antimalarial medication.

Also remember the South Pacific sun is hot all year, so protect your youngsters from it with ample sunscreen.

Some other tips: Frequent handwashing can reduce their chances of catching respiratory and intestinal illnesses. If they do contract severe diarrhea, seek medical attention. Some tropical plants and animals may resemble rocks or vegetation, so teach your youngsters to avoid touching or brushing up against rocks, seaweed, and other objects. If your child is prone to swimmer's ear, use vinegar or preventive drops before they go swimming in freshwater streams or lakes. Have them shower soon after swimming or suffering cuts or abrasions.

Some of the more exclusive resorts do not accept children under the ages of 12 or 13. I point those out in the establishments listings, but you may want to ask to make sure. Also inquire if the hotel can provide cribs, bottle warmers, and other needs.

Rascals in Paradise, 650 Fifth Street, San Francisco, CA 94107 (tel. 415/978-

9800, or toll free 800/872-7225), specializes in organizing South Pacific tours for families with kids, including visits with local families and schoolchildren.

6. ALTERNATIVE/SPECIALTY TRAVEL

HOMESTAYS

French Polynesia and American Samoa are the only South Pacific islands with systems of homestays; that is, you stay in the home of a local family. See Chapters 4 and 9. You can get a feel for local life at guesthouses in Western Samoa and Tonga. See Chapters 8 and 10.

ADVENTURE/WILDERNESS TRAVEL

Scuba diving is far and away the South Pacific's most widely available form of adventure, primarily because the diving is some of the world's best. Every island country now has at least one diving operation.

Sailors can charter yachts and explore many islands in French Polynesia, Tonga, Fiji, and New Caledonia.

Fiji has white-water rafting and hiking expeditions into the mountains, plus organized overnight trips to Fijian villages in the highlands. Walking to the lip of the Mount Yasur volcano on Tanna in Vanuatu is a soft adventure, as is an excursion to see that nation's Pentecost Island land divers.

World War II veterans—or anyone else interested in that conflict—can tour the battlefields of Guadalcanal and the other Solomon Islands. Plans were in the works as we went to press for the 50th anniversary commemoration of the Battle of Guadalcanal in August 1992.

See the specific country chapters for more details.

7. GETTING THERE

The romantic days of great passenger ships crossing the South Pacific are gone. A few cruise ships visit the islands, and you can sail your own yacht or hitch a ride on someone else's (see below), but today more than 98% of all visitors to the islands arrive by air. Since the distances are great and the populations small, however, flights are not nearly as frequent in the islands as we Westerners are accustomed to at home. There may be only one flight a week between some countries, and flights that are scheduled today may be wiped off the timetables tomorrow. Accordingly, it's always wise to consult a travel agent or contact the airlines to see what's happening at present.

A recent development in the airline industry is known as "code sharing." That means two carriers use their own airline codes (Air New Zealand's code is NZ, for example) over a route, but only one provides the plane. Let's say you buy a ticket from Air New Zealand in Vancouver, British Columbia. Instead of an Air New Zealand jet, however, you ride a Canadian International Airlines plane from Vancouver to Honolulu, then switch to an Air New Zealand craft for the flight to Fiji. Your ticket, however, says Air New Zealand all the way. I mention code sharing so you won't be surprised when, for example, an Air Pacific flight ends up being on a Solomon Airlines plane.

THE AIRPORTS

With the exception of Fiji, where **Nadi** is the major airport but a few international flights also arrive at **Suva,** all island countries have just one international airport each. These are **Papeete** on Tahiti in French Polynesia; **Rarotonga** in the Cook Islands; **Pago Pago** in American Samoa; **Apia** in Western Samoa;

Tongatapu, the main island in Tonga; **Port Vila** in Vanuatu; **Nouméa** in New Caledonia; and **Honiara** in Solomon Islands. You will land at one of these airports in order to get anywhere else in the South Pacific. Nadi (pronounced and sometimes spelled Nandi) is the only major regional hub.

More than likely you will fly to smaller airports on the outer islands. ***Always* reconfirm your return flight** as soon as you arrive on an outer island, primarily so that the carrier will know where to reach you in case of a schedule change. Avoid booking a return flight from an outer island on the same day your international flight is due to leave for home; give yourself plenty of leeway in case the plane can't get to the outer island on the day it's supposed to arrive for your return flight.

THE AIRLINES

Here are the international carriers serving the South Pacific island countries and territories and their North American telephone numbers:

Air New Zealand (tel. 213/642-0196 in Los Angeles, or toll free 800/262-1234), consistently one of the world's top-rated airlines, and the New Zealand national flag carrier, has the most extensive network in the islands. Its planes fly directly from Los Angeles to Papeete, Rarotonga, and Nadi on their way to its home base in Auckland, New Zealand. From Auckland, the system fans out to serve Nouméa, Tonga, Apia, and several Australian cities (which means that Australians can reach most of the South Pacific islands through Auckland). Air New Zealand also has flights from Frankfurt and London to Los Angeles, where connections can be made to the islands, and it has nonstop service between Japan and Fiji. In Asia, it flies from Singapore and Hong Kong to Auckland.

Air Calédonie International (tel. 213/670-7302, or toll free 800/677-4277), has a fleet of two modern Boeing 737 aircraft which link New Caledonia to Tahiti, Fiji, Vanuatu, Auckland, and Melbourne, Sydney, and Brisbane in Australia. The most direct way to fly from North America to New Caledonia is with Air France or UTA French Airlines (UTA) to Papeete and from there directly to Nouméa on Air Calédonie International (with stops at the French island of Wallis and at Fiji). Connections to Nouméa can also be made in Fiji.

Air Pacific (tel. 213/417-2236), Fiji's national airline, connects its base at Nadi to Tonga (eight times a week), Western Samoa (four times), Vanuatu (three times), and Solomon Islands (twice a week), as well as flying several times daily between Nadi and Suva, Fiji's capital. It also links Fiji to Auckland, Sydney, and Melbourne and has nonstop service twice a week between Fiji and Japan. Given these frequencies and its special airfares for visitors from North America (see below), Air Pacific's flights are one of the most economical ways to get around the South Pacific once you're gotten to Nadi.

Polynesian Airlines (tel. 213/642-7487), the flag carrier of Western Samoa, is expertly managed by Ansett Airlines of Australia. It links Apia with New Zealand, Australia, Tonga, Rarotonga, and Fiji, and as we went to press it was planning to give Hawaiian Airlines competition on the Apia-Honolulu route. It's Polypass fare (see below) is a bargain for Aussies and Kiwis.

Solomon Airlines (tel. 213/670-7302, or toll free 800/677-4277), the national airline of Solomon Islands, has taken over several segments in the Southwestern Pacific during recent years. It now flies between Honiara and Nadi, Port Vila, Auckland, Papua New Guinea, and Brisbane and Cairns in Australia. The most direct way from North America to the Solomons is to Nadi, then on Solomon Airlines to Honiara via Port Vila.

Air France (tel. 212/247-0100 in New York City, or toll free 800/237-2747 outside New York City), which now owns UTA French Airlines (see below), flies to Tahiti from Paris, Los Angeles, and Tokyo.

Air Vanuatu (tel. 408/865-8901) owns one Boeing 727 plane which flies between Port Vila in its home country and Nadi, Auckland, Sydney, Melbourne, and Brisbane.

Canadian Airlines International (tel. toll free 800/426-7000 in the U.S.) no longer flies its own planes to the South Pacific, but as indicated above, shares the service with Air New Zealand and Qantas Airways. Nevertheless, you can still get on

Canadian in Vancouver or Toronto and end up in Fiji, albeit with a change to an Air New Zealand or Qantas plane in Honolulu. The airline has a toll-free telephone number in each Canadian city; check your local phone directory.

Hawaiian Airlines (tel. 808/537-5100 in Honolulu, toll free 800/882-8811 in the other Hawaiian islands, or toll free 800/367-5320 in the continental U.S., Alaska, and Canada) has two sets of South Pacific flights from Los Angeles, San Francisco, and Seattle through Honolulu. One goes to Tahiti and Rarotonga; the other, to American Samoa, Western Samoa, and Tonga.

Lan-Chile Airlines (tel. toll free 800/735-5526) can get you from the United States to Tahiti, a roundabout routing made possible by its weekly flights between Santiago and Papeete by way of Easter Island.

Qantas Airways (tel. 415/761-8000 in San Francisco, 604/684-8231 in Vancouver, B.C., toll free 800/227-4500 in the U.S., toll free 800/663-3411 in British Columbia and Alberta, or toll free 800/663-3423 in the rest of Canada), stops at Tahiti and Fiji on its flights between Los Angeles and San Francisco and Sydney. From Australia, it also goes to New Caledonia and Solomon Islands.

Samoa Air (no telephone in North America), a carrier based in American Samoa, flies its small planes between Pago Pago and Vava'u in Tonga.

UTA French Airlines (tel. 212/247-0100 in New York City, or toll free 800/237-2747 outside New York City) is now owned by Air France (hence, both carriers share the same telephone numbers). As we went to press, UTA still was flying from San Francisco to Tahiti.

AIRFARES

The Pacific Ocean hasn't shrunk since it took 10 days and more than 83 hours in the air for Charles Kingsford Smith to become the first person to fly across it in 1928. Even though you can now board a jetliner in Los Angeles in the evening and be strolling under the palm trees by the crack of dawn, the distances still run into the thousands of miles. Coupled with the small size of the islands and their populations, this translates into some of the most expensive air miles on earth. Consequently, transportation costs will be the largest single expense of a trip to the South Pacific. There are ways, however, to keep these costs from going completely through the ceiling.

FROMMER'S SMART TRAVELER: AIRFARES

1. Shop all the airlines that fly to the South Pacific.
2. Don't ask just for a discounted fare; request the lowest.
3. Ask about special fares such as Air New Zealand's excursion, Air Pacific's Pacific Pass, Polynesian Airlines' Polypass, Solomon Airlines Discover Pacific Pass, and the Triangle Fare on several South Pacific carriers.
4. Keep an eye peeled for promotional fares offered by Air New Zealand, Qantas, Hawaiian Airlines, Air France, and UTA French Airlines, especially during slack seasons in the South Pacific.
5. Wholesalers and groups often reserve blocks of low-cost seats in advance but release some of them near the date of departure. Keep calling the airlines to see if anything has opened up.
6. Check consolidators ("bucket shops") to see if any last-minute flights have opened up at reduced fares.
7. Ask about frequent-flyer programs that award bonus miles for South Pacific flights.
8. Look into airline hotel booking services, such as Air New Zealand's Hotpac hotel service, and packages which provide discounted land arrangements.
9. Ask your travel agent to see if there are charter flights going to the islands.

THE SEASONS

Depending on the carrier, the South Pacific has four airfare seasons: High or "peak" season is from December through February. One "shoulder" season includes March and April; a second runs from September through November. Low or "basic season" is from May through August. Fares will be 10% to 25% higher during peak season when compared to the basic months. Accordingly, the less expensive time to fly is during the northern summer months of May, June, July, and August. That's also when the weather is at its finest in the South Pacific islands.

REGULAR FARES

Purchasing your tickets 2 weeks or a month in advance usually results in significant savings off the normal fare. This type of fare is known as **Advance Purchase Excursion (APEX),** and most carriers serving the South Pacific offer some form of it. *Always* ask about advance-purchase fares.

Here's just one example: Air New Zealand's regular round-trip coach fare from Los Angeles to Fiji or Rarotonga is about $1,500 peak season, $1,250 in low. If you purchase a ticket 14 days in advance of departure, however, this fare drops to about $1,365 during the peak season and $1,100 during the rest of the year. A Los Angeles–Tahiti round-trip APEX ticket on Air New Zealand can cost as little as $950 during the basic season.

SPECIAL FARES

Another deal to ask about is Air New Zealand's **excursion fare,** which includes stops at Papeete, Rarotonga, Nadi, and Honolulu (one of my recommended itineraries). This ticket costs about $1,500 in peak season, $1,350 during the shoulders, and $1,250 in basic season. In other words, you get Tahiti and the Cook Islands thrown in for the regular APEX round-trip fare from Los Angeles to Fiji.

Air Pacific offers a **Pacific Air Pass** to North American travelers. This permits trips from Nadi to Port Vila, Apia, and Tonga for $449. For another $100 they will throw in Honiara. Air Pacific flies "spoke" routes among the islands; like the spokes of a wheel, its planes fly from Nadi or Suva to another country, then turn around and come back. That means you will have to return to Fiji in order to get from Tonga to Samoa, but it also means you can fan out from Nadi to the other countries at a great price. For example, Air Pacific's normal round-trip excursion fare between Nadi and Tonga alone is about $300. For another $149 you get two more countries; for $249 you can go to four more. The Pacific Pass must be bought in North America, is good for 30 days after departure on the first leg, and is subject to a $50 cancellation penalty.

Another variation on the same theme is a **Triangle Fare** on Air Pacific, Air New Zealand, Air Calédonie International, Qantas, or Air Vanuatu. These come in three variations: (1) Fiji-Tonga–Western Samoa for $448; (2) Fiji-Vanuatu–New Caledonia for about $525; and (3) Australia-Fiji-Vanuatu for about $850 to $1,000. The exact prices depend on exchange rates and which Australian city is included.

Air Pacific also has a joint fare with Qantas, Canadian International Airlines, United Airlines, and American Airlines which allows Australia-bound travelers on those carriers to visit Fiji free via Air Pacific's services between Australia or New Zealand and Nadi.

Polynesian Airlines sells a **Polypass** which permits unlimited travel for 30 days (beginning with the first flight) among Western Samoa, American Samoa, Fiji, Tonga, and Rarotonga, plus one round-trip from Australia (Sydney and Brisbane) or New Zealand (Auckland) to the islands. Among the restrictions: Travel cannot begin during December or January, the tickets must be written for the complete itinerary before the first flight, they may be changed only once during your 30-day trip, and they are not transferable or refundable after travel has begun. A Polypass costs $999 for adults, $500 for children under 12 years old, and $100 for children under 2. That's a good deal for Pacific islanders, Australians, and New Zealanders.

Solomon Airlines has a **Discover Pacific Pass,** which represents big savings if you're going from Fiji to Vanuatu and the Solomons. Two flights cost $399; three, $499; and four, $599. That means Fiji-Vanuatu-Honiara-Fiji will cost $499.

Remember, most if not all special fares have restrictions. Be sure to ask the airline or your travel agent what these are.

FEEDER FARES

If you don't live in Los Angeles, San Francisco, Honolulu, Vancouver, Sydney, Brisbane, Auckland, or another city where flights to the South Pacific originate, then you will have to pay to get there in order to make a connection. Most carriers offer a "feeder" fare—or "add-on"—to cover the connecting flights. Be sure to ask about the feeder fares offered by your choice of airline.

CONSOLIDATORS

Sometimes called "bucket shops," consolidators are discount firms which sell seats on the major international carriers that otherwise would go unfilled, especially during the slow seasons. Some discount firms run small ads in the Sunday travel sections of newspapers, and you should look into the fares they offer. Generally, however, it's best to go through a travel agent. Ask the agent to comparison-shop for you, but always match the deals they come up with to those offered directly by the airlines.

Consolidator deals can be riskier than buying directly from a carrier, since the agent will deal with a middleman. On the other hand, they can result in substantial savings on tickets that have fewer restrictions than you would get with an advance purchase ticket bought from an airline. In any event, inquire as to any and all restrictions there may be.

Here are a few American consolidators:

UniTravel Corp., 1177 N. Warson Rd., P.O. Box 12485, St. Louis, MO 63132 (tel. 314/569-0900, or toll free 800/325-2222).

Euram Tours, 1522 K St. NW, Washington, DC 20005 (tel. 202/789-2255, or toll free 800/848-6789).

Travac Tours and Charters, 989 Sixth Ave., New York, NY 10018 (tel. 212/563-3303, or toll free 800/872-8800).

TFI Tours International, 34 W. 32nd St., New York, NY 10001 (tel. 212/736-1140).

Council Charter, 205 E. 42nd St., New York, NY 10017 (tel. 212/661-0311).

Access International, Inc., 101 W. 31st St., Suite 1104, New York, NY 10107 (tel. 212/333-7280, or toll free 800/333-7280).

CHARTER FLIGHTS

At press time, only **Minerve,** Club Med's charter airline, had regular charter flights from the United States to the South Pacific, and those primarily were to take customers to the region's three Club Meds. Ask your travel agent or call Club Med (tel. toll free 800/528-3100 in the U.S. and Canada) for details. **Air Pacific** (tel. 213/417-2236) has announced plans to begin Los Angeles–Fiji charter flights in 1993, with an eye to starting a regularly scheduled service in 1995.

PACKAGE TOURS

Quite often a package tour will result in savings, not just on airfares but on hotels and other activities as well. You pay one price, usually in advance, for a package that varies from one tour operator to the next. Airfare and accommodations are always covered, and sometimes meals and specific activities are thrown in. The costs are kept down because wholesale tour operators (known as "wholesalers" in the travel industry) can make volume bookings on the airlines and at the hotels. The packages are then sold through retail travel agents who deal directly with the public.

This could mean that you'll end up at the large resort hotel and not in your own bungalow at a small, more intimate establishment. You may find that once you're in the islands, you want to shift to that cozy bungalow down the road; if you do, you may lose the money you've already paid. And since the tour prices are based on double occupancy, the single traveler is almost invariably penalized. You could end up traveling with strangers who become friends for life; they also could be loudmouthed bores.

On the other hand, some wholesalers offer group prices to independent travelers, so smart shopping could pay off. Look for deals that save you money without compromising your ability to go when you want. Go to a knowledgeable travel agency, explain exactly where you want to go and how long you want to stay there, and see what's available at present.

Wholesalers usually take bookings from retail agents, not from the public. But since I know from personal experience that not all retail agents are familiar with the South Pacific, here are a few of the leading wholesalers who specialize in the islands:

Hawaiian Sunspots: tel. 503/666-3893 in Portland, Oregon, toll free 800/422-4315 in Oregon, or toll free 800/334-5623 outside Oregon. Owner John T. Smith and family are experts on Rarotonga and Samoa but will arrange an itinerary for you anywhere in the islands.

Ted Cook's Islands in the Sun: tel. 714/645-8300, in Costa Mesa, California, or toll free 800/854-3413. Ted Cook, who pioneered group tours to Tahiti, has sold out to Accor, the French company that runs the Sofitel, Ibis, and Novotel hotels. Guess where you're likely to stay.

Tahiti Vacations: tel. 213/553-3477 in Los Angeles, California, or toll free 800/337-1040. John Biggerstaff's firm also represents Air Tahiti in the U.S.

Tahiti Nui's Island Dreams: tel. 415/453-9121 in San Anselmo, California, toll free 800/922-6851 in California, or toll free 800/824-4976 elsewhere.

Island Vacations: tel. toll free 800/287-6722 in California, or 800/426-1713 elsewhere in the U.S. Has packages to Tahiti, the Cook Islands, and Fiji using Air New Zealand's services.

United Touring Company: tel. 215/923-8700 in Philadelphia, Pennsylvania, or toll free 800/223-6486. Specialists in Fiji, where the company is based.

SO/PAC: tel. 213/393-8262 in Santa Monica, California, toll free 800/455-0190 in California, 800/551-2012 elsewhere in the U.S., 800/235-8222 in Canada.

South Pacific Tour Planners: tel. 213/427-1787 in Long Beach, California, toll free 800/624-7926 in California, 800/421-3197 elsewhere.

If you decide to go, read the fine print carefully. You may not want all the "extras" that are included, such as all meals (why pay in advance for all meals in places like Tahiti and New Caledonia, where eating out is a major extracurricular activity?). And don't think the free manager's welcoming party is any big deal; you're likely to be invited anyway, whether you're on the tour or not.

JET LAG

Any way you cut it, flying to the South Pacific islands from anywhere other than Australia and New Zealand translates into jet lag. Most flights are so long that frequent travelers don't speak in terms of miles but in hours. Compounding the problem are the five time zones between the U.S. West Coast and Solomon Islands.

There are probably as many theories about what to do for jet lag as there are travelers. Some people advise trying to adjust to destination time before leaving home by getting up early or sleeping late. Others say you shouldn't eat or drink alcoholic beverages on the plane. Still others advise not sleeping during the flight. Air New Zealand says you should drink lots of nonalcoholic fluids to counter dehydration that takes place at high altitudes, eat lightly, and exercise occasionally by walking up and down the aisle (all those fluids probably will send you to the rear of the plane whether you're in the mood to exercise or not).

As for me, I try to break my transpacific trips by laying over for a day or so en route. I stop for at least one good night's sleep in Los Angeles or Honolulu, for example, between my East Coast home and the South Pacific. I also make every effort to schedule flights during the daylight hours; however, I sometimes think that the airlines' schedulers must be a bunch of sadists, since so many transpacific flights are overnighters. When I have no choice but to fly overnight, I eat lightly and try to sleep as much as possible, comforted by the knowledge that I can recover by lazing the next morning away on a South Pacific beach.

Once you get across the Pacific, hopping from one South Pacific island to another is much easier. With a few exceptions, most interisland flights last no more than 3 hours and take place during the day.

8. GETTING AROUND

The great transoceanic passenger liners may be gone, but it's still possible to sample some of the romance of the South Pacific by sea, primarily by an island-hopping cruise ship or—for the really adventurous who have lots of time—a private yacht.

BY CRUISE SHIP

Occasionally it may be possible to cross the Pacific on a ship making an around-the-world cruise or on one being repositioned, say, from Alaska to Australia. Most of them, however, steam through the islands for a week or two at a time from a home port such as Papeete or Sydney. They are usually under way at night, with visits to the islands during the day.

Passengers fly to the home port, enjoy the cruise, and fly home, which means that cruises are no longer only for the idle rich with time on their hands. The cruise companies usually offer some form of reduced airfares on these "fly-and-cruise" vacations, so you'll save over the cost of booking the air and cruise separately. Many operators also offer land packages that enable their passengers to stay over for a few days or a week at a hotel at or near the home port, usually for a reduced rate.

The cruise price ordinarily includes all meals and double-occupancy stateroom or cabin, although the fare varies with the size and position of the quarters. You can save money by booking one of the smaller interior cabins on the lower decks. You won't have a porthole, but I can tell you from having served in the U.S. Navy that the lower amidship cabins tend to ride more smoothly than those on the outside of the upper decks.

Two very popular cruises operate year-round in French Polynesia and Fiji—the *Wind Song* out of Papeete and the six vessels of Blue Lagoon Cruises out of Lautoka, respectively. See the chapters on French Polynesia and Fiji for details.

Most of the other cruise ships sail from ports in Australia and New Zealand, and visit the islands in the western South Pacific such as Vanuatu, Fiji, and Tonga. Their itineraries tend to change from season to season, and there's not space here to describe every possibility and price. For more information, contact a travel agent or the following companies which operate cruise ships in the South Pacific:

Princess Cruises, 10100 Santa Monica Blvd., Los Angeles, CA 90067 (tel. 213/553-1700, or toll free 800/521-0522).

Royal Cruise Line, One Maritime Plaza, Suite 1400, San Francisco, CA 94111 (tel. 415/956-7200, or toll free 800/792-2992 in California, 800/227-4534 elsewhere in the U.S.).

Royal Viking Line, 95 Merrick Way, Coral Gables, FL 33134 (tel. 305/447-9660, or toll free 800/634-8000).

Windstar Sail, 300 Elliott Ave. West, Seattle, WA 98119 (tel. 206/281-3535, or toll free 800/258-7245).

Society Expeditions, 1520 Kensington Rd., Suite 212, Oak Brook, IL 60521 (tel. 708/954-2944, or toll free 800/323-7308).

Euro Lloyd Tours, 1640 Hempstead Tpk., East Meadow, NY 11554 (tel. 516/466-1262, or toll free 800/334-2724).

International Cruise Center, 250 Old Country Rd., Mineola, NY 11501 (tel.

516/747-8880, or toll free 800/221-3254), a company that handles bookings for Soviet cruise ships operating out of Sydney under management of an Australian company.

Cunard Line, 555 Fifth Ave., New York, NY 10017 (tel. 212/880-7500, or toll free 800/528-6273).

BY YACHT

A partner and I once set out from the U.S. East Coast to sail a yacht through the South Pacific and on around the world. After transiting the Panama Canal, we met a young German who was looking for a ride west. He became a temporary member of our crew and sailed with us to such out-of-the-way places as the Galápagos, the Marquesas, and the Tuamotu islands. Two months later we put him ashore in Tahiti. That trip of 4,000 miles cost him the price of the food he ate and the case of beer he drank before we were halfway across.

Our young friend was not alone in hitching a ride on a private yacht. The South Pacific is a popular destination for cruising yachts from the U.S. West Coast, Australia, and New Zealand, and it's right on the route that follows the trade winds around the world. Hundreds of boats pass through Papeete, Pago Pago, Vava'u, Suva, and Port Vila each year, and many of their skippers need crew from port to port. They particularly like persons who have sailed before, although adventurous young women are always in demand—whether they've been to sea or not.

Caution is in order before you commit, however, for the passages are long, the quarters confined, the sea always bumpy, and the company sometimes unbearable. Try to get to know your comrades before signing on, and be certain that the terms—whether you are to pay for your food, for example—are spelled out in advance. You can be sure that you'll have to stand watch during the nights at sea (there's no place to anchor, after all) and to share in the chores that never seem to end. In other words, it's not like a cruise liner on which you sit back and relax. And don't expect the skipper to turn around and go back into port if you get seasick.

Many South Pacific countries require persons entering on yachts to have in their possession an air ticket back to their home country or the money to cover the cost of such a ticket. You'll need either a ticket or the money or you won't be allowed to leave the boat.

Few yachts move about during the South Pacific hurricane season, from November through April. Those coming down from North America or Panama leave early in the year so that they'll arrive in French Polynesia after the hurricane season ends, so that's a good time to find them. Look in the classified ads in *Yachting, Sail, Cruising World,* and other boating magazines, and check at the coastal yacht clubs for boats that might be leaving. Most yacht clubs have bulletin boards where you may find messages from skippers looking for crew and crew looking for skippers.

The usual route across the South Pacific is from the West Coast to a Mexican port such as Manzanillo, thence to the Marquesas Islands northeast of Tahiti. Yachts leaving Panama usually arrive at the Marquesas via the Galápagos, where they are allowed to stop for no more than 48 hours. From the Marquesas, the route continues through the Tuamotu Archipelago, Tahiti, Moorea, Bora Bora, Rarotonga, Pago Pago, Vava'u, and Suva. From there some boats go south to New Zealand or Australia for the cyclone season. Others hole up until all's clear and then head west on the around-the-world route via Port Moresby and the Torres Strait between Australia and Papua New Guinea.

CHARTERING YACHTS

There are a number of yachts available for charter in the South Pacific, both with and without skipper and crew. If you want a "bareboat" charter (that is, one without professional captain or crew), you must have had enough experience and skill with yachts ranging between 30 feet and 60 feet in length to satisfy the charter company. No experience is required to charter a boat with captain. Details are in the chapters on French Polynesia, Tonga, Fiji, Vanuatu, and New Caledonia. The conditions in those countries make them ideal places to go boating.

SUGGESTED ITINERARIES

Not surprisingly, my friends often ask where I would go on a vacation in the South Pacific. It's a difficult question for me to answer. I am fond of the dramatic, breathtaking scenery in French Polynesia and American Samoa, the enormously friendly people in Tonga, Fiji, and Solomon Islands, the charm and warmth of Western Samoa and the Cook Islands, the fascinating mix of cultures in Vanuatu, the excitement of a relocated Riviera in New Caledonia. There are few experiences in the world quite like standing at dusk on the lip of Yasur volcano in Vanuatu and watching its sulfur cloud turn pink over the exploding earth in the caldera far below.

If you want to see it all, give yourself several busy months of island hopping. If you have only 1 week, then your time will best be spent in just one island country (internal intineraries will be found in the chapters devoted to the larger countries). If you have 2 or 3 weeks, here are some suggestions—I repeat, *suggestions*—to consider. I put them here in the transportation chapter because getting off the beaten track in the South Pacific requires keeping a sharp eye on the airline schedules.

FIJI-RAROTONGA-TAHITI

One of the easier and less expensive ways to sample the South Pacific is to fly with Air New Zealand over its "Coral Route," from Fiji to Rarotonga to Tahiti, or vice versa. Air New Zealand pioneered this route in the days of flying boats, and one of its Boeing 767s now does it once a week, leaving Auckland early in the morning and ending in Papeete about midnight. The plane turns around and returns by the same route the following day, so it's possible to do this trip in either direction.

Since the Coral Route is a once-a-week proposition, you will have to spend 7 days in the Cook Islands. For a 3-week trip, add to that a week in Fiji and another in French Polynesia. Depending on flight connections, you can shorten your stays in Fiji and Tahiti. As a variation, you can cut out Tahiti altogether and reduce your time in the Cook Islands by flying directly to Rarotonga from Los Angeles, Honolulu, or Auckland. See the section on airline fares (above) for information about Air New Zealand's excellent excursion fare over this route.

I highly recommend this itinerary because it gives a good sampling of Melanesia and the transplanted Indian culture in Fiji, of English-speaking Polynesia in the Cook Islands, and of Polynesia with a French overlay in Tahiti and its islands.

THE SAMOAS & TONGA

A tour through the "Bible Belt" of Polynesia includes American Samoa, nearby Western Samoa, and the Kingdom of Tonga, the last of the South Pacific's monarchies. All three are very conservative (on Sunday the sidewalks roll up and you could be stoned for swimming), but by being conservative they have maintained their traditional Polynesian cultures.

American Samoa has become a blend of Samoa and modern Hawaii, but the scenery there is definitely major-league tropics, with mountains dropping spectacularly into Pago Pago Harbor. You can tour American Samoa in a day, so make your base in Western Samoa with its relatively unchanged Polynesian way of life. You may have to backtrack to Pago Pago to get on to Tonga, but it's worth it just to see King Taufa'ahau Tupou IV, all 300-plus pounds of him, riding his bicycle.

Hawaiian Airlines flies to the Samoas and Tonga from Honolulu, or you can work the countries in either on Air Pacific's Pacific Pass or on the Triangle Fare using Air Pacific and Polynesian Airlines.

FIJI-TONGA—THE SAMOAS

These three countries offer diversity—Melanesia, Polynesia, and the Indian side of Fiji—plus friendly people, fine beaches, reefs, and tropical scenery. Fiji is by far the larger of the countries, so give yourself more time there.

Air Pacific's Pacific Pass and the Triangle Fare using Air Pacific to Tonga and Apia (see above) make visits combining Fiji, Tonga, and Western Samoa attractive, as do each country's reasonably priced accommodation and restaurants. The most expeditious routing is Fiji-Tonga on Air Pacific, Tonga-Apia on Polynesian Airlines, and Apia-Fiji on Air Pacific or Polynesian Airlines.

FIJI-VANUATU–SOLOMON ISLANDS–FIJI

This side trip from Nadi takes you into the heart of Melanesia. Start with a week in Fiji, then take either Air Pacific or Solomon Airlines to Port Vila for a visit to Vanuatu. Plan an overnight side trip to Tanna to see Mount Yasur and the custom villages and a day-trip to Santo where James A. Michener wrote his popular *Tales of the South Pacific*.

Honiara on Guadalcanal is not that far from Port Vila, but you'll have to backtrack and stay overnight in Nadi in order to get to Solomon Islands on Air Pacific with its Pacific Pass fare. The alternative is a shortcut between the two towns on Solomon Airlines. Air Pacific and Solomon Airlines each return to Nadi from Honiara.

FIJI-VANUATU–NEW CALEDONIA–FIJI

Another attractive combination is the same week in Vanuatu mentioned above, then on to New Caledonia on its airline, Air Calédonie International. Plan to get outside Nouméa, where the country is very Melanesian. The Isle of Pines is a fine example of unspoiled beauty and has some of the most spectacular beaches to be found anywhere. Spend at least a day there. This routing can be done with a Triangle Fare using Air Pacific, Air Calédonie International, and Air Vanuatu.

9. WHERE TO STAY

The South Pacific has a wide range of accommodations, from deluxe resort hotels to mom-and-pop guesthouses and dormitories with bunk beds. The establishments are covered in the chapters which follow. Here are some general observations about what you will find.

My favorite type of South Pacific hotel accommodates its guests in individual bungalows set in a coconut grove beside a sandy beach and quiet lagoon. Some of these bungalows—always expensive—even stand on stilts out over the reef; others are as basic as a tent. In between they vary in size, furnishings, and comfort. In all, you enjoy the privacy of your own place, one usually built or accented with thatch and other native materials but containing most of the modern conveniences. Few of these accommodations are air conditioned, but ceiling fans create a cooling breeze and an appropriate tropical atmosphere. Hotels of this style are widespread in the South Pacific.

The major tourist markets for the South Pacific island countries, with the exception of French Polynesia, are Australia and New Zealand. Accordingly, the vast majority of hotels are tailored to Aussie and Kiwi tastes, expectations, and uses of the English language.

Unlike the usual American hotel room, which likely has two humongous beds, the standard "Down Under" room has a double bed and a single bed that also serves as a settee. It may or may not have a bathtub but always has a shower. There may be no washcloths (bring your own), but there will be tea and instant coffee and an electric "jug" to heat water for same. Televisions are not yet common (broadcast television in the South Pacific is in its infancy); many hotels have radios, but the selections will be limited to the one, two, or three stations on the island.

Rooms are known to South Pacific reservation desks as "singles" if one person books them regardless of the number and size of beds they have. They are "doubles" if they have a double bed and are reserved for two persons who intend to sleep together in that bed. On the other hand, "twins" have two twin beds; if two

FROMMER'S SMART TRAVELER: HOTELS

1. You can save on many hotel rooms by booking them through the airlines. One example: Air New Zealand's **Hotpac** offers savings at a number of establishments in Fiji, French Polynesia, the Cook Islands, Western Samoa, Tonga, and New Caledonia. You book the rooms and pay for them when you buy your Air New Zealand ticket. You also can book rooms ahead through Air New Zealand's offices and agents as you go along. Ask Air New Zealand for one of its Hotpac brochures listing the hotels and rates.
2. If business is slow, many hotels will accept less than the "rack" rates they charge independent travelers, and some even have "local" rates for islanders. Most rack rates include commissions of up to 30% for travel agents, which you might save if you make your own reservations and bargain a little. It never hurts to ask politely for a lower rate. This tactic works best in the slower seasons (see "When to Go" in this chapter).
3. Some less expensive hotels which take credit cards may reduce their rates if you offer to pay cash.
4. Ask how much the hotel charges for local and long-distance calls. In some cases this surcharge can more than double the cost. If so, make your calls at a post office or pay phone.
5. Most South Pacific countries charge a room tax. Inquire if it is included in the quoted rate. The "Fast Facts" sections of the following chapters give the amount of tax charged in each country.
6. If you're going to spend a week in a country, ask about long-term rates or discounts.

unmarried people book them, they are known as "shared twins." Third and fourth occupants are usually charged an additional few dollars, on top of the double or shared twin rates.

Some hotel rooms, especially in Rarotonga and the Cook Islands, are modeled on the New Zealand "motel" concept; that is, they have kitchenettes equipped with a small refrigerator (the "fridge"), hotplates (the "cooker"), pots, pans, crockery, silverware, and cooking utensils. Establishments with this type of room usually call themselves "motels" rather than hotels. Having the kitchenette can result in quite a saving on breakfasts and light meals.

Very few hotels raise their rates during the busy periods, such as during Australian school holidays (see "When to Go," above).

10. WHAT TO BUY

Take some extra money along, for there are many things to spend it on throughout the islands. The business hours vary greatly from country to country, so check the "Fast Facts" in the individual chapters for the local hours.

DUTY-FREE SHOPPING

Fiji has the most developed duty-free shopping industry in the region by far, with scores of stores and wide selections. Every country and territory except Solomon Islands, however, has at least a small duty-free shop at its international airport. Ordinarily, the choice of cigarettes is limited to those manufactured in New Zealand, Australia, Fiji, or Western Samoa, and generally only the most popular brands of liquors will be stocked. Otherwise, items and prices offered vary from country to country, with perfumes, watches, electronic equipment, and cameras leading the list.

A word to the wise about duty-free shopping in the South Pacific: Shop around carefully before leaving home. Quite often you can find better prices and selections at the larger-volume dealers at home. If it's a Sony Walkman, a Nikon camera, or Chanel perfume you're looking for, find it at home first so you can compare the price in the South Pacific. Also compare the models offered in the duty-free shops with those available at home. Those in the South Pacific may not be the latest editions.

The Fiji National Duty Free Merchants Association recommends that customers request receipts that accurately describe their purchases; that they make sure all guarantee and warranty cards are properly completed and stamped by the merchant; and that they examine all items before making payment. If you later find that the item is not what you expected (or, God forbid, is not what you think you actually bought), return to the shop immediately with the item and your receipt. As a general rule, purchases are not returnable and deposits are not refundable.

Personally, I pay for my duty-free purchases by credit card. That way, if something goes wrong after I'm back in the United States, at least I have the large financial institution that issued my card to call on for help.

WHAT YOU CAN BRING HOME

U.S. residents are normally allowed to bring back, duty free, 200 cigarettes and 100 cigars, 1 liter of alcoholic beverages, and $400 worth of other goods purchased overseas. A flat 10% duty is charged on the next $1,000 worth of purchases. You need declare only the total value up to $1,400; if you are over that amount, you must list every item you bought. (For goods purchased in American Samoa these figures are $1,200, $2,400, and $3,200, respectively, provided you were there at least 48 hours.) I always keep my purchase receipts and carry them through Customs to prove how much I paid for my goodies. You must also tell the Customs people if you are taking more than $10,000 in U.S. or foreign currency or monetary instruments (including traveler's checks) into or out of the United States.

More information about U.S. duties and exemptions is available from the U.S. Customs Service, P.O. Box 7407, Washington, DC 20044 (tel. 202/566-8195).

More than 700 endangered species of plants and animals—or any parts thereof—cannot be imported into the United States and most other countries. These are protected by U.S. laws and by a treaty known as the Convention on International Trade in Endangered Species of Wild Fauna and Flora. As far as the South Pacific is concerned, the major prohibited items are large parrots, sea-turtle shells, crocodile skins, wild bird feathers, and whales' teeth. Most of the shell and coral jewelry you'll see can be brought home, but make sure that the scrimshaw you buy in Tonga is on a bone or tooth of some animal other than a whale. The importation of live animals and most plants is either prohibited or subject to permits that must be obtained in advance.

For more information about what animals you can and cannot bring into the United States, contact the Federal Wildlife Permit Office, 4401 North Fairfax Drive, Arlington, VA 22203 (tel. 703/358-2104).

BEST BUYS

HANDCRAFTS

Locally produced handcrafts are the South Pacific's best buys. The most widespread are hats, mats, and baskets woven of pandanus or other fibers, usually made by the local women who have maintained this ancient art to a high degree. Tonga has the widest selection of woven items and the best prices. The finely woven mats made in Tonga and the Samoas are still highly valued as ceremonial possessions and are seldom for sale to tourists.

Before the coming of European traders and printed cotton, many South Pacific islanders wore garments made from the beaten bark of the paper mulberry tree. The making of this bark cloth, widely known as *tapa,* is another preserved art in Polynesia and Fiji (where it is known as *masi*). The cloth is painted with dyes made from natural substances, usually in geometric designs whose ancestries date back thousands of years. Tapa is an excellent souvenir, since it can be folded and brought back in a suitcase.

Wood carvings are also popular. Spears, war clubs, knives made from sharks' teeth, canoe prows, and cannibal forks are some examples. Many carvings, however, tend to be produced for the tourist trade and often lack the imagery of bygone days. Carved tikis are found in most South Pacific countries, but many of them resemble the figures of the New Zealand Maoris rather than figures indigenous to those countries. The carvings from the Marquesas Islands of French Polynesia and from Solomon Islands are the best of the lot today.

Note: Some governments restrict the export of antique carvings and other artifacts of historic value. If the piece looks old, check before you buy.

Jewelry made of shells and of pink or black coral is available in many countries, as is scrimshaw. Pearls are produced in several South Pacific atolls, including those in French Polynesia and the Cook Islands. The prices in Rarotonga usually are less than those in Tahiti.

CLOTHING

Colorful hand-screened, -blocked, and -dyed fabrics are very popular in the islands for making dresses or the wraparound skirts known as *pareus* in Tahiti and Rarotonga, *lavalavas* in the Samoas and Tonga, *sulus* in Fiji, and *laplaps* in Melanesia. Heat-sensitive dyes are applied by hand to gauzelike cotton, which is then laid in the sun for several hours. Flowers, leaves, and other designs are placed on the fabric, and as the heat of the sun darkens and sets the dyes, the shadows from these objects leave their images behind on the finished product.

French Polynesia produces the greatest variety of tropical clothing products, but Rarotonga and Western Samoa aren't far behind.

FAST FACTS: SOUTH PACIFIC

American Express American Express Company has full-service representatives in Tahiti, Fiji, and New Caledonia. One of the travel agents in Western Samoa also collects card-members' mail and will help with lost or stolen cards, but it does not offer other services such as personal-check cashing. If you lose your American Express credit card or traveler's checks in the Cook Islands, American Samoa, Tonga, Vanuatu, or Solomon Islands, have the international operator place a collect call to American Express's number in your home country. In the U.S., green-card holders should phone 919/668-6666; gold-card members should call 305/474-0108. American Express also has a "Global Assist" service, which provides advice and referrals to its members who need help when traveling. Card members can call collect from overseas (tel. 202/783-7474) for assistance.

Banks Every main town has at least one bank where traveler's checks can be cashed. This is not always the case in the rural areas, especially on the outer islands; always carry sufficient local currency when traveling away from town.

International transfers of funds to the South Pacific can take more time than you have to spend there. I always use my major credit cards and carry enough funds in traveler's checks to cover my anticipated expenses. When I need extra money from home, I use American Express's personal check–cashing service or get a cash advance with one of my VISA or MasterCard.

Business Hours See the "Fast Facts" in the individual country chapters.

Camera/Film Availability and price of film vary from place to place, so take some with you. The security devices at many South Pacific airports are somewhat less than state-of-the-art, so ask to pass your film around the X-ray machine.

Climate See "When to Go," above.

Crime See "Safety," below.

Currency See "Information, Entry Requirements & Money," above, for general information and in each country chapter for specifics.

Customs Most countries allow the "usual" carton of cigarettes and 10 rolls of film to be brought in duty free, although the permissible volume of alcoholic beverages tends to vary. Plants are subject to inspection and fumigation, and animals are either forbidden altogether or subject to quarantine.

Documents Required See "Information, Entry Requirements & Money," above, for general information and in the country chapters for specifics.

Driving Rules See the "Getting Around" sections in the individual country chapters.

Drug Laws Although the islands do not have the draconian drug laws found in some Southeast Asian countries, you can get a stiff term in a very uncomfortable jail for possession and sale of illegal narcotics and dangerous drugs. Some Customs officials use dogs to sniff luggage for such contraband.

Drugstores See the "Fast Facts" sections of the individual country chapters.

Electricity With the exception of American Samoa, where 110-volt power and American plugs are used, electrical current throughout the South Pacific is 220 volts to 240 volts and either 50 cycles or 60 cycles, depending on the island. French Polynesia and New Caledonia use French plugs, which have two round, skinny prongs. The other countries use Australian-style plugs, which have two heavy, angled prongs. There are switches on most wall outlets, so if the lights or your hairdryer won't work at first, try flipping the switch next to the plug. Many hotels have outlets for 110-volt electric razors in their bathrooms, but you'll need a converter and adapter plug for any other appliances.

Embassies/Consulates See the "Fast Facts" in the individual country chapters.

Emergencies See the "Fast Facts" in the individual country chapters.

Etiquette See the "People" descriptions in the individual country chapters.

Firearms All South Pacific countries severely restrict or prohibit outright the importation of firearms. If you really must take a firearm along, write well in advance to the Customs department of the country.

Gambling The only gambling casinos in the area are in New Caledonia and Vanuatu. Only tourists are allowed past the slot machines.

Hitchhiking See the "Fast Facts" in the individual country chapters.

Holidays See "When to Go," above, for general information and in the individual country chapters for specifics.

Information See "Information, Entry Requirements & Money," above, for general information and in the individual country chapters for specifics.

Languages More than 300 languages are spoken in the South Pacific islands covered in this book, some of them by just a few hundred people. Solomon Islands and Vanuatu each have so many dialects that forms of Pidgin English have become the common languages in those countries. Thanks to the former British, New Zealand, and Australian colonial regimes and the American presence in American Samoa, however, English is used as an official language and is spoken in addition to the indigenous tongues of the Cook Islands, the Samoas, Fiji, Vanuatu, and Solomon Islands. It also is used alongside Tongan in the Kingdom of Tonga. French is spoken in French Polynesia and New Caledonia, although English is understood by most hotel and many restaurant staffs. While English has gained an upper hand, French is also used widely in Vanuatu. See "Recommended Books" in Chapter 1 for a general phrasebook; others are recommended in the individual country chapters.

Laundry See the "Fast Facts" in the individual country chapters.

Liquor Laws Each country and territory has its own liquor laws. See the "Fast Facts" in the individual country chapters.

Mail/Postage The postal systems are reliable but sometimes slow. Allow 1 to 2 weeks for an airmail letter to reach the islands from the U.S. mainland and vice versa, more from Europe, less from Australia and New Zealand. It will help expedite your letter or parcel if you write "(South Pacific)" to the right of the country name. For example: Fiji Islands (South Pacific).

Surface mail leaves each island on the next ship out; allow at least 3 months for the handcrafts you purchased to arrive home by surface mail. Post offices in the main towns all have a poste restante (general delivery) section that will hold mail for 30 days.

Maps See "Getting Around" in the individual country chapters.

Newspapers/Magazines Two very fine regional news magazines are published in Fiji: *Pacific Islands Monthly* and *Islands Business Pacific*. They cover recent events throughout the Pacific islands. The Australian and New Zealand editions of *Time* are sold in most island bookshops. *Newsweek* is included in the Australian newsmagazine *The Bulletin*.

Passports See "Information, Entry Requirements & Money," above.

Pets All South Pacific islands have stringent restrictions on the importation of all animals. My advice is: Don't even consider taking your pet to the South Pacific. More than likely it will end up in quarantine for the duration of your vacation.

Police See the "Fast Facts" in the individual country chapters.

Radio/TV Every country has at least one radio station, but at present only French Polynesia, the Cook Islands, American Samoa, Tonga, and New Caledonia have broadcast TV. Most of Western Samoa receives the station in American Samoa. Fiji was planning television as we went to press. Video movies can be found in all the towns, and even on some of the most remote islands.

Rest Rooms See the "Fast Facts" in the individual country chapters.

Safety With the exceptions of Suva and Nouméa, the South Pacific is relatively free of such street crime as holdups and purse snatchings. This does not mean, however, that you should be careless, for it's your responsibility to be alert even in the most heavily touristed areas. You alone are responsible for your safety. Always be aware of your immediate surroundings, and stick to well-traveled, lighted streets after dark. Wear a moneybelt if you're carrying cash or other valuables, and keep a close eye on your possessions. Be particularly careful with cameras, purses, and wallets, all favorite targets of thieves and pickpockets.

Burglary and other crimes against property have increased significantly in some islands in recent years. Do not leave valuable papers or other items in your hotel room; put them in safekeeping with the front desk. Furthermore, communal ownership of property is prevalent in the South Pacific, which means that local residents may simply walk off with your camera or other items if you leave them unattended. Always keep a list of your traveler's checks and a photocopy of your passport identifying information separate from the actual documents.

As noted above, women should not wander alone on deserted beaches. In some South Pacific countries, women should not visit a native village without a male companion.

See the specific chapters for more information.

Taxes See the "Fast Facts" in the individual country chapters.

Telephone/Telegraph/Telex/Fax In general, the communications systems in the South Pacific countries are very good by so-called third world standards, but they are neither as efficient nor as inexpensive as those in the U.S. and other Western countries. The systems vary from country to country. Most now have direct international dialing to most of the world. You can place international telephone calls and telegrams through or at a central office in each of the capital towns, although many hotels will place them for you (ask about those surcharges). Be prepared to wait several minutes while your call goes through.

By the time you get this book, you should be able to dial directly to any phone in the South Pacific (depending on which long-distance carrier you use). Where international direct dialing is available in the U.S., you dial 011, the country code (which is given in the "Fast Facts" section of each country chapter in this book), and the local number. Calls dialed directly from the U.S. can cost about a third as much as calls placed from the South Pacific countries. Consult your long-distance carrier for the most inexpensive times to call.

Facsimile machines are used widely in the islands; in fact, they are very quickly replacing telexes.

Time The Pacific Ocean from the U.S. West Coast to Solomon Islands spans five time zones, and there are three additional ones from the East Coast to California. In addition to jet lag, that translates into some intellectual gymnastics if you decide to call home from Honiara and not wake your loved ones at 3am.

In addition, the international date line runs right through the South Pacific, splitting the area from one day to the next (see Chapter 10 on Tonga for more about the date line). French Polynesia, the Cook Islands, and the Samoas are on the east side of the date line and share the same day as the U.S. and Canada. Tonga, Fiji, Vanuatu, New Caledonia, and Solomon Islands lie to the west and are 1 day ahead, along with Australia and New Zealand.

As a practical matter, this means travelers leaving Los Angeles on Fri for an overnight flight to Fiji will arrive on Sun morning, not on Sat. Never fear, you get the day back when you leave Fiji on Sat and arrive back in Los Angeles the next day, which is not Sun but Sat all over again. Don't worry—you'll get the hang of it when there's no one waiting for you at the airport back home.

Tipping Tipping is considered contrary to both the Polynesian and Melanesian traditions of hospitality and generosity. That's not to say that some small gratuity isn't in order for truly outstanding service, or that you won't get that "Where's-my-tip?" look from a porter as he sheepishly delays leaving your room. But American-style tipping officially is discouraged throughout the South Pacific. Nor will you be socked with a service charge on your hotel and restaurant bills. So forget that hidden 15% your vacation could cost elsewhere.

Tourist Offices Each island country has a tourist information office. See "Information, Entry Requirements & Money," above and in the individual country chapters.

Visas See "Information, Entry Requirements & Money," above and in the individual country chapters.

Water See "Health & Insurance," above, and the "Fast Facts" in the individual country chapters.

CHAPTER 3

GETTING TO KNOW FRENCH POLYNESIA

No other names ring quite the South Pacific bell as do legendary Tahiti and its bustling, noisy port city of Papeete. Although it's the largest and most heavily populated, and its name often is used synonymously with the territory, Tahiti is only one of hundreds of islands that make up this overseas possession of France.

While Tahiti has its charms, islands like Moorea and Bora are what you see on the postcards and in the movies. Accordingly, keep one thought in mind as we get to know French Polynesia: You must visit not only Tahiti but what are known locally as "Her Islands." That's where you will find the real Polynesian charm that has spellbound Europeans for two centuries.

1. HISTORY

The discovery of Tahiti by Wallis in 1767 and the subsequent visits of Bougainville, Cook, and Bligh (see the brief history in Chapter 1) brought many changes to Tahiti, starting with iron, which the Tahitians had never seen, and barter, which they had never practiced. The Tahitians figured out right away that iron was much harder than stone and shells, and that they could swap pigs, breadfruit, bananas, and the affections of their young women for it. Iron cleats, spikes, and nails soon took on a value of their own, and so many of them disappeared from the *Dolphin* that Wallis finally restricted his men to the ship out of fear it would fall apart in Matavai Bay. A rudimentary form of monetary economy was introduced to Polynesia for the first time. The English word "money" soon entered the Tahitian language as *moni*.

WHAT'S SPECIAL ABOUT FRENCH POLYNESIA

Great Towns/Villages
- ☐ Papeete: Tahiti's storied port, now a bustling little city.
- ☐ Fare: Huahine's main village has old South Seas charm.

Ancient Monuments
- ☐ Polynesian *marae:* Temples of rock and stone hauntingly evoke the old religion.

Museums
- ☐ Museum of Tahiti and Her Isles: one of the South Pacific's best.
- ☐ Gauguin Museum: not many of the great painter's works, but it captures his time in Polynesia.

Events
- ☐ *Heiva I Tahiti:* Bastille Day turned into a rollicking, month-long good time with incredible dancing.

Natural Spectacles/Beaches
- ☐ Mountains on Moorea and Bora Bora: Green-shrouded ridges and jagged peaks soar to the clouds.
- ☐ Lagoons of Bora Bora and Rangiroa: Water shouldn't be this colorful.
- ☐ Surf on Tahiti's black sand beaches.

Shopping
- ☐ Black pearls: a wide selection of the world's best, produced in the Tuamotu Archipelago.
- ☐ Tropical clothing: a rainbow of colors on every body.

After Dark
- ☐ Tahitian dance shows: Find out why there was a mutiny on the *Bounty.*

DATELINE

- **ca. 6th Century A.D.** Polynesians arrive.
- **1595** Alvaro de Mendaña discovers the Marquesas Islands.
- **1606** Pedro Fernández de Quirós sails through the Tuamotus.
- **1765** Searching for *terra australis incognita,* Capt. John Byron in HMS *Dolphin* finds some Tuamotu islands but misses Tahiti.
- **1767** Capt. Samuel Wallis, also in HMS *Dolphin,* discovers Tahiti, claims it for King

(continues)

Another type of metal was soon introduced by the *Bounty* mutineers: firearms. Wars were fought hand-to-hand with sticks and clubs until the mutineers hiding on Tahiti loaned themselves and their guns to rival chiefs, who for the first time were able to extend their control beyond their home valleys. With the mutineers' help, chief Pomare I came to control half of Tahiti and all of Moorea.

THE FIRST MISSIONARIES

The first missionaries sent to Tahiti by the London Missionary Society arrived in 1797 aboard the ship *Duff.* They toiled for 15 years before they made their first convert, and even that was only accomplished with the help of the powerful chief Pomare II. The missionaries thought Pomare II was king of Tahiti, but in reality he was locked in battle to extend his father's old rule and to become just that. He converted to Christianity primarily to win the missionaries' support, and with it, he quickly gained control of the entire island. The people then made the easy intellectual transition from their old god Taaroa to the missionaries' supreme being.

The Protestant missionaries then had a free hand on Tahiti for almost 30 years. There were few ordained ministers among them, however, for most were tradesmen sent to Tahiti to teach the natives useful Western skills, which the London Missionary Society considered essential for the Tahitians' successful transition to devout, industrious Christians in the mold of working-class English men and women. Some of the missionaries stayed and went into business on their own (some cynics in the islands insist some missionaries "came to do good and stayed to do well").

FRANCE CLAIMS THE ISLANDS

The Protestant monopoly ended when the first Roman Catholic priests arrived on the scene from France in the 1830s. The Protestants immediately saw a threat and in 1836 engineered the expulsion of the interlopers from the island by Queen Pomare IV, the illegitimate daughter who by then had succeeded to the throne created by her father Pomare II.

When word of this outrage reached Paris, France sent a warship to Tahiti to demand a guarantee that the French would thereafter be treated as "the most favored foreigners" in Tahiti. Queen Pomare IV politely agreed, but as soon as the warship left Papeete, she sent a letter to Queen Victoria asking for British protection. Britain, more interested in its profitable colonies in Australia and New Zealand and at loggerheads with the United States over the location of the U.S.-Canadian border, declined to interfere. That opened the door for a Frenchman to trick several Tahitian chiefs into signing a document requesting that Tahiti be made a protectorate of France. The French were in fact interested in a South Pacific port for their warships and whalers, and when word of the document reached Paris, a ship was dispatched to Papeete. Tahiti was then claimed by France and the protectorate declared in 1842.

Queen Pomare, who did not know of the document signed by the chiefs, continued to resist along with her followers, and the Tahitians launched an armed rebellion against the French troops, who surrounded Queen Pomare's palace and forced her to retreat to Raiatea. The fighting continued until 1846, when the last Tahitian stronghold was captured and the remnants of their guerrilla bands retreated to Tahiti Iti. A monument to the fallen Tahitians now stands beside the round-island road near the airport at Faaa, a village noted for its strong pro-independence sentiment today.

Queen Pomare finally gave up the struggle in 1847. She returned to Papeete and ruled as a figurehead until her death 30 years later. Her son, Pomare V, who liked the bottle more than the throne, ruled 3 more years until abdicating in return for a sizable pension from the French government for him, his family and his mistress. Tahiti was then declared a full-fledged French colony. In 1903 all of eastern Polynesia was consolidated into a single colony known as French Oceania, which it remained until 1957, when its status was changed to an overseas territory known as French Polynesia.

DATELINE

George III.

- **1768** Capt. Antoine de Bougainville also discovers Tahiti.
- **1769** Capt. James Cook arrives to observe the transit of Venus on the first of his three voyages of discovery.
- **1788** HMS *Bounty* under Capt. William Bligh arrives to take breadfruit to the Caribbean.
- **1789** Lt. Fletcher Christian leads the munity on the *Bounty*.
- **1791** HMS *Pandora* captures mutineers left on Tahiti.
- **1792** Capt. Bligh returns, gets breadfruit he came for in the *Bounty*. Slaves in the Caribbean refuse to eat it.
- **1797** London Missionary Society emissaries arrive looking for converts.
- **1812** King Pomare II becomes the first Tahitian to convert to Christianity. With European help, he begins wars that make him King of Tahiti 3 years later.
- **1824** King Pomare III crowned European-style. New civil code prohibits dancing.
- **1827** Queen Pomare IV succeeds to the throne.

(continues)

DATELINE

- **1834** Queen Pomare signs pledge against sale of liquor. Tahiti quiets down, becomes an important trading port.
- **1837** French Catholic priests arrive, are refused permission to land by the Protestants. France demands full reparations.
- **1838** Admiral du Petit-Thouars arrives in warship, hands ultimatum to the queen. She reluctantly signs.
- **1841** French traders trick Tahitian chiefs into signing document asking for French protection. They later disavow it.
- **1842** Admiral du Petit-Thouars returns, threatens to occupy Tahiti, and demands 10,000 Spanish dollars. Chiefs agree to pay, and Tahiti becomes a French protectorate. Herman Melville jumps ship, spends time in the *Calaboosa Beretane* (British jail). He later writes *Omoo* about his adventures.
- **1844** Guerrilla war erupts between Tahitians and the French, lasts 4 years.
- **1847** Queen Pomare acquiesces in full French protection.
- **1862** Irish adventurer William

(continues)

Except for periodic invasions by artists and writers, French Polynesia remained an idyllic backwater from the time France took complete possession until the early 1960s. French painter Paul Gauguin gave up his family and his career as a Parisian stockbroker and arrived in 1891; he spent his days reproducing Tahiti's colors and people on canvas until he died of syphilis on Hiva Oa in the Marquesas Islands. Stories and novels by writers such as W. Somerset Maugham, Jack London, Robert Louis Stevenson, and Rupert Brooke added to Tahiti's romantic reputation during the early years of this century. In 1932 two young Americans—Charles Nordhoff and James Norman Hall—published *Mutiny on the Bounty,* which quickly became an enormous best-seller. Three years later MGM released an enormously successful movie version with Clark Gable and Charles Laughton in the roles of Christian and Bligh, respectively. Although the movie contained background shots of 40 Tahitian villages, most of the movie was filmed on Santa Catalina off the California coast; neither Gable nor Laughton visited Tahiti. (It actually was the second film to be based on the *Bounty* story; the first was an Australian production which starred Errol Flynn in his first movie role.)

The book and movie brought fame to Tahiti, but any plans for increased tourism were put on hold during World War II. French Polynesia had sided with the Free French, who gave permission for the United States to use the islands in the war against Japan. In 1942 some 6,000 U.S. sailors and marines quickly built the territory's first airstrip on Bora Bora and remained there throughout the war. A number of mixed-race Tahitians are descended from those American troops.

THE 1960s & BEYOND

Even after the war, the islands were too far away and too difficult to reach to attract more than the most adventurous or wealthy travelers who arrived by ocean liner or by seaplane. Then in the early 1960s two events brought rapid changes to most of French Polynesia.

First, Tahiti's new international airport opened at Faaa in late 1960. Shortly thereafter Marlon Brando and a movie crew arrived to film a remake of *Mutiny on the Bounty.* This new burst of fame, coupled with the ability of tourists to reach Tahiti overnight on the new long-range jets, transformed the island into a major destination, and hotel construction began in earnest.

Second, France established the *Centre d'Expérimentation du Pacifique,* its nuclear testing facility in the Tuamotus about 700 miles southeast of Tahiti. A huge support base was constructed on the outskirts of Papeete.

Together, tourism and the nuclear-testing facility brought a major boom to Tahiti almost overnight. Thousands of Polynesians flocked to Papeete to take the new construction and hotel jobs, which enabled them to earn good money and experience life in Papeete's fast lane.

In addition, some 15,000 French military personnel and civilian technicians swarmed into the territory to staff the new nuclear-testing facility, all of them with money and many with an inclination to spend it on the local women. The Tahitian men struck back, brawls erupted, and for a brief period in the 1960s the island experienced one of its rare moments of open hostility between the Tahitian majority and the French.

That's not to say there weren't hard feelings all along. An independence movement had existed since the guerrilla skirmishes of the 1840s, and by the 1970s it forced France to choose between serious unrest or granting the territory a much larger degree of control over its internal affairs. In 1977 the French parliament passed a law that created an elected Territorial Assembly with powers over the local budget. The vice president of the Assembly was the highest elected local official. A high commissioner sent from Paris, however, retained authority over defense, foreign affairs, immigration, the police, civil service, communications, and secondary education. This system lasted 7 years.

2. GOVERNMENT & THE ECONOMY

Honoring a previous promise of more local autonomy (if not independence), and with its eye on the pro-independence disturbances in New Caledonia, the government of French president François Mitterrand in 1984 enacted another constitution for French Polynesia, which set up the present territorial government. Rather than some sinister plot to rip off tourists, it's this government, and in particular the way it is financed, that is responsible for the relatively high prices you will pay.

GOVERNMENT

The 30 members of the Territorial Assembly now elect their own president, who is the highest-ranking official in the territory and is referred to as the president of French Polynesia. The assembly and its Council of Ministers participate in decisions far more than under more direct French rule, and they govern most matters affecting the territory—except defense, justice, national police, and foreign affairs.

Technically an overseas territory of France, French Polynesia sends two elected deputies and a senator to the French parliament in Paris. Residents of the territory vote in French presidential elections.

The French also still play a significant role in law enforcement. The city of Papeete and a few other *communes* have their own police forces, but the French *gendarmes* are in control of most parts of the territory. The

DATELINE

Stewart starts a cotton plantation at Atimaono.

- **1865** The first 329 Chinese arrive from Hong Kong to work Stewart's plantation. It fails, but most of them stay.
- **1872** Pierre Loti (Julien Viaud) spends several months on Tahiti. His *The Marriage of Loti* is published 8 years later.
- **1873** William Stewart declared bankrupt, dies the next night.
- **1877** Queen Pomare IV dies at age 64.
- **1880** King Pomare V abdicates in return for pensions for him, his family and mistress. Tahiti becomes a French colony.
- **1884** Fire destroys Papeete. Thatch outlawed as building material.
- **1888** Robert Louis Stevenson spends 2 months at Tautira on Tahiti Iti.
- **1891** "Fleeing from civilization," the painter Paul Gauguin arrives, soon moves to Mataiea on Tahiti's south shore.
- **1897** France annexes the Leeward Islands.
- **1903** Paul Gauguin dies at Hiva Oa in the Marquesas, apparently of syphilis. His last painting sold at Ni-

(continues)

DATELINE

agara Falls for 7 francs. All of eastern Polynesia becomes one French colony.
- **1906** Hurricane does severe damage to Tahiti.
- **1914** Two German warships shell Papeete, sink the French navy's *Zélée*.
- **1917** W. Somerset Maugham spends several months on Tahiti.
- **1933** *Mutiny on the Bounty* by Charles Nordhoff and James Norman Hall is published, becomes a best-seller.
- **1935** Clark Gable and Charles Laughton star in the movie *Mutiny on the Bounty*. Neither visit Tahiti.
- **1942** U.S. Marines build the territory's first airstrip on Bora Bora. Tahiti sides with the Free French.
- **1960** Faaa International Airport opens, turning Tahiti into a jet-set destination. Marlon Brando arrives to film a second movie version of *Mutiny on the Bounty*.
- **1963** France chooses Moruroa as its nuclear-testing site. Many Tahitians object, pro-autonomy party wins majority.
- **1966** France explodes the first nuclear bomb aboveground at

(continues)

man wearing the round de Gaulle hat who stops you for riding a motorbike without a helmet is more likely to be from Martinique than from Moorea.

The independence movement hasn't gone away. The village of Faaa surrounding the airport on Tahiti is a hotbed of pro-independence sentiment. You'll also hear more English used in Faaa than anywhere else, as evidenced by stores with American-sounding English names, such as "Cash and Carry," "Fare (Home) Center," and "Kiddy Shop."

Although many of them gripe about the French, most Tahitians readily accept the largesse sent their way by the French government, which supplies more than half the money spent by the Territorial Assembly on modern schools, roads, hospitals, airports, and other public projects that are as good as any in the South Pacific. On a per capita basis, only the American money poured into Pago Pago rivals the amount spent by the French on their South Pacific territories.

THE ECONOMY

Very little is produced locally—even most foodstuffs are imported into French Polynesia. The local share of governmental services is paid for by heavy duties levied on these imports—which translates into high prices for everything except bread, rice, sugar, and a few other basics. The import tax on tobacco alone supplies 7% of the local revenue, which explains why a package of American cigarettes costs about $5.

The cost of living soared when the American dollar rose significantly against the French franc in the early 1980s, and merchants, restaurateurs, and hoteliers raised their prices to make up for the increased cost of imports. But when the American dollar fell by 25% from 1984 to 1985, the prices didn't come down with it.

Tahiti very quickly became known as an outrageously expensive destination, especially when visitors went home with tales of paying up to $6 for a beer in a hotel bar, even more for a mixed drink, on top of the most expensive hotel room rates in the region. Compounding the problem for the territory's tourist industry, about 70 stores and shops in downtown Papeete were burned in October 1987 during a riot ignited by a labor dispute. Accordingly, the number of visitors dropped precipitously in 1988.

Faced with scores of unoccupied rooms, the owners of many small hotels have held their rates steady or even dropped them in recent years. The territorial government also decided in 1988 to control prices charged by hotels, restaurants, and some bars. As a result, most prices stabilized during the late 1980s and early 1990s, while the rest of the South Pacific tended to catch up with Tahiti. From a traveler's standpoint, since the sales tax already is included in the price and there is no need to tip (a combined saving of about 23%), a carefully planned, moderately priced visit should cost about what one would in Hawaii, excluding the more expensive airfare.

Nevertheless, you'll find prices of basic items expensive when compared to the going rate in most Western nations. Just remember that you are not alone; the local residents pay the same inflated prices in their grocery stores as you will.

DATELINE

Moruroa.
- **1973** Quinn's Bar closes; replaced by a shopping center.
- **1977** France grants limited self-rule to French Polynesia.
- **1984** Local autonomy statute enacted by French parliament.

3. GEOGRAPHY

French Polynesia sprawls over an area of two million square miles in the eastern South Pacific. That's about the size of Europe excluding the Soviet Union or about two-thirds the size of the continental United States. The 130 main islands, however, consist of only 1,500 square miles, an area smaller than Rhode Island.

Within this huge area lie five major archipelagos which differ in terrain, climate, and to a certain extent, people. With the exception of the Tuamotus, an enormous chain of low coral atolls northeast of Tahiti, all but a few are high islands, the mountainous tops of ancient volcanoes that have been eroded into jagged peaks, deep bays, and fertile valleys. All have fringing or barrier coral reefs and blue lagoons worthy of postcards.

THE SOCIETY ISLANDS

The most strikingly beautiful and most frequently visited are the **Society Islands,** so named by Capt. James Cook because they lay relatively close together. These include **Tahiti** and its nearby companion **Moorea,** which together are known also as the Windward Islands because they sit to the east whence comes the prevailing trade wind. To the northwest lie **Bora Bora, Huahine, Raiatea, Tahaa, Maupiti,** and several smaller islands. Because they are downwind of Tahiti, they also are called the Leeward Islands.

To James A. Michener's eye, Bora Bora is the most beautiful island in the world. To mine, that title goes to Moorea in a close race. It's all a matter of degree, for the Society Islands definitely are the most dramatically beautiful collection of islands in the world.

THE TUAMOTUS

One of the world's largest collections of atolls, the 69 atolls of the low-lying **Tuamotu Archipelago** run for 720 miles on a line from northwest to southeast across the approaches to Tahiti from the east. The early European sailors called them the "Dangerous Archipelago" because of their tricky currents and because they virtually cannot be seen until a ship is almost on top of them. Even today they are a wrecking ground for yachts and interisland trading boats. Two of them, Moruroa and

IMPRESSIONS

The people of the south-easterly clusters—concerning whom, however, but little is known—have a bad name as cannibals; and for that reason their hospitality is seldom taxed by the mariner.

—HERMAN MELVILLE, 1847

No Sort of Iron, or any thing that is made of Iron, or any sort of Cloth or other usefull or necessary articles are to be given in exchange for any thing but provisions.

—JAMES COOK, 1769

IMPRESSIONS

It is no exaggeration to say, that to a European of any sensibility, who, for the first time, wanders back into these valleys—away from the haunts of the natives—the ineffable repose and beauty of the landscape is such, that every object strikes him like something seen in a dream; and for a time he almost refuses to believe that scenes like these should have a commonplace existence.

—Herman Melville, 1847

Fangataufa, are used by France to tests its nuclear weapons. Others provide the bulk of Tahiti's well-known black pearls. **Rangiroa,** the world's second-largest atoll, is the most frequently visited.

THE MARQUESAS

The **Marquesas,** a group of 10 high islands, sit beyond the Tuamotus some 750 miles northeast of Tahiti. They are younger than the Society Islands, and protecting coral reefs have not enclosed them. As a result, the surf pounds on their shores, there are no encircling coastal plains, and the people live in a series of deep valleys that radiate from central mountain peaks. The Marquesas have lost their once-large populations to 19th-century disease and the 20th-century economic lure of Papeete; today their sparsely populated, cloud-enshrouded valleys have an almost haunted air about them.

THE AUSTRAL ISLANDS

The **Austral Islands** south of Tahiti are part of a chain of high islands that continues on into the Cook Islands to the west. The people of the more temperate Australs, which include Rurutu, Raivavae, and Tubuai (where the *Bounty* mutineers tried to settle), once produced some of the best art objects in the South Pacific, but these skills have passed into time.

THE GAMBIER ISLANDS

Far on the southern end of the Tuamotu Archipelago, the **Gambier Islands** are part of a semisubmerged, middle-aged high island similar to Bora Bora. The hilly remnants of the old volcano are scattered in a huge lagoon, which is partially enclosed by a barrier reef marking the original outline of the island before it began to sink. The largest of these remnant islands is Mangareva.

4. PEOPLE & CULTURE

About 70% of French Polynesia's population of 190,000 is Polynesian, 4.2% is of pure Asian descent (primarily Chinese), 14.2% are of mixed races, and the remaining 11.5%

IMPRESSIONS

He had once landed there, and found the remains of a man and a woman partly eaten. On his starting and sickening at the sight, one of Moipu's young men picked up a human foot, and provocatively staring at the stranger, grinned and nibbled at the heel.

—Robert Louis Stevenson, 1890

N
0
100 km
62 mi
Apataki
Niau
Arutua
Kaukura
TUAMOTU ISLANDS
Tiputa
Rangiroa
Mehitia
Makatea
Tikehau
Mataiva
South Pacific Ocean
Tetiaroa
Windward Islands
Papeete
Tahiti
Moorea
SOCIETY ISLANDS
Maiao
Leeward Islands
Fare
Huahine
Uturoa
Tahaa
Raiatea
Tupai
Bora Bora
Vaitape
Maupiti

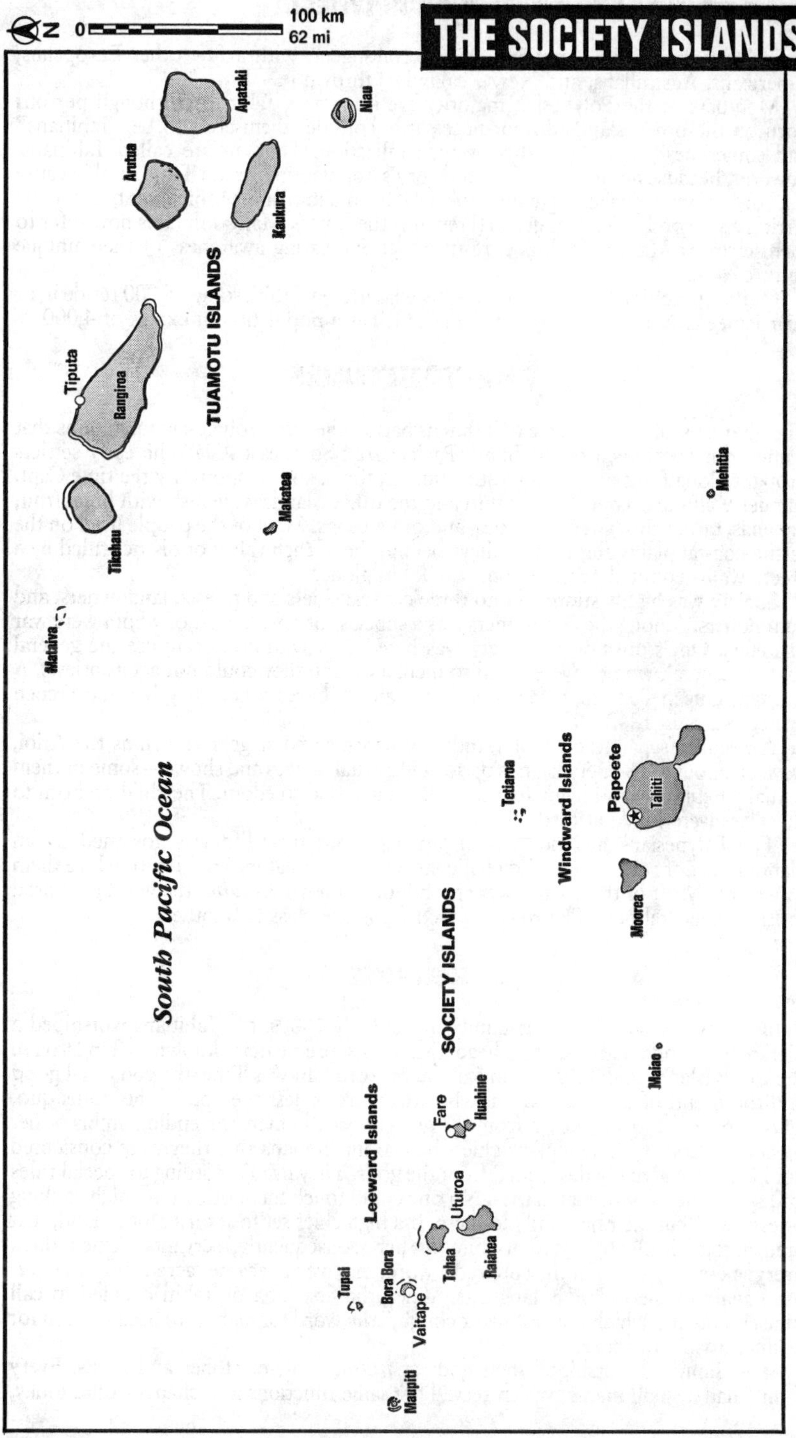

is made up mostly of a growing French contingent, with a few other Europeans, Americans, Australians, and New Zealanders thrown in.

Members of the Polynesian majority are known as Tahitians, although persons born on the other islands do not necessarily consider themselves to be "Tahitians" and sometimes gripe about this overgeneralization. They all are called Tahitians, however, because about 70% of the territory's population lives on Tahiti, and because the Polynesian language originally spoken only on Tahiti and Moorea has become the territory's second official language (French is the other). Many Tahitians now refer to themselves as *Maohi* (Maori), a result of an increasing awareness of their unique culture.

Of the approximately 120,000 persons who live on Tahiti, some 85,000 reside in or near Papeete. No other village in the islands has a population in excess of 4,000.

THE TAHITIANS

The Tahitians' ancestors came to Tahiti as part of the great Polynesian migrations that fanned out over much of the South Pacific from Southeast Asia. The early settlers brought along food plants, domestic animals, tools, and weapons. By the time Capt. Samuel Wallis arrived in 1767, Tahiti and the other islands were lush with breadfruit, bananas, taro, yams, sweet potatoes, and other crops. Most of the people lived on the fertile coastal plains and in the valleys behind them, each valley or district ruled by a chief. Wallis counted 17 chiefdoms on Tahiti alone.

Society was highly stratified into three classes: chiefs and priests, landowners, and commoners. Among the commoners was a subclass of slaves, most of whom were war prisoners. One's position in society was hereditary, with primogeniture the general rule. In general, women were equal to men, although they could not act as priests. A woman, Queen Pomare, ruled over Tahiti and Moorea when they became French protectorates in 1842.

A peculiar separate class of wandering dancers and singers known as the Arioi, traveled about the Society Islands performing ritual dances and shows—some of them sexually explicit—and living in a state of total sexual freedom. The children born to this class were killed at birth.

The Polynesians had no written language, but their life was governed by an elaborate set of rules that would challenge modern legislators' abilities to reduce them to writing. Most of these rules were prohibitions known as *tabu,* the word now used in English as "taboo." The rules differed from one class to another.

RELIGION

Before they converted to Christianity in the early 1800s, the Tahitians worshiped a hierarchy of gods that had at its head Taaroa, a supreme deity known as Tangaroa in the Cook Islands and Tangaloa in Samoa. Next to him was Tane, the god of all good and the friend of armies, and Tu, who was more or less the god of the status quo. *Mana,* or power, came down from the gods to each human, depending on his or her position in society. The highest chiefs had so much mana that they were considered godlike, if not actually descended from the gods. They lived according to special rules and spoke their own vocabularies. No one could touch them other than high-ranking priests, who cut their hair and fed them. If a high chief set foot on a plot of land, that land automatically belonged to him or her (consequently, servants carried them everywhere they went). If they uttered a word, that word became sacred and was never used again in the everyday language. When the first king of Tahiti decided to call himself Pomare, which means "night cough," the word for night (*po*) became tabu for a time. It isn't anymore.

The Tahitians worshiped their gods at *marae* built of stones and rocks. Every family had a small marae, which served the same functions as a chapel would today,

IMPRESSIONS

I was pleased with nothing so much as with the inhabitants. There is a mildness in the expression of their countenances which at once banishes the idea of a savage, and an intelligence which shows that they are advancing in civilization.

—CHARLES DARWIN, 1839

---

and villages and entire districts—even islands—built large marae that served not only as places of worship but also as meeting sites. Elaborate religious ceremonies were held on the large central marae. Priests prayed that the gods would come down and reside in carved tikis and other objects during the ceremonies (the objects lost all meaning afterward). Sacrifices were offered to the gods, sometimes including humans, most of whom were war prisoners or troublemakers. Despite the practice of human sacrifice, cannibalism apparently was never practiced on Tahiti, although it was fairly widespread in the Marquesas Islands.

The souls of the deceased were believed to be taken by the gods to Havaiki, the homeland from which their Polynesian ancestors had come. In all Polynesian islands, Havaiki always lay in the direction of the setting sun, and the souls departed for it from the northwest corner of each island.

SEX

The sexual freedom that intrigued the early European explorers permeated Tahitian society, although it was not without its limits. Except for the nobility, sex was restricted to one's own class. Children generally were encouraged to have as many partners as they wanted from puberty to marriage, so they would learn the erotic skills necessary to make a good marriage. Even within marriage there was a certain latitude. Married men and women, for example, could have extramarital affairs with their sisters-in-law and brothers-in-law, respectively. Since first cousins were considered brothers and sisters, the opportunities for licensed adultery were numerous.

The old rules have disappeared and sexual relations in Tahiti today are governed by a mishmash of morals. The coming of Christianity and its ethics has left Tahitians with as much guilt over adultery as anyone else. On the other hand, the European moral code was not accepted as readily as was the belief in God, and premarital sex has continued to be practiced widely in French Polynesia. Prostitution, which was unknown before the coming of the Europeans and their system of sex-for-nails (see "History," above), is widespread in Papeete's cash economy.

As in other Polynesian societies, homosexuality was accepted among a class of transvestites known as *mahu,* a fact that startled the early explorers and shocked the missionaries. Mahus still abound in Papeete, especially at several nightclubs that cater to all sexual preferences and at the resort hotels, performing as women in some dance reviews. Women were not considered equal in this respect in ancient times, however, and lesbianism was discouraged.

IMPRESSIONS

The dance competitions—and other events of the Heiva festival—are unexpectedly tourist-free, a genuine people's celebration on which it is a privilege to eavesdrop.

—RON HALL, 1991

. . . they wear a sort of gown, open in front, very loose, and as negligent as you please. The ladies here never dress for dinner.

—HERMAN MELVILLE, 1847

Note that the acquired immune deficiency syndrome (AIDS) virus has been detected in French Polynesia. Accordingly, visitors should exercise at least the same degree of care in the choice of their sexual partners and safe-sex practices as they would at home.

THE CHINESE

The outbreak of the American Civil War in 1861 and the subsequent blockading of the Confederacy resulted in a worldwide shortage of cotton. In September 1862 an Irish adventurer named William Stewart arrived in Tahiti and shortly thereafter founded a cotton plantation at Atimaono, the island's only large tract of flat land. The Tahitians weren't the least bit interested in working for Stewart, so he used laborers imported from the Cook Islands to clear the land. He then arranged to import a contingent of Chinese laborers to put the plantation into full production; the first 329 of them arrived from Hong Kong in February 1865.

Stewart ran into difficulties, both with finances and with his workers. At one point, a rumor swept Tahiti that he had built a guillotine, practiced with it on a pig, and then executed a recalcitrant Chinese laborer. That was never proved, although a Chinese immigrant, Chim Soo, was the first person to be executed by guillotine in Tahiti. Stewart's financial difficulties, which were compounded by the drop in cotton prices after the American South resumed production after 1868, led to the collapse of his empire.

Nothing remains of his plantation at Atimaono (a golf course and public park now occupy some of the land), but many of the Chinese who came to work decided to stay in Tahiti. They grew vegetables for the Papeete market, saved their money, and invested in other businesses. Their descendants and subsequent immigrants from China now make up about 10% of the territory's population and influence the economy far in excess of their numbers. They run nearly all of French Polynesia's grocery and general merchandise stores, which in French are called *magasins chinoises,* or Chinese stores.

5. LANGUAGE

The official languages in the territory are French and Tahitian. English is also taught as a second language in the schools, so communication is usually not a problem in shops, hotels, and restaurants. Once you get away from the beaten path, however, some knowledge of French or Tahitian is very helpful.

Tahitian is the language spoken in most homes in the Society Islands, although the old local dialects are used on a daily basis in the far outer islands. Nearly everyone—with the exception of some older Polynesians—speaks French, which was the only medium of instruction in the schools until the mid-1980s. Only after the French gave the Tahitians control over their own internal affairs in 1984 was Tahitian taught in the schools along with French. This is one reason many pro-independence Tahitians view French as a symbol of colonial control over their islands.

TAHITIAN PRONUNCIATION

A little knowledge of Tahitian is important for two reasons: First, most of the place names are Tahitian, so you'll want to know how to pronounce your destinations; and second, you can score some brownie points with the locals by saying a few words in their language.

No Polynesian language was written until Peter Heywood jotted down a Tahitian

IMPRESSIONS

Tahiti has unique sex freedom. A bitter critic of the island has sneered that its charm is explainable solely in terms of the "erotic mist" that hangs over the island. . . . I remember as a boy poring over the accounts of early navigators and coming repeatedly upon that cryptic phrase "so we put into Tahiti to refresh the men."

—James A. Michener, 1951

---

vocabulary while awaiting trial for his part in the mutiny on the *Bounty*. The early missionaries who later translated the Bible into Tahitian decided which letters of the Roman alphabet to use to approximate the sounds of the Polynesian languages. These tended to vary from place to place. For example, they used the consonants *t* and *v* in Tahitian. In Hawaiian, which is similar, they used *k* and *w*. The actual Polynesian sounds are somewhere in between.

The consonants used in Tahitian are *f, h, m, n, p, r, t,* and *v*. There are some special rules regarding their sounds, but you'll be understood if you say them as you would in English.

The Polynesian languages, including Tahitian, consist primarily of vowel sounds, which are pronounced in the Roman fashion, that is, *ah, ay, ee, oh,* and *ou*—not *ay, ee, eye, oh,* and *you,* as in English. Almost all vowels are sounded separately. For example, Tahiti's airport is at Faaa, which is pronounced Fah-ah-ah, not Fah. Papeete is Pah-pay-*ay*-tay, not Pa-pee-tee. Paea is Pah-*ay*-ah.

Westerners have had their impact, however, and today some vowels are run together. Moorea, for example, technically is Moh-oh-*ray*-ah, but nearly everyone says Mo-*ray*-ah. The Punaauia hotel district on Tahiti's west coast is pronounced Poo-*nav*-i-a.

Look for *Say It in Tahitian* by D. T. Tryon (Pacific Publications, 1977) in the local bookshops and hotel boutiques. This slim volume will teach you more Tahitian than you can use in one vacation.

USEFUL WORDS

To help you impress the local residents with what a really friendly tourist you are, here are a few Tahitian words you can use on them. Note that *u* is pronounced like the *oo* in "kangaroo"; *i* as *ee,* as in "hee haw."

ENGLISH	TAHITIAN	PRONUNCIATION
hello	**Ia orana**	ee-ah oh-*rah*-na (sounds like "your honor")
welcome	**maeva**	mah-*ay*-vah
goodbye	**parahi**	pah-*rah*-hee
good	**maitai**	*my*-tie
very good	**maitai roa**	*my*-tie-*row*-ah
thank you	**maruru**	mah-*roo*-roo
thank you very much	**maruru roa**	mah-*roo*-roo *row*-ah
good health!	**manuia**	mah-*new*-yah
woman	**vahine**	vah-*hee*-nay
man	**tane**	*tah*-nay
sarong	**pareu**	pah-*ray*-oo
small islet	**motu**	*moh*-too
take it easy	**hare maru**	*ha*-ray *mah*-roo
fed up	**fiu**	few

6. INFORMATION, ENTRY REQUIREMENTS & MONEY

INFORMATION

Other than this guide, your best sources of information are the **Tahiti Tourist Promotion Board's** offices in Papeete and elsewhere. In the **U.S. and Canada,** contact the board at 9841 Airport Boulevard, Suite 1108, Los Angeles, CA 90045 (tel. 213/649-2884, fax 213/649-3825). Ask specifically for "Tahiti and Her Islands," a booklet with all the latest information.

In **New Zealand,** the board has an office at No. 4 Ophir Street, Newton, P.O. Box 5172, Wellesley Street, Auckland (tel. 732-649, fax 732-415). In **France and Europe,** contact the board under it's French name, Office du Tourisme de Tahiti et Ses Iles, 28 bd. Saint Germain, 75005 Paris (tel. 46-34-50-59, fax 46-33-82-54).

In French Polynesia, the board is referred to by its French acronym **OPATTI.** The main office is in Fare Manihini, the Polynesian-style building along the waterfront on boulevard Pomare at the foot of rue Paul-Gauguin (tel. 42-96-26, fax 43-66-19). The staff members all speak English and are very helpful to visitors, especially in providing such information as when trading boats will leave for the distant islands groups. The schedules and fares are posted on a bulletin board in the welcome center. Hours are 7:30am to 5pm Monday to Friday, 8am to noon on Saturday.

You won't find them sitting out on display, but low-budget travelers can request lists of all the territory's less expensive "unclassified" hotels, pensions, and campgrounds at Fare Manihini. They are compiled by island, so ask for the lists applicable to your specific destinations.

Local tourism committees have information booths on Moorea, Raiatea, Huahine, Bora Bora, and Rangiroa. Details are in Chapter 5.

ENTRY REQUIREMENTS

Most visitors are required to have a valid **passport** and a return or ongoing ticket. The immigration official may ask to see both.

No **vaccinations** are required unless you are coming from a yellow fever, plague, or cholera area.

Visas valid for 90 days are issued upon arrival to most visitors. At the time of writing, visas were being issued to New Zealanders upon arrival at Tahiti; however, Australians still needed to get a visa before leaving home. French embassies and consulates overseas can issue visas valid for stays of between 1 and 3 months, and they will forward applications for longer visits to the local immigration department in Papeete. There are French consulates in Boston, Chicago, Detroit, Houston, Los Angeles, New York, San Francisco, New Orleans, and Honolulu. Residents of those cities are required to apply there. If there is no French consulate in your hometown, contact the Embassy of France, 4102 Reservoir Road NW, Washington, DC 20007 (tel. 202/944-6000).

As a practical matter, your initial visa can be extended to 6 months if you still have your return air ticket, sufficient funds, aren't employed in French Polynesia, and have kept your nose clean. Applications for extensions must be made at the immigration office. To find it, go into the alley nearest boulevard Pomare off rue Jeanne-d'Arc across from the Vaima Centre in Papeete, enter the first door on the left, and proceed to the top floor.

In addition to personal effects, duty-free **Customs** allowances are 200 cigarettes or 50 cigars, 2 liters of spirits or 2 liters of wine, 50 grams of perfume, two still cameras and 10 rolls of unexposed film, one video camera, one cassette player, and sports and camping equipment. Narcotics, dangerous drugs, weapons, ammunition, and copyright infringements (that is, those video- and audiotapes you have pirated) are prohibited. Pets and plants are subject to stringent regulations. If your flight arrives from American Samoa or Fiji, your bags will be fumigated (pack your carry-on bag for an overnighter).

MONEY

French Polynesia uses the French Pacific franc (CFP), which is pegged directly to the French franc (5.5 CFP per franc) and used interchangeably with the French Pacific francs printed or coined in New Caledonia. Prices in this chapter are quoted in Pacific francs followed in parentheses by the U.S. dollar equivalent.

The U.S. dollar has fluctuated considerably in recent years on either side of 100 CFP. On my most recent visit, $1 was worth 90 CFP. When I arrived in New Caledonia a few weeks later, the U.S. buck had risen to 105 CFP—a difference of 15%. I have used the rate of **$1 = 100 CFP** to compute the U.S. dollar prices.

To find out how many Pacific francs you will get for one U.S. dollar, look in the financial section of your hometown newspaper, locate the number of French francs per dollar, and multiply that amount by 18.18. Since many banks are not the least bit familiar with the Pacific franc, you may get a better rate if you wait to change your money in French Polynesia rather than before you leave home.

No decimals are used in dealing with Pacific francs, so the amounts can seem staggering. As long as the U.S. dollar is worth around 100 CFP, it's helpful to think of 100 CFP as $1, 1,000 CFP as $10, and so on. In other words, drop two zeros, and you have the approximate amount of U.S. dollars.

Don't bargain, for to haggle over a retail price is to offend the integrity of the seller, especially if he or she is a Polynesian.

WHAT THINGS COST IN FRENCH POLYNESIA	U.S. $
Taxi from airport to Papeete (at night)	25.00
Local phone call	.50
Ride on *le truck*	1.00
Overwater bungalow at Hotel Moana Beach (deluxe)	498.00
Double bungalow at Résidence Les Tipaniers (moderate)	100.00
Double bungalow at Moorea Village (inexpensive)	55.00
Hostel bunk at Hiti Mahana Beach Club (budget)	15.00
Lunch for one at La Pizzeria (moderate)	9.00
Lunch for one at Snack Vaiete (budget)	4.00
Dinner for one, without wine, at Auberge du Pacific (expensive)	50.00
Dinner for one, without wine, at Lou Pescadou (moderate)	30.00
Dinner for one, without wine, at *les roulettes* (budget)	9.50
Beer (at a hotel bar)	3.50
Coca Cola (in a snack bar)	1.20
Cup of coffee	1.50
Roll of ASA 100 Kodacolor film, 36 exposures	11.50
Admission to Gauguin Museum	4.50
Movie ticket	7.00

THE FRANC & THE DOLLAR

At this writing, $1 = approximately 100 CFP, the rate of exchange used to calculate the U.S. dollar prices given in this chapter. This rate has fluctuated widely and may not be the same when you visit. Accordingly, use the following table only as a guide.

$ CFP	$ U.S.	$ CFP	$ U.S.
100	1	1,000	10
150	1.50	1,500	15
200	2	2,000	20
300	3	3,000	30
400	4	4,000	40
500	5	5,000	50
600	6	6,000	60
700	7	7,000	70
800	8	8,000	80
900	9	9,000	90
1,000	10	10,000	100

7. WHEN TO GO — CLIMATE, HOLIDAYS & EVENTS

There is no bad time to go to French Polynesia, but some periods are better than others. For the best combination of weather and availability of hotel rooms, the months of May, June, September, and October are best.

CLIMATE

Tahiti and the Society Islands have a typical balmy tropical climate. There are two seasons. November through April is the summer **wet season,** when the average maximum daily temperature is 86°F and rainy periods can be expected. Nighttime lows are about 72°F. May through October is the austral winter **dry season,** when midday maximum temperatures average a delightful 82°F, with early morning lows of 68°F often making a blanket necessary. Some winter days, especially on the south side of the islands, can seem quite chilly when a strong wind blows from Antarctica. Tropical showers can pass overhead at any time of the year. Humidity averages between 77% and 80% throughout the year.

The central and northern Tuamotus have much the same climate except that the amount of rainfall is lower. Since there are no mountains to create cooling night breezes, they can seem desertlike hot between November and April. The Marquesas are closer to the equator and temperatures and humidity tend to be slightly higher than in Tahiti. The climate in the Austral and Gambier islands is more temperate.

French Polynesia is on the far eastern edge of the South Pacific cyclone (hurricane) belt, and for 70 years did not experience a devastating storm until 1983, when six of them raked the islands. As of 1991, there had not been another.

HOLIDAYS

Public holidays are New Year's Day, Good Friday and Easter Monday, Ascension Day, Whitmonday, Assumption Day, Labor Day (May 1), Bastille Day (July 14), Internal

Automomy Day (September 8), All Saints Day (November 1), Armistice Day (November 11), and Christmas.

From a visitor's standpoint, July is the busiest month because of the *Heiva I Tahiti* festival (see below). Hotels on the outer islands are usually full during August, the traditional French vacation month when many Papeete residents do their own version of getting away from it all.

FRENCH POLYNESIA CALENDAR OF EVENTS

JANUARY

☐ **Chinese New Year.** Parade, musical performances, demonstrations of martial arts, Chinese dances, and handcrafts. Between mid-January and mid-February.

FEBRUARY

☐ **Tahitian International Billfish Tournament.** Moorea. Last week in February.

MARCH

☐ **Boat Show.** Boats of various sizes are displayed at the Lotus Center in Punaauia, Tahiti. 1st week in March.

☐ **National Women's Day.** French Polynesia's own version of Mother's Day. 2nd Sunday in March.

APRIL

☐ **Moorea International Triathlon.** Swimming, cycling, running competition. A smaller version of the famous Hawaii triathlon. Moorea. Mid-April.

MAY

☐ **Maire Fern Day.** Celebrates the many uses of the sweet-scented Maire fern. Concludes with a ball. Mid-May.

JUNE

☐ **World Environment Day.** Program at Point Venus emphasizes campaign to clean up the islands. Early June.

JULY

✪ ***HEIVA I TAHITI*** *The festival to end all festivals in French Polynesia. Originally a celebration of Bastille Day on July 14, this shindig has been extended into a month-long blast (it is commonly called* Tiurai*, the Tahitian word for July). They pull out all the stops, with parades, outrigger-canoe races, javelin-throwing contests, fire walking, games, carnivals, festivals, reenactments of ancient Polynesian ceremonies at restored marae. Highlight: An extraordinarily colorful contest to determine the best Tahitian dancing troupe for the year. The winning groups then tour the other islands for a series of small festivals. Airline and hotel reservations are difficult to come by during July, so book early and take your written confirmation with you. Contact the Tahiti Tourist Promotion Board for details (See "Information, Entry Requirements & Money," above).*

AUGUST

☐ **International Marathon of Tahiti-Moorea.** 42-km race on Tahiti, 20km on Moorea attract runners from around the world. Late August.

SEPTEMBER

☐ **Floralies Day.** In biggest flower show of the year, the Territorial Assembly Hall is bedecked in flowers and tropical plants in honor of Harrison W. Smith, the American who created the botanical gardens next to the Gauguin Museum in Papeari. Late September.

OCTOBER

☐ **Stone Fishing Ceremony.** A 4-day celebration on Tahaa includes sports, music, speedboat and sailing races around the island, fire walking, and stone fishing festival climaxed by a huge Tahitian feast on a small islet. Late October, early November.

NOVEMBER

☐ **All Saints Day.** Flowers are sold everywhere to families who put them on graves after whitewashing the tombstones. November 1.

DECEMBER

☐ **Tiare Tahiti Day.** Everyone on the streets of Papeete and in the hotels receives a *tiare Tahiti,* the fragrant gardenia that is indigenous only to Tahiti. December 1.

8. GETTING AROUND FRENCH POLYNESIA

All but a few visitors arrive at Faaa International Airport on Tahiti's northwest corner about 7 miles from downtown Papeete. For details about the airport and getting into town or to the suburban hotels on Tahiti, see Chapter 4, "Orientation." For information about getting to French Polynesia, see Chapter 2, "Getting There."

ISLAND HOPPING

FROM TAHITI TO MOOREA

Moorea, 12 miles away from Papeete, is not yet a suburb of Tahiti, but if transportation between the islands continues to improve, it may soon be. At present, you can choose between a 7-minute shuttle flight or a 1-hour ferry ride.

Air Tahiti (tel. 42-24-44) has service between Papeete and Moorea 4 days a week, usually but not always in the mornings in order to connect with arriving international flights. Air Tahiti's terminal is on the west end of Faaa airport—that's to the right as you exit Customs.

Air Moorea (tel. 42-44-29) flies a shuttle between Faaa and Moorea. They leave Faaa every half hour from 6 to 9am and from 3 to 6pm daily, and once an hour between those periods. From Moorea, they depart on the half hour. There are no flights after dark or before dawn. Air Moorea does not take reservations. Its little terminal is on the east end of Faaa airport (to the left as you come out of Customs). The pathway between the two terminals is painted red; it's a long hoof, so grab one of the free carts in the baggage-claim area.

The fare is 2,750 CFP ($27.50) one-way on both Air Tahiti and Air Moorea.

Note: The **baggage limit** on both airlines is 10kg (22 lb.) per person. You may get around that limit by booking Air Tahiti as a connection to your international flight, in which case the limit is 20kg (44 lb.). Otherwise, you may have to leave some extra belongings in the storage room at your hotel or at Faaa airport (see "Fast Facts: Tahiti" in Chapter 4).

If you didn't do that and your bags are too heavy, you'll be riding the **Moorea Ferry** (tel. 43-76-50). Actually there are two automobile-passenger ferries, *Tamarii Moorea VIII* and *Tamarii Moorea 2-B*. Together they make 5 trips daily in each direction between 5:30am and 5pm, with an extra voyage added on Friday and Sunday (Moorea is a popular weekend retreat for Papeete's residents). Ordinarily the first ferry leaves Papeete at 7am Monday through Saturday and at 8am on Sunday. Pick up a schedule at the booth next to the ferry landing on the Quay. Reservations are required only for automobiles. One-way fares are 700 CFP ($7) for adults, half that for children. You can take your rental car to Moorea from Papeete for 2,000 CFP ($20) one-way, plus 700 CFP ($7) for your own passage.

Ferries depart from the Quay opposite the Royal Papeete Hotel (whose bar is a popular watering hole for Mooreans awaiting the next boat home) and from Vaiare on Moorea's southeast coast. From Vaiare, one of the company's trucks will transport you to your hotel or other destination for another 200 CFP ($2). The ferry takes about 1 hour; add another hour if you're going near Club Med on the opposite side of Moorea.

The passage between Tahiti and Moorea is over open water, so the ferries can tend to pitch and roll. The prevailing trade winds blow toward Moorea, which means that the trip from Tahiti to Moorea usually is smoother than the return voyage; the rule-of-thumb is to ride the ferry to Moorea and fly back to Tahiti if you're inclined to turn more than the usual shade of green.

TO THE OTHER ISLANDS BY PLANE

Air Tahiti (tel. 42-24-44) has a monopoly on air service to more than 40 islands beyond Moorea. It has daily flights between Papeete and Bora Bora in its comfortable twin-engine, 42-passenger planes, but flights to the other islands are less frequent. In other words, reserve as early as possible.

Air Tahiti's central reservations office in Papeete is on the second level (the French call it the first floor, or *premier étage*) of the building just west of the Vaima Centre on boulevard Pomare (go through the shopping arcade and up the stone stairs flanked by palm trees). Its airport ticketing booth is on the west end of Faaa airport. The mailing address is B.P. 314, Papeete, Tahiti, French Polynesia. Air Tahiti also has a representative at 9841 Airport Boulevard, Suite 1124, Los Angeles, CA 90064 (tel. 213/337-1040).

Some sample one-way Air Tahiti fares on the usual visitor's circuit (double the fare for round-trips between any two islands):

Papeete to Huahine	8,400 CFP ($84)
Huahine to Raiatea	4,200 CFP ($42)
Raiatea to Bora Bora	4,600 CFP ($46)
Bora Bora to Papeete	11,550 CFP ($115)
Bora Bora to Rangiroa	19,000 CFP ($190)
Rangiroa to Papeete	12,950 CFP ($129)

An alternative to taking Air Tahiti's scheduled flights is to charter a plane and pilot from **Air Moorea,** B.P. 6019, Faaa, Tahiti (tel. 42-44-29). When split among a large enough group, the price per person could be less than the regular airfare.

TO THE SOCIETY ISLANDS BY BOAT

Reliable ferry service exists not only between Tahiti and Moorea but also between Tahiti and Huahine, Raiatea, and Bora Bora. On the other hand, when you head by boat to the other island groups—the Tuamotus, Marquesas, Gambiers, and

Australs—you will relive the days of old when "copra schooners" plied the seas in search of trade; trips can take several weeks or even months.

The modern **Raromatai Ferry** (tel. 43-90-42) carries passengers and vehicles twice weekly between Papeete and Huahine, Raiatea, and Bora Bora. It has a covered promenade deck with benches, a large salon with airline-style seats and video movies, a snack bar, a dining room, cabins with two bunks, and cabins with four bunks. The salon and cabins are air conditioned. It normally leaves from the ferry wharf on the Papeete waterfront at 8:30pm on Tuesday, arrives at Huahine the next morning, goes on to Raiatea and Tahaa 2 hours later, and from there to Bora Bora at midday. The beautiful, 3-hour passage from Raiatea through the Tahaa lagoon and across blue water to Bora Bora is more than worth the 1,000 CFP ($10) cost. Consider it as an alternative to flying.

The *Raromatai Ferry* usually leaves Bora Bora at noon on Thursday and returns by the same route, sailing overnight between Huahine and Papeete, and returning at dawn on Friday. The ferry also leaves Papeete at 8:30pm on Friday, follows the same route, and returns at dawn on Sunday.

For the voyage from Papeete to Huahine, Raiatea, or Bora Bora, fares for seats in the salon or on deck are 3,800 CFP ($38) for adults and 1,900 CFP ($19) for children under 12. Two-bunk cabins are 8,000 CFP ($80) per person with a two-person minimum. Four-bunk cabins are 6,000 CFP ($60) per person. Deck or salon fare between Huahine, Raiatea, and Bora Bora is 1,000 CFP ($10). For information or reservations contact **Compagnie Maritime des Isles Sous le Vent,** 85 rue des Remparts-Prolongées, in Fare Ute (tel. 43-90-42). The mailing address is B.P. 9012, Papeete, Tahiti, French Polynesia.

Two other ships make the same Papeete to Bora Bora trip via Huahine and Raiatea, the **Temehani II** and the **Taporo IV.** Both leave the interisland shipping wharf in Motu Uta, usually on Monday and Friday (*Taporo IV* at 5am, *Temehani II* at 5pm). They are primarily cargo ships, and their cabins are not as clean or as comfortable as those on the *Raromatai*. Most passengers bring their own food, drinks, blankets, and rain gear, and sleep on deck. Fares from Papeete to Bora Bora are about 1,500 CFP ($15) on deck and about 2,500 CFP ($25) for cabin space. The current fares and schedules are posted in the Tahiti Tourist Promotion Board's welcome center at Fare Manihini in Papeete and usually at the wharfs on the islands. For more information about the *Temehani II,* contact **Société de Navigation Temehani** in Motu Uta (tel. 42-98-83). *Taporo IV* is operated by **Compagnie Française Maritime de Tahiti,** B.P. 368, Papeete (tel. 42-63-93).

These two ships usually arrive at Huahine from Papeete in the middle of the night or the crack of dawn, do their loading, and depart for the short passage to Raiatea. As a result, you won't see much of the beautiful Society Islands from their decks. Their fares between each of the Society Islands are relatively few francs less than their more speedy and comfortable counterparts—800 CFP ($8) compared to 1,000 CFP ($10). Even if you are trying to visit French Polynesia on as little money as possible, don't hesitate to spend that extra 200 CFP ($2) to see Raiatea, Tahaa, and Bora Bora in the daylight. You won't regret it.

TO THE OUTER ISLANDS BY BOAT

Unlike the three ships traveling twice a week among the Society Islands, most vessels that voyage to the more remote island groups keep schedules in terms of weeks or even months, not days. Their primary mission is trade—retail goods for copra (dried coconut meat)—with passenger traffic a secondary source of income. Accordingly, they leave an island when the cargo is loaded, not necessarily when their schedules dictate. They also are at the mercy of the weather and mechanical breakdowns. I knew a young Australian who once took a boat to Rapa in the Austral Islands, expecting to return with it in a few weeks to Papeete. However, the ship broke down and went into the repair yard on Tahiti. He stayed on Rapa for 3 months.

One ship, however, not only is reasonably reliable but is comfortably outfitted for 90 passengers: the **Aranui,** a 343-foot freighter that makes regularly scheduled, 17-day round-trips to six of the 10 Marquesas Islands from Papeete, stopping at

Rangiroa and Takapoto in the Tuamotus on the way out. Accommodation is in air-conditioned deluxe cabins with their own showers and toilets, in first-class cabins (some of which share shower and toilets), or on a mattress laid on deck. Showers are provided for the deck-class passengers. Fares for the complete voyage, including meals, range from 143,000 ($1,430) for deck passage to 384,450 CFP ($3,845) for deluxe cabins. For more information about the *Aranui*'s schedule for the coming year or for reservations, contact **Compagnie Polynésienne du Transport Maritime,** B.P. 220, Papeete, Tahiti (tel. 42-62-40 or 43-76-60 in Papeete; 415/541-0674 in San Francisco).

There are more than 20 other ships that journey to the Tuamotu, Marquesas, Gambier, and Austral groups, and there is a charm to riding them from one remote island to the next. The sea is an incredible shade of royal blue, and the sun setting through the clouds will split the horizon into colors that span the spectrum. Your fellow passengers will be the salt of the Polynesian earth, with straw sleeping mats and cardboard suitcases. However, many passengers (perhaps even you) will spend the entire voyage with seasick heads slung over the rail. You will often experience choking diesel fumes, and will seldom escape the acrid odor coming from sacks of copra. Your shipmates will include cockroaches large enough to steal the watch off your wrist, and some of the cabins—if you can get one—could pass for outhouses. In other words, you'll need lots of flexible time, tolerance born of adversity, and the patience of Job.

If you're still interested, write to the Tahiti Tourist Promotion Board (see "Information, Entry Requirements, and Money," above) and ask for a list of interisland schooners operating at the time you want to go. That won't tell you when the ships will depart Papeete, but it will give you the addresses and phone numbers of the companies that operate them. You can also show up in Papeete, get a list from the tourist board's office, and start looking around (the tourist board's staff is quite helpful in this respect). Tickets should be purchased at least a day in advance of scheduled departure. Make sure you have obtained a 3-month visa to stay in French Polynesia—the chances are great that you'll need more than 30 days for one of these trips.

BY CRUISE SHIP

At the opposite extreme from simple deck passage on interisland trading boats are tours on deluxe cruise ships. Some of the companies mentioned in the "Getting Around by Cruise Ship and Yacht" section in Chapter 2 send their vessels to French Polynesia from time to time. Although it's mentioned above as a working cargo ship, the comfort of its cabins and quality of its food qualifies the *Aranui* for this category.

On a regular basis, the 440-foot, four-masted sail cruiser ***Wind Song*** carries up to 148 passengers in 74 spacious cabins from Papeete to Moorea and Bora Bora—with peeks at Huahine and Raiatea along the way. This unusual vessel, whose companion ships *Wind Star* and *Wind Spirit* operate elsewhere in the world, provides all the amenities of a luxury yacht. Guests won't get their hands chafed hauling lines, however, for all sails are set mechanically. The ship also spends most nights in port; none of this trying to sleep while the boat rolls on the open sea. Double-occupancy rates for the 1-week cruises range from $2,195 to $2,595 per person most of the year but jump to as much as $4,295 at New Year's. Add another $95 to $120 per person for port fees. For more information or reservations contact Windstar Sail, 300 Elliott Avenue West, Seattle, WA 98119 (tel. 206/286-3535, or toll free 800/258-7245).

BY CHARTERED YACHT

Boating enthusiasts can charter their own yacht—with or without skipper and crew—and knock around some of the French Polynesian islands as the wind and their own desires dictate.

The Moorings, a Florida firm that helped pioneer yacht chartering in the Caribbean, now operates a small fleet of sailboats based on Raiatea, which shares the same lagoon with Tahaa and is within sight of Huahine and Bora Bora, all of which are within the approved "cruising grounds." Boats available are Moorings 51, Moorings 43, Moorings 432, Moorings 50, and Moorings 38, all built in France.

Bareboat rates (that is, you rent the "bare" boat without skipper or crew) range from $4,500 per week (or $600 a day) for the 51-footer to $2,177 a week (or $260 a day) for the smaller yachts. That's per boat, not per person. Provisions are about $29 per person per day if you want your shopping done for you. The agency will check you out to make sure you and your party can handle sailboats of these sizes; otherwise, a skipper rents for $95 a day. If you don't want to prepare your own meals, they'll throw in a cook for $60 a day. For more information or bookings, contact the **The Moorings,** 19345 U.S. 19 North, Suite 402, Clearwater, FL 34624 (tel. 813/535-1446, or toll free 800/535-7289).

BY CAR

The major car-rental firms (*locations de voiture* in French) have licensees on Tahiti and Moorea. Reputable local firms operate there and on Huahine, Raiatea, and Bora Bora. See chapters 4 and 5 for details.

As noted above, automobile ferries operate between Tahiti and Moorea and from Tahiti to Huahine, Raiatea, and Bora Bora. Not all rental firms permit their cars to be taken on the ferries; check with them before doing it.

Valid **driver's licenses** from your home country will be honored in French Polynesia.

Gasoline (*essence* in French) was selling during my recent visit for about 100 CFP ($1) per liter (that's about $4 per U.S. gallon). Service stations are fairly common on Tahiti, but only in the main villages on the other islands.

Motorbikes and scooters are rented on the other islands but not on Tahiti. As soon as you see the traffic in Papeete, you'll understand why no insurer in its right mind will underwrite that risk.

DRIVING RULES

Driving is on the right-hand side of the road, as in North America and continental Europe.

All persons in a vehicle **must wear seat belts.**

Helmets (*casques,* pronounced "casks") are mandatory if you drive or ride on a scooter or motorbike.

Speed limits are 40kmph (24 m.p.h.) in the towns and villages, 80kmph (48 m.p.h.) on the open road. The limit is 60kmph (36 m.p.h.) for 8km (5 miles) on either side of Papeete. The general rule on the RDO freeway between Papeete and Punaauia on Tahiti's west coast is 90kmph (54 m.p.h.), although there is one short stretch going down a hill where it's officially 110kmph (66 m.p.h.).

Drivers on the main rural roads have the right-of-way. In Papeete, priority is given to vehicles entering from the right side unless an intersection is marked with a traffic light, stop, or yield sign. This rule is contrary to most other countries, so be especially careful at all intersections, especially those marked with a *priorité à droite* (priority to the right) sign, and give way accordingly.

Drivers are required to stop for pedestrians in marked crosswalks, but don't trust them if you're trying to cross a busy street.

Traffic lights in Papeete may be difficult to see, since some of them are on the far left-hand side of the street instead of on the driver's side of the intersection.

SUGGESTED ITINERARIES

Much depends on your personal interests and pocketbook. As is true throughout the South Pacific, your exact itinerary will depend on the airlines' schedules.

IF YOU HAVE 1 DAY

Some visitors have a 1-day layover between flights. If this is your case, spend at least half of it on Moorea. Head into downtown Papeete for breakfast and an early morning look at the Municipal Market. Take the 9am ferry to Moorea. Tour Moorea (including a trip to the Belvédère overlook) by rental car, scooter, or simply by riding the bus from the ferry landing to the Club Méditerranée area. Return to Papeete by an afternoon plane. Make a walking tour of downtown, with some shopping thrown in. Ride a late afternoon *le truck* to the Tahiti Beachcomber Parkroyal for sunset over Moorea. Catch a Tahitian dance show in the evening.

IF YOU HAVE 2 DAYS

Day 1 Visit the Papeete Municipal Market during early morning. After breakfast make a walking tour of downtown. After lunch, spend the afternoon on a tour around Tahiti, either by car or with an organized tour. End the day by watching sunset over Moorea from a hotel on the west coast, followed by a Tahitian dance show. Overnight on Tahiti.

Day 2 Take an early-morning ferry to Moorea. Drive or take a tour around the island. After lunch and some midday beach time, take a walk in Cook's Bay and savor some of the South Pacific's most enchanting scenery. Return to Papeete by plane or on a late-afternoon ferry.

IF YOU HAVE 7 DAYS (LEISURELY)

Days 1 and 2 Tour Tahiti on the first day and Moorea on the second, as suggested above, but spend your second night on Moorea.

Days 3 and 4 Spend these 2 full days on Moorea. There's plenty to do (see Chapter 5).

Days 5 and 6 Fly to Bora Bora on the morning of your fifth day. Stay there 2 days. Be sure to tour the island and take a trip on the lagoon.

Day 7 Return to Papeete in time for your international flight.

IF YOU HAVE 7 DAYS (BUSY)

Days 1 and 2 Tour Tahiti and Moorea, as suggested above.

Day 2 Spend an extra day on Moorea.

Day 4 Fly to Huahine. Tour the island and its historical marae in the afternoon. Spend some time looking around the village of Fare; it has lots of old South Seas charm.

Day 5 Fly to Raiatea. Tour the island, including the great Taputapuatea marae, and Uturoa, French Polynesia's second-largest town.

Day 6 Fly to Bora Bora. Tour the island and take a trip on the lagoon.

Day 7 Return to Papeete for your flight home.

FRENCH POLYNESIA

American Express The territory's one full-service representative is in Papeete. See "Fast Facts: Tahiti" in Chapter 4.

Area Code The **international country code** is 689.

Banks **Westpac, Banque de Polynésie, Banque de Tahiti,** and **Banque Socredo** have offices on the main islands (for specific locations and banking hours, see "Fast Facts" for the individual islands in chapters 4 and 5). In recent years all of them except Banque Socredo charged a 350 CFP ($3.50) fee for each exchange transaction, but competition may have forced them to stop doing so by the time you arrive (Banque Socredo had long lines at the exchange counters, the others didn't). Ask if there is a fee; if so, head for Banque Socredo or shop around. Although Banque Socredo used a slightly lower exchange rate, you usually saved money except on very large transactions. This still may be the case when you get there.

Business Hours Although some shops now stay open over the lunch period, general shopping and business hours are Mon–Fri 7:30–11:30am and 2–5pm, Sat

8am–noon. In addition to regular hours, most small general stores also are open Sat 2–6pm and Sun 6–8am.

Camera/Film Photographic film is expensive, so bring 10 rolls with you. Papeete has several camera and film processing shops where you can get your color-print film developed in 1 hour (it will be much less expensive to have your developing done at home). On the other islands, the hotel boutiques usually carry color-print film.

Climate See "When to Go—Climate, Holidays, & Events" in this chapter.

Clothing Lightweight summer clothing is in order throughout the year, although a light jacket or sweater will come in handy for evenings during the cooler months, June–Aug. Evening attire for men is usually a shirt and slacks; for women, a long, brightly colored dress. The rules of modesty prevalent elsewhere in Polynesia are relaxed here, especially on the resort hotel beaches where topless sunbathing is the norm. Compared with Tonga and Samoa, even some of the chic, see-through outfits worn by the women in Papeete seem risqué. Shorts are acceptable during the day almost everywhere. Outside Papeete, the standard attire for women is the colorful wraparound sarong known in Tahitian as a pareu, which can be tied in a multitude of ways into dresses, blouses, or skirts. If you don't have a pareu, there will be plenty of opportunities to buy one.

Credit Cards American Express, VISA, MasterCard, and Diners Club credit cards are accepted widely by the hotels, airlines, rental-car firms, most restaurants, and shop's that cater to tourists.

Crime See "Safety" below and in the "Fast Facts: South Pacific" section in Chapter 2.

Currency See "Information, Entry Requirements & Money" in this chapter.

Customs See "Information, Entry Requirements & Money" in this chapter.

Dentist French-trained dentists are available on Tahiti and the other more-visited islands. Ask your hotel staff to recommend one who speaks English.

Doctor Medical care is reasonably good, but relatively expensive. The public hospitals tend to be crowded with local residents, who get their care for free. Most visitors use private doctors or clinics where they are available. Some English-speaking physicians are on call by the hotels in and around Papeete. Each of the smaller islands has at least one infirmary, although the doctor is likely to be of a higher caliber than his equipment. See the "Fast Facts" for the individual islands in chapters 4 and 5.

American health-insurance plans are not recognized, so remember to get receipts at the time of treatment.

Documents Required See "Information, Entry Requirements & Money" in this chapter.

Driving Rules See "Getting Around: By Car" in this chapter.

Drug Laws Possession and use of dangerous drugs and narcotics are subject to heavy fines and jail terms.

Drugstores A few pharmacies are known as *drugstores* even in French; most are called *pharmacies* just as in English. Several are in Papeete, and most islands have one. See the "Fast Facts" sections for the individual islands in chapters 4 and 5 for details.

Electricity Electrical power is 220 volts, 50 cycles, and the plugs are those French kind with two round, skinny prongs. Most hotels have 110-volt outlets for shavers only, so you will need a converter and adapter plugs for your other appliances. Some hotels, especially those on the outer islands, have their own generators, so ask at the reception desk what voltage is supplied.

Embassies/Consulates Austria, Chile, Denmark, Finland, Italy, South Korea, Monaco, Norway, the Netherlands, Sweden, and West Germany have consuls in Papeete. The nearest full-service U.S. embassy is in Auckland, New Zealand.

Emergencies If you are in a hotel, contact the staff. Otherwise, the **emergency phone number is 17** throughout the territory.

Etiquette Even though European and some Tahitian women go topless and wear the skimpiest of bikini bottoms at the beach, the Tahitians have a sense of propriety that you find in any Western nation. Don't offend them by engaging in behavior that would be impermissible at home. See the "People and Culture" section of this chapter and the "The Islands Today" section of Chapter 1 for more information.

Firearms All weapons except bush knives (machetes) and BB guns are prohibited, but don't try to bring either into the territory.

Gambling There are no casinos in French Polynesia.

Hitchhiking Thumbing rides is possible in the rural parts of Tahiti and on the outer islands. Women traveling alone should be extremely cautious (see "Safety," below).

Holidays See "When to Go—Climate, Holidays, & Events" in this chapter.

Information See "Information, Entry Requirements & Money" in this chapter.

Insects There are no dangerous insects in French Polynesia; the only real nuisances are mosquitoes and tiny black sand flies known locally as "no-nos." If you forget to bring insect repellent along, look for the Dolmix Pic brand at the pharmacies.

Language See the "Language" section of this chapter.

Laundry Only Papeete has commercial laundries and dry cleaners (see "Fast Facts: Tahiti" in Chapter 4). The hotels provide laundry service for their guests. It's expensive.

Liquor Laws Regulations about where and when you can drink are liberal, and some bars stay open until the very wee hours on weekends. The prime restraint is the relatively high price of alcoholic spirits (see "Government and the Economy" in this chapter).

Mail Airmail postage from French Polynesia to the U.S. starts at 76 CFP (76¢) for letters and postcards. Letters usually take about a week to 10 days to reach overseas destinations in either direction. If you need it quicker than that, United Parcel Service has 2- to 3-day service; contact J. A. Cowan & Fils at Faaa Airport (tel. 42-44-25). Americans should remember that although first-class postage travels by air at home, letters to French Polynesia must be sent via airmail or they will end up on a ship.

Most mailing addresses in French Polynesia consist of a post office box (*bôite postale* in French, or B.P. for short) but no street numbers or names.

Maps The Tahiti Tourist Promotion Board distributes free maps of each island. Most useful are those of downtown Papeete and of Tahiti showing key points on the circle-island tour. Each weekly edition of the free *Tahiti Beach Press* carries artistic island and Papeete maps. **Librairie Hachette,** Tahiti's largest bookseller, carries several *cartes touristiques.* The best is map number 513, *Archipel de la Société,* published by the Institut Géographique National. It shows all the Society Islands in detail, including all roads and topographic features, and costs about 500 CFP ($5). The full-color *Tahiti et ses Isles: 39 Cartes Touristiques* shows the precise locations of all hotels and pensions. It costs about 1,000 CFP ($10) but is a useful tool if you're hunting for cheap hotel rates. One Hachette store is on the second level of the Vaima Centre; another is on avenue Bruat off boulevard Pomare. Look in the sections where books on Tahiti are displayed.

Newspapers/Magazines Librairie Hachette also carries the *International Herald Tribune, Time,* and *Newsweek* (the latter is the back section of the *Bulletin,* an Australian newsmagazine). The *Tahiti Beach Press,* an English-language weekly tabloid devoted to news of Tahiti's tourist industry, runs features of interest to tourists and advertisements for hotels, restaurants, real estate agents, rental-car firms, and other businesses that cater to tourists and have English-speaking staffs. It is given away free by the establishments that buy ads in it. The daily newspapers *La Dépêche de Tahiti* and *Les Nouvelles* are in French.

Passports See "Information, Entry Requirements & Money" in this chapter.

Pets Don't even think about it. Your pet will be placed in quarantine.

Police The emergency number for police is 17.

Radio/TV French Polynesia has one AM radio station, which is owned and operated by the government and carries programming in French and Tahitian. Several FM stations in Papeete are privately owned and play as many American and British musical numbers as they do those from France. The announcers, however, speak

French. The one television station is government-owned and broadcasts entirely in French, except for the news in Tahitian at 6:45pm. Both the government-owned radio station and TV can be received throughout the territory via satellite.

Religious Services More than half of the French Polynesians are Protestant, most belonging to an evangelical denomination descended from the early London Missionary Society, known as the *Eglise Evangélique de Polynésie Française.* Nearly every village in the islands has a whitewashed evangelical *temple Protestant* as its centerpiece. There are also a considerable number of Roman Catholics and some Jews, Mormons, Seventh-Day Adventists, and Jehovah's Witnesses. A significant portion of the Chinese population is Buddhist.

The hotel activities staff or receptionist will direct you to the service of your choice.

Rest Rooms Public rest rooms are not common in French Polynesia, so most likely you'll have to rely on the hotels and restaurants. See "Fast Facts" in chapters 4 and 5 for rest rooms on the individual islands.

Safety Although crimes against tourists are rare in French Polynesia, stay alert whenever you're traveling in an unfamiliar city or country. Be aware of your immediate surroundings. Wear a moneybelt. This will minimize the possibility of your becoming a victim of crime. Every society has its criminals. It's your responsibility to be aware and alert, even in the most heavily touristed areas. Women should be extremely cautious and should not wander alone on deserted beaches. See "Health & Insurance" and "Fast Facts" in Chapter 2.

Taxes All hotel bills will have a 7% government tax added to them. There are no other direct taxes, but you'll be paying an indirect import tax every time you buy, drink, or eat something in French Polynesia that isn't locally produced.

Telephone/Telex/Fax French Polynesia's telephone system is reliable and very expensive. Direct international dialing is available into and out of Tahiti.

International calls can be placed through your hotel, though with a surcharge that often doubles the fee. It's less expensive to make them from a post office or even a pay phone (see below). In the post offices, place your call at the desk and wait for it to come through to one of the booths or phones across the room.

The minimum charge for operator-assisted calls to the U.S. is about 700 CFP ($7) per minute. Compare: A call to Tahiti dialed directly from the U.S. after 11pm local time costs about $2 for the first minute, less than $1 for each minute thereafter.

Public pay phones are located at all post offices and are fairly numerous elsewhere on Tahiti. They sit in large glass-and-metal booths with black lettering on a yellow background. Many are like the older phones used in France: You lift the receiver, listen for the dial tone, deposit your coins in the slots across the top of the phone (which match the size of the coins), watch them stack up behind the glass window under each slot, dial your number, and start talking when the party answers. A light on the upper left-hand front of the phone will flash 12 seconds before your time runs out, giving you just enough time to fumble and drop the rest of your money on the ground before your party is cut off.

An increasing number of pay phones now come equipped with digital displays instead of coin stacks. You put your money in the slot on top, listen for a dial tone, then *composez* (dial) your number on the pushbutton pad. The readout tells you how many francs you have used and will give you a 12-second warning before your money is exhausted. In other words, keep an eye on the display, or your party may be unceremoniously cut off in mid-sentence.

Of newer vintage, some pay phones now take only a *télécarte,* a credit card you buy at a post office. The disadvantage is that you can't just walk up and put in a coin; the advantage is that you don't have to stand there and feed the machine's voracious appetite while calling home.

Local calls on Tahiti cost 50 CFP (50¢) for the first five minutes. Calls to Moorea cost 50 CFP (50¢) per minute. Calls to the other islands cost at least 100 CFP ($1) a minute.

Calls within Tahiti, Moorea, and the other main islands can be dialed direct without going through a long-distance operator. To get the operator for other interisland calls, dial 10. The **international operator** is at 19. The **emergency** (*secours*) police number is 17. For **directory information** (*service des renseignements*), dial 12.

Time Local time in the most-visited islands is 11 hours behind Greenwich mean time. I find it easier to think of it as 5 hours behind U.S. Eastern standard time or 2 hours behind Pacific standard time. Translated: When it's noon Pacific standard time in California, it's 10am in Tahiti. When it's noon Eastern standard time on the East Coast, it's 7am in Tahiti. Add 1 hour for daylight saving time.

The Marquesas Islands are 30 minutes ahead of the rest of the territory.

French Polynesia is on the west side of the international date line; therefore, Tahiti has the same date as the U.S., the Cook Islands, and the Samoas, and is 1 day behind Australia, New Zealand, Fiji, and Tonga.

Tipping Despite inroads made by uniformed American tourists, tipping is considered contrary to the Polynesian custom of hospitality. In other words, tipping is not expected unless the service has been truly exceptional.

Tourist Offices See "Information, Entry Requirements & Money" in this chapter.

Visas See "Information, Entry Requirements & Money" in this chapter.

Water Although the tap water on most of the main islands is considered safe to drink, it is untreated and can become muddy during heavy rains. French mineral waters are available at every grocery and are served by restaurants. Eau Royale, derived from a spring on Tahiti, is the least expensive brand. Well water in the Tuamotus tends to be brackish; rainwater is used there for drinking.

CHAPTER 4

TAHITI

Tahiti has experienced considerable change during the past two decades, and some modern explorers may be disappointed to find a bustling city where a few native huts once stood. From a languid little port, Papeete has grown into a busy city clogged with cars, trucks, motorbikes, and scooters. Most of the sleazy bars and stage-set wooden Chinese stores have been replaced by chic bistros and high-rise shopping centers of glass and concrete. The cheap waterfront hotels with their ceiling fans and balconies overlooking the harbor have been replaced by air-conditioned resorts featuring high prices to match their luxurious modern conveniences.

Others find charm in Papeete's frantic pace and are invigorated by its mix of French, Polynesian, and Chinese cultures. Whether you are enchanted or disenchanted, you will have to spend at least a few hours on Tahiti, since all international flights land there. So let's make the most of it.

1. ORIENTATION: ARRIVING & GETTING AROUND

ORIENTATION

The largest and most populous of the French Polynesian islands, Tahiti lies about halfway between the U.S. and Australia going in one direction and halfway between Japan and Chile going in another. It's status as a large and abundant island centrally located in the eastern South Pacific made Tahiti a gateway and natural base for the early explorers who came into the area from Europe around the tip of South America. It was from Tahiti that most of the rest of the South Pacific was explored and added to the world maps in the 18th century, and Papeete became a major shipping crossroads in later years. Although it now shares the distinction with other destinations, Tahiti is still a major gateway to the South Pacific.

Tahiti is shaped like a figure eight lying on its side. The "eyes" of the eight are two extinct, eroded volcanoes joined by a narrow, flat isthmus known as Taravao. The northern part is known as Tahiti Nui ("Big Tahiti" in Tahitian), while the smaller southern section below the isthmus is named Tahiti Iti ("Little Tahiti"). Together they comprise about 416 square miles, about two-thirds the size of the island of Oahu in Hawaii.

The volcano on Tahiti Nui has been eroded over the eons so that now long ridges, separating deep valleys, fan out from the crater's ancient rim to the coast far below. The rim itself is still intact, except on the north side where the Papenoo River has cut its way to the sea. The highest peaks, Mount Orohena (7,353 ft.) and Mount Aora

WHAT'S SPECIAL ABOUT TAHITI

Great Towns
- ☐ Papeete, the renowned South Seas port of yesterday has grown into a bustling little city with modern charms.

Ancient Monuments
- ☐ Arahurahu Marae: Polynesia's only restored temple with exhibit boards explaining why it's there.
- ☐ Mahaiatea Marae: Most of Polynesia's tallest temple has been removed, but its beachside setting is impressive.

Literary Shrines/Buildings
- ☐ Home of James Norman Hall: See where *Mutiny on the Bounty*'s coauthor lived and worked.

Buildings
- ☐ Papeete Town Hall: An accurate recreation of Queen Pomare's mansion shows what colonial mansions were like.

Museums
- ☐ Museum of Tahiti and Her Isles: Learn about Polynesian culture and history at one of the region's best.
- ☐ Gauguin Museum: Don't expect to see many of the painter's works, but learn about his life in Polynesia.

Natural Spectacles
- ☐ Faarumai Waterfalls: Cool off in the pool at the bottom of this refreshing cascade.

Festivals
- ☐ *Heiva I Tahiti:* Most of the rip-roaring July festival happens in Papeete.

Film Location
- ☐ Matavai Bay: Now over developed, Bligh's 1788–89 landing place was used in 1960 for the Marlon Brando version of *Mutiny on the Bounty.*

(6,817 ft.), tower above Papeete. Another peak, the toothlike Diadème (4,360 ft.) can be seen from the eastern side of Papeete but not from downtown.

With the exception of the east coast of Tahiti Iti, where great cliffs fall into the lagoon, and a few places where the ridges end abruptly at the water's edge, the island is skirted by a flat coastal plain. The majority of Tahiti's residents live on this plain or in the valleys or on the foothills adjacent to it.

Most of Tahiti's resort hotels are on its northwest corner, which faces Moorea across the Sea of the Moon. Below the hotels, down through Punaauia and Paea, the west coast is Tahiti's high-rent suburban district favored by its French residents. Befitting this status, it is connected to Papeete by the RDO freeway, which cuts across the ridges above the congestion near the airport.

Away from Papeete, the island's highway system consists primarily of a paved two-lane road that runs for 72 miles around Tahiti Nui and halfway down each side of Tahiti Iti. From the isthmus, a road partially lined with trees wanders up to the high, cool Plateau of Taravao, whose pastures and pines give it an air more of provincial France than of the South Pacific.

ARRIVING

French Polynesia's international airport sits on the northwest corner of Tahiti at **Faaa,** 7km (4 miles) west of downtown Papeete. Most overseas flights arrive in the middle of the night. Once through immigration and Customs, you will see a booth straight ahead sometimes staffed by the **Tahiti Tourist Promotion Board.** Start there for maps and other information. If you are traveling with a group tour, the operators will have signs announcing their presence. A branch of **Westpac Bank** is to the left; in addition to its regular daytime hours, it opens 1 hour before an international flight is due to arrive or depart and stays open until the last passengers have changed enough money to get to their hotels. A snack bar to the right opens for night flights and is a good place to idle away the hours until 6am when the taxi fares go down and *le truck* starts running.

The airport's **baggage storage room** to the right at the Air Tahiti terminal is open from 8am to 5pm everyday and 2 hours before each international flight regardless of departure time. Charges are 160 CFP ($1.60) per day for bags, 450 CFP ($4.50) for large items such as surfboards and bicycles. (The hotels will keep your baggage for free.)

Many passengers transiting on to the other islands will wander over to **Air Tahiti**'s domestic terminal and wait until the planes start flying at dawn. If you are going directly to Moorea on **Air Moorea,** its terminal is to the far left on the east end of the terminal (follow the red pathway).

If you arrive between 10pm and 6am and are not part of a tour, your only choice of transportation to your hotel will be a **taxi.** Fares are nearly doubled during these hours, and you may have to bargain a little on top of that. The official late-night fare for a ride into Papeete or to the hotels on the west coast is 2,500 CFP ($25). Daytime fare is 1,500 CFP ($15).

If you arrive any other time, you can haul your baggage across the parking lot in front of the terminal, climb the stairs to the main road, and flag down **le truck** (see "Getting Around," below). The fares are 100 CFP ($1) during the day and 150 CFP ($1.50) after 6pm.

If you are driving a rental car, watch for the RDO signs directing you to the freeway that connects Papeete to the west coast. You can take it or the old road that runs along the inland side of the airport. The RDO is not a toll road.

Check-in time for departing flights is 90 minutes before flight time. There is no airport departure tax.

GETTING AROUND

The choices for getting around Tahiti are taxis (which primarily operate in and around Papeete and the hotels), rental cars, and the local buses known singularly and collectively as le truck.

BY LE TRUCK

Although it may appear from the number of vehicles scurrying around Tahiti that everyone owns a vehicle, the average citizen gets around by **le truck.** They are called "truck" instead of "bus" because the passenger compartments are brightly painted wooden cabins mounted on the rear of flatbed trucks. Each compartment has a padded bench, windows of Plexiglas that slide down when it isn't raining, and at least one monstrous speaker from which Tahitian or reggae music often blares at incredible volume; you can hear some of the trucks coming from blocks away.

In Papeete, look for official bus stops (called an *arrêt le truck* in French). Elsewhere the trucks will stop for you anywhere, even if it means coming to a screeching halt in the middle of rush-hour traffic. The vehicles all are privately owned, and a 100-franc ($1) fare won't be missed. Wave to catch the driver's eye. To get off at your destination, search around for one of the doorbell buttons mounted over or behind your head and give it a good push. Pay the driver in his cab after you have dismounted.

As disorganized as the trucks may appear, there really is a system to their madness. Most of them begin their initial runs before the crack of dawn (let's say 5am) from their owner's residence and proceed to the market in Papeete. Successive runs are made from the market to the end of their route and back during the course of the day. The villages or districts served by each truck are written on the sides and front of the passenger cabin.

Trucks going west from Papeete line up beside the market on rue du 22 Septembre. They proceed along rue du Général de Gaulle, which becomes rue du Commandant Destremeau and later route de l'Ouest, the road that circles the island.

There is frequent service from dawn to 10pm along this route as far as the Hotel Sofitel Maeva Beach. Trucks labeled FAAA and MAEVA BEACH will pass the airport and the hotels Tahiti, Tahiti Beachcomber Parkroyal, and Te Puna Bel Air. The long-distance trucks going down the west coast to Paea, Papara, Mataiea, Papeari, and beyond tend to be larger than those that go only to Maeva Beach, and the service much less frequent the farther one gets from Papeete. In general, the last long-distance runs of the day leave the market shortly after everyone gets off work at 5pm.

Trucks going east from Papeete gather just off boulevard Pomare on rue François Cardella, the 1-block-long street on the east side of the market. There is frequent service as far as the Hotel Hyatt Regency Tahiti but not beyond there after dark.

No trucks go all the way around the island, but you can make a circle-island tour on them. To do so, find one that is making a return trip in the morning from Papeete to Taravao, Vairao, or Teahupoo on the west side. Get off at Taravao, walk across the isthmus, and find a truck that's returning to Papeete in midafternoon. There are no set schedules, so you'll be on your own to find that return truck. If you get stranded, it's relatively easy for tourists to hitch a ride back to Papeete. Confused? Never fear, for all you really have to do to ride le truck is to show up at the market in Papeete and look like a tourist who wants a ride. The drivers or their assistants will find you and tell you which vehicle to get in.

Fares between Papeete and Maeva Beach in one direction and the Hotel Hyatt Regency Tahiti in the other are 100 CFP ($1) until 6pm and 150 CFP ($1.50) thereafter. The price goes up the farther you travel from Papeete. A trip to the end of the line will cost between 300 CFP and 500 CFP ($3 and $5).

BY TAXI

Papeete has a large number of taxis, although they can be hard to find during the morning and evening rush hours, especially if it's raining. You can flag one down on the street or find them gathered at one of several stations. The largest of these gathering stations are at the market (tel. 42.02.92) and at the Vaima Centre (tel. 42.98.35). Most taxi drivers understand some English.

Taxi fares are set by the government, and all cabs now have meters. Be sure the driver turns it on or that you and the driver have agreed on a fare before you get in. Note that *all fares are nearly doubled between 10pm and 6am.* A trip anywhere within downtown Papeete will start at 800 CFP ($8) and go up 100 CFP ($1) for every kilometer after the first one. As a rule of thumb, the fare from the Papeete hotels to the airport or vice versa is about 1,500 CFP ($15) during the day; from the west coast hotels to the airport, about 1,000 CFP ($10); from the Hotel Hyatt Regency Tahiti to Papeete, about 1,500 CFP ($15); and from the Hyatt Regency Tahiti to the airport, about 3,000 CFP ($30). A trip to the Gauguin Museum on the south coast will cost 6,500 CFP ($65) one-way. The fare for a journey all the way around Tahiti is about 15,000 CFP ($150).

BY RENTAL CAR

Budget (tel. 43.80.79, or toll free 800/527-0700 in the U.S.) is slightly less expensive than the other Big Three rental firms present on Tahiti. Expect to pay 1,980 CFP ($20) a day plus 32 CFP (32¢) per kilometer for a small Ford Fiesta. Add to that the cost of gasoline and 1,100 CFP ($11) a day for full insurance coverage. The unlimited-kilometer rate of 6,600 CFP ($66) per day represents a savings if you are driving around the island and intend to wander off on Tahiti Iti. Ask about special ½-day rates, applicable between 11am and 5pm, and 3-day weekends for the price of 2 days. Budget's main office is at the end of rue des Remparts in Fare Ute, but the staff will deliver to any hotel in and around Papeete. They answer the phone 24 hours a day.

Avis (tel. 42.09.26, or toll free 800/331-1212 in the U.S.) has desks at the airport, the Sofitel Maeva Beach Hotel, Tahiti Beachcomber Parkroyal, and Hyatt Regency Tahiti. Its main office is on rue Charles Vienot between rue DuMont d'Urville and rue

IMPRESSIONS

The journals of its [Tahiti's] first visitors, containing as they did, such romantic descriptions of a country and people before unheard of, produced a marked sensation throughout Europe; and when the first Tahitians were carried thither, Omai in London, and Aootooroo in Paris, were carressed by nobles, scholars, and ladies.

—Herman Melville, 1847

Nansouty. Avis also has an agency on Moorea. **Hertz** (tel. 42.04.71, or toll free 800/654-3001 in the U.S.) has its office on route de-l'Ouest in Tipaerui on the west end of Papeete and desks at the airport, Tahiti Beachcomber Parkroyal, the Hyatt Regency Tahiti, and Hotel Royal Papeete.

You can save about 600 CFP ($6) a day by renting cars from **Pacificar** (tel. 42.43.64), a reputable local firm whose office is on rue des Remparts at the pont de l'Est traffic circle. It rents Fiats, Ford Fiestas, Peugeots, and Suzukis starting at 1,300 CFP ($13) plus 26 CFP (26¢) per kilometer and 800 CFP ($8) for full insurance. Pacificar also has an agency on Huahine.

Driving Hints

As noted in Chapter 3, in Papeete priority is given to vehicles entering an intersection from the right side. This rule does not apply on the four-lane boulevard Pomare along the waterfront, but be careful everywhere else because drivers on your right will expect you to yield the right-of-way at intersections where there are no stop signs or traffic signals. Outside of Papeete, priority is given to vehicles already on the round-island road.

Parking

Finding a parking space can be difficult in downtown Papeete. Some large buildings, such as the Vaima Centre, have garages in their basements. I usually resort to the lots on the waterfront by the Moorea Ferry docks, especially in front of the Hotel Royal Papeete. The spaces there are not metered, but many of them are reserved at night for *les roulottes,* the mobile restaurants and food stalls that gather there in the evenings. Be safe and find a space close to boulevard Pomare.

FAST FACTS: TAHITI

American Express The full-service American Express representative is **Tahiti Tours,** on rue Jeanne d'Arc (tel. 42-78-70) across from the Vaima Centre in downtown Papeete. The mailing address is B.P. 627, Papeete, Tahiti, French Polynesia. Go in the morning if you want to exchange a personal check for traveler's checks in any currency other than French francs; the office has to telex Australia for approval, which takes about 30 minutes.

Baby-Sitters Most hotels can arrange for baby-sitters who speak English.

Bookstores **Librairie Hachette,** the major bookseller on Tahiti, has stores on the second level of the Vaima Centre and on avenue Bruat just off boulevard Pomare, near the monument to General de Gaulle on the waterfront. It also operates a magazine and newspaper kiosk on the northeast corner of the Vaima Centre. Its stores carry the *International Herald Tribune, Time,* and *Newsweek.* They also have a wide selection of books on French Polynesia, many of them in English, and a few English-language novels and other paperback books. In addition, they sell the excellent *Carte Touristique,* or **Tourist Map,** published by the Institut

Géographique Nationale. It shows geographical features (in topographical relief) and the system of roads and trails on all the Society Islands. It's a handy item to have on a tour around these islands. Both Hachette stores are open Mon–Sat 8am–5pm.

Business Hours Although some shops now stay open over the long lunch break, most businesses are open 8–11:30am and 2–5pm, give or take 30 minutes. Sat hours are 8–11:30am, although some shops in the Vaima Centre keep Sat afternoon hours. The Papeete Municipal Market is a roaring beehive Sun 5–7am, and many of the nearby general stores are open during those hours. Except for some small groceries that have variable hours, most other stores are closed on Sun.

Camera/Film A wide range of film is available at high prices. Bring your own supply. One-hour color-print processing is available at several stores in downtown Papeete. One of the best is QSS, at the back of the Vaima Centre (they also do watch repairs).

Car Rentals See "Getting Around," above.

Climate See "When to Go—Climate, Holidays, & Events" in Chapter 3.

Clothing See "Fast Facts: French Polynesia" in Chapter 3.

Currency See "Information, Entry Requirements & Money" in Chapter 3.

Currency Exchange **Westpac, Banque de Polynésie, Banque de Tahiti,** and **Banque Socredo** all have at least one branch on boulevard Pomare in Papeete and in many suburban locations. Banque Socredo does not charge a fee for each transaction. The others may have stopped the practice by the time you get to Tahiti.

Banking hours on Tahiti generally are Mon–Thurs 8am–3:30pm, Fri 8am–4:30pm; however, Banque Socredo's office on boulevard Pomare in the block west of the Vaima Centre, is open for currency exchanges Sat 8am–11:30am.

Dentist Ask your hotel to recommend an English-speaking dentist.

Doctor Some English-speaking physicians are on call by the hotels in and around Papeete. See "Hospitals," below.

Drugstores There are a number of pharmacies in and around Papeete, most of which carry French products. Pharmacie Central is downtown on boulevard Pomare, across from the Tahiti Tourist Promotion Board's information office and the Banque de Polynésie. The pharmacies rotate night duty, so ask your hotel staff to find out which one is open after dark.

Embassies/Consulates See "Information, Entry Requirements, and Money" in Chapter 3.

Emergencies The best thing to do in case of emergency is to contact your hotel staff. Otherwise, the number for **police** is **17.** Don't expect the person on the other end of the line to speak English.

Eyeglasses One of the larger dealers, **Pacific Optique** (tel. 42.70.78), is on rue Emile Martin at rue Yves Martin. **Optique Surdit** (tel. 42.77.52) upstairs in the Vaima Centre specializes in designer frames.

Hairdressers/Barbers There is no shortage of *coiffeuses* (hairdressers) in Papeete, although few speak English fluently. The beauty salons at the Sofitel Maeva Beach, Tahiti Beachcomber Parkroyal, and Hyatt Regency Tahiti hotels are popular with both local English-speaking residents and visitors alike.

Holidays See "When to Go—Climate, Holidays & Events," in Chapter 3.

Hospitals The public hospital usually is crowded with local residents, who get their care free. Both **Clinique Cardella** (tel. 42.80.10) on rue Anne Marie Javouhey and **Clinic Paofai** (tel. 43.77.00) on boulevard Pomare accept visitors as patients.

Information The **Tahiti Tourist Promotion Board's** main office and welcome center is in Fare Manihini, the Polynesian-style building on the waterfront on boulevard Pomare at the foot of rue Gauguin (tel. 42.96.26). The staff members all speak English and are helpful, especially in providing such information as when trading boats will leave for the distant island groups. See "Information, Entry Requirements & Money" in Chapter 3 for addresses of overseas offices.

Laundry/Dry Cleaning You can send your laundry and dry cleaning out through your hotel or take it directly to **Central Pressing** on rue Albert LeBoucher near rue Clappier, behind the Royal Papeete Hotel in Papeete. Prices are about 300 CFP ($3) per shirt or blouse, 500 CFP ($5) per trousers or skirt.

Libraries The **Territorial Cultural Center** (*Office Territorial d'Action Culturelle*) on boulevard Pomare west of downtown Papeete (tel. 42.88.50) has a small library of mostly French books on the South Pacific and other topics. Hours are Mon–Tues and Thurs–Fri 8am–5pm, Wed 8am–4pm.

Liquor Laws See "Fast Facts: French Polynesia" in Chapter 3.

Lost Property Report stolen articles at the nearest gendarmerie. In downtown Papeete, it's at the end of avenue Braut.

Luggage Storage/Lockers Most hotels have storage rooms where you can leave your extra belongings while touring the islands. Faaa airport has a storage room (see "Arriving" in this chapter).

Newspapers/Magazines The Hachette bookshops sell some international newspapers and newsmagazines. See "Bookstores," above, and "Fast Facts: French Polynesia" in Chapter 3.

Police The emergency number is 17. Otherwise, contact the nearest gendarmerie, whose numbers are listed in the blue pages of the phone book.

Post Office The **main post office** in Papeete, on boulevard Pomare a block west of the Vaima Centre, is open Mon–Fri 7am–3pm. The postal clerks are on the second floor; take the escalators. Mail may be picked up at the poste restante counter on the ground floor next to the international telephone counter. Be prepared to show the clerk your passport and pay a small fee for each letter and newspaper you receive.

The branch post office at the Faaa airport terminal is open Mon–Fri 5–9am and 6:30–10:30pm, Sat–Sun 5am–noon and 6:30–10:30pm. Mail departs Tahiti more quickly if it's posted at the Faaa branch.

Radio/TV See "Fast Facts: French Polynesia" in Chapter 3.

Religious Services There is a large beige Protestant church (*Eglise Evangélique*) on Papeete's waterfront across from the racing-canoe landing. Catholic services are held at the Cathédrale de l'Immaculée Conception at the end of rue Jeanne-d'Arc behind the Vaima Centre.

Rest Rooms Public rest rooms are not common in French Polynesia, and by and large visitors must rely on the hotels and restaurants for relief. One exception in Papeete are the public toilets and showers in a concrete building on the Quay across from Bougainville Park and the main post office. They are open from dawn to dark and are used by the "yachties" who tie up along the Quay. The water from the shower heads, by the way, is fresh off the mountain and bone-numbing cold.

Safety See "Fast Facts: French Polynesia" in Chapter 3. Exercise caution when on the streets of Papeete at night.

Shoe Repairs Try **Hélène Chaussures** (tel. 42.80.52) a shoe and shoe-repair shop on rue Gauguin in front of the Papeete Town Hall. Shoe-repair shops are known as *cordonneries* in French. Shoes are *chaussures*. If you break a heel on another island, forget it. Wear your shower sandals.

Taxes See "Fast Facts: French Polynesia" in Chapter 3.

Taxis See "Getting Around" in this chapter.

Telegrams/Telex See "Telephone," below.

Telephone The telephone, telegraph, and telex office on the second floor of the main post office in Papeete is open Mon–Fri 7am–6pm, Sat–Sun 8–10am. You place your call at the desk and wait for it to come through to one of the booths across the room. Out of town, check with the local post office. See "Fast Facts: French Polynesia" in Chapter 3 for more information about pay phones and international calls.

Local calls on Tahiti cost 50 CFP (50¢) for the first 5 minutes. Calls to Moorea are 50 CFP (50¢) per minute. Calls to the other islands cost at least 100 CFP ($1) a minute.

To get the operator for other interisland calls, dial 10. The **international**

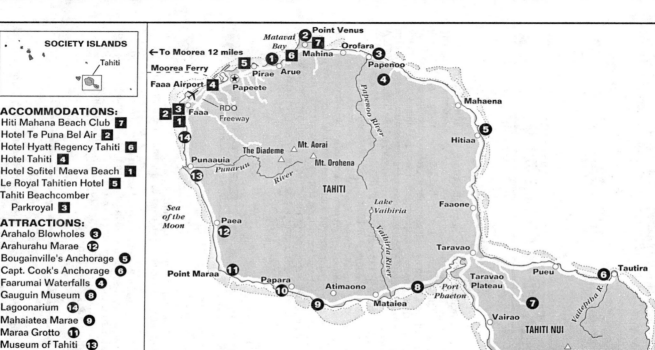

TAHITI

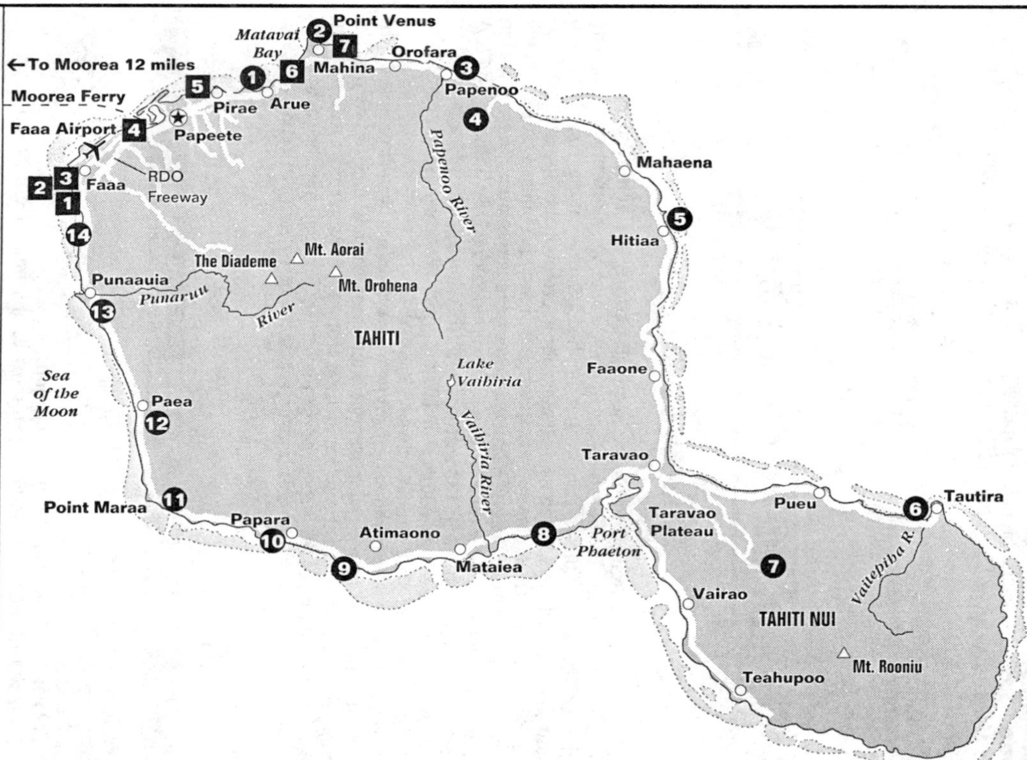

SOCIETY ISLANDS

Tahiti

ACCOMMODATIONS:

- Hiti Mahana Beach Club 7
- Hotel Te Puna Bel Air 2
- Hotel Hyatt Regency Tahiti 6
- Hotel Tahiti 4
- Hotel Sofitel Maeva Beach 1
- Le Royal Tahitien Hotel 5
- Tahiti Beachcomber Parkroyal 3

ATTRACTIONS:

- Arahalo Blowholes 3
- Arahurahu Marae 12
- Bougainville's Anchorage 5
- Capt. Cook's Anchorage 6
- Faarumai Waterfalls 4
- Gauguin Museum 8
- Lagoonarium 14
- Mahaiatea Marae 9
- Maraa Grotto 11
- Museum of Tahiti 13
- Point Venus 2
- Shell Museum 10
- Taravao Lookout 7
- Tomb of Pomare V 1

operator is at 19. The **emergency** (*secours*) police number is 17. For **directory information** (*service des renseignements*), dial 12.

Time See "Fast Facts: French Polynesia" in Chapter 3.

Tipping Except at La Romana Restaurant, tipping is not customary and is not expected.

2. WHAT TO SEE & DO

PAPEETE

Located on the flat coastal plain on the northwest corner of Tahiti, Papeete curves around one of the South Pacific's busiest harbors. There wasn't even a village here until the 1820s, when Queen Pomare set up headquarters along the shore and merchant ships and whalers began using the harbor in preference to the less protected Matavai Bay to the north. A claptrap town of stores, bars, and billiard parlors sprang up quickly, and between 1825 and 1829 it was a veritable den of iniquity. It grew even more after the French made it their headquarters upon taking over Tahiti in 1842. A fire nearly destroyed the town in 1884, after which thatch was outlawed as a building material. A cyclone did severe damage in 1906, and in 1914 two German warships shelled the harbor and sank the French navy's *Zélée*.

Otherwise, Papeete was perhaps best known for Quinn's, a waterfront establishment whose reputation as the quintessential South Seas bar has survived its demise. For many, the watershed in Papeete's transition from a backwater port to a modern city was not the building of the airport or the nuclear testing facility in the early 1960s; it was the tearing down of Quinn's and its replacement by modern retail stores in 1973.

WALKING TOUR — Papeete

Start: Tourist board office.
Finish: Papeete Town Hall.
Time: 2 hours.
Best Time: Early morning or late afternoon.
Worst Time: Midday, or Sunday when most establishments are closed.

A stroll through downtown Papeete is a good way to get the lay of the land. You will pass not only most of the sights in town but also the shops to which you may want to return (or duck into if there's a passing shower).

Begin at the Tourist Board's office at the foot of rue Paul-Gauguin and stroll westward along boulevard Pomare to:

IMPRESSIONS

Without qualification I can say that the waterfront of Papeete, with Moorea in the background, is unequaled.
—JAMES A. MICHENER, 1951

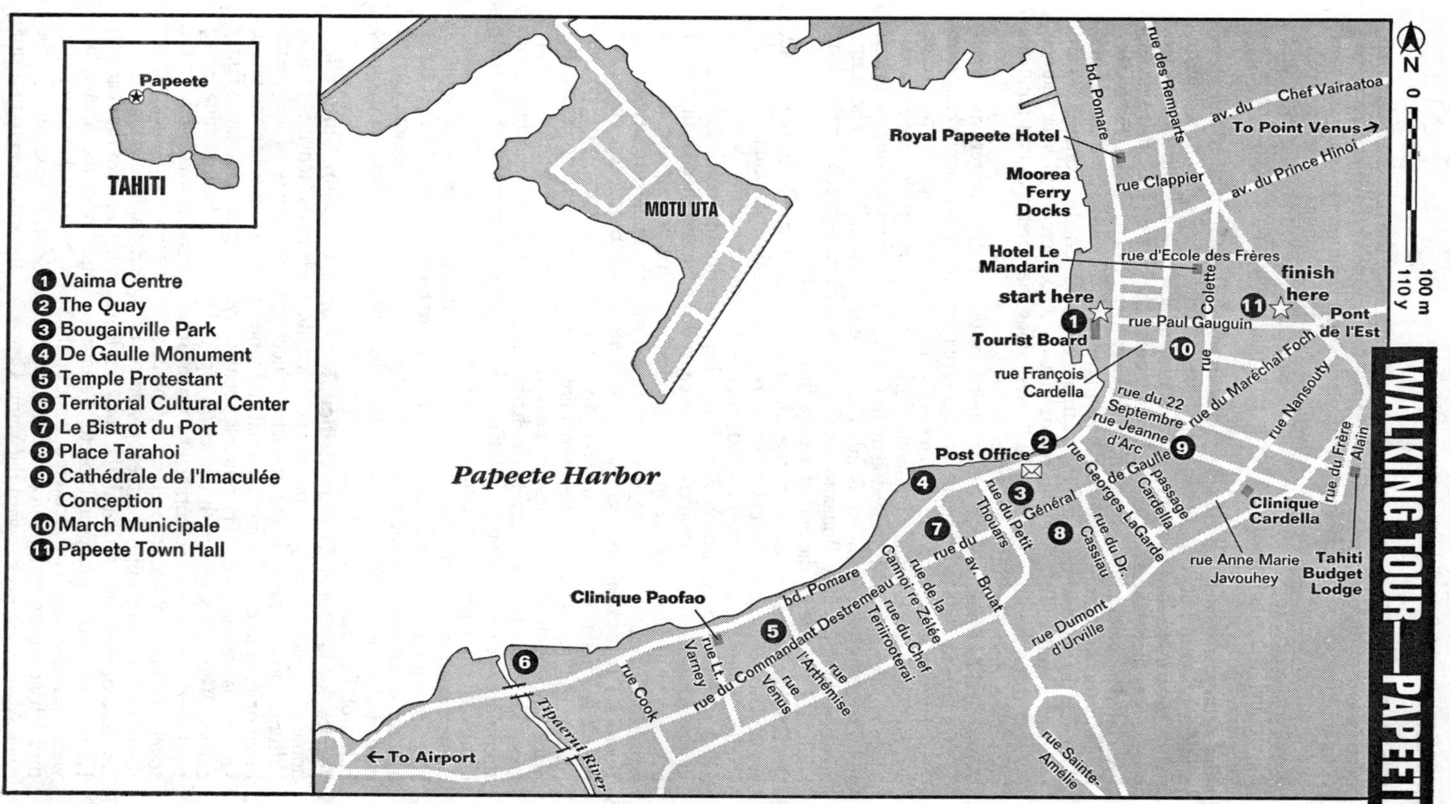

WALKING TOUR—PAPEETE
N
0
100 m
110 y
Papeete
TAHITI
1 Vaima Centre
2 The Quay
3 Bougainville Park
4 De Gaulle Monument
5 Temple Protestant
6 Territorial Cultural Center
7 Le Bistrot du Port
8 Place Tarahoi
9 Cathédrale de l'Imaculée Conception
10 March Municipale
11 Papeete Town Hall
MOTU UTA
Papeete Harbor
Royal Papeete Hotel
Moorea Ferry Docks
Hotel Le Mandarin
start here
Tourist Board
finish here
Pont de l'Est
To Point Venus→
av. du Chef Vairaatoa
av. du Prince Hinoi
bd. Pomare
rue des Remparts
rue Clappier
rue d'Ecole des Frères
rue Colette
rue Paul Gauguin
rue François Cardella
rue du Maréchal Foch
rue Nansouty
rue du Frère Alain
rue du 22 Septembre
rue Jeanne d'Arc
passage de Gaulle Cardella
Post Office
rue Georges LaGarde
rue du Dr. Cassiau
rue du Petit Thouars
rue Général
Clinique Cardella
Tahiti Budget Lodge
rue Anne Marie Javouhey
rue du av. Bruat
rue de la Cannoi re Zélée
rue du Chef Teriirooterai
rue Dumont d'Urville
rue Sainte-Amélie
rue du Commandant Destremeau
rue l'Arthémise
rue Venus
rue Lt. Varney
Clinique Paofao
rue Cook
Tipaerui River
←To Airport

1. **Vaima Centre.** The modern shopping center opposite the tuna boat dock has become one of the centers of town, especially for Papeete's French and European communities (the municipal market still serves this function for most Tahitians and Chinese). Quinn's Bar stood in the block east of the Vaima Centre, where the Noa Noa boutique is now. The Vaima Centre takes its name from the Vaima Restaurant, everyone's favorite eatery in those days, which it replaced. Across the four-lane boulevard from the Vaima, is:
2. **The Quay,** a mecca for cruising yachts from April to September and some resident boats in between. Beyond the boats, on the other side of the harbor, stands **Motu Uta,** once a small natural island but now home of the wharves and warehouses that serve as Papeete's shipping port. The reef on the other side has been filled to make a breakwater and to connect Motu Uta by road to **Fare Ute,** the industrial area and French naval base to the right. The interisland boats dock alongside the filled-in reef, and their cargoes of copra (dried coconut meat) are taken to a mill at Fare Ute, where coconut oil is extracted and later shipped overseas to be used in cosmetics. Walk west along the waterfront past the main post office, next to which you come to:
3. **Bougainville Park,** a shady block named for the French explorer who found Tahiti a little too late to get credit for discovering it. Two naval cannons hang over the sidewalk: One was on the French navy's *Zélée;* the one nearest the post office was on Count von Luckner's infamous World War I German raider, the *Seeadler,* which ran aground at Mopelia atoll in the Cook Islands after terrifying the British and French territories in the South Pacific during World War I. The statue between the guns is of Bougainville. On the waterfront a block farther along boulevard Pomare, at the end of avenue Bruat, stands:
4. **De Gaulle Monument.** After the fall of France to Nazi Germany in 1940, French Polynesia quickly went over to the Free French side under Gen. Charles de Gaulle. When Japan entered the war in 1941, local authorities permitted the Allies to build an airstrip on Bora Bora. The majority of French Polynesians supported de Gaulle as president of France, and the conservative Gaullist party has been an important force in local politics ever since. Keep going along the waterfront to rue l'Arthémise, where you can't miss the impressive steeple of:
5. **Temple Protestant,** the largest *Eglise Evangélique* (Evangelical church) in French Polynesia. The protestant sect grew out of the early work by the London Missionary Society. Today the pastors are Tahitian. Across the boulevard, the black-sand beach backed by shade trees is where sleek outrigger racing canoes are kept. They can be seen cutting the harbor during lunchtime and in the late afternoons—canoe racing is Tahiti's major indigenous sport. The partially completed stone gateway is a monument to the Hokule'a, a traditional voyaging canoe which toured the South Pacific in the 1980s, setting off a wave of Polynesian pride. Boulevard Pomare continues west for 6 more blocks, the canoes and harbor on one side and a few remaining stately colonial homes interspersed with modern office buildings on the other. Near the end of the boulevard, on the banks of Tipaerui Stream, stands the:
6. **Territorial Cultural Center (Office Territorial d'Action Culturelle),** home of Papeete's civic auditorium and town library. Periodic activities include cultural shows, classical and modern concerts, reenactments of Polynesian ceremonies, and exhibits of traditional and modern art. A snack bar and public rest rooms are just inside. The center is open from 8am to 5pm Monday to Friday except Wednesday, when it closes at 4pm. Do some backtracking along boulevard Pomare to the corner of avenue Bruat, taking in what's left of the stately old colonial homes on the "mountain side" of the street. When you get there, sit down and enjoy a refueling stop on the covered sidewalk of:
7. **Le Bistrot du Port.** Although the noisy traffic has stolen much of the charm of French-style outdoor cafés in Papeete, it's easy to imagine what the quieter days were like. After you have recovered, walk up the shady, tree-lined avenue Bruat, turn left at the stoplight, and proceed along rue du Général de Gaulle. To the right as you walk back toward the Vaima Centre are the spacious grounds of:
8. **Place Terahoi,** Papeete's governmental center, which was royal property in the

old days. Queen Pomare built a fine mansion here, long gone but replicated by the Papeete Town Hall. As you face the grounds, the buildings on the right house the French part of the government, including the high commissioner's office and home. The modern building on the left houses the local part, the Territorial Assembly. You can walk around hallways of the Assembly building during business hours. In front of it is a monument to Pouvanaa a Oopa, a Tahitian who became a hero fighting for France in World War I and then spent the rest of his long life (1895–1977) battling for independence for his homeland. At one point in the 1960s and 1970s he spent 15 years in prison in France but returned home in time to see more local autonomy granted the territory. In fact, his fellow Tahitians promptly sent him back to Paris as a member of the French Senate. Continue 2 more blocks along rue du Général de Gaulle past the rear of the Vaima to Tahiti's oldest Catholic church:

9. **Cathédrale de l'Immaculée Conception,** which, houses a series of paintings of the Crucifixion. It's a very cool, quiet, and comforting place to worship or just to comtemplate. Rue du Général de Gaulle becomes rue du Maréchal Foch past the church, but follow it for a block until rue Colette angles off to the left. The honking *le truck* horns at this intersection accounce the presence of the:
10. **Marché Municipale,** Papeete's Municipal Market. Take a stroll under the large tin pavilion and examine the multitude of fruits and vegetables offered for sale. Unwritten rules dictate that Tahitians sell fruits and traditional vegetables, such as taro and breadfruit, Chinese sell European and Chinese vegetables, and Chinese and Europeans serve as butchers and bakers. If your stomach can handle it, look for hogs' heads hanging in the butcher stalls. The market is busiest early in the mornings, but the local fishermen set off a new wave of activity when they arrive with their daily catch about 4pm. The busiest time of all is from 5 to 7am every Sunday, when people from the outlying areas of Tahiti, and even from the other islands, arrive to sell their produce. By 8am the pickings are slim. After sampling the market and the marvelous handcraft stalls upstairs, walk along rue Colette 2 more blocks to:
11. **Papeete Town Hall.** This magnificent replica of Queen Pomare's mansion which once stood at place Tarahoi captures the spirit of the colonial South Pacific. The *Hôtel de Ville* or *Fare Oire* (French and Tahitian, respectively, for town hall) was dedicated in 1990 by French president François Mitterrand during an elaborate celebration. It's worth a walk up the grand entrance steps and to catch a cool breeze from its all-encompassing balconies.

TOURING TAHITI

ORGANIZED TOURS

Several companies offer circle-island tours of Tahiti. The prices for the same tour may vary from one operator to the next, so some shopping around is in order. Expect to pay about 4,000 CFP ($40), not including lunch. The major operators are **Paradis Tours** (tel. 42.49.36), **Tahiti Tours** (tel. 42.50.50), and **Tahiti Nui Travel** (tel. 42.68.03). They have reservations desks in several of the hotels.

Optional buffet lunches at the Restaurant du Musée Gauguin are about 2,000 CFP ($20) per person.

Excursions into Tahiti's interior are growing in popularity. **Paradis Tours** offers a ½-day trip up the valleys and across the ridges for 5,000 CFP ($50) per person. Reservations may be made at the activities desks of most hotels.

Day-trips to Moorea with lunch and sightseeing cost about 15,000 CFP ($150) per person, depending on whether you take the ferry both ways or fly one or both ways. That's almost twice the amount two people would pay to do it on their own, including the cost of the ferry, rental car for ½ day, and lunch (which means that you pay a steep price for the guide and for the luxury of not having to make your own arrangements).

The companies also offer day trips to Huahine, Bora Bora, and Tetiaroa (Marlon

Brando's atoll, which lies 30 miles north of Tahiti). These range from 29,000 CFP to 37,000 CFP ($290 to $370).

It's far from inexpensive, but one way to see Tahiti's interior mountains, valleys, and waterfalls is by helicopter with one of two "flightseeing" companies based at Faaa Airport: **Tahiti Helicoptères,** (tel. 43.34.26, or 42.61.22 after business hours) or **Pacific Helicopter Service** (tel. 43.16.18 or 43.84.25). Both have several tours ranging in length from 30 minutes to 1 hour. It's a spectacular way to see Tahiti and nearby Moorea, but pick a day when clouds aren't hanging around the mountain tops. Usually early in the day is the best time.

THE CIRCLE-ISLAND TOUR

Most of Tahiti's tour companies (see "Organized Tours," above) offer around-the-island trips—known locally as "circle-island tours"—in air-conditioned coaches for about 4,000 CFP ($40) per person, and all of them have knowledgeable guides to explain what you're seeing. But in case you want to do it on your own, here's what you will find, proceeding clockwise from Papeete on the road skirting the shore. For a more detailed description, look for Bengt Danielsson's *Tahiti: Circle Island Tour Guide* in the local shops.

On the land side of the road are red-topped concrete markers (*Pointes kilomètres* in French, or "PK" for short) that tell you the distance in kilometers between Papeete and the isthmus of Taravao. The end of each kilometer is marked with a PK. The markers give the distance from Papeete to Taravao in each direction—not the total number of kilometers around the island. The large numbers facing the ocean are the number of kilometers from Papeete; the numbers facing you as you drive along are the number of kilometers you have to go, either to Papeete or Taravao, depending on your direction. Distances between the PKs are referred to in tenths of kilometers; for example, PK 35.6 would be 35.6 kilometers from Papeete. Once you've mastered these facts, they make handy frames of reference.

The road around the island is 72 miles long, not counting side trips on Tahiti Iti. It's 54km (32 miles) from Papeete to Taravao along the east coast and 60km (40 miles) back along the west coast. If your car has an odometer, reset it to zero; if not, make note of the total kilometers at the outset.

Give yourself half a day at least, a full day to do it leisurely.

THE NORTH & EAST COASTS

First you have to find your way out of town. The broad **avenue du Prince Hinoi,** which runs off boulevard Pomare at the Hotel Prince Hinoi on the waterfront, is the start of the road that eventually circles the island. Therefore, turn at the Prince Hinoi and go straight.

Loti's Pool (PK 2.5) A road goes right into the Fautaua Valley and the Bain Loti, or Loti's Pool. Julien Viaud, the French merchant mariner who wrote under the pen name Pierre Loti, used this pool as a setting for his novel, *The Marriage of Loti,* which recounted the love of a Frenchman for a Tahitian woman. The pool, now part of Papeete's water-supply system, is covered in concrete and is not worth the trip. The road goes into the lower part of the valley and terminates at the beginning of a hiking trail up to the **Fautaua Waterfall,** an arduous 3-hour walk away.

Tomb of Pomare V (PK 4.7) Turn left at the sign and drive a short distance to a Protestant churchyard that commands an excellent view of Matavai Bay to the right. The tomb on the right with a Grecian urn on top was built in 1879 for Queen Pomare. Her remains were removed a few years later, however, by her son, King Pomare V, who abdicated in return for a French pension and later died of too much drink. Now he is buried there, and tour guides like to say the urn is not an urn at all but a liquor bottle.

Home of James Norman Hall (PK 5.4) The lovely tin-roofed home, now a museum, was built by James Norman Hall, coauthor with Charles Nordhoff of

IMPRESSIONS

The village of Papeete struck us all very pleasantly. Lying in a semicircle round the bay, the tasteful mansions of the chiefs and foreign residents impart an air of tropical elegance, heightened by the palm-trees waving here and there, and the deep-green groves of bread-fruit in the background. The squalid huts of the common people are out of sight, and there is nothing to mar the prospect.

—Herman Melville, 1847

Mutiny on the Bounty. (See "History" in Chapter 3.) Nordhoff and Hall served together in World War I, moved to Tahiti to write, and produced three novels on the mutiny (*Men Against the Sea* and *Pitcairn's Island* are the others) and several more books about French Polynesia. Hall died in 1951 and is buried on the hill above his home. His home and library are open to the public 8am to 5pm Tuesday to Sunday. Admission is free.

✪ **Point Venus** (PK 10) Turn left at the road sign marking the turnoff to Point Venus, Tahiti's northernmost point. If the sign's not there, turn left just before the Mobil service station at the "Y" intersection at PK 10. The low, sandy peninsula covered with casuarina trees is about 2km (1.2 miles) from the main road. Captains Wallis, Cook, and Bligh landed here and anchored behind the reef in Matavai Bay offshore. Captain Cook made his observations of the transit of Venus across the sun in 1769 from a point between the black-sand beach and the meandering river that cuts the peninsula in two. The beach and the parklike setting around the tall white lighthouse, which was completed in 1868 (notwithstanding the 1867 date over the door), are popular for picnics. There's a snack bar, souvenir and handcraft shop, and pay toilets.

The heavily rusted cannons beside the Tahitian-style meetinghouse were recovered from the reefs at Amanu Island in the Tuamotu Archipelago, where they reputedly were lost in 1526 by J. S. Elcano, Magellan's pilot, who took over command of the first circumnavigation after Magellan was killed in the Philippines in 1522 (Elcano thus became, for the record, the first man to sail around the world). Australian author Robert Langdon believes that a Spanish ship that disappeared in the early 1500s actually ran aground on one of the Tuamotu Islands and that the survivors were responsible for the red-haired Tahitians seen by Captain Cook 250 years later.

Note that it's possible to reach Point Venus from Papeete by taking a le truck bound for Mahina, the village nearby.

Papenoo Valley (PK 17.1) Tahiti's longest bridge crosses its longest river at the end of its largest valley at one of its largest rural villages—all named Papenoo. The river flows down to the sea through the only hole in the wall of the old volcanic crater that once topped the island. A dirt track used by four-wheel-drive vehicles leads into the valley from the east side of the bridge. A hiking trail continues from the end of the vehicular track up the valley, across the old crater wall, and down to Tahiti's only lake, **Vaihiria.** Another trail leads from there down to the south shore, so it's possible to walk from Papenoo across to Mataiea—do it only with a guide and proper equipment.

The Blowholes (PK 22) The north coast has more dramatic seascapes than any other part of Tahiti, as the road winds along one surf beach after another and around one rocky headland after another. The surf pounding against the headland at Arahoho has formed overhanging shelves with holes in them. As waves crash under the shelves, water and air are forced through the holes, resulting in a geyserlike phenomenon. The largest blowhole is just over the concrete railing on the ocean side of the road, but you can listen for air escaping through cracks at the base of the cliff on the land side.

✪ **Faarumai Waterfalls** (PK 22.1) A sign on the right just past the blowhole marks a formerly paved road that leads 1.3km (¾ mile) up a small valley to the *Cascades de Faarumai,* Tahiti's most accessible waterfalls. Park near the stand of bamboo trees and follow the signs to the falls: Vaimahuta falls are an easy walk to the right after crossing a footbridge; Haamaremare Iti and Haamaremarerahi falls are up a more difficult trail to the left. There is a covered picnic table overlooking the shallow pool at the base of Vaimahuta falls, which plunge straight down several hundred feet from a hanging valley above. Bring insect repellent.

Mahaena Battlefield (PK 32.5) The Tahitian rebellion after the French annexed Tahiti came to a head on April 17, 1844, when 441 French troops charged several times that many poorly armed Tahitians dug in near the village of Mahaena. The Tahitians lost 102 men; the French, 15. It was the last set battle of the rebellion, although the Tahitians struggled on with guerrilla actions for 2 more years before the French captured their headquarters.

Bougainville's Landing (PK 37.6) Bougainville anchored just offshore when he arrived in Tahiti in 1768. The two small islands on the reef, Oputotara and Variararu, provided slim protection against the prevailing trade winds, and Bougainville lost six anchors in 10 days trying to keep his ships off the reef. In fact, he was lucky not to have lost his ships in the process. One of the anchors was recovered by the Tahitians, who gave it to the high chief of Bora Bora, who in turn gave it to Captain Cook in 1777. A plaque mounted on a rock on the northern end of the bridge at Hitiaa commemorates Bougainville's landing.

View of Tahiti Iti (PK 39) Once past Hitiaa, the road heads due south, and the green mountains of Tahiti Iti, the southern part of the island, come spectacularly into view across the water. The terrain as well as the view changes. Sharp ridges give way to narrow valleys that reach down to rocky black beaches pounded by foaming white surf. In many respects this east coast of Tahiti Nui resembles the Marquesas Islands, which are more rugged and geologically newer than Tahiti.

Vaiharuru Waterfall (PK 41.8) In fact, some of the valleys look so much like those in the Marquesas that in 1957 director John Huston chose one of them, picturesque Faatautia, as a location for a movie version of *Typee,* Herman Melville's novelized account of his ship-jumping adventures among the Marquesans in the 1840s. The project was scrapped after another of Huston's Melville movies, *Moby Dick,* bombed at the box office. As you round the curve into Faatautia, you can see Vaiharuru Waterfall cascading into the uninhabited valley, which must look today much as it did 1,000 years ago.

Taravao (PK 53) After passing the small-boat marina, the road climbs up onto the Taravao isthmus. At the top are the stone walls of Fort Taravao, which the French built in 1844 to bottle up what was left of the rebellious Tahitians on the Tahiti Iti peninsula. It is now used as a French army training center. Germans stuck on Tahiti during World War II were interned there. The village of Taravao with its shops, suburban streets, and churches has grown up around the military post. There are Chinese stores, two gas stations, a new car dealer with two automobiles on display under a tin roof, and two reasonably priced restaurants on the main road: One serves French and Chinese cuisine, the other specializes in pizza.

TAHITI ITI

The isthmus joins the larger Tahiti Nui to its smaller Siamese twin, the peninsula of Tahiti Iti. The latter is much more sparsely populated, and paved roads dead-end about halfway down its north and its south sides. A series of cliffs plunges into the sea on Tahiti Iti's rugged east end.

IMPRESSIONS

It came upon me little by little. I came to like the life here [Tahiti], with its ease and its leisure, and the people, with their good-nature and their happy smiling faces.

—W. Somerset Maugham, 1921

The North Coast

The road on the north coast of Tahiti Iti goes for 18km (11 miles) to the sizable village of Tautira, which sits on its own little peninsula built up by sediment washed down from the mountains by the Vaitepiha River. Captain Cook anchored in the bay off Tautira on his second visit to Tahiti in 1773. "Anchored" may not be entirely accurate, for Cook's ships apparently ran aground on the reef while their crews were partying one night. He managed to get them off, but lost several anchors in the process. One of them was found in 1978 and is now on display at the Museum of Tahiti and Her Islands, which we will come to on the west side of the island.

A year after Cook landed at Tautira, two Franciscan priests were put ashore there by the *Aguila*, a Spanish ship from Peru, whose captain, Don Domingo de Boenechea, claimed the island for Spain. It was the third time Tahiti had been claimed for a European power. The *Aguila* returned a year later, but the priests had had enough of Tahiti and sailed back to Peru. When Cook returned again in 1777, he found a wooden cross outside the priests' abandoned European-style house which was inscribed CHRISTUS VINCIT CAROLUS III IMPERAT 1774. Cook understood the cross to be a grave marker, but rather than leave it to be interpreted as a possible claim of possession, he had his carpenter carve on the back, GEORGIUS TERTIUS REX ANNI 1767 69 73 74 & 77. No question, it was King George's island.

As far as anyone knows, Tautira's next famous visitor was Robert Louis Stevenson, who spent 2 months there in 1888 working on *The Master of Ballantrae*, a novel set not in Tahiti but in Scotland. Stevenson's mother was with him in Tautira. After she returned to London she sent the local Protestant church a silver communion service, which is still being used today.

The Taravao Plateau

Another dead-end paved road runs high up into the rolling pastureland of the Taravao Plateau. To find the road, turn on the north coast at Taravao village as if going to Tautira, turn right into the paved street just before the school in the village, and follow the pavement as it makes a sharp left turn at the end of the suburban residential section and heads up the hill. If you have to choose one of three roads on Tahiti Iti, take this one. There is a pavilion shortly before the road ends, and from there you'll have a spectacular view of the entire isthmus and down both sides of Tahiti Nui. In addition, the plateau is more than 1,200 feet high at this point, which gives it a refreshing climate—springlike rather than tropical; the surrounding pastures and tree lines are more reminiscent of provincial France than of Tahiti.

Down the South Coast

The picturesque road along the south coast of Tahiti Iti skirts the lagoon and passes through small settlements. After a few kilometers you come to a marina at the edge of the lagoon, across from which a very steep paved road leads to the Hotel Puunui, which has a nice view over the isthmus and both sides of Tahiti Nui.

Zane Grey, author of many western novels, had a deep-sea fishing camp from 1928 to 1930 at 7.3km (4½ miles), near the village of Toahotu. In 1930 he caught a silver marlin that was about 14 feet long and weighted more than 1,000 pounds—even after the sharks had had a meal on it while Grey was trying to get it aboard his boat. He wrote about his adventures in *Tales of Tahitian Waters*.

According to Tahitian legends, the demigod Maui once made a rope from his sister Hina's hair and used it to slow down the sun long enough for Tahitians to finish cooking their food in their earth ovens (a lengthy process). He accomplished this feat while standing on the reef at a point 8.5km (5 miles) along the south coast road, and his footprints are still there (though personally I've never been able to find them). The **Bay of Tapueraha,** beyond Maui's alleged footprints, is the best natural harbor on Tahiti and was used as a base by a large contingent of the French navy during the aboveground nuclear tests at Moruroa atoll in the 1960s. Some of the old mooring pilings still stand just offshore.

The village of Taravao on the isthmus is a good place for lunch or refreshment. Several snack bars and restaurants sit on the main road. Try **Pâtisserie Taravao** (tel. 57.19.30) for delightful pastries and tasty pizzas. In fact, owner Gotthard "Hardy" Wusseng often supplies pizzas to the Club Med on Moorea. For something more elaborate, wait until the Gauguin Museum and its nearby restaurant.

THE SOUTH COAST OF TAHITI

As you leave Taravao heading back to Papeete along Tahiti's south coast, note the PK markers begin to decrease the nearer to Papeete you get. The road rims casuarina-ringed **Port Phaeton,** another deep-water harbor that cuts nearly halfway across the isthmus. Port Phaeton and the Bay of Tapueraha to the south are Tahiti's finest harbors, yet European settlement and most development have taken place on the opposite side of the island, around Papeete.

Apparently Tahiti's initial residents recognized the advantages of the south coast and its deep lagoons and harbors, for word-of-mouth history says that the first Polynesians to arrive came through the Hotumatuu Pass in the reef and settled at **Papeari** (PK 52). Their arrival would have been sometime between A.D. 400 and 500. Today Papeari is a thriving village whose residents often sell fruit and vegetables at stands along the road.

✪ **Gauguin Museum** (PK 51.2) Tahiti's most famous artist gave up a career as a stockbroker in Paris, left his family, and in 1891 moved to Tahiti to devote himself to painting, free of what he saw as the chains of civilization. His life in Tahiti was marked by poverty and sickness for 12 years, but during this time he produced a series of paintings of Tahiti and Tahitians that brought new fame to the islands. Unfortunately for Gauguin, his works were not fully appreciated during his lifetime: In 1903, nearly penniless, he died of syphilis at Atuona on Hiva Oa in the Marquesas Islands, where he was living with the last in a series of teenaged mistresses/models.

On the rare occasion when his paintings come on the market today, they fetch in millions of dollars. At those prices, it's no wonder that Tahiti's Musée Gauguin does not own even one of his major paintings (it owns a lesser painting and some sculptures, woodcuts, engravings, and a ceramic vase). The museum does have an active program to borrow Gauguin's major works, and one might be on display during your visit. Otherwise, the exhibits are dedicated to the history of the period when Gauguin lived on Tahiti. Excellent reproductions of his works are available at the museum's gift shop. The museum is open from 9am to 5pm 7 days a week. Admission is 450 CFP ($4.50) for adults, 250 CFP ($2.50) for children between the ages of 2 and 18.

The museum sits in lush **Harrison Smith Botanical Gardens,** started in 1919 by Harrison Smith, an American who followed in Gauguin's footsteps by leaving a career (teaching physics at the Massachusetts Institute of Technology) and moving to Tahiti; he died here in 1947. His gardens, which now belong to the public, have a plethora of tropical plants from around the world. The large tiki in front of the modern building is believed to be cursed because it was removed from its home on Raivavae in the Austral Islands.

IMPRESSIONS

Tahiti was in those days a veritable paradise to the seaman—one of the richest islands in the world, with a mild and wholesome climate, abounding in every variety of delicious food, and inhabited by a race of gentle and hospitable barbarians. . . . And as regards the possibilities of dissipation, to which seamen are given in every port, the island could only be described as a Mohammedan paradise.

—Charles Nordhoff and James Norman Hall, 1933

IMPRESSIONS

The young girls when ever they can collect 8 or 10 together dance a very indecent dance which they call Timorodee *singing most indecent songs and useing most indecent actions in the practice of which they are brought up from their earlyest Childhood . . .*

—James Cook, 1769

Restaurant du Musée Gauguin (PK 50.5) The organized circle-island tour groups usually stop for lunch at this restaurant, which sits across a small bay from the museum and shares its name. An extensive buffet is offered for lunch at 2,000 CFP ($20) per person. Main courses, which primarily feature shrimp and steak, range from 1,500 CFP to 1,800 CFP ($15 to $18), and there is a wide assortment of salads and appetizers. The restaurant is open from noon to 3pm, 7 days a week. For reservations, phone 57.13.80.

Vaihiria River (PK 48) A hiking trail leads from the bridge over the Vaihiria River to **Lake Vaihiria,** Tahiti's only lake, which is at 1,560 feet above sea level and is noted for its freshwater eels (the same species can be seen at the Hotel Te Puna Bel Air). Cliffs up to 3,000 feet tall drop to the lake on its north side. Tahitians make the trek to the lake on a regular basis to tend their banana plantations, but it's not advisable for visitors to make the trip without a guide.

Atimaono (PK 41) The largest parcel of flat land on Tahiti is now the site of Olivier Bréaud International Golf Course, French Polynesia's only links at present. During the American Civil War, William Stewart started his cotton plantation here. Nothing remains of the plantation, but it was Stewart who brought the first Chinese indentured servants to Tahiti. Behind the golf course, **Atimaono Park** has hiking trails leading to views from the ridges above.

Mahaiatea Marae (PK 39.2) The first paved road to the left after you pass Chez Mahaitea leads to the beach and a huge overgrown pile of boulders that was once Tahiti's most imposing Polynesian temple, the Mahaiatea Marae. Capt. James Cook described its dimensions as about 100 yards long, 30 yards across, and 15 yards high. One reason it's no longer that large today is that William Stewart apparently raided it for stones to use on his cotton plantation at Atimaono. The setting on the beach is worth the short drive from the main road. Judging from the surrounding beer cans and other litter, it's a popular gathering spot for local residents.

Dorence Atwater's Grave (PK 36) The United States once had a consul in Tahiti, and after the Civil War the post was occupied by Dorence Atwater. Atwater had been a Union Army soldier held as a prisoner of war by the Confederates. He was assigned to a Southern hospital, where he recorded the names of Union soldiers who died while in captivity. He later escaped and brought to the federal government's attention his lists, which proved that the Confederacy was keeping inaccurate records; the action made him a hero in the eyes of the Union Army. He later moved to the south coast of Tahiti, married the daughter of a chief of the Papara district, and at one time invested in William Stewart's cotton venture. He is buried in the Protestant churchyard.

Also in Papara village is a local **Centre Artisanal,** next to the *mairie* (town hall). A handcraft shop has quilted pillows, quilts, baskets, pareus, and a large selection of shell jewelry. The shop is open from 7:30am to 4pm. An adjoining ***Musée de Coquillage*** (**Seashell Museum**) has a collection of polished shell collages and dried sea snakes, sea-turtle shells, and crabs—many of which are for sale as well as for viewing (remember, however, that sea turtles cannot legally be imported into the United States and many other countries). The museum is open Monday through Saturday from 8am to 5pm. Admission is free.

Maraa Grotto (PK 28.5) Near the southwest corner of Tahiti the road runs at the base of a series of headlands that drop precipitously to the lagoon. Deep into one of these cliffs goes the Maraa Grotto, also called the Paroa Cave. It usually has a lake inside and goes much deeper into the hill than appears at first glance. The mouth of the cave is clearly visible from the road. Park in the parking lot, not along the road.

THE WEST COAST

Once the road turns northward at Maraa, it runs through the Paea and Punaauia districts, which are rapidly becoming crowded suburbs of Papeete. The west coast is the driest part of Tahiti, and it's very popular with Europeans, Americans, and others who have built homes along the lagoon and in the hills overlooking it.

✪ **Arahurahu Marae** (PK 22.5) A small road on the right of the Chinese store known as Magasin Laut leads to a narrow valley, on the floor of which sits the Arahurahu Marae. This particular marae (temple) apparently had no special historical importance, but it was restored in 1954, complete with exhibit boards explaining the significance of each part. For example, the stone pens near the entrance were used to keep the pigs to be sacrificed to the gods. This is the only marae in all of Polynesia that has been fully restored and is maintained like a museum. Arahurahu is used during the July celebrations for the reenactment of old Polynesian ceremonies.

✪ **Tahiti Museum** (PK 15.1) Turn left at the gas station and follow the paved road through a residential area to the lagoon and the museum, which is officially known as the **Musée de Tahiti et Ses Isles** (Museum of Tahiti and Her Islands). One of the best museums in the South Pacific, it has displays of the geological history of the islands, their sea life, flora, and fauna, and the history and culture of their peoples. There are exhibits devoted to traditional weaving, tapa-cloth making, early tools, body ornaments, fire making, tattooing, fishing and horticultural techniques, religion and marae, games and sports, warfare and arms, deaths and funerals, writers and missionaries. Most, but not all, of the display legends are translated into English. The museum is open from 9:30am to 5:30pm Tuesday through Sunday; admission is 300 CFP ($3).

Punaruu Valley (PK 14.8) Driving back from the museum to the main road provides a view up the Punaruu Valley toward the **Diadème,** the huge jagged tooth of a mountain that sits on a ridge. An unpaved road up the valley from the bridge over the Punaruu River leads to a plateau covered with orange trees. The French built a fort on the north side of the river mouth during the rebellion of 1842–46, but the site is occupied today by a television relay station.

North of the bridge the road widens to four lanes with speedy traffic, which always distracts me from the gorgeous view across the lagoon toward Moorea. If you started your tour in the morning, you should be arriving on the west coast just in time to have a cold drink and watch the sun go down over Moorea. As you continue on your journey, the road soon splits: the right lane feeds into the RDO freeway, which roars back to Papeete, while the left lane will take you along the old road past the west coast hotels and the Faaa airport before returning to town.

3. WHERE TO STAY

Most of Tahiti's hotels are grouped in two areas: downtown Papeete and the northwest coast facing Moorea. The major exceptions are the Hotel Hyatt Regency Tahiti and Le Royal Tahitien Hotel, both east of town. The establishments on the northwest coast have more of a beachside resort atmosphere than do the businesslike hotels in Papeete. The choice of location, therefore, depends to a large extent on whether you're looking for a resort environment or the convenience of being in Papeete, close to its restaurants, shops, nightclubs, and a quick escape on the Moorea ferries.

For years the territorial government encouraged only well-to-do tourists and prohibited camping altogether. That changed in the late 1980s, however, when some

IMPRESSIONS

Edward called for him in a rickety trap drawn by an old mare, and they drove along a road that ran by the sea. On each side of it were plantations, coconut and vanilla; now and then they saw a great mango, its fruit yellow and red and purple among the massy green of the leaves, now they had a glimpse of the lagoon, smooth and blue, with here and there a tiny islet graceful with tall palms.
—W. Somerset Maugham, 1921

Tahitian families realized they could help make ends meet during hard economic times by tapping the low-budget, backpacking market. Although it will be more expensive than elsewhere in the South Pacific, today's backpacking traveler can find clean accommodations in Tahiti and the other islands of French Polynesia. On the other hand, there is a much bigger difference in quality than price between Tahiti's moderate and budget accommodation. These are basic, roof-over-your-head establishments. Period.

A reminder: The Tahiti Tourist Board has a list of pensions, private homes, and camping facilities. See "Information, Entry Requirements & Money" in Chapter 3.

EXPENSIVE

HOTEL HYATT REGENCY TAHITI, B.P. 1015, Papeete, Tahiti. Tel. 48-11-22, or toll free 800/228-9000. Fax 45.25.44. Telex 225. 200 rms. A/C MINIBAR TEL **Location:** On round-island road in Mahina, 8km (5 miles) east of Papeete. Take a Mahina truck.

$ Rates: 21,000 CFP–27,500 CFP ($210–$275) single or double. AE, DC, MC, V.

Also referred to locally by its former name, the Hotel Tahara'a, the Hyatt virtually hangs off the steep headland Captain Cook named One Tree Hill. Its 10 stories are set into the side of the hill, with the reception and other public areas on top. From this high, clifflike perch, the entire complex has a breathtaking view over Matavai Bay and down Tahiti's north coast to Moorea on the horizon. Even if you have no other reason to visit the Hyatt, stop in to enjoy this grand vista. While there, check out the collection of Tahitian antiques on display in the main lobby.

Each room has a terrace that offers the spectacular view over a railing covered with magenta bougainvillea. Since the floors are staggered going down the hill, the rooms and their terraces have an atmosphere of privacy. Americans will feel right at home, since most rooms have combination tub-showers and two double beds.

A path from the 10th floor (that's the bottom level of this upside-down hotel) leads to a black-sand beach on which the Hyatt has a Beach Club with sun chairs and other beach paraphernalia; snacks and drinks are also available. A free "beach buggy" shuttles between reception and the beach once an hour.

Dining/Entertainment: Under a big thatch roof on the top level are the Captain Cook Restaurant and Discovery Bar, used on Friday and Saturday nights for buffet dinners and one of Papeete's top Tahitian floor shows (see "Evening Entertainment," below). The Mahana Café, on the next level down, is open for breakfast from 6:30 to 9am and for snacks and light meals from 11:30am to 10pm.

Services: A shopping shuttle runs into Papeete three times a day Monday through Friday and twice a day on weekends and holidays.

Facilities: Shops; swimming pool with adjacent bar; two tennis courts; spa and fitness center; car-rental, tour, and activities desks; beauty salon.

HOTEL SOFITEL MAEVA BEACH, B.P. 6008, Papeete, Tahiti. Tel. 42-80-42, or toll free 800/763-4835. Fax 41.05.05. Telex 214. 230 rms. A/C MINIBAR TEL TV **Location:** On the round-island road in Punaauia, 7.5km (4½ miles) west of Papeete. Take any Faaa or Maeva Beach truck.

$ Rates: (in U.S. dollars only) $210–$240 single; $225–$255 double. AE, DC, MC, V.

Half a kilometer south of the Tahiti Beachcomber Parkroyal, this terraced high-rise building surrounded by tropical gardens sits beside Maeva Bay and a half-moon, black-sand beach of the same name. The lagoon off the beach isn't quite as good for swimming and snorkeling as for anchoring numerous cruising yachts. The rooms on the upper floors on the beach side enjoy the views of Moorea from their balconies, while those on the garden side look south along Tahiti's west coast. All have carpets, two single beds or one king-size bed, television movies in French and English, tropical furnishings, and a supply of toiletries. They do not, however, have tea- or coffee-making facilities.

The Maeva Beach offers a wide range of daily activities and demonstrations—weaving and handcraft-making, preparation of *poisson cru* (marinated fish), and Tahitian dancing.

Dining/Entertainment: The elegant, intimate, and air-conditioned Le Gauguin Restaurant serves some of Tahiti's best French cuisine by candlelight under its rose-colored ceilings. It's open 7 to 10pm 7 days a week except during January, when the staff takes a holiday. Restaurant L'Amiral de Bougainville is under a large thatch roof on the ground level next to the pool and Moorea Bar. You can get snacks and light meals from 6:30am to 10pm. The Sakura Restaurant offers tappanyaki-style Japanese dishes cooked by your table. Paper walls framed in blond wood separate several small dining nooks. The Sakuna is open every day except Thursday from noon to 1:30pm and from 7 to 10pm. Evening entertainment features Tahitian dance shows in the Restaurant L'Amiral de Bougainville on the beach level.

Services: Laundry, baby-sitting.

Facilities: Shops; beauty salon; car-rental, tour, and activities desks; swimming pool; pontoon for swimming and sunbathing; tennis courts and pro; golf driving range; free water sports provided by Richard Johnson's Tahiti Aquatique (see "Water Sports," below).

TAHITI BEACHCOMBER PARKROYAL, B.P. 6014, Faaa, Tahiti. Tel. 42-51-10, or toll free 800/835-7742. Fax 43.61.06. Telex 276. 182 rms, 17 bungalows. A/C MINIBAR TEL TV **Location:** On the round-island road in Faaa, 7km (4 miles) west of Papeete. Take any Faaa or Maeva Beach truck.

$ Rates (in U.S. dollars only): $210–$225 single; $240–$255 double; $320 overwater bungalows. AE, DC, MC, V.

Known locally as "The Beachcomber," this extraordinarily well-maintained property sits on Tataa Point at Tahiti's northwest corner. In the old pre-Christian days, souls leaped from this point on their journey to the ancient homeland; today the hotel's visitors get one of Tahiti's best views of Moorea—from both the guest rooms and the thatched-roof bungalows, which extend out over the lagoon from an artificial, manicured island joined to the hotel by a wooden footbridge. This is one of the best places to watch the sun set over Moorea—get a drink at the Motu Bar on the ground level, wander out to the beach, and as the French say, watch the sun go to bed while a group of Tahitians strum their guitars.

The Beachcomber's reception is on the top level of one of the five three-story buildings that house its Australian-style hotel rooms.

Each room has its own private patio or balcony with an ocean view, tropical decor with lots of rattan and bamboo furniture and flower-print spreads, drapes, and upholstery. This hotel began life as a TraveLodge, so don't expect the largest rooms in Tahiti (the Hyatt has those). Tahitian women spread mats in the grand foyer 3 days a week and sell colorful pareus and handcraft items.

Dining/Entertainment: Open-air Te Tiare Restaurant serves full or continental breakfasts from 7 to 9:30am daily, lunch from 11am to 3pm, and dinner from 7 to 9:30pm. The lunch menu consists of burgers, spaghetti, and grilled mahi mahi (dolphin fish) filets; evening meals might feature a light mousse of fresh fish with saffron butter, grilled mahi mahi, crabe farci créole style, and veal sautéed with morels and black mushrooms. Evening entertainment features nightly Tahitian string bands or dance shows at Le Motu Bar.

Services: Laundry service, baby-sitting.

Facilities: Swimming pool; tennis courts; boutique; beauty salon; tour and rental-car desks; water-sports equipment provided by Activities Rainbow (see "Water Sports," below).

MODERATE

HOTEL LE MANDARIN, 51 rue Colette, P.O. Box 302, Papeete, tel. 42-16-33. Fax 42.16.32. Telex 467. 37 rms. A/C MINIBAR TEL TV **Location:** Downtown Papeete near Municipal Market. From bd. Pomare, walk inland on rue des Ecoles des Frères 2 blocks to rue Colette.

$ Rates: 11,000 CFP–13,000 CFP ($110–$130) single; 12,500 CFP–14,500 CFP ($125–$145) double. DC, V.

Papeete's newest hotel, the six-story Le Mandarin has its lobby and coffee shop at the street level, a Chinese restaurant on the second floor, and basically two grades of rooms in the upper stories. Those on the top two floors are larger and have views overlooking the city. Lower-level rooms are smaller and less expensive. All rooms have sliding glass doors opening to very skinny balconies. As befits its name (and ownership), most decor and furnishings are Chinese or have Chinese overtones, with the restaurant and conference room qualifying as ornate.

In addition to its coffee shop and on-premises restaurant, guests also can dine at Le Mandarin Restaurant next door. The two establishments are joined by a hallway. Business services are available.

ROYAL PAPEETE HOTEL, B.P. 919, Papeete, Tahiti. Tel. 42-01-29, or toll free 800/252-0211 in California, 800/421-0000 elsewhere in the U.S., 800/368-0900 in Canada. Fax 43.79.09. Telex 384. 85 rms. A/C TEL **Location:** On bd. Pomare directly across from Moorea Ferry docks in downtown Papeete.

$ Rates: 8,000 CFP–9,500 CFP ($80–$95) single; 9,500 CFP–11,000 CFP ($95–$110) double. AE, DC, MC, V.

(S) This is my usual base of operations because of its proximity to the Moorea Ferry docks and the mobile snack bars that gather there at night. Most of the Royal Papeete's furnishings are from the United States, even the plumbing fixtures. About half the rooms are in the old wing facing the boulevard and half are in a new wing in the rear of the building. The older rooms have two twin beds and Tudor-style windows overlooking the Papeete waterfront; street noise is drowned out by the low hum of the air-conditioning units in each room. The smaller rooms in the old wing are the least expensive and are usually taken, but if you reserve one well in advance, you may get a larger room at the same rate. Rooms in the newer wing are much larger and have double beds, but be sure to ask for one on the west or south side. Those on the north and east are located next to Papeete's diesel-powered electric generating plant or directly over the Friday-night beat of La Cave nightclub downstairs. In other words, avoid Rooms 221 through 227 and 321 through 327.

Le Gallieni Restaurant, on the ground level, serves American-style breakfasts, French and continental lunches and dinners. It's often packed at lunch and is a popular watering hole for Moorea residents waiting for the ferry.

LE ROYAL TAHITIEN HOTEL, B.P. 5001, Pirae, Tahiti. Tel. 42-81-13, or 818/843-6068 in the U.S. Fax 41.05.35. 40 rms. A/C TEL **Location:** In suburb of Pirae, 4km (2½ miles) east of downtown. Take a Mahina truck or follow av. du Prince Hinoi 2 miles east. Get off truck and turn left into first lane past Total and Mobil stations opposite each other. Follow lane almost to beach, then turn left into unmarked parking lot.

$ Rates (in U.S. dollars only): $150 single or double. AE, DC, MC, V.

The Royal Tahitien enjoys a quiet garden setting beside a black-sand beach in the residential suburb of Pirae. Contemporary two-story wood and stone buildings look more like an American condominium complex than a tropical hotel. They hold spacious, carpeted rooms with comfortable European-style furniture. The rooms have coffee- and tea-making facilities, something seldom found in French Polynesia. Each has a patio or balcony with views of an expansive lawn which separates the rooms from a dining-bar complex beside the beach. Although the beach is very narrow, guests can lounge and sunbathe on a waterside wooden deck.

A long building covered with shingles and thatch houses the restaurant and bar; both are popular with local businesspeople. The cuisine is French and American.

HOTEL TAHITI, B.P. 416, Papeete, Tahiti. Tel. 42-95-50, or toll free 800/252-0211 in California, 800/421-0000 elsewhere in the U.S., 800/368-0900 in Canada. Fax 41.31.51. Telex 406. 92 rms and bungalows. A/C TEL **Location:** On route de l'Ouest, the old round-island road, 1.6km (1 mile) west of downtown Papeete. Take a Faaa or Maeva Beach truck.

$ Rates: 6,000 CFP ($60) single; 7,000 CFP ($70) double; 8,000–9,000 CFP ($80–$90) bungalow. AE, DC, MC, V.

Before the Hotel Maeva Beach was built in the 1960s, the Hotel Tahiti was the island's premier establishment. It sits on prime land that belonged to Princess Pomare, daughter of Tahiti's last king. Though it's now far from modern, lots of old South Seas charm still permeates its 2 acres of picturesque garden grounds, and especially the huge thatch-roofed public buildings. Guest bungalows of native materials and colonial-style hotel rooms with gingerbread fretwork on their balconies and patios are good value for travelers not looking for all the modern conveniences. There's no sandy beach, but the swimming pool is near the lagoon; both the pier and the pool command a view of the northern half of Moorea.

Twin-bedded hotel rooms are less expensive and are located in the colonial-style blocks. Although the furniture is beginning to show its age, the paneling was installed in the 1980s, and the hotel's owners make sure the rooms are kept clean. Ask for a room away from the main road, which runs along the rear of some of the buildings (rush hour comes very early in Tahiti).

What the rooms may lack in modernity, the hotel makes up for in the charm and coolness of its public areas. Carved tiki poles support large thatch roofs, from which dangle lamps of bamboo fish traps and chandeliers of cowry shells, over the airy bar and restaurant. The bar features live Tahitian entertainment several nights a week, and the restaurant serves French, American, and Polynesian dishes at lunch from 11:30am to 1:30pm and at dinner from 6:30 to 9:30pm daily. A separate thatch building sits over the reef and is the site of barbecue buffet dinners.

HOTEL TE PUNA BEL AIR, B.P. 6634, Faaa Airport, Tahiti. Tel. 42-09-00. Fax 41.31.84. Telex 215. 48 rms, 28 bungalows. A/C (deluxe rooms only) TEL (rooms only) **Location:** On the round-island road in Faaa, 7.2km (4 miles) west of Papeete. Take any Faaa or Maeva Beach truck.

$ Rates: 8,000 CFP–9,000 CFP ($80–$90) single room or bungalow, 12,000 CFP ($120) single bungalow with kitchenette; 9,000 CFP–10,000 CFP ($90–$100) double room or bungalow, 13,000 CFP ($130) double bungalow with kitchenette. AE, DC, MC, V.

Known simply as the Bel Air, this comfortable establishment is tucked between the Beachcomber and Maeva Beach hotels. There is no view of Moorea, however, since it's screened off by the headland separating the Bel Air and the Beachcomber, and the Bel Air's section of Maeva Beach has been eroded almost into nonexistence. Nevertheless, it's a short stroll to the more luxurious neighbors and their beaches and views.

The Bel Air has oval duplex bungalows sitting among tall palms in a tropical garden. They are far from fancy, but each unit has a porch on its end, tile floors and baths, three single beds, walls of woven pandanus over plywood, and screened windows. They aren't air conditioned, but each has a ceiling fan. The deluxe bungalows have kitchens and a double bed in a sleeping loft. The Bel Air's most comfortable accommodation is in regular motel-style rooms in two two-story buildings near the beach. The "deluxe" models have air conditioners; "standard" rooms only have ceiling fans. All rooms have balconies or patios.

A small restaurant in the center of the complex features adequate French cooking.

A fixed-price, three-course dinner is served between 6:30 and 9pm for 2,300 CFP ($23). Guests can use a swimming pool and tennis courts next to the restaurant.

BUDGET

CHEZ COCO, B.P. 8039, Puurai, Faaa, Tahiti. Tel. 42-83-60. 4 rms (none with bath), 12 bunks. **Location:** In Puurai, a hillside suburb above Faaa. From downtown, take a Puurai truck. From the airport, take any truck east toward Papeete for 1km (½ mile), then inland on the Puurai road another kilometer.

$ Rates: 3,000 CFP ($30) single; 4,000 CFP ($40) double; 1,500 CFP ($15) bunk. No credit cards.

Close to the international airport, it has four bedrooms, each with two single beds, and a living room with 12 bunks; all share two communal baths and a kitchen. Guests can use the swimming pool and washing machine. A taxi driver, Coco Dexter provides free airport transfers.

HITI MAHANA BEACH CLUB, B.P. 11580, Mahina, Tahiti. Tel. 48-16-13. 4 rms (all with bath), 30 bunks, 50 tent sites. **Location:** In Mahina, 10.5km (6.3 miles) east of Papeete. Take any Mahina truck. Tell driver you're going to Hiti Mahana; some may take you all the way there. If not, get off at the Hiti Mahana sign near Faty grocery, walk 1.5km (1 mile) to beach.

$ Rates: 700 CFP ($7) tent site per person, 1,500 CFP ($15) bunk, 3,000 CFP–5,000 CFP ($30–$50) single room; 4,000 CFP–6,000 CFP ($40–$60) double room. No credit cards.

Tahitian Coco Pautu and his American-born wife, Patricia, have three of their four rooms in a somewhat dilapidated, century-old plantation house with high ceilings and tall doors which swing open to a wraparound veranda on the ground level and a matching covered balcony upstairs. The 30 hostel beds are foam mattresses lined up on the balcony (insect repellent is a must). Guests share the mansion's kitchen. The Pautus also have one large room with kitchen in a modern building and 50 tent sites in 10 acres next to a black-sand beach. A communal kitchen and outdoor toilets and showers are included in the price of a campsite. The entire establishment actually is a beach club popular with local windsurfing enthusiasts. The club has a bar and restaurant.

MOTEL MAHINA TEA, rue Sainte-Amélie, B.P. 17, Papeete, Tahiti. Tel. 42-00-97. 22 rms (all with shower). **Location:** In the Sainte-Amélie neighborhood of downtown Papeete. From bd. Pomare, go up av. Bruat, bear right at the gendarmerie onto rue Sainte-Amélie. The hotel is on the right side of the street.

$ Rates: 3,000 CFP–3,500 CFP ($30–$35) single or double for each of first 2 nights; 2,800 CFP–3,200 CFP ($28–$32) single, 3,000 CFP–3,300 CFP ($30–$33) double per night for longer stays. No credit cards.

This plain, simple Tahitian-owned property has been around for years. Despite its name, the three-story establishment is more residential pension than motel, to which the nearby families' roosters will attest well before the crack of dawn. The basic but clean rooms have large louvered but unscreened windows, bathrooms with showers separated from the toilets by curtains, and double beds. Hot water is more or less available except between the hours of 6 and 10pm, and the two rooms on the front are slightly larger than the others. The management speaks just enough English to collect your money in advance.

TAHITI BUDGET LODGE, rue du Frère Alain, B.P. 237, Papeete, Tahiti. Tel. 42-66-82. 7 rms (3 with bath). 12 bunks. **Location:** Downtown Papeete on rue du Frère Alain at the end of rue Edouard Ahnne. From bd. Pomare or the market, go inland 5 blocks on rue du 22 Septembre, which becomes rue Edouard Ahnne.

$ Rates: 3,200 CFP–4,500 CFP ($32–$45) single or double; 1,500 CFP ($15) bunk. No credit cards.

Conveniently located, this establishment opened in 1990 in a low-slung white building with green trim on the edge of Papeete's business district. The small rooms are clean but have neither air conditioners nor fans. Preferable rooms are at the rear away from the al fresco communal kitchen and lounge, where guests gather along one side of the building. Dormitory beds are in four rooms with three bunks each. There's a TV in the lounge. Laundry facilities are available.

4. WHERE TO DINE

Visitors face two dilemmas when dining out on Tahiti. One is choosing among a wide selection of excellent French, Italian, and Chinese restaurants, for Papeete ranks along with Nouméa in New Caledonia at the top of South Pacific cuisine. The restaurants recommended in this section are but a few of many on Tahiti; don't hesitate to strike out on your own. The second dilemma is how to eat (and drink) well while not blowing your entire wad of francs on one meal, for like everything else, food is relatively expensive in French Polynesia.

TAHITIAN CUISINE

Before the Europeans' arrival, the Polynesians' diet consisted primarily of fruits, such as bananas, breadfruit, and coconuts, and starchy root crops, such as taro, arrowroot, yams, and sweet potatoes. Pig, dog, fish, shellfish, green leafy vegetables, and coconut cream were used as complements. The reefs and lagoons provided abundant seafood to augment food provided by the domesticated animals that were brought to the islands from the West.

Since the Tahitians had given up the use of pottery or other cooking vessels, their meals were cooked in an earth oven known as a *himaa,* in which the individual food items were wrapped in leaves, placed on a bed of heated stones, covered with more leaves and earth, and left to steam for several hours. When the meal was done, the Tahitians would uncover the oven, unwrap the food, sit down for a feast of *ma'a Tahiti* (or island) food, and dance the night away. The results of the himaa are quite tasty, with the steam spreading the aroma of one ingredient to the others.

The Tahitians have adopted many Western and Chinese foods (Chinese food is *ma'a Tinito*), but use of traditional foods remains popular. The himaa is used on special occasions, such as feasts, which are known as *tama'ara'a,* and even big family meals after church on Sunday. Some restaurants, including those in the resort hotels, prepare tama'ara'a in the traditional way for their guests, and I recommend that visitors give it a try in order to sample a little of what island life was like more than 200 years ago.

Tahiti's three big resort hotels usually have at least one feast a week, depending on the number of tourists in town; check the *Tahiti Beach Press* or phone the hotels to see if and when one will be offered. They usually run about 4,000 CFP ($40) a person, but they include a Tahitian dance show after the meal (see "Evening Entertainment," below).

Many individual Tahitian dishes are offered by restaurants whose cuisine may otherwise be French, Italian, or Chinese. One you will see on almost every menu is *poisson cru,* French for "raw fish"; it's a Tahitian-style salad of fresh fish, such as tuna marinated in lime juice and served with cucumbers, onions, and often tomatoes in coconut cream. Another is local freshwater shrimp (or imported prawns if the local variety isn't available) sautéed and served in a sweet sauce of curry and coconut cream.

MAKING YOUR OWN MEALS

One method of saving money on food is to make your own snacks or perhaps a picnic lunch to enjoy at the beach. Every village has a Chinese grocery, and there is a supermarket right in the heart of Papeete, in Fare Tony on the west side of the Vaima Centre. Fresh sticks of French bread cost about 35 CFP (35¢), and the markets carry cheeses, deli meats, vegetables, and other sandwich fixings.

Locally brewed Hinano beers sell for 130 CFP ($1.30) versus 350 CFP ($3.50) at the hotel bars, and bottles of decent French wine cost about 500 CFP ($5) versus somewhere between 1,300 CFP and 3,000 CFP ($13 and $30) or more at the restaurants. Even less expensive are Margot and Faragui wines, which are Algerian and Moroccan wines shipped in bulk to Tahiti and bottled in plastic containers (these vintages are sometimes jokingly referred to as "Château Plastique"). Add a little water to make them more palatable.

You will find that most items grown or produced in French Polynesia are more expensive than their imported counterparts. Frozen vegetables from California, for example, cost less than locally grown produce. Tender beef and lamb from New Zealand are less costly than the fish caught offshore and sold in the markets. Chicken is much less expensive than pork, the traditional "Sunday meal" throughout Polynesia. Butter is cheaper than margarine. The prices of flour, sugar, and rice are tightly controlled by the government; therefore, bread is cheap, as is rice, the Tahitians' main modern staple. Although we are talking here of Tahiti, the same holds true throughout French Polynesia.

LES ROULETTES

The best food bargain in Papeete literally rolls out every night on the Moorea Ferry docks: *les roulettes.*

These portable, family-owned and -operated meal wagons have assigned spaces in the waterfront parking lots. The entire waterfront takes on a carnival atmosphere as some owners set up charcoal grills behind their trucks and small electric generators in front to provide plenty of light for the diners, who sit on stools along either side of the vehicle.

The normal menu includes charbroiled steaks or chicken with french fries (known, respectively, as *steak frites* and *poulet frites*), Chinese dishes, and poisson cru for about 700 CFP ($7) per plate. Glassed-in display cases along the sides of some trucks hold actual examples of what's offered at each (not exactly the most appetizing exhibits, but you can just point to what you want rather than fumbling in French). Other trucks specialize in crêpes, pizzas, couscous, and waffles (*gaufres*). Even if you don't eat an entire meal at les roulettes, stop for a crêpe or waffle and enjoy the scene.

A NOTE ABOUT LIQUOR PRICES Faced with growing complaints from tourists

FROMMER'S SMART TRAVELER: RESTAURANTS

1. Take advantage of *plats du jour* (daily specials), especially at lunch. These three-course offerings usually are made from fresh produce direct from the market and represent a significant savings over ordering from the menu.
2. Look for *prix-fixe* (fixed-priced) menus, sometimes called "tourist menus" by Tahiti's restaurants. These three-course meals usually are much less expensive than if you ordered *à la carte*.
3. Patronize restaurants subscribing to the government's "tourist rates" on alcoholic beverages; beer and wine in these establishments cost significantly less than elsewhere.
4. Order *vin ordinaire* (table wine) served in a carafe. The chef buys good quality wine in bulk; you get the savings.
5. For less expensive meals, stick to the cafeterias at lunch and *les roulettes*, the mobile canteens, on the Papeete waterfront at night.
6. Ask if the hotel has a Modified American or other meal plan, or if the wholesale travel agents mentioned in Chapter 2 offer discounted meals as part of their packages. Remember, however, that you won't save if you plan to dine out every night.

about the exorbitant prices of alcoholic beverages in French Polynesia—not to mention Tahiti's resulting bad reputation as a tourist ripoff—in late 1980s the territorial government devised a scheme under which the hotels and restaurants could gain relief from the high import duties otherwise imposed on beer, wine, and spirits. All of the hotels and many eateries agreed to charge "tourist rates" for their alcoholic beverages. The price of a small, locally brewed Hinano beer dropped from 500 CFP ($5) and more to 350 CFP ($3.50), and a bottle of ordinary French wine came down from 3,000 CFP ($30) or more to about 1,300 CFP ($13).

Some restaurants did not go along, and you may wander into an establishment still charging the old prices. All of the nightclubs do, so you will be in for an old-time Tahiti price shock after you finish dinner and hit the town for some nightlife.

RESTAURANTS

FRENCH

AUBERGE DU PACIFIQUE, PK 11.2, Punaauia. Tel. 43-98-30.

Cuisine: FRENCH/TAHITIAN. **Reservations:** Recommended, especially on weekends. **Location:** 3.7km (2.2 miles) south of Hotel Sofitel Maeva Beach on the round-island road. The Paea trucks go by it during the day. Take a taxi at night.

$ Prices: Appetizers 1,000 CFP–2,000 CFP ($10–$20); main courses 1,600 CFP–2,800 CFP ($16–$28); special tourist menu 2,500 CFP ($25). V.

Open: Lunch Wed–Mon 11:30am–2pm; dinner Wed–Mon 6:30–9:30pm.

This lagoonside restaurant has been one of Tahiti's finest since 1974. Owner Jean Galopin was named a *Maître Cuisinier* (Master Chef) *de France* in 1987, in large part because of his unique blending of French and Tahitian styles of cooking. He has shared many of his techniques in a popular cookbook, *La Cuisine de Tahiti et des Iles*.

In addition to offering traditional French fare at Auberge du Pacifique, he also prepares many Tahitian-style dishes, such as *fafa* (chicken and taro leaves steamed in coconut milk). The gourmet quality, however, is in marked contrast to what ordinarily comes out of a Tahitian earth oven on a Sunday afternoon. The special three-course "tourist menu" features poisson cru, chicken fafa, and fruit salad. It's good value for the quality. The restaurant itself occupies a memento-decorated room whose roof slides open to reveal the twinkling stars above.

CAPTAIN BLIGH RESTAURANT AND BAR, PK 11.4, Punaauia, at the Lagoonarium. Tel. 43-62-90.

Cuisine: FRENCH. **Reservations:** Recommended on weekends. **Location:** 3.9km (2.3 miles) south of Hotel Sofitel Maeva Beach on the round-island road. The Paea trucks go by it during the day. Take a taxi at night or reserve for the "tourist menu," which includes transportation.

$ Prices: Appetizers 800 CFP–1,500 CFP ($8–$15); main courses 1,400 CFP–2,900 CFP ($14–$29); set prix-fixe "tourist menu" 3,500 CFP–4,500 CFP ($35–$45) including transportation. AE, V.

Open: Lunch Tues–Sun 11:30am–2pm; dinner Tues–Sat 7–9pm.

One of Tahiti's most unusual restaurant settings, this large thatch-roofed building extends over the lagoon (you can toss bread crumbs to the fish swimming just over the railing, or you can stroll along a pier to a tiny artificial island and dine al fresco under the stars). The pier goes on out to the Lagoonarium, an underwater viewing room surrounded by pens containing reef sharks, sea turtles, and many tropical fish. Specialties of the house are grilled steaks and lobster plus a few seafood dishes, such as curried shrimp and mahi mahi under a creamed pepper sauce.

Admission to the **Lagoonarium,** open from 9am to 6pm, is included with the meal; it's 500 CFP ($5) for adults, 300 CFP ($3) for children under 12 if you don't eat there. When I was last there, the Captain Bligh staged Tahitian dance shows at 8:45pm on Wednesday, Friday, and Saturday. The bar opens at 6:30pm for sundowner cocktails.

LE BELVEDERE, Fare Rau Ape Valley. Tel. 42-73-44.

Cuisine: FRENCH. **Reservations:** Imperative. **Location:** Perched high on a ridge overlooking Papeete and Moorea. Transportation provided by restaurant from your hotel.

$ **Prices:** 3,900 CFP ($39) per person including full meal, wine, and ride. AE, MC, V.

Open: Lunch Thurs–Tues 11:30am–2pm; dinner Thurs–Tues 6:30–9:30pm.

Dinner at Le Belvédère is a highlight of Tahiti for many visitors, because this innlike establishment sits 2,000 feet up in the cool hills behind Papeete and has a spectacular view of the city and Moorea beyond. Best of all, the restaurant provides free round-trip transportation from your hotel up the narrow, one-lane, winding, switchback road that leads to it. The ride itself is worth the price of the meal, and I don't encourage anyone to attempt it in a rental car. Le Belvédère's truck makes several runs for lunch or dinner, but the one to take leaves the hotels about 5pm and reaches the restaurant in time for sunset over Papeete and Moorea. Once you're there, the specialty of the house is fondue bourguignonne, which is served with six sauces. Other choices are mahi mahi grilled with butter, steak in green-pepper sauce or "any way you like it," shish kebab, and chicken with wine.

ACAJOU RESTAURANT, bd. Pomare in Fare Tony. Tel. 42-87-58.

Cuisine: FRENCH. **Reservations:** Recommended at dinner. **Location:** Opposite the west side of Vaima Centre on the Papeete waterfront.

$ **Prices:** Appetizers 350 CFP–1,800 CFP ($3.50–$18); main courses 1,300 CFP–1,800 CFP ($13–$18). AE, DC, V.

Open: Mon–Sat 5am–11pm.

The flagship of chef Acajou's (he goes only by his nickname), this is consistently the most popular French restaurant on Tahiti. The food is excellent, the prices fairly reasonable, and the setting alongside the Quay and Vaima Center convenient. A sidewalk terrace faces the yachts moored along the Quay; a more formal dining room re-creates the atmosphere of a French country inn. The sidewalk terrace is a nice place to have a cool beer or a mixed drink after a day of shopping in Papeete. All of the waiters speak English.

The choices of appetizers include hearts-of-celery salad and poisson cru. Acajou's delicious specialties emphasize fresh seafood. Try his fabulous freshwater shrimp with coconut-curry sauce; you will see this extraordinary dish on many menus in French Polynesia, but Acajou's is as good as it gets.

RESTAURANT MOANA ITI, bd. Pomare. Tel. 42-65-24.

Cuisine: FRENCH. **Reservations:** Recommended at dinner. **Location:** On bd. Pomare 2 blocks west of Vaima Centre.

$ **Prices:** Appetizers 500 CFP–1,700 CFP ($5–$17); main courses 1,200 CFP–1,700 CFP ($12–$17). AE, V.

Open: Lunch Mon–Sat 11:30am–2pm; dinner Mon–Sat 6:30–9:30pm.

This is on the street level of an office building 2 blocks west of the Vaima Centre, next to the more easily recognizable La Pizzeria Restaurant. A bar runs down one side of Moana Iti, and the other wall is covered with a photograph of Papeete's waterfront in the early 1900s. There's a mezzanine dining area up a curving flight of stairs. Moana Iti is best known for its very well prepared meat dishes. Specialties of the house are filet mignon sautéed with artichokes, rabbit in white wine sauce, and roast lamb with herbs. There is always a plat du jour at lunch.

READERS RECOMMEND

Le Belvédère, *Fare Rau Ape Valley. Tel. 42-73-44. "In Papeete we found the Belvédère to be all you said and then some more and we do recommend the sunset hour not only for the view up and back and from the restaurant but we decided we wouldn't want to make the drive in the dark."*—Mr. and Mrs. Frank R. Souza, Guadalajara, Mexico.

ITALIAN

Tahiti might be a French territory, but some of its most popular—and best-value—restaurants are Italian. In fact, they present Papeete's best opportunity for local residents as well as us value-conscious travelers to enjoy a fine meal in pleasant surroundings without exhausting all our CFPs.

LA ROMANA, av. du Commandant Destremeau. Tel. 41-33-64.

Cuisine: ITALIAN. **Reservations:** Recommended for dinner, especially weekends. **Location:** Just off av. Bruat, 1 block from de Gaulle Monument.

$ **Prices:** Appetizers 400 CFP–1,500 CFP ($4–$15); pizzas and pastas 700 CFP–1,100 CFP ($7–$11); meat courses 1,300 CFP–2,200 CFP ($13–$22). AE.

Open: Lunch Mon–Fri 11:30am–2pm; dinner Mon–Sat 6:30–9:30pm.

La Romana opened its doors in 1988 and quickly became one of Papeete's favorite Italian eateries—both for its fine food and its nightly entertainment. When I was there, a guitar quartet from Latin America, of all places, made the rounds among the tables (going against Polynesian tradition, La Romana has introduced the custom of tipping to Tahiti; if you like the music, you tip the band). Between songs you can pay attention to the excellent pizzas and pasta dishes; grills of sausages, steaks, or lamb chops with mustard, Roquefort, pepper, or tartar sauce; or the house specialties, such as shrimp à la niçoise (tomato and garlic sauce).

LOU PESCADOU, rue Anne Marie Javouhey at passage Cardella. Tel. 43-74-26.

Cuisine: ITALIAN. **Reservations:** Not accepted. **Location:** Take narrow passage Cardella, a 1-block street that looks like an alley directly behind the Vaima Centre.

$ **Prices:** Appetizers 500 CFP–1,300 CFP ($5–$13); pizzas and pastas 450 CFP–800 CFP ($4.50–$8); meat courses 1,300 CFP–1,600 CFP ($13–$16). No credit cards.

Open: Lunch Mon–Sat 11:30am–2pm; dinner Mon–Sat 6:30–9:30pm.

Although La Romana took away some of its business, the always popular Lou Pescadou continues to roll along. It will remind you of Italian restaurants back home: red-and-white-checked tablecloths, dripping candles on each table, Ruffino bottles hanging from every nook and cranny, a backlit stained-glass window, ceiling fans circulating the aroma of garlic and oregano, shuttered windows thrown open so passersby can look in, friendly waiters running hither and yon carrying pizzas. This ambience is one reason for its popularity, excellent food is another, and the cost of a meal is a third. The individual-size pizzas are cooked in a wood-fire oven range, and the pasta dishes include spaghetti, fettuccine, and lasagne.

LA PIZZERIA, bd. Pomare. Tel. 42-98-30.

Cuisine: ITALIAN. **Reservations:** Not accepted. **Location:** West of the Vaima Centre and post office, on the waterfront.

$ **Prices:** Appetizers 650 CFP–1,000 CFP ($6.50–$10); pizzas and pastas 350 CFP–950 CFP ($3.50–$9.50); meat courses 1,400 CFP–1,600 CFP ($13–$16). No credit cards.

Open: Daily 11:30am–10pm. **Closed:** Sun lunch and holidays.

This small building sitting among a grove of trees across from the harbor resembles an Elizabethan waterfront tavern. The exposed-beam Tudor interior has been accented with nautical relics, such as a ship's brass compass in one corner and a large pilot wheel used as a table divider. The food, on the other hand, is definitely Italian. Both pizzas and steaks are cooked in a wood-fired oven. The menu features spaghetti, fettuccine, lasagne, steak milanese, veal in white or marsala wine sauce, and grilled homemade Italian sausage. You can dine inside or outside under large shade trees beside boulevard Pomare.

CHINESE

JADE PALACE, bd. Pomare in the Vaima Centre. Tel. 42-02-19.

Cuisine: CANTONESE CHINESE. **Reservations:** Recommended. **Location:** East side street level of Vaima Centre.

$ **Prices:** Appetizers 500 CFP–1,500 CFP ($5–$15); main courses 1,200 CFP–2,200 CFP ($12–$22). AE, V.

Open: Lunch Mon–Sat 11am–1:40pm; dinner daily 6:30–9:40pm.

The most elegant and pricy of Papeete's Chinese restaurants, the Jade Palace serves a relatively limited number of excellent Cantonese dishes, with emphasis on soups, chicken, and beef. Of the seafood dishes, try the crystal prawns (shrimp are known as prawns in this part of the world), which are served almost raw with flavorings of ginger and spring onions.

LE MANDARIN, rue des Ecoles des Frères, near rue Colette. Tel. 42-99-03.

Cuisine: CANTONESE CHINESE. **Reservations:** Not necessary. **Location:** Near the Town Hall in the heart of Papeete, 2 blocks from bd. Pomare on rue des Ecoles des Frères.

$ Prices: Appetizers 600 CFP–1,100 CFP ($6–$11); main courses 900 CFP–1,800 CFP ($9–$18). DC, MC, V.

Open: Lunch daily 11am–1:30pm; dinner daily 6–9:30pm.

A good moderate choice, Le Mandarin and the hotel of the same name (it's just around the corner on rue Colette) are joined by a passageway and share the same owners. Chinese decor disguises the storefront location of the dining rooms. A wide-ranging menu lists well-prepared vegetable, chicken, duck, beef, pork, and seafood dishes.

TE HOA, rue du Maréchal Foch. Tel. 42-99-27.

Cuisine: CANTONESE CHINESE. **Reservations:** Not accepted. **Location:** Behind the Municipal Market.

$ Prices: Appetizers 450 CFP–600 CFP ($4–$6); main courses 700 CFP–900 CFP ($7–$9). No credit cards.

Open: Lunch Mon–Sat 11:30am–2pm; dinner daily 6:30–9:30pm.

(S) This rock-bottom but clean family-style restaurant is extraordinarily popular at lunch. Don't expect any frills, just good food served up in larger portions than is usually the case in French Polynesia's Chinese restaurants.

CAFETERIAS

Cafeterias are a relatively new development in Tahiti, but they represent the island's best values for breakfast and lunch (none are open for dinner).

POLYSELF, rue Paul Gauguin in Banque de Polynésie Building. Tel. 43-75-32.

Cuisine: CHINESE. **Location:** ½ block off bd. Pomare near the Municipal Market.

$ Prices: Dishes 800 CFP–900 CFP ($8–$9). No credit cards.

Open: Daily 5am–1:30pm.

Chinese dishes such as chow mein, sweet-and-sour pork, and fried rice are displayed in a stainless-steel counter in this air-conditioned establishment. No English is necessary; just point to what you want. Dim sum dumplings augment such traditional French breakfast fare as croissants and coffee.

ACAJOU NUMERA HOE, rue François Cardella. Tel. 43-19-22.

Cuisine: CHINESE. **Location:** Just off bd. Pomare near the Municipal Market.

$ Prices: Dishes 750 CFP–850 CFP ($7.50–$8.50). No credit cards.

Open: Daily 5am–1:30pm.

Not to be confused with the Acajou restaurant mentioned above, this cafeteria has the same owner who insists on offering quality food, hearty portions, and reasonable prices. In this case, Acajou's marketing strategy translates into both good food and volume: It's always packed with local residents. Like at the Polyself cafeteria, the selections here are Cantonese dishes that can be prepared in bulk.

SELF-SERVE IO TATA, bd. Pomare at rue l'Arthémise, in the Foyer des Jeunes Filles. Tel. 42-65-75.

Cuisine: FRENCH/TAHITIAN. **Location:** Ground floor of the Foyer des Jeunes Filles (Girls' Hostel) next to the large Protestant church.

$ **Prices:** Appetizers 250 CFP–500 CFP ($2.50–$5); main courses 650 CFP–850 CFP ($6.50–$8.50). No credit cards.

Open: Lunch Mon–Sat 11am–1pm; dinner Mon–Sat 6–8pm. **Closed:** Holidays.

Equivalent to a YWCA cafeteria at home, this clean establishment is one of the best food deals in Tahiti. Daily specials include a meat and two vegetables, and there are soups, salads, and desserts. The reasonably priced portions are large. The cafeteria and hostel are operated by the Evangelical church, so alcoholic beverages are not served.

SNACK BARS

You won't find a McDonald's or any of the other well-known fast-food chains in French Polynesia. Instead of hamburgers, the most popular quick-snack item is the *casse-croûte,* a sandwich made from a crusty French-bread baguette and slivers of such ingredients as ham, lettuce, tomatoes, and cucumbers. These are available at numerous snack bars and most Chinese groceries all over Tahiti and the other islands, and usually cost about 150 CFP ($1.50) or less.

The snack bars listed below are open during the morning and lunchtime hours. For nighttime fare, see the description above of *les roulettes,* the portable meal wagons that gather after dark each evening near the Moorea ferry docks in Papeete.

D. HILLAIRE PATISSIER, rue du Général de Gaulle in the Vaima Centre. Tel. 42-68-22.

Cuisine: PATISSERIE. **Location:** At street level, rear side of Vaima Centre.

$ **Prices:** Pastries and sandwiches 150 CFP–500 CFP ($1.50–$5). No credit cards.

Open: Mon–Sat 7am–5pm.

One of several pâtisseries in Papeete, this spotless establishment has been my favorite breakfast haunt since the late 1970s. Order at the cash register, then sit down. The staff will bring your selections to your table.

SNACK VAEITE, rue Emile Martin. Tel. 42-80-38.

Cuisine: SNACK BAR. **Location:** Downtown, in the first block off bd. Pomare.

$ **Prices:** Sandwiches and burgers 150 CFP–300 CFP ($1.50–$3); meals 650 CFP–900 CFP ($6.50–$9). No credit cards.

Open: Mon–Sat 6am–5pm.

For lunch you often find me at this very clean establishment operated by a Chinese family. Try the casses-croûtes, burgers, or fish-and-chips. Plate lunches feature ma'a Tinito, the Tahitians' version of Chinese food. Coca-Colas in small plastic bottles cost 150 CFP ($1.50); compare that with the price in some hotel bars: 350 CFP ($3.50).

SNACK ROGER, place Notre Dame opposite the Catholic cathedral. Tel. 42-19-69.

Cuisine: SNACK BAR. **Location:** On the east side of Cathédrale de l'Immaculée Conception, rear of the Viama Centre.

$ **Prices:** Sandwiches and burgers 150 CFP–300 CFP ($1.50–$3); meals 650 CFP–900 CFP ($6.50–$9). No credit cards.

Open: Mon–Sat 6am–5pm.

This establishment is comparable to Snack Vaiete in price, quality, and cleanliness. The main difference is that it's closer to the Vaima Centre, while Snack Vaiete is convenient to the Moorea Ferry. It's also darker inside.

SNACK EPI D'OR, rue du Maréchal Foch.

Cuisine: SNACK BAR. **Location:** Behind the Municipal Market, same block as Te Hoa Chinese restaurant.

$ **Prices:** Sandwiches 120 CFP–160 CFP ($1.20–$1.60). No credit cards.

Open: Mon–Sat 4am–6pm, Sun 2am–10am.

The casse-croûtes don't get any fresher than at Epi d'Or because this establishment is actually an upstairs bakery. Stand on the sidewalk in front of the carry-out counter (there's no place to sit here) and watch the hot sticks of French bread come down the dumb waiter. You can buy the plain, crispy baguettes by themselves or as sandwiches. Note the unusual hours on Sunday.

5. SPORTS & RECREATION

GOLF

The 18-hole, 6,950-yard **Olivier Bréaud International Golf Course,** PK 40.2, Atimaono (tel. 57-40-32), sprawls over the site of William Stewart's cotton plantation. A clubhouse, pro shop, restaurant, bar, locker rooms, showers, swimming pool, spa pool, and driving range are on the premises. Chez Mahiatea snack bar (tel. 57-41-03), less than a mile before the entrance to the course, also rents equipment at slightly higher fees. Call to reserve a starting time.

HIKING

Tahiti has a number of hiking trails, such as the one that cuts across the island via Lake Vaihiria and another that ascends to the top of Mount Aorai, but very few of them should be undertaken without the proper equipment and a guide. Downpours can occur in the higher altitudes, swelling the streams that most trails follow, and the nights can become bitterly cold and damp. The "rainy side" of the island can shift from one day to the next, depending on which way the wind blows. In addition, the quick-growing tropical foliage can quickly obscure a path that was easily followed a few days before. Permits are required to use some trails that cross government land. With all this in mind, check with the Tahiti Tourist Board's information office on the waterfront for the names of guides available for hire.

HORSEBACK RIDING

Hotel Puunui (tel. 57-19-20), high up on Tahiti Iti's pastureland, has horses for rent. Call the hotel for details.

SAILING

Mer et Loisirs, B. P. 3488, Papeete, Tahiti (tel. 43-97-99), in a floating office on the quay across from the main post office, is agent for several charter sail- and powerboats. Most of these come with or without a skipper and rent for at least 30,000 CFP ($300) a day. Day-trips or weekend voyages to Marlon Brando's **Tetiaroa** atoll, about 30 miles north of Papeete, cost 14,500 CFP ($145) per person for a day-trip, 24,000 CFP ($240) for a weekend, including food and drinks.

TENNIS

Visitors are not encouraged to use Tahiti's public tennis courts, so if you're a tennis buff, stay at a hotel that has courts available for its guests.

WATER SPORTS

Tahiti Aquatique, at the Hotel Sofitel Maeva Beach, B.P. 6008, Papeete, Tahiti (tel. 42-80-42, ext. 0951), offers a comprehensive list of water-sports activities. Tahiti Aquatique is owned and operated by Richard Johnson, an American marine biologist who has lived in French Polynesia for a number of years. Here are some sample prices (per person, unless otherwise indicated): scuba diving, per dive including equipment and a guide, 5,000 CFP ($50); introductory dive, 8,000 CFP ($80); fin, mask, and snorkel rental, 800 CFP ($8); glass-bottom-boat tour, 1,500 CFP ($15); waterskiing, per hour, 1,600 CFP ($16); sport-fishing charters, 45,000 CFP ($450) for ½ day or 65,000 CFP ($650) for a full day, per boat; Sunfish or Hobie Cat sailboats, 2,500 CFP ($25) per hour per boat; and Windsurfers, 1,500 CFP ($15) per hour per boat.

Activities Rainbow, at the Tahiti Beachcomber Parkroyal (tel. 42-51-10, ext. 551), offers a less comprehensive list at similar prices. See Jugel Gilles at the water-sports booth to the far right as you look out over the Beachcomber's beach.

6. SHOPPING

There's no shortage of things to buy in Tahiti, especially in Papeete, which is one of the South Pacific's better-stocked shopping cities. Visitors are most likely to be interested in black pearls, both French and Tahitian fashions, handcrafts, and duty-free items. The selection and prices on some items may be better on Moorea, but here are some hints on what to look for and where to find it on Tahiti.

DUTY-FREE SHOPPING

French Polynesia may be heaven in some respects, but not when it comes to duty-free shopping. The **airport departure lounge** has four duty-free shops whose prices are the same as those in their downtown branches. French perfumes are the best duty-free deal in Tahiti.

Duty Free Tahiti (tel. 42-61-61), on the street level, water side of the Vaima Centre, is the largest duty-free shop. Its specialties are Seiko, Lorus, and Cartier watches and Givenchy, Yves St. Laurent, Chanel, and Guerlain perfumes. Cigarettes are $9 to $11 per carton, and liquor is cheap when compared to regular Tahiti prices but costs about the same as in most U.S. cities.

WHAT TO BUY

BLACK PEARLS

The Japanese stranglehold on the cultured-pearl market has been loosened somewhat over the past two decades, and French Polynesia has stepped into the competition with black pearls, most of which are grown at pearl farms in the clear, clean lagoons of the Tuamotu Archipelago east of Tahiti. Pearls are cultured by implanting a small nucleus into the shell of a live oyster, which then coats it with nacre, the same lustrous substance that lines the mother-of-pearl shell. The nacre of the oysters used in French Polynesia, the *Pinctada margaritifera,* produces dark pearls that are known as "black" but whose actual color ranges from black with shades of rose or green, which are the rarest and most valuable, to slightly grayer than white. The bulk of the crop is black with bluish or brownish tints. Most range in size from 10mm to 17mm (slightly less than half an inch to slightly less than three-quarters of an inch).

A pearl's value is determined by its size, color, luster, cleanliness, and shape. No two are exactly alike, but the most valuable are the larger ones that are most symmetrical, have few dark blemishes, and whose color is dark with the shades of a peacock showing through a bright luster. A high-quality pearl 13mm or larger will sell for $10,000 or more, but there are thousands to choose from in the $500 to $1,000 range. Some small, imperfect-but-still-lovely pearls cost much less.

National Geographic carried a very informative article on cultured pearls in its August 1985 issue, so dig it out of the attic before heading off to Tahiti. And if you are going to Moorea, look in **Island Fashions** and the other shops over there before making a purchase in Tahiti; the selection may not be as wide, but you may find better prices. See the Moorea section in Chapter 5 for details.

Papeete has scores of *bijouteries* (jewelry shops), and most of them carry black pearls in a variety of settings. Most are in or around the Vaima Centre or along boulevard Pomare. Here's a few to get you started; poke your head into any others you pass.

Start at ✪ **Tahiti Perles Center** (tel. 43-85-44) on boulevard Pomare next to the Temple Protestant. This shop has not only a fine selection but also a museum explaining the history of pearls back to antiquity, the method by which they are cultured, and the things to look for when making your selection. The center carries only excellent-quality pearls and uses only 18-karat gold for its settings, so the prices tend to be high.

Now walk along boulevard Pomare to the Vaima Centre. At the street level, check **Polynésie Perles** (tel. 45-05-05) and **Tahitian South Sea Pearl** (tel. 42-56-68), two small, upmarket shops. On the second level, **Or et Perles (Les Artisans Réunis)** (tel. 42-44-55) has grown in recent years and now has a large selection, including some smaller, less expensive pearls which may not be readily available elsewhere.

HANDCRAFTS

Economic hard times in recent years had one salutary effect: Strapped for income, many local residents began producing handcrafts. Now you can find a wide range, especially of jewelry made from seashells. You also can find a reasonably good selection of homemade quilts, rag dolls, needlework, and straw hats, mats, baskets, and handbags.

The most popular item by far, however, is the cotton pareu or wraparound sarong, which is screened, blocked, or printed by hand in the colors of the rainbow. The same material is made into other tropical clothing and various items, such as bedspreads. Pareus are sold virtually everywhere a visitor might wander.

A must stop is upstairs at ✪ **Papeete Municipal Market,** where various women's associations operate stalls. They offer a wide selection of handcrafts at fairly reasonable prices for Tahiti. The market is one of the few places where you can regularly find pareus for 1,000 CFP ($10), bedspreads made of the colorful tie-dyed and silk-screened pareu material, and *tivaivai,* the colorful appliqué quilts stitched together by Tahitian women as their great-grandmothers were shown by the early missionaries.

If you're staying on the west coast, the local women have stalls in **Punaauia Nui Centre Artisinal** (tel. 41-00-52), the large thatch-roof building next to the Mobil service station at the Euromarché shopping mall south of the Sofitel Maeva Beach. Their prices are the same as those at the Papeete market.

For finer-quality handcrafts, such as wood carvings from the Marquesas Islands, shell chandeliers, tapa lampshades, or mother-of-pearl shells, try **Manuia Curios** (tel. 42-04-94) on place Notre Dame opposite the Catholic cathedral. Manuia Curios carries some artifacts from several South Pacific countries, including large basket masks from the Sepik River area of Papua New Guinea and jade and porcelain from China.

TROPICAL CLOTHING

You've arrived in Tahiti and you notice that everyone under the sun is wearing print sundresses or flowered aloha shirts. Where do you go to get yours?

Each hotel has at least one boutique that carries tropical clothing, including pareus. The prices there reflect the heavy tourist traffic, but they aren't much worse than at the stores in Papeete. Clothing, to put it bluntly, is dear in French Polynesia.

On boulevard Pomare, stop in **Marie Ah You** (tel. 42-03-31) and **Aloha Boutique** (tel. 42-87-52), both in the block east of the Vaima Centre. Their selections for women are trendy and a bit expensive. In the Vaima Centre, **Anemone** (tel. 43-02-66) and **Vaima Shirts** (tel. 42-48-80) have excellent creations for both

---

IMPRESSIONS

"It's a comfort to get into a pareo when one gets back from town," said Jackson. "If you were going to stay here I should strongly recommend you to adopt it. It's one of the most sensible costumes I have ever come across. It's cool, convenient, and inexpensive."

—W. Somerset Maugham, 1921

men and women. You can save by exploring the plethora of Chinese shops behind the Vaima Centre and around the Papeete market.

For unusual dresses, blouses, shirts, and pareus, visit **Tahiti Art** (tel. 42-97-43) in Fare Tony on boulevard Pomare just west of the Vaima Centre. This shop specializes in block-printed traditional designs (as opposed to the swirls and swooshes with leaves and flowers popular on most pareus).

7. EVENING ENTERTAINMENT

A 19th-century European merchant once wrote of the Tahitians, "Their existence was in never-ending merrymaking." In many respects this is still true, for once the sun goes down Tahitians like to make merry as much today as they did in the 1830s, and Papeete has lots of good choices for visitors who want to join in the fun.

TAHITIAN DANCING

Like all Polynesians—the Hawaiians and their hula are one example—Tahitians are renowned for their dancing. Before the Europeans came, they would stage *heivas,* entertainments that featured dancing, for almost any reason, from blessing the harvest to celebrating a birth. After eating meals cooked in their earth ovens, they would get out the drums and nose flutes and dance the night away. As described by Captain Cook and other early European visitors, some of the dances involved elaborate costumes, while others were quite lasciviously and explicitly danced in the nude or seminude, which only added to Tahiti's reputation as an island of love.

The puritanical Protestant missionaries, however, managed to get laws enacted in the early 1820s to end all dancing. Of course, strict prohibition never works, and Tahitians—including a young Queen Pomare—would sneak into the hills to dance. Only after the French took over in 1842 was dancing permitted again, and then only with severe limitations on what the dancers could do and wear. A result of these various restrictions was that most of the traditional dances performed by the Tahitians prior to 1800 were totally forgotten within a period of 100 years.

You'd never guess that Tahitians ever stopped dancing, for after tourists started coming in 1961 they went back to the old ways—or so it would seem. Today traditional dancing is a huge part of their lives—and of every visitor's itinerary. No one goes away without vivid memories of the elaborate and colorful costumes, the thundering drums, and the swinging hips of a Tahitian *tamure* in which young men and women provocatively dance around each other.

The tamure is one of several dances performed during a typical dance show. Others are the *o'tea,* in which men and women in spectacular costumes dance certain themes, such as spear throwing, fighting, or love; the *aparima,* the hand dance, which emphasizes everyday themes, such as bathing and combing one's hair; the *hivinau,* in which men and women dance in circles and exclaim "*hiri haa haa*" when they meet each other; and the *pata'uta'u,* in which the dancers beat the ground or their thighs with their open hands. It's difficult to follow the themes without understanding Tahitian, but the color and rhythms (which have been influenced by faster, double-time beats from the Cook Islands) make the dances thoroughly enjoyable—and leave little doubt as to the temptations that faced the *Bounty*'s mutineers.

Traditional dance shows usually are staged along with the Tahitian feasts mentioned in "Where to Dine," above. Bear in mind that the schedules can and do change, so a little detective work on your part is in order.

CAPTAIN BLIGH RESTAURANT AND BAR, PK 11.4, Punaauia, at the Lagoonarium. Tel. 43-62-90.

The big thatch roof over this restaurant's lagoonside dining room adds an appropriate atmosphere for dance shows Wednesday, Friday, and Saturday at 8:40pm. The entertainment follows dinner at the restaurant, but you can order a drink and

IMPRESSIONS

The air was full of that exquisite fragrance of orange blossom and gardenia which is distilled by night under the thick foilage; there was a great silence, accentuated by the bustle of insects in the grass, and that sonorous quality, peculiar to night in Tahiti, which predisposes the listener to feel the enchanting power of music.

—PIERRE LOTI (JULIEN VIAUD), 1880

---

watch from the bar. Note that the trucks don't run this far down the west coast at night. See "Where to Dine," above, for details about the Captain Bligh's menu offerings.

Prices: Drinks 450 CFP–700 CFP ($4.50–$7).

HOTEL HYATT REGENCY TAHITI, PK 8.1, Mahina. Tel. 48-11-22.

The Hyatt stages a *Grande Revue du Pacifique* in its Captain Cook Restaurant every Friday and Saturday at 7pm. The best of the traditional hotel shows, this one features the Ia Ora Tahiti dance troupe, which has toured the world promoting French Polynesia. A buffet featuring some Tahitian dishes follows the show.

Prices: Dinner 4,200 CFP ($42). Drinks 450 CFP–700 CFP ($4.50–$7).

HOTEL SOFITEL MAEVA BEACH, PK 7.5, Punaauia. Tel. 42-80-42.

The hotel stages a dance show at 8pm every day except Sunday in the Amiral Bougainville dining room on the ground level. You don't have to have dinner to watch the show; merely have a drink at the adjacent bar. The hotel also has a camera show every Sunday at 1pm, accompanied a Tahitian feast.

Prices: Dinner 4,200 CFP ($42). Drinks 450 CFP–700 CFP ($4.50–$7).

PUB CRAWLING

Papeete has a nightclub or watering hole to fit anyone's taste, from upscale private (*privé*) discotheques to down-and-out bars and dance halls where Tahitians strum on guitars while sipping on large bottles of Hinano beer. If you look like a tourist, you'll be allowed into the private clubs. Generally, everything gets to full throttle after 9pm (except on Sunday, when most are closed).

None of the clubs is cheap. Expect to pay about 1,000 CFP ($10) cover charge, which will include your first drink. After that, beers cost at least 500 CFP ($5), with most mixed drinks in the 1,000 CFP to 1,500 CFP ($10 to $15) range.

As in all South Pacific towns, Papeete's nightclubs go up and down in popularity. I mention a few clubs and bars that have been around for years. I hope they are still there when you are.

Before you head out, stroll down boulevard Pomare near the Tahiti Tourist Board's office. There you will find Tahitian women weaving flower crowns, traditional headwear for Papeete's female merrymakers. Buy one if you want to look the part. The Tahitians will love you for it; everyone else will think you're a silly tourist.

TAMURE HUT, bd. Pomare in the Royal Papeete Hotel. Tel. 42-01-29.

One of the few nightclubs designed for visitors as well as locals, the Royal Papeete's

---

IMPRESSIONS

They have several negative comments on the beachcombing life in Tahiti: Not much cultural life. No intellectual stimulus. No decent library. Restaurant food is disgraceful. (An average Texas lunch: $1.40.) But I noticed that Saturday after Saturday they turned up at Quinn's with the most dazzling beauties on the island. When I reminded them of this they said, "Well that does compensate for the poor library."

—JAMES A. MICHENER, 1951

Tamure Hut also charges tourist rates for its drinks. The decor evokes the earlier period when Quinn's Bar dominated Papeete's nightlife scene. Live bands crank out various styles of dance music, from Tahitian to 1950s rock-and-roll. The clientele usually is mature and well behaved. It's open Wednesday to Saturday 9pm to 3am.

Admission: 1,200 CFP ($12) Fri–Sat, including one drink (hotel guests free). **Prices:** Drinks 700 CFP–800 CFP ($7–$8).

MANYANA CLUB, av. Bruat just off bd. Pomare. Tel. 43-82-29.

A posh private club on the second floor of Centre Bruat, the Manyana's sophisticated decor and atmosphere traditionally attract an affluent younger crowd. European and American popular disco music is featured by recordings during the week, by live band on Friday and Saturday. Open Monday to Saturday from 9pm to 2am.

Admission: 1,000 CFP ($10) Fri–Sat, including one drink. **Prices:** Drinks 1,000 CFP–1,500 CFP ($10–$15).

PIANO BAR, rue des Ecoles des Frères. Tel. 42-88-24.

The narrow rue des Ecoles des Frères is the heart of Papeete's mahu district, where the male transvestites described earlier hang out. The Piano Bar is popular with local residents of all sexual persuasions, especially for its late-night strip shows featuring female impersonators. When you've had enough of the Piano Bar, go next door to **Lido Nightclub** (tel. 42-95-84), which has the same hours, cover charge, and drink prices.

Admission: 1,000 CFP ($10), including one drink. **Prices:** Drinks 1,000 CFP–1,500 CFP ($10–$15).

LA CAVE, bd. Pomare in the Royal Papeete Hotel. Tel. 42-01-29.

The Royal Papeete's La Cave has loud Tahitian music for dancing on Friday and Saturday from 9pm to 2am. It's dark inside and popular with mahus, so one cannot always be sure at first glance of every stranger's gender. Enter through the hotel's lobby.

Admission: 700 CFP ($7); hotel guests free. **Prices:** Drinks 800 CFP–1,200 CFP ($8–$12).

THE PITATE, at the corner of av. Bruat and bd. Pomare. Tel. 42-80-54.

The venerable Pitate is today's version of the late Quinn's, a dark Tahitian dance hall with electrified Polynesian music (heavy on guitars, light on notes) blaring from very large speakers. The clientele is mostly young Tahitian working-class men and women, but tourists who smile usually will be accepted. The later it gets, however, the rougher the Pitate can become. Open daily from 9pm to 2am.

Admission: 1,000 CFP ($10) Fri–Sat and holidays, including one drink. **Prices:** Drinks 700 CFP–1,000 CFP ($7–$10).

TIKI D'OR BAR AMERICAIN, rue Georges LaGarde, behind the Vaima Centre. Tel. 42-07-37.

This plain and simple Tahitian drinking establishment draws its heaviest crowd just after work on weekdays. Someone likely will be playing a guitar and singing Tahitian songs. It's a good place if you want to mingle with the locals without paying the hefty cover charges. It's open Monday through Saturday from 10am to midnight.

Admission: Free. **Prices:** Drinks 500 CFP–1,000 CFP ($5–$10).

SALOON BAR, rue Emile Martin 2 blocks from bd. Pomare. No phone.

Another no-frills Tahitian establishment, this one has no name other than "Bar" and "Saloon" written on its streetside sign (look for the red star). It's a smoky beer hall as opposed to a loud dance hall, but someone usually brings a guitar and leads the crowd in Tahitian songs, and a few hips may sway to the beat before the night is out. Open 5 to 11pm Monday to Saturday, until 2am Friday and Saturday.

Admission: Free. **Prices:** Beer 350 CFP ($3.50).

CHAPTER 5

MOOREA, BORA BORA & OTHER ISLANDS

Now that we have had our sojourn in Tahiti, let's head to the other islands and their picture-postcard white-sand beaches, deep blue lagoons, and soaring mountains. Each is different; each has its own attractions.

Because of its proximity to Papeete, Moorea is a must for anyone visiting French Polynesia. Many visitors then go on to see Bora Bora's tombstonelike central mountain, and incredible lagoon. Between Moorea and Bora Bora lie the three other major Society Islands: Huahine, Raiatea, and Tahaa. Each has its own blend of quiet, undeveloped charm.

The low atolls of the Tuamotu Archipelago lie in flat contrast to the high, rugged Society Islands. The most frequently visited is Rangiroa, one of the world's largest atolls.

1. MOOREA

Moorea's jagged mountains, deep bays, and emerald lagoons are so stunning that Hollywood often uses "stock shots" of them to create a South Seas setting for movies that don't even take place in French Polynesia. It's also a peaceful island where a hint of old Polynesia coexists with modern resort hotels and fine restaurants.

Geologists say that the triangle-shaped, 53-square-mile Moorea of today is what remains of a great volcano that once loomed more than 11,000 feet above the sea. Over time the volcano's northern half either fell into the sea or was blown away in a cataclysmic explosion, leaving only its southern half standing above water. Today Moorea's tallest point is just under 4,000 feet high.

As you enter **Cook's Bay,** you can't help but notice on your right **Mount Rotui,** whose buttresses of black basalt seem to fall into the bay. It stands in the center of the old crater; the serrated peaks, spires, and cliffs circling from your left and disappearing behind it are what's left of the crater's interior wall.

Mount Rotui is surrounded on three sides by Cook's Bay, Opunohu Bay, and the valley that lies between them on what was the floor of the crater. The two bays are scenic wonders and reach into the heart of Moorea's soaring mountains. The land rises gradually from the head of the bays and then abruptly leaps to the jagged peaks sitting atop the crater's walls.

One of these peaks, cathedrallike **Mount Mouaroa** (or the "Shark's Tooth"), is Moorea's trademark and shows up in innumerable travel posters and photographs and on the 100-CFP coin. Another, thumblike **Mount Tohivea,** has a hole in its top; legend has it that this hole was made by the spear of the Tahitian hero Pai when Hiro, god of thieves, attempted to steal Mount Rotui in the middle of the night and take it away to Raiatea. The gods alerted Pai, who rushed to the west coast of Tahiti and threw his spear toward Moorea. It pierced the top of Mount Tohivea and woke up all of Moorea's roosters, whose crowing alerted the citizenry to put a stop to Hiro's dastardly plan.

Moorea's mountains, like those of Tahiti, have been eroded into a series of valleys, and a narrow, flat coastal strip surrounds the island. The entire island is ringed by a coral reef that sits offshore, leaving a calm, blue lagoon between it and the shore. Long stretches of white-sand beaches, which sharply contrast with Tahiti's limited beaches of black volcanic sand, extend for miles along the lagoon on Moorea's northeast and northwest corners. There are no towns on Moorea; most of its 6,000 or so residents live on the coastal plain, many of them in settlements where the valleys meet the lagoon.

A paved coastal road runs through coconut groves around the island's 60-km (36-mile) circumference, and another paved road climbs from the head of Opunohu Bay to the **Belvédère,** a scenic point partway up the crater's wall. The spectacular view from the Belvédère encompasses both Cook's and Opunohu bays, Mount Rotui, and the jagged old crater rim curving off to left and right.

The mountains tend to suck moisture from the southeast trade winds and screen the north and northwest coasts from inclement weather. Consequently, the north side is popular not only with hoteliers but also with a number of Europeans and Americans who have built homes here.

Vanilla was the island's big crop early in the 20th century, and many clapboard "vanilla houses" built with the profits still stand, surrounded by wide verandas trimmed with Victorian fretwork. Tourism is the base of the economy today, but vegetables, pineapples, and copra are still produced and are shipped to market in Papeete. Opunohu Bay has an agricultural-experiment station and a pineapple cannery.

GETTING THERE

The **Moorea Ferry** makes the 12-mile trip between the ferry dock in downtown Papeete and **Vaiare,** 5km (3 miles) south of the airport on Moorea's southwest coast several times a day.

Air Moorea runs a shuttle service between Faaa International Airport and Moorea's airstrip at **Temae** on the island's northwest tip. **Air Tahiti** also flies between Faaa and Temae several times a week. Moorea's airport is not lighted, so planes arrive and take off only during daylight hours. The Moorea telephone number for both airlines is 56-10-34.

See "Getting Around French Polynesia" in Chapter 3 for more details.

GETTING AROUND

There is no regular public transportation system on Moorea, but the ferries do have their own **trucks** that meet them at the Vaiare wharf and carry their passengers to their final destinations on Moorea. These trucks also make runs around the island, stopping at the hotels or flagged down along the road, to pick up passengers for the ferries' next departure for Papeete. In other words, it's possible to get rides from the ferry wharves to your hotel, or vice versa, on these trucks. The one-way fare is 200 CFP ($2) regardless of the length of the ride.

Otherwise, you'll have to depend on rental cars or scooters, a few taxis, bicycles, foot, or organized tours.

IMPRESSIONS

From Tahiti, Moorea seems to have about forty separate summits: fat thumbs of basalt, spires tipped at impossible angles, brooding domes compelling to the eye. But the peaks which can never be forgotten are the jagged saw-edges that look like the spines of some forgotten dinosaur.

—JAMES A. MICHENER, 1951

RENTAL CARS & SCOOTERS

The largest rental-car company on Moorea is **Arii Rent-a-Car** (tel. 56-11-03), which has offices at the airport, the Vaiare ferry wharf, Hotel Bali Hai, Club Bali Hai, and the Club Med. Small Peugeots and Renaults start at 5,000 CFP ($50) for 4 hours and go up to 6,500 CFP ($65) for a full day. The rates include unlimited kilometers and liability insurance but not gasoline or collision damage insurance. Scooters and mopeds are 4,000 CFP ($40) for a full day, including gasoline, full insurance, and unlimited kilometers. Reservations are a very good idea, especially on weekends, when many Tahiti residents come to Moorea for a day or two. The firm is open daily from 7:30am to 5:30pm.

The only international firm on Moorea, **Avis** (tel. 56-12-58, or toll free 800/331-1212 in the U.S.) has offices at the Total gas station at the airport junction, the airport itself, Hotel Sofitel Ia Ora, and the Viare ferry wharf. Four-passenger Renaults and Peugeots rent for 7,800 CFP ($78) for 24 hours, including unlimited kilometers and liability insurance but excluding gasoline. Add another 1,300 CFP ($13) a day for collision-damage insurance. The agency is open daily from 7:30am to 5:30pm.

Albert Rent-a-Car (tel. 56-13-53), across from the Club Bali Hai in Cook's Bay, rents Fiats and Ford Fiestas for 6,500 CFP ($65) for 24 hours and 5,000 CFP ($50) for ½ day, including unlimited kilometers and liability insurance but not gasoline or collision insurance. Scooters rent for 4,000 CFP ($40) for all day and 3,000 CFP ($30) for ½ day. Albert also is open daily from 7:30am to 5:30pm. If there's no one in the booth, inquire at the house behind it.

If you rent a scooter, make sure that the brakes, headlight, and horn work before you drive off. None of the companies like to rent their scooters overnight, since local youths can easily jump-start them and go for joyrides.

TAXIS

Taxis are far from inexpensive on Moorea. Expect to pay about 3,500 CFP ($35) one-way for the 17-mile ride from the airport to the Club Med area, less for stops along the way. Be sure that you understand—in simple, plain English if you don't speak French—what the fare will be before you get in.

The only taxi stand is at the airport (tel. 56-10-18), and that's open only during daylight hours. Moorea's taxis are owned by individuals who don't run around looking for customers. The hotel desks can call one for you. Make advance reservations for service between 6pm and 6am.

IMPRESSIONS

I saw it first from an airplane. On the horizon there was a speck that became a tall, blunt mountain with cliffs dropping sheer into the sea. And about the base of the mountain, narrow fingers of land shot out, forming magnificent bays, while about the whole was thrown a coral ring of absolute perfection. . . . That was Bora Bora from aloft. When you stepped upon it the dream expanded.

—JAMES A. MICHENER, 1951

BICYCLES

The 60km (36-mile) road around Moorea is relatively flat. The two major hills are on the west side of Cook's Bay and just behind the Hotel Sofitel Ia Ora (which has a stupendous view of Tahiti). The above-mentioned **Arii Rent-a-Car** (tel. 56-11-03) and **Albert Rent-a-Car** (tel. 56-13-53) both rent bicycles. They cost 800 CFP ($8) for ½ day, 1,000 CFP ($10) for all day, and 1,500 CFP ($15) if you keep them overnight.

FAST FACTS MOOREA

Bookstores The island's sole bookstore (or *librairie* in French) is just west of the bridge in Pao Pao, Cook's Bay.

Business Hours Give or take half an hour, most shops are open Mon–Fri 7:30–11:30am and 2–5pm, Sat 9am–noon. The grocery stores stay open daily until 6pm except on Sun, when hours are 6:30–8am.

Car Rentals See "Getting Around," above.

Currency Exchange French Polynesia's four big banks all have offices on Moorea. Hours are Mon–Fri 8am–noon and 1:30–4:30pm. Banque Socredo, which does not charge a transaction fee to change currency or traveler's checks, had been operating in Vaire during my recent visit but was expected to move to a new shopping center near Hotel Bali Hai in Maharepa. Banque de Polynésie is at Pao Pao at the head of Cook's Bay. Westpac and the Banque de Tahiti have offices virtually side by side in Maharepa near Hotel Bali Hai. Westpac has a second office in Le Petit Village across from the Club Med.

Dentist Ask your hotel for a recommendation.

Doctor Dr. Christian Joinville (tel. 56-11-04) has an office in Pao Pao in Cook's Bay. He has lived on Moorea many years, speaks English fluently, and has treated many visitors, including me.

Drugstores Moorea's only drugstore, Pharmacie Tran (tel. 56-10-51), is in Maharepa. The owners, Mr. and Mrs. Tran Thai Thanh, are Vietnamese refugees who speak English. Their hours are Mon–Sat 7:30–11:45am, Mon–Fri 2–5pm, and Sun and holidays 8–10am.

Emergencies The telephone number for the gendarmerie at Afareaitu is 56-13-44. Local police have offices at Pao Pao (tel. 56-13-63) and at Haapiti (tel. 56-10-84) near the Club Med.

Hairdressers/Barbers Moorea has two hairdressers. Harmony Coiffure (no phone) is in a small storefront shop across the road from the Club Bali Hai. Vaitiare Coiffure (tel. 56-18-04) is near the Club Med in Haapiti.

Hospitals The island's infirmary, which has an ambulance, is at Afareaitu on the southwest coast (tel. 56-24-24).

Information The local tourism committee has an information office near the Hotel Baie de Cook. Hours are irregular.

Laundry/Dry Cleaning There is no commercial laundry or dry cleaners on Moorea. The hotels will take care of your laundry.

Lost Property See "Police," below.

Photographic Needs Supersonics (tel. 56-14-96), in Le Petit Village shopping center opposite the Club Med in Haapiti sells film and camera batteries. The hotel boutiques sell color-print film.

Police See "Emergencies," above.

Post Office Moorea's main post office is at Temae just past the airport junction heading toward the Hotel Sofitel Ia Ora. It's open Mon–Thurs 7am to 3pm, Fri till 2pm. You place long-distance and international telephone calls at the counter. A small post office in Papetoai village is open Mon–Thurs 7:30am–3:30pm, Fri 7:30am–2:30pm.

Religious Services A small Catholic church is on the west side of Cook's Bay, 10km (6 miles) from the airport; another is in Haapiti on the west coast. A Protestant church is in the village of Papetoai, on a road off the coastal road, right by the post office. The village of Haapiti has a Catholic church and a Protestant church, and there is a village church in Afareaitu.

Taxis See "Getting Around," above.

Telegrams/Telex Send telegrams and telexes at the Temae post office (see "Post Office," above).

WHAT TO SEE & DO

SIGHTSEEING

The sights of Moorea may lack great historical significance, but the physical beauty of the island makes a tour—at least of the north shore around Cook's and Opunohu bays—a must.

As on Tahiti, the road that circles the island is marked every kilometer with a PK post. Distances are measured between the intersection of the airport road with the main round-island coastal road and the village of Haapiti on Moorea's opposite side. In other words, the distances indicated on the PKs increase from the airport in each direction, reaching 30km near Haapiti. They then decrease as you head back to the airport.

A Road Tour

Few things give me as much pleasure in the South Pacific as riding around Moorea, its magnificent peaks hanging over my head one minute and plunging into its two great bays the next. I've done it by bicycle, scooter, car, and foot. You can take an organized tour, but if you decide to do it on your own, here's what you will see.

Begin at the **airport** turnoff in Temae and head west along the north shore. The airstrip is on Moorea's only sizable area of flat land. At one time it was a *motu*, or small island, sitting on the reef by itself. The lagoon has since been filled by people and nature except for Lake Temae, which you can see from the air if you fly to Moorea.

Temae, 1km from the airport junction, supplied the dancers for the Pomare dynasty's court and is still known for the quality of its performers. Herman Melville spent some time here in 1842 and saw the famous, erotic *upaupa,* which he called the "lory-lory," performed clandestinely, out of sight of the missionaries.

The relatively dry north shore between the airport and the entrance to Cook's Bay is known as **Maharepa.** The road skirts the lagoon and passes the Hotel Bali Hai and the businesses that have grown up around it before curving left into ✪ **Cook's Bay,** a fingerlike body of water virtually surrounded on three sides by the jagged peaks that line the semicircular "wall" of Moorea. **Mount Tohivea** is the large thumb with a small hole in its top made by Pai's spear. **Mount Mouaroa,** the "Shark's Tooth," is the cathedrallike mountain buttressed on its right by a serrated ridge.

IMPRESSIONS

Seen for the first time by European Eyes, this coast is like nothing else on our workaday planet; a landscape, rather, of some fantastic dream.

—CHARLES NORDHOFF and JAMES NORMAN HALL, 1933

The village of **Pao Pao,** huddled along the curving beach at the head of the bay, is one of Moorea's economic centers. The *marché municipale* (municipal market) is open every day but, like Papeete's, does its best business between 5 and 7am on Sunday. Otherwise, the pickings are slim. The paved road that seems to run through the school next to the bridge cuts through the valley between Cook's Bay and Opunohu Bay. Its surface soon turns to dirt, but it intersects with the main road between Opunohu Bay and the Belvédère lookout.

A small **Catholic church** sits on the shore on the west side of Cook's Bay, at 10km (6 miles) from the airport. Inside is a large mural painted by artist Peter Heyman in 1946 and an altar decorated with mother-of-pearl.

Mount Rotui will tower to your left as you proceed around the peninsula that separates Cook's and Opunohu bays. The road passes a gorgeous plantation-style house on the right and you go deep into Opunohu. As soon as the road levels out, watch for pathways through the woods on the right. These lead a few feet to **Robinson's Cove,** one of the world's most photographed yacht anchorages.

For the 1983 production of *The Bounty,* starring Mel Gibson and Anthony Hopkins, the curving beach backed by shade trees and the valley at the head of ✪ **Opunohu Bay** were turned into Matavai Bay on Tahiti. Many of the replica canoes made for the film can still be seen around Moorea. They look remarkably like dugout log canoes but in reality are fiberglass. Such a pristine backdrop may not be available much longer, for plans have been announced for a Sheraton hotel development at this magnificent and heretofore totally undeveloped spot.

The paved road to the left runs up the central valley through the agricultural-experiment station (the ponds are for breeding those shrimp you may have eaten with coconut-curry sauce) and through pastureland stocked with cattle. This, too, may have changed before you arrive; the Sheraton development is to have an 18-hole golf course on these fields.

The road soon curves sharply and steeply to the ✪ **Titiroa Marae** and the **Belvédère** lookout, with its remarkable view of the valley and both bays. The marae, which is marked by a large sign, has been restored. It was part of a concentration of marae and other structures, including an archery platform used for competition (archery was a sport reserved for high-ranking chiefs and was never used in warfare in Polynesia). The remains of these structures can be seen by taking a short stroll among the towering Tahitian chestnut trees that have grown up around and through them.

Back on the coastal road, the village of **Papetoai,** which has more than its share of "vanilla houses" (so named because they were built by vanilla planters in the early 20th century), was the retreat of the Pomare dynasty in the 1800s. It was the base from which Pomare I launched his successful drive to take over all of Tahiti and Moorea. It also was headquarters for the London Missionary Society's work throughout the South Pacific, and the road to the right by the post office leads to an octagonal **Temple Protestant** built on the site of a marae dedicated to Oro, son of the supreme Taaroa and the god of war. The original church was constructed in the 1820s, and although advertised as the oldest European building still in use in the South Pacific, the present structure dates from the late 1880s.

From Papetoai, the road runs through the hotel district on the northwest corner and then heads south through the rural parts of Moorea. The 300-bungalow Club Med and the businesses it has generated, including Le Petit Village shopping center across the road, dominate the northwest corner of the island.

REFUELING STOP The Club Med area is your last chance to stop for refreshment before you travel the sparsely populated southern half of Moorea. My favorite stop is **Snack Michel** west of the Club's entrance. Other possibilities are the pleasant beachside restaurants at **Hotel Moorea Village** and **Maohi Beach.** The latter is a few kilometers beyond the Club Med. Your absolute last stop will be **Linareva Floating Restaurant and Bar** near Haapiti village 7km (4 miles) beyond Club Med. See "Moorea: Where to Dine," below for details.

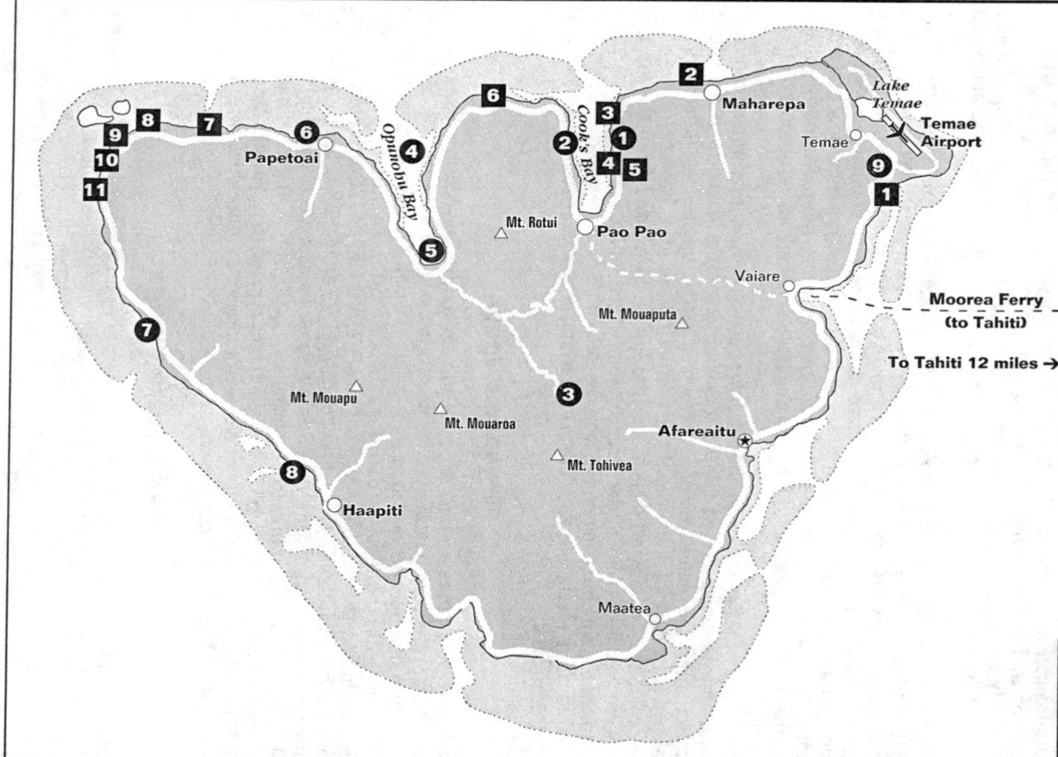

ACCOMMODATIONS:

- Camp Grounds 10
- Club Mediterranee 9
- Club Bali Hai 4
- Hotel Baie de Cook 3
- Hotel Bali Hai 2
- Hotel Moorea Lagoon 6
- Hotel Moorea Village 11
- Hotel Sofitel la Ora 1
- Moorea Beachcomber Parkroyal 7
- Motel Albert 5
- Residence Les Tipaniers 8

ATTRACTIONS:

- Belvédère Lookout 3
- Cook's Bay 2
- Island Fasions 1
- Linareva Floating Restaurant 8
- Opunohu Bay 4
- Papetoai Village 6
- Robinson's Cove 5
- Tahiti Lookout 9
- Tiki Theatre Village 7

Two kilometers (1.2 miles) beyond the club, look for the **Tiki Theatre Village,** a cultural center consisting of thatch huts on the coastal side of the road. Demonstrations of traditional Polynesian life take place at various times, with the main show usually at noon. It's the only place to see what a Tahitian village looked like when Captain Cook arrived, so pull in. See below for details and admission fees.

When those first Europeans arrived, the lovely village of **Haapiti** was home of the powerful Marama family, which was allied with the Pomares. It became a center of Catholic missionary work after the French took over the territory and is one of the few villages whose Catholic church is as large as its Protestant counterpart. South of Haapiti, just as the road curves sharply around a headland, is a nice view of a small bay with the mountains towering overhead. In contrast to the more touristy north shore, the southeast and southwest coasts have retained an atmosphere of old Polynesia.

The village of **Afareaitu,** on the southwest coast, is the administrative center of Moorea, and the building that looks like a charming hotel across from the village church actually is the island's mairie, or town hall. Farther up the coast is the small bay of **Vaiare,** a beehive of activity when the ferries pull in from Papeete.

The road then climbs a hill just past the Ia Ora hotel, and from the top is a magnificent view of the hotel, the green lagoon flecked with brown coral heads, the white line of the surf breaking on the reef, the deep blue of the Sea of the Moon, and all of Tahiti rising on the horizon. There's a parking area at the overlook, so stop and use up some film.

Organized Tours

Most hotels offer tours around Moorea and up to the Belvédère lookout in the interior. Most require a minimum of six passengers. **Albert's Tours** (tel. 56.13.53), the same firm that operates as Albert Rent-a-Car in Cook's Bay across from the Club Bali Hai, has ½-day round-island tours for 1,500 CFP ($15). The afternoon tour of the interior, including the Belvédère lookout, costs 1,200 CFP ($12). **Paradis Tours,** operating out of Arii Rent-a-Car's offices (tel. 56.11.03 or 56.12.86), has round-island and interior tours for the same prices. In addition, Paradis has a shopping tour for 1,200 CFP ($12), a guided hike to a waterfall for 3,000 CFP ($30), and a hike across the mountains for 3,500 CFP ($35). For a different type of tour, **Maohi Beach** (tel. 56.17.70) has ½-day "safari" tours of Moorea's interior in four-wheel-drive vehicles. They cost 4,000 CFP ($40) per person.

Tiki Theatre Village

Another way to see Moorea is on the circle-island tour sponsored by **Tiki Theatre Village** (tel. 56.18.97), but the highlight will be the visit to Tiki Village itself. Built in the fashion of old Tahitian villages, this cultural center—2km (1.2 miles) south of Club Med—stages various demonstrations of traditional Polynesian life-styles. The main "show" takes place at noon each day, but guides will lead you through the village at any time between 10:30am and 3:30pm. Included are examples of house construction, handcraft making, and food preparation.

Admission fees to the village vary. A tour with a guide and an explanation of the many uses of the coconut palm costs 700 CFP ($7). Entrance, including the noontime show, is 1,000 CFP ($10). Lunch of native foods is another 2,000 CFP ($20). For a total of 4,000 CFP ($40), they will come and get you in a canoe, lead you around the

---

IMPRESSIONS

Nothing on Tahiti is so majestic as what faces it across the bay, for there lies the island of Moorea. To describe it is impossible. It is a monument to the prodigal beauty of nature.

—James A. Michener, 1951

village, let you watch the show at noon, and feed you lunch. Children between 3 and 12 years old pay half of all fees.

SPORTS & RECREATION

Most hotels have active water-sports programs for their guests, such as glass-bottom-boat cruises and snorkeling in or sailing on Moorea's beautiful lagoon.

Scuba diving is available from **Moorea Underwater Scuba-diving Tahiti (M.U.S.T.)** (tel. 56.17.32), whose office is on the dock next to the Hotel Baie de Cook. Owner Philippe Molle and his instructors take up to 12 divers out in the morning, 12 in the afternoon. One dive costs 4,500 CFP ($45), including all equipment. Lessons cost 6,000 CFP ($60) for one person or 20,000 CFP ($200) for a group of four.

When he's not on a charter to the Leeward Islands, English-born David Parkin keeps his 50-foot trimaran sailboat ***Esprit*** (tel. and fax 56.17.90) anchored in the lagoon between Cook's and Opunohu bays. The boat sleeps eight and is always crewed. Chartering season runs from March to November. Rates are $1,200 per person a week, $2,000 for 2 weeks.

Horseback riding along the beach and in Moorea's interior is available at **Tiahura Ranch** (tel. 56.28.55) opposite Snack Michel in Haapiti. Rates are 1,500 CFP ($15) for 1 hour and 2,000 CFP ($20) for 90 minutes.

Avid hikers can look for a trail that runs from the ferry wharf at Vaiare up across a pass on the old crater's rim and down to Pao Pao on Cook's Bay. This trail is best followed from the Vaiare side, since that's the way the red-paint markers face.

SHOPPING

You will pass a number of boutiques and other shops on your tour of Moorea—don't hesitate to stop in and have a look. In general, handcraft items and tropical clothing, including pareus, are less expensive at the handcraft stalls on the second level of the Papeete Municipal Market. On the other hand, you are likely to find better deals on black pearls on Moorea than on Tahiti or any other island.

The economic recession of the late 1980s and early 1990s dealt some heavy blows to Moorea's boutiques, hotels, and restaurants. I will mention those that have been in business for many years and which I have found to give good value for your money. If they aren't there when you arrive, you can't say I didn't warn you.

FROMMER'S FAVORITE MOOREA EXPERIENCES

View from the Belvédère The scene from this lookout is awesome, with jagged Mount Rotui separating the fingers of Cook's and Oponohu bays in the foreground and the serrated wall of the old volcanic crater circling behind you.

View from Above the Sofitel Ia Ora My neck strains every time I cross the hill behind the Hotel Sofitel Ia Ora, for there across the Sea of the Moon sits fabled Tahiti in all its green glory. Whenever possible I stop at the lookout and reflect on what amazement the early explorers must have felt when those mountains appeared over the horizon.

Happy Hour at Club Bali Hai To my mind the scene from the shores of Cook's Bay is unsurpassed in the South Pacific, and the jagged mountains and deep blue waters are at their haunting best as the setting sun changes their colors from green against the blue sky to purple against pink to a mystical black against gray. The waterside bar has half-price drinks from 6 to 7pm Tuesday and Friday, a balm for the pocketbook.

GALERIE VAN DER HEYDE, Cook's Bay. Tel. 56.14.22.

Just north of the Kaveka Beach Club, this is the domain of Dutch artist Aad van der Heyde, who has lived and worked on Moorea since 1964. One of his bold, impressionist paintings of a Tahitian woman was selected for French Polynesia's 100-CFP postage stamp in 1975. Aad will sell you a lithograph of the painting for 8,900 CFP ($89) and will autograph it for free. You may find him playing chess if he's not busy showing off his paintings, which are displayed in the gallery's garden, or the multitude of pearls, wood carvings, tapa cloth, shell and coral jewelry, and primitive art from Papua New Guinea in his boutique. His prices, especially on black pearls, are reasonable for the quality. Aad's hours are somewhat irregular.

HEIMATA BOUTIQUE, Pao Pao, Cook's Bay. Tel. 56.18.51.

Next to the old wharf and municipal market, seamstress Micheline Tetuanui's shop has reasonable prices on pareus and souvenir items, such as soap made with tiare-scented Monoi oil and Hinano beer glasses, and its prices on books about French Polynesia are the best to be found anywhere. It also has a good selection of tablecloths and napkins printed with tapa designs. You may find Micheline sewing away on a fine selection of tropical fashions, many of them in traditional Tahitian fabrics and styles.

ISLAND FASHIONS, Cook's Bay. Tel. 56.11.06.

Just a few yards from the Galerie van der Heyde, this is an essential establishment for anyone shopping for black pearls. American Ron Hall sailed down to Tahiti with the actor Peter Fonda in 1974; Peter went home, Ron didn't. Now Ron and Canadian Peter Ringland are partners in a black-pearl farm at Manihi atoll in the Tuamotus. Peter manages production and sales. Ron runs the air-conditioned Moorea retail outlet, and in 15 minutes he will show you the basics of picking a pearl. He also will have your selection set in a mounting of your choice, and his prices are fair (don't hesitate to bargain politely). In addition to stylish pearls, Island Fashions derives its name from a small but excellent selection of aloha shirts, dresses, bathing suits, and T-shirts.

LA MAISON BLANCHE, in Maharepa Tel. 56.13.26.

Opposite Hotel Bali Hai, a whitewashed vanilla planter's house with railing enclosing a magnificent front veranda is now home to this shop carrying an array of pareus, tropical dresses, bathing suits, T-shirts, shell jewelry, and other handcrafts. Prices reflect the high quality of the merchandise. La Maison Blanche (The White House) is open daily from 8:30am to 5:30pm.

LE PETIT VILLAGE, Haapiti. No phone.

This shopping center in the neocolonial buildings across from the Club Med has several shops worth a look. **Vanille Boutique** has hand-silk-screened pareus and pillowcases and an interesting collection of handcrafts and souvenirs. **Lagon Bleu** is an upscale shop featuring jewelry of black pearls, shark's teeth, black coral, and scrimshaw. **Arts Polynésiens** on the far left as you face the center carries souvenirs and a wide selection of T-shirts. **Supersonics** carries film, watch and camera batteries, stamps, and other items. Upstairs, **Tiki Pearls** has expensive black pearls and other jewelry.

TEVA'S MOOREA PERLES CENTRE, Cook's Bay. Tel. 56.13.13.

In a low-slung thatch building opposite Club Bali Hai, this quality shop carries some large black pearls, finely polished seashells, and very well made handcrafts, especially shell necklaces and mother-of-pearl earrings. In addition to regular shopping hours, it's open Saturday from 2 to 5pm.

WHERE TO STAY

Most of Moorea's hotels and restaurants are huddled on the eastern shore of Cook's Bay or in the Haapiti district on the northwest corner of the island around the Club Med. With the exceptions of the luxury Bali Hai and Sofitel Ia Ora hotels, those in or near Cook's Bay do not have the best beaches on the island, but their views of the mountains are unsurpassed in the South Pacific. Those on the northwest corner, on the other hand, have fine beaches, lagoons like giant swimming pools, and unobstructed views of the sunset if not of Moorea's mountains. The two areas are relatively far apart, so you may spend most of your time near your hotel unless you rent transportation or otherwise make a point to see the sights. An alternative is to split your stay between the two areas.

EXPENSIVE

CLUB BALI HAI, B.P. 26, Temae, Moorea. Tel. 56.13.68, toll free 800/282-1402 in California, 800/282-1401 elsewhere in the U.S. Fax 56.19.22. Telex 331. 20 rms, 19 bungalows. A/C **Location:** Cook's Bay, near Pao Pao.

$ Rates (in U.S. dollars only): $93 single or double room; $295 single or double bungalow. AE, DC, MC, V.

Under the same management as the Hotel Bali Hai (see below), the Club sits deep in Cook's Bay and has an incredible view of Moorea's ragged mountains across the water. It offers 13 over-the-water bungalows and 6 set on the beach. The 20 hotel-style rooms (which really belong in the moderate category below) are in a two-story building. They are rather ordinary but comfortable; each has a private patio or balcony. The bungalows and rooms have been converted to time-share units, which meant a complete refurbishment and the addition of kitchenettes (a money-saving feature given the territory's high food costs) during the 1980s.

Dining/Entertainment: The restaurant and main bar are in a large thatch-roofed building, and you can have a drink at a smaller bar by the swimming pool and beach while taking in the great view. The restaurant's menu is similar to that of the Hotel Bali Hai, and the price range is comparable. A Tahitian string band plays during dinner. Happy hours from 6 to 7pm Tuesday and Friday are popular with Moorea's expatriate residents.

Services: Boutique, laundry, baby-sitting. Guests share all the activities of the Hotel Bali Hai.

Facilities: Laundromat, swimming pool, water-sports equipment, tennis, glass-bottom boat for snorkeling expeditions and sunset cruises, video room; activities desk.

HOTEL BALI HAI MOOREA, B.P. 26, Temae, Moorea. Tel. 56.13.59, or toll free 800/282-1402 in California, 800/282-1401 elsewhere in the U.S. Fax 56.19.22. Telex 331. 54 rms, 9 overwater bungalows. **Location:** Maharepa, between airport and Cook's Bay.

$ Rates (in U.S. dollars only): $118–$175 single or double; $215 single or double beachfront bungalow; $325 single or double overwater bungalow. AE, DC, MC, V.

This is the flagship of the small hotel chain founded by Californians Jay Carlisle, Don "Muk" McCallum, and Hugh Kelley, the legendary "Bali Hai Boys." They gave up their budding business careers to buy an old vanilla plantation on Moorea. When they realized there was little money to be made in vanilla, however, they refurbished an old hotel on the property and opened it as the Bali Hai in 1961. With the international airport opening just across the Sea of the Moon on Tahiti, their timing couldn't have been better: They quickly had a success on their hands. By the 1970s they had opened two more Bali Hai hotels, one on Huahine and one on Raiatea, and in the 1980s they spearheaded the conversion of the Aimeo Hotel in Cook's Bay to the time-share operation now known as the Club Bali Hai. In addition, they put the old vanilla plantation to work producing chickens, eggs, and milk.

One notable innovation of the Bali Hai Boys was the over-the-water bungalow, and the Hotel Bali Hai Moorea has nine of them, standing on pilings over the lagoon. Spotlights under each shine into the water at night, so you can watch through a glass panel in the bungalow's floor as the fish swim among the coral heads below you. You can join the fish by walking down steps from your private porch and jumping right into the water. (If you don't want to mingle with the sea life, there's a swimming pool complete with waterfall on one end and a bar on the other, from which you can get a cool tropical drink without leaving the water.)

The Bali Hai's other rooms sit in a coconut grove, although a few have porches that extend over the beach to the water. There are beachfront bungalows and garden bungalows, a few of which have two or more units in them. All have thatch roofs, tile baths with showers (but no tubs), ceiling fans, small fridges, double and single beds, and tea- and coffee-making facilities.

Dining/Entertainment: The central building on the beach contains the Boom Boom Bar and the airy Bali Hai Canoe Club and Grill, whose menu features fish, steaks, and lamb in various sauces. A band provides Tahitian music for cocktails and dinner, and the hotel stages a Sunday-afternoon barbecue and traditional dance show.

Services: Laundry, baby-sitting.

Facilities: Swimming pool; tennis; boutique; Liki Tiki, a pontoon boat with its own thatch roof that offers snorkeling, picnics, and sunset cruises; video room; snorkeling and other water-sports equipment; activities desk.

CLUB MEDITERRANEE, B.P. 575, Papeete, Tahiti. Tel. 56.15.00, 42.96.99 in Papeete, or toll free 800/528-3100 in the U.S. Fax 42.16.83. Telex 256. 350 bungalows. **Location:** Haapiti, on island's northwest corner.

$ Rates (including meals): 13,000 CFP ($130) double per person. AE, CB, DC, MC, V.

(S) This huge playground is the center of activity on the northwest corner of Moorea (17 miles from the airport). The setting is exceptional, with an azure lagoon lying between the beach and a private motu on the reef offshore, which the club's guests can use for sunbathing in the buff (the skimpiest of bottoms are required on the main beach). The club is such a world unto itself that it even marches to its own clock, set an hour earlier than Moorea's in order to give the guests extra time in the sun. Casual guests are not welcomed by the guards who stand watch at the main gate and patrol the premises. All but a few of the club's guests are Americans and Australians.

As at all Club Meds, you pay one price for everything, including a shared bungalow, meals with wine, and a wide range of mile-a-minute activities—from snorkeling to scuba diving and from nightclub shows to classical music as the sun sets. The only extras are drinks at the bar (for which you pay with color-coded plastic beads purchased in advance), tours of the island, and a snorkeling extravaganza to Marlon Brando's Tetiaroa atoll. Also, the club's guests can take advantage of charter airfares.

The club's bungalows are a cross between traditional and colonial styles. Instead of thatch, the roofs are made of shingles, the walls of tongue-in-groove lumber, the floors of polished hardwood; the ceiling fans, mirrors, and other items are trimmed in brass. Each bungalow is a double room with two oversize twin beds; if you don't have a roommate, one of the same sex may be assigned.

Dining/Entertainment: Although good, the food is better known for its substantial quantity than outstanding quality. Breakfasts and lunches are all-you-can-eat buffets. Dinners are sit-down affairs. The staff performs nightclub-style floor shows several nights a week. Disco dancing takes place every evening after dinner or the show.

Services: Laundry, baby-sitting.

Facilities: Swimming pool, glass-bottom boat, snorkeling gear, scuba diving, waterskiing, outrigger canoes, boutique.

MOOREA BEACHCOMBER PARKROYAL, B.P. 1019, Papetaoi, Moorea. Tel. 56.19.19, or toll free 800/252-2155 in California, 800/421-0536 elsewhere in the U.S., 800/251-2166 in Canada. Fax 56.18.88. Telex 441. 52 rms, 102 bungalows. A/C (rooms only) MINIBAR TV TEL **Location:** Between Papetaoi and Haapiti.

$ Rates: 21,000 CFP ($210) single room; 23,000 CFP ($230) double room; 26,500 CFP ($265) beach bungalow; 32,500 CFP ($325) overwater bungalow. AE, DC, MC, V.

Situated in a flat, almost swampy coconut grove, and known formerly as the Sofitel Tiare Moorea Hotel, this property was troubled financially in the late 1980s until taken over by Southern Pacific Hotels. Much of the reef was dredged to form fingerlike islands separated by narrow channels and joined by footbridges. Most of the bungalows extend partially over the water from unpainted concrete supports anchored on the islands. They are of European construction and feature mat walls;

carpeted lounges with sofa beds and chairs; separate toilets and sleeping and dressing areas; combination tub-showers; ceiling fans, and indirect lighting. Wood-frame doors open to porches, but only small windows in the rear of each unit give ventilation. The air-conditioned hotel rooms are in a curving two-story building. Some of these have king-size beds; others, two doubles. Furniture, spreads, drapes, and carpets follow a forest green theme throughout all bungalows and rooms.

Dining/Entertainment: A large central building with a shingle roof built at several angles houses the hotel's reception and indoor activities areas. The adjoining dining room offers French cuisine in a tropical setting under a large thatch roof supported by white beams. A more formal restaurant was under construction during my recent visit. A string band plays Tahitian songs from sunset through dinner nightly except on Wednesday, which are devoted to a barbecue and Tahitian dance show at a reasonable 2,600 CFP ($26) per person, and Saturday, which see dinner-dances at 5,100 CFP ($51) a head.

Services: Laundry, baby-sitting.

Facilities: Adults and children's swimming pools; parasailing; snorkeling gear; glass-bottom boat; scuba diving; activities and car-rental desks; small boutique; conference room.

HOTEL SOFITEL IA ORA MOOREA, B.P. 28, Temae, Moorea. Tel. 56.12.90, 41.04.04 in Papeete, or toll free 800/763-4835. Fax 41.05.05. Telex 214. 80 bungalows. **Location:** Temae, on northeast coast facing Tahiti.

$ Rates: 22,400 CFP–28,100 CFP ($224–$281) single, 24,400 CFP–30,100 CFP ($244–$301) double; 39,700 CFP ($397) single suite, 41,700 CFP ($417) double suite. AE, DC, MC, V.

★ Formerly known as the Kia Ora, this collection of thatch-roofed buildings sits beside one of the island's most picturesque lagoons and a long beach over which grape-leaf and casuarina trees hang. At present, it's the only hotel on Moorea with a view of Tahiti, whose green, cloud-topped mountains seem to climb out of the horizon beyond the reef.

Most of the Ia Ora's comfortable bungalows are in rows in a coconut grove, although a few are on a ridge above the trees and have an unobstructed view of Tahiti. Almost all have a large tile bathroom with shower, carpeted floors, a ceiling fan over twin beds that can be made into a king, a lounge chair and coffee table, and sliding glass doors leading to a porch under an extension of the thatch roof. A few large suite bungalows have these same features plus two separate bedrooms.

Dining/Entertainment: Its bungalows may not be built over the water, but one of the Ia Ora's two restaurants is. The Molokai Restaurant and Bar are in a large thatch-roofed building sitting on pilings just beyond the beach. The restaurant, which is open for breakfast and lunch, has captain's tables and chairs under mother-of-pearl chandeliers that tinkle in the trade winds sweeping through the large building. A rectangular hole in the floor lets you watch the fish swim in the lagoon below. Lunch is served from noon to 2pm. The menu changes occasionally but usually features salads, sandwiches, burgers, omelets, fettuccine, and spaghetti, and main courses of steak, lamb, veal, or fresh fish.

Dinners, usually barbecue buffets costing about 4,500 CFP ($45) per person, are served in La Pérouse Restaurant; it's in a large thatch building in the coconut grove. On nonbarbecue nights, diners choose from an à la carte menu. Tahitian dance shows follow dinner 3 nights a week; other evenings, a string band performs.

Services: Laundry, baby-sitting.

Facilities: Water-sports activities center; tennis; pearl shop; boutique; bicycles; video room; volleyball; activities, tour, and car-rental desks.

MODERATE

HOTEL MOOREA LAGOON, B.P. 11, Temae, Moorea. Tel. 56.14.68. Fax 56.26.25. Telex 327. 45 bungalows. **Location:** Between Cook's Bay and Opunohu Bay.

$ Rates: 11,000 CFP–16,000 CFP ($110–$160) single; 12,000 CFP–17,000 CFP ($120–$170) double. AE, DC, MC, V.

Owned by the same local family that operates the Hotel Te Puna Bel Air on Tahiti and Hotel Baie de Cook on Moorea, this establishment represents good value for couples seeking a more isolated setting, since no other hotels or restaurants are within an easy walk. A bulkhead holds the lagoon away from most of the property, but there are patches of excellent beach partially overhung by shade trees. Beachfront bungalows, with the water virtually at their front porches, are the choice. Those in the somewhat sparse garden are shaded by few palms or other trees. All identical, the bungalows have thatch roofs, mat throw rugs on tile floors, ceiling fans, rattan furnishings, and double beds. There are no screens on the windows or doors.

Guests enjoy reasonably good French cuisine under a large, beachside thatch roof. Unless you intend to rent a car or scooter to get to distant restaurants, consider buying a Modified American Plan at 3,600 CFP ($36) per person a day. A string band plays during happy hour and dinner. Across the road, Moorea's only disco rocks and rolls on Saturday nights. Facilities include a swimming pool, tennis court, and water-sports equipment.

HOTEL MOOREA VILLAGE, P.O. Box 1008, Papetoai, Moorea. Tel. 56-10-02. Fax 56.22.11. 48 bungalows. **Location:** In Haapiti, near the Club Med.

$ Rates: 5,000 CFP ($50) single, 5,500 CFP ($55) double without kitchen; 8,500 CFP ($85) single, 10,500 CFP ($105) with kitchen. Add 2,000 CFP ($20) for beachfront; add 10% during July–Aug. AE, MC, V.

One of the island's better values, and my long-standing favorite for the money, this is also known as Fare Gendron. It has 48 bungalows situated on a grassy lawn under coconut palms. Fifteen of these fares have kitchenettes, but the majority consist of one room and a bath under a peaked thatch roof from which hangs a ceiling fan.

The restaurant/bar is perched on a bank next to the beach. Breakfast is served on a long porch that hangs over the sand along the waterfront side of the restaurant. Evening meals in the restaurant emphasize both French and Chinese cooking at moderate prices. A Tahitian band entertains every evening, but the highlight entertainments are a barbecue with pareu show on Saturday evening and an authentic earth-oven feast and dance show Sunday afternoons. Facilities include a swimming pool next to the beach, snorkeling gear, and canoes.

RESIDENCE LES TIPANIERS, B.P. 1002, Papetaoi, Moorea. Tel. 56-12-67, or toll free 800/521-7242 in the U.S. and Canada. Fax 56.12.67. 21 bungalows. **Location:** Haapiti, east of Club Med.

$ Rates: 7,500 CFP ($75) single, 9,500 CFP ($95) single with kitchenette; 10,000 CFP ($100) double, 12,000 CFP ($120) double with kitchenette. AE, DC, MC, V.

Another northwest-corner hotel, this shares the sandy beach that runs along the Club Med. The thatch bungalows are set back from the edge of the beach, which gives the small complex an open, airy atmosphere. The bungalows are clean and comfortable, and the flowered-print bedspreads and sofa covers give them an authentic Tahitian feel. Except for those in the bathrooms, the windows are not screened; this side of Moorea is dry and mosquitoes are relatively few in number, but if they bother you, keep the nonscreened windows in mind. A few newer, larger bungalows have kitchenettes.

Les Tipaniers has a pleasant snack bar with a deck over the beach from which a long pier runs to deep water out in the lagoon. The snack bar is open from 7am to 6pm and serves pizza, sandwiches, and hot dogs, plus main courses from noon to 2pm. The hotel is also home of the excellent Les Tipaniers restaurant, which is known for its Italian food (see "Moorea: Where to Dine," below). Facilities include outrigger canoes, snorkeling gear, volleyball, and table tennis.

BUDGET

MOTEL ALBERT, Post Office, Temae, Moorea. Tel. 56-12-76. 19 cottages (all with bath) **Location:** In Cook's Bay opposite Club Bali Hai.

$ Rates: 3,000 CFP ($30) 1 bedroom and kitchen for one or two; 4,000 CFP ($40)

2 bedrooms and kitchen for up to four, or 1,500 CFP ($15) per person for large group. 2-night minimum stay required.

For years the only inexpensive place to stay on Moorea was Albert Haring's collection of European-style cottages across the road from the Club Bali Hai in Cook's Bay. Eight of the houses have one bedroom, a kitchen, and a bath; 11 larger houses have two bedrooms, a kitchen, and a bath. All houses have porches, and linen and kitchen equipment are provided. None has hot water.

HOTEL BAIE DE COOK, B.P. 30, Temae, Moorea. Tel. 56-10-50. 76 rms. A/C **Location:** Cook's Bay.
$ Rates: 3,000 CFP ($30) single or double. AE, MC, V.

Ⓢ Formerly an Ibis hotel, this two-story building was being run as a budget property during my last visit by the same family which has the Hotel Te Puna Bel Air on Tahiti and the Hotel Moorea Lagoon. The two-story, L-shaped, colonial-style building surrounds a pool. A short bridge links a restaurant and bar. The small motel-style rooms have twin beds and shower-only baths.

Camping

MOOREA CAMPING, Papetaoi, Moorea. Tel. 56-14-47. 12 rms, 24 bunks, 20 tent sites. **Location:** In Haapiti, near Club Med.
$ Rates: 500 CFP ($5) per camper; 600 CFP ($6) dorm bunk; 1,500 CFP ($15) per person in rooms. No credit cards.

For considerably less shade but a better beach upon which to camp than at Chez Nelson and Josiane's Backpackers' Beach Club (see below), where a rock ledge can interfere with swimming, this establishment in a coconut grove has it. A beachside thatch pavilion covers picnic tables and a communal kitchen. Twelve small plywood houses—actually little more than permanent tents—contain foam mattresses and are considered "rooms." The management provides free fruit, outrigger canoes, and snorkeling equipment.

CHEZ NELSON AND JOSIANE'S BACKPACKERS' BEACH CLUB, PK 27.1, Haapiti, Moorea. Tel. 56-15-18. 2 bungalows, 15 bunks. **Location:** Haapiti, near Club Med.
$ Rates: 500 CFP ($5) per camper; 1,500 CFP ($15) bunk; 3,000 CFP ($30) double bungalow the first night, 2,500 CFP ($25) thereafter; 1,500 CFP ($15) dorm bunk (includes two meals).

Josiane and Nelson Flohr have a roaring campground and hostel business in a beachside coconut grove about 200 yards west of the Club Med. All guests share adequate toilets, cold-water showers, and communal kitchen facilities. In recent years the Flohrs have added seven very small bungalows for couples, a block of 10 tiny dorm rooms (two bunks each) that looks like it might belong in a migrant labor camp, and three other thatch-roofed hostel bungalows down the road (and still on the beach). Each of the latter has a kitchen, modern bathroom, and porch.

WHERE TO DINE

Just as Moorea's hotels suffered during the economic recessions of recent years, so did its restaurants. Several of the best closed shop; others changed owners or chefs. Remarkably, a few new ones opened. Under these circumstances, I hesitate to tell you much more than where to find the ones that were operating during my recent visit. On the other hand, you aren't likely to get a bad meal on Moorea, so feel free to strike out on your own.

A ✪ **feast** cooked Tahitian-style in an earth oven should be on the agenda of anyone with the least bit of culinary curiosity. Since several hotels and one restaurant have weekly feasts, you should have several opportunities to sample ma'a Tahiti while on Moorea. Details are under each individual establishment's listing. Remember that these schedules can change, so call ahead. Here's a summary.

Hotel Sofitel Ia Ora (tel. 56.12.90) has a buffet of Tahitian foods Saturday at

6:30pm, followed by a dance performance at 8pm. **Tiki Theatre Village** (tel. 56.18.97) has a feast and show 2 nights a week, usually on Tuesday and Saturday. **Hotel Bali Hai Moorea** (tel. 56.13.59), **Hotel Moorea Village** (tel. 56.10.02), and **The Other Place** at Maohi Beach (tel. 56.17.70) all have their feasts and shows just after noon on Sunday. Prices for feast and show range from 3,300 CFP ($33) at Maohi Beach to 4,500 CFP ($45) at the hotels.

RESTAURANTS

LINAREVA FLOATING RESTAURANT AND BAR, Haapiti. Tel. 56-15-35.

Cuisine: SEAFOOD. **Reservations:** Recommended on weekends. **Location:** 7km (4 miles) south of Club Med near Haapiti village.

$ **Prices:** Appetizers 600 CFP–1,200 CFP ($6–$12); main courses 1,400 CFP–1,900 CFP ($14–$19). AE, MC, V.

Open: Lunch daily 11:30am–2pm; dinner daily 6:30–9pm; bar daily 9am–10pm.

This restaurant and bar holds title to Moorea's most unusual home: the hull of the original *Tamarii Moorea,* the first ferry to ply between Papeete and Moorea. Owner Eric Lussiez completely rebuilt the old vessel (twice, actually, for it sank at its dock due to a plumbing error after the job was finished) and outfitted the dining room with polished wood, large windows, and plenty of bright brass and other nautical decor. The menu changes, as does availability of local produce, but house specialties feature seafood in a selection of traditional French sauces.

RESTAURANT DOUME ET ROGER, Cook's Bay. Tel. 56-29-65.

Cuisine: FRENCH/ITALIAN/CHINESE. **Reservations:** Recommended on weekends. **Location:** Cook's Bay between Club Bali Hai and Pao Pao village.

$ **Prices:** Appetizers 700 CFP–1,200 CFP ($7–$12); pastas and Chinese dishes 700 CFP–1,200 CFP ($7–$12); French main courses 1,300 CFP–1,900 CFP ($13–$19). AE, V.

Open: Daily 11:30am–10pm.

For years Moorea's leading butcher, the Doumé half of this partnership joined with restauranteur Roger in 1990 to offer a mix of French, Italian, and Chinese cuisines. Formerly the home of Le Hakka restaurant, the pleasant building has windows as walls on three sides of the dining room. Ceiling fans augument the tropical breezes. Highlights of their menu are the homemade pastas and main courses of steak, veal, mussels, shrimp, and salmon in a variety of traditional French sauces. The Chinese dishes are of the Cantonese variety. Try the fettuccine seafood special.

AUBERGE MICHEL ET JACKIE, Maharepa. Tel. 56-11-08.

Cuisine: FRENCH/PIZZA. **Reservations:** Recommended on weekends. **Location:** In Maharepa between the Hotel Bali Hai and the airport. Free or reduced taxi fares available at dinner.

$ **Prices:** Appetizers 600 CFP–1,200 CFP ($6–$12); main courses 1,500 CFP–2,000 CFP ($15–$20); pizzas 1,500 CFP–2,500 CFP ($5–$25); lunch 750 CFP–1,400 CFP ($7.50–$14). AE, MC, V.

Open: Lunch Tues–Sun 11:30am–2:30pm; dinner Tues–Sun 6–9:30pm.

Jeanine and Daniel Serventi have taken this establishment over from former owners Michel and Jackie, who departed for Chile, and specialize in French cuisine—except for two person-size pizzas, which come with a variety of toppings from plain cheese to seafood. Lunches include burgers, sandwiches, omelets, and salads. The dinner menu features seafood, steak, veal, and rabbit in a variety of excellent sauces. You can dine inside the low building or al fresco under sprawling trees in a garden.

FARE MANAVA, Cook's Bay. Tel. 56-14-24.

Cuisine: CHINESE. **Reservations:** Recommended for a waterside table. **Location:** In Pao Pao village just east of the bridge.

$ **Prices:** Appetizers 700 CFP–800 CFP ($7–$8); main courses 900 CFP–2,500 CFP ($9–$25). MC, V.

Open: Lunch Thurs–Tues 11am–2:30pm; dinner Thurs–Tues 6–10pm.

Picturesquely situated under a large thatch roof on the banks of Cook's Bay, Fare Manava should not be confused with Restaurant Manava Nui, which used to be here but is now about a mile away. The two share only the Cantonese style of cooking, not owners. Fare Manava's small room to one side has tables virtually at the water's edge and are worth waiting for if you haven't made a reservation. Tablecloths and folded napkins give a certain class to the restaurant's otherwise plain atmosphere. Meat and chicken dishes are considerably less expensive than those with fish and lobster.

MANAVA NUI RESTAURANT, Cook's Bay. Tel. 56-22-00.

Cuisine: CHINESE/CONTINENTAL. **Reservations:** Recommended on weekends. **Location:** In Cook's Bay just north of Club Bali Hai.

$ Prices: Appetizers 700 CFP–800 CFP ($7–$8); main courses 700 CFP–1,000 CFP ($7–$10). DC, V.

Open: Lunch Mon–Sat 11:30am–2pm; dinner Mon–Sat 6:30–9pm.

Tahiti's first Chinese immigrants were of Hakka descent, and this restaurant puts the Hakka accent on its Cantonese fare, served under a magnificent thatch-roofed building. You can get a meal of fried rice or *kai fan* (boiled chicken and rice); beef, pork, chicken, or prawn; or European-style dishes. Add 130 CFP ($1.30) for a bowl of steamed rice.

THE OTHER PLACE, Maohi Beach, Haapiti. Tel. 56-17-70.

Cuisine: FRENCH. **Reservations:** Recommended on weekends or anytime for free transportation. **Location:** In Haapiti, west of Club Med.

$ Prices: Appetizers 400 CFP–1,200 CFP ($4–$12); main courses 1,200 CFP–1,800 CFP ($12–$18).

Open: Lunch daily 11:45am–2:15pm; dinner daily 7–10pm; bar daily 10am–midnight.

Maohi Beach is a park reserved for clients of this bar and restaurant, both under a thatch pavilion beside the lagoon. Guests can eat inside or at waterside picnic tables under cabanas. Steaks and seafood are grilled and served either plain or with traditional French sauces. The house specialty is *paru,* a deep-sea fish cooked in paper. An earth-oven feast at noon Sunday is followed by Tahitian dancing; cost is 3,300 CFP ($33) per person. Free transportation is provided from Haapiti hotels and campgrounds upon reservation.

RESTAURANT LES TIPANIERS, Haapiti. Tel. 56-12-67.

Cuisine: FRENCH/ITALIAN. **Reservations:** Recommended. **Location:** At entrance to Résidence Les Tipaniers, just east of Club Med.

$ Prices: Appetizers 400 CFP–1,300 CFP ($4–$13); pasta and pizza 1,000 CFP ($10); main courses 1,400 CFP–1,900 CFP ($14–$19). AE, DC, MC, V.

Open: Dinner Wed–Mon 6:30–9:30pm.

Although this excellent restaurant is in a hotel, I'm including it here because it's popular with guests at the other establishments as well as with Moorea's permanent residents. Most people come here for pizzas with a variety of toppings. And when owner Ione Chiari is on the island (usually from April to November), everyone orders her homemade spaghetti, lasagne, and fettuccine served with bolognese, carbonara, or napoletana sauce. Year-round features include fine traditional French dishes, such as pepper steak, fondue bourguignonne, and filets of mahi mahi in pepper sauce or spiced butter.

SNACK BARS

LA CREPERIE, Cook's Bay. Tel. 56-12-06.

Cuisine: SNACK BAR/CREPES/WAFFLES. **Location:** Cook's Bay near Club Bali Hai.

$ Prices: Crêpes and waffles 120 CFP–400 CFP ($1.20–$4); sandwiches, burgers, fried chicken, omelets, and steaks 250 CFP–900 CFP ($2.50–$9). No credit cards.

Open: Tues–Sun 8am–5pm.

Patrick and Maïté Bretault's clean little establishment specializes in sweet crêpes and waffles for breakfast. At lunch time, the crêpes come filled with eggs, curry, cheese, ham, or other stuffings. They also serve sandwiches, burgers, omelets, and steak with french fries.

LE SYLESIE PATISSERIE, Cook's Bay. Tel. 56-15-18.

Cuisine: PATISSERIE. **Location:** 1km (.6 mile) north of Club Bali Hai in Cook's Bay.

$ **Prices:** Quiches, pizzas, croissant sandwiches, and omelets 350 CFP–500 CFP ($3.50–$5). No credit cards.

Open: Daily 6:30am–noon, Tues–Sun 2–6pm.

This little shop has an excellent selection of pastries, pizzas, salads, omelets, ice cream, sundaes, and other goodies. Try the croissants with ham and cheese fillings. There are few tables on a patio where you can have breakfast, but note that the place is not open for lunch.

LE SYLESIE PATISSERIE II, Haapiti. No phone.

Cuisine: PATISSERIE. **Location:** West of Club Med in Haapiti.

$ **Prices:** Quiches, pizzas, croissant sandwiches, and omelets 350 CFP–500 CFP ($3.50–$5). No credit cards.

Open: Tues–Sun 6:45am–noon and 2–6pm.

This little shop serves the same croissants-and-coffee breakfasts on the northwest coast as does its companion institution in Cook's Bay (see above). The low-slung building has a few tables under cover in front, but it's primarily a take-out establishment.

SNACK MICHEL, Haapiti. No phone.

Cuisine: SNACK BAR. **Location:** Walking distance west of Club Med in Haapiti.

$ **Prices:** Meals 600 CFP–700 CFP ($6–$7). No credit cards.

Open: Wed–Mon 8am–7pm.

This clean little establishment near Haapiti's campgrounds is run by Swiss-born Michel and his Tahiti-born wife, Julienne. They offer sandwiches, burgers, and daily specials at reasonable prices. I am particularly fond of their ragoût of beef, a filling stew served over rice. Eat inside or outside.

SNACK ROTUI, Cook's Bay. No phone.

Cuisine: SNACK BAR. **Location:** Near the bridge in Pao Pao.

$ **Prices:** Sandwiches 150 CFP ($1.50); plate lunches 500 CFP ($5). No credit cards.

Open: Tues–Sun 7am–6pm.

Located on the shore of Cook's Bay, this is run by a Chinese family, and for 300 CFP ($3) you can get a casse-croûte sandwich, a soft drink, and a slice of delicious homemade cake topped with chocolate pudding. Daily plate lunches, usually a Chinese dish with rice, are prepared earlier in the day and served without refrigeration. A few tables under a roof beside the beach catch the breezes off the bay.

SNACK TE HONU ITI, Cook's Bay. Tel. 56-19-84.

Cuisine: SNACK BAR. **Location:** Just north of Pao Pao on east side of Cook's Bay.

$ **Prices:** Plat du jour 1,200 CFP ($12); sandwiches 300 CFP ($3); breakfast 400 CFP ($4). No credit cards.

Open: Tues–Sun 8am–5pm.

"The Little Turtle," next to the Heimata Boutique near the old wharf in Pao Pao, offers a selection of burgers, sandwiches, salads, poisson cru, ice cream, cakes, and a daily homemade Tahitian-style special. The hamburgers are delicious. The plat du jour sometimes includes steak in green-pepper sauce. Tables beside the bay make for pleasant midday dining.

EVENING ENTERTAINMENT

Unfortunately the One Chicken Inn, Moorea's version of Quinn's infamous Tahitian-style bar in Papeete, closed several years ago. Since then, no one has gone to Moorea just for its nightlife. The island's evening entertainment now is limited to activities at the hotels. Since they were covered above in the "Where to Stay" section, I will merely recap here.

Remember that these schedules change, so do your detective work. Call the hotels before striking out.

Club Méditerranée (tel. 56.14.09) has nightly skits, floor shows, and other entertainments for its guests. When business is slow, it may open its doors to outsiders and charge them about 5,000 CFP ($50) per person for dinner, wine, and the show.

Hotel Sofitel la Ora (tel. 56.12.90) has Tahitian dance shows at 8pm several nights a week (Tuesday, Thursday, and Saturday during my recent visit). The meal costs about 4,500 CFP ($45), but you can get a drink in the bar and watch the dancers.

Tiki Theatre Village (tel. 56.18.97), when enough visitors are on hand, stages an authentic feast and dance show, including transfer to the village by canoe. Admission, transfers, meal, and show usually cost about 5,000 CFP ($50) per person.

Moorea Beachcomber Parkroyal (tel. 56.19.19) has a barbecue and Tahitian dance show once a week, usually on Wednesday evening for 2,600 CFP ($26) a head and a dinner-dance on Saturday for 5,100 CFP ($51).

Hotel Moorea Village (tel. 56.10.02) has a barbecue with a pareu fashion show Saturday at 7:30pm.

Club Bali Hai (tel. 56.13.68) has a very popular happy hour Tuesday and Friday from 6 to 7pm; most of the island's English-speaking expatriate residents show up to take advantage of half-price drinks.

2. BORA BORA

As you arrive, you'll appreciate why James A. Michener called this half-atoll/half-mountain the world's most beautiful island. Lying 143 miles northwest of Tahiti in the Leeward Islands, which include Huahine, Raiatea, Tahaa, Maupiti, and several smaller dots of land, Bora Bora is one of those middle-aged islands that consist of a high center completely surrounded by a lagoon enclosed by coral reef. What makes it so beautiful is the combination of sand-fringed motus sitting on the outer reef, the multihued lagoon cutting deep bays into the central high island, and the basaltic tombstone known as Mount Otemanu towering over it all.

Be first to board the plane if you fly to Bora Bora, for all this will be visible from the left side of the aircraft as you fly up from Papeete and descend to the island's airport on Motu Mute, a flat island on the northern edge of the barrier reef. Beyond Motu Mute the lagoon turns deep blue because it's deep—deep enough for the U.S. Navy to have used Bora Bora as a way station during World War II. The airstrip you land on is another legacy of that war, built by the U.S. Navy as part of Operation Bobcat, during which 6,000 American sailors and soldiers were stationed on this tiny island. Bora Bora never saw combat during World War II, but it was a major refueling base on the America-to-Australia supply line.

You'll get to see the lagoon close up soon after landing, for all passengers are ferried across it from the airport to **Vaitape,** the main village on the west coast, sitting opposite Teavanui Pass, the only entrance through the reef into the lagoon.

As is the case on Tahiti and Moorea, a road runs around the shoreline of Bora Bora, cutting in and out of the bays and skirting what seem like a thousand white-sand beaches lapped by the waters of the lagoon. The best of the beaches—in fact, one of the best in French Polynesia—stretches for more than 2 miles around a flat, coconut-studded peninsula known as Matira Point.

The island is so small that the road around it covers only 17 miles from start to finish. All the 3,500 or so Bora Borans live on a flat coastal strip that quickly gives way to the mountainous interior. The highest point on the island is the unusual slab, **Mount Otemanu** (2,379 ft.), Bora Bora's trademark. Next to it is the more normal **Mount Pahia** (2,165 ft.). These two mountains never quite seem the same from any two different viewpoints. Mount Otemanu can look like a tombstone from one direction, a needle from another. Because these mountains are relatively low, Bora Bora doesn't get as much rain as the taller Tahiti, Moorea, or Raiatea. Water shortages can occur, especially during the drier months from June through September (consequently, most hotels have their own desalinization facilities).

GETTING THERE

Air Tahiti has at least one flight a day from Papeete, but the connections from Huahine and Raiatea are less frequent. Originally built by the Americans during World War II, Bora Bora's airport is on a motu. Unless they are picked up by a hotel boat, all passengers take a launch to Vaitape, where they then board buses for the hotels.

The Air Tahiti office is in the white building adjacent to the wharf in Vaitape (tel. 67.70.35). It is open from 7:30 to 11:30am and from 1 to 5pm Monday to Friday, from 8 to 11am on Saturday.

The *Raromatai Ferry* and the interisland freighters land about 2 miles north of Viatape at the entrance to Faanui Bay, not at Vaitape.

See "Getting Around French Polynesia" in Chapter 3 for details.

GETTING AROUND

There is no public transportation system on Bora Bora. The larger hotels provide **le truck** service for their guests to get to town and back, but the frequency can vary depending on how many tourists are on the island. Some restaurants will pick up dinner guests who call for reservations.

Two companies rent cars, scooters, and bicycles. The larger of the two is **Maeva Locations** (tel. 67.76.78), whose office is about a mile north of Vaitape (it may move when the Club Med relocates). It also has a small booth across the main road from the wharf in Vaitape. Small French cars rent from 4,500 CFP ($45) for 2 hours to 7,500 CFP ($75) for 24 hours, including insurance and unlimited kilometers. Automatic-shift Peugeot scooters, which look like something out of a *Star Wars* movie, range from 3,000 CFP ($30) for 2 hours to 4,500 CFP ($45) for 24 hours, including insurance, unlimited kilometers, and gasoline. Bicycles cost from 500 CFP ($5) for 2 hours to 1,500 CFP ($15) for 8 hours. *Credit cards are not accepted, so bring cash.* Your driver's license will be kept as a security deposit on both car and scooter rentals (if you're stopped by the police, show them your rental receipt). Maeva Locations is open daily from 7am to 7:30pm.

Bora Bora Car Rentals (tel. 67.70.03) has an office in Vaitape south of the village wharf, plus a booth that doubles as a snack bar across from the Vaitape wharf. Its prices are the same as at Maeva Locations. It is open from 8am to noon and from 2 to 6pm every day.

The 17-mile-long road around Bora Bora is paved for only about two-thirds of the way. Most of it is flat, but be very cautious on the steep hill on the east side of the island. Also watch out for pedestrians and dogs; always drive or ride slowly and carefully.

FAST FACTS: BORA BORA

Currency Exchange Banks are located in Vaitape; each has its own business hours but all are open Mon–Fri 8–11am and 2–4pm. Banque Socredo is north of the wharf behind the basketball court.

Doctor An infirmary (tel. 67.70.77) and a doctor are available in Vaitape, but consult your hotel staff if you have a problem.

Drugstores A pharmacy north of the town wharf in Vaitape is open Mon–Fri 8–11:30am and 3:30–6pm, Sat 8–11:30am and 5:30–6pm, and Sun 9–9:30am.

Information The Bora Bora Tourism Committee (tel. 67.70.10) has an office in the large building on the north side of Vaitape wharf. Hours are Mon–Sat 8–11am and 1:30–4:30pm. The address is B.P. 144, Vaitape, Bora Bora.

Police The telephone number of the gendarmerie is 67.70.58.

Post Office The post office in Vaitape is open Mon 8am–3pm, Tues–Fri 7am–3pm, and Sat 7–9am.

WHAT TO SEE & DO

SIGHTSEEING

✪ A **tour** around Bora Bora is a must on every visitor's schedule. Since the island is only 17 miles around, many visitors do it on bicycle (give yourself 4 hours), by scooter, by car, or by an organized tour. Either way, don't miss a tour of this incredibly beautiful island. Here's what you'll see.

Touring the Island

AROUND THE ISLAND Begin at the wharf in **Vaitape,** where there's a monument to French yachtsman Alain Gerbault, who sailed his boat around the world between 1923 and 1929 and lived to write about it (thus adding to Bora Bora's fame); then head south (counterclockwise) around the island.

You will soon pass a weathered clapboard mansion sitting behind two thatch buildings on the mountain side of the road; this was built as a replica of the governor's residence at Pago Pago for the movie *Hurricane* in 1977. The road then curves along the shore of **Povai Bay,** where Mounts Otemanu and Pahia tower over you. Take your time along this bay; the views are the best on Bora Bora. When you reach the area around Bloody Mary's Restaurant and Bar, stop for a look back across the water at **Mount Otemanu.**

The road climbs the small headland at the Hotel Bora Bora on **Raititi Point,** then runs smoothly along curving **Matira Beach.** Some of the best snorkeling in French Polynesia is just off the end of the beach closest to the hotel. When the road curves sharply to the left, look for a narrow paved road to the right. This leads to **Matira Point,** the low, sandy, coconut-studded peninsula that extends out from Bora Bora's south end. Down this track about 50 yards is a **public beach** on the west side of the peninsula opposite Hotel Moana Beach. The lagoon is shallow all the way out to the reef at this point, but the bottom is smooth and sandy. When I first came to Bora Bora in 1977, I camped a week on Matira Point; the Moana is only one of many structures in what was then a deserted coconut grove completely surrounded by unspoiled beach.

Up the east coast you'll pass the Beach Club Bora Bora and Sofitel Marara hotels and the construction site for a new Club Méditerranée, then a long stretch of coconut plantations before entering **Anau,** a typical Polynesian village with a large church, a general store, and tin-roofed houses crouched along the road. The east-coast road beyond Anau is unpaved and can be treacherous, especially on the steep hill north of the village (get off and walk your bicycle over it, or go very slowly if on a scooter). A trail cuts off to the right just before the hill and goes to the **Aehautai Marae,** one of several old temples on Bora Bora. This particular one has a great view of Mount Otemanu and the blue outlines of Raiatea and Tahaa islands beyond the motus on the reef.

Except for a few native homes and the Revatua Club (tel. 67.71.67), which makes an excellent refueling stop, the northwest coast is deserted. Here you ride through several miles of coconut plantations pockmarked by thousands of holes made by the land crabs known as *tupas.* After rounding the northernmost point, you soon pass a group of over-the-water bungalows and another group of houses, which climb the hill. Some of these are condominiums; the others are part of defunct project that was to have been a Hyatt resort. Across the lagoon are Motu Mute and the airport.

Faanui Bay was used during World War II as an Allied naval base, and you'll pass the remains of a wharf and seaplane ramp built by the U.S. Navy on the north side of the bay. Farther along beside the road is the **Fareopu Marae,** which has petroglyphs of turtles, considered sacred in ancient Polynesia, carved on some of its stones. A road cuts off into the **Faanui valley,** from which an unmarked hiking trail leads over the saddle to Bora Bora's east coast.

Just beyond the main shipping wharf at the point on the south side of Faanui Bay is the restored **Marotetini Marae.** In his novel *Hawaii,* James Michener had his fictional Polynesians leave this point to discover and settle the Hawaiian Islands. Nearby are tombs in which members of Bora Bora's former royal family are buried. If you look offshore at this point, you'll see the only pass into the lagoon; a path up to two of the American guns that guarded it begins near the Club Med. Ask around for directions.

Near the end of your round-island tour you will pass **Magasin Chin Lee,** Bora Bora's largest general store and grocery and a major gathering place for local residents. It's the best place to put together a picnic lunch or just have a soft drink or, if you've been riding a bike, a cold bottle of Eau Royale.

ORGANIZED TOURS If you want a guide to fill you in on local legends, join **Otemanu Tours** (tel. 67.70.49) for a trip around the island. It costs 1,800 CFP ($18) per person and usually last from 2 to 4:30pm (it could be longer if the group is interested enough to ask questions). Not only will you see the scenery, you'll be told of local history and traditions and shown how flowers and fruits are grown. The tour stops at boutiques along the way for the spending of money.

LAGOON TOURS Bora Bora has one of the world's most beautiful lagoons, and getting out on it, snorkeling and swimming in it, and visiting the islands on its outer edge is an absolute must. Invariably the excursions take in ✪ **Lagoonarium,** a fenced-in area just off one of the motus out on the reef's edge. Willing guests are put overboard in snorkeling gear to be pushed by the current along the fence. On the other side swim schools of tropical sea life, including black-tipped reef sharks. You can even hitch a ride on an anything-but-harmless–looking manta ray.

Your hotel or pension can recommend one of several guides for lagoon trips. Some ½-day excursions cost as little as 1,000 CFP ($10) per person; if you take one of these, be sure to bring along a bottle of Eau Royale water to drink. Others cost 2,000 CFP ($20) and include refreshments. At the top end, the **Blue Lagoon Restaurant** (tel. 67.70.54) has two tours. One takes all day and includes a stop on a deserted island for a scrumptious lunch, including wine to calm your nerves after the manta-ray ride. This trip follows the lagoon all the way around the island and costs 5,000 CFP ($50) a head. A shorter, 3-hour version is good value at 2,700 CFP ($27) per person. **Teremoana** (tel. 67.71.38) at Chez Nono pension has an all-day boat tour including lunch on a motu for 4,000 CFP ($40) per person.

Divers can swim among the coral heads, sharks, and fishes with two scuba operators: **Moana Aventure Tours** (tel. 67.70.28) at the Hotel Bora Bora's activities desk, and **Nirvana Dive** (tel. 67.71.16) at Beach Club Bora Bora. The former is operated by photographer Erwin Christian. Expect to pay at least 6,000 CFP ($60) for a one-tank dive.

Another way to see the lagoon is on ***Vehia,*** a 46-foot catamaran owned and skippered by American expatriate Richard Postma. The name *Vehia* comes from a legendary woman surfer who defeated her much stronger male competitors in a royal match; one of the last Polynesian families to oppose French rule symbolically took the name. *Vehia* is docked at the Hotel Bora Bora, goes on picnic cruises 3 days a week and sunset cruises on the other days. The all-day picnic cruise costs 6,500 CFP ($65) per person; the sunset cruise is 2,500 CFP ($25) per person. Reservations can be made at the Hotel Bora Bora's activities desk (tel. 67.76.62) or by calling Richard direct (tel. 67.70.79).

BORA BORA

N 0 2.5 km 1.5 mi

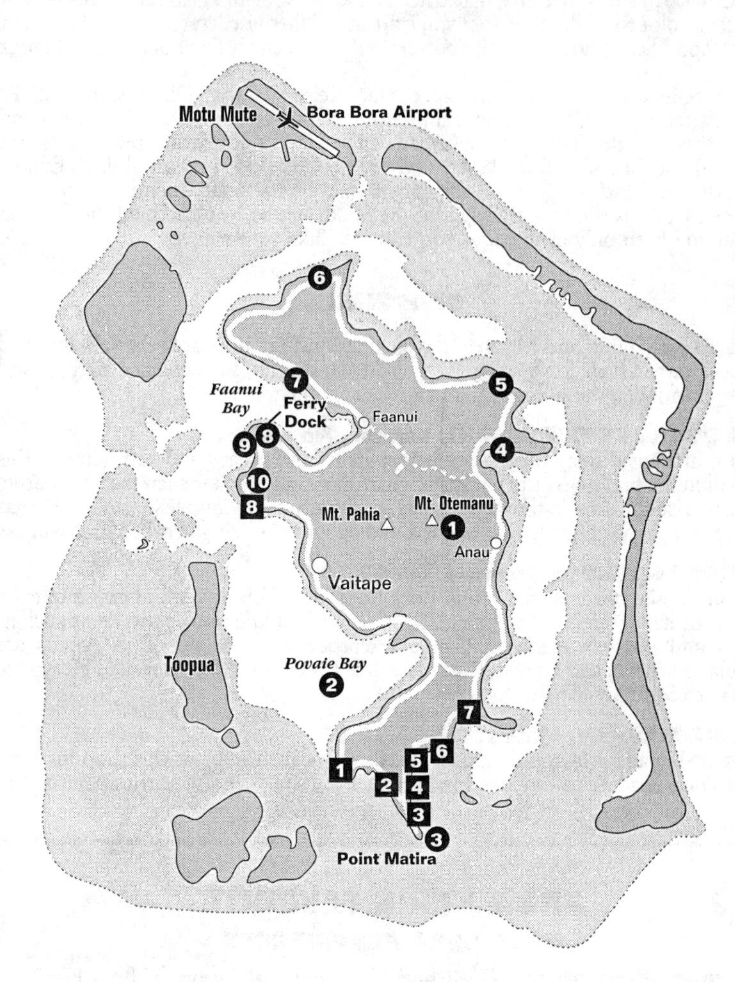

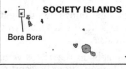

SOCIETY ISLANDS

Bora Bora

ACCOMMODATIONS:

- Beach Club Bora Bora 5
- Chez Pauline 4
- Club Med (old site) 8
- Club Med (new site) 7
- Hotel Bora Bora 1
- Hotel Matira 2
- Hotel Moana Beach 3
- Sofitel Marara 6

ATTRACTIONS:

- Aehautai Marae 4
- Mareotetini Marae 8
- Matira Beach 3
- Mt. Otemanu 1
- Old Hyatt Site 6
- Povaie Bay 2
- Revatua Club 5
- U.S. Wharf 7
- U.S. Guns 10
- Yacht Club 9

You can rent your own motorboat from **Southern Cruises** (tel. 67.74.45) for 7,000 CFP ($70) a day, but take my advice and know something about the relation of the water's color to its depth before you start out. Otherwise, you may run the risk of hitting a coral head and tearing the bottom out of the craft. The boats can hold four persons.

For excellent deep-sea game fishing, contact Keith "Taaroa" Olson, skipper of ***Te Aratai II*** (tel. 67.71.96). An American, Keith has lived on Bora Bora since 1968 and supplies much of the fresh fish consumed at the island's hotels and restaurants. He charges 40,000 CPF ($400) for ½ day and 55,000 CFP ($550) for a full day's fishing. Note that the *Wind Song* cruise ship often charters the boat when it's in port, so inquire early. As is the case throughout the South Pacific, you catch all the fish you can, but you keep only as much as you can eat. Take your camera.

SHOPPING

Compared with Tahiti and Moorea, the pickings on Bora Bora are relatively slim and the prices rather high for black pearls, most handcrafts, silk-screened pareus, and clothing. However, the following are worth examining.

BORA BORA I TE FANAU TAHI, Vaitape. No phone.

Local artisans display their straw hats, pareus, and other handcraft items in this large hall in the buildings at the Vaitape wharf. It's always open when the *Wind Song* or other cruise ships are in the lagoon. The local tourism committee (tel. 67.70.10) has its offices on the waterfront side of the building and can tell you when that will be.

BOUTIQUE GAUGUIN, Nuunue. Tel. 67.76.67.

About a mile north of the Hotel Bora Bora, this shop in a white house offers a selection of handcrafts, clothing, and black pearls in addition to curio items such as ashtrays and coasters featuring Gauguin reproductions. Some of its pareus are particularly artistic, and its handbags made like tivaivai quilts are unusual. Hours are Monday to Saturday 8:30am to 6pm.

GALERIE MASSON, Matira. Tel. 67.72.04

Rosine Temauri Masson designs and sells tropical clothing at this shop just past Matira Point heading toward the Hotel Sofitel Marara. She also carries paintings of

FROMMER'S FAVORITE
BORA BORA EXPERIENCES

Lagoon Excursions With both deep and shallow water, Bora Bora's lagoon is one of the most varied in the world, and a boat trip with swimming and snorkeling should not be missed. The Lagoonarium is a bit touristy, but at least it guarantees you will see plenty of sea life.

Snorkeling Some of the Hotel Bora Bora's over-water bungalows sit right on the edge of a reef face that drops precipitously to dark depths. It's like flying when you snorkel from the shallow reef out over the cliff.

Sunset Cruise Some of my most vivid photographs in the 1970s were taken of sunsets at Bora Bora while anchored in the lagoon. Now I recapture those gorgeous sundown colors from the deck of Richard Postma's *Vehia*.

Bike Riding There's no better way to see Bora Bora than to ride around it on a bicycle. I halt where I want for as long as I want; with the big tombstone central peak and incredible lagoon offering such spectacular views, I stop often just to have a look.

island scenes by herself and her late husband, Jean Masson. Her business hours can be irregular, so call ahead.

MARTINE CREATIONS, Matira. Tel. 67.70.79.

Martine Postma, wife of sailor Richard Postma, designs her own hand-painted clothing, which she sells in a neocolonial house just south of the Hotel Bora Bora. She also carries a good selection of quality black pearls. Open Monday to Saturday 8am to 5pm.

MOANA ARTS, Matira. Tel. 67.70.33.

Noted photographer Erwin Christian owns this boutique virtually next door to the Hotel Bora Bora. You will see his spectacular photographs in numerous books and on many postcards, and here you can buy some of his most dramatic works mounted and framed. If he's there, he'll autograph them for you. Open Monday to Saturday 9am to noon and 2 to 6pm.

POKALOLA BOUTIQUE, Vaitape. Tel. 67.71.82.

Yves Bastien's shop over Bora Bora Burger in Vaitape has the island's largest selection of T-shirts, pareus, tropical clothing, wood carvings, black pearls, shell jewelry, and curios such as Hinano beer glasses. Stop in on your visit to Vaitape. Open Monday to Saturday 8am to 6pm.

WHERE TO STAY

Bora Bora has a fairly wide range of well-established, quality hotels. Most share the beach around Matira Point.

EXPENSIVE

HOTEL BORA BORA, B.P. 1, Bora Bora. Tel. 67.70.28, 45.10.45 in Papeete for reservations, or toll free 800/262-4220 in California, 800/421-1490 elsewhere in North America. Fax 67.74.38. 80 bungalows. MINIBAR **Location:** 4.4 miles from Vaitape on island's southwest point.

$ Rates: 27,500 CFP ($275) garden single or double; 34,125 CFP ($341) beachside single or double; 41,000 CFP–47,250 CFP ($410–$472) overwater single or double. May be less if booked and paid in advance in U.S. dollars. AE, DC, MC, V.

Guests pay a steep price to stay here, but this is in some respects the finest hotel in the South Pacific. The central building of this American-managed establishment sits atop a low headland with comfortable Tahitian-style bungalows among the palm trees on the flat shoreline on either side. On the north, 15 of them are set on pilings over the reef, some actually perched right on the edge where the reef gives way to deep blue water; many of them have views of Mount Otemanu across Povai Bay. To the south of the main building begins magnificent Matira Beach, whose coral gardens provide some of the best snorkeling in French Polynesia. The entire complex faces west, so the sunsets over Motu Toopua, a hilly remnant of Bora Bora on the other side of the lagoon, can be gorgeous.

The roomy bungalows all have roofs of heavy thatch that sweep down low over the sides, providing ample protection for the windows and front porches from occasional wind and rain. There is a boutique on the main level, with prices that can be almost twice those on Tahiti or Moorea. A shop across the road from the hotel resembles a 7-Eleven back home.

Dining/Entertainment: The hotel's restaurant, on the upper level of the main building, overlooks the lagoon on three sides. You can have your lunch brought to a pool- and beachside bar just below the restaurant. A bar adjoins the restaurant, and Tahitians strum their guitars and sing there every evening, when a dress code (no shorts, tank tops, or shower sandals) is in effect. Traditional dance shows occur at least 2 nights a week.

Services: Laundry, baby-sitting, twice-daily shuttle to Vaitape, afternoon tea.

Facilities: Swimming pool, tennis courts, water sports including scuba diving, bicycles, boutique, TV and video lounge, activities and car-rental desks.

HOTEL MOANA BEACH, B.P. 156, Vaitape, Bora Bora. Tel. 67.73.73, or toll free 800/346-6262 in the U.S.; 800/387-8842 in Canada. Fax 67.71.41. Telex 445. 40 bungalows. MINIBAR TEL **Location:** Matira Point.

$ Rates: 36,800 CFP ($368) single or double; 49,800 CFP ($498) overwater single or double. May be less if booked and paid in advance in U.S. dollars. AE, DC, MC, V.

This is the newest addition to the island's pricey over-the-water establishments. Its bungalows—30 of them linked by a pier that meanders over the reef—have exquisitely crafted interiors. You can remove the top of a glass coffee table and actually feed the fish swimming in the turquoise lagoon below. A Japanese-style sliding wall separates the king-size bed from the lounge area, the bath has two sinks and an American-size tub (a rarity in French Polynesia), and you can sunbathe in the buff on a private deck with steps leading down to the lagoon. Bedside tables have built-in stereo tape players. Ashore on Point Matira peninsula, four thatch-roofed buildings surround a small courtyard and house reception, a lounge complete with a TV equipped to play any type of videotape, and the bar and restaurant.

Dining/Entertainment: The airy, beachside dining room offers very fine French selections with emphasis on seafood. Complete meals cost 1,800 CFP ($18) for a full breakfast, 2,000 CFP ($20) for a set-menu lunch, and 3,700 CFP ($37) for a set dinner, 4,500 CFP ($45) if you order à la carte. If you want to eat in your bungalow, your food will be delivered by canoe-borne room service. A Tahitian string band entertains every evening.

Services: Laundry, baby-sitting, room service by canoe.

Facilities: Swimming pool, water sports including scuba diving and waterskiing, activities and car-rental desks, TV-video lounge, boutique.

SOFITEL MARARA BORA BORA, B.P. 6, Bora Bora. Tel. 67.70.46, 41.04.04 in Papeete, or toll free 800/763-4835 in the U.S. Fax 67.74.03. Telex 214. 64 bungalows. MINIBAR TEL **Location:** North of Matira Point on east side.

$ Rates: 23,400 CFP ($234) single, 25,400 CFP ($254) double garden; 32,400 CFP ($324) single, 34,100 CFP ($341) double beachside; 41,200 CFP ($412) single, 43,200 CFP ($432) double overwater. AE, DC, MC, V.

Known locally as "The Marara," this well-managed, French-owned hotel was built in 1977 by Italian movie producer Dino De Laurentis to house the crew working on his box-office bomb *Hurricane*. It has 64 oval bungalows facing a curving beach of white sand, the lagoon, and Raiatea and Tahaa on the horizon. A long pier joins 21 over-the-water bungalows to the shore. Just outside the restaurant is a swimming pool sunken into a deck built out over the beach and lagoon.

Dining/Entertainment: The central building houses La Pérouse Restaurant, open on three sides to the lagoon, where French and Chinese cuisines reign. Dinner is served buffet-style several nights a week. The bar fronts a fascinating wall inlaid with layers of shaved mother-of-pearl. Evening entertainment features a Tahitian string band every night. A traditional dance show is held once a week, usually Saturday evening when a buffet featuring earth-oven foods costs about 4,500 CFP ($45).

Services: Laundry, baby-sitting, shuttle bus to Vaitape.

Facilities: Swimming pool; water sports, including Windsurfers; tennis courts; boutique; activities and car-rental desks.

MODERATE

BEACH CLUB BORA BORA, B.P. 252, Bora Bora. Tel. 67.71.16, 43.08.29 in Papeete. Fax 41.09.28. Telex 428. 36 rms. A/C **Location:** North of Matira Point on east side.

$ Rates: 13,000 CFP ($130) beachside single, 15,000 CFP ($150) beachside double; 11,000 CFP ($110) mountainside single, 13,000 CFP ($130) mountainside double. Add 4,000 CFP–5,000 CFP ($40–$50) for air conditioning. AE, DC, MC, V.

Originally an Ibis hotel but now locally managed, this property had begun to show need of refurbishment when I was last there. Nevertheless, it is a short stroll along the beach to the Hotel Sofitel Marara. Nine bungalows each hold four hotel-style rooms, each of which has a private terrace. Twenty of the rooms are in a coconut grove next to the central building, which houses a restaurant and bar next to the beach. The other 16 rooms are across the road and are classified as "mountain view."

Burgers, sandwiches, omelets, salads, and steaks with french fries are served all day at the bar in the U-shaped central building. The restaurant on the other side of the building features French and Italian cuisine for dinner. The hotel provides water-sports equipment, and a scuba-dive operation is on the premises.

HOTEL MATIRA, B.P. 31, Bora Bora. Tel. 67.70.51. 28 bungalows. **Location:** Matira Point.

$ Rates: 9,000 CFP ($90) single, 10,500 CFP ($105) double without kitchenette or mountain side with kitchenette; 9,900 CFP ($99) single, 12,600 CFP ($126) double beachside with kitchenette. Airport transfers cost extra. AE, V.

The reception desk is just inside Matira Restaurant and Bar, but basically what you get here is your own bungalow and chamber service once a day but little else in the way of hotel service or amenities. All have thatch roofs, porches on the front, baths with showers, and a double bed or two singles. Some also have kitchenettes. About half are on Matira Point, while the others are about 500 yards away, across the road from the restaurant.

CLUB MEDITERRANEE, B.P. 575, Papeete, Tahiti. Tel. 67.70.57, 42.96.99 in Papeete, or toll free 800/528-3100 in the U.S. Fax 42.16.83. Telex 256. 57 rms. **Location:** 1 mile north of Vaitape.

$ Rates (including meals): 13,000 CFP ($130) double per person. AE, DC, MC, V.

Sometimes still referred to as the Hotel Noa Noa, this establishment should be replaced in 1992 or early 1993 by a much larger and more appealing facility north of the Hotel Sofitel Marara on Bora Bora's east coast. In the meantime, the old Club has several tons of sand behind a stone breakwater to make up for its lack of a natural beach. Guests can do their serious beaching during trips to a small, uninhabited motu near the entrance to the lagoon. Of its 57 rooms, 36 are in duplex bungalows that extend out over the reef and have over-the-water porches. Six more bungalows sit on a small island connected to the complex by a footbridge. As at all Club Meds, one price pays for the room and three hearty meals a day (with wine at lunch and dinner), in this case served family-style in a central bar-lounge-dining room beside the lagoon. Evening entertainment consists of floor shows and skits, plus a Tahitian dance show 2 nights a week. Nonguests can come for dinner and the show for about 4,500 CFP ($45) a head. Many guests divide their time between the clubs on Bora Bora and Moorea.

BUDGET

CHEZ NOEL "NONO" LEVERD, B.P. 282, Bora Bora. Tel. 67.71.38. 6 rms, 2 bungalows, 1 apartment. **Location:** Matira Point. Take the paved road past Hotel Moana Beach to a small sign on the right.

$ Rates: 3,000 CFP ($30) single, 5,000 CFP ($50) double; 4,000 CFP ($40) single, 6,000 CFP ($60) double bungalow or apartment. No credit cards.

The Leverd family's pension-style establishment enjoys an idyllic location right on Matira Beach. Indeed, two bungalows sit almost on the sand; both have their own baths and one is big enough for four persons. The apartment has its own kitchen as well as bath. The six rooms are in a house next to the family's home; you share the bath and kitchen with your fellow guests.

CHEZ PAULINE, B.P. 217, Vaitape, Bora Bora. Tel. 67.72.16. 2 bungalows, 6 huts, 10 bunks, 20 tent sites. **Location:** North of Matira Point between Moana Beach and Sofitel Marara hotels.

$ Rates: 1,000 CFP ($10) tent site; 1,500 CFP ($15) bunk in hostel; 3,500 CFP ($35) single or double hut; 9,000 CFP ($90) single or double bungalow. No credit cards.

English-speaking Pauline Youseff and her husband spent nearly 30 years operating a small hotel in New Caledonia, but when they returned to Bora Bora in the late 1980s, she very quickly cornered a large share of the low-budget travelers arriving on her home island. The huts contain one double bed each (they resemble pup tents made of wood and covered with thatch). Occupants of the huts, hostel, and tents share communal toilets, showers, and kitchen facilities. The bungalows are self-contained. Bookings are advised.

WHERE TO DINE

EXPENSIVE

BAMBOO HOUSE, Matira. Tel. 67.76.24.

Cuisine: SEAFOOD. **Reservations:** Recommended. **Location:** About a mile north of Hotel Bora Bora.

$ **Prices:** Appetizers 500 CFP–1,200 CFP ($5–$12); main courses 1,800 CFP–2,300 CFP ($18–$23). AE, MC, V.

Open: Sun–Fri 6:30–10pm; bar Sun–Fri noon–10pm.

That's exactly what this little establishment is: a bamboo house, and a charming one at that. The entire building is made of varnished split bamboo, and lots of dried bamboo leaves are stacked or hung here and there to render a jungly effect. Japanese lanterns provide subdued lighting. Prime tables are on a small front porch. The menu depends on what seafood is caught in local waters but usually features parrot fish, tuna, and shrimp, all well prepared in French sauces. Free transportation from the hotels if reservations are made by 5pm.

BLOODY MARY'S RESTAURANT AND BAR, Matira. Tel. 67.72.86.

Cuisine: SEAFOOD. **Reservations:** Recommended. **Location:** Just around the bend north of Hotel Bora Bora.

$ **Prices:** Appetizers 900 CFP–1,100 CFP ($9–$11); main courses 2,300 CFP–2,500 CFP ($23–$25). AE, MC, V.

Open: Mon–Sat 7–9:30pm; Tupa Bar opens at 5pm.

You won't be on Bora Bora long before you hear of this place. Although some readers have commented that the quality of the food has slipped in recent years, it's worth the price of a drink to soak up the atmosphere of the building. If it looks like a stage set from a South Seas movie, it's with good reason. Polish-born Australian George von Dangel came to Bora Bora from Papeete to act in the movie *Hurricane,* and after watching the set designers do their work, he and his partners designed this restaurant to look like a South Seas building of yesteryear. A floor of fine white sand is covered by a large thatch roof from which hang ceiling fans, colored spotlights, and stalks of dried bamboo. The butcher-block tables are made of coconut-palm lumber, and the seats are sections of palm trunks cut into stools. George was running the Bamboo House (above) when I saw him recently. He sold Bloody Mary's to Americans, which explains the Californian—as opposed to Tahitian—greeting you will receive. As for the food, you order after inspecting the fresh seafood laid out on a bed of ice. It will be charbroiled and served on large round plates covered with banana leaves, with a sauce on the side if you want one. Free transportation from hotels if reservations are made by 5pm.

MODERATE

BLUE LAGOON RESTAURANT, Vaitape. Tel. 67.70.54.

Cuisine: FRENCH. **Reservations:** Recommended. **Location:** Just south of Vaitape on the lagoon.

$ **Prices:** Appetizers 850 CFP–1,200 CFP ($8.50–$12); main courses 1,200 CFP–1,800 CFP ($12–$18). AE, MC, V.

Open: Lunch daily 11:30am–2pm; dinner daily 6:30–10pm.

This charming eatery beside the lagoon specializes in paella valenciana, which you must order at least 20 minutes in advance; it costs 2,900 CFP ($29) per person. Other main courses feature steaks and seafood in various French-style sauces, such as Roquefort or pepper. The owners also operate all-day boat trips to an offshore motu, including Spanish-style picnic lunches, for 4,900 CFP ($49) per person (book a day in advance). Free transportation from hotels if reservations are made by 5pm.

MATIRA BAR AND RESTAURANT, Matira. Tel. 67-70-57.
Cuisine: CHINESE. **Reservations:** Not usually necessary. **Location:** Between Hotel Bora Bora and Matira Point.
$ Prices: Appetizers 600 CFP–1,100 CFP ($6–$11); main courses 1,100 CFP–1,500 CFP ($11–$15). AE, V.
Open: Lunch Tues–Sun 11am–1:30pm; dinner Tues–Sun 5:30–8:30pm.
This literally hangs over the beach at the Hotel Matira about a mile south of the Hotel Bora Bora and is an excellent place to have a lagoonside lunch or sunset drink before dinner. The menu offers a selection of beef, pork, chicken, duck, and seafood dishes done in the Cantonese fashion with Hakka overtones.

BUDGET

BORA BORA BURGERS, Vaitape. No phone.
Cuisine: FAST FOOD. **Location:** Next to the post office in Vaitape.
$ Prices: Meals 350 CFP–650 CFP ($3.50–$6.50). No credit cards.
Open: Mon–Sat 7:30am–5pm.
This is a fast-food bar with coconut-palm trunks as stools and a few tables on the sidewalk. The reasonably priced sandwiches, burgers, and hot dogs make this one of Bora Bora's few real food bargains. It calls itself the "3B."

CHEZ BEN'S, Matira. Tel. 67.74.54.
Cuisine: SNACK BAR. **Location:** Between Hotel Bora Bora and Matira.
$ Prices: Sandwiches, salads, and pizzas 300 CFP–950 CFP ($3–$9.50); meals 900 CFP–1,500 CFP ($9–$15). No credit cards.
Open: Daily 11am–8pm.
Bora Bora–born Ben Teraitepo and his Oklahoma-born wife, Robin, hold fort just across the road from a shady portion of Matira Beach. They serve sandwiches, poisson cru, pizzas, and lasagne. Robin's tuna-salad sandwiches are delicious. Ben's mother, who lived 20 years in Hawaii, makes colorful pareus, which they sell for 1,000 CFP ($10), another bargain on Bora Bora.

LA TABLE DU MANDARIN, Matira. No phone.
Cuisine: VIETNAMESE/CHINESE. **Location:** Matira near Beach Club Bora Bora.
$ Prices: Main courses 800 CFP–900 CFP ($8–$9). No credit cards.
Open: Daily noon–5pm.
A cross between a carry-out and a restaurant, this tiny little establishment prepares tasty meals in the Saigon style of Vietnamese cooking and Cantonese version of Chinese. Customers often gather around the lone table even when they don't know each other; if there's no room, you can order to carry out.

EVENING ENTERTAINMENT

Like Moorea, things are quiet on Bora Bora after dark. You may want to listen to a Tahitian band playing at sunset or watch the furious hips of a Tahitian dance show. If so, you will be limited to whatever is going at Hotel Bora Bora (tel. 67.70.28), Hotel Sofitel Marara (tel. 67.70.46), and Club Méditerranée (tel. 67.70.57). See "Bora Bora: Where to Stay" for their general entertainment schemes. Remember that schedules change; call ahead.

La Récife Discothèque (no phone), about 2 miles north of Vaitape, is the island's one nightclub, and it opens only on Friday and Saturday at 11pm (that's right, 11pm) and closes sometime around dawn the following mornings. The clientele is mostly Tahitians between 18 and 24 years old, and fights have been known to break out at that late hour. Admission is 500 CFP ($5). Beers cost about 700 CFP ($7) each.

3. HUAHINE

The first of the Leeward group of islands you come to from Tahiti, mountainous Huahine is notable for its serrated coastline, long beaches, ancient marae, picturesque main town, and independent-spirited residents.

About 106 miles northwest of Papeete, Huahine (pronounced Wa-*ee*-nee by the French, who-a-*hee*-nay by the Tahitians) is actually two islands enclosed by the same reef and joined by a bridge. About 4,000 people live on the two islands, and most of them earn a living growing cantaloupes and watermelons and harvesting copra for the Papeete market. Huahine was not annexed by France until 1897—more than 50 years after Tahiti was taken over—and its people are still independent in spirit. Pouvanaa a Oopa, the great leader of French Polynesia's independence movement, was born on Huahine. At the time the first Europeans arrived, Huahine was governed as a single chiefdom and not divided into warring tribes as were the other islands, and this spirit of unity is still strong.

The chiefs built a series of marae on the shores of Maeva Lake, which separates the north shore from a long motu on the barrier reef, and on Matairea Hill above the lakeside village of Maeva. These have been restored and are some of the most impressive in French Polynesia.

The main village of **Fare,** hardly more than a row of clapboard stores opposite a quay, is nestled alongside the lagoon on the northwest shore opposite the main pass in the reef. When the *Raromatai Ferry* and the other boats put in from Papeete, Fare comes to life before the crack of dawn—or long before. Trucks and buses arrive from all over Huahine with passengers and cargo bound for the other islands. The rest of the time, however, Fare lives at the lazy, slow pace of the South Seas of old as a few people amble down its tree-lined main street and browse through the Chinese general stores that face the town wharf.

GETTING THERE

Huahine is 40 minutes' flying time northwest of Papeete via Air Tahiti. The airport is on the north end of the island 3km (2 miles) from Fare; the terminal has a bar and what sometimes passes as a tourist information desk (it is seldom staffed, but the posters and brochures tacked to the wall give a substantial amount of information about the island).

Air Tahiti has a reservations office in Fare (tel. 68.82.89).

The *Raromatai Ferry* stops at the wharf in Fare four times a week, twice after its overnight passages from Papeete and twice on the return voyages. As I have pointed out earlier, the short trips between Huahine, Raiatea, and Bora Bora are so beautiful that they should not be missed if they can be worked into your schedule. The fare between each island is 1,000 CFP ($10).

See "Getting Around French Polynesia" in Chapter 3 for more information.

GETTING AROUND

Unless you have reserved a rental car or are willing to walk the 3km (1.8 miles) into Fare, take your hotel minibus or **Enite's Taxi** (tel. 68.82.37), apparently the only cab authorized to pick up tourists arriving by plane. The fare into Fare (no pun intended) is 300 CFP ($3), 500 CFP ($5) to the Hotel Sofitel Heiva, and 600 CFP ($6) to Relais Mahana on Huahine's south end.

Pacificar (tel. 68.81.81) and **Kake Rent-a-Car** (tel. 68.82.59) both have offices on the main road between the airport and Fare. They charge the same prices for tiny Fiat Pandas and larger cars. The little Pandas, which is all the car you will need on Huahine, cost 3,500 CFP ($35) for 4 hours, 4,500 CFP ($45) for 8 hours, and 5,500 CFP ($55) if you keep it overnight. Scooters start at 2,200 CFP ($22) for 4 hours. Add 800 CFP ($8) for insurance plus the cost of the gasoline you use. Bicycles run 600 CFP ($6) for 4 hours, 800 CFP ($8) for 8 hours, and 1,000 CFP ($10) for 24 hours.

Only part of Huahine's roadways are paved, but the rest should be in reasonably good shape—except for the *traversière,* a road that traverses the mountains from Maroe Bay to Faie Bay on the east coast. Other than during periods of heavy rain, this road is passable but is very steep and rough; travelers have been killed trying to ride bicycles down it. The island's only **gasoline stations** are in the center of Fare.

Each district has its **le truck,** which runs into Fare at least once a day, but the schedules are highly irregular. If you take one from Fare to Parea, for example, you may not be able to get back on the same day.

HUAHINE

Currency Exchange Banque Socredo is in Fare on the road that parallels the main street and bypasses the waterfront. Banque de Tahiti, Westpac, and most other businesses are along Fare's waterfront.

Doctor The government infirmary is in Fare (tel. 68.82.48).

Information The local tourism committee has a booth at the airport, but it seldom is staffed. Check the brochures and other materials posted there for information.

Police The phone number of the gendarmerie in Fare is 68.82.61.

Post Office The post office is in Fare on the bypass road. Hours are Mon–Thurs 7am–3pm, Fri 7am–2pm.

Rest Rooms The building at the wharf in Fare has public toilets. Otherwise, rely on the hotels and restaurants.

Safety Campers have reported thefts from their tents on Huahine, so don't camp.

Telegrams/Telex See "Post Office," above.

WHAT TO SEE & DO

TOURING THE MARAE

A tour of the many 16th-century **marae** near the village of Maeva can be made on your own or arranged through your hotel. Start east of Maeva village where the large, reed-sided meetinghouse sits over Maeva Lake. The stones sitting at the lake's edge and scattered through the adjacent coconut grove were family marae. More than 200 stone structures have been discovered between there and Matairea Hill, which looms over Maeva, including some 40 marae (the others were houses, paddocks, and agricultural terraces). Six marae and other structures on Matairea Hill can be reached by a trail that starts between two houses on the mountain side of the road in the village (both have concrete block walls in front; one had a yellow gate during my recent visit, the other's gate was painted black). If you can't find the trail, ask around. The track can be muddy and slippery during wet weather, and the steep climb is best done in early morning or late afternoon.

A large and easier marae to reach stands on the beach about a ½-mile across the bridge on the east end of Maeva. To find it, follow the left fork in the dirt road after crossing the bridge. The setting is impressive.

From the bridge you will see several stone fish traps, which were restored by Dr. Shinoto of the Bishop Museum in Honolulu. They work as well today as they did in the 16th century, trapping fish as the tide ebbs and flows in and out of the narrow passage separating the lake from the sea.

When construction began on the Hotel Bali Hai Huahine (see below) in 1973, workers discovered some old artifacts while excavating the lily ponds. Dr. Yoshiko H. Sinoto, the chairman of the anthropology department of the Bernice P. Bishop Museum in Honolulu and the man responsible for restoring many marae throughout

Polynesia, just happened to be on the island and took charge of further excavations. During the next 2 years the diggers uncovered adzes, fishhooks, and ornaments that had been undisturbed for more than 1,000 years, according to radiocarbon dating of a whale bone found with the other items. So far it's the earliest evidence of habitation found in the Society Islands. If the hotel has reopened, you may find some of the artifacts exhibited in a display in the public areas.

RECREATION

Horseback Riding

La Petite Ferme ("The Little Farm," tel. 68.82.98), on the main road north of Fare just before the airport turnoff, has Marquesas-bred horses that can be ridden with English or western saddles for 1,200 CFP ($12) an hour. Co Siorat and partners also organize 2- and 3-day horseback camping trips into Huahine's interior. When not riding, they produce pareus and other items for sale in a shop.

Scuba Diving

Pacific Blue Adventures (tel. 68.87.21) at the Hotel Sofitel Heiva charges 4,000 CFP ($40) for a one-tank dive, a bargain compared to 6,000 CFP ($60) on Bora Bora. The guide often feeds the sharks and pets the moray eels on their heads.

WHERE TO STAY

For many years the Hotel Bali Hai Huahine just north of Fare was the premier establishment on the island, but it was closed several years ago. Reports during my last visit indicated that a deal was in the works to sell the entire Bali Hai chain to Japanese interests, who might enlarge the Huahine version after major renovations. To see if it has reopened, call 56.13.59 on Moorea or toll free 800/282-1402 in California, 800/282-1401 in the rest of the U.S.

Campers have reported thefts from their tents on Huahine, so don't camp.

HOTEL SOFITEL HEIVA, B.P. 38, Fare, Huahine. Tel. 68.85.86, 41.04.04 in Papeete, or toll free 800/763-4835. Fax 41.05.05. Telex 214. 22 rms, 2 suites, 23 beach bungalows, 6 overwater bungalows. MINIBAR TEL **Location:** On Maeva Motu, 10km (6 miles) from airport. If driving, go over bridge at Maeva and bear right on dirt path.

$ **Rates:** 18,000 CFP ($180) single, 20,000 ($200) double room; 28,000 CFP ($280) single, 30,000 CFP ($300) double beachside bungalow; 44,000 CFP ($440) single, 46,000 CFP ($460) double overwater; 38,000 CFP ($380) single, 40,000 CFP ($400) double suite. AE, DC, MC, V.

This well-managed, luxury hotel opened in 1990 at the end of Maeva Motu where a pass lets the sea into Maeva Lake. The flat almost-island is joined to the main island by a one-lane bridge. A large, airy thatch-roofed building holds reception, dining room, and bar-lounge with glass doors opening to adult and children's swimming pools between which water pours from a giant clamshell. White-sand beaches and bungalows flank this central complex. The spacious bungalows are tastefully furnished with comfortable bamboo chairs and tables; each has sliding doors opening to a covered porch, ceiling fan, polished wooden floors, and bath with large shower. In addition, the six overwater models—joined to the shore by a curving pier—have glass panels for fish watching and balconies with steps to the lagoon. Although in long buildings, the rooms are as spacious as the bungalows.

Dining/Entertainment: The dining room, known as the Omai Restaurant in honor of the Tahitian who went to London with Capt. James Cook, specializes in French cuisine and offers abundant buffets twice a week when the staff performs traditional Tahitian dances.

Services: Laundry, baby-sitting.

Facilities: Children's and adults' swimming pools, water-sports equipment, scuba diving, double-hull canoe with glass bottom for lagoon excursions, TV-video lounge, boutique, small library.

RELAIS MAHANA, B.P. 30, Fare, Huahine. Tel. 68.81.54. Fax 68.85.08. Telex 300. 12 bungalows. **Location:** On Avera Bay near Parea on Huahine's south end, 30 minutes from airport.

$ Rates: 12,300 CFP ($123) single or double garden bungalow; 13,800 CFP ($138) single or double beach bungalow. AE, DC, MC, V.

Although it may soon grow in size, this little property has the best beach-lagoon combinations of any resort in French Polynesia. It sits right on the long white beach that stretches down a peninsula on Huahine's south end; a pier runs from the Mahana's main building right over a giant coral head around which fish and guests swim. The peninsula blocks the brunt of the southeast trade winds, so the lagoon is usually as smooth as glass. Just climb down off the pier and step right in or go for a ride on a paddleboat or Hobie Cat.

The French-operated Mahana has bungalows on the beachfront and bungalows with views of the water; all have shingle roofs, one double or two single beds, baths with showers (very hot water), and porches. Excellent French-style meals on the Modified American Plan (breakfast and dinner) are 3,200 CFP ($32) per person a day. Friday evenings usually feature Tahitian entertainment; reservations are essential. Facilities include a bar, TV-video lounge, Laundromat, tennis court, and water-sports equipment including paddle- and sailboats.

At press time, the owners were planning to enlarge the Mahana by adding 12 new bungalows, including five over the water. The resort may be closed during some of the construction.

CLUB BED (GUYNETTE'S PENSION), Fare, Huahine. Tel. 68.83.75. 6 rooms (all with bath), 7 bunks. **Location:** On the main street in Fare opposite the quay.

$ Rates: 1,500 CFP ($15) bunk first night, 1,000 CFP ($10) bunk after first night; 3,000 CFP ($30) single or double. 300 CFP ($3) extra for fans. No credit cards.

Alain and Helen Geurineau (he's French, she's French Canadian) bought this friendly establishment—formerly known as Guynette's Pension—in 1991, and in a play on the Club Med name, renamed it Club Bed. A corridor runs down the center of the building to a communal kitchen and lounge at the rear. The simple rooms and dorms flank the hallway to either side. The rooms have baths with cold-water showers. The Geurineaus offer hearty dinners for 800 CFP ($8) but no other meals.

HOTEL HUAHINE, B.P. 121, Fare, Huahine. Tel. 68-82-69. 10 rms (all with bath). **Location:** On Fare's waterfront next to Club Bed.

$ Rates: 2,500 CFP ($25) single; 3,500 CFP ($35) double. No credit cards.

If Club Bed is full, consider this cold-water hotel in a three-story concrete building next door. It's nothing to write home about, but the plain rooms are clean and have private shower-only baths. A bar at street level is a popular local watering hole (it's one of the few on Huahine), and the restaurant serves meals if you reserve in advance.

WHERE TO DINE

For rock-bottom prices and restaurants with no frills whatsoever, try any of the basic Chinese eateries on Fare's waterfront.

TE MARARA SNACK BAR, Fare. Tel. 68.87.66.
Cuisine: REGIONAL. **Reservations:** Not necessary. **Location:** On the beach, north end of Fare's waterfront.

$ Prices: Burgers and meals 650 CFP–1,100 CFP ($6.50–$11). No credit cards.
Open: Mon–Sat 8:30am–9:30pm, Sun 8:30am–4pm.

Guy Flohr's pleasant waterside establishment is Fare's best place to have a drink or meal while listening to the lagoon lap ashore or watching another tremendous tropical sunset. He changes the menu almost daily but usually includes steak, veal, fish, and lobster (order the latter well in advance). Special fixed-price meals for about 1,100 CFP ($11) are served Friday and Saturday from 6:30pm, when a band plays Tahitian music. Guy speaks excellent English.

PENSION ENITE, Fare. Tel. 68.82.37.

Cuisine: FRENCH/TAHITIAN. **Reservations:** Required. **Location:** Down the alley behind Te Marara Snack Bar.

$ Prices: Full meals 2,000 CFP–2,500 CFP ($20–$25). No credit cards.

Open: One sitting, usually 7pm.

Enite Temaiana serves renowned home-cooked meals featuring local as well as French dishes. Diners sit under a thatch pavilion right on the lagoon at her pension. Enite can be busy on her many other projects, such as operating the airport bus, so reservations are essential. She speaks limited English.

TIARE TIPANIE RESTAURANT-SNACK, Fare. Tel. 68.80.52.

Cuisine: FRENCH. **Reservations:** Not necessary. **Location:** North end of Fare at intersection of bypass and main street.

$ Prices: Snacks 250 CFP–350 CFP ($2.50–$3.50); appetizers 150 CFP–250 CFP ($1.50–$2.50); main courses 600 CFP–900 CFP ($6–$9). No credit cards.

Open: Wed–Mon 6:30am–9pm.

The Pommier family started out running a pastry shop but now have a small restaurant on their hands. In addition to their pastries (excellent for breakfast) they serve omelets, sandwiches, hamburgers, salads, and main courses such as steak in bordelaise sauce and smoked salmon with eggs, plus a daily plat du jour. The original take-out counter is still there, but guests now sit at tables on a pleasant veranda.

4. RAIATEA & TAHAA

The mountainous land you can see on the horizon from Huahine or Bora Bora is actually two islands, Raiatea and Tahaa, which are enclosed by a single coral reef. There are no beaches on either Raiatea or Tahaa, and tourism is not considered an important part of their economies, which are based on agricultural produce and, in the case of Raiatea, government salaries.

Raiatea, the largest island in the Leeward group, is by far the more important of the two, both in terms of the past and the present. In the old days Raiatea was the religious center of all the Society Islands, including Tahiti. Polynesian mythology has it that Oro, the god of fire and war, was born in Mount Temahani, the extinct flat-top volcano that towers over the northern part of Raiatea. Taputapuatea, on its southeast coast, was the most important marae in the islands. Legend also has it that the great Polynesian voyagers who discovered and colonized Hawaii and New Zealand left from Raiatea's Faaroa River (the only navigable river in French Polynesia). Recent archeological discoveries have substantiated the link with Hawaii.

Today Raiatea (pop. 6,500) is still important as the economic and administrative center of the Leeward Islands. Next to Papeete, the town of **Uturoa** (pop. 3,500) is the largest settlement and most important transportation hub in French Polynesia.

Tahaa (ta-*ha*) is much smaller than Raiatea in terms of land area, population (about 1,000), and the height of its terrain. It's a lovely island, with a few very small villages sitting deep in bays which cut into its hills. Although sailors can circumnavigate it without leaving the lagoon, most visitors see it on day-trips from Raiatea.

GETTING THERE

Air Tahiti has several flights a week from Papeete to Raiatea and also links the island directly to Huahine, Bora Bora, and Maupiti. The Raiatea airstrip is 3km (2 miles) north of Uturoa. The small, modern terminal has a snack bar and small boutique in a building to the right as you exit the terminal. The snack bar is open from sunrise to sundown. Air Tahiti's Raiatea office is at the airport (tel. 66.32.50).

There is no airport on Tahaa; connections are by boat from Raiatea. Speedy canoes leave the villages Wednesday and Friday mornings—occasionally more often—for the quai des Pêcheurs in Uturoa. They return to Tahaa about 11am. The pensions will make transfer arrangements for their guests with advance reservations.

The *Raromatai Ferry* and other interisland trading boats land at the wharf in the center of Uturoa. They stop at Tahaa only if there are vehicles or cargo to land or pick up.

See "Getting Around French Polynesia" in Chapter 3 for more information.

GETTING AROUND

There is no regular public transportation system on Raiatea and no public transport whatsoever on Tahaa.

There are **trucks** on Raiatea, but they leave the outlying villages for Uturoa at the crack of dawn and return in the afternoon. The trucks gather around the market on the waterfront in the heart of town. Asking around is the only way to find out when they leave, where they go, and when (and if) they return to Uturoa.

Hotel Le Motu (tel. 66.34.06), on the main street in the heart of Uturoa, rents cars for 6,500 CFP ($65) for 8 hours and 7,500 CFP ($75) for 24 hours, including insurance and unlimited kilometers but not gasoline. MasterCard and VISA are accepted.

An assortment of French cars is available to rent from **Guirouard Location de Voitures,** B.P. 139, Uturoa, Raiatea (tel. 66.33.09), whose office is in Garage Motu Tapu, a large tin building on the mountain side of the main road between town and the airport (look for the yellow Renault sign). Rates are the same as at Hotel Le Motu. Manager Suzanne Guirouard speaks English, but she doesn't accept credit cards.

Location Apetahi (tel. 66.32.15), which in reality is Charles Brotherson's barbershop opposite Banque de Tahiti on Uturoa's main street, rents **scooters** for 4,000 CFP ($40) per day, plus a 5,000 CFP ($50) deposit. The rate drops to 3,000 CFP ($30) if you take it for more than 1 day. Charles also rents **bicycles** for 1,000 CFP ($10) a day. If he isn't in his barbershop, check at Apetahi Mobil station north of town (tel. 66.39.04).

A major road-improvement program has been in the works on Raiatea for the past several years. Ask about the road conditions before heading out around the island.

There is a **taxi stand** near the market in Uturoa (tel. 66.20.60), or contact René Guilloux (tel. 66.31.40).

FAST FACTS: RAIATEA & TAHAA

Bookshop Librairie d'Uturoa (tel. 66.30.80) on the inland side of the main street, center of town, carries French books and magazines. Polycentre (tel. 66.31.13) next door has picture books about French Polynesia.

Car Rentals See "Raiatea & Tahaa: Getting Around," above. There are no rentals available on Tahaa.

Currency Exchange French Polynesia's four banks have offices on Uturoa's main street. The noncommission-charging Banque Socredo is at the south end of the business district. There is no bank on Tahaa.

Dentist Ask your hotel for the name of a dentist in private practice.

Doctor See "Hospitals," below.

Drugstores Pharmacie de Raiatea (tel. 66.34.44) in Uturoa carries French products.

Emergencies See "Police," below.

Eyeglasses For repairs or new glasses go to Pacifique Optique next to Banque Socredo.

Hairdressers/Barbers Ask at your hotel for the name of a hairdresser who speaks English. Men can get a trim at Charles Bortherson's barbershop in Uturoa (tel. 66-32-15). Charles speaks English fluently.

Hospitals The hospital at Uturoa (tel. 66-32-92) serves all the Leeward Islands. Tahaa has an infirmary at Patio (tel. 65-63-31).

Information The local tourism committee has a tourist information office in Uturoa at the corner of the city park nearest the waterfront. The friendly, English-speaking staff is quite helpful. Open Mon–Fri 8–11am, Tues–Thurs 1:30–3:30pm, and Sat 7–9am.

Lost Property See "Police," below.

Police The telephone number of the gendarmerie is 66.31.07. On Tahaa, the gendarmerie is at Patio, the administrative center, on the north coast (tel. 65-64-07).

Post Office The post office is in a modern building north of Uturoa on the main road (as opposed to a new road that runs along the shore of reclaimed land on the north side of town) and is open Mon–Fri 7am–3pm. The telecommunications section stays open for phone calls Mon–Fri until 6pm; it's open Sat–Sun 8–10am.

Rest Rooms *Sanitaires public* are on the wharf behind Restaurant Le Quai des Pêcheurs.

Taxis See "Raiatea & Tahaa: Getting Around," above.

WHAT TO SEE & DO

Highlights of a visit to Raiatea include day-trips to and around Tahaa, picnics on small islands on the outer reef, canoe adventures up the Faaroa River, and hikes into the mountains to see the *tiare apetahi,* a white flower found nowhere else on earth. Legend says that the five delicate petals are the fingers of a beautiful Polynesian girl who fell in love with a prince but couldn't marry him because of her low birth. Just before she died heartbroken in her lover's arms, she promised to give him her hand to caress each day throughout eternity. At daybreak each morning, accordingly, the five petals pop open.

SIGHTSEEING

✪ **Taputapuatea Marae,** on the outskirts of Opoa village 35km (21 miles) from Uturoa, is worth a look, not only for the marae itself but for the scenery along the way. The road skirts the southeast coast and follows Faaroa Bay to the mouth of the river. Taputapuatea was the most important marae in French Polynesia and is one of the largest that has been preserved. Its huge *ahu,* or raised altar of stones for the gods, is more than 50 yards long, 10 yards wide, and 3½ yards tall. Flat rocks, used as backrests for the chiefs and priests, still stand in the courtyard in front of the ahu. The entire complex is in a coconut grove on the shore of the lagoon opposite a pass in the reef, and legend says that bonfires on the marae guided canoes through the reef at night.

A **stroll through Uturoa** will show you what Papeete must have been like a few generations ago. A number of Chinese stores line the main street, which parallels the waterfront a block inland, but Raiatea is not the place to shop except for handcrafts made on Tahaa. Check the vendors' stalls on the harbor side of the city park for pareus and handcrafts, including brassieres made of two polished coconut shells. The market on the waterfront is busiest early on Wednesday, Friday, and Sunday mornings. The *Raromatai Ferry* and the other interisland boats arrive on Wednesday, Thursday, Friday, and Saturday, bringing extra life to the waterfront.

The road beside the gendarmerie, just north of downtown Uturoa, leads to a trail that ascends to the television towers atop 970-foot-tall **Papioi Hill.** The view from the top includes Uturoa, the reef, and the islands of Tahaa, Bora Bora, and Huahine. Another trail begins with a Jeep track about 200 yards south of the bridge, at the head of Pufau Bay on the northwest coast. It leads up to the plateau atop **Mount Temehani.** The mountain itself actually is divided in two by a deep gorge.

Almost Paradise Tours (tel. 66-23-64) has road tours including Taputaputea and other archeological sites. This company is operated by Bill Kolans, an American who has lived on Raiatea since 1979. He is well versed in Polynesian legends. His 3-hour island tour by minibus costs 2,500 CFP ($25).

Raiatea Safari Tours (tel. 66-37-10), the touring part of Pension Marie-France (see below), has a ½-day tour of Raiatea's highlights by four-wheel-drive vehicle. It costs 3,000 CFP ($30) per person.

LAGOON TOURS

If you can put together your own group (because a minimum of four persons is required), you can take a variety of excursions on the ✪ Raiatea-Tahaa lagoon.

Delphine Harris's **Havai'i Tours** (tel. 66-27-98) has boat tours to nearby Tahaa, including a visit to the French Polynesia's first pearl farm outside the Tuamotus and a picnic on a motu. Prices range from 1,000 CFP ($10) per person for just a motu picnic to 3,500 CFP ($35) for the longer excursion all the way around Tahaa.

Raiatea Safari Tours (tel. 66-37-10) also has several boat trips, including one by canoe up the Faaroa River. A full-day trip to Tahaa includes snorkeling over a coral garden, a visit to a fish park, and stops at white-sand beaches on two deserted islets. Prices range from 2,500 CFP to 4,000 CFP ($25 to $40). For 600 CFP ($6) the company will take you to a motu off Pension Marie-France; you bring your own supplies.

The Moorings (tel. 66-35-93) charter sailboat operation is based at Marina Apooti, just north of the airport (see "Getting Around: By Chartered Yacht" in Chapter 3). If a boat is available, it can be chartered on a daily basis for about 7,000 CFP ($70) a person including lunch. Arrangements for longer charters should ordinarily be made before leaving home. The boats can be sailed across the "blue water" of the open ocean between Raiatea and Bora Bora or Huahine. If you don't have good sea legs, it's easy to spend a week inside the reef exploring the various anchorages of Tahaa, the only French Polynesian island that can be circumnavigated without actually putting out to sea.

Raiatea may not have beaches, but the reef and lagoon are excellent for **scuba diving.** Patrice Philip, husband of Marie-France Philip, does most of the diving for **Raiatea Safari Tours** (tel. 66-37-10) at Pension Marie-France.

WHERE TO STAY

HOTEL BALI HAI RAIATEA, B.P. 26, Temae, Moorea. Tel. 66-31-49, 56-13-59 on Moorea, or toll free 800/282-1402 in California, 800/282-1401 elsewhere the U.S. Fax 56-19-22. Telex 331. 36 bungalows (all with bath). **Location:** 2km (1.2 miles) south of Uturoa.

$ **Rates** (in U.S. dollars only): $93–$155 garden single or double; $200 overwater single or double. AE, DC, MC, V.

(S) The only real tourist hotel on either island, this is the fourth creation of Moorea's "Bali Hai Boys" (hence, the Moorea address, telephone and fax numbers). Like everywhere else on Raiatea, there is no beach, but eight of its bungalows sit over the lagoon on pilings. Their porches extend out over the clifflike reef face. The others, some of which have two units under their thatch roofs, are either along the seawall or in the gardens beyond. Also sitting on the seawall is a central building housing a restaurant and a lounge whose bar looks like the hull of an oceangoing canoe. A pier extends out to a dock from which you can climb into the water and get the sensation of flying as you snorkel along the face of the reef. Facilities include a swimming pool and tennis courts.

HOTEL RAIATEA VILLAGE, B.P. 282, Uturoa, Raiatea. Tel. 66-31-62 or 66-33-60. 12 bungalows (all with bath). **Location:** 11km (6.6 miles) south of Uturoa.

$ Rates (including 7% government room tax): 5,900 CFP ($59) single; 8,300 CFP ($83) double. V.

This is a locally owned and -operated establishment at the mouth of the Faaroa River. The bungalows have thatch roofs but are otherwise of modern construction. Paneled walls separate a bedroom and large bathroom from the living area, which has a kitchen complete with gas range, refrigerator, and stainless-steel double sink. There are no ceiling fans, but the complex faces directly into the prevailing southeast trade winds. The staff will prepare meals if you reserve in advance. A small bar sits under a thatch pavilion on a artificial sandy beach behind a seawall.

The staff will take guests on snorkeling and picnic excursions to a motu directly offshore on the reef; up the Faaroa River; or on all-day trips to Tahaa—provided there are four people to make the trips. Le truck departs for Uturoa from a depot across the road at 6 and 7am each morning and returns in the afternoon.

SUNSET BEACH MOTEL, B.P. 397, Uturoa, Raiatea. Tel. 66-33-47. 16 bungalows (all with kitchens). TV **Location:** Apooiti, 5km (3 miles) northwest of Uturoa.

$ Rates: 6,000 CFP ($60) single, 7,000 CFP ($70) double for first night; 5,000 CFP ($50) single, 6,000 CFP ($60) double 2 nights or more; 1,000 CFP ($10) per person campsite. Discounts for stays of 15 days or longer. No credit cards.

One of the best values in French Polynesia for anyone wanting to do their own cooking, this property occupies a coconut grove on a skinny peninsula sticking out west of the airport. The bungalows sit in a row just off a palm-draped beach. The lagoon here is very shallow, but the beach enjoys a gorgeous westward view toward Bora Bora. The lagoon excursion companies mentioned above pick up their guests off a long pier which stretches to deep water. Although of European construction rather than Polynesian, the modern bungalows are spacious, comfortably furnished, and have fully equipped kitchens. Each has a large front porch with lagoon view. Solar panels provide hot water for cleaning and showering. Part of the grove is set aside for campers, who have their own building with toilets, showers, and kitchen. Manager-owner Eliane Boubée speaks English.

PENSION GREENHILL, B.P. 598, Uturoa, Raiatea. Tel. 66-37-64. 3 rms, 1 apartment, 1 bungalow (with bath). **Location:** Faaroa Bay, 10km (6 miles) south of Uturoa.

$ Rates (including lodging, meals, and outings): 6,500 CFP ($65) single; 7,900 CFP ($79) double. No credit cards.

The climb to Marie-Isabelle and Jason Chan's establishment takes you up a steep driveway to a stunning view across Faaroa Bay to the soaring mountains beyond. The Chans accommodate their guests either in three bedrooms of their own modern villa, in an apartment with its own bathroom, or in a bungalow with its own gorgeous view from its perch above the main house. Three meals a day are served family-style on their spacious terrace. Guests are taken on several tours and lagoon excursions without additional charge.

PENSION MARIE-FRANCE, B.P. 272, Uturoa, Raiatea. Tel. 66-37-10. Fax 66-20-94. 5 rms, 1 rustic bungalow, 28 bunks (none with bath). **Location:** 2km (1.2 miles) south of Uturoa, 200 yards from Hotel Bali Hai Raiatea.

$ Rates: 1,200 CFP ($12) bunk. MC, V.

Low-budget travelers will find a friendly and well-informed home here. Hosts Marie-France and Patrice Philip also run Raiatea Safari Tours out of this establishment. They have been enlarging their hostel since 1988, and it may be even bigger when you arrive. Couples can have one of five rooms with twin beds (easily pushed together); everyone else piles into the dorm facilities. All guests share toilets, showers, communal kitchen, and TV lounge. Meals are available.

WHERE TO DINE

For rock-bottom eats, the shops in the little shacklike buildings bordering the city park look unappetizing from the outside, but their owners prepare reasonably good

Chinese fare and sell casse-croûtes for about 100 CFP ($1). They are open for breakfast and lunch. In addition, Raiatea's version of Papeete les roulettes congregate on the waterfront after dark; they stay open past midnight on Friday and Saturday.

RESTAURANT LE QUAI DES PECHEURS, Uturoa. Tel. 66-36-86.

Cuisine: FRENCH/PIZZA. **Reservations:** Recommended weekend evenings and Sun lunch. **Location:** Uturoa's waterfront.

$ **Prices:** Appetizers 600 CFP–1,100 CFP ($6–$11); main courses 1,000 CFP–2,500 CFP ($10–$25); pizzas 650 CFP–900 CFP ($6.50–$9). V.

Open: Daily 7am–10pm.

Lea Constant, who was Miss Tahiti back when we both were young, operates this somewhat less than gourmet yet pleasant restaurant on the quay where the fishing boats land. Usually right off the boat, the seafood selections are best, especially the poisson cru. A wood-fired oven is sometimes used to produce tasty pizzas at lunch. You can eat right on the veranda by the dock. At night the restaurant becomes Utuora's most civilized watering hole.

JADE GARDEN RESTAURANT, Uturoa's main street. Tel. 66-34-40.

Cuisine: CHINESE. **Reservations:** Recommended on weekends. **Location:** In a storefront on mountain side of Uturoa's main street.

$ **Prices:** Appetizers 600 CFP–1,800 CFP ($6–$18); main courses 1,000 CFP–1,800 CFP ($10–$18). V.

Open: Lunch Wed–Sat 11am–1pm; dinner Wed–Sat 6:30–9pm.

(S) On first impression, this appears to be just another family-run Chinese restaurant, but those who try it are in for a pleasant surprise. My most recent meal there consisted of ginger beef, chicken with fresh water chestnuts, and pork with cashew nuts. All three dishes were delicately seasoned in the Cantonese style and were worthy of the more sophisticated (and far more expensive) Chinese restaurants in Papeete. The upstairs dining room is more pleasant than the one on the street level. Both are air conditioned.

SNACK MOEMOEA, Uturoa waterfront, in the Toporo Building. Tel. 66-39-84.

Cuisine: SNACK BAR. **Location:** Opposite the small-boat harbor.

$ **Prices:** Sandwiches 250 CFP–400 CFP ($2–$4); main courses 700 CFP–1,200 CFP ($7–$12). No credit cards.

Open: Mon–Sat 5am–5pm.

(S) While there are several snack bars open for breakfast and lunch near the Uturoa market, this is the most pleasant of the lot. The old corner storefront has been completely remodeled, with tables both outside on the sidewalk and inside on the ground floor or on a mezzanine platform. The menu includes casse-croûte sandwiches and fine hamburgers, poisson cru, grilled fish, and steaks.

LE GOURMET PATISSERIE, Uturoa's main street. Tel. 66-21-51.

Cuisine: PASTRIES. **Reservations:** Not accepted. **Location:** In Westpac Bank building on main street near market.

$ **Prices:** Pastries 150 CFP–400 CFP ($1.50–$4); meals 600 CFP–900 CFP ($6–$9). No credit cards.

Open: Mon–Sat 6am–6pm.

This little bakery has excellent breads and pastries for breakfast and plats du jour such as steak with vegetables for lunch on weekdays (only pastries and breads are served on Saturday). The goodies are on display in a case; point and order.

IMPRESSIONS

At Rangiroa you pick up a hundred natives with pigs, guitars, breadfruit and babies. They sleep on deck, right outside your bunk, and some of them sing all night.

—James A. Michener, 1951

5. RANGIROA

The largest and most popular of the great chain of atolls known as the Tuamotu Archipelago, Rangiroa lies 194 miles northeast of Tahiti. It consists of a chain of low, skinny islets that enclose a tadpole-shaped lagoon more than 46 miles long and 14 miles wide. This means that when you stand on one side of the lagoon, you cannot see the other. In fact, the entire island of Tahiti could be placed in Rangiroa's lagoon with room left over.

The islets are so low—never more than 10 feet above sea level, not including the height of the coconut palms growing all over them—that ships cannot see them until they're a few miles away. For this reason, Rangiroa and its companions in the Tuamotu are also known as the Dangerous Archipelago. Hundreds of yachts and ships have been wrecked on the reefs, either unable to see them until it was too late or dragged ashore by tricky currents. Rangiroa has two navigable passes into its interior lagoon, and currents of up to 6 knots race through them as the tides first fill the lagoon and then empty it during their never-ending cycle. Even at slack tide, watching the coral rocks pass a few feet under your yacht is a tense experience. Once inside the lagoon, however, you anchor in a huge bathtub whose crystal-clear water is stocked with an incredible amount and variety of sea life. People come to Rangiroa primarily to swim, snorkel, or enjoy some of the best scuba diving in French Polynesia.

GETTING THERE

Air Tahiti has at least one flight from Papeete to Rangiroa Sunday through Friday, and two nonstop flights a week from Bora Bora. Otherwise, you will have to take a freighter or charter a yacht. Rangiroa is a regular stop on the monthly voyages of the *Aranui.* For details see "Getting Around French Polynesia" in Chapter 3.

GETTING AROUND

Rangiroa's airstrip and most of its hotels and pensions lie on a perfectly flat, 7-mile-long island on the north side of the lagoon. The airport is about equidistant between the village of Avatoru on the west end and Tiputa Pass on the east. The hotels and pensions meet their guests; if you don't have reservations, ask around for the establishments' representatives or at the information desk in the airport.

Most hotels and pensions have bicycles for their guests' use, and they may be able to arrange motorbike or scooter rentals. There are no car-rental agencies on Rangiroa.

RANGIROA

Currency Exchange Banque de Tahiti has a branch in Tiputa village, which is a boat ride across Tiputa Pass from the main island. An agent comes to Avatoru on Wednesday and to the Tiputa side of the island on Tuesday. In other words, take enough cash with you if you are staying at a pension.

Doctor See "Hospitals," below.

Drugstores Avatoru also has a small pharmacy.

Emergencies See "Police," below.

Hospitals There are infirmaries at Avatoru (tel. 96-03-75) and across the pass at Tiputa (tel. 96-03-96).

Information The Tahiti Tourist Promotion Board has an information desk at the airport which is staffed only when planes arrive.

Photographic Needs For film, check the boutique at the Kia Ora Village or the pharmacy in Avatoru.

Police The phone number for the gendarmerie is 96.03.61.

Post Office The small post office in Avatoru is open Mon–Fri 7:30am–3pm, Sat 7:30–8:30am.

Taxis There is no taxi service on Rangiroa.

Telegrams/Telex See "Post Office," above.

WHAT TO SEE & DO

Except for a walk around Avatoru, a typical Tuamotuan village with whitewashed stone walls lining the main street in the oldest section nearest the pass, plan on enjoying the fantastic lagoon. The hotels and pensions either have or can arrange outings by boat. One favorite destination is the so-called Blue Lagoon, an area of colorful corals and plentiful sea life.

Yves Lefèvre of **Raie Manta Club** (as in manta ray), B.P. 55, Avatoru, Rangiroa (tel. 96-04-80), has a monopoly on scuba diving and normally operates from the Kia Ora Village or from a base near Avatoru. Any of the hotels or pensions can arrange dives, which cost 4,500 CFP ($45) including all equipment. Divers must be certified in advance and bring a medical certificate with them.

WHERE TO STAY

Ask at the Tahiti Tourist Board office in Papeete for a list of Rangiroa's nine or more pensions. There are no restaurants on Rangiroa outside the hotels, so the American Plan or *pension complet* (three meals) should be purchased. Modified American or *demi pension* plans (breakfast and dinner) are available if you want to take one meal a day at another establishment.

Don't be disappointed if you find the beaches to consist of gravelly coral instead of fine white sand; Rangiroa is known for its lagoon, not the quality of its beaches.

Except at Kia Ora Village and La Bouteille à la Mer, which have bilingual staffs or owners, a knowledge of French is a must on Rangiroa.

KIA ORA VILLAGE, B.P. 706, Papeete, Tahiti. Tel. 96-03-84 on Rangiroa, 42-86-72 in Papeete for reservations, or toll free 800/221-4542 in the U.S. Fax 41-30-40. Telex 306. 25 bungalows, 5 suites (all with bath). **Location:** About 3km (2 miles) from the airport near the east end of the island.

$ Rates (including three meals): 27,800 CFP ($278) single, 37,600 CFP ($376) double; 30,800 CFP ($308) single suite, 40,600 CFP ($406) double suite. Add 10% July–Aug. AE, DC, MC, V.

This romantic, first-class establishment has been Rangiroa's premier hotel for two decades and remains so today despite the emergence of deluxe models now found elsewhere in French Polynesia. The thatch-roofed buildings look like a Polynesian village set in a coconut grove directly on the lagoon. White sand has been trucked over from the ocean side of the island, but the beach still is a bit rocky; however, a long pier reaches out into deep water for excellent swimming and snorkeling. The beachside main building features an open-air dining room, and a round bar sitting over the beach provides spectacular sunsets.

Dining/Entertainment: Excellent French cuisine in the dining room features local fish and meats imported from New Zealand. Depending on the number of guests, local villagers stage Tahitian dance shows.

Services: Laundry, baby-sitting.

Facilities: Boutique, bicycles, water-sports equipment, and activities, including a wild ride in snorkeling gear on the riptide through Tiputa Pass. The hotel arranges boat trips to Tiputa village across the pass and tours by *le truck* to Avatoru.

LA BOUTEILLE A LA MER, B.P. 17, Avatoru, Rangiroa. Tel. 96-03-34, or

43-99-30 in Papeete. Fax 96-02-90. 11 bungalows (all with bath). **Location:** 1km (.6 mile) from airport, 4km (2.4 miles) from Avatoru.

$ Rates (including three meals): 13,250 CFP ($132.50) single; 22,950 CFP ($229.50) double. Discounts for stays of more than 2 weeks or if booked directly. AE, DC, MC, V.

Jean-Michel and Sylvia Deloubes' place also sits in a coconut grove by the lagoon. Their spacious bungalows have thatch roofs and plenty of island charm despite showing some wear and tear. One of the bungalows is large enough for five people. French food is served in large portions in a dining room–bar complex right by the water. Bicycles are provided to guests free. Other facilities include video lounge, snorkeling equipment, outrigger canoes. Lagoon excursions and scuba diving can be arranged. Bring your tennis racket; there is an all-weather court.

RAIRA LAGON, B.P. 42, Avatoru, Rangiroa. Tel. 96-04-23. 3 bungalows (all with bath). **Location:** 1km (.6 mile) from airport, 4km (2.4 miles) from Avatoru, adjacent to La Bouteille à la Mer.

$ Rates: 3,000 CFP ($30) single, 6,000 CFP ($60) double; 4,500 CFP ($45) per person including two meals; 5,000 CFP ($50) per person including three meals. No credit cards.

Mareva Bennet and Didier Tehina have built three basic bungalows and a lagoonside dining pavilion at their homestead. The small bungalows have thatch roofs, plywood walls, small front porches, and small baths with cold-water showers. Mosquito nets hanging over the platform beds give a romantic charm to an otherwise basic establishment. Mareva cooks hearty and very tasty home-style meals featuring fresh fish when available. Despite her English surname, Mareva does not speak the language. Nor does Didier.

6. OTHER ISLANDS

Several other French Polynesian islands have accommodations and restaurants, and they offer a slice of the old Polynesia that is rapidly disappearing under the tourist onslaught on the more developed islands. These islands are very small both in geographical area and number of inhabitants. Once there, you will be able to find your way around. A working knowledge of French or Tahitian, however, will be essential for full enjoyment of what they have to offer: lovely beaches and lagoons, and friendly Polynesian inhabitants.

See "Getting Around French Polynesia" in Chapter 3 for information on flights and boats to the islands.

Changing currency could be difficult on some islands, so do your banking elsewhere and take plenty of local money with you.

MANIHI

Known for its black-pearl farms, Manihi lies 520km (312 miles) northeast of Tahiti in the Tuamotus. Although not nearly as large as Rangiroa, it has a clear lagoon filled with tropical sea life and colorful coral.

The only hotel is the **Hotel Kaina Village,** B.P. 2560, Papeete, Tahiti (tel. 42-75-53, or toll free 800/346-6262 in the U.S.; fax 43-46-94; telex 276). This lagoonside establishment has a restaurant and bar and 12 modern, overwater bungalows on the main islet near the airport. Rates including three meals are 23,600 CFP ($236) single, 29,100 CFP ($291) double. American Express, Diners Club, MasterCard, and VISA cards are accepted. Free activities include a visit to a pearl farm, windsurfing, snorkeling both in the lagoon and with the strong current through one of the passes in the reef, fishing, reef walking, and visits to a native village by speedboat. You pay to rent a boat or be taken to a remote island for a picnic.

Check with the Tahiti Tourist Board in Papeete about the possibility of staying with local families.

Gilles Petre's **Manihi Blue Nui Dive Center** is located at the Hotel Kaina Village. He charges 3,500 CFP ($35) per dive.

MAUPITI

Just 40km (25 miles) west of Bora Bora, Maupiti is like a junior version of its more glamorous neighbor. A mountain rises in the center of a colorful lagoon partially enclosed by a chain of islands on the outer edge of the barrier reef. Unlike Bora Bora, however, Maupiti has seen little tourism development and remains unspoiled.

Most of the island's inhabitants live in Vaiea, Petei, and Pauma, three villages on the east side of the central island.

Air Tahiti flies to Maupiti twice a week from Raiatea—not from Bora Bora. The airstrip is on Tuanai, one of the reef islands. *Toporo I,* a small freighter based at Uturoa on Raiatea, visits Maupiti every 2 weeks, weather permitting. Check with the Toporo offices in Raiatea (tel. 66-30-29) or Papeete (tel. 43-79-72).

Activities are limited to swimming, boat excursions, hiking, and getting to know as many of Maupiti's 1,000 or so residents as you can.

There are no hotels or restaurants on Maupiti, so accommodations and meals are limited to pensions. The owners meet the incoming flights and actively promote their businesses.

Chez Mareta, Vaiea, Maupiti (tel. 67-80-25) occupies a four-bedroom house in the main village. Rates are 4,000 CFP ($40), including two meals. It's owned by Mme Mareta Anua.

At **Hotel Auira,** B.P. 2, Vaiea, Maupiti (tel. 67-80-26), Mme Edna Terai has eight thatch bungalows at a beachside setting on Motu Auira, the reef island enclosing the western side of the lagoon. Her rates, including three meals, are 6,000 CFP ($60) per person with shared bath, 7,500 CFP ($75) per person in a self-contained bungalow.

For others, check with the Tahiti Tourist Board's offices.

TETIAROA ATOLL

About 30 miles north of Tahiti and Moorea is the small atoll Tetiaroa (*teshi*-roah), a circular necklace of low islands enclosing a lagoon. Once a retreat for Tahiti's royalty, it has been owned since the 1960s by Marlon Brando, who fell in love with French Polynesia and with one of his Tahitian costars while filming the 1963 version of *Mutiny on the Bounty.* For some years Brando operated a hotel consisting of bungalows made of native materials but lacking most modern conveniences. The 1983 hurricanes did extensive damage to the island, however, and now it's used primarily for day-trips or short weekend excursions from Papeete. Do not go to Tetiaroa expecting to meet the great actor; he seldom is there. For more information, see "What to See & Do" in Chapter 4 or contact the Tetiaroa office, B.P. 2418, Papeete, Tahiti (tel. 42-21-10).

CHAPTER 6

RAROTONGA & THE COOK ISLANDS

Perhaps it's the rugged beauty, rivaling that of the more famous Tahiti. Maybe it's the warmth and friendliness of a proud Polynesian people who love to talk about their islands, and do so in English. It could be the old South Seas charm of a small island nation relatively unaffected by the hustle and bustle of modern civilization. Whatever the reason, there are few old South Pacific hands who aren't absolutely enraptured with Rarotonga and the other Cook Islands. As soon as you get there, you'll see why the local tourist authority isn't far wrong in calling the country "Heaven on Earth."

Cook Islanders also like to boast that Rarotonga, their main island, is the way Tahiti used to be. Since they use New Zealand currency, it's like Tahiti used to be in one very important respect: For anyone spending U.S. dollars, the prices of most things in the Cook Islands are as reasonable as will be found in the South Pacific. Given their unique combination of beauty, beaches, charm, facilities, and prices, the Cooks easily qualify as the all-around pick of eastern Polynesia for value-conscious travelers.

1. GETTING TO KNOW THE COOK ISLANDS

GEOGRAPHY

Rarotonga and the other 14 Cook Islands are tiny specks scattered between Tahiti and Samoa in an ocean area about a third the size of the continental United States, yet all together they comprise only 93 square miles of land. Rarotonga is by far the largest, with 26 of those square miles.

The Cook Islands are divided both geographically and politically into a Southern and a Northern Group. Most of the nine islands of the Southern Group, including Rarotonga, are volcanic, with lush mountains or hills. The islands of the remote Northern Group, except Nassau, are typical atolls, with circles of reef and low coral

WHAT'S SPECIAL ABOUT THE COOK ISLANDS

Beaches/Natural Spectacles
- ☐ Muri Beach: White sands stretch 8 miles around one corner of Rarotonga.
- ☐ Aitutaki Lagoon: Shallow but colorful and stocked with sea life, it's one of the South Pacific's best.

Events/Festivals
- ☐ Constitution Week: Cook Islands dancing at its hip-swinging best during 10 days in August.
- ☐ Island Dance Festival: another week of drums and hips, this time in April.

Great Towns/Villages
- ☐ Avarua: evokes the South Seas era of traders and beachbums.

After Dark
- ☐ Banana Court Bar: One of the last old South Seas institutions just keeps on rocking.
- ☐ Dancing: For Cook Islanders, dancing is *the* thing to do.

Shopping
- ☐ Black pearls: Get them at a fraction of what you pay in French Polynesia.
- ☐ Handcrafts: Bring home a finely woven, white straw hat to wear to church.

Sunday Selections
- ☐ Church services: You'll never hear such lovely, unpracticed harmony anywhere else.

islands enclosing central lagoons. The sandy soil and scarce rainfall support coconut palms, scrub bush, and a handful of people. Although they can be reached by plane, the remote Northern Group receives few visitors.

Rarotonga, the only high, mountainous island, in many ways is a miniature Tahiti: It has jagged peaks and steep valleys surrounded by a flat coastal plain, white sandy beaches, an azure lagoon, and a reef about ¼-mile offshore. In most places the shoreline consists of a slightly raised sandy bar backed by a swampy depression, which then gives rise to the valleys and mountains. Before the coming of missionaries in 1823, Rarotongans lived on the raised ground beyond the swampy flats, which they used for growing taro and other wet-footed crops. They built a remarkable road, actually paved in part with stones, from village to village almost around the island. That "back road" still exists, although the paved round-island road now runs near the shore. The area between the two roads appears to be bush but is in fact heavily cultivated with a variety of crops and fruit trees.

While Rarotonga masquerades as a small version of Tahiti, **Aitutaki** plays the role of Bora Bora in the Cook Islands. Although lacking the spectacular mountains that Bora Bora has, little Aitutaki is nearly surrounded by a large, shallow lagoon whose multihued beauty and abundant sea life rival its French Polynesian counterpart and make this charming, atoll-framed outpost the second most-visited of the Cooks.

The vegetation of the southern islands is typically tropical: The mountains and hills are covered with native brush, while the valley floors and flat coastal plains are studded with coconut and banana plantations and a wide range of flowering trees and shrubs.

IMPRESSIONS

At last I came to Maungapu, the highest point on Aitutaki. At 407 feet high, Maungapu is no Everest, but it offered me a view that, I submit, could not have been improved upon by Everest itself.

—LAWRENCE MILLMAN, 1990

DATELINE

- **A.D. 1200** First Polynesians arrive.
- **1595** Mendaña discovers Pukapuka.
- **1606** De Quirós finds Rakahanga.
- **1773–77** Capt. James Cook discovers more islands, names them the Herveys.
- **1789** Capt. Bligh finds Aitutaki shortly before mutiny on the *Bounty*.
- **1814** American sandalwood trader discovers Rarotonga.
- **1821** Tahitian missionaries covert Aitutaki to Christianity.
- **1823** Rev. John Williams rediscovers Rarotonga, lands missionaries.
- **1824** Missionaries divide Rarotonga into five villages.
- **1862** William Marsters arrives, starts his unique family on Palmerston Island.
- **1888** Residents on Manihiki trick French warship into turning away; Britain declares protectorate.
- **1901** Cook Islands included in boundaries of newly independent New Zealand.
- **1942** U.S. troops build airstrip on Aitutaki.
- **1965** Cook Islands become independent in association with New Zealand. Sir

(continues)

HISTORY

Legend says that the first Polynesians arrived in the Cook Islands by canoe from the islands of modern-day French Polynesia about A.D. 1200, although anthropologists think the first of them may have come much earlier. In any event, they discovered the Cook Islands as part of the great Polynesian migrations that settled all of the South Pacific long before the Spanish explorer Alvaro de Mendaña laid the first European eyes on any of the Cook Islands when he discovered Pukapuka in 1595.

The Spanish at that time were more interested in getting from Peru to the riches of Manila than in general exploration. Thus, except for Rakahanga, which was discovered by Pedro Fernández de Quirós during a later voyage along the same general route in 1606, the islands did not appear on European maps for another 170 years.

And then, as happened in so many South Pacific island groups, along came Capt. James Cook, who stumbled onto some of the islands during his voyages in 1773 and 1777; he named them the Hervey Islands. In 1824 the name was changed to the Cook Islands by the Russian cartographer John von Krusenstern.

Captain Cook sailed around the Southern Group but missed Rarotonga, which apparently was visited first by the mutineers of HMS *Bounty*, under Fletcher Christian. There is no official record of the visit, but oral history on Rarotonga has it that a great ship arrived offshore about the time of the mutiny. A Cook Islander visited the ship and was given some oranges, the seeds of which became the foundation for the island's citrus industry.

When the first Europeans arrived, the local Polynesians were governed by feudal chiefs, who owned all the land within their jurisdictions and held life-and-death power over their subjects. Like other Polynesians, they believed in a hierarchy of gods and spirits, among them Tangaroa, whose well-endowed carved image is now a leading handcraft item.

CHRISTIANITY

The man who claimed to have discovered Rarotonga was the same man who brought Christianity to the Cook Islands, the Rev. John Williams of the London Missionary Society. Williams had come from London to Tahiti in 1818 as a missionary, and he soon set up a base of operations on Raiatea in the Society Islands, from which he intended to spread Christianity throughout the South Pacific. He set his sights on the Hervey Islands after a canoeload of Polynesians from there was blown by a storm to Raiatea. They were receptive to Williams's teachings and asked that missionaries be sent to the Herveys.

In 1821 Williams sailed to Sydney and on the way dropped two teachers at Aitutaki. One of them was a Tahitian named Papeiha. By the time Williams returned 2 years later, Papeiha had converted the entire island. Pleased with this success, Williams and a newly arrived missionary named Charles Pitman headed off in search of Rarotonga.

It took a few weeks, during which Williams stopped at Mangaia, Mauke, Mitiaro, and Atiu, but he eventually found Rarotonga in July 1823. Never mind the visit of the *Bounty* mutineers or the fact that an American sandalwood trader almost certainly had been there in 1814: Williams went into the earth oven on Erromango claiming to be the discoverer of Rarotonga.

Williams, Pitman, and Papeiha were joined a year later by Aaron Buzacott, another missionary. Pitman soon left for the village of Ngatangiia on the east coast, Papeiha went to Arorangi in the west, and Buzacott took over in Avarua in the north. Williams spent most of the next 4 years using forced native labor to build a new ship, *The Messenger of Peace,* and eventually sailed it west in search of new islands and more converts.

Meanwhile, the missionaries quickly converted the Cook Islanders. They overcame the powerful feudal chiefs, known as *ariki,* whose titles but not their power have been handed down to their present-day heirs. On Rarotonga, the missionaries divided the island into five villages and split the land into rectangular parcels, one for each family. Choice parcels were set aside for the church buildings and rectories. Rarotongans moved down from the high ground near their gardens and became seaside dwellers for the first time.

DATELINE

Albert Henry elected first prime minister.

- **1974** Queen Elizabeth II dedicates new Rarotonga International Airport. Islands opened to tourists.
- **1978** Sir Albert Henry indicted, stripped of office and knighthood.
- **1990** Rarotonga gets television.

The religion the missionaries taught was rock-ribbed and puritanical. They blamed the misdeeds of the people for every misfortune, from the epidemics of Western diseases that came with the arrival of more Europeans to the hurricanes that destroyed crops. They preached against sexual permissiveness and cut off the hair of wayward women. The Rarotongans took it all in stride, and whenever a woman had her locks shorn, she would appear in public wearing a crown of flowers and continue on her merry way. For the most part, however, the transition to Christianity was easy, since in their old religion the Rarotongans, like most Polynesians, believed in a single, all-powerful god who ruled over lesser gods.

Out of the seeds planted by Williams and the London Missionary Society grew the present-day Cook Islands Christian Church, to which about 60% of all Cook Islanders belong. The churches, many of them built by the missionaries in the 19th century, are the center of life in every village, and the Takamoa College Bible school that the missionaries established in 1837 still exists in Avarua. The Cook Islands Christian Church still owns the land under its buildings; the churches of other denominations sit on leased property.

WILLIAM MARSTERS

Another Englishman arrived in 1862 and proceeded to have quite another impact on the Cook Islands. William Marsters, a farmhand from Gloucester, took a local wife, and, with her and her sister, settled on tiny, isolated, and uninhabited Palmerston Island. Within a year he had declared himself a minister of the Anglican church, married himself to two of his wife's sisters (the second sister had come to assist during

IMPRESSIONS

The pre-missionary law was that no one under the age of eighteen should wear clothing; but the precise age is somewhat doubtful, for my neighbor Bones says that it was twenty-five when he was a child, and furthermore, that the fathers at one time decided that even this age was too early for the wearing of clothing. Therefore, instead of raising the age limit, they lengthened the year, making it fifteen moons long instead of twelve.

—Robert Dean Frisbie, 1928

the pregnancy of wife number one), and proceeded to start a family with each of his three new wives.

Marsters divided the island into three parts, one for each of his families, and within 18 years he fathered 60 children. Today his descendants number in the thousands and live throughout the Cook Islands and in New Zealand.

COLONIALISM

It was almost inevitable that the Cook Islands would be caught up in the wave of colonial expansion that swept across the South Pacific in the late 1800s. The French, who had established Tahiti as a protectorate, wanted to expand their influence west, and in 1888 a French warship was sent to Manihiki in the Northern Group of the Cooks. The locals quickly sewed together a British Union Jack and ran it up a pole. The French ship turned away. Shortly thereafter the British declared a protectorate over the Cook Islands and the Union Jack went up officially.

The islands were small and unproductive, and in 1901 Britain gladly acceded to a request from New Zealand's prime minister, Richard Seddon, to include the Cook Islands within the boundaries of his newly independent country. And there they remained until 1965.

In addition to engineering the transfer, Seddon is best remembered in the Cook Islands for his vehement hatred of the Chinese. He instituted the policy that has effectively barred the Chinese—and most other Asians, for that matter—from settling in the Cook Islands.

Otherwise, New Zealand, itself a former colony, was never interested in becoming a colonial power, and it never did much to exploit—or develop—the Cook Islands or Western Samoa (over which it exercised a League of Nations trusteeship from the end of World War I until 1962). For all practical purposes, the Cook Islands remained a South Seas backwater for the 72 years of New Zealand rule, with a brief interlude during World War II when U.S. troops built and manned an airstrip on Aitutaki.

INDEPENDENCE

The situation began to change after 1965, when the Cook Islands became self-governing in association with New Zealand. Under this arrangement, New Zealand provides for the national defense needs of the islands and renders financial aid amounting to about one-fifth the revenues of the Cook Islands government. There is an official New Zealand "representative" in Avarua, not an ambassador or consul. For all practical purposes the Cook Islands are independent, although the paper ties with New Zealand deprive them of a seat in the United Nations. The Cook Islanders hold New Zealand citizenship, which means they can live there. New Zealanders, on the other hand, are not citizens of the Cook Islands.

The first prime minister of the newly independent government was Sir Albert Henry, one of the South Pacific's most colorful modern characters. He came to power in 1965, when his Cook Islands Party won a majority of the first parliament and ruled for a controversial 13 years, during which the Cook Islands were put back on the map.

That came in 1973. Using aid from New Zealand, which wanted to provide an independent source of revenue for its former colony, the government enlarged Rarotonga's airport. In return for its assistance, Air New Zealand received exclusive landing rights and began regularly scheduled service, initially using 747 jumbo jets (this has since been scaled back to 767 service). Four years later the first-class Rarotongan Resort Hotel opened, and the Cook Islands became an international destination.

Sir Albert ruled until the national elections in 1978. Even though his party won a majority, he and it were indicted for bribery. Allegedly, government funds had been used to pay for charter flights that ferried Cook Islands Party voters home from New Zealand on election day. The chief justice of the High Court agreed, and Sir Albert and his party were booted out of power. Queen Elizabeth then stripped him of his knighthood. He remained highly popular with his supporters, however, and many

Cook Islanders still refer to him as "Sir Albert." When he died in 1981, his body was taken around Rarotonga on the back of a pickup truck; the road was lined with mourners for the entire 20 miles.

GOVERNMENT & ECONOMY

The Cook Islands **government** is based on the Westminster system, with 24 elected members of parliament led by a prime minister chosen by members of the majority party. Parliament meets twice a year, in February and March and from July to September. There is also a House of Ariki (hereditary chiefs), which advises the government on matters of traditional custom and land tenure. Each island has an elected Island Council and a Chief Administrative Officer (CAO), who is appointed by the prime minister.

The **economy** is based on tourism and exports: tropical fruit and fruit juices, copra, and clothes made at two factories on Rarotonga. Some revenue is derived from the Cook Islands' status as a tax-free financial haven. Without New Zealand aid and the money earned from tourism, however, the country would be in serious financial trouble.

PEOPLE

About half of the 18,000 people who live in the Cook Islands live on Rarotonga, and of these 9,000 people, about 4,000 live on the north coast in Avarua, the only town in the country. Some 80% to 85% of the entire population is pure Polynesian; they call themselves Cook Islands Maoris. In culture, language, and physical appearance, this great majority is closely akin to both the Tahitians and the Maoris of New Zealand. Only on Pukapuka and Nassau atolls to the far northwest, where the residents are more like the Samoans, is the cultural heritage significantly different.

Modern Cook Islanders have maintained much of the old Polynesian way of life, including the warmth, friendliness, and generosity that characterize Polynesians everywhere. Like their ancestors, they put great emphasis on family life. Within the extended family it's share and share alike, and no one ever goes without a meal or a roof over his or her head. In fact, they may be generous to a fault, since many of the small grocery stores they run reputedly stay on the verge of bankruptcy.

Although not a matriarchy, Cook Islands culture places great importance on the roles of wife and mother. The early missionaries divided all land into rectangular plots (reserving choice parcels for themselves and their church buildings, of course), and women are in charge of the section upon which their families live. They decide which crops and fruit trees to plant, they collect the money for household expenses, and, acting collectively and within the churches, they decide how the village will be run. The land cannot be sold, only leased, and when the mother dies, it passes jointly to her children. Since many women prefer to build simple homes so as not to set off squabbles among their offspring when they die, most houses provide basic shelter and are not constructed with an eye to increasing value. In fact, when a woman dies, the house occasionally is left vacant by succeeding generations.

The burial vaults you will see in many front yards are the final resting places of the mothers who built the houses. Their coffins are sealed in concrete vaults both for sanitary reasons and because to shovel dirt on a woman's dead body is to treat her with disrespect. (Likewise, striking a woman is the quickest way for a Cook Islands man to wind up in prison.) The survivors care only for the graves of persons they

---

IMPRESSIONS

Compared with French Polynesia, the Cook Islands are the South Seas demystified—more approachable, more friendly, more affordable, more intimate, more relaxed, but perhaps just a touch less magical.

—RON HALL, 1991

knew, which explains the many overgrown vaults. Eventually, when no one remembers their occupants, the tops of the old vaults will be removed and the ground plowed for a new crop.

Christianity as taught by the Protestant missionaries, most sent from the London Missionary Society's outposts in what is now French Polynesia, was taken to heart by the Cook Islanders in the early 19th century, and their descendants virtually close the country down on Sunday—except the hotels and the churches that are at the center of life in every village.

Cook Islanders have retained that old Polynesian tradition known as "island time." The clock moves more slowly here, as it does in other South Pacific Islands. Everything will get done in due course, not necessarily now. So service is often slow by Western standards, but why hurry? You're on vacation.

In addition to those who are pure Polynesian, a significant minority are of mixed European-Polynesian descent. There also are a number of New Zealanders, Australians, Americans, and Europeans, most of whom live on Rarotonga and seem to move to the beat of "island time," too. There are very few Chinese or other Asians in the Cook Islands—thus the relative scarcity of Asian cuisine here.

LANGUAGE

Nearly everyone speaks English, the official language. All signs and notices are written in it. The everyday language for most people, however, is Cook Islands Maori, a Polynesian language similar to Tahitian and New Zealand Maori. A little knowledge of it is helpful, particularly since nearly all place names are Maori.

Cook Islands Maori has eight consonants and five vowels. The vowels are pronounced in the Roman fashion: *ah, ay, ee, oh, oo* instead of *a, e, i, o, u* as in English. The consonants used are *k, m, n, p, r, t,* and *v*. These are pronounced much as they are in English. There also is *ng,* which is pronounced as the *ng* in "ring." The language is written phonetically; that is, every letter is pronounced. If there are three vowels in a row, each is sounded. The name of Mangaia Island, for example, is pronounced "mahn-*gah*-ee-ah."

More than likely Cook Islanders will speak English to all Europeans, but here are some helpful expressions with suggested pronunciations.

ENGLISH	MAORI	PRONUNCIATION
Hello	**kia orana**	*kee*-ah oh-*rah*-nah
Good-bye	**aere ra**	ah-*ay*-ray rah
Thank you	**meitaki**	may-ee-*tah*-kee
How are you?	**peea koe**	*pay*-ay-ah *ko*-ay
Yes	**ae**	*ah*-ay
No	**kare**	*kah*-ray
Good luck	**kia manuia**	*kee*-ah mah-*nu*-ee-ah
European person	**Papa'a**	pah-*pah*-ah
Wraparound sarong	**pareu**	pah-*ray*-oo
Keep out	**tapu**	*tah*-poo
Small island	**motu**	*moh*-too

2. INFORMATION, ENTRY REQUIREMENTS & MONEY

INFORMATION

The excellent staff at the **Cook Islands Tourist Authority** will provide information upon request. The address is P.O. Box 14, Rarotonga, Cook Islands, South Pacific (tel. 29-435, fax 21-435). The main office and visitors center is beside the Banana

Court Bar next to the traffic circle in the heart of Avarua. Maps and brochures are available there.

In **North America** the authority has a representative at 1000 San Clemente Way, Camarillo, CA 93010 (tel. 805/338-4673, fax 805/338-8086).

Other offices are:

New Zealand: Travel Industry Services, Ltd., P.O. Box 3647, Auckland (tel. 09/371-546).

Australia: Cook Islands Tourist Authority, 11th Floor, 39 York St., Sydney, NSW 2000 (tel. 02/262-5200, fax 02/262-5202).

Hong Kong: Pacific Leisure, Tung Ming Building, 40 Des Voeux Rd., Central, Box 2582, Hong Kong (tel. 247-076).

Once you get to Rarotonga, pick up a copy of *What's On In The Cook Islands,* a skinny book full of facts and advertisements. It's distributed free by the tourist authority and most hotels.

ENTRY REQUIREMENTS

Visitors with valid passports, onward or return air tickets (they will be examined at the immigration desk upon arrival), and sufficient funds are allowed to stay for 31 days. Extensions are granted on a month-to-month basis for up to 5 months beyond the initial 31-day visa upon application to the Immigration Department near the airport in Avarua and payment of NZ$30 ($18) per month. Visitors intending to stay more than 6 months must apply from their home country to the Principal Immigration Officer, Ministry of Labour and Commerce, P.O. Box 61, Rarotonga, Cook Islands.

At one time the government required all visitors to have a confirmed hotel reservation before arrival; that was no longer the case during my last visit. There were reports, however, that the government was planning to review its policy regarding low-budget, backpacking travelers.

Customs allowances are 2 liters of spirits or wine, 200 cigarettes or 50 cigars, two cameras, 10 rolls of film, and other goods up to a value of NZ$50 ($30). Arriving passengers can purchase items from the duty-free shop at the airport before clearing immigration. Firearms, ammunition, and indecent materials are prohibited. Personal effects are not subject to duty. All food and other agricultural products are subject to inspection and must be declared, and live animals are prohibited entry. The dog hanging around the baggage-claim area may be sniffing for drugs.

MONEY

The New Zealand dollar is the medium of exchange, although the Cook Islands government prints its own colorful notes and mints unusual coins, such as a triangular $2 piece and the famous Tangaroa dollar. The latter bears the likeness of Tangaroa—well-defined private part and all—on one side and Queen Elizabeth II on the other (the queen reportedly was not at all pleased about sharing the coin with Tangaroa in all his glory). So both the New Zealand and Cook Islands currencies are used and have the same values, but the Cook Islands currency cannot be exchanged outside the islands.

At the time of this writing, the New Zealand dollar was worth about U.S. 60¢, give or take a few cents. The exchange rate is carried in the business sections of most daily newspapers.

WHAT THINGS COST IN THE COOK ISLANDS	U.S. $
Hotel bus from airport to Avarua	5.00
Local phone call	.06
Ride on The Bus	1.80
Double room at Manuia Beach Hotel (expensive)	150.00
Double room at Rarotongan Sunset Motel (moderate)	75.00
Double room at Are-Renga Motel (budget)	30.00

THE NEW ZEALAND & U.S. DOLLARS

At this writing, NZ$1 = approximately U.S. 60¢, the rate of exchange used to calculate the U.S. dollar prices given in this chapter. This rate has remained fairly stable during the past few years but may change by the time you visit. Accordingly, use the following table only as a guide.

$ NZ	$ U.S.	$ NZ	$ U.S.
.25	.15	15	9.00
.50	.30	20	12.00
.75	.45	25	15.00
1.00	.60	30	18.00
2.00	1.20	35	21.00
3.00	1.80	40	24.00
4.00	2.40	45	27.00
5.00	3.00	50	30.00
6.00	3.60	75	45.00
7.00	4.20	100	60.00
8.00	4.80	125	75.00
9.00	5.40	150	90.00
10.00	6.00	200	120.00

	US$
Lunch for one at Trader Jack's (expensive)	15.00
Lunch for one at Hibiscus Restaurant (moderate)	7.00
Lunch for one at Cook's Corner Cafe (budget)	4.00
Dinner for one, without wine, at the Flame Tree (expensive)	30.00
Dinner for one, without wine, at Kaena Restaurant (moderate)	20.00
Dinner for one, without wine, at Metua's Cafe (budget)	10.00
Beer	2.50
Coca-Cola	1.00
Cup of coffee	.60
Roll of ASA 100 Kodacolor film, 36 exposures	6.00
Movie ticket	3.00

3. WHEN TO GO — CLIMATE, HOLIDAYS & EVENTS

CLIMATE

The islands of the Southern Group, which are about as far south of the equator as the Hawaiian Islands are north, have a very pleasant tropical climate. Even during the summer months of January and February, the high temperatures on Rarotonga average a comfortable 84°F, and the southeast trade winds usually moderate even the hottest day. The average high drops to 77°F during the winter months, from June to

August, and the ends of Antarctic cold fronts can bring a few downright chilly nights during those months. It's a good idea to bring a light sweater or jacket for evening wear anytime of the year.

December through April is both the cyclone (hurricane) and rainy season. There always is a chance that a cyclone will wander along during these months, but most of the rain comes in short, heavy cloudbursts that are followed by sunshine. Rain clouds usually hang around Rarotonga's mountain peaks, even during the dry season, from June to August.

In short, there is no bad time weatherwise to visit the Cook Islands, although the "shoulder" months of April, May, September, and October usually provide the best combination of sunshine and warmth. Frankly, I much prefer cool and dry Rarotonga in July and August to the hot and steamy Mid-Atlantic state where I live.

HOLIDAYS

Legal **holidays** are New Year's Day, ANZAC (Memorial) Day (April 25), Good Friday, Easter Monday, the Queen's Birthday (in June), Constitution Day (August 4), Christmas Day, and Boxing Day (December 26).

The busiest **season** used to be July and August when New Zealanders and Australians escaped their own winters; however, more and more Americans, Canadians, and Europeans have been visiting in recent years, which means that all year is fairly busy, especially for the smaller hotels and motels. Make your hotel reservations early. Many Cook Islanders live in New Zealand and come home for Christmas; airline seats may be hard to come by during that holiday season.

Note: Rarotonga will host the South Pacific Arts Festival in October 1992, when hotel rooms will be at a premium.

COOK ISLANDS CALENDAR OF EVENTS

FEBRUARY

- ☐ **Cultural Festival Week.** Features various cultural, arts-and-crafts displays, and a giant canoe race. 3rd week in February.

APRIL

- ☐ **Island Dance Festival Week.** Features one of the South Pacific's great traditional dance competitions; villages from all over the country send their young people to Rarotonga to compete for the coveted Dancers of the Year award. 2nd week in April.
- ☐ **ANZAC Day.** Cook Islanders killed in the two world wars are honored with parades and church services. April 25.

AUGUST

- ☐ **Constitution Week.** Honoring the attainment of self-government on August 4,

IMPRESSIONS

It would be a fitting way for an island trader to end his days; and when he closed his eyes for the last time and he was snugly buried in the clean coral sand, how well he would sleep there, the trade-wind rocking the palms over his grave and the long Pacific rollers thundering along the reef offshore.

—Robert Dean Frisbie, 1928

1965, this biggest Cook Islands celebration is highlighted by a week-long Polynesian dance contest. There are also parades and sporting events. Begins Friday before August 4, runs for 10 days.

SEPTEMBER

- ☐ **Cook Islands Art Exhibition Week.** Works of local artists and sculptors are displayed at a variety of exhibitions. 2nd week in September.

OCTOBER

- ☐ **Cook Islands Fashion Week.** Local fashions and accessories are featured at various displays and shows. 3rd week in October.
- ☐ **Gospel Day.** Honors the arrival of the first missionaries and features outdoor religious plays known as *nuku*. Last Sunday in October.

NOVEMBER

- ☐ **Round Rarotonga Road Run.** Marathoners race completely around Rarotonga—all 32km (20 miles) of it. 1st week in November.
- ☐ **Tiare Festival Week.** A float parade and floral arrangement competition spotlights the islands' favorite flower. 3rd week in November.

4. GETTING THERE & GETTING AROUND

GETTING TO RAROTONGA

Air New Zealand has direct service from Los Angeles to Rarotonga via Honolulu. It also has weekly service to Rarotonga from Tahiti and Fiji on the Coral Route, making possible the Los Angeles–Tahiti-Rarotonga-Nadi (or vice versa) route I recommend in Chapter 2 as a suggested itinerary. In addition, Air New Zealand has several flights a week between Auckland and Rarotonga. Polynesian Airlines connects Rarotonga to both Pago Pago and Apia. Hawaiian Airlines flies to Rarotonga from Los Angeles, San Francisco, and Seattle, with a change of planes in Honolulu. For more information, see "Getting There" in Chapter 2.

The small terminal at **Rarotonga International Airport,** the country's only gateway, is 2.2km (1.3 miles) west of Avarua. Westpac Bank's terminal office is open 1 hour before and after all international flights. Small shops in the departure lounge sell handcrafts, liquor, cigarettes, and stamps. Arriving passengers can purchase duty-free

IMPRESSIONS

I arrived late on a Saturday. Next day I decided to explore the island, but that next day was Sunday, and even Aitutaki's ubiquitous mynah birds seem inclined toward indolence on a Sunday.

—Lawrence Millman, 1990

IMPRESSIONS

For my taste, there are few approaches anywhere on this planet more exhilarating than when your plane sweeps down out of the clouds and, suddenly, miraculously, you see the lush green mountains of Rarotonga rising out of the sea like a landscape from a childhood fairy tale, like a lost world.

—LAWRENCE MILLMAN, 1990

---

items before clearing immigration. Air New Zealand and the other airlines have their Rarotonga offices in the terminal.

Transportation from the airport is by hotel bus, taxi, or rental car. Most hotels tack from NZ$5 to NZ$12 ($3 to $7) per person to your hotel bill for the round-trip transfer.

A **departure tax** of NZ$20 ($12) for adults and NZ$10 ($6) for children between the ages of 2 and 12 is payable in New Zealand or Cook Islands currency; check in at the airline counter first, then pay at the window beside the entrance to immigration.

GETTING AROUND THE COOKS

BY PLANE

Air Rarotonga (tel. 22-88) has two flights a day (except Sunday) to Aitutaki and once a day to Atiu, Mauke, Mangaia, and Mitiaro. Round-trip fares are about NZ$285 ($170) to Aitutaki, NZ$255 ($152) to Atiu, NZ$260 ($156) to Mangaia, and NZ$284 ($170) to Mauke or Mitiaro. Air Rarotonga will also book hotels and most activities on the other islands free of charge. You can save as much as NZ$100 ($60) by buying a package of airfare and accommodation.

Air Rarotonga has day-trips to Aitutaki for about NZ$270 ($162), which includes airfare and a lagoon excursion with a barbecue lunch. When I was there its lagoon trips were in a boat whose deck was shaded by a canopy.

Don't forget to reconfirm your flights.

BY SHIP

"Adventures in Paradise," the 1950s television series, may have glorified the South Pacific "copra schooners" that still ply the South Seas trading corned beef and printed cotton for copra, but those operating in the Cook Islands have experienced anything but glory in recent years. In fact, several of them have run aground; one even stopped

FROMMER'S SMART TRAVELER: AIRFARES

Air Rarotonga often has discounts of up to 25% on selected off-peak flights, and its Island Hopper Pass includes reduced fares to two or more islands. Its day and overnight trips to Aitutaki cost less than if you do it yourself.

working while at sea and drifted several hundred miles before being towed to safety by a passing tanker. To put it bluntly, you can't count on getting anywhere in the Cooks by ship these days. If you want to see if any are running, check in with the Harbour Office at the wharf in Avatiu, the western half of Avarua. The daily *Cook Islands News* prints the local shipping schedules each morning.

GETTING AROUND RAROTONGA

Only 20 miles around by road, Rarotonga is so small that the runway at the international airport stretches almost a quarter of the way across its northern coast. In fact, the Cross Island Track can be hiked in less than a ½-day. Nevertheless, some form of transportation is necessary in order to get around and see the sights of this lovely island. There are several modes available, but avoid hitchhiking, which is frowned upon by the government.

THE BUS

When someone says "catch the bus" on Rarotonga, they mean the Cook's Corner Island Bus (no phone) that leaves the Cook's Corner shopping center in Avarua on the hour going clockwise and on the half hour going counterclockwise from 8am to 4:30pm Monday to Friday, from 8am to noon Saturday. The two buses each take 50 minutes to circle the island, arriving back in Avarua in time to start another trip. The fare is NZ$3 ($1.80) regardless of the length of the ride, but most hotels sell day passes for NZ$5 ($3) and 10-ride books for NZ$16 ($9.60). The receptionist will know approximately when a bus will pass your hotel, but it will stop anywhere. Just wave to get on board.

The same buses operate a "Raro by Nite" service every evening except Sunday. The buses depart Cook's Corner at 6, 8, 9, and 10pm Monday to Saturday. Additional departures are at midnight on Friday and Saturday and at 1:30am Friday (that is, Saturday morning). Round-trip fares are NZ$4 ($2.40).

The Rarotongan Resort Hotel operates a gaily painted minibus shuttle between the hotel and Avarua between 9:45am and 4:10pm Monday to Saturday. Fares are NZ$2 ($1.20) one-way, NZ$3 ($1.80) round-trip.

RENTAL CARS

Visitors are required to have a valid Cook Islands driver's license before operating any motorized vehicle. To get one, you just have to go to Police Headquarters (on the main road just west of the Avarua traffic circle), present your valid overseas license, and pay NZ$2.50 ($1.50). It's valid for the same class of vehicles covered by your home-country license. If you want to rent a motorbike or scooter and you aren't licensed to drive them at home, you will have to take a driving test and pay an additional NZ$2.50 ($1.50). Tests are given from 11am to 1pm Monday through Saturday. All drivers must be at least 21 years old.

Driving Rules: Driving is on the left, and the speed limit is 50kmph (30 m.p.h.) in the countryside and 25kmph (15 m.p.h.) in Avarua and the villages. Gasoline is available from service stations in Avarua and at some village shops. The road around the island is paved but somewhat rough, and drivers must be on the alert at all times for dogs, chickens, potholes, and pigs.

I usually rent from Winton Pickering at **Budget Rent-A-Car** (tel. 20-895, or toll free 800/527-0700 in the U.S.), which has an office in Avarua a block off the main road (turn at the colonial house next to the Hibiscus Bar and Cafe), a booth on Avarua's main road, and desks at the Edgewater Resort and Rarotongan Resort Hotel. Subaru sedans rent for NZ$50 ($30) per day with unlimited kilometers plus NZ$5 ($3) for a collision damage waiver—even with this insurance, however, the renter is responsible for the first NZ$600 ($360) of any damage. Budget provides free delivery and drop-off at the hotels or airport.

Ace Rent-a-Car (tel. 21-901, or toll free 800/331-1212 in the U.S.) is the local **Avis** licensee. Its rates are approximately the same as Budget's. The main office is in Arorangi between the Edgewater Resort and Manuia Beach Hotel.

Tipani Rentals (tel. 22-327 or 22-328), on the main road in Avarua and in Arorangi opposite the Edgewater Resort, and **Rental Cars (C.I.) Ltd.** (tel. 24-442) on the main road in town both rent cars of various vintages at the same rates charged by Budget and Avis. In addition, some hotels have cars that they rent.

SCOOTERS & BIKES

Cook Islanders are as likely to travel by motorbike or scooter as they are by automobile. **Polynesian Bike Hire Ltd.** (tel. 20-895) and **Tipani Rentals** (tel. 22-327) both rent them on a daily or weekly basis. Rates start at NZ$20 ($12) per day. Polynesian Bike Hire Ltd. and Budget Rent-A-Car share offices (see above).

There are no hills on the round-island road, so touring by bicycle ("push-bikes" they're called in the Cook Islands) is a pleasure. Several hotels have bicycles available for their guests to use. **Polynesian Bike Hire Ltd.** (tel. 20-895) and **Tipani Rentals** (tel. 22-327) have them for NZ$10 ($6) per day.

TAXIS

There are a number of cars and minibuses scurrying around Rarotonga with "taxi" signs on top, but there are no meters. Service is available daily from 7am to midnight. As a rule of thumb, taxi fares should be about NZ$1 (60¢) per kilometer. If a taxi doesn't have a meter, be sure to settle on a fare before getting in. To call a taxi, phone either 27-021, 23-510, 20-213, or 22-238.

DISTANCES

Here are some distances from the traffic circle in Avarua.

Going East (clockwise)	**Km**	**Miles**
Tamure Resort Hotel	2.4	1.4
Kii Kii Motel	2.8	1.6
Sailing Club/Pacific Resort	10.7	6.4
Muri Beachcomber Motel	10.9	6.5
Welland Studio	12.0	7.2
Little Polynesia Motel	14.1	8.5
Moana Sands Beach Hideaway	14.3	8.6
Going West (counterclockwise)		
Airport terminal	2.2	1.3
Parliament	3.2	1.9
Golf Course	5.1	3.0
Rarotonga Sunset Motel	6.3	3.8
Edgewater Resort	6.8	4.1
Dive Rarotonga	7.2	4.3
Manuia Beach Hotel	8.0	4.8
Are-Renga Motel	8.5	5.1
Puaikura Reef Lodges	11.5	6.9
Lagoon Lodges	13.1	7.8
The Rarotongan Resort	13.5	8.1
Vaima Restaurant	18.0	10.8

RAROTONGA

American Express There is no American Express representative in the Cook Islands. See the "Fast Facts: South Pacific" in Chapter 2 for how to report lost or stolen American Express credit cards or traveler's checks. The local banks may be able to assist in reporting lost checks.

Area Code The international country code is 682.

Baby-sitters Contact the hotel reception desks to arrange baby-sitters.

Banks See "Currency Exchange," below.

Bookstores **The Bounty Book Shop,** in the high-rise C.I.D.B. Building in Avarua, and the **Cook Islands Trading Corporation** (C.I.T.C.), on the waterfront, both sell paperback novels, maps of Rarotonga and Aitutaki, and books about the Cook Islands and the South Pacific in general. The Bounty Bookshop also carries the international editions of *Time* and *Newsweek,* the latter incorporated into the *Bulletin,* an Australian newsmagazine.

Business Hours Most shops on Rarotonga are open Mon–Fri 8am–4pm and Sat 8am–noon. Some small grocery stores in the villages are open in the evenings and for limited hours on Sun. The only shop open on Sun afternoon is the boutique in the Rarotongan Resort Hotel.

Camera/Film A reasonable selection of color-print film is available at many shops in Avarua. One-hour processing of color-print film is available at **Rarotonga Pharmacy Ltd.** in the Cook Islands Trading Corp. (C.I.T.C.) shopping center in Avarua. **Cocophoto,** next to South Seas Duty Free near Avatiu harbor, offers a 4-hour developing service. Color slides are sent to New Zealand for processing.

Car Rentals See "Getting Around Rarotonga" in this chapter.

Climate See "When to Go—Climate, Holidays, and Events," in this chapter.

Clothing Dress in the Cook Islands is informal. Shorts of respectable length (that is, not of the short-short variety) are worn during the day by both men and women, but beach attire should be reserved for the beach only. Nude or topless sunbathing is not permitted anywhere. The colorful wraparound pareu is popular with local women. Evenings May–Sept can be cool, so trousers, skirts, light jackets, sweaters, or wraps are in order after dark. The only neckties to be seen are at church on Sun.

Credit Cards American Express, VISA, MasterCard, and Diners Club credit cards are accepted at the hotels, restaurants, duty-free shops, and rental-car firms.

Crime See "Safety," below.

Currency See "Information, Entry Requirements & Money" in this chapter.

Currency Exchange Two banks operate on Rarotonga, and both are open Mon–Fri 9am–3pm. **Westpac Bank** has its main office west of the traffic circle on the main road in Avarua, as well as a branch in Arorangi on the west coast. **ANZ Bank** has an office at the rear of the first-floor shopping arcade in the C.I.D.C. Building, the large modern structure west of the traffic circle in Avarua (it has wooden stairs ascending in front). If you go to the outer islands, you can cash traveler's checks at the local post offices.

Customs See "Information, Entry Requirements & Money" in this chapter.

Dentist Dental care on Rarotonga is good and relatively inexpensive (many residents of French Polynesia come to Rarotonga for their dental work rather than pay the high prices on Tahiti). Ask at your hotel desk for the name of a private practitioner or go to the Tupapa Outpatient Clinic on the east end of Avarua. Hours are Mon–Fri 8am–4pm, Sat 8–11am.

Doctor Medical care in the Cook Islands is relatively good by South Pacific standards but by no means sophisticated. Most doctors and dentists were trained in New Zealand, and several of them are in private practice. See "Hospital," below.

Documents Required See "Information, Entry Requirements & Money" in this chapter.

Driving Rules See "Getting Around Rarotonga" in this chapter.

Drug Laws Dangerous drugs and narcotics are illegal; possession can land you in a very unpleasant jail for a very long time.

Drugstores **Rarotonga Pharmacy Ltd.** (tel. 29-292), in the Cook Islands Trading Corp. shopping center in Avarua, is the only commercial pharmacy. The clinics on the outer islands have a limited supply of prescription medicines.

Electricity Electricity is 230 volts, 50 cycles, so converters are necessary in order to operate American and Canadian appliances. The plugs, like those of New Zealand and Australia, have two angled prongs, so an adapter will also be needed. If your appliances or the table lamps in your room don't work, check to see if the switch on the wall outlet is turned on.

Embassies/Consulates No foreign government maintains an embassy or consulate in the Cook Islands. In case of a problem, seek advice from the travel facilitation and consular officer in the Ministry of Foreign Affairs (tel. 20-507). The New Zealand government has a representative, whose office is across the street from the Chief Post Office in Avarua. The U.S. embassy in Wellington, New Zealand, has jurisdiction.

Emergencies The emergency number for the **police** is 999; for an **ambulance** or the hospital, 998; for **fire,** 996.

Eyeglasses There is no optician on Rarotonga, but Nev Pearson of Nev's Services (tel. 25-477) in Brown's Arcade, Avarua, can make repairs to frames and possibly replace a lens.

Firearms Don't even think about it—they're illegal!

Gambling There are no gambling casinos in the Cook Islands, but a lot of money reportedly changes hands on bingo games and on New Zealand horse races, cricket, and rugby matches.

Hairdressers/Barbers Douglas & Company (tel. 20-770) is located in Brown's Arcade in Avarua.

Hitchhiking Technically hitchhiking is frowned upon by the government.

Holidays See "When to Go—Climate, Holidays, and Events," in this chapter.

Hospital The hospital (tel. 22-664, or 998 in case of emergency) is located behind the golf course. The cost of care is relatively reasonable—a day in the hospital costs about NZ$30 ($18). For minor problems, go to the Tupapa Outpatient Clinic on the east end of Avarua; it's open Mon–Fri 8am–4pm, Sat 8–11am.

Information See "Information, Entry Requirements & Money" in this chapter.

Insects There are no poisonous insects in the Cook Islands. Mosquitoes are plentiful, especially during the summer months and in the inland areas, so bring a good repellent. Mosquito coils can be bought at most village shops.

Language See "Language" in this chapter, under "Getting to Know the Cook Islands."

Laundry/Dry Cleaning **Blue Pacific Laundry and Dry Cleaning** (tel. 26-884) is in a white building next to the petroleum storage tanks across from the airport terminal; same-day service is available on weekdays if items are brought in by 8am. Most hotels offer laundry service or facilities to their guests. **Sunbird Laundry** has Laundromats at Avarua in the Empire Theatre building and in Arorangi.

Libraries The Cook Islands Library and Museum is open Mon–Fri 9am–4:30pm, Sat 8:30–11:30pm, and Tues and Thurs 7–8:30pm. The library has a fine collection of works on the South Pacific, including many hard-to-find books.

Liquor Laws When it's open during regular business hours (see above), the government-owned Cook Islands Liquor Supplies has a corner on sales of beer, wine, and liquor by the bottle. Some village shops sell beer when it's closed. The hotel bars can sell alcoholic beverages to their guests on Sun, but most other bars and nightclubs close promptly at midnight Sat.

Mail The Chief Post Office is located at the traffic circle in Avarua and is open Mon–Fri 8am–4pm. There's a branch post office opposite Titikaveka College on Rarotonga's south coast. Each of the other islands has a post office. International airmail rates for letters are NZ$1.05 (65¢); postcards and airgrams are NZ85¢ (50¢). There is no mail delivery, so all addresses include a post office box.

Maps The little tourist publication, *What's On In The Cook Islands* contains maps of Rarotonga and the town of Avarua. Get a copy at the tourist authority's office or at most hotels. The government Department of Surveys (tel. 29-433) behind the Chief Post Office sells excellent topographic maps prepared by the New Zealand surveyor general.

Newspapers/Magazines A tiny tabloid, the *Cook Islands News,* is published Mon–Sat. It contains local, regional, and world news, radio and TV schedules, shipping schedules, a weather map for the South Pacific, and notices of local events (including advertisements for "island nights" at the hotels). It even has two comic strips. Copies are available at the Bounty Bookshop and the large Cook Islands Trading Corp. (C.I.T.C.) store in the center of Avarua.

Pets All animals brought into the country must be declared for inspection. As a practical matter, the next time you see your quarantined pet will be when you leave Rarotonga.

Police See "Emergencies," above and "Safety," below.

Radio/TV Rarotonga has one AM and one FM radio station; both broadcast Polynesian and Western music, and most programming is in English. International news from Radio Australia is broadcast at 8am. One TV channel broadcasts the news at noon and entertainment programs 5–11pm nightly.

Religious Services In addition to the 60% of all Cook Islanders who belong to the Cook Islands Christian Church, the major Protestant denomination, there are Roman Catholics, Mormons, Baha'is, and Seventh-Day Adventists in the islands.

Rest Rooms In Avarua, Cook's Corner shopping center has clean rest rooms. There are also public facilities in the shedlike building on the waterfront by the old wharf in Avarua. Otherwise, visitors should use the facilities in the hotels, bars, and restaurants.

Safety Although crimes against tourists are rare, do not offer temptation by leaving your belongings untended. Stay alert whenever you're traveling in an unfamiliar city or country. See the "Fast Facts: South Pacific" in Chapter 2 for more warnings.

Taxes In addition to the NZ$20 ($12) airport departure tax, the government imposes a 10% tax on all hotel, restaurant, and rental-car bills.

Telephone/Telex/Fax International telephone calls, telegrams, and telex messages can be made or sent from most hotels or from Telekom Cook Islands, Ltd., on the street between the Cook Islands Trading Corp. and the Cook's Corner shopping centers in Avarua. The communications office is open 24 hours a day, including Sun.

There is a minimum charge of NZ$19 ($11.40) for the first 3 minutes of all calls to North America. Each additional minute costs NZ$6.50 ($4). Payment is made after the call is completed, in cash or by credit cards issued by one of the American Bell System telephone companies.

Direct dialing to the Cook Islands from most parts of the world has been available for some time, and it should be available from North America by the time you use this book. The **country code is 682.** If you can't get through, contact your telephone company's international operator.

Red **public telephones** are located at Telekom Cook Islands, at the post offices, and in booths in many villages. To operate, lift the receiver, listen for a dial tone, deposit a New Zealand or Cook Islands 10-cent coin, and dial the local number. Dial 010 for local directory assistance, 015 for international calls, and 020 for calls to the outer islands. Emergency numbers are listed above.

Time Local time is 10 hours behind Greenwich mean time. Translated, that's 2 hours behind California during standard time, 3 hours behind during daylight saving time. The Cook Islands are on the east side of the international date line, which puts them in the same day as the U.S. and a day behind New Zealand and Australia.

Tipping Tipping is considered contrary to the Polynesian way of life and is frowned upon.

Tourist Offices See "Information, Entry Requirements & Money" in this chapter.

Visas See "Information, Entry Requirements & Money" in this chapter.

Water Generally, tap water on Rarotonga is safe to drink, although it can become slightly muddy after periods of heavy rain. Many hotels have their own filtration systems. If in doubt, boil it in the electric "jug" in your hotel room. The tap water on Aitutaki is *not* safe to drink.

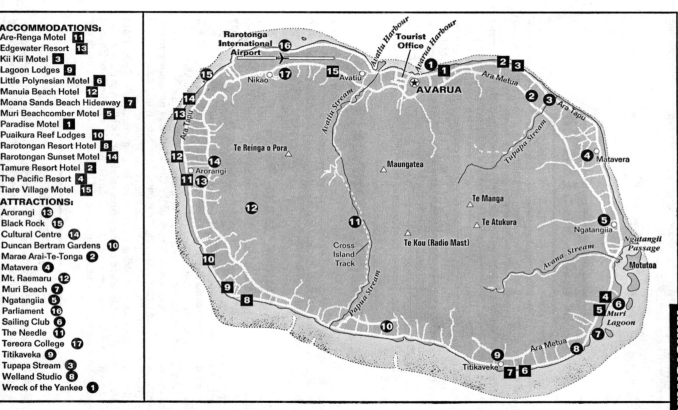

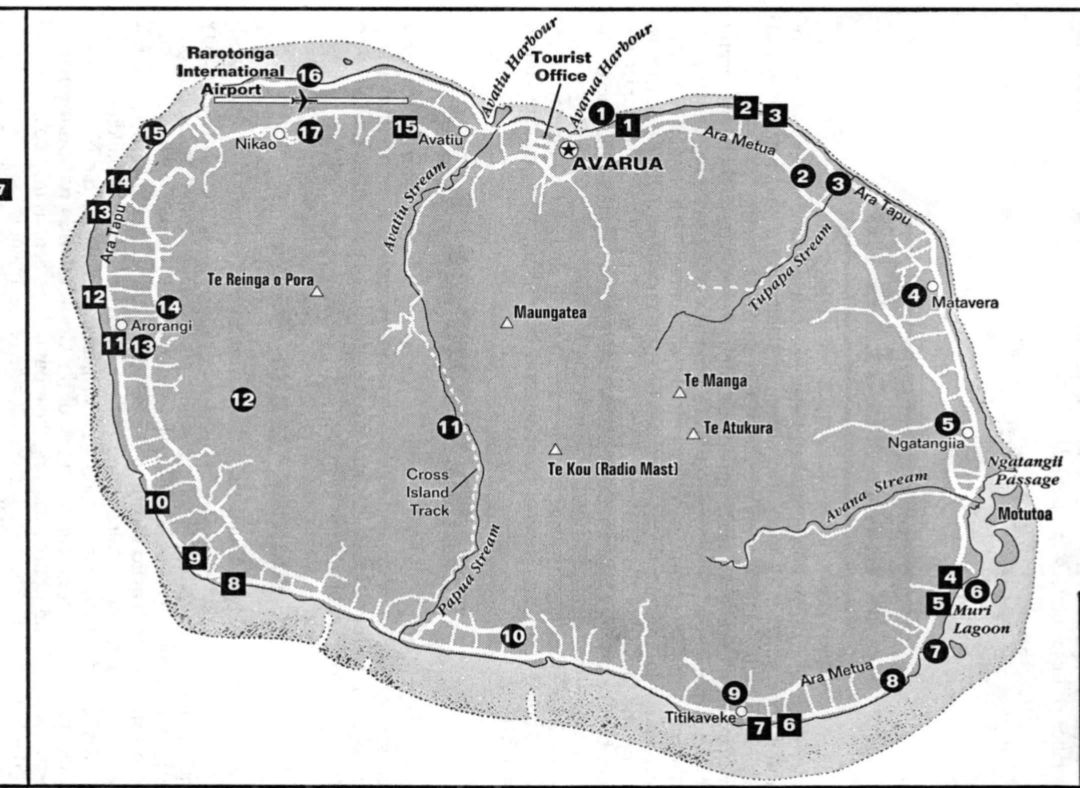
RAROTONGA
N
0
2.5 km
1.5 mi
ACCOMMODATIONS:
Are-Renga Motel 11
Edgewater Resort 13
Kii Kii Motel 3
Lagoon Lodges 9
Little Polynesian Motel 6
Manuia Beach Hotel 12
Moana Sands Beach Hideaway 7
Muri Beachcomber Motel 5
Paradise Motel 1
Puaikura Reef Lodges 10
Rarotongan Resort Hotel 8
Rarotongan Sunset Motel 14
Tamure Resort Hotel 2
The Pacific Resort 4
Tiare Village Motel 15
ATTRACTIONS:
Arorangi 13
Black Rock 15
Cultural Centre 14
Duncan Bertram Gardens 10
Marae Arai-Te-Tonga 2
Matavera 4
Mt. Raemaru 12
Muri Beach 7
Ngatangiia 5
Parliament 16
Sailing Club 6
The Needle 11
Tereora College 17
Titikaveka 9
Tupapa Stream 3
Welland Studio 8
Wreck of the Yankee 1
Rarotonga International Airport
Avatiu Harbour
Tourist Office
Avarua Harbour
AVARUA
Nikao
Avatiu
Ara Metua
Ara Tapu
Avatiu Stream
Tupapa Stream
Matavera
Te Reinga o Pora
Maungatea
Arorangi
Te Manga
Te Atukura
Te Kou (Radio Mast)
Ngatangiia
Ngatangii Passage
Cross Island Track
Avana Stream
Motutoa
Papua Stream
Muri Lagoon
Ara Metua
Titikaveke

Weights/Measures The Cook Islands are on the metric system; only the post office still uses ounces and pounds.

5. WHAT TO SEE & DO

A microcosm of modern Polynesia, Rarotonga has enough island activities to satisfy almost anyone, whether it's snorkeling, shopping, sightseeing, scuba diving, or several other pastimes. Its cultural tours are the best in the South Pacific.

Regardless of bleary eyes and splitting heads left over from the night before, nearly everyone in the Cook Islands puts on his or her finest white straw hat and goes to ✪ **church** on Sunday morning. Visitors should give serious consideration to joining them, and not just because there isn't much else to do on Sunday in the Cook Islands. No one who attends a Cook Islands Christian Church service will ever forget the magnificent harmony of a hundred Polynesian voices, and a rousing sermon never did hurt anyone—even if it's delivered in thundering Maori.

Services at Rarotongan village churches are normally at 10am on Sunday; buses leave the hotels at 9:30am. Reserve at the activities desk or just show up at any church on the island.

SEEING RAROTONGA

All one has to do to see a beautiful sight on Rarotonga is look up at the green razor ridges soaring to lofty mountain heights or out at the turquoise lagoon with the deep blue sea beyond. But there is much more to see, and the island is small enough to do so by car, motorbike, bicycle, or even on foot.

WALKING TOUR OF AVARUA

Avarua is best seen by walking, since this picturesque little South Seas town winds for only a mile along the curving waterfront between its two harbors. Virtually every sight and most of the shops sit along or just off the main around-the-island road, which for this mile serves as Main Street.

Let's start at the **traffic circle** in the heart of town at the old harbor, which is more or less both the beginning and end of the road. The old building on the southeast corner of this intersection was once headquarters for the New Zealand colonial government. It now houses most of the **Cook Islands national government,** with the Land Court occupying the ground floor. Serious map collectors will find the Department of Surveys at the back side of the building.

Behind the government building on the street heading inland is the **Chief Post Office,** over which is the **office of the prime minister.** Look across the street for his reserved parking space in front of the Philatelic Bureau and the New Zealand representative's office. At 10am on Tuesday and Thursday you can walk a block past

IMPRESSIONS

People here honor the Sabbath even more virtuously than Scottish Highlanders, but they also honor Tangaroa, ancient god of fertility, whose well-endowed figure appears on their own one-dollar coin.

—Lawrence Millman, 1990

the post office and have a tour of the local **brewery,** which includes a taste of Rarotonga's own Cooks Lager.

About 200 yards east on the main road, just beyond Brown's Arcade, are the ruins of what once was a Sunday school. A path on the right side of this relic leads to another sad hulk: The steel hull of the brigantine ✪ ***Yankee*** lies high and almost dry on the reef just offshore, the rusting carcass of one of the most famous ships of the postwar era. Irving and Electra Johnson sailed it around the world seven times between 1948 and 1957 and wrote books and several *National Geographic* articles about their exploits. After they sold it, *Yankee* was put to use by a cruise firm and arrived at Rarotonga in 1964 with its engines out of action and in bad need of repairs. These couldn't be made, and one night when the crew was partying on board and paying scant attention to the weather, the wind shifted to the north. *Yankee* dragged anchor, and the pounding surf put it on the reef with a series of grinding thuds that sent shudders through the hearts of onlookers ashore. All efforts to remove it from the reef failed, and all that remains today is the rusting skeleton, a grim reminder of how quickly the Pacific can turn violent.

In a shady parklike setting across the road from the *Yankee* wreck stands **Taputapuatea,** the restored "palace" of Queen Makea Takau Ariki. Don't enter the grounds without permission, for they are taboo to us commoners. Queen Makea is long dead, but when she was around in the 19th century, the palace reputedly was a lively place.

Facing the palace grounds across the road running inland is the tall, white ✪ **Cook Islands Christian Church,** which was built in 1855. Just to the left of the main entrance is the grave of Albert Henry, the late prime minister. A bust of "Sir Albert" sits atop the grave, complete with shell lei, crown, and his reading glasses. Robert Dean Frisbie, the American-born writer and colorful South Seas character, is buried in the inland corner of the graveyard next to the road. (See "Recommended Books" in Chapter 1.)

To the right near the end of the road is the **Cook Islands Library and Museum.** The museum is small but worth a visit; it has excellent examples of Cook Islands handcrafts, a canoe from Pukapuka built in the old style with planks lashed together, the island's first printing press (brought to the islands by the London Missionary Society in the 1830s and used until the 1950s by the government printing office), and *Yankee*'s bell and compass. No admission fee is charged, but there is a box for donations.

Farther up the inland road is the **Takamoa Mission House,** built as a school in 1842 by the London Missionary Society. It also can be visited from 9am to 4:30pm Monday through Friday, from 8:30 to 11:30am on Saturday, and from 7 to 8:30pm on Tuesday and Thursday.

Return to the main road and continue east to the next inland road. This leads to **Constitution Park** on the right, site of many of the Constitution Week festivities each year, and the **Tupapa Sports Ground** on the left, scene of fierce rugby matches during the austral winter months. Like other South Pacific islanders who once were under New Zealand or Australian rule, the Cook Islanders take their rugby seriously. Although much of the action has shifted to the stadium at Tereora College near the airport, Tupapa may still see a brawl or two on Saturday afternoons.

The inland road ends where it intersects with the **Ara Metua,** also known as the Great Road of Toi, which apparently was constructed centuries ago when the people of Rarotonga lived inland. When the first Europeans arrived, they were startled to find

---

IMPRESSIONS

If I could vacation on only one Pacific island I would choose Rarotonga. It's as beautiful as Tahiti, much quieter, much stuffier and the food is even worse. But the climate is better and the natives are less deteriorated.

—James A. Michener, 1951

it, paved with rocks in many sections, nearly encircling the island. Much of it is still passable, and it's paved from Avarua to the west coast below the airport.

This brings us to the east end of Avarua. From the traffic circle west to **Avatiu Harbour** is a lovely walk, with canoes pulled up under casuarina trees in the park along the beach side of the road and various shops along the other. Have a pleasant stroll. I'll save the details for "Shopping," described below.

A CIRCLE-ISLAND TOUR

Traveling completely around Rarotonga and seeing the sights should take about 4 hours—with the help of a motorized vehicle. As mentioned below, several tour companies operate circle-island tours. A tour can also be made independently by car or motorbike. I would give myself all day to do it on a bicycle.

Let's travel in a clockwise direction from Avarua.

A small dirt road about 1km (½-mile) past the Kii Kii Motel and almost in front of Delmar Services Garage leads to the **Marae Arai-Te-Tonga,** one of the most sacred spots on the island. In the old days before the coming of Europeans, these stone structures formed a *koutu,* or royal court. The investiture of high chiefs took place here amid much pomp and circumstance; also, offerings to the gods and the "first fruits" of each season were brought here and presented to the local *ariki,* or chief. The basalt investiture pillar, the major remaining structure, stands slightly offset from a rectangular platform about 12 feet long, 7 feet wide, and 8 inches high. Such temples, or marae, still are considered sacred by some Cook Islanders, so don't walk on them.

The old Ara Metua road crosses by Arai-Te-Tonga and leads south a few yards to a small marae on the banks of **Tupapa Stream.** A trail follows the streambed up to the peaks of Mounts Te Ikurangi, Te Manga, and Te Atukura, but these are difficult climbs; it's advisable to make them only with a local guide.

Back on the main road, **Matavera** village begins about 2km (1.2 miles) beyond Tupapa Stream. Notable for the picturesque Cook Islands Christian Church and graveyard on the mountain side of the road, it's worth a stop for a photograph before continuing on to historic **Ngatangiia** village. Legend has it that a fleet of canoes left Ngatangiia sometime around A.D. 1350 and sailed off to colonize New Zealand, departing from a point across the road from where the Cook Islands Christian Church now stands in the center of the village. Offshore is **Ngatangiia Passage,** between the mainland and Motutapu, a low island, through which the canoes left on their voyage.

Ngatangiia also had its day in the sun in the early 1800s, when it was the headquarters of Charles Pitman, the missionary who came with the Rev. John Williams and later translated *Pilgrim's Progress* into Cook Islands Maori. Unlike many of his fellow missionaries, Pitman carefully avoided becoming involved in local politics or business, and he objected strongly when Williams forced the Cook Islanders to build the *Messenger of Peace.*

The **courthouse** across from the church was the first one built in the Cook Islands.

The shore at Ngatangiia, with three small islands sitting on the reef beyond the lagoon, is one of the most beautiful parts of Rarotonga. An old stone **fish trap** is visible underwater between the beach and the islands. Such traps were quite common throughout eastern Polynesia: Fish were caught inside as the tide ebbed and flowed through Ngatangiia Passage.

South of Ngatangiia begins magnificent **Muri Beach,** whose white sands stretch for 14km (8 miles) around the southeast corner of Rarotonga. The beach is used during holidays for bareback horse races—the thunder of hooves is a marked contrast to the silence of sailboats gliding across the crystal-clear lagoon. A fine place to enjoy the beach and go for a swim in the lagoon is the **Rarotonga Sailing Club** and, above it, Sails Restaurant.

Farther along the main road is the **Welland Studio,** where American-born artist

IMPRESSIONS

I have hunted long for this sanctuary. Now that I have found it, I have no intention, and certainly no desire, ever to leave it again.
—Robert Dean Frisbie, 1928

Rick Welland displays and sells his work. Rick has been considered Rarotonga's artist-in-residence almost since settling there in the early 1960s. The gallery is in a small building along the road. If he's not there, knock on the door of his home on the beach.

Beyond the Little Polynesian Motel is the village of **Titikaveka.** The Cook Islands Christian Church here was built in 1841 of coral blocks hand-cut from the reef almost a mile away and carried to the building site. The lagoon at Titikaveka is the best on the island for snorkeling, and the tour companies use it for their Muri Beach picnic outings.

From Titikaveka, the road runs along the south coast and passes another old stone fish trap just inside Avaavaroa Passage, the **Duncan Bertram Memorial Botanical Gardens** on the Ara Metua just past Taipara Stream, and the late Albert Henry's white beachside home. **Mount Te Rua Manga,** the rock spire also known as "The Needle," can be seen clearly from the main road between the Vaima Restaurant and the Rarotongan Resort Hotel. Also in the Viama region you may see what looks like a modern ruin; it's the site of an aborted and highly controversial Sheraton hotel site.

The road turns at the Rarotongan Resort and heads up the west coast to the village of **Arorangi,** which was founded as a peacemaking "Gospel Village" by the missionary Aaron Buzacott when a dispute over land boundaries broke out in 1828. Arorangi replaced the old inland village, Puaikura, where the Tahitian missionary Papeiha went to teach Christianity after being put ashore by John Williams. Papeiha is buried in the yard of Arorangi's Cook Islands Christian Church, which was built in 1849. According to Polynesian legend, the canoes that left Ngatangiia in the 1300s stopped in Arorangi before heading off west to New Zealand. There is no reef passage near Arorangi, but the story enables the people on both sides of Rarotonga to claim credit for sending settlers to New Zealand.

The flat-topped mountain behind Arorangi is **Mount Raemaru.** Another legend says that mighty warriors from Aitutaki, which had no mountain, stole the top of Raemaru and took it home with them. There is a steep and somewhat dangerous trail to the top of Raemaru.

The area north of Arorangi is well developed with hotels, restaurants, and shops. The shore just before the golf course is known as **Black Rock** because of the volcanic outcrop standing sentinel in the lagoon offshore. According to ancient Maori belief, the souls of the dead bid farewell to Rarotonga from this point before journeying to the fatherland, which the Cook Islanders called *Avaiki.*

There are two ways to proceed after passing the golf course. The main road continues around the west end of the **airport** runway (be careful—there are more road accidents on this sharp curve than anywhere else on Rarotonga). The airstrip was originally built by the New Zealand government during World War II. It was enlarged in the early 1970s to handle jumbo jets, and Queen Elizabeth II officially opened the new strip, which was renamed Rarotonga International Airport, on July 29, 1974. The **Parliament Building** is located on the shore about halfway along the length of the runway. Parliament meets from February to March and from July to September. Visitors can observe the proceedings from the gallery from 1 to 5pm on Monday, Tuesday, and Thursday, and from 9am to 1pm on Wednesday and Friday. The cemetery along the road just before town is where some of the cancer patients who came to Rarotonga in the 1970s to see Milan Brych, the controversial specialist who claimed to have discovered a cure, were buried.

The other way to return to Avarua from Black Rock is to turn right on the first paved road past the golf course and then left at the dead-end intersection onto the **Ara**

Metua or "back road," as the section running from Black Rock to town is called. About halfway to town is **Tereora College,** established as a mission school in 1865. An international stadium was built on the college campus for the 1985 South Pacific Mini Games held on Rarotonga and is now the site of rock 'em, sock 'em rugby games on Saturday afternoons from June through August.

The short ride back to town concludes the circle-island tour.

CULTURAL TOURS

Given their use of English and their pride in their culture, the Cook Islanders themselves offer a magnificent glimpse into the life-style of eastern Polynesia. They are more than happy to answer questions put to them sincerely by inquisitive visitors. Some of them also do it for money, albeit in a low-key fashion, by offering some of the finest ✪ **cultural tours** in the South Pacific.

Your money will be well spent on several hours with **Hugh Henry Tours** (tel. 25-320 or 25-321). The extraordinarily knowledgeable son of the late Prime Minister Albert Henry, Hugh Henry leads tours around the island that cover local customs and traditions, marae and other prehistoric sites, fauna and flora, politics and history. His 4-hour historic tour usually leaves at 9:30am several days a week and costs NZ$18 ($11). Depending on the weather, Hugh or one of his associates also lead hikes over the Cross Island Track (see "Hiking," below) for the same price.

For an examination of old Polynesian ways and skills, visit the **Cook Islands Cultural Village** (tel. 21-314), on the back road in Arorangi. The village consists of 9 thatch huts, each one featuring a different aspect of life, such as the making of crafts, cooking, and even dancing. Guests are guided through the huts and then enjoy a lunch of island-style foods. The gates open at 9:45am and close at 11:30am, after which lunch is served and the staff stages a Cook Islands dance show. Cost for the entire morning and lunch is NZ$22 ($13), plus NZ$2 ($1.20) for bus transportation if required. The Cultural Village also does its own circle-island historical tour; it costs NZ$20 ($12) and includes lunch and the show.

More energetic souls can climb up to the base of "The Needle" with **Pa's Mountain Trek** or take a more leisurely time of it on **Pa's Nature Walk,** both conducted by Cook Islander Pa. He points out various plants, such as wild vanilla, candlenuts, mountain orchids, and the shampoo plant, and explains their everyday uses in the days before corned beef and trading stores. The mountain trek costs NZ$20 ($12) and requires good walking or running shoes. The less strenuous nature walk costs NZ$15 ($9). Both last about 4 hours. Book at any of the hotel activities desks.

To learn everything you ever wanted to know about the various uses of the coconut palm in old Polynesia, including a lengthy demonstration of old-time fire-starting, catch a **Piri Puruto's Show** at the various hotels. Dressed in a loincloth and cap made of fibers from the top of a palm, Piri scales one of the tallest trees around and throws down several coconuts and various other materials for his fire-starting demonstration. He then whacks open the nuts with a bush knife and gives everyone a taste (the texture and flavor change with the age of each coconut). Look for one of Piri's brochures or call 20-309 to find out where he's appearing. Some hotels charge nonguests to see his show, others don't.

In addition to his tree-climbing exhibitions, Piri also stages **Piri's Umukai Picnic** twice a week on a small island off Muri Beach. This full-day excursion includes a meal actually cooked in an umu. His boats leave the Pacific Resort at 9:30am, usually on Monday and Thursday. Cost is NZ$23 ($14) per person. Bookings are essential (tel. 20-309). He also leads walks over the Cross Island Track for NZ$18 ($11), lagoon and reef fishing expeditions for NZ$20 ($12), and will administer 1 hour of coconut-oil massage for NZ$30 ($18).

FLIGHTSEEING

Another way to see Rarotonga is by plane. **Air Rarotonga** (tel. 22-888) offers 20-minute sightseeing flights around the island. Flights can be arranged at the customers' choice of time if two or more people fly. Departures are usually at 2pm, but try to go early in the morning before the clouds have built up over the mountains. The prices have varied with the price of crude oil in recent years, so inquire first.

SPORTS & RECREATION

Rarotonga has enough sporting and other outdoor activities to occupy the time of anyone who decides to crawl out of a beach chair and move the muscles.

Fishing

Deep-sea fishing begins as soon as the charter boat clears the reef, and there have been some world-class catches of skipjack tuna (bonita), mahi mahi, blue marlin, wahoo, and barracuda in Cook Islands waters. You can try your luck on the MV ***Seafari,*** P.O. Box 148, Rarotonga (tel. 20-328), a 34-footer, or on the *Te Manu Ka Rere,* a 26-footer operated by **Pacific Marine Charters,** P.O. Box 770, Rarotonga (tel. 21-237). Both like to have a day's notice, and both may also be chartered for sightseeing trips around the island. Standard cost for a day's fishing usually is less than NZ$100 ($60) per person, one of the lowest rates in the South Pacific. Don't expect to take the catch back to the hotel, however, for fresh fish are expensive in Rarotonga and will be sold by the boat operator on the local market. Bring a camera.

Golf

Visitors are welcome to take their shots at the radio towers and guy wires that give the **Rarotonga Golf Club's** nine-hole course some of the world's most unusual obstacles. The course was once located on what is now the international airport; club members had to move it when the runway was expanded. It now lies under Rarotonga's radio station antennae—balls that hit a tower or wire can be replayed at the player's option. Greens fees are NZ$5 ($3). Rental equipment and drinks are available in the clubhouse (tel. 27-360). The club is open Monday through Saturday from 8am until dark.

Hiking

There are a number of hiking trails on Rarotonga, but the most popular by far is the ✪ **Cross Island Track** that runs from Avarua to the south coast. It begins in the Avatiu valley and follows the stream high up to the base of **Mount Te Rua Manga** ("The Needle"). It's a very steep, muddy, and often slippery climb up to Te Rua Manga, and the trail is not well marked. Nevertheless, hundreds of visitors make the trek each year, most of them accompanied by a guide. The tour companies mentioned above (see "Cultural Tours," above) offer cross-island trips, which take about 4 hours.

Lawn Bowls

The **Rarotonga Bowling Club** (tel. 26-277) has an international-standard bowling green on Moss Road in Avarua. Visitors are welcome, and there's a licensed bar on the premises.

Running & Jogging

The "Hash House Harriers" organization meets once a week for a fun run and sponsors an annual Round Rarotonga Road Run in November each year. Information is available from David Lobb (tel. 22-000). Really, all one has to do for a jog on Rarotonga is to run down the road or beach.

Sailing

Aqua Sports (tel. 27-350) at the Rarotonga Sailing Club on Muri Beach (Muri Lagoon offshore is the island's best spot for sailing) rents a variety of water-sports equipment. Rates range from NZ$8 ($5) to NZ$20 ($12) per hour for sailboats,

Windsurfers, and canoes. Snorkeling gear costs NZ$10 ($6) for ½ day. Aqua Sports is open Monday through Saturday from 9am to 5pm.

Scuba-Diving

Rarotonga's lagoon is only 4 to 10 feet deep, but depths easily reach 100 feet outside the reef, and a drop-off starts at 80 feet and descends to more than 12,000 feet. There are canyons, caves, tunnels, and many varieties of coral. Visibility usually is in the 100- to 200-feet range. Two wrecks, a 100-foot fishing boat and a 150-foot cargo ship, sit in depths of 80 feet and 60 feet, respectively.

Barry and Shirley Hill, owners of **Dive Rarotonga,** P.O. Box 38, Rarotonga (tel. 21-873), make dive trips daily. They charge NZ$35 ($21) per dive including tank, air, weight belt, and boat; NZ$45 ($27) if you rent the rest of the equipment. The Hills expect to have a PADI instructor on board in 1992. Their office is roadside in Arorangi.

Greg Wilson and Trev Bergman of **Cook Island Divers,** P.O. Box 1002, Rarotonga (tel. 22-483), operate out of Greg's house in Arorangi (watch for the roadside signs) and from the Mana Court Dive Shop in Avarua. They charge NZ$50 ($30) per dive including all equipment. They also teach a 4-day NAUI course for NZ$400 ($240) including all equipment. (That's a very reasonable price by South Pacific standards.)

Squash

The **Edgewater Resort** (tel. 25-435) in Arorangi has the island's only squash courts. Rates are NZ$10 ($6) per hour for outsiders; racket rental is NZ$4 ($2.50). The courts are open from 7am to 10pm Monday through Saturday, and reservations are essential.

Swimming & Snorkeling

Obviously, getting into the water has to have high priority during a visit to the South Pacific, and Rarotonga is certainly no exception. Most hotels have snorkels, fins, and masks for their guests to use while snorkeling. They also can be rented for NZ$10 ($6) per day from **Dive Rarotonga** (tel. 21-873) in Arorangi or from **Aqua Sports** (tel. 27-350) on Muri Beach. It's not wise to snorkel off an unfamiliar beach or in water that is too shallow—as it often is at low tide.

Tennis

The **Rarotongan Resort Hotel** (tel. 25-800) and the **Edgewater Resort** (tel. 25-435) both allow nonguests to play on their tennis courts. Their rates are NZ$10 ($6) per hour, and NZ$4 ($2.50) per hour for rackets. There are **public tennis courts** in Avarua and at Titikaveka College on the south coast, but ask at your hotel before dashing off with racket in hand; many Rarotongans take their tennis seriously and don't look kindly on tourists who hog the public courts.

SHOPPING

As long as the New Zealand dollar remains devalued against its U.S. counterpart, Rarotonga will offer some bargains for those of us carrying American bucks, especially on black pearls, native handcrafts, and silk-screened or tie-dyed cotton garments.

For the most part, you can do your shopping during your visit to Avarua, for most shops line the town's waterfront on either side of the traffic circle. **Cook Islands Trading Corporation (C.I.T.C.)** is the largest trader. It's low-slung complex with the parking lot in front is the center of the town's business district. The building holds the company's large department store as well as Rarotonga Pharmacy, and Rarotonga Duty Free. On the west side, the modern **Cook's Corner** shopping center houses many of the island's upscale clothing, handcraft, and pearl shops. It definitely is worth a visit. To the east across the bridge, **Brown's Arcade** has a few small shops.

Residents of most developed Western countries are not likely to find many **duty-free** bargains on Rarotonga. The largest shop is **Rarotonga Duty Free** (tel. 22-240, ext. 207) in the C.I.T.C. building on the Avarua waterfront. It carries handcrafts, jewelry, perfumes, curios, film, and some electronic equipment. Duty-free cigarettes and liquor can be purchased only at the airport, either before clearing formalities upon arrival, or after clearing immigration upon departure.

WHAT TO BUY

Handcrafts

Cook Islanders may not produce island handcrafts in the same volume as Tongans, but there is a fine assortment to choose from, especially items made on the outer islands. Particularly good if not inexpensive buys are the delicately woven *rito* (white straw hats) the women wear to church on Sunday and the fine Samoan-style straw mats from Pukapuka in the Northern Group. Carvings from wood are plentiful, as is jewelry made from shell, mother-of-pearl, and pink coral. The most popular wood carvings are small totems representing Tangaroa—they may be more appropriate for the nightstand than the coffee table, for Tangaroa has not a shy bone in his body.

BEACHCOMBER, LTD., Cook's Corner, Avarua. Tel. 21-939.

In addition to black pearls, Joan Rolls sells some handcrafts, including wood carvings, excellent black- and pink-coral jewelry, and exquisite rito hats. She even carries Cook Islands dance costumes complete with grass skirt.

COOK ISLANDS WOMEN'S HANDCRAFT CENTRE, Traffic Circle, Avarua. Tel. 28-033.

You should look here first. Some of the best work is sold through the cooperative outlet, especially from the outer islands, and the prices tend to be reasonable. Although the other shops now buy most of the best items directly from the producers, you should find some fine woven mats, grass skirts, straw hats, handbags, fans, brooms, headbands, purses made from coconut shells, wood carvings, and jewelry. The center is on the main road opposite the Banana Court Bar at the traffic circle.

ISLAND CRAFTS, Centrepoint Building, Avarua. Tel. 22-010.

A must stop, this large shop is located on the main street next to Westpac Bank. It has Rarotonga's largest selection of handcrafts—some from other parts of the South Pacific—and a wide selection of carved wooden Tangaroa tikis in various sizes. You can even buy a 9-karat gold pendant of the well-endowed god.

MANU MANEA FASHIONS, Cook's Corner, Avarua. Tel. 24-477.

Although primarily a clothing store, this shop has tapa cloth from Fiji and some tie-dyed pareus. The **Kenwall Gallery** in the shop sell art supplies and the works of local artists such as Michael Tavioni and Judith Kunzle.

RAROTONGAN RESORT HOTEL BOUTIQUE, in the Rarotongan Resort Hotel. Tel. 25-800.

The hotel's boutique is reasonably well stocked with handcrafts as well as tropical clothing, film, and the usual curios, toiletries, and other merchandise found in most hotel shops. The prices are somewhat inflated, but it's the only place to shop on Sunday.

Tropical Clothing

The craze for tie-dyed or silk-screened clothing has swept from Tahiti to Rarotonga, where—in U.S. dollars—the prices for these colorful cotton garments can be considerably less than in French Polynesia. The wraparound pareus range from

NZ$12 ($7) for those of average quality to NZ$18 ($11) for fine examples of the craft. In other words, average works sell for less than in Tahiti, while the really good examples cost about the same. Dresses, skirts, blouses, and shirts made from pareu material are available in many shops on Rarotonga at reasonable prices.

JOYCE PEYROUX GARMENTS, Arorangi. Tel. 20-202.

The island's largest tropical-clothing manufacturer and retailer, Mrs. Peyroux has her factory outlet on the ocean side of the road in Arorangi and shops in the C.I.D.C. Building in the middle of Avarua. Her tie-dyed pareus at NZ$12 ($7) are very good value. Other specialties include unusual airbrushed T-shirts.

KRISTY & KENDRICK APPAREL, Cook's Corner, Avarua. Tel. 28-223.

This shop has pareus, shirts for men, blouses and dresses in tropical flower prints, and other quality items. The T-shirts have some clever designs, but be careful how you wash the shirts made in China; they may shrink.

MANU MANEA FASHIONS, Cook's Corner, Avarua. Tel. 24-477.

At the rear of the Cook's Corner shopping center, this shop has women's wear and shoes, including some silk-screened items. The company's factory and showroom (tel. 20-477) between Avatiu Harbour and the airport is worth a look. They will alter their stock dresses for free or, for a reasonable price, make one for you from scratch.

TAV LTD., Cook's Corner, Avarua. Tel. 21-802.

Check out TAV for the island's best selection of tie-dyed pareus, sundresses, and other items for men, women, and children. During my last visit it sold the pick of Rarotonga's colorful pareus; the NZ$18 ($11) price was very reasonable for the quality. TAV's workshop (tel. 23-202) on the back road behind the Hibiscus Bar and Cafe will alter items for free or will make them for you from scratch.

Perfume & Soaps

See John Abbott at his **Ariki Perfume Factory** (tel. 20-964), on the back road between Avarua and Avatiu harbors, for delightful perfumes, soaps, body oils, and after-shave lotions made of local gardenia, jasmine, aloe vera, and coconut oils. The factory is open from 8am to 5pm Monday through Saturday.

Black Pearls

Manihiki and Penrhyn atolls in the Northern Group of the Cook Islands produce a fair number of pearls, many of them of the same black variety seen in French Polynesia. Although they have yet to reach the quantity produced in the Taumotus, in U.S. dollar terms, Cook Islands pearls are considerably less expensive. For example, a medium-size pearl set as a necklace might sell for 50,000 CFP ($500) in Tahiti. On Rarotonga this same size and quality pearl necklace might be priced at NZ$500 ($300). That's a 40% savings just from the exchange rate.

I strongly encourage anyone interested in buying pearls in the South Pacific to do some research beforehand. Also see "Shopping" in Chapter 4.

BEACHCOMBER LTD., Cook's Corner, Avarua. Tel. 21-939.

In addition to carrying the handcraft items mentioned above, Joan Rolls also has a small but excellent selection of pearls. Some are loose, others are set. Loose pearls start at NZ$100 ($60); those in settings begin at NZ$200 ($120) and go up to NZ$7,000 ($4,200) if they are mounted alongside diamonds.

PEARLS OF POLYNESIA (THE PEARL SHOP), Cook's Corner, Avarua. Tel. 21-902.

Mike and Marge Bergman helped start the pearl industry in the Cook Islands, and their shop is the place to see Rarotonga's largest selection, whether loose or incorporated into jewelry. Both they and Joan Rolls of Beachcomber Ltd. carry small pearls still attached to their gold-trimmed shells and sold as necklaces.

Coins & Stamps

For years the Cook Islands government has earned a considerable portion of its revenue from the sale of its stamps to collectors and dealers overseas. The **Philatelic**

Bureau, across the road from the Central Post Office in Avarua, issues between three and six new stamps a year. All are highly artistic and feature birds, shells, fish, flowers, and historical events and people, including the British royal family. For whatever reason—perhaps the remoteness of the islands or the beauty of the stamps—they are popular worldwide.

As noted earlier in this chapter, the Cook Islands government prints its own colorful notes and mints some unusual coins, including the triangular $2 piece and the famous Tangaroa dollar. They cannot be spent outside the Cooks, but they do make interesting souvenirs. You will get plenty of them in change, and there is no limit on how many you can take out of the Cook Islands.

6. WHERE TO STAY

Rarotonga may be a small island, but it has a wide range of accommodations. With the exception of the two big resorts, most of the properties are small, owner-operated motels. They call themselves "motels" because they're modeled after the typical New Zealand motel, in which each room has a small but quite complete kitchen to make up for the lack of a restaurant on the premises. Rooms in all establishments, whether hotel or motel, are equipped with electric "jugs" and tea and coffee.

In terms of accommodations and restaurants, the west coast near Arorangi is the most developed part of Rarotonga. It is somewhat drier than the other sides, and the sunsets can be glorious. The beach is fine, but the lagoon tends to be very shallow, especially at low tide. The southeast coast, on the other hand, boasts the marvelous Muri Beach and a lagoon that's wider, deeper, and better for snorkeling and sailing, but the prevailing southeast trade winds can make it chilly, especially during the austral winter months of June through August. The hotels on the north coast are near Avarua and its shops and restaurants, but the beaches are rocky and the lagoon more walkable than swimmable.

When making your choice, take into consideration these factors as well as the

FROMMER'S FAVORITE
COOK ISLANDS EXPERIENCES

Cultural Touring One of my fondest South Pacific memories is of a ½ day spent exploring Rarotonga with the entertaining and highly informative Exham Wichman. He told me much of what this chapter has to say about the Cook Islands' life-style. Exham has retired from the cultural tour business, leaving a clear field for the equally informative Hugh Henry.

Cook Islands Dancing I never visit the Cook Islands without watching the hips swing at a traditional dance show. Take my word for it: Had the crew of HMS *Bounty* seen the dancing on Rarotonga instead of Tahiti, they might have staged their mutiny before the ship even left port.

Banana Court Bar Anyone who laments the loss of Quinn's infamous Tahitian bar in Papeete can join me at the Banana Court Bar, one of the last old-time South Seas bars anywhere. Compared to the Cook Islanders, the French have much to learn about *joie de vivre.*

Aitutaki Although physically not as awe inspiring as Bora Bora, the Cooks' second most-visited island still has a friendliness that is disappearing in some more-touristed parts of the South Pacific. Like many others, I plan my trips to include an island night at Aitutaki's Rapae Cottage Hotel.

expected weather during your stay. Unless noted otherwise, every hotel or motel sits in a tropical garden setting complete with coconut palms and flowering plants.

THE BIG RESORTS

THE RAROTONGAN RESORT HOTEL, P.O. Box 103, Rarotonga. Tel. 25-800. Fax 25-799. Telex 62003. 151 rms. A/C TEL **Location:** Southwest corner of the island, 13km (8 miles) from Avarua.

$ Rates: NZ$125–NZ$165 ($75–$99) single or double. AE, DC, MC, V.

Opened in 1977 when the Cooks themselves were first opened to tourists, the Rarotongan Resort Hotel has begun to show some wear and tear. In fact, reports have persisted that the Cook Islands government has been trying to sell it to investors with enough capital to make needed renovations. It still is the island's flagship hotel and is the only one built in the typical big-resort fashion. An island-style central building houses the reception and activities desks, boutique, restaurant, and bar. Even the lagoon was designed to please tourists: A number of coral heads were removed by dynamite to improve the lagoon as a swimming hole (Cook Islanders have since prohibited further destruction of the reefs).

The location, on the island's southwest corner is superb. The hotel gets the cooling trade winds from one direction and a view of the setting sun from the other.

Its air-conditioned rooms (the only ones in the Cook Islands) are on the ground levels of nine two-story buildings surrounded by tropical gardens; some face the beach, and some face the garden. Rooms on the upper floors have ceiling fans hanging from peaked ceilings instead of air conditioners. All rooms are equipped like those found throughout the South Pacific. Each has a double bed and a single (that serves as a settee), radio, and a private balcony or patio beyond sliding glass doors. The decor, needless to say, is tropical.

More charming are 30 "Paradise Rooms." Although joined, these one-story units are staggered so that each has the feel of an individual bungalow. They come complete with a ceiling fan, a private patio, and a large tile shower.

Dining/Entertainment: Although the Rarotongan once had three restaurants, food service has shrunk in recent years to one dining room, the Manava Terrace at ground level near the swimming pool. Noted primarily as a place to have Sunday brunch, it's open from 7am to 10pm daily. The hotel usually stages its island night buffet and dance show on Friday for NZ$25 ($15) per person.

Services: Laundry, baby-sitting.

Facilities: Tennis courts (NZ$10 [$6] per hour for outsiders), boutique, games and conference rooms, swimming pool, beach, jogging, aerobics, windsurfing, water volleyball, coconut husking, tree climbing, bingo, and backgammon.

EDGEWATER RESORT, P.O. Box 121, Rarotonga. Tel. 25-435. Fax 25-475. Telex 62059. 171 rms, 2 apartments. TEL **Location:** Arorangi, 6.8km (4 miles) from Avarua.

$ Rates (including 10% tax): NZ$85–NZ$150 ($51–$90) single; NZ$95–NZ$200 ($57–$120) double. AE, DC, MC, V.

In number of rooms, the Edgewater is the island's largest resort, although it's on a relatively small parcel of land—just four beachside acres hold all the rooms, three central buildings, swimming pool, and three tennis courts. One of its two-story motel-style blocks of rooms was originally built as a clinic by the controversial cancer specialist Milan Brych, who was kicked out of the country in the 1970s after making a lot of money but curing no cancer. Several more concrete block structures have been added. The shoreline is rocky; you have to walk a ways north to reach a sandy bottom.

Each room has a kitchenette, ceiling fan, private patio or balcony, and radio. Only the newer rooms have phones. Rooms 400 to 411, 500 to 511, and 600 to 611 are closest to the beach and farthest from the restaurant-bar–swimming pool, which can be crowded and noisy when the house is full.

Dining/Entertainment: The Reef Restaurant in the central building serves three meals a day at moderate prices. Entertainment features a buffet and Cook Islands dance show 2 nights a week, usually Thursday and Saturday.

Services: Laundry, baby-sitting.

Facilities: Swimming pool; snorkeling equipment; squash courts (Rarotonga's only ones) and tennis courts (for NZ$5 [$3] per game—balls and rackets are available to rent); Laundromat; TV/video-rental shop; activities and car-rental desks.

HOTELS ON THE WEST COAST

MANUIA BEACH HOTEL, P.O. Box 700, Rarotonga. Tel. 22-461, or toll free 800/448-8355. Fax 22-464. Telex 62060. 20 rms. MINIBAR TV TEL **Location:** Arorangi, 8km (5 miles) from Avarua.

$ Rates (including a full breakfast): NZ$250 ($150) garden single or double; NZ$320 ($192) beachfront single or double. AE, DC, MC, V.

Owners Peter Heays and Jolene Bosanquet completely remodeled this little property in the late 1980s and turned the former Beach Motel into an intimate "boutique" hotel where emphasis is on comfort and service for an upmarket adult clientele (no children under age 15 are accepted as guests). The 20 rooms are in 10 duplex bungalows set rather close together on a narrow strip of beachfront land; however, tropical foilage helps give each unit a feeling of privacy. Three of the rooms have water beds; the others boast queen-size mattresses. There are ceiling fans, white tile floors, and sliding glass doors that lead to wooden verandas. Angled shower stalls in one corner and lavatories in another maximize space in rather small baths. The choice beachfront units have a view of the reef across a kidney-shaped swimming pool.

Dining/Entertainment: Although none of the rooms has a kitchen, you can amble down to the Right on the Beach Bar and dig holes in its white-sand floor while enjoying a bistro-style meal under a low-slung thatch roof. The intimate Bounty Restaurant serves quality dinners amid nautical decor. One night a week is devoted to a fixed-menu meal featuring local produce prepared in unusual ways—spices add zest to normally bland taro and kumera (sweet potato). Diners are then transported to another hotel for a traditional dance show.

Services: Laundry; evening turn-down; sleeping attire; some outside restaurants and activities can be billed to clients' hotel account.

Facilities: Swimming pool, Jacuzzi, free golf at Rarotonga Golf Club, snorkeling equipment, activities and car rentals, telephones and TV/videos in rooms on request.

LAGOON LODGES, P.O. Box 45, Rarotonga. Tel. 22-020. Fax 22-021. Telex 62067. 15 units. TV TEL **Location:** On southwest corner near Rarotongan Resort Hotel, 13.1km (7.8 miles) from Avarua.

$ Rates: NZ$82 ($49) single or double garden studio; NZ$95 ($57) 1- or 2-bedroom garden bungalow for up to four persons; NZ$128 ($77) oceanview villa up to six persons; NZ$195 ($117) executive villa for up to seven persons. AE, MC, V.

Those who agree with me that bungalow living is the way to go in the South Pacific will find it at these lodges, which are less than a mile north of the Rarotongan. Owner/managers Des and Cassey Eggelton have six studio units, each of which has a queen-size and a single bed, bath with shower, ceiling fan suspended from a peaked roof, kitchenette, dining table, and porch. Even though each cottage has two units, there is a feeling of privacy. In addition, four one-bedroom units and four two-bedroom cottages are like small houses with sizable verandas. They also have one real house: a three-bedroom villa with its own enormous veranda and private swimming pool, all set on ¼ acre of land. The spacious grounds of the bungalow complex contain a swimming pool, grass tennis court, and barbecue area, and the beach is just across the road.

RAROTONGAN SUNSET MOTEL, P.O. Box 377, Rarotonga. Tel. 28-028, or toll free 800/334-5623. Fax 28-026. Telex 62074. 20 units. MINIBAR TV TEL **Location:** Arorangi, 6.3km (3.8 miles) from Avarua.

$ Rates: NZ$110 ($66) single or double garden; NZ$125 ($75) single or double beachfront. AE, DC, MC, V.

New Zealand moteliers Nigel and Irene Purdie put a lot of thought into their motel, and it shows. Although the furnishings are European as opposed to tropical, each unit has a well-designed and -equipped kitchen and thick pile carpeting in the lounge area and separate bedroom. Net curtains double as mosquito netting across the sliding glass fronts at night. In addition to videos and Rarotonga's broadcast programs, a satellite dish (the island's first) brings in Cable News Network and other programs. There are 9 beachfront units, all in one-story buildings, and most of the 11 garden units are situated to provide at least partial views of the beach and lagoon from the verandas (those with a view are filled first). There's an odd-shaped swimming pool with a bridge over it, a shallow end for children, and adjacent "Bird Cage Bar" (it has colorful wooden parrots suspended from its peaked ceiling) at which the Purdies stage Sunday-evening barbecues. Rental cars and bikes are available.

PUAIKURA REEF LODGES, P.O. Box 397, Rarotonga. Tel. 23-537. Fax 21-537. 12 units. TV **Location:** Southeast corner of island, 11.5km (6.9 miles) from Avarua.

$ Rates (including 10% tax): NZ$82.50 ($49.50) single or double. AE, DC, MC, V.

Paul and Susan Wilson's recently refurbished motel units are situated in two one-story buildings facing a grassy lawn, swimming pool, and barbecue area. Half the units have a separate bedroom, and all have a double bed and two singles, tile bath with shower, clock radio, ceiling fan, kitchen, and patio with table and chairs. Rental cars and scooters are available, and a shady park with covered picnic tables is across the road along the beach.

ARE-RENGA MOTEL, P.O. Box 223, Rarotonga. Tel. 20-050. 20 units. **Location:** Arorangi village.

$ Rates: NZ$25 ($15) single; NZ$30 ($18) double. No credit cards.

This good budget choice is located in the village of Arorangi and is popular with Canadian travelers. The entire property enjoys a beautiful view of the mountains, and a path leads to the beach through a churchyard across the road. Cook Islander Jim Estall and family run a basic but clean establishment; the motel's units make up for a complete lack of frills with ample space. Nine units are in a newer, motellike block at the rear of the property. An older building has six units in which the bedroom is separated from the living-cooking area by a curtain; the three upstairs apartments share a large veranda while a patio does double duty for the three downstairs. All units have kitchen facilities. In addition, a small house has three bedrooms; house guests share communal kitchen facilities, lounge, and veranda. Low-budget travelers can share a room or unit for NZ$15 ($9) each.

HOTELS ON MURI BEACH

The southeast coast of Rarotonga may not have a view of the sunset, and it may be breezy and cool in the winter months (refreshing in summer), but it does have great sunrises over the white sands of Muri Beach. The lagoon here is wide and relatively deep.

THE PACIFIC RESORT, P.O. Box 790, Rarotonga. Tel. 20-427. Fax 21-427. Telex 62041. 34 units, 3 villas. MINIBAR (villas only) TV (villas only) TEL **Location:** Muri Beach, 10.7km (6.4 miles) from Avarua.

$ Rates: NZ$151–NZ$161 ($90.50–$96.50) single or double garden; NZ$175 ($105) single or double beachside; NZ$190 ($114) single or double beachfront; NZ$350 ($210) villa. AE, DC, MC, V.

Sitting in a spacious coconut grove alongside the island's best beach and lagoon, this property comes closest of any Rarotonga hotel or motel to capturing the appearance and ambience of French Polynesia's small resorts. In fact, it's three luxurious seaside villas are considered by most observers to be at the top of Rarotonga's accommodations. These spacious houses have two bedrooms with king-size beds, private entertainment areas, full kitchens, laundry facilities, minibars, and TVs with video players. Each of the 34 one- and two-bedroom units has a kitchenette in addition to ceiling fans, modern bath with shower, attractive wicker furnishings, and its own patio or balcony. Most units are in two-story motel-style buildings on either side of a tropical garden complete with a stream crossed by two footbridges. More bungalowlike, the beachside and beachfront suites give the impression of having your own cottage. Four of the beachfront suites have water beds.

Dining/Entertainment: The Barefoot Bistro Bar beside the beach offers an "All-Day Food List" of soups, salads, burgers, sandwiches, and fish-and-chips. Island Night usually is on Friday when the staff cooks a Polynesian feast in an earth oven; the resulting buffet is followed by a traditional dance performance. Other evening meals feature buffets and barbecues.

Services: Laundry, baby-sitting.

Facilities: Swimming pool, volleyball court, children's playground, boutique, activities desk, snorkeling gear, Windsurfers, canoes (other water-sports equipment available for rent at the Rarotonga Sailing Club next door), rental cars, and bikes.

MURI BEACHCOMBER MOTEL, P.O. Box 379, Rarotonga. Tel. 21-022. Fax 21-323. Telex 62000. 12 units, 1 4-bedroom house. **Location:** Muri Beach, 10.9km (6.5 miles) from Avarua.

$ Rates (including 10% tax): NZ$102 ($61) single; NZ$120 ($72) double; NZ$238 ($143) single or double, NZ$21 ($12.50) each additional person up to seven in "Lodge." Discount of 10% if booked direct. AE, DC, MC, V.

(S) This pleasant motel is conveniently located near the Pacific Resort, the Rarotonga Sailing Club, and the Flame Tree restaurant, which more than makes up for the lack of on-site restaurant and other facilities. Spotlights illuminate the tropical foliage of the grounds at night, and the rising moon over the lagoon is a sight to see. One of two New Zealander couples who manage the Muri Beachcomber—Helen and Peter Kemp, Lynley and Bill Tillick—is always available to lend assistance and advice. They have cars, scooters, and 12-speed bicycles to rent.

Ten of its one-bedroom, full-kitchen units are in five duplex units grouped around a grassy lawn fronting Muri Beach. Two other, larger family units stand next to a swimming pool, making it easy for parents to keep an eye on the kids from their shady verandas. For larger groups or anyone who just wants a lot of space, the Muri Beachcomber has a four-bedroom house next door. Called "The Lodge," this modern home has a massive, breezy veranda overlooking a lawn right on the beach. Huge doors open to the veranda from the living room and from two of the four bedrooms.

MOANA SANDS BEACH HIDEAWAY, P.O. Box 1007, Rarotonga. Tel. 26-189. Fax 22-189. Telex 62044. 14 rms. **Location:** Muri Beach, 14.3km (8.6 miles) from Avarua.

$ Rates (including 10% tax): NZ$120 ($72) single or double. AE, DC, MC, V.

Right on the beach at the deepest part of Muri Lagoon, this two-story motel has six rooms upstairs and six on the ground level. Each has a balcony or patio facing the lagoon, ceiling fan, tiled shower-only bath, bright flower-print drapes and spreads, and Pullman kitchens. A small dining room provides breakfasts (brought to your room if you wish) and two- or three-course fixed-menu dinners (eaten under a beachside thatch pavilion if weather permits). No lunch is served, but guests have access to the dining room and "honesty" bar at all times. The guest lounge has a small library and games and other distractions for children. Guests can play golf and tennis at other facilities for free. Snorkeling equipment and sailboats are provided on-site.

LITTLE POLYNESIAN MOTEL, P.O. Box 366, Rarotonga. Tel. 24-280. Fax 21-585. Telex 62065. 9 units. MINIBAR **Location:** Muri Beach, 14.1km (8.5 miles) from Avarua.

$ Rates: NZ$86 ($51.50) single or double. AE, DC, MC, V.

(S) Reminiscent of the small hotels on Moorea or Bora Bora but without the restaurant and bar, this establishment has an idyllic coconut-grove location right on the beach and some of the deeper waters of Muri Lagoon. Jeannine Peyroux recently renovated all eight of her duplex units in four cottages and a "honeymoon" bungalow that stands romantically by itself beside the beach. Each unit has a king-size bed, ceiling fan in case the trades die down, cooking facilities, and its own veranda. There's a small swimming pool surrounded by a rock ledge. Motorbike rentals are available.

HOTELS IN OR NEAR TOWN

Although the beaches on Rarotonga's north shore are very rocky and the lagoon fit for walking rather than swimming, staying near Avarua saves money on transportation, since the town's restaurants and shops are close at hand.

TAMURE RESORT HOTEL, P.O. Box 483, Rarotonga. Tel. 22-415. Fax 24-415. Telex 62007. 35 rms. TEL **Location:** 2.4km (1.4 miles) east of Avarua.

$ Rates: NZ$66 ($40) single, NZ$78 ($47) double if booked through travel agent; NZ$45 ($27) walk-in rate or if booked direct or through airline; NZ$40 ($24) walk-in rate for rooms nearest bar and restaurant. AE, MC, V.

Although this establishment usually has the best Island night buffets and dance shows (Wednesday and Saturday during my recent visit), it is not for anyone who seeks peace and quiet. The hotel-style rooms—no cooking facilities—are in two long, one-story buildings which stretch from the road to a very rocky beach (sand has been imported to make up for nature's lack thereof). A central structure between the two buildings houses the hotel's restaurant and bar; hence, the noise from the bar can infiltrate the rooms to either side. In fact, the noisier rooms adjacent to the bar area are rented on a walk-in basis at budget rates. Near the shore is a sunken, thatch-roofed bar snuggled next to a swimming pool. The hotel also has tennis courts and a gift shop.

KII KII MOTEL, P.O. Box 68, Rarotonga. Tel. 21-937. Fax 21-450. Telex 62008. 20 units. TV TEL **Location:** 2.8km (1.6 miles) east of Avarua.

$ Rates: NZ$37–NZ$59 ($22–$35.50) single; NZ$46–NZ$74 ($27.50–$44.50) double. AE, DC, MC, V.

(S) Harry and Pauline Napa's motel is one of Rarotonga's better bargains if you don't need a great beach. They have 8 units in a new building facing the lagoon and 12 older units—which are spotlessly maintained and spacious—only a few steps from the water. All units have full kitchens, including electric ranges with ovens, and they all face a swimming pool (which helps compensate for the absence of sand on the beach). The lower-priced budget rooms have the same amount of space as the newer units but do not have phones or TVs. There is no restaurant or bar, but the Tamure Resort Hotel is a short walk away.

PARADISE MOTEL, P.O. Box 674, Rarotonga. Tel. 20-544. Fax 22-544. 12 rms. **Location:** Avarua, east of traffic circle.

$ Rates: NZ$47 ($28) single; NZ$54 ($32.50) double; NZ$37 ($22) single in budget rooms. AE, MC, V.

This is not only the sole hotel located right in Avarua, but it's also Rarotonga's most unusual accommodation. Until 1986 the warehouse-size pink building on the main road east of the traffic circle was a dance hall. Then American David Gragg divided it into 12 split-level rooms. Most have Pullman kitchens, lavatories, large glass doors opening out to a narrow walkway alongside the hotel, and spiral staircases leading to sleeping lofts. Two small budget rooms have only one story; a lack of ventilation can make them hot and stuffy unless the outside door is left open. The common areas at the rear of the building are split-level, with a bar and patio next to the beach and a guest lounge with honesty bar upstairs. Except for this common area, there are no grounds; the building occupies almost all the hotel's land. The Paradise is popular with businesspeople and overseas volunteers serving in the Cook Islands.

TIARE VILLAGE MOTEL, P.O. Box 719, Rarotonga. Tel. 23-466. Fax 20-969. 3 rms, 3 chalets. **Location:** On Back Road behind airport, 2km (1.2 miles) west of Avarua.

$ Rates (including 10% tax and airport transfers): NZ$15 ($9) per person. MC, V.

(S) Much of the low-budget brigade congregates at this hostel that has a guesthouse and three A-frame chalets in a thick tropical garden. The house does triple duty as lounge (usually on a large covered veranda), office, and communal kitchen. Each of the chalets has its own kitchen, small bath with shower stall, living room, and covered veranda downstairs, plus a bedroom with double platform bed, a tiny hallway with a single bed, and a half bath upstairs. The guesthouse has three bedrooms, one with a double bed for couples. Although basic, the establishment is clean, comfortable, and friendly. Guests can help themselves to fruit growing on the property.

7. WHERE TO DINE

About half of Rarotonga's visitors come from New Zealand, where the cuisine is renowned for its superb basic ingredients but somewhat lackluster seasonings. However, as a result of the growth of the island's tourist industry, a number of restaurants offer fare of appeal to more discriminating palates. The cuisine of Italy, France, and East Africa have been added to the steaks, roasts, and chops of New Zealand.

P. J.'s Cafe and the hotel restaurants are the only ones open on Sunday.

Like their counterparts throughout Polynesia, in pre-European days the Cook Islanders cooked their food in an earth oven known here as an *umu.* The local produce—pig, fish, octopus, chicken, breadfruit, taro roots and leaves, arrowroot (tapioca), sweet potatoes, and bananas—were carefully wrapped in leaves and placed in layers over hot stones in a pit. Everything was covered with palm fronds and earth and then left to steam for several hours. When the dirt was removed, the piping hot food was placed on a table of banana leaves. There were no pots, no pans, no dishes, and no utensils to clean afterward. Eating with their fingers, members of an entire clan or village would partake of a feast known as an *umukai.* When they had finished eating, the thundering of drums would announce the beginning of all-night dancing and revelry.

The food is as finger-licking good today as it was hundreds of years ago, although now it's eaten with knives and forks during ✪ **"island nights"** at Rarotonga's hotels. At least one of these is a visitor's must, if not for the experience of eating native foods, then certainly for the dancing that follows. The hotels provide a wide assortment of salads and cold cuts for those who are not particularly fond of taro, arrowroot, and octopus cooked in coconut milk.

Check the daily *Cook Islands News* (especially the Friday edition) or with the hotels to find out when the feasts are on. The buffets cost about NZ$25 ($15), and reservations are essential at all the establishments. Some of them may charge a small admission to see the dance show if you don't have dinner.

When I was in Rarotonga recently, the **Tamure Resort Hotel** (tel. 22-415) had the most popular island buffets on Wednesday nights (its Saturday-night dance show followed a buffet of Chinese foods). **The Rarotongan Resort Hotel** (tel. 25-800) and **The Pacific Resort** (tel. 20-427) had their feasts and shows on Friday night. The **Edgewater Resort** (tel. 25-435) staged its versions on Saturday evening.

RESTAURANTS ON THE WEST COAST

OUTRIGGER RESTAURANT, Arorangi. Tel. 27-378.

Cuisine: SEAFOOD. **Reservations:** Recommended. **Location:** Arorangi, opposite Manuia Beach Hotel, 8km (4.8 miles) from Avarua.

$ Prices: Appetizers NZ$6–NZ$12.50 ($3.50–$7); main courses NZ$17.50–NZ$25.50 ($10.50–$15.50). AE, DC, MC, V.

Open: Dinner Mon–Sat 6–9:30pm.

Cook Islanders Hugh and Helen Henry (he's the tour leader and son of Sir Albert) specialize in local seafood, including freshly caught tropical lobsters from Aitutaki. Fishnets and ship's lights set the proper tone in this redecorated old store. Try the Henrys' "seafood pot" of mussels, oysters, scallops, prawns, and filets of fish in a fresh tomato-and-wine sauce. You may find Garth Young on the piano entertaining the Outrigger's guests on Friday and Saturday evenings.

TUMANU TROPICAL RESTAURANT AND BAR, Arorangi. Tel. 20-501.

Cuisine: REGIONAL. **Reservations:** Recommended. **Location:** Arorangi, near Edgewater Resort.

$ **Prices:** Appetizers NZ$6–NZ$14 ($3.50–$8.50); main courses NZ$19–NZ$28 ($11.50–$17). AE, MC, V.

Open: Dinner Mon–Sat 6–10pm; bar open till midnight.

With its low-slung thatch roof and lush outdoor gardens, this is the only restaurant and bar on Rarotonga that looks like it genuinely belongs in the South Seas. Julie and Eric Bateman's cozy place has subdued lighting inside, dividers of driftwood separating the tables, foreign flags hanging on split bamboo walls, and various paraphernalia stuck around the bar area, including old license plates from Texas, Oregon, Iowa, and Alaska. Colorful tablecloths help spice up otherwise plain dining-room furniture. The menu is heavy on seafood served braised or fried, but you can also get baked chicken or steaks in pepper or mushroom sauce. A special vegetarian platter comes with fruit salad, vegetables, and cheese omelet. Eric tends a friendly and popular bar; if you smoke, he will hand you a long piece of bamboo for your ashes.

VIAMA RESTAURANT AND BAR, Vaima. Tel. 26-123.

Cuisine: REGIONAL/CONTINENTAL. **Reservations:** Recommended, required for transportation. **Location:** Southwest coast, 2km (1.2 miles) east of Rarotongan Resort.

$ **Prices** (including 10% tax): Appetizers NZ$5.50–NZ$10.50 ($3.50–$6.50); main courses NZ$18.50–NZ$23 ($11–$14). AE, DC, MC, V.

Open: Dinner Mon–Sat 6:30–10pm.

The Viama sits between the main road and the lagoon, and dining is either inside the island-style building or outside under a semicircular thatch roof. German-born Renaldo (he uses no last name "because it's too difficult to pronounce") has several interesting features on his menu; chicken breasts, for example, are grilled and served with bananas and coconut flakes, and beef médaillons can be sliced with a fork through a pineapple and melted-cheese sauce. Want something German? Renaldo imports veal for his weinerschnitzel. Round-trip transportation from your hotel or motel costs NZ$5 ($3) per person.

KAENA RESTAURANT AND BAR, Arorangi. Tel. 25-433.

Cuisine: REGIONAL. **Reservations:** Recommended. **Location:** Southwest coast, north side of Rarotongan Resort Hotel, 13.5km (8.1 miles) from Avarua.

$ **Prices:** Appetizers NZ$4–NZ$9 ($2.50–$5.50); main courses NZ$13–NZ$18 ($8–$11). AE, DC, MC, V.

Open: Dinner Mon–Sat 6–10pm.

Tauei and Lynne Solomon's little place offers a home-style dining alternative to guests of the nearby Rarotongan Resort, Lagoon Lodges, and Puaikura Reef Lodges—or to anyone else looking for good food at a reasonable price. In business since 1982, the Kaena shares a building with a mom-and-pop grocery; don't be misled by the outside appearance, for inside their restaurant is quite charmingly decorated. You can dine inside or in an enclosed veranda room with flowering vines growing under its tin roof. Main courses feature charbroiled steaks either plain or with sauce, chicken in wine and cream, and steamed New Zealand mussels in white wine.

P. J.'S CAFE AND PIANO BAR, Arorangi. Tel. 20-367.

Cuisine: TAKE-OUT/EUROPEAN/CHINESE. **Reservations:** Seldom needed. **Location:** Arorangi, near Edgewater Resort and Rarotongan Sunset Motel, 6.3km (3.8 miles) from Avarua.

$ **Prices:** Appetizers NZ$5–NZ$12 ($3–$7); main courses NZ$13.50–NZ$25 ($8–$15). AE, MC, V.

Open: Mon–Thurs noon–2am, Fri noon–Sat 10pm, Sun 9am–10pm.

The only nonhotel restaurant open on Sunday, P. J.'s has a take-out counter on one side featuring burgers with various dressings and Cantonese dishes. A plain but tastefully decorated dining room offers lunches and dinners of steak, fish, chicken, or lamb, as well as the Cantonese dishes. The bar on the right-hand side of the establishment is a very popular watering hole, especially in the wee hours of Saturday morning (it stays open right through from Friday to Saturday).

RESTAURANTS ON MURI BEACH

FLAME TREE RESTAURANT, Muri Beach. Tel. 25-123.

Cuisine: INTERNATIONAL. **Reservations:** Required. **Location:** On Muri Beach, 10.5km (6.3 miles) from Avarua.

$ Prices: Appetizers NZ$8–NZ$16 ($5–$9.50); main courses NZ$18–NZ$25 ($11–$15). AE, DC, MC, V.

Open: Dinner Tues–Sat 6:30–9:30pm.

Yachties-turned-restaurateurs Bill and Sue Carruthers showed up in Rarotonga a few years ago and immediately transformed the island's eating scene by opening Portofino (see below) and the Flame Tree. They have since separated; Bill carries on at Portofino, Sue operates the Flame Tree. Located within walking distance of the Muri Beachcomber Motel and the Pacific Resort, the Flame Tree enjoys a pleasant beachside setting. Calling on the cuisines of her native Kenya and others she ran across during her extensive voyages, Sue whips together a wide range of selections, all displayed on a huge chalkboard menu, such as Thai ginger fish and an absolutely delightful East African dish of chicken served under a spicy tomato-and-peanut sauce. I particularly enjoy one of her nightly specials: fresh parrot fish breaded, fried, and served over rice and under a mound of taro-top spinach sweetly cooked in coconut sauce.

SAILS RESTAURANT, Muri Beach. Tel. 27-350.

Cuisine: EUROPEAN. **Reservations:** Advised for dinner. **Location:** Above Rarotonga Sailing Club, Muri Beach, 10.7km (6.4 miles) from Avarua.

$ Prices: Lunch NZ$5.50–NZ$10.50 ($3.50–$6.50); two-course dinner NZ$20 ($12). AE, DC, MC, V.

Open: Lunch Mon–Sat 11am–2pm; dinner Mon–Sat 6:30–9:30pm. Bar Mon–Sat 11am–11pm, happy hour 4–6pm.

Hoteliers/restaurateurs Jolene Bosanquet and Peter Heays took over the upstairs rooms of the Rarotonga Sailing Club and opened this breezy, nautically decorated establishment in 1991. They were serving only lunches of sandwiches and salads when I was there, but plans were to open evenings and offer two-course dinners of roasts or seafood for a reasonable fixed price of NZ$20 ($12). Call to make sure they are open at night.

RESTAURANTS IN TOWN

Avarua has a few places to get snacks and light meals at very reasonable cost, and anyone suffering from a McDonald's "Big Mac attack" and in need of a fast-food fix can seek relief at one of the canteen trucks that line up along the waterfront and at Avatiu Harbour from dawn until midnight, later on Friday.

PORTOFINO RESTAURANT, Avarua. Tel. 26-480.

Cuisine: ITALIAN. **Reservations:** Recommended. **Location:** In town, east of traffic circle.

$ Prices: Appetizers NZ$6.50–NZ$9.50 ($4–$5.50); main courses NZ$13.50–NZ$25 ($8–$15). AE, DC, MC, V.

Open: Dinner Mon–Sat 6:30–9:30pm.

Bill Carruthers serves up the best homemade pastas and tomato sauce between Tahiti and New Caledonia in this cozy old clapboard store dressed up with a cross between Mediterranean and Polynesian decor. An open-air pavilion to one side makes room for a few fresh-air tables. Spaghetti or rigatoni is served with Neapolitan, bolognese, Florentine, or Alfredo sauces, either as a heavy appetizer or as a main course. Tender charbroiled New Zealand–bred steaks are cooked plain or under pizzaiola, garlic, or pepper sauce. Daily specials feature such tempting dishes as a seafood lasagne with fish, crabmeat, and smoked mussels.

HIBISCUS BAR AND CAFE, Avarua. Tel. 20-824.

Cuisine: REGIONAL. **Reservations:** Recommended for dinner. **Location:** Avarua waterfront, west end of business district.

$ Prices: Appetizers NZ$6.50–NZ$10 ($4–$6); main courses NZ$13.50–NZ$14.50 ($8–$9); fixed-price meals NZ$20–NZ$25 ($12–$15); lunch NZ$3–NZ$8 ($2–$5). AE, MC, V.

Open: Lunch Mon–Sat 10:30am–2:30pm; dinner Mon–Sat 6–9pm.

Brendan and Megan Glassey's establishment resides in a colonial-style house that is almost below sea level on the land side of Avarua's main street. Lunches include a hamburger-and-beer combination, and daily specials, such as Indonesian-style beef satay. A blackboard menu features dinners such as grilled steaks and fried fish. An open-air bar has a shady courtyard to one side and serves libations (it's a popular watering hole) as well as morning and afternoon teas on Monday through Saturday from 10am; the courtyard can be packed during happy hour—4:30 to 6:30pm—on weekdays. The Glasseys have some form of entertainment Friday evenings and hold a games night on Wednesday.

TRADER JACK'S BAR AND GRILL, Avarua. Tel. 26-464.

Cuisine: EUROPEAN. **Reservations:** Recommended at dinner. **Location:** At the old wharf in Avarua, opposite the traffic circle.

$ Prices: Appetizers NZ$6.50–NZ$8 ($4–$5); main courses NZ$10.50–NZ$20 ($6.50–$12). AE, DC, MC, V.

Open: Lunch Mon–Sat noon–2pm; dinner Mon–Sat 7–10pm; bar Mon–Sat 11am–midnight.

"Trader Jack" Cooper opened this modern establishment in 1986 after spending a small fortune on a building with floor-to-ceiling windows on three sides facing the water and giving nearly everyone in the large bar and split-level dining area a view of the harbor, the reef, and the sea and sunsets beyond. Then in 1987 a cyclone destroyed the whole thing, along with a substantial portion of Avarua's business district. He rebuilt the establishment pretty much as was, and it is as popular as ever with local business and professional folk. There actually are three waterside decks, which can be packed at happy hour Monday through Friday and the rest of Friday night. The chalkboard menu changes daily but usually features roasts, charbroiled steaks, sashimi, and shrimp salad.

COOK'S CORNER CAFE, Avarua. Tel. 22-345.

Cuisine: SNACK BAR. **Location:** In Cook's Corner shopping center, across side street from C.I.T.C. store.

$ Prices: Meals NZ$5–NZ$9 ($3–$5.50). No credit cards.

Open: Mon–Sat 7am–4pm.

You will find me having a cooked breakfast at Maureen Young's little sidewalk café. She also serves snacks, morning and afternoon teas, and light lunches which include daily specials listed on a blackboard. They are purchased at a counter and eaten on the covered sidewalk of the small shopping center. Maureen's husband, Garth, plays the piano at the Outrigger Restaurant most evenings.

MAMA'S CAFE, Avarua. No phone.

Cuisine: SNACK BAR. **Location:** Next to Foodland on Avarua's waterfront, heart of business district.

$ Prices: Sandwiches and pastries NZ$2–NZ$3 ($1.20–$2). No credit cards.

Open: Mon–Fri 8am–4:30pm, Sat 8am–12:30pm.

Look for Mama's clean cafeteria-style café at the big Foodland grocery store. Walk along the cafeteria line and choose from a variety of snacks in the cold or hot cabinets. Then, if you can find one vacant, eat at one of the plastic tables in the seating area pleasantly accented with potted plants.

METUA'S CAFE, Avarua. Tel. 20-850.

Cuisine: REGIONAL/EUROPEAN. **Location:** In Brown's Arcade, just east of the traffic circle.

$ Prices: Sandwiches and burgers NZ$2.50–NZ$6 ($1.50–$3.50); meals NZ$10–NZ$12 ($6–$7). No credit cards.

Open: Mon–Thurs 8am–10pm, Fri 8am–3am, Sat 8am–midnight.

Metua's is another good place for full American breakfasts, sandwiches and hamburgers, fish-and-chips, salads and soups, and hot meals, such as grilled scallops, steaks, or chops. All-you-can-eat barbecues start Friday and Saturday at 6:30pm and go until the food's exhausted; they are excellent value at NZ$10 ($6). There's also a bar and patio with picnic tables right on the waterfront. Dancing to live island and rock music accompanies the Friday and Saturday barbecues.

8. EVENING ENTERTAINMENT

Sunday might be a *very* quiet day on Rarotonga, but the local residents seem to make up for it almost every other night—especially on Thursday, Friday, and Saturday (but never on Sunday). Visitors are more than welcome to join in the fun.

COOK ISLAND DANCING

No one should miss an "island night" Polynesian dance show on Rarotonga—or for that matter, anywhere else in the South Pacific. Cook Islanders are particularly famous for their dancing. A New Zealander once told me in jest that all Cook Islanders are deaf because they grow up three feet from a drum whose beats you can hear from 3 miles away.

The hip-swinging tamure is very much like that in Tahiti, except it tends to be faster (which I found hard to believe the first time I saw it) and more suggestive (which I had even more trouble believing). The costumes generally aren't as colorful as those in Tahiti.

Even though the dance shows at the hotels are tailored for tourists, the participants go at it with an enthusiasm that is too seldom seen in the French Polynesian hotel shows these days. Dancing is *the* thing to do in the Cook Islands, and it shows every time the drums start their suggestive tattoo.

Unadulterated Cook Islands dancing is best seen on the outer islands (I've known some travelers who have planned a side trip to Aitutaki around the Rapae Cottage Hotel's Friday island night) or when the outer islanders come to dance on Rarotonga during the annual Dance Week in April or during the Constitution Week celebrations in early August.

In the absence of one of these celebrations, make do with a show or two at the hotels. There will be a performance every night from Wednesday through Saturday, and sometimes two or three. A little detective work is required, but you'll easily find out where the next island night is being staged. Ask at your hotel tour desks or the tourist authority, or check for advertisements in the daily *Cook Islands News*.

Back in the "Where to Stay" and "Where to Dine" sections I set out the schedule when I was on Rarotonga recently. Here's a repeat: The **Tamure Resort Hotel** (tel. 22-415) had the most popular island dance shows Wednesday and Saturday nights. **The Rarotongan Resort Hotel** (tel. 25-800) and **The Pacific Resort** (tel. 20-427) had their feasts and shows on Friday night. The **Edgewater Resort** (tel. 25-435) staged its versions on Saturday evening. In addition, the **Banana Court Bar** (tel. 20-043) at the traffic circle in Avarua (see below) interrupts its rock-and-roll band long enough to have Cook Island dancing at least 1 night a week, often on Thursday.

The Banana Court extracts a NZ$3 ($1.80) cover charge for its show. Some others may charge a small admission to see the dance show if you don't have dinner, but it will be worth it. The buffets cost about NZ$25 ($15), and reservations are essential if you are having the buffet at one of the hotels.

PUB CRAWLING

When Rarotongans aren't dancing in a show, they seem to be dancing with each other at one or more of the most colorful bars in the South Pacific. Let's join them in Avarua and hit a few of these pubs.

BANANA COURT BAR, Avarua at the traffic circle. Tel. 20-043.

"The B.C." is one of the last old-time South Seas bars anywhere. In fact, it is as much of an institution as the Cook Islands government across the street, since the Banana Court is owned by the government (the Cook Islands Tourist Authority is responsible for its operation and is supported by its profits).

The building is as interesting as the mob that jams it on Thursday, Friday, and Saturday nights. It was built by the government as the Cook Islands' first hotel, and the interior is still divided into a number of rooms now used for drinking. A dance floor in the rear is usually packed as visitors and islanders alike gyrate to the beat of rock music well into the early morning—except on Saturday, of course, when the Banana Court and nearly everything else on Rarotonga comes to a screeching halt as midnight announces the arrival of Sunday. There's hardly room to move anywhere, especially on Friday night, but some fancy footwork will result in a spot at the bar in the far-right corner near the dance floor. Forget about ordering a complicated mixed drink; settle for a locally brewed Cooks Lager. Almost everyone else will be guzzling one. The action really gets going after 9pm, although the bar opens Monday through Friday at 11am (Saturday at 8pm). *Caution:* Things have been known to get a bit rowdy after midnight on Friday.

Admission: Thurs–Sat NZ$3 ($1.80). **Prices:** Beers NZ$3 ($1.80), drinks NZ$3.50 ($2).

FIRST CLUB, Avarua, behind the Hibiscus Restaurant. Tel. 21-110.

This dark disco features island and soft rock music, which attracts a more affluent and older crowd than the Banana Court or T. J.'s Niteclub. The seating areas are carpeted, and the building is air conditioned throughout. Stylish island attire is the order of the day. It's open Monday through Saturday 9pm to midnight, to 2am on Friday.

Admission: NZ$3 ($1.80). **Prices:** Drinks NZ$3.50 ($2).

METUA'S CAFE, Avarua, in Brown's Arcade. Tel. 20-850.

This café, mentioned above in "Where to Dine," turns into an outdoor nightclub on Friday and Saturday at 9pm when a live band starts playing island and rock music for dancing. The evenings really get going at 6:30pm, however, with Metua's famous all-you-can-eat barbecues.

Admission: Free. **Prices:** Drinks NZ$3.50 ($2). Dinner NZ$10 ($6).

P.J.'S CAFE & PIANO BAR, Arorangi, near Edgewater Resort. Tel. 20-367.

The cozy piano-bar side of the café draws a crowd of locals and visitors every night, including Sunday when it's the only nonhotel eating or drinking establishment with Sabbath hours. It's also the last stop on Friday night/Saturday morning, when it stays open all night. Otherwise, hours are Monday through Thursday noon to 2am, Saturday and Sunday 9am to 10pm.

Admission: Free. **Prices:** Drinks NZ$3.50 ($2).

T. J.'S NITECLUB, Avarua, east of the traffic circle. Tel. 20-576.

The pub-crawling path leads from the Banana Court to T. J.'s, as the first floor of the large building behind Brown's Arcade is another mecca for Rarotonga's young people. Like the Banana Court, it can get rowdy after midnight. Open Wednesday through Friday 9pm to 2am, Saturday 9pm to midnight.

Admission: NZ$2 ($1.20). **Prices:** Drinks NZ$3.50 ($2).

TERE'S BAR, Avatiu Harbour. Tel. 20-352.

Under the thatch cabana across from the fishing-boat harbor at Avatiu, Tere has a live band on Friday night and draws a somewhat older and more sedate—if not more sober—crowd than does the Banana Court or T. J.'s. Tere's Bar is open Monday through Thursday 10am to midnight, Friday 10am to 2am, and Saturday 10am to midnight. It's a pleasant place to have a cold Cooks Lager after a walking tour of Avarua.

Admission: Free. **Prices:** Drinks NZ$3 ($1.80).

TRADER JACK'S BAR AND GRILL, Avarua, at the old wharf. Tel. 26-464.

The well-known restaurant and watering hole becomes a gathering spot for the more affluent on Friday and Saturday, when a band plays island songs and light rock numbers. Many locals start their weekend evenings with a bite to eat at Trader Jack's or Metua's Cafe, then hit the hard-rock places later.

Admission: Free. **Prices:** Drinks NZ$4 ($2.50).

9. AN EASY EXCURSION TO AITUTAKI

The farther away visitors get from the South Pacific's international airports, the more likely they are to find an island and a way of life that have escaped relatively unscathed by the coming of Western ways—remnants of "old" Polynesia or Melanesia, as the case may be. This is certainly true of Aitutaki, the most frequently visited of the outer Cook Islands.

Lying 155 miles north of Rarotonga, Aitutaki is often referred to as "the Bora Bora of the Cook Islands" because it consists of a small, hilly island at the apex of a triangular barrier reef dotted with skinny flat islands. This reef necklace encloses one of the South Pacific's most beautiful lagoons, which appears at the end of the 1-hour flight up from Rarotonga as a turquoise carpet spread on the deep blue sea. The view from the air is memorable.

The central island, only 8 square miles in area, is dotted with the coconut, pineapple, banana, and tapioca plantations that are worked by most of the island's 2,500 residents. A few Aitutakians make their living at the island's three hotels, but the land and the lagoon still provide most of their income. Aitutaki is a major supplier of produce and seafood to Rarotonga. Much of the fresh fish, lobster, and octopus consumed at Rarotonga's restaurants is harvested here.

The administrative center, most of the shops, and the main wharf are on the west side of the island at **Arutanga** village, where a narrow, shallow passage comes through the reef. Trading boats cannot get through the pass and must remain offshore while cargo and passengers are ferried to land by barge. A network of mostly unpaved roads fans out from Arutanga to **Viapai** and **Tautu** villages on the east side, and to the airport on a flat hook at the northeast end of the island. The airport's two long runways were paid for by New Zealand and built by the Americans during World War II.

The uninhabited palm-fringed small islands out on the reef have white-sand beaches on their lagoon sides and pounding surf on the other; they're perfect for picnics and snorkeling expeditions.

GETTING THERE

Air Rarotonga (tel. 22-888 on Rarotonga) has several flights a day to and from Aitutaki. Air Rarotonga also offers day- and overnight trips with discounts on lodging. It will make reservations at any of the outer-island accommodations.

For fares and more information, see "Getting Around the Cooks" above in this chapter.

Air-hotel packages to Aitutaki can vary in price but always represent a savings over do-it-yourself arrangements, so check with the travel agents in Avarua to see if they have deals. **Island Hopper Vacations** (tel. 22-026) and **Stars Travel** (tel. 23-699) both specialize in outer-island trips. Their offices are in the heart of Avarua's business district.

Since Aitutaki's airport sits on the northeast corner of the island, you more than likely will fly over the lagoon on the approach; if possible, get a seat on the left side of the aircraft.

GETTING AROUND

The airport is about 7km (4 miles) from most hotels and guesthouses. Air Rarotonga provides **airport transfers** for NZ$4 ($2.50) each way. The Aitutaki office is in Ureia village just north of Arutanga. The rattletrap minibuses pick up passengers from the hotels prior to departing flights. Ask the hotel desk to reconfirm your return to Rarotonga; otherwise, the bus won't stop for you.

There is no public transportation system on Aitutaki.

Scooters and **bicycles** are available from Rino's Rentals (tel. 31-197) and Josie's Lodge (tel. 31-111) for NZ$20 ($12) a day. Both establishments are on the main road about ½ mile south of the Rapae Cottage Hotel.

If she isn't busy taking visitors on island tours, **Mama Tereu** at the Tiare Maori Guest House (tel. 31-119) provides transfers from the Arutanga area to the Aitutaki Lagoon Hotel for NZ$5 ($3) a person.

FAST FACTS

Currency Exchange Traveler's checks can be cashed at Westpac Bank's little agency or at the post office, both in Arutanga, Mon–Fri 8am–3pm.

Dentist/Doctor See "Hospital," below.

Drugstores Some prescription drugs are available at the island's hospital near Arutanga—there is no private pharmacy on Aitutaki.

Emergencies In case of emergency, contact your hotel staff. The police station is in Arutanga.

Hospital Medical and dental treatment are available at the island's hospital near Arutanga. There are two doctors and a dentist, all of them trained in New Zealand.

Liquor Laws The post office in Arutanga houses the bond store, where liquor and beer can be purchased Mon–Thurs 8am–3pm, Fri 8am–2:30pm (no liquor is sold during Fri-afternoon rugby and cricket games).

Police See "Safety," below.

Post Office The post office at Arutanga is open Mon–Fri 8am–3pm.

Safety The police station is in Arutanga. See the "Fast Facts" for Rarotonga earlier in this chapter for general warnings and precautions.

Telegrams/Telex International telephone calls can be made at the post office daily 7am–midnight.

Water Visitors should not drink the tap water on Aitutaki unless they are sure it comes from a rainwater catchment. Ask first.

WHAT TO SEE & DO

Most activities on Aitutaki focus on its magnificent lagoon and barrier reef, but there are also golf, a short hiking trail leading to a panoramic view, and island tours. Nightlife on Aitutaki centers on its famous "island night" dance shows.

SEEING AITUTAKI

The hotels have organized ½-day land tours of the island for NZ$20 ($13) per person. Entertaining and informative, Mama Tereu of **Tiare Maori Guest House** (tel. 31-119) does a 2-hour tour of the island for that same price.

If you decide to rent a bicycle or scooter and tour Aitutaki yourself, here's what you will see. It should take about 2 hours on a scooter, about ½ day on a bicycle. Begin at the Rapae Cottage Hotel and proceed north.

The North Shore

The towering cliff is **Mount Maungapu,** Aitutaki's highest point. Legend says that in the beginning the island was completely flat, but then Aitutaki warriors went to Rarotonga and stole the top of Mount Raemaru. Pitched battles were fought on the way home, and parts of the mountain fell into the sea: Black Rock, on Rarotonga's northwest point; Rapota and Moturakau islands, in the south of Aitutaki's lagoon;

and the black rocks along Aitutaki's west coast. In the end, the Aitutakian warriors were victorious, and the top of Raemaru is now Mount Maungapu. There's a walking trail to the top (see "Hiking," below).

The volcanic part of Aitutaki is joined to the reef on the island's north end, and it was here that the American forces—with a lot of help from the local residents—built the large **airstrip** during World War II. About 1,000 Americans were stationed at the strip, which was used as a refueling stop on the route between North America and New Zealand. Many present-day Aitutakians reportedly are the children and grandchildren of those American sailors.

The road runs around the western end of the runway, through a coconut grove, and past the golf course and the airport terminal building before following the edge of the larger and longer southeast-northwest strip. Small paths go off to the beach, which is rocky and pounded by the surf along the north coast.

The road splits at the end of the airport. The right fork follows the shore to an old jetty used by Air New Zealand (known then as Tasman Empire Air Lines) on its famous Coral Route in the 1950s. For about 8 years Aitutaki was a refueling stop for the giant airships that flew from Auckland to Suva in Fiji, Apia in Western Samoa, and Papeete in Tahiti. Before the international airport at Faaa opened in 1961, these so-called flying boats were the only way to get to Tahiti by plane. The planes would land in the lagoon at Aitutaki, and passengers could disembark and enjoy a swim and picnic on the beach while the plane was refueled and prepared for the next leg. The lagoon off the dock is about as deep as it gets on Aitutaki and is one of the best places on the island to snorkel.

Akitua Island

The left fork leads to Ootu Passage, beyond which lie Akitua island and The Aitutaki Lagoon Hotel. According to legend, the first Polynesians to reach Aitutaki came in through this pass. They were led by the mighty warrior and navigator Ru, who brought four wives, four brothers, and a crew of 20 young virgins from either Tubai or Raiatea (the legend varies as to which one) in what is now French Polynesia. Akitua island, where they landed, originally was named Urituaorukitemoana, which means "where Ru turned his back on the sea." The first European to visit Aitutaki was Capt. William Bligh, who discovered it a few weeks before he was set adrift in Tonga by the mutinous crew of HMS *Bounty* in 1789.

The road ends at the pass. The narrow footbridge leads to the Aitutaki Lagoon Hotel, a property that has had its troubles in recent years (see "Where to Stay & Dine," below). Nevertheless, it makes a decent refueling stop before we backtrack to the western end of the airport.

The East Coast

Take the track to the left (that is, east) at the fork on the south side of the runway and turn left at the rock quarry. This road runs through coconut, banana, taro, and tapioca **plantations** along the east coast. The tin sheds along the way are for drying copra before it is shipped to Rarotonga and on to the coconut-oil mill in Tahiti. There are some nice views of the lagoon and the islets on the reef as the road skirts the shore.

Turn left at the T intersection and bear left at the next fork in the road to arrive at **Vaipae** village, whose Vaipaepae-O-Pau meeting hall is the second largest on the island. The village of Reureu on the east coast set off a meeting-hall competition in the 1970s when it constructed what was then the largest on the island. Suddenly big halls became the rage, and each village on Aitutaki vied to see who could build the biggest. Thousands of dollars, many of them coming from Aitutakians living in New Zealand, were spent on the competition. There apparently has been no similar competition to see who can build the biggest church—the Cook Islands Christian Church in Vaipae has a new roof, but the building itself is more than a century old.

Between Vaipae and Tautu villages stands the **Vaitau School,** which was named for both communities. The big banyan tree past the school, which marks the boundary between the two villages, is believed to be more than 2,000 years old. The first dirt track to the left past the tree leads to **Tautu jetty,** built by the Americans during World War II as a landing and hurricane shelter for boats. There's another nice view of the lagoon and reef islands from the jetty, which is used by Tautu villagers as a fishing-boat harbor.

The West Coast

The road to the right in Tautu leads across the island to the west coast and to **Arutanga,** the main village, where the island's post office sits in the middle of "town." The divided road from the post office to the wharf has two names. The southern part is Sir Albert Henry Drive, in honor of Albert Henry, who was born and raised on Aitutaki. The northern part is named Lady Elizabeth Drive, in honor of the late prime minister's wife.

South of Sir Albert Henry Drive is the large banana-packing shed where Aitutaki's crop is prepared for shipment to New Zealand. The main wharf at the end of the two drives was built by the Americans during World War II. Plans were to extend the wharf to the deep water and enlarge and deepen the pass through the reef. The war ended, however, and the project was never completed.

Just south of the post office is the **Cook Islands Christian Church,** the country's oldest, built in 1839 of coral and limestone. The monument in front is to John Williams, the exploring missionary who came to Aitutaki in October 1821, and to Papeiha, the Tahitian teacher who came with him and stayed for 2 years—during which he converted the entire island. Papeiha then went to Rarotonga and helped the missionaries do the same thing there. The interior of the church is unusual in that the altar is on one side rather than at one end. Worshipers from each village sit together during services, but visitors can take any vacancy during services at 10am on Sunday. An anchor is suspended from the ceiling in the middle of the building in reference to Hebrews 6:19.

Across from the church is the meeting ground where the kings (that is, the high chiefs, or *ariki*) of Aitutaki are installed. The nearby **Ngapuariki Meeting Hall** is named for Ru's canoe, and the modest green house next to it is the home of Tamatoa, the island's reigning ariki. From here the paved road continues south a few hundred yards, then becomes dirt until terminating at a beautiful beach backed by coconut palms and casuarinas. It then becomes a narrow track to the island's southernmost point.

The road from Arutanga back to the Rapae Cottage Hotel passes most of the island's stores and businesses, the rugby and cricket field, and the three guesthouses.

SPORTS & RECREATION

✪ **LAGOON EXCURSIONS** The big attraction on Aitutaki is at least one day spent on the lagoon and the small islands out on the reef. The "standard" day-trip begins at 9am and ends about 4pm. The boat leaves from the main wharf for a morning of cruising and fishing on the lagoon. Midday is spent on one of the reef islands, where guests swim, snorkel, and sun while the crew cooks the day's catch and the local vegetables in an island-style earth oven. The itinerary changes from day to day depending on the weather and the guests' desires.

A common destination is Tapuaetai, or "One Foot," island. According to Teina Bishop, who runs Blue Water Cruises, this tiny motu got its name when an ancient chief prohibited his subjects from fishing there on pain of death. One day the chief and his warriors saw two people fishing on the reef and gave chase. The two were a man and his young son. They ran onto the island, the father carefully stepping in his son's footprints as they crossed the beach. The son then hid in the top of a coconut tree. The chief found the father, who said he was the only person fishing on the reef. After a search proved fruitless, the chief decided it must have been rocks he and his men saw on the reef. He then killed the father. Ever since, the island has been known as Tapuaetai (in the local dialect, *tapuae* means footprint, *tai* is one).

Those dark things that look like cucumbers dotting the bottom of the lagoon, by the way, are *bêches-de-mer* (sea slugs). Along with sandalwood, they brought many traders to the South Pacific during the 19th century because both brought high prices in China. Sea slugs are harmless—except in China, where they are considered to be an aphrodisiac.

Your hotel can book a day-trip for you. **Clive's Tours** (tel. 31-025) uses a powerboat with a canopy, which provides much-needed shade (you will go with Clive if you book Air Rarotonga's day-trip). He charges NZ$35 ($21) per person. **Viking Lagoon Cruises** (tel. 31-180) has day cruises using open boats powered by outboard engines. They cost NZ$30 ($18) a day. Teina Bishop of **Blue Water Cruises** (tel. 31-009) takes his guests on Hobie Cats. His prices are NZ$30 ($18) for a ½ day, NZ$50 ($30) for a full day. When I was there recently, Teina was planning to put a large, covered motorboat into operation; it will be worth checking out.

Whatever way you go, bring a hat and plenty of sunscreen. The sun on the lagoon can be blistering, even if your boat has a canopy.

DIVING Divers can contact Neil Mitchell of **Aitutaki Scuba,** P.O. Box 40, Aitutaki (tel. 31-103), for underwater adventure. Neil operates from his home just south of the Rapae Cottage Hotel. He charges NZ$45 ($27) per one-tank dive, NZ$50 ($30) with equipment, and will teach a 4-day certification course for NZ$395 ($237). Neil also can tell you how to go deep-sea fishing.

GOLF Golfers who missed hitting the radio antennae and guy wires on the Rarotonga course can try again at the nine-hole course at the **Aitutaki Golf Club,** on the north end of the island between the airport and the sea. One hole runs along the runway, but a ball hit there is now considered to be out of bounds—it used to be playable, but broken clubs and increasing air traffic put an end to that. You can rent equipment at the clubhouse. The club doesn't have a phone, but the hotels and guesthouses can arrange rentals and a tee-off time. Greens fees are NZ$5 ($3).

HIKING Hikers can take a trail to the top of **Mount Maungapu,** Aitutaki's highest point at 124 meters (410 ft.). It begins about a mile north of the Rapae Cottage Hotel, across from the Paradise Cove Guest House (the home with a water tank in front). The trail starts under the power lines and follows them up the mountain for about a mile. The tall grass is sharp and can be soaked after a rain, but the track is usually well tramped and should be easy to follow. Nevertheless, wear trousers. The view from the top includes all of Aitutaki and its lagoon.

SHOPPING

The **Women's Handicraft Center,** behind the post office, offers a few mats and other woven items at prices below those on Rarotonga (after all, most Cook Islands handcrafts are made in the outer islands). Paula and Terepai Maoate, Jr., sell souvenirs and tie-dyed T-shirts and pareus at **Maina Traders** in Arutanga.

WHERE TO STAY & DINE

There are a number of good places to stay, but when it comes to dining, other than the hotel and guesthouse dining rooms, the pickings are slim. In fact, there is no restaurant as such on Aitutaki, although two of the nightspots mentioned in "Evening Entertainment," below, sell what amounts to "counter meals" to their customers. Otherwise, you're limited to **Big Jay's Snack Bar** (no phone) just south of the post office in Arutanga. It has burgers, hot dogs, and fried fish with either breadfruit or taro chips. Prices range from NZ$2.50 to NZ$5 ($1.50 to $3). It's open Monday through Saturday from 9am to 5pm.

THE AITUTAKI LAGOON HOTEL, P.O. Box 342, Rarotonga. Tel. 20-234.
Fax 20-990. Telex 62048. 25 bungalows. **Location:** On Akitua Island, 2km (1.2 miles) south of airport, 9km (5.4 miles) from Arutanga.

$ Rates: NZ$130 ($78) single; NZ$155 ($93) double. AE, DC, MC, V.

Originally named the Aitutaki Resort Hotel, this property had a few good years until a cyclone inflicted heavy damage in 1987. At the time of my recent visit, the government had been trying to sell the property without success. It was limping along primarily on the good graces of its friendly Cook Islander staff. Given the capital for renovation, this could again be a first-class property, and that could happen by the time you plan your trip. A thatch central building and surrounding bungalows sit on Akitua, the little motu south of the airport (see "Seeing Aitutaki," above, for the island's legend).

The ocean surf breaks on one side, the magnificent lagoon laps a white-sand beach on the other. The shingle-roofed bungalows have cane lounge furniture, double and single beds, large windows on two sides, and porches with entrances both to the main rooms and to shower-only baths.

The restaurant serves plain meals with an emphasis on buffets and barbecues at dinner. One evening usually sees an island dance show after dinner. Facilities include a boutique, tour desk, and some water-sports equipment.

AITUTAKI LODGES, P.O. Box 70, Aitutaki. Tel. 31-334. Fax 31-333. 6 bungalows. MINIBAR **Location:** East side of island between Vaipai and Tautu villages.

$ Rates (including 10% tax): NZ$114 ($69) single or double; NZ$182 ($109) single, NZ$226 ($136) double with evening meal and scooter. AE.

Two of your fellow readers, Tony Carter and Kathy Bisset, stayed a week on Aitutaki while escaping the frigid winter climes in their hometown of Whitehorse in the Yukon Territory, Canada. They found Wayne and Aileen Blake's establishment before I did. I've seen it since, but here's what they accurately reported:

"Located on the east side of the island just south of Tautu jetty, it is within a 10-minute drive of Arutanga village. Accommodations consist of six immaculate A-frame-style bungalows set into a hillside sloping to the edge of the lagoon. Each bungalow has a queen-size and single bed, bathroom with a shower, ceiling fan, full kitchen including a stocked minibar, and a porch offering spectacular views across the lagoon to the islands and the reef. They are quiet and private.

"Although the water in front of the hotel is too shallow to be considered good swimming, there is a launch available to take guests out on the lagoon. A lagoon cruise including a beach barbecue leaves at 9:30am and returns at 4pm, and snorkel gear may be hired. For the traditionalists, and the stout of palm, there is an authentic dugout canoe that may be poled around the lagoon. Motor scooters are also available to guests."

I might add that the launch, lagoon cruise and barbecue, and motor scooters all cost extra.

Since Tony and Kathy were there, the Blakes have added a small thatch-roofed dining room and bar where guests have a grand view down a lawn to the lagoon. They serve three meals a day.

RAPAE COTTAGE HOTEL, P.O. Box 4, Aitutaki. Tel. 31-320. Fax 31-321. 12 rms. **Location:** 1km (.6 mile) north of Arutanga.

$ Rates: NZ$60 ($36) single; NZ$65 ($39) double. AE, MC, V.

The government was in the process of selling this hotel during my recent visit. It was in need of renovation planned by the new owners, so some changes in quality—and rates—may have occurred by the time you plan your trip. The Rapae has rooms in six duplex bungalows and two other family-size units, each in a separate bungalow. The rooms all have a double and a single bed, a bathroom with a shower, a ceiling fan, and a porch running across the front. Although a little shopworn, they're clean. The most serious drawback is that the walls are thin and every snore in one room can be heard on the other side of the duplex bungalow.

The thatch-roofed central building sits in a beachside casuarina grove. The bungalows are built on higher ground behind the building, and all of them face the lagoon. Black lava rocks on the beach just north of the hotel offer a fine sunset view. The lagoon off the Rapae's beach is shallow enough for a walk out to the reef at low tide but is one of the island's best snorkeling spots when the tide is in.

Home-cooked meals are served in the main building. Dinner consists of a buffet of European and island-style selections at NZ$18 ($11) a head. Outsiders should book no later than 3pm for the night's sitting at 7pm sharp. Everyone gets a plate and sits down before someone says grace. The Rapae's island night, held every Friday at 7pm, is the most authentic in the Cook Islands, both in terms of the local foods in the buffet and the Polynesian dance show. The NZ$20 ($12) per-person cost is well worth it.

JOSIE'S LODGE, Post Office, Aitutaki. Tel. 31-111, 22-225, or 21-314 on Rarotonga. 6 rms. **Location:** 10-minute walk north of Arutanga.

$ Rates: NZ$28 ($17) single; NZ$33 ($20) single with breakfast; NZ$38 ($23) double; NZ$48 ($29) double with breakfast. No credit cards.

Mrs. Josie Sadaraka has turned her typical island home into a guesthouse, but don't expect frills. Her six bedrooms, once used by her family, flank a central hallway; each has a double bed and single bed with mosquito nets (the house has no screened windows). Guests share two bathrooms and the kitchen. Josie will prepare home-cooked dinners for NZ$10 ($6) per person. She also has motorbikes and bicycles to rent.

TIARE MAORI GUEST HOUSE, P.O. Box 16, Aitutaki. Tel. 31-119. 7 rms.

Location: 10-minute walk north of Arutanga.

$ Rates: NZ$28 ($17) single; NZ$38 ($23) double. NZ$2.50 ($1.50) for use of stove. No credit cards.

Known for years simply as "Mama's" in honor of its gregarious proprietor, Mrs. Tunui Tereu, this guesthouse sits about 100 yards inland from the main road (turn off near Josie's Lodge). You should be able to spot it by the umbrella tables in the front yard. Inside, the rooms all have double beds but no screened windows. Breakfasts and dinners are available at NZ$5 ($3) and NZ$15 ($9), respectively. No shoes, alcoholic beverages, or smoking is allowed inside the house, but guests can wear shoes, drink, and smoke in the carport lounge.

TOM'S BEACH COTTAGE, P.O. Box 51, Aitutaki. Tel. 31-051. 8 rms.

Location: 10-minute walk north of Arutanga.

$ Rates: NZ$28 ($17) single; NZ$38 ($23) double. 1 free night for a week's stay. No credit cards.

Aitutaki's three guesthouses (Josie's, Tom's, and Tiare Maori) all are within a very short walk of each other. Tom's distinguishing feature is that it sits right on the beach (the other two are on the mountain side of the road). In fact, the lounge's big louvered windows look right out on the lagoon. Otherwise, you get a room and share two bathrooms and the kitchen.

EVENING ENTERTAINMENT

Nightlife on Aitutaki essentially centers on its "island night" dance shows, one on Thursday night, two on Friday.

RAPAE COTTAGE HOTEL, 1km (½-mile) north of Arutanga. Tel. 31-320.

As I said earlier, Friday night at the Rapae is what a lot of people come to Aitutaki for. Things kick off at 7pm with a buffet of island foods cooked in an umu. Once everyone has eaten, the show goes on. The quality of the dance will depend on which troupe performs, but it always will be energetic. It seems that the entire island turns out once the drums start to beat.

Prices: Dinner NZ$20 ($12). Show free. Drinks NZ$3.50 ($2).

RINO'S BAR, opposite the Rapae Cottage Hotel. No phone.

Once the Friday night show is over at the Rapae, everyone staggers directly across the road to Rino's (pronounced "Reno's") for another traditional Cook Islands dance performance at 9pm. On Thursday and Saturday nights, Rino's has live music for dancing. Aitutaki occasionally runs out of beer if the trading boat is late, but Rino seldom lets that interfere with his Thursday-to-Saturday bashes—he flies in emergency shipments. Rino also serves up basic fish-and-chips (taro or breadfruit, depending on the season) for about NZ$10 ($6) a plate.

Prices: Show free. Drinks NZ$3.50 ($2).

THE CRUSHER BAR, 1 mile north of Rapae Cottage Hotel. No phone.

If you couldn't get to Aitutaki on a Friday, then the Crusher has its island feast and floor show on Thursday, with the feast starting at 7pm, the floor show at 8:30pm. Cost for the meal and show is NZ$20 ($12). The bar opens Monday to Thursday at 10pm, Saturday at 8pm, and goes most nights until there is no more business (until midnight Saturday). I haven't sampled them, but I've heard that the fish-and-chips are very good.

CHAPTER 7

GETTING TO KNOW THE SAMOAS

Western Samoa and American Samoa, which share a people if not a flag, present a sharp contrast in how modern development has affected the oldest Polynesian culture.

On the one hand, the larger but poorer **Western Samoa,** an independent nation since 1962, is a cultural storehouse, where *fa'a Samoa*—The Samoan Way—remains alive and well. Its inhabited islands are living museums of the old life-style and traditions, and to visit its villages is to get a glimpse of what life could have been like three millennia ago, when the first humans settled in Samoa, "The Cradle of Polynesia."

In contrast, **American Samoa**—the only United States territory south of the equator—has been made relatively prosperous by money from Washington and the earnings of two fish canneries sitting deep in famous **Pago Pago,** the South Pacific's best harbor. In American Samoa the ancient, traditional way of life hangs on, but constantly adapts to modern American ways.

American Samoa suffers a serious lack of first-class accommodations. On the other hand, Western Samoa's picturesque capital, **Apia,** is blessed with quite comfortable and charming hotels and adequate guesthouses. Accordingly, I recommend you read these next three chapters with an eye toward making Apia your base of operations and treat American Samoa as a side trip from Western Samoa.

This chapter covers what the two Samoas have in common (plus a few items that make them different). For details about traveling in Western Samoa, see Chapter 8; for American Samoa, see Chapter 9.

Go with an eye to meeting the people while exploring some of the South Pacific's most beautiful outposts. If approached with this goal in mind, these two little gems will fascinate and enchant you, just as they did Robert Louis Stevenson, W. Somerset Maugham, and Margaret Mead, who all found plenty in Samoa to write home about.

1. GEOGRAPHY

Located in the central South Pacific some 1,200 miles west of Tahiti and 2,600 miles southwest of Hawaii, the Samoas consist of 16 islands between them. The seven islands of American Samoa are located on the eastern end of the 300-mile-long archipelago and comprise a land area of 77 square miles, 53 of which are on **Tutuila.** The nine islands of Western Samoa have a land area of 1,090 square miles, 703 of

SAMOA ISLANDS

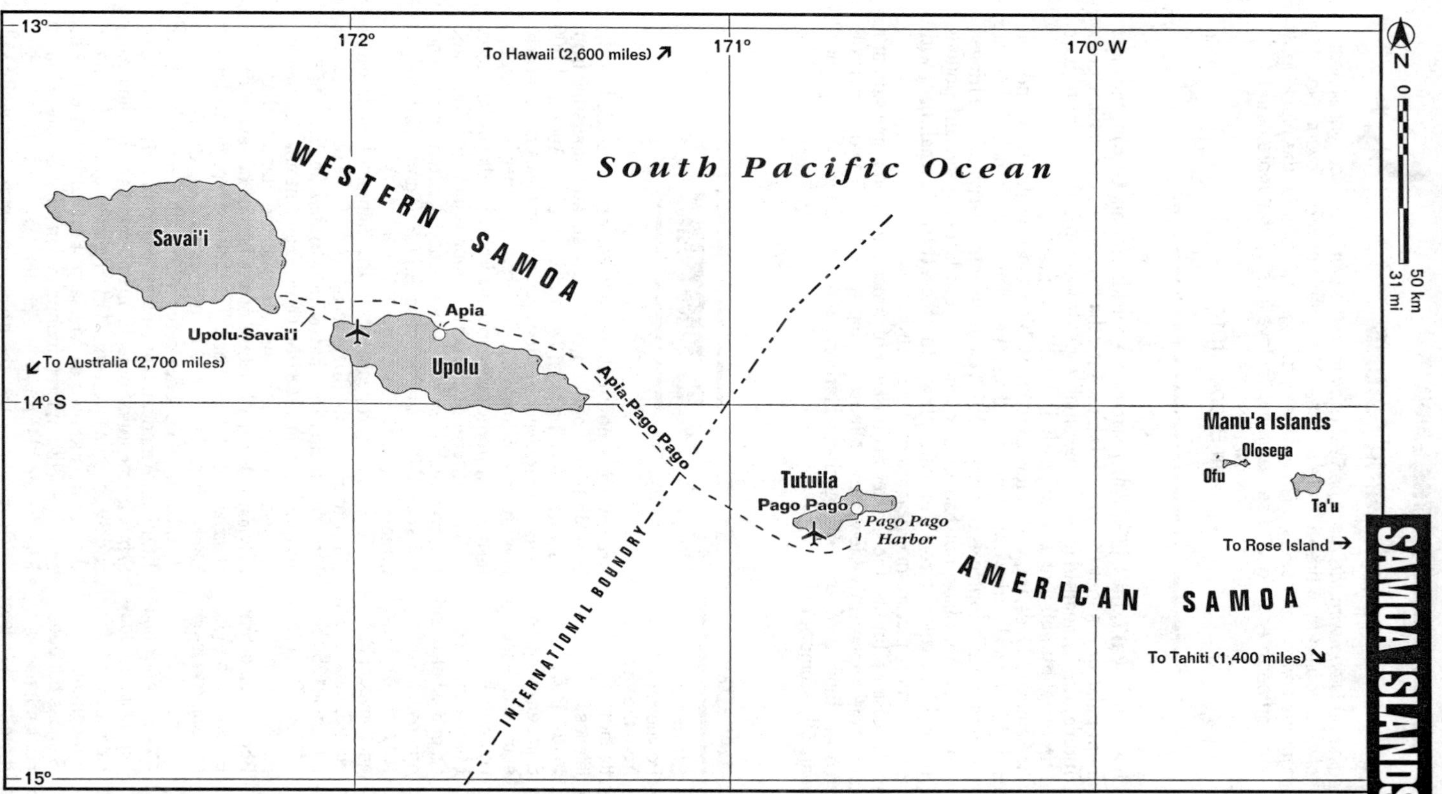

IMPRESSIONS

Imagine an island with the most perfect climate in the world, tropical yet almost always cooled by a breeze from the sea. No malaria or other fevers. No dangerous snakes or insects. Fish for the catching, and fruits for the plucking. And an earth and sky and sea of immortal loveliness. What more could civilisation give?

—Rupert Brooke, 1914

---

which are on **Savai'i,** the largest Polynesian island outside Hawaii. **Upolu,** the most heavily populated, is about the size of Tahiti. With the exceptions of Savai'i, Upolu, and Tutuila, the Samoan islands are the small tops of volcanoes that seem to have given up the ghost and quit growing early in life.

The Samoan islands are, with a few exceptions, high and volcanic, lush, and well watered. Geologically they are younger than the islands in French Polynesia. Volcanoes on Savai'i erupted as recently as 1911. Consequently, the islands are fringed with coral reefs that have not had time to enclose deep lagoons; the surf pounds directly on black volcanic rocks in many places. In others there are small bays with some of the most picturesque beaches in the South Pacific.

In the case of Tutuila, the slender main island of American Samoa, one side of a volcanic crater apparently blew away, almost cutting the island in two. Thus was created the long, bent arm of Pago Pago Harbor, one of the South Pacific's most dramatically scenic spots.

2. HISTORY

Archeologists now believe that Polynesians settled in the Samoan Islands about 3,000 years ago, after migrating from Southeast Asia through Melanesia and Fiji. Another 1,000 years or more went by, however, before voyagers went on to colonize the Marquesas, Society, and other island groups farther east in the great triangle known today as Polynesia.

The universe of the early Samoans included Tonga and Fiji, to which they regularly journeyed, often waging war. For some 300 years between A.D. 950 and 1250 Tongan invaders ruled the Samoas.

The first European to see the Samoan Islands was a Dutchman, Jacob Roggeveen, who in 1722 sighted the Manu'a Islands in what is now American Samoa. After visiting Tahiti in 1768, the Frenchman Antoine de Bougainville sailed through the Samoas and named them the Navigator Islands because of the natives he saw in canoes chasing tuna far offshore. The first Europeans to land in Samoa were part of a French expedition under Jean La Pérouse in 1787. They came ashore on the north coast of Tutuila in American Samoa and were promptly attacked by Samoan warriors. Some 12 members of the landing party and 39 Samoans were killed during the skirmish. The site of the battle is known as Massacre Bay. La Pérouse and his entire expedition later disappeared in what is now Solomon Islands (see "History" in Chapter 1).

To the Samoans, the great ships with their white sails seemed to have come through the slit that separated the sky

DATELINE

- **3000 B.C.** Polynesians arrive from the west, settle in the Samoan islands.
- **2000 B.C.** Samoans venture south and west, colonize Tonga, Marquesas, Society, and other island groups.
- **A.D. 950** Tongans invade, conquer Samoans, and rule until 1250.
- **1722** Dutch explorer Jacob Roggeveen is first European to sight the Samoan islands.
- **1768** After finding Tahiti, de Bougainville sails through the Samoas but does not land; names them the Navigator

(continues)

from the sea, and they named the strange people sailing them *papalagi,* "sky bursters." The name, shortened to *palagi,* now means Westerners with white skin.

The Rev. John Williams, who roamed the South Pacific in *The Messenger of Peace* discovering islands and preaching the Gospel, landed the first missionaries in Samoa in 1830. Shortly afterward came traders—including John Williams, Jr., son of the missionary. European-style settlements soon grew up at Apia on Upolu and on the shores of Pago Pago Harbor on Tutuila. By the late 1850s German businessmen had established large copra plantations on Upolu, and by the 1870s, when steamships started plying the route between San Francisco and Sydney, American businessmen cast an eye on Pago Pago. The U.S. Navy negotiated a treaty with the chiefs of Tutuila in 1872 to permit the United States to use Pago Pago as a coaling station. The U.S. Congress never ratified this document, but it served to keep the Germans from penetrating into Eastern Samoa, as present-day American Samoa was then known.

COLONIALISM

Meanwhile, German, British, and Americans jockeyed for position among the rival Samoan chiefs on Upolu, with the Germans gaining the upper hand when they staged a coup in 1887, backed up (unofficially) by German naval gunboats. Two years later the Samoans revolted. Their armed rebellion turned into a major international incident—fiasco is a better word—when the U.S., Britain, and Germany all sent warships to Apia. Seven vessels arrived, anchored in the small and relatively unprotected harbor, and proceeded to stare down each other's gun barrels. It was March 16, 1889, near the end of the hurricane season. When one of the monster storms blew up unexpectedly, only the captain of the British warship *Calliope* got his ship under way; his was the sole ship to escape. In all, four ships were sunk, two others were washed ashore, and 146 lives were lost despite heroic efforts by the Samoans on Upolu, who stopped their feuding long enough to pull the survivors through the roaring surf. Of the three American warships present, the *Trenton* and the *Vandalia* were sunk, and the *Nipsic* was beached. Another beached ship, the Germans' *Adler,* rested half-exposed until the reef was covered by landfill 70 years later. (A newspaper story of the time is mounted in the lounge of Aggie Grey's Hotel in Apia.)

Cooler heads prevailed after the disaster, and in December 1889 an agreement was signed in Berlin under which Germany was given Western Samoa, the United States was handed the seven islands to the east, and Britain was left to do what it pleased in Tonga (it created a protectorate). After many years of turmoil, the two Samoas were split apart and swept into the colonial system.

WESTERN SAMOAN HISTORY

Although the Germans were given Western Samoa under the Berlin agreement of 1889, they didn't establish a full-fledged colony until 1900. In the meantime, they governed through Malietoa, one of the island's four para-

DATELINE

Islands.

- **1787** Thirty-nine Samoans and 12 members of French exploring team under Jean La Pérouse killed during skirmish at Massacre Bay on Tutuila.
- **1830** Rev. John Williams lands first missionaries at Leone on Tutuila. European-style settlements soon established at Pago Pago and Apia.
- **1850s** Germans start plantations on Upolu in Western Samoa.
- **1872** American navy negotiates treaty with Tutuila chiefs for American coaling station at Pago Pago.
- **1887** German residents on Upolu stage a coup, set off an argument between U.S., Britain, and Germany.
- **1888** Ousted chief Mataafa leads bloody rebellion at Apia but loses to German-backed chief Malietoa.
- **1889** Warships arrive at Apia to back claims of Western powers; hurricane sinks four, drives two aground, kills 146 sailors. Treaty of Berlin is negotiated and signed. Robert Louis Stevenson settles in Apia.
- **1890** Treaty goes into effect giving Western

(continues)

mount chiefs, who had thrown in his lot with them in the pre-1889 disturbances and was recognized as king of Western Samoa by the Berlin treaty. One of his rivals, Mataafa, lost a brief but bloody rebellion in 1888, during which heads were taken in Samoan style, and was subsequently exiled to the German Marshall Islands. Similar unrest continued until the German flag was raised on March 1, 1900, after which several stern governors sent more of Mataafa's followers and other resisters into exile. Malietoa remained as the chosen chief, and the Germans residing in Western Samoa proceeded to make fortunes from their huge, orderly copra plantations.

German rule came to an abrupt end, however, in August 1914. With the outbreak of World War I that month, New Zealand sent an expeditionary force to Apia and the German governor surrendered without a fight. The Germans in Samoa were interned for the duration of the war, and their huge land holdings were confiscated. The plantations are still owned by the Western Samoa Trust Estates Corporation (WSTEC), a government body whose name you will see all over the country.

New Zealand remained in charge until 1962, first as warlord, then after World War I as trustee, initially under the League of Nations and then under the United Nations. The New Zealand administrators did relatively little in the islands except keep the lid on unrest, at which it was generally successful. In 1929, however, the Mau Movement under Tupua Tamasese Lealofi III created an uprising. The movement was crushed when the New Zealand constables fired on Tamasese and a crowd of his followers gathered outside the government building in Apia, killing him and eight other Samoans.

Twenty years later, after opposition to colonialism flared up in the United Nations, a legislative assembly of matais was established to exercise a limited degree of internal self-government. A constitution was drafted in 1960, and the people approved it and their own independence a year later by referendum. On January 1, 1962, Western Samoa became the first South Pacific nation to regain its independence from the Western powers.

For most of its life as a colony and trusteeship territory, Western Samoa remained in the backwaters of the South Pacific. Only during World War II did it appear on the world stage, and then solely as a training base for thousands of Allied servicemen on their way to fight the Japanese in the islands farther west and north. Tourism increased after the big jets started landing at Pago Pago in the early 1960s, but significant numbers of visitors started arriving only after Faleolo Airport was upgraded to handle large aircraft in the 1980s.

AMERICAN SAMOAN HISTORY

The prosperity we see today was a long time coming to the beautiful Territory of American Samoa, for with the exception of the World War II years, the United States did very little with its share of the Samoan Islands.

Eleven years after the Berlin agreement gave it an unrestricted hand in Eastern Samoa, the United States

DATELINE

Samoa to Germany, Eastern Samoa to U.S., free hand in Tonga to Britain.

- **1894** Robert Louis Stevenson dies at Vailima, his home above Apia; is buried at end of "Track of Loving Hearts."
- **1900** Germany officially establishes colony of Western Samoa, raises its flag at Apia. U.S. negotiates treaty with Tutuila chiefs to cede their island; U.S. flag raised at Pago Pago.
- **1905** Chief of Manu'a finally cedes his islands to the U.S., completing American possession of Eastern Samoa.
- **1914** New Zealand expeditionary force seizes Western Samoa from Germany at outbreak of World War I, confiscates German lands.
- **1920** League of Nations establishes New Zealand trusteeship over Western Samoa.
- **1929** New Zealand constables put down rebellion, kill nine Samoans. U.S. Senate ratifies treaties of 1900 and 1905 turning Eastern Samoa over to U.S.
- **1942** Allied troops use both Samoas as training areas for World War II battles in

(continues)

entered into a treaty with the chiefs on Tutuila, who ceded control of their island; another 5 years went by before the Tu'i Manu'a, the paramount chief of the Manu'a Group of islands east of Tutuila, entered into a similar agreement. The Tu'i Manu'a was so distraught over what he had done that he willed that his title go to the grave with him. To this day it has not been revived.

Those treaties, finally ratified by the U.S. Senate in 1929, are the legal foundation for the U.S. presence in American Samoa. "Presence" is the accurate term, for under those treaties the United States does not "possess" American Samoa as it does, say, the U.S. Virgin Islands, which it literally bought from Denmark during World War I. Instead, the United States is present in American Samoa subject to the conditions of the treaties, one of the most important of which is a U.S. obligation to preserve the system of matais and to retain the traditional ways of fa'a Samoa, including the communal ownership of Samoan land.

Legally, American Samoa is an "unincorporated territory" of the United States, which means that certain provisions of the U.S. Constitution may be subservient to those of the treaties. For example, ownership of most land is restricted to persons of American Samoan ancestry. If American Samoa were a state, such a racially discriminatory restriction would be on shaky Constitutional grounds. As it stands, however, American Samoa's leaders see such restrictions as having prevented them from losing control of their land to wealthy Americans. "If the land was open to sale to American citizens, then the Rockefellers and the Fords would come in and buy it up," one of American Samoa's highest ranking chiefs once told me. "It would be gone, and we would be just another Hawaii. In Hawaii, the political power rests with the Japanese, the money with the Chinese, and the land with the Americans. The poor Hawaiians have nothing."

American Samoans are U.S. nationals, not U.S. citizens, and they often refer to the islands—not to the United States—as their "country." Although they carry American passports, have unrestricted entry into the United States, and can serve in the U.S. armed forces, they cannot vote in American presidential elections. At the present time, only half as many American Samoans live in their home islands as reside in the United States, where a number of them have made names for themselves as college and professional football players.

DATELINE

central and southwestern Pacific. Aggie Grey starts her hamburger business in Apia.

- **1949** New Zealand creates local legislative assembly in Apia, grants Western Samoa limited internal self-government.
- **1951** U.S. Government transfers administration of American Samoa from Navy to Interior Department.
- **1960** Western Samoans vote for independence, draft a constitution.
- **1961** *Reader's Digest* criticizes American Samoa as "America's Shame in the South Seas." H. Rex Lee named by John F. Kennedy as governor to clean up the mess. U.S. aid starts flowing to Pago Pago.
- **1962** Western Samoa becomes first South Pacific country to regain independence after colonial era.
- **1977** Peter Tali Coleman chosen first locally elected governor of American Samoa.
- **1991** Universal suffrage comes to Western Samoa after 30 years of chiefs-only voting for parliament.

THE BACKWATER YEARS

Unlike Western Samoa, which has ample land suitable for large copra plantations, the American islands are small, rugged, and comparatively unproductive. There was little reason, therefore, for American planters to invade or for the U.S. government to take much interest in the islands except to keep a coaling station at Pago Pago.

From the time the Samoan chiefs signed the treaties until 1951, American authority in Samoa rested with the U.S. Navy, which maintained the refueling station at Pago Pago and for the most part left the local chiefs alone to conduct their own affairs in their own fashion. All but a small fraction of land remained in communal hands, and justice was carried out at the village level. Life in American Samoa went on as it had for thousands of years, the people living in their turtle-shaped open-sided thatched houses (known as *fales* in Samoan), growing taro in the hills, and conducting themselves in accordance with fa'a Samoa.

Only in World War II, when the Japanese cast their eyes on the Samoas as bases from which they could cut the supply line between the United States and Australia and New Zealand, did the United States pay much attention to Pago Pago. When the war broke out, Tutuila became a major forward training base for the U.S. Marine Corps. Shore batteries were installed in the hills above the harbor's entrance and concrete pillboxes were built all along Tutuila's shoreline. Many of them can be seen still standing. The only hostile action American Samoa saw, however, occurred when a Japanese submarine pulled up offshore and lobbed a few shells toward the land. Ironically, they hit only one building: a store owned by Frank Shimasaki, the island's only resident of Japanese descent.

Thousands of American Samoans joined the U.S. Marines during the war, and thousands of others formed a home guard militia. Enlisting in the U.S. armed forces—especially the Marines—is to this day considered an honorable undertaking for American Samoans.

World War II brought the first taste of American ways—and of a cash economy—to American Samoa. After the war, however, things returned to normal in the islands. They lost their global strategic value when the nuclear age dawned in 1945, and control of the territory was shifted from the navy to the U.S. Department of the Interior in 1951. American Samoa now has little military value to the United States, although some officials admit they would not want the excellent harbor or the international airport to fall into unfriendly hands.

PROSPERITY ARRIVES

The Interior Department did little to change things in American Samoa until 1961, when *Reader's Digest* ran a well-publicized article about "America's Shame in the South Seas." It described the lack of roads and adequate schools, medical care, and housing. What the magazine really described was a virtually untouched Polynesian society, complete with thatch houses and subsistence farming, smiling faces, and few motor vehicles. By contemporary American standards, that was a "shame."

The U.S. government reacted as it so often has in the past when it attempts to solve a social problem—by throwing money at it. Along with the money came H. Rex Lee, appointed governor of the territory by Pres. John F. Kennedy. A professional government employee with years of experience with the Interior Department's Bureau of Indian Affairs, Lee set about to reform the territory. Using the money to augment a massive effort by the Samoans themselves, he built sealed roads and an airstrip capable of handling intercontinental airliners, improved the water and electrical systems, built the modern Rainmaker Hotel and nearby Convention Center (Lee Auditorium is named for him), and revamped the school system. In the absence of trained Samoan teachers, he strung a mile-long cable across Pago Pago Harbor and used it to build a television transmitter atop 1,610-foot Mount Alava to beam education programming to the outlying schools.

To provide jobs, Lee used the territory's duty-free status and relatively low wages to entice two American firms—Star-Kist Tuna Company and Van Camp Seafood Company—to build tuna canneries at Pago Pago. Even more money came with Pres. Lyndon B. Johnson's Great Society programs, many of which were made applicable to the U.S. territories as well as to the states. Other programs followed during the Nixon administration, and Mr. Nixon's appointed governor, John P. Haydon, turned up the money tap even higher than before. (The museum at Pago Pago is named for Haydon's wife, Jean P. Haydon.)

With all that money and all those jobs coming their way in the 1960s and '70s, American Samoans were reluctant to tinker with their political relationship with Washington for fear of losing all federal funds. They remained content to have the Interior Department send governors and other territorial officials out from Washington. That changed, however, in the mid-1970s, when one appointed governor, a former congressman from North Carolina, turned out to be very unpopular. In 1976, after twice previously having turned down the proposal, American Samoans voted in favor of electing their own governor. Peter Tali Coleman, a federal official of part-Samoan descent and a former appointed governor of the territory, was chosen its first elected governor in 1977.

3. PEOPLE

At present there are about 170,000 people living in Western Samoa and 38,000 in American Samoa. The vast majority are full-blooded Samoans, the second-largest group of pure Polynesians in the world (the Maoris of New Zealand are the largest).

Although divided politically in their home islands, the Samoans share the same culture, heritage, and in many cases, family lineage. Despite the inroads that Western influences have made—especially in American Samoa—they are a proud people who fiercely protect their old ways.

"Catch the bird but watch for the wave" is an old Samoan proverb that expresses the basically cautious approach followed in the islands. This conservative attitude is perhaps responsible for the extraordinary degree to which Samoans have preserved fa'a Samoa—the Samoan Way—while adapting it to the modern world. Even in American Samoa, where most of the old turtle-shaped fales have been replaced with structures of plywood and tin, the firmament of the Samoan way lies just under the trappings of the territory's commercialized surface.

THE EXTENDED FAMILY

The foundation of Samoan society is the extended family unit, or *aiga* (ah-*eeng*-ah); unlike the Western family, it can include thousands of relatives and in-laws. In this basically communal system, everything is owned collectively by the aiga; the individual has a right to use that property but does not personally own it. As stated in a briefing paper prepared for the government of American Samoa by the Pacific Basin Development Council, "the attitude toward property is: If you need something which you don't have, there is always someone else who has what you need." This notion is at odds with Western concepts of private ownership, and visitors may notice the difference directly when a camera or other item left unattended suddenly disappears.

At the head of each of the more than 10,000 aigas is a *matai* (*mah*-tie), a chief who is responsible for the welfare of each member of the clan. Although the title of matai usually follows bloodlines, the family can choose another person—man or woman—if the incumbent proves incapable of handling the job. The matai settles family disputes, parcels out the family's land, and sees that everyone has enough to eat and a roof over his or her head.

Strictly speaking, all money earned by a member of an aiga is turned over to the matai, to be used in the best interest of the entire clan. Accordingly, the system has been threatened as more and more young Samoans move to the United States or New

IMPRESSIONS

How impossible it would be for us, with our notions of so-called civilisation and style, to exist in our northern city suburbs with open spaces for walls and the camouflage of the night our only privacy. Yet here it seemed the most natural thing in the world, a picture of harmony and a vivid example of what they call fa'a Samoa, the Samoan Way.

—JOHN DYSON, 1982

Zealand, earn wages in their own right, and spend them as they see fit. Nevertheless, the system is still remarkably intact in both Samoas. Even in expatriate Samoan outposts in Hawaii, California, Texas, and Auckland (which collectively have a larger Samoan population than do the islands), the people still rally around their aiga, and matais play an important role in daily life in those faraway places.

As is true throughout the South Pacific, landownership is a touchy subject. In Samoa land is held by the aiga and is passed down from generation to generation. There are very strict laws prohibiting non-Samoans from owning land, although it is possible for them to lease property under certain circumstances.

ORGANIZATION & RITUAL

Samoan life is ruled above the aiga level by a hierarchy of matais known in English as high talking chiefs, high chiefs, and paramount chiefs, in ascending order of importance. The high talking chiefs do just that: talk on behalf of the high chiefs, usually expressing themselves in great oratorical flourishes in a formal version of Samoan reserved for use among the chiefs. The high chiefs are senior matais at the village or district level, and the paramount chiefs can rule over entire island groups. The chiefly symbol, worn over the shoulder, is a short broom resembling a horse's tail.

The conduct and relations between chiefs are governed by strict rules of protocol. Nowhere is ritual more obvious or observed than during a *kava* (pronounced ava in Samoan) ceremony. Cups of brew made by crushing the roots of the pepper plant *Piper methysticum* are scooped from a large wooden bowl and passed around. In the old days the roots were chewed and spit into the bowl by the virgin daughter of a chief. That method of kava preparation has disappeared in the face of modern notions of disease control. Each participant holds out the cup, spills a little on the mats covering the floor, and says "*Manuia*" ("Good health") before gulping down the slightly narcotic drink. It's all a show of respect to host and honored guest. Of course, kava works on the lips like Novocain, which must do wonders for the conversation that follows.

Although some Samoans can become unruly after imbibing too much of potions containing not kava but alcohol, the showing of respect permeates their life. They are by tradition extremely polite to guests, so much so that some of them tend to answer in the affirmative all questions posed by a stranger. The Samoans are not lying when they answer wrongly; they are merely being polite. Accordingly, visitors who really need information should avoid asking questions that call for a yes or no answer.

RELIGION

Like other Polynesians, the Samoans in Pre-European days worshiped a hierarchy of gods under one supreme being, whom they called Le Tagaloa. When the London Missionary Society's Rev. John Williams arrived in *The Messenger of Peace* in 1830, he found the Samoans willing to convert to the Christian god. It was a strict, puritanical Christianity that Williams and his Tahitian teachers brought, and his legacy can be seen both in the large white churches that dominate every settlement in Samoa and in the fervor with which the Samoans practice religion today. Along with Tonga and the Cook Islands, the Samoas make up the South Pacific's "Bible Belt."

The majority of Samoans are members of the Congregational Christian church, a Protestant denomination that grew out of the London Missionary Society's work. Western Samoa almost closes down on Sunday, and even in more Westernized American Samoa things come to a crawl on the Sabbath. Although Samoans threw

---

IMPRESSIONS

All life is to be seen on the stage of the Samoan fale. *In the evening, when television sets as well as electric lights are switched on, the scene is surreal.*

—Ron Hall, 1991

stones at the son of the chief justice of American Samoa a few years ago for surfing on Sunday, swimming is now tolerated in both countries at the hotels and, after church, at beaches frequented by overseas visitors.

Christianity has become an integral part of fa'a Samoa, and every day about 6:30pm each village observes *sa,* 10 minutes of devotional time during which everyone goes inside to pray, read the Scriptures, and perhaps sing hymns. A gong (usually an empty acetylene tank hung from a tree) will be struck, once to announce it's time to get ready, a second time to announce the beginning of sa, and a third time to announce that all's clear. It is permissible to drive on the main road during sa, but it's not all right to turn off into a village or to walk around.

Even if you can't understand the sermon, the sounds of Samoans singing hymns in harmony makes going to church a rewarding experience.

SEX & THE SAMOANS

Despite their ready acceptance of much of the missionaries' teaching, the Samoans no more took to heart their puritanical sexual mores than did any other group of Polynesians. In 1928 anthropologist Margaret Mead published her famous *Coming of Age in Samoa,* which was based on her research in American Samoa. She described the Samoans as a peaceable people who showed no guilt in connection with ample sex during adolescence, a view that was in keeping with practices of Polynesian societies elsewhere. Some 55 years later, New Zealand anthropologist Derek Freeman published *Margaret Mead and Samoa: The Making and Unmaking of an Anthropological Myth,* in which he took issue with Mead's conclusions and argued instead that Samoans are jealous, violent, and not above committing rape. The truth may lie somewhere in between.

As noted in Chapter 1, the Samoans share with other Polynesians the practice of raising some boys as girls, especially in families short of household help. They dress as girls, do a girl's chores around the home, and often grow up to be transvestites. They are known as *fa'afafines* in Samoan.

RULES OF CONDUCT

Visitors should be aware of several customs of this conservative society. The briefing paper prepared by the Pacific Basin Development Council for the American Samoan Office of Tourism gives some guidelines that may be helpful.

First, in a Samoan home don't talk to people while standing, and don't eat while walking around a village.

Second, avoid stretching your legs straight out in front of you while sitting. If you can't fold them beneath you, then pull one of the floor mats over them.

Third, if you are driving through a village and spot a group of middle-aged or elderly men sitting around a fale with their legs folded, it's probably a gathering of matais to discuss business. It's not polite to drive past the meeting place. If going past on foot, don't carry a load on your shoulders or an open umbrella (even if several of Pago Pago's 200 inches of annual rainfall are pouring on you).

Fourth, if you arrive at a Samoan home during a prayer session, wait outside until the family is finished with its devotions. If you are already inside, you will be expected to share in the service. If you go to church, don't wear flowers.

Fifth, if you are invited to participate in a kava ceremony, hold the cup out in front of you, spill a few drops on the mat, say "Manuia," and take a sip. In Samoa you do not bolt down the entire cup in one gulp as you would in Fiji; instead, save a little to pour on the floor before handing back the empty cup. And remember, this is a solemn occasion—not a few rounds at the local bar.

Sixth, whenever possible, consult a Samoan about appropriate behavior and practices. They will appreciate your interest in fa'a Samoa and will take great pleasure in explaining their unique way of life.

I would add a seventh: Don't wear bathing suits, short-shorts, halter tops, or other skimpy clothing away from the beach or hotel swimming pool. Although shorts of respectable length are worn by some young Samoan men and women, it is considered very bad form for a Samoan to display his or her traditional tattoos, which cover many of them from knee to waist. Even though Samoan women went bare-breasted before the coming of Christianity, that is definitely forbidden today. Traditional Samoan dress is a wraparound *lavalava,* which reaches below the knee on men and to the ankles on women.

Finally, should you be invited to stay overnight in a Samoan home, let them know at the beginning how long you will stay. Upon leaving, it's customary to give a small gift known as a *mea alofa.* This can be money—between $5 and $10 a day per person—but make sure your hosts understand it is a gift, not a payment.

Some Samoan villages have adopted the practice of charging small **"custom fees"** to visitors who want to use their beaches or swim under their waterfalls. These usually are a dollar or two and are paid by local residents from other villages as well as by tourists.

In all cases, remember that almost everything and every place in the Samoas is owned by an aiga, and it's polite to ask permission of the nearby matai before crossing the property, using the beach, or visiting the waterfall. They will appreciate your courtesy in doing so.

4. LANGUAGE & LITERATURE

LANGUAGE

Although English is an official language in both countries and is widely spoken, Samoan shares equal billing and is used by most people for everyday conversation. It is a Polynesian language somewhat similar to Tahitian, Tongan, and Cook Islands Maori, but with some important differences.

The vowels are pronounced not as in English (*ay, ee, eye, oh,* and *you*) but in the Roman fashion: *ah, ay, ee, oh,* and *oo* (as in "kangaroo"). All vowels are sounded, even if several of them appear next to each other—although there have been some modern corruptions. The village of Nu'uuli in American Samoa, for example, is pronounced new-*oo*-lee. The apostrophe which appears between the vowels indicates a glottal stop—a slight pause similar to the tiny break between "Oh-oh!" in English. The consonants *f, g, l, m, n, p, s, t,* and *v* are pronounced as in English with one major exception: the letter *g* is pronounced like "ng." Therefore, *aiga* is pronounced "ah-*eeng*-ah." Pago Pago is pronounced "Pango Pango."

If you're interested in learning more about the Samoans' language and their legends, I recommend Joan Galea'i Holland's *Samoan for the Visitor,* available at the boutique in the Rainmaker Hotel in Pago Pago.

Meanwhile, here are some words that may help you win friends and influence your hosts.

ENGLISH	SAMOAN	PRONUNCIATION
Hello	**talofa**	tah-*low*-fah
Welcome	**afio mai**	ah-*fee*-oh my
Good-bye	**tofa**	*tow*-fah
Good luck	**manuia**	mah-*new*-yah
Please	**fa'amolemole**	fah-ah-*moly*-moly
Man	**tamaloa**	tah-mah-*low*-ah
Woman	**fafine**	fah-*fi*-ni
Transvestite	**fa'afafine**	fah-fah-*fi*-ni
Thank you	**fa'afetai**	fah-*fee*-tie
Kava bowl	**tanoa**	tah-*no*-ah
Good	**lelei**	*lay*-lay
Bad	**leaga**	lay-*ang*-ah
Happy/feast	**fiafia**	fee-ah-*fee*-ah
House	**fale**	*fah*-lay

Wraparound skirt	**lavalava**	**lava-lava**
Dollar	**tala**	**tah-lah**
Cent	**sene**	**say-nay**
High chief	**ali'i**	**ah-*lee*-ee**
Small island	**motu**	***mo*-too**
White person	**palagi**	**pah-*lahng*-ee**

Many words in Samoan—as in most modern Polynesian languages—have European roots. Take the word for corned beef, *pisupo* (pee-*soo*-poh). The first Western canned item to reach Western Samoa was pea soup. *Pisupo,* the Samoan version of pea soup, was adopted as the word for corned beef, which also came in cans and was much more popular than pea soup.

LITERATURE

ROBERT LOUIS STEVENSON

The salvage crews were still working on the hulks of the British, American, and German warships when Western Samoa's most famous temporary resident arrived in Apia. He was a thin, tubercular writer from Scotland named Robert Louis Stevenson.

Not yet 40 years old but already made famous and wealthy by novels, such as *Treasure Island* and *Dr. Jekyll and Mr. Hyde,* Stevenson had given up the cold climate of Europe and had traveled across the United States and a good part of the Pacific, including the Marquesas Islands, Tahiti, and Hawaii, in search of a climate more suitable to his ravaged lungs.

Stevenson was accompanied by his wife, Fanny (an American divorcée 11 years his senior), his stepmother, and stepson; his mother, who had been along in Tahiti and Hawaii, had stayed in Honolulu but would later join him in Samoa. They intended to stay in Apia for a few weeks while Stevenson caught up on a series of columns he was writing for an American newspaper syndicate; however, they all stayed on to build a mansion known as Vailima up on the slopes of Mount Vaea overlooking Apia, and remained in Samoa until Stevenson died on December 3, 1894.

Over the course of the 5 years he lived above Apia, Stevenson wrote and published more than 750,000 words. He learned the Samoan language and translated into it "The Bottle Imp," his story about a genie. It was the first work of fiction translated into Samoan.

Stevenson loved Samoa. "Day after day the sun flamed; night after night the moon beaconed, or the stars paraded their lustrous regiment," he wrote. And the Samoans loved Stevenson. Great orators and storytellers in their own right, they called him Tusitala, "Teller of Tales." Their descendants later gave the government's hotel the same name in his honor. When he died, more than 200 grieving Samoans hacked a "Track of Loving Hearts" up Mount Vaea to a little knoll below the summit, where they placed him in a grave with a perpetual view overlooking the mountains, the town, the reef, and the sea that he loved. Carved on his grave is his famous requiem:

This be the verse you grave for me:
Here he lies where he longed to be;
Home is the sailor, home from the sea,
And the hunter home from the hill.

5. GOVERNMENT & ECONOMY

GOVERNMENT

WESTERN SAMOA

The 1960 referendum was the first time all Western Samoans had a chance to vote for anything; the next time came in 1991 when universal suffrage went into effect. During those intervening 31 years, the country was ruled by a Parliament made up of 47 members, of whom 45 were chosen by the matais, not by the people as a whole. The other two members were elected by Non-Samoans living in the country. With more and more Samoans exposed to Western political ways, this system was changed in 1991 to include universal suffrage. Ironically, the people then decided not to change the government, returning the Human Rights Protection party to power.

There are two political parties, with the Christian Democratic party once again serving as the opposition.

The titular head of state is Malietoa Tanumafili II, one of Western Samoa's four paramount chiefs and a descendant of the Malietoa who chose sides with the victorious Germans in 1888–89. Malietoa II will hold the job for life, which in effect makes Western Samoa a constitutional monarchy at present. Under the constitution, however, parliament will choose his successor from among Western Samoa's four paramount chiefs. That person will serve not for life but for a term of 5 years.

AMERICAN SAMOA

In addition to the executive branch and the courts, American Samoa has a bicameral legislature known as the Fono. Members of the Fono's lower House of Representatives are elected by universal suffrage, while senators are chosen in accordance with Samoan custom by the matais. Although both the Interior Department and the governor have veto power over the laws it passes, the Fono has considerable authority over the budget and local affairs. Local government is organized by counties and villages under a secretary of Samoan affairs, a position traditionally held by a ranking matai. The High Court of American Samoa has a special branch that deals exclusively with landownership and matai titles.

American Samoans choose their leaders every 4 years. They also elect a nonvoting delegate to the U.S. House of Representatives.

The government, which receives about half its revenue from Washington (but still runs in the red), employs about 46% of the local work force. Its annual budget is considerably larger than that of the government in Western Samoa, which has a population five times larger than American Samoa's.

ECONOMY

WESTERN SAMOA

Once a large exporter of fresh bananas to New Zealand, Western Samoa has lost that market to Ecuador and other Latin American countries. Although some bananas, taro, and other fresh produce are still shipped overseas (primarily to American Samoa), the largest export now is coconut oil. There is some light manufacturing, including cigarettes and beer (try a Vailima brew while you're there), but the industrial sector is in its infancy. Furthermore, the country's exclusive fishing zone is one of the smallest in the Pacific. Only foreign aid and some $30 million to $35 million shipped home each year by Samoans living in American Samoa or overseas keep the country out of bankruptcy.

To correct its huge trade imbalance, the Western Samoan government has devalued its currency and imposed heavy duties on most imports. The result has been that stores in Apia generally are poorly stocked. Consequently, Western Samoans who can afford it regularly go to Pago Pago to buy items such as mayonnaise. (When I was last there, Polynesian Airlines flew its jet aircraft to American Samoa 1 day a week and allowed huge free baggage allowances; it was known as "the shoppers' jet.")

Western Samoan hotels, rental-car firms, and some tour operators quote their prices in U.S. dollars in order to avoid the "price shock" that would be caused if they were stated in tala. Although expensive by local standards, travelers using U.S. dollars will find most prices in Western Samoa are among the more reasonable in the South Pacific.

A majority of the work force is employed by the government. Even in those jobs, wages are so low that several thousand Western Samoans regularly live and work in American Samoa.

AMERICAN SAMOA

Although you would never guess it judging from the size of some of their relatively large retail stores, American Samoans produce very little for export except canned tuna; in fact, they import most of their foodstuffs either from the U.S. mainland or from Western Samoa.

Other than the local government, the largest employers are Pago Pago's two tuna canneries, which together have about 20% of the work force on their payroll. Most other workers are employed by retail establishments, service businesses, and a few small manufacturers. With so many American Samoans living in the United States rather than in their home islands, about a third of the work force is made up of Western Samoans, Tongans, and other Pacific islanders who have come to Pago Pago to take their place and to earn wages that are often more than triple those they can earn at home.

6. WHEN TO GO — CLIMATE, HOLIDAYS & EVENTS

CLIMATE

"It did not pour, it flowed," wrote W. Somerset Maugham in his 1921 short story "Rain," the famous tale of prostitute Sadie Thompson, who seduces a puritanical missionary while stranded in American Samoa. This description, however, applies mainly to Pago Pago, which, because of its location behind appropriately named Rainmaker Mountain, gets an average of more than 200 inches of rain per year. For the most part, both Samoas enjoy a typically tropical climate, with lots of very intense sunshine even during the wet season (December to May). Average daily high temperatures range from 83°F in the drier and somewhat cooler months of June through September to 86°F from December to April, when midday can be hot and sticky. Evenings are usually in the comfortable 70s all year round.

HOLIDAYS & EVENTS

Western Samoa takes off both January 1 and January 2 for New Year's. Other major holidays are Easter Monday, ANZAC Day (April 25, as a memorial to those who died in the two world wars), June 1 through 3 (Independence Anniversary), Arbor Day (November), Christmas Day, and Boxing Day (December 26).

The independence celebrations in June feature dances, outrigger-canoe races, marching competitions, and horse racing. The second Sunday in October is observed as White Sunday, during which children go to church dressed in white, lead the services, and are honored at family feasts. The week of Christmas is celebrated with great gusto.

American Samoa observes U.S. holidays plus one big one of its own: New Year's Day, President's Day (the third Monday in February), Good Friday, Flag Day (April 17), Memorial Day (the last Monday in May), the Fourth of July, Labor Day (the first Monday in September), Columbus Day (the second Monday in October), Veterans Day (November 11), Thanksgiving (the fourth Thursday of November), and Christmas Day.

The biggest celebration is on April 17, when Flag Day commemorates the raising of the Stars and Stripes over Tutuila in 1900. The second Sunday in October is observed as White Sunday, when children attend church dressed in white and later are honored at family feasts.

In addition to the holidays and events, late October or early November will see hundreds if not thousands of Samoans out on the reefs of both countries with lanterns and nets to snare the wiggly *palolo*, a coral worm that comes out to mate on the seventh day after the full moon. Palolo are considered by Pacific islanders to be the caviar of their region.

7. GETTING THERE & GETTING AROUND

GETTING THERE

Both Western Samoa and American Samoa have international airports: **Faleolo International Airport** about 19 miles from Apia, and **Pago Pago International Airport** about 7 miles west of Pago Pago. Since the two are about 20 minutes flying time apart, many international flights will land at both.

Hawaiian Airlines provides service from North America to both Apia and Pago Pago through its base at Honolulu. As we went to press, Western Samoa's national carrier, **Polynesian Airlines,** was planning to begin serving the Honolulu-Apia route. Polynesian also links the Samoas with Australia, New Zealand, Tonga, and the Cook Islands, and it and **Air Pacific** have joint service between Apia and Fiji. **Air New Zealand** has at least two flights a week from Auckland to Apia. One of those flights stops in Tonga on its way to Apia, but the return trip is nonstop back to Auckland; that is, you can go from Tonga to Apia on Air New Zealand but not the other way around. **Samoa Air,** a carrier based in Pago Pago, flies small aircraft between Pago Pago and Vava'u in Tonga.

For more information, see the "Getting There" section in Chapter 2.

GETTING AROUND

Polynesian Airlines (tel. 22-737 in Apia or 633-4331 in Pago Pago) and **Samoa Air** (tel. 22-321 or 22-901 in Apia, 699-9106 in Pago Pago) both shuttle back and forth between Apia and Pago Pago several times a day.

Round-trip fares on both airlines are WS$153 ($76.50) if purchased in Apia but $95 if bought in American Samoa. In other words, thanks to an exchange rate of about 2-to-1 for the Western Samoan tala against the U.S. dollar (see "Information, Entry Requirements & Money" in Chapter 8), it is less expensive to fly from Apia to Pago Pago and return than the other way around. That's one more reason to make your Samoan base in Apia.

Plans were in the works during my recent visit to use **Fagali'i Airstrip** near Apia as an international airport for Apia–Pago Pago flights, which will shorten the transit time between the Samoas by eliminating the long drive from Apia to Faleolo International Airport.

For the adventurous, a relatively modern **ferry,** the *Queen Salamasina,* makes the 8-hour voyage between Pago Pago and Apia twice a week, usually leaving the main wharf in Apia about 10pm on Tuesday and Thursday and departing Pago Pago's marine terminal the following afternoon. Tickets should be bought at least a day ahead of time; they cost WS$20 ($10) if purchased in Apia but $20 in Pago Pago, one-way. The *Queen Salamasina* is operated by the Western Samoa Shipping Corporation, whose ticket office is over the Ministry of Transport, across Beach Road from the main wharf in Apia (tel. 20-935). The agent in Pago Pago is M&S Shipping Company (tel. 633-5728), whose office is on the dock between the Jean P. Haydon Museum and the Amerika Samoa Bank. Since the trade winds prevail from the southeast, the trip going west with the wind toward Apia is usually somewhat smoother.

See the "Getting Around" sections of chapters 8 and 9 for information about transportation within Western Samoa and American Samoa.

CHAPTER 8

WESTERN SAMOA

Major differences between the two Samoas are quickly evident on the scenic 19-mile drive from Faleolo Airport, near the western end of Upolu, into historic Apia, capital of Western Samoa. Instead of ridges reaching down to the sea between steep valleys as on Tutuila, the land on western Upolu slopes gently down from old volcanic cones in the center of the island. On one side of the road lies the lagoon; on the other, coconut plantations with palms planted in the orderly, straight rows favored by the Germans who took over Western Samoa in 1889 and ruled it until World War I.

Instead of shopping centers and modern homes, the road passes hundreds of Samoan *fales* (thatch houses), their big turtle-shaped roofs sitting on poles, their sides open to the breeze and to the view of passersby, except when mats are lowered from the eaves to keep out the rain. Village lawns, their grass carefully mowed and trimmed with boulders painted white, make the entire route seem like an unending park. Samoans wrapped in lavalavas go about their daily routines, to most appearances as they have for 3,000 years. Chickens wander onto the road, daring drivers to turn them into meals, which would then deprive their owners of a much more valuable commodity, eggs.

Even Apia, which has a population of about 35,000, has the appearance of a slightly dilapidated old South Seas town. White clapboard stores and government buildings sleep along a tree-lined street curving along the waterfront. Compared with the relative bustle of Pago Pago and its Americanized ways, life in Apia is slow and easy.

A series of volcanoes on a line running roughly east to west formed the island of Upolu, which is about 39 miles long and 13 miles wide. Some 75% of Western Samoa's population lives on Upolu, although it's considerably smaller than Savai'i, 13 miles to the west.

1. INFORMATION, ENTRY REQUIREMENTS & MONEY

INFORMATION

The very friendly and helpful staff at the **Western Samoan Visitors Bureau,** P.O. Box 2272, Apia, Western Samoa (tel. 20-878 or 20-180, fax 20-886), have maps, brochures, and other publications available at their office in a handsome Samoan fale on the harbor side of Beach Road east of the Town Clock (you can't miss it, since the structure dominates that side of Beach Road). Make the visitors bureau a stop early in your visit.

WHAT'S SPECIAL ABOUT WESTERN SAMOA

Beaches

- ☐ Return to Paradise Beach: so lovely it was used for Gary Cooper's 1951 movie *Return to Paradise.*
- ☐ Vavau: You actually can snorkel in the shade at this incredible site.

Literary Shrines

- ☐ Vailima: Head of state now resides in Robert Louis Stevenson's last home.
- ☐ Stevenson's Grave: Overlooking Apia, the author's famous requiem is carved in stone.

Great Towns/Villages

- ☐ Apia: Century-old clapboard buildings give this seafront town the old South Seas look.

Cultures

- ☐ Fa'a Samoa: The Samoan Way, Polynesia's oldest culture, continues its ancient ways into the present and future.

Natural Spectacles

- ☐ Volcanoes: Now dormant, volcanoes have left lava fields with tunnels on Savai'i, the country's largest island.

In addition to the invaluable *Western Samoa: Tourist Map Guide,* be sure to pick up copies of two informative and up-to-date brochures: *Western Samoa Visitors Information* and *Western Samoa Tariffs.*

The bureau's hours are 8am to noon and 1 to 4:30pm Monday through Friday, 8am to 12:30pm on Saturday.

The **Embassy of Western Samoa,** 1155 15th Street NW, Suite 510, Washington, DC 20005 (tel. 202/833-1743), also can provide information for visitors.

ENTRY REQUIREMENTS

No **visa** or entry permit is required for visitors who intend to stay 30 days or less and who have a valid passport, a return or ongoing airline ticket, and a place to stay in Western Samoa. Those who wish to stay longer must apply, prior to arrival, to the Immigration Office, Government of Western Samoa, Apia, Western Samoa (tel. 20-291). Americans can get more information from the Embassy of Western Samoa in Washington, DC (see above). Citizens or subjects of other countries should contact the Western Samoan High Commissions in their countries or if there is none, any New Zealand diplomatic post or British consulate.

Vaccinations are not necessary unless arriving within 6 days of being in a yellow fever or cholera-infected area.

Customs exemptions for visitors are 200 cigarettes, either a 26-ounce or a 40-ounce bottle of liquor, and their personal effects. Firearms, ammunition, illegal drugs, and pornography are prohibited—so leave your *Playboy* magazine in Pago Pago. Plants, live animals, or products of that nature, including fruits, seeds, and soil, will be confiscated unless you have obtained prior permission from the Western Samoa government's Department of Agriculture and Forest.

MONEY

Western Samoa uses the *tala* (the Samoans' way of saying "dollar"), which is broken down into 100 *sene* ("cents"), although most people will refer to them as dollars and cents when speaking to visitors. The official abbreviation for the currency is SAT, but I have used **WS$** in this chapter. As noted in Chapter 7, Western Samoa's major hotels and most rental-car firms quote their prices in U.S. dollars. To avoid confusion, their U.S. dollar prices are given in this chapter as **U.S. $.**

At presstime, the **exchange rate** was about WS$2.30 for each U.S. $1. I have computed the equivalent values based on an exchange rate of two tala for one U.S. dollar (WS$2 = U.S.$1). If you get more, then good for you.

Since the tala is virtually worthless outside Western Samoa, you won't be able to buy any before arriving there. Remember, too, to change your talas back to another currency before leaving Western Samoa. There is no quick way of finding out in advance the exchange rate that will be applicable when you arrive in Apia short of calling the Bank of Western Samoa (tel. 22-422). The Western Samoan embassy in Washington, D.C., or a travel agent should be able to give you an approximate figure.

WHAT THINGS COST IN WESTERN SAMOA	U.S. $
Taxi from airport to Apia	13.00
Bus from airport to Apia	3.00
Double room at Aggie Grey's Hotel (expensive)	100.00
Double bungalow at Vaiala Beach Cottages (moderate)	65.00
Double room at Seaside Inn (budget)	17.50
Lunch for one at Amigo's (moderate)	6.00
Lunch for one at Daphne's (budget)	3.00
Dinner for one, without wine, at The Waterfront (expensive)	29.00
Dinner for one, without wine, at Amigo's (moderate)	17.50
Dinner for one, without wine, at The Godfather's (budget)	6.00
Beer	1.50
Coca-Cola	.60

THE TALA & U.S. DOLLAR

At this writing, WS$1 = approximately U.S.50¢, the rate of exchange used to calculate the U.S. dollar prices given in this chapter. This rate has remained fairly stable during the past few years but may change by the time you visit. Accordingly, use the following table only as a guide.

$ WS	**$ U.S.**	**$ WS**	**$ U.S.**
.25	.13	15.00	7.50
.50	.15	20.00	10.00
.75	.38	25.00	12.50
1.00	.50	30.00	15.00
2.00	1.00	35.00	17.50
3.00	1.50	40.00	20.00
4.00	2.00	45.00	22.50
5.00	2.50	50.00	25.00
6.00	3.00	75.00	37.50
7.00	3.50	100.00	50.00
8.00	4.00	125.00	62.50
9.00	4.50	150.00	75.00
10.00	5.00	200.00	100.00

	US$
Cup of coffee	.75
Roll of ASA 100 Kodacolor film, 36 exposures	9.00
Movie ticket	1.00

2. GETTING THERE & GETTING AROUND

GETTING THERE

A modern, open-air terminal building greets visitors from overseas at **Faleolo Airport,** on the northwest corner of Upolu about 19 miles from Apia.

The Bank of Western Samoa and Pacific Commercial Bank have small booths where you can change money while waiting to clear Customs; you will need at least WS$6 ($3) to pay the bus fare to town. If you forget to change before clearing, both banks have booths in the center concourse (turn right after exiting Customs). There is no bank in the departure lounge, so change those talas before clearing immigration.

Relatively small buses meet international flights and take passengers to the Apia hotels (you will be astounded how many passengers and their baggage can be crammed into one of these vehicles). Don't count on a bus being there if you're flying a small aircraft over from Pago Pago; they don't always meet the small flights. The bus ride costs WS$6 ($3) each way. The government-regulated taxi fare into town is WS$28 ($14), so don't let the drivers rip you off.

The airline buses also transport passengers from the Apia hotels to the airports for departing international flights. They arrive at the hotels 2 hours before departure time. Be sure to reconfirm your flight (even if Air New Zealand says you don't have to) and tell your hotel what flight you are leaving on; otherwise, the bus could leave you behind. If you drive a car to the airport, you will be hit with a WS50¢ (25¢) parking fee at the gate.

When leaving the country, get your boarding pass and then pay WS$20 ($10) **departure tax** at a booth to the right of the check-in counters. Travelers need pay the tax only once every 30 days, so save your receipt if you are going to American Samoa and will return to Apia.

Remember, Western Samoan currency cannot be exchanged outside the country, even in Pago Pago, so change any talas you have left before departing.

GETTING AROUND

You will have several choices of transportation options in Apia. Daily air service and ferries run between Opolu, Savai'i, and the small islands in between (see "An Easy Excursion to Savai'i," at the end of this chapter). Some domestic flights from Apia to Savai'i use Fagali'i Airstrip, 2 miles east of town.

BY RENTAL CAR

The car-rental firms will arrange to pick you up at the airport if you have reservations. Most of them quote their rates in U.S. dollars, and all accept American Express, VISA, MasterCard, and Diners Club credit cards. Insurance policies do not cover damage to

ACCOMMODATIONS:

- Aggie Grey's Hotel 5
- Harbour Light Hotel 3
- Hotel Kitano Tusitala 6
- Le Godinet Beachfront Hotel 7
- Oliva Yandall Accommodations 1
- Seaside Inn 4
- Vaiala Beach Cottages 2

ATTRACTIONS:

- American, British and German Memorials 10
- Apia Market 7
- Apia Weather Observatory 13
- Congregational Church 2
- Court House 4
- John Williams Memorial 3
- Malietoa Tombs 12
- Palolo Deep 1
- Parliament (Fono) 11
- St. Mary's Convent and School 8
- Tamasese Tomb 14
- Town Clock 6
- Visitors Bureau 5
- WSTEC Headquarters 9

the vehicles' undercarriages, which may occur on Western Samoa's heavily potholed or rocky roads. Don't count on buying gasoline outside of Apia. Depending on your own insurance policies, you may also want to buy optional personal-accident coverage, which covers you and your passengers.

Budget Rent-A-Car has an office in the National Provident Fund building opposite the Town Clock in Apia (tel. 20-561, or toll free 800/527-0700 in the U.S.). Rates range from U.S. $48 to U.S. $65 a day, depending on whether the car is air conditioned or not, including full insurance and unlimited miles. For the cost of 6 days, you can keep the car for a week.

As with all of Apia's rental-car firms, Budget will not allow you to take its vehicles on the ferry to Savai'i, nor can you drive them on unpaved roads. You pay for the gasoline; bring it back full.

Le Car Rentals (tel. 22-754) is a local firm which specializes in four-wheel-drive vehicles. You will need one of them if you're going off the (allegedly) paved roads.

The **Avis** licensee is **Rentway,** also known as Apia Motors (tel. 22-468, or toll free 800/331-1212 in the U.S.). Rates range from WS$160 to WS$180 ($80 to $90) for 2 days, including unlimited mileage and liability insurance.

Other local rental companies to investigate are **Pavitt's U-Drive** (tel. 21-766), **Billie's Car Rentals** (tel. 21-724), and **G&J Rentals** (tel. 21-078). Their rates could be less than Budget's or Avis's, but be sure to look their cars over carefully before agreeing to a contract.

BY MOTORCYCLE

The term "allegedly" paved is not used above guardedly. In fact, Western Samoa's roads were hit hard by Cyclone Ofa in February 1990 and were still in serious disrepair during my recent visit (the country simply doesn't have money for adequate repairs). Accordingly, I cannot recommend motorcycles outside the immediate environs of Apia. If you want to rent one in town, contact **McGarret Tourist Rentals** (tel. 20-998 or 24-590), **G&J Rentals** (tel. 21-078), or **Sky Tour Bikes** (tel. 24-145). Rates at all three are about U.S. $25 a day plus U.S. $50 deposit.

Driving Rules

You drive on the right-hand side of the road in the American fashion, stopping for pedestrians in crosswalks marked with well-worn white stripes, and not exceeding the speed limits of 35 m.p.h. on the open road or 15 m.p.h. in Apia and the villages. Western Samoans and their dogs, chickens, and pigs have a habit of walking in the middle of the roads that pass through their villages, so proceed with care. Even if the way is clear, local courtesy dictates that you slow down when going through the villages so as not to kick up a lot of dust. Special care is required on Sunday when Samoans usually lounge around the village after going to church.

Visitors technically are required to get a local **driver's license** from the Ministry of Transport on Beach Road opposite the wharf. They may be obtained upon presentation of a valid home driver's license, WS$10 ($5) in cash, and two passport photos. You neglect this technicality at your own risk (that having been said, I've never bothered to get one, and I don't know anyone who ever has).

BY BUS

Western Samoa has a system of "aiga buses" (similar to those in American Samoa), most of which have wooden passenger compartments built on the back of flatbed trucks. They have the names of their villages written on the front. The first buses leave their villages usually between 5 and 7am and use the market in Apia as their terminal, fanning out from there to return to their villages. Ordinarily the last bus leaves the villages for town between 2 and 2:30pm; last departure from Apia is about 4:30pm. They do not run on Saturday afternoon or Sunday.

The Western Samoan Visitors Bureau keeps a list of key buses posted in its office on the waterfront. Here are the destinations most often visited, followed by the names of the village buses that go there:

Piula Cave Pool: Falefa, Luatuanuu, Lufilufi. They run about every 30 minutes.

Return to Paradise Beach: Lefaga, Safata, Siumu, Falealili. They run about once an hour.

Papase'a Sliding Rocks: Se'ese'e. About every 30 minutes.

Fares are set by the government and are available from the visitors bureau or the Ministry of Transport. In general, 50 sene (25¢) will take you around Apia and into the hills above the town. The maximum fare is about WS$4 ($2) to the most distant villages and to Mulifanua Wharf, where the Savai'i ferries land on Upolu's western end (see "An Easy Excursion to Savai'i," below).

BY TAXI

Silver Star Taxis (tel. 21-770), **Marlboro Taxis** (tel. 20-808), **Vailima Taxis** (tel. 22-380), **Heini Taxis** (tel. 24-431), and **Town Taxis** (tel. 21-600) all provide taxi service in Apia. Unlike the others, **Town Taxis** also has a stand at the airport.

Aggie's Taxis is the collective name of cabdrivers who wait across Beach Road for customers coming out of Aggie Grey's Hotel. Generally, they charge more than the other taxis.

The cabs do not have meters, but **fares** are set by the government. A pamphlet listing them is available at the visitors bureau or at the Ministry of Transport. In general, WS$1.70 (85¢) will take you around Apia and its hotels. From Apia to Vailima costs W$3.50 ($1.75); to Fagali'i Airstrip, WS$5 ($2.50); to Faleolo Airport, WS$28 ($14); to Lefaga and Return to Paradise Beach, WS$45 ($22.50); and to Piula College and Cave Pool, WS$25 ($12.50), all one-way.

FAST FACTS: WESTERN SAMOA

American Express The American Express representative in Western Samoa is Retzlaff Travel & Tours, P.O. Box 1863, Apia, Western Samoa (tel. 21-724 or 21-725), but it does not offer full card-member services. It will receive and hold your mail and will help if you lose your card or traveler's checks, but that's the extent of its services. The office is on Vaea St. in the second block inland from the Town Clock.

Area Code The international country code is 685.

Baby-sitters Like their counterparts in American Samoa, the Western Samoans are very good with children, and your hotel can arrange for qualified baby-sitters.

Bookstores The Wesley Bookstore, in the Wesley Arcade next to the Methodist Church on Beach Rd., carries books on Samoa and the South Pacific and a few paperback novels, as does Aggie's Gift Shop at Aggie Grey's Hotel. Also, check Aggie's for copies of the international newsmagazines. Educational Bookshop, at the end of Vaea St., is not as convenient, but it has some novels and maps of the Samoas.

Business Hours Most shops and government offices are open Mon–Fri 8am–noon and 1:30–4:30pm, Sat 8am–noon. Except for the major hotels, the only businesses open on Sun are the scores of mom-and-pop grocery shops in Apia and some villages. Several of these inhabit small shacks on the waterfront side of Beach Rd. near the Town Clock.

Car Rentals See "Getting Around" in this chapter.

Climate See "When to Go—Climate, Holidays & Events" in Chapter 7.

Clothing Lightweight, informal summer clothing is best throughout the year, although a light sweater or wrap could come in handy for evening wear June–Sept. Men can wear shorts and shirts almost anywhere, but women should stick to dresses away from the hotels and should never wear bathing suits or skimpy clothing away from the beach or swimming pool. Topless or nude bathing is outlawed. Outside Apia most Samoans still wear wraparound lavalavas, which come well below the knees of men and to the ankles on women.

Credit Cards American Express, VISA, MasterCard, and Diners Club credit cards are accepted by the major hotels and rental-car firms. Elsewhere, carry enough cash to cover your anticipated expenses.

Currency See "Information, Entry Requirements & Money," above.

Currency Exchange The Bank of Western Samoa and the Pacific Commercial Bank both have main offices in the block of Beach Rd. west of the Town Clock in Apia. Banking hours are Mon–Fri 9:30am–3pm. No bank fees are charged to exchange foreign currency or traveler's checks, but you will have a few sene deducted for stamp tax. As noted in "Getting There," above, the banks have offices at Faleolo International Airport.

Dentist Two dentists are in private practice. Soonalole Dental Surgery (tel. 21-145) is upstairs over Apia Pharmacy on Beach Rd. Leavai Dental Surgery (tel. 20-172) is in the area of town known as Three Corners.

Doctor There are doctors with private clinics in Apia; ask your hotel staff to recommend one. For American-trained doctors, you will have to go to the Lyndon B. Johnson Tropical Medical Clinic in Pago Pago. Also see "Hospital," below.

Documents Required See "Information, Entry Requirements & Money," above.

Driving Rules See "Getting Around" in this chapter.

Drugstores Two pharmacies ("chemists") on Beach Road near the Town Clock carry cosmetics, nonprescription remedies, and prescription drugs—most of New Zealand or Australian manufacture. Don't expect to find sophisticated medications; bring your own prescription drugs with you.

Electrical Appliances Electricity in Western Samoa is 240 volts, 50 cycles, and most plugs have angled prongs like those used in New Zealand and Australia. Aggie Grey's Hotel and the Hotel Kitano Tusitala supply 110-volt current for electric shavers only; you will need a converter and adapter plugs for other American and Canadian appliances.

Embassies/Consulates The U.S. Embassy is in the John Williams Building on Beach Rd. in Apia (tel. 21-631). New Zealand and Australia both have "high commissions" (they would be called "embassies" outside the British Commonwealth) on Beach Rd.

Emergencies The emergency phone number for police, fire, and ambulance is **999.**

Eyeglasses Try the National Hospital (see "Hospital," below); if it can't be fixed there (replacements must be ordered from New Zealand) try the Lyndon B. Johnson Tropical Medical Center in Pago Pago.

Gambling There are no casinos or other types of organized gambling in Western Samoa.

Hairdressers/Barbers Aggie Grey's Hotel has a beauty parlor (tel. 23-277).

Hospital The National Hospital, on Ifi'ifi St. in Apia (tel. 21-212), has an outpatient clinic open daily 8am–noon and 1–4:30pm. If you have something seriously wrong, however, head for the Lyndon B. Johnson Tropical Medical Center in Pago Pago.

Information See "Information, Entry Requirements & Money," above.

Insects There are no dangerous insects in Western Samoa, and the plentiful mosquitoes do not carry malaria. Bring a good insect repellent with you and consider burning mosquito coils at night.

Laundry/Dry Cleaning The hotels will take care of your dirty clothes, or you can wash and dry them yourself at Fuapepe's Laundro-Mat, behind the Bank of Western Samoa branch opposite the National Hospital on Ifi'ifi St., or at Sapolu Laundrette, near the inland end of Vaea St. A load costs WS$2 ($1) to wash and WS$3 ($1.50) to dry. Faupepe's is open daily 9am–11pm; Sapolu's hours are Mon–Sat 6am–10pm, Sun 6am–8pm.

Libraries Nelson's Public Library, opposite the Town Clock on Beach Rd., is open Mon–Tues and Thurs 9am–5pm, Wed 8am–8pm, Fri 8am–4pm, and Sat 9am–noon.

Liquor Laws Except for the prohibition of Sun sale of alcoholic beverages outside the hotels or licensed restaurants, the laws are fairly liberal. Spirits, wine, and beer are sold at private liquor stores. Try Samoa Wine & Spirits 3 blocks inland on Vaea St.

Lost Property Report to the police station (tel. 22-222) on Ifi'ifi St. a block inland from the prime minister's office.

Luggage Storage/Lockers There are none in Western Samoa. The hotels will store your extra gear.

Maps The Western Samoa Visitors Bureau distributes *Western Samoa: Tourist Map Guide,* a one-sheet collection of maps of the Samoa Islands, Upolu, and Savai'i. See "Information, Entry Requirements & Money" in this chapter. The best commercial map available is *Islands of Samoa,* by cartographer James A. Bier. Published by the University Press of Hawaii, it can be purchased for about U.S. $4.50 at the bookshops in Apia. See "Bookstores," above. The Department of Lands and Surveys, on Beach Rd. next to the Australian High Commission, also has excellent maps, most of them produced by the Surveyor General of New Zealand.

Newspapers/Magazines Two tabloids, *The Samoa Times* and the *Samoa Observer,* carry local and world news. The larger *Samoa Observer* also has shipping schedules, international flight timetables, movies playing at Apia's two cinemas (Tivoli and Starlight 2), and programs on KVZK-TV, the Pago Pago station. Check Aggie's Gift Shop at Aggie Grey's Hotel for copies of the international newsmagazines.

Photographic Needs Quantity and selection of film available in Western Samoa are limited, so bring some with you from home or from Pago Pago. Try the two pharmacies, Aggie's Gift Shop, or the photo shop in Forsgren's. The latter is just west of the Town Clock.

Police The police station (tel. 22-222) is on Ifi'ifi St. inland from the prime minister's office.

Post Office The Chief Post Office is located on Beach Rd. east of the Town Clock. Airmail letters to North America cost 65 sene (35¢); postcards and airgrams, 55 sene (30¢). Hours are Mon–Fri 9am–4:30pm.

Radio/TV Western Samoa does not have broadcast television, but many homes receive the American Samoan channels. The government operates only one AM radio station, on which most programming is in Samoan. The world news is rebroadcast from Radio Australia at 7am, 9am, and 7pm daily. The country's first privately owned FM station began broadcasting on FM 98.8 in 1991. American Samoa's AM station, WVUV, can be picked up fairly well on Upolu's north shore.

Religious Services The Congregational Christian church, a Protestant denomination that grew from the London Missionary Society's early work in the islands, is the largest church in Western Samoa. Others are the Assembly of God church, the Baha'i Faith, the Baptist church, the Roman Catholic church, the Church of Christ, the Church of God of Prophecy, Jehovah's Witnesses, the Seventh-Day Adventist church, the Methodist church, and a large mission of the Church of Jesus Christ of Latter-Day Saints.

Rest Rooms You will have to rely on the hotels, restaurants, and bars.

Safety Although crimes against tourists have been rare in Western Samoa, remember that the communal-property system still prevails in both Samoas. Items such as cameras and bags left unattended may disappear, so take the proper precautions. Street crime has not been a serious problem, but be on the alert if you walk down dark streets at night. Women should not wander alone on deserted beaches. Western Samoans take the Sabbath seriously, and there have been reports of local residents tossing stones at tourists who drive through some villages on Sun. If you plan to tour by rental car, do it during the week. See the "Fast Facts: South Pacific" in Chapter 2 for more warnings.

Shoe Repairs Try Fale Seevae Co. Ltd. (tel. 22-543) on Vaea St.

Taxes Western Samoa imposes a 10% tax on all hotel, restaurant, and bar bills. Also, an airport departure tax of WS$20 ($10) is levied on all passengers leaving Western Samoa (see "Getting There," above). Travelers need pay the tax only once every 30 days, so save your receipt if you expect to depart Western Samoa again within a month. No such tax is imposed on domestic flights or on the ferry to Pago Pago.

Taxis See "Getting Around," above.

Telegrams/Telex See "Telephone," below.

Telephone Western Samoa's telephone system is operated by the post office. Domestic long-distance and international calls may be placed at the International Telephone Bureau just inside the Chief Post Office on Beach Rd. You place your call with the clerk at the central booth and wait to be paged to one of the side booths. The bureau does not accept credit cards; you must reverse the charges or pay cash in advance of having your call placed. Station-to-station calls to North America cost WS$13.50 ($6.75) for the first 3 minutes, then WS$4.50 ($2.25) a minute thereafter. Calls to Australia and New Zealand cost about half that amount. The bureau is open 24 hours every day.

Pay telephones are in post offices in the villages. They are the same red phones used in Fiji and are operated by lifting the handset from its cradle atop the device, depositing a 20-sene coin, and dialing your call.

The number for **directory assistance** is 933; for the **international operator,** 900; for the **domestic long-distance** operator, 920.

Calls to Western Samoa from the U.S. and most Western nations may be dialed directly. The **country code is 685.**

Time Local time in Western Samoa is 3 hours behind Pacific standard time (4 hours behind during daylight saving time). In other words, if it's noon standard time in California and 3pm in New York, it's 9am in Apia. If daylight saving time is in effect, it's 8am in Western Samoa.

The islands are east of the international date line; therefore, they share the same date with North America and are 1 day behind Tonga, Fiji, Australia, and New Zealand. That's worth remembering if you are going on to those countries or will be arriving in Western Samoa from one of them.

Tipping There is no tipping in Western Samoa except for extraordinary service, and the practice is discouraged as being contrary to the traditional way of life, fa'a Samoa. One exception is the growing practice of throwing money on the dance floor to show appreciation of a show well performed.

Weights/Measures Western Samoa officially is on the metric system of weights and measures, but most residents are familiar with the British system used in American Samoa and in the U.S. Speed limits are posted in miles per hour.

3. WHAT TO SEE & DO

ORGANIZED TOURS

Given the condition of many roads in Western Samoa, consider an organized tour as one of the best ways to see and enjoy Upolu's sights. Here are some of the companies; their offerings and prices are listed in the visitors bureau booklet, *Western Samoa: Tariffs*.

Samoa Scenic Tours, based at Aggie Grey's Hotel (tel. 22-880), offers a different tour each day. Most stop along the way for photographs and a swim at beautiful beaches and waterfalls, and they include a beachside barbecue lunch (beers and soft drinks, too). Prices range from WS$20 ($10) for ½ day to WS$50 ($25) for full-day trips. Each day's offerings are scrawled on a notice board in the lobby at Aggie's.

Other companies to call are **Annie's Tours** (tel. 21-550 or 20-744), **Gold Star Tours** (tel. 20-466), **Janes Tours** (tel. 20-942), **Oceania Tours** (tel. 24-443), and **Retzlaff's Tours** (tel. 21-724). Among them you will find something interesting, especially for Sunday, which, except for church services, will be a slow day in Samoa.

TOURING UPOLU

A DRIVING TOUR

To travel along the roads of Upolu away from Apia is to see Polynesia relatively unchanged from the days before the Europeans arrived in the islands. There are very few road signs in Western Samoa, so make sure you have a good map in hand (see "Fast Facts," above). Also, the roads were severely damaged by Cyclone Ofa in early 1990 and still may be in very rough shape. A four-wheel-drive vehicle is recommended.

From Apia to the East

A paved road follows the north coast for 16 miles to the village of **Falefa,** skirting the lagoon and black-sand surf beaches at Lauli'i and Solosolo. Look for **Piula College,** a Methodist school on a promontory overlooking the sea about 2 miles before Falefa. Cut into the cliff below the church on the school grounds is the freshwater ✪ **Piula Cave Pool.** You can use snorkeling gear to swim through an underwater opening at the back of the pool into a second cave. The cave pool is open from 8am to 4:30pm Monday through Saturday; admission is WS$2 ($1), and there are changing rooms for visitors.

Just beyond Falefa village lie **Falefa Falls,** impressive during the rainy season. The pavement continues for another 2 miles past Falefa, after which a rugged dirt road climbs toward **Le Mafa Pass** in the center of the island. Another road to the left just before the pass leads down to picturesque **Fagaloa Bay.** These roads should be traveled with caution, especially following rainy periods. After crossing the 950-foot-high pass, the road descends on a gradual incline toward the south coast. Look for a sign on the left side of the road, and be prepared to walk about 300 yards and to pay a custom fee of WS$1 (50¢) to see **Fuipisia Falls,** which plunges 185 feet into a valley. A dirt road goes off to the right about 2 miles farther along; there is no sign marking it, but this is the main road to the south and west coasts. Don't take this road yet; instead, go straight a short distance to a viewpoint overlooking 175-foot-high **Bopo'aga Falls.** The road you are on continues to the south shore and on to Aleipata District on the east end of Upolu, a very scenic area with cliffs, white sandy beaches, lagoons, and small islands offshore.

A highlight along the southeast shore is ✪ **Vavau,** a charming village sitting beside an incredibly beautiful white-sand beach with rocky outcrops along the shore; you can actually snorkel in the shade. The South Pacific Tourism Commission is working with the villagers to create a modest, locally owned and operated resort. It was not up and running when I was in Western Samoa, but the beach alone should make it a target, at least for a day-trip.

Central Upolu

The cross-island road runs from the John Williams Building on Beach Road in Apia for 14 miles to the village of Si'umu on the south coast. Along the way it passes first Vailima and then the modern, nine-sided **House of Worship,** one of six Baha'i Faith temples in the world. Open for meditation and worship, the temple was dedicated in 1984. An information center outside the temple makes available materials about the Baha'i Faith.

IMPRESSIONS

Many an English village is bigger by far than Apia. And the whole place had an air of faded obsolescence, as if somebody had decided that it was hardly worth nailing the buildings to the ground or giving them a lick of paint because the inevitable hurricane was bound to blow them away.

—JOHN DYSON, 1982

After passing the temple, the road winds its way through cool, rolling pastureland and then starts its descent to the east coast. Watch on the left for a scenic overlook. **Tiavi Falls,** which plunges 300 feet, are off to the right, but you'll have to ask directions to them from a clerk in one of the small grocery stores along the way.

The South Coast

A few miles east of Si'umu village on the south coast is **O Le Pupu-Pue National Park** and the **Togitogiga Recreational Reserve.** A visitor's center sits under a fale made in the traditional manner of natural materials; an exhibit board details the method of construction. The park contains the best remaining tropical rain forest on Upolu, but you'll have to hike into the valley to reach it. Some 51 species of wildlife live in the park: 42 species of birds, 5 of mammals, and 4 of lizards. Lovely **Togitogiga Falls** is a short walk from the visitors center. A trail to **Peapea Cave** also starts at the visitors center; it's a 2-hour round-trip hike. **Mount Le Pu'e,** in the northwest corner of the park, is a well-preserved volcanic cinder cone. The park and reserve are open during the daylight hours 7 days a week, and there's no admission fee.

The most beautiful beaches on Upolu are along the southwest coast, particularly in the Lefaga district. One of these is at the village of **Salamumu.** Farther on the south coast road, watch for the ✪ **RETURN TO PARADISE BEACH** sign nailed to a coconut tree on the left. Turn there and follow the dirt road to the beach, left through Matautu village and along a track to one of the most gorgeous coves in the South Pacific. Palms hang over a sandy beach punctuated by large boulders that confront the breaking surf. The movie made from James A. Michener's *Return to Paradise,* starring Gary Cooper, was filmed on this beach in 1951. It has been known ever since as "Return to Paradise Beach." The WS$2 ($1) per-person custom fee charged by Matautu village is well worth it.

From Matautu you have the choice of following the coastal road along the beaches and lagoon around the western end of Upolu before heading back to Apia. This road skirts the lagoon in places and passes **Mulifanua Wharf,** where the ferries leave for Savai'i. Offshore lie the blue outlines of **Manono** and **Apolima** islands, and beyond them the hovering presence of **Savai'i.** The other option is to follow the main road, which winds across the center of the island to the north coast.

TOURING APIA

A WALKING TOUR

Like most South Pacific towns, Western Samoa's capital and only town has expanded from one small Samoan village to include adjacent settlements and an area of several square miles, all of which is now known collectively as Apia (the name of the village where Europeans first settled). The town now has a population approaching 35,000. For the visitor, most points of interest lie along **Beach Road,** the shady avenue which curves along the harbor, the water on one side and churches, government buildings, and businesses on the other.

We start our walking tour of downtown at **Aggie Grey's Hotel,** on the banks of the Vaisigano River on the east end of Apia, and proceed west along Beach Road. This famous hotel and its founder are stories unto themselves, which I recount in the accommodation listings below. Head west, or to the left as you face the sea from Aggie's.

The two large churches on the left are both Protestant, legacies of the Rev. John Williams, for whom the modern high-rise office building at the corner of Falealili Road is named. On the waterfront across Beach Road is a memorial to this missionary who brought Christianity to Samoa and many more of the South Pacific islands. Williams's bones are reputedly buried beneath the clapboard **Congregational Christian Church,** directly across Beach Road from the memorial. The missionary was eaten after the natives did him in on Erromango in what now is Vanuatu; the story has it that his bones were recovered and brought to Apia.

During business hours there's usually a line outside the **New Zealand High Commission** office, just beyond the church, as Western Samoans wait to apply for visas. Like their American Samoan cousins who flock to the United States, they migrate in droves to Auckland for better jobs and higher pay. Unlike them, however,

Western Samoans do not have unrestricted access to the larger country and must apply for visas to enter New Zealand, their former "Mother Country."

Next door to the high commission is the **Foreign Ministry.** The clapboard, colonial-style **courthouse** on the next corner houses the Supreme Court and prime minister's office. It was headquarters of the New Zealand trusteeship administration, and site of the Mau Movement demonstration and shootings in 1929. Cars are stopped at 7:50am weekdays while the flag is raised at the courthouse to the strains of the police band. The police station is behind the courthouse.

The Marist Brothers' Primary School is on the banks of Mulivai Stream. Across the bridge stands **Mulivai Catholic Cathedral,** begun in 1885 and completed some 20 years later. Farther along, the imposing **Matafele Methodist Church** abuts the shops in the **Wesley Arcade.** According to a monument across Beach Road, Chief Saivaaia of Tafua in Tonga brought Methodism to Samoa in 1835. The Methodist Church of Australia had responsibility for the Samoas from 1859 until an independent conference was established in Western Samoa in 1964.

The remains of the German warship *Seeadler* are buried under the reclaimed land jutting into the harbor across from the churches. On the water side of Beach Road stands a memorial to the Western Samoans who fought alongside the New Zealanders during World War II. A fire in June 1986 destroyed the colonial-style post office opposite the memorial (it was replaced by the modern Bank of Western Samoa building).

The center of modern Apia's business district is the **Town Clock,** the World War I memorial at the foot of Vaea Street. Behind the clock on the reclaimed land is a large Samoan fale known as Pulenu'u House, where local residents can be seen lounging or eating their lunches. Next to the clock on the water side is **Nelson's Public Library,** which has a collection of South Pacific literature in the Pacific Room, to the right after you enter. The clock and library were gifts from the family of Olaf Nelson, a Swede who arrived in 1868 and built a sizable trading empire.

Beyond lies the sprawling **Apia Market,** known in Samoan as *Marketi Fou,* a beehive of activity 24 hours a day. Samoan families practically camp under the market's pavilion rather than risk losing their prized spaces. They sell a wide variety of tropical fruits and vegetables, all of which have the prices clearly marked (there is no bargaining). Some stalls in the rear of the market carry handcraft items, although selections probably will be better elsewhere. I haven't had the stomach for such local fare since my days as a young backpacker, but at WS$2 to WS$3 ($1 to $1.50) a plate, the food stalls along the market's water side are the cheapest places in town to get a meal.

As in most South Pacific towns, the market also serves as the bus terminal, and the crowded machines will be lined up outside belching fumes and gathering riders.

Fugalei Street, which leaves Beach Road across from the market, goes to the airport and west coast. A block down it is picturesque **St. Mary's Convent and School.**

The Mulinu'u Peninsula

Beyond the market, Beach Road becomes Mulinu'u Road. It runs about a mile to the end of Mulinu'u Peninsula, a low arm separating Apia Harbor to the east and shallow Vaiusu Bay on the west.

Just beyond the market on the left is the **Western Samoan Trust Estates Corporation,** which took over ownership of the copra plantations when the Germans were kicked out of the islands at the beginning of World War I. The WSTEC building was originally headquarters of the German firms that owned and managed the plantations. The Kitano Tusitala Hotel just up the way was built where once stood a boardinghouse for the German employees of the original company.

About halfway out on the peninsula are **three memorials,** one to the Germans who died in the 1889 hurricane, one to the British and American sailors who were drowned during that fiasco, and one to commemorate the raising of the German flag in 1900.

The end of Mulinu'u Peninsula is home of the **Fono,** Western Samoa's parliament. The new Fono building sits across from a memorial to Western Samoa's indepen-

IMPRESSIONS

Our place is in a deep cleft of Vaea Mountain, some six hundred feet above the sea, embowered in a forest, which is our strangling enemy, and which we combat with axes and dollars.

—Robert Louis Stevenson, 1890

---

dence, the two separated by a wide lawn. The Fono's old home is next to the road in the same park. The large **tomb** to the left of the new Fono building holds the remains of Iosefa Mataafa, one of the paramount chiefs. Beyond the Apia Yachting Club rest the remains of the reigning Malietoa family of paramount chiefs, which makes this the **burial grounds** of Western Samoa's "royalty."

At the end of the peninsula you'll find the **Apia Weather Observatory,** originally built by the Germans in 1902 (they apparently learned a costly lesson from the unpredicted, disastrous hurricane of March 1889). Beyond the observatory are the tombs of two more of Western Samoa's paramount chiefs, Tuimaleai'ifano and Tupua Tamasese.

Stevenson's Vailima

When Robert Louis Stevenson and his wife, Fanny, decided to stay in Samoa in 1889, they bought 314 acres of virgin land on the slopes of Mount Vaea above Apia and named the estate **Vailima**—"five waters"—because of the five streams that crossed it. They cleared about 8 acres and lived there in a small shack for nearly a year. The American historian Henry Adams dropped in unannounced one day and found the Stevensons dressed in lavalavas, doing dirty work about their hovel. To Adams, the couple's living conditions were repugnant. Their Rousseauian existence didn't last long, however, for in 1891 they built the first part of a mansion that was to become famous throughout the South Pacific.

When completed 2 years later, the big house had five bedrooms, a library, a ballroom large enough to accommodate 100 dancers, and the only fireplace in Samoa. A piano sat in one corner of the great hall in a glass case to protect it from Samoa's humidity. All the building materials were imported from the United States or Australia, and the Stevensons shipped 72 tons of furniture out from England, all of which was hauled the 3 miles from Apia on sleds pulled by bullocks. There were leather-buttoned chairs, mahogany tables, a Chippendale sideboard, Arabian curtains of silver and gold, paintings by the masters, a Rodin nude that was a gift from the sculptor, a damask tablecloth that was a gift from Queen Victoria, and a sugar bowl that had been used by both Robert Burns and Sir Walter Scott.

The Stevensons' life-style matched their surroundings. Oysters were shipped on ice from New Zealand, Bordeaux wine was brought by the cask from France and bottled at Vailima, and 1840 vintage Madeira was poured on special occasions. They dressed formally for dinner every evening—except for their bare feet—and were served by Samoans dressed in tartan lavalavas, in honor of the great author's Scottish origins.

Vailima and this lavish life-style baffled the Samoans. As far as they could tell, writing was not labor; therefore, Stevenson had no visible way of earning a living. Yet all this money rolled in, which meant to them that Stevenson must be a man of much mana. He was also a master at one of their favorite pastimes—storytelling—and he took much interest in their own stories, as well as their customs, their language, and their politics. Even though Stevenson picked the losing side, the grateful followers of the defeated Mataafa (paramount chief) built a road from Apia to Vailima in appreciation for his support in their struggle for power during the time the Germans were establishing their colony.

On December 3, 1894, almost 5 years to the day after he arrived in Apia, Stevenson was writing a story about a son who had escaped a death sentence handed down by his own father and had sailed away to join his lover. Leaving the couple embraced, Stevenson stopped to answer letters, play some cards, and fix dinner. While preparing mayonnaise, he suddenly clasped his hands to his head and fell to the floor. He died not of the tuberculosis that had dogged him most of his adult life, but of a stroke.

Stevenson's wife, Fanny, died in California in 1914, and her ashes were brought back to Vailima and buried at the foot of his grave on Mount Vaea, overlooking Vailima. Her Samoan name, Aolele, is engraved on a bronze plaque, which also bears Stevenson's ode:

A fellow-farer true through life,
Teacher, tender comrade, wife,
A fellow-farer true through life
Heart-whole and soul-free
The August Father gave to me.

Vailima is 3 miles south of Apia on the cross-island road (turn off Beach Road at the high-rise John Williams Building in Apia and go straight). The mansion, now the residence of Western Samoa's head of state, is not open to the public, but permission to visit its grounds may be obtained from the prime minister's office (in the courthouse on Beach Road). The remainder of the estate is a national park.

The "Track of Loving Hearts" leading to **Stevenson's grave** is open every day and begins at the end of a road to the right of the entrance to the estate. Before climbing Mount Vaea it passes by a lovely cascade, which Stevenson turned into a swimming pool (now open—no admission—to the public). A short, rather steep walking track to the grave takes about 30 strenuous minutes; a longer but easier path takes about 1 hour. Mount Vaea is best climbed in the cool of early morning. A thatch pavilion and benches provide (temporary) rest for the weary at the gravesite.

SHOPPING IN APIA

Although the quantity produced is not what it used to be, Western Samoans still produce a reasonable amount of quality handcrafts: baskets, sewing trays, purses, floor mats, napkin rings, placemats, and fans woven from pandanus and other local materials, plus some wood carvings. The country also produces some excellent items of tropical clothing.

By and large, your stroll along Beach Road will take you past most of the shops worth poking your head into. In addition to those listed below, some of the Samoan families who have booths in the rear of the vegetable-and-fruit market sell handcraft items, and local women offer lavalavas, dresses, and T-shirts in an alley in the block west of the Town Clock on Beach Road.

ADVENTURE GIFTS, next to John Williams Building, Beach Rd. No phone.

Although somewhat poorly stocked, you might find a choice handcraft item such as a kava bowl or tapa among the tie-dyed dresses and T-shirts which are Adventure Gifts' specialty. In addition to this shop near Aggie Grey's Hotel, the company has a small outlet next to Tinoa's Barbeque in the block west of the Town Clock.

AGGIE'S GIFT SHOP, next to Aggie Grey's Hotel, Beach Rd. Tel. 22-880.

The hotel's gift shop has a wide range of handcrafts and Samoan products such as sandalwood soap, small bags of kava, and watercolors by local artists. The handcrafts include shell and black-coral jewelry, tapa cloth (*siapo* in Samoan) and large laundry baskets (most imported from Tonga), and carved wooden war clubs,

---

IMPRESSIONS

Western Samoa is different. Of all the Polynesian nations, it is the one with the most peculiar life-style, the strangest customs, the greatest resistance to foreign encroachment; and yet, paradoxically, it is the nation that offers itself most proudly for public inspection.

—Ron Hall, 1991

ceremonial kava bowls, and high talking chiefs' staffs (known as *tootoo*). Among clothing items are hand-screened lavalavas, T-shirts, shorts, and dresses. The shop also carries books about the Samoas and has a snack bar just inside the front door.

AMY'S GIFT SHOP, Leung Wai Arcade, Vaea St. Tel. 22-092.

Although Western Samoans have all but given up making tapa, some local artists are now using the original boards to press the geometric designs onto cloth made from cotton rather than mulberry bark. One of these is Kalolo Steffany, who often can be found in his own little shop across the walkway from this one, which is owned by his mother-in-law, Amy Leung Wai. She carries his designs as well as tie-dyed jumpsuits, dresses, and blouses. The arcade is in the second block inland on Vaea Street.

FORSGREN'S, Beach Rd., west of Town Clock. Tel. 21-009.

This general store, which also includes a photography studio, carries a small selection of handcrafts such as tapa, wood carvings, baskets, black-coral and shell jewelry, grass skirts, straw hats, and T-shirts.

CAROL 'N' MARK BOUTIQUE, off Beach Rd., west of Town Clock. Tel. 21-038.

Frieda Paul's little boutique is a required stop for anyone looking for unusual and very high-quality tropical clothing. Like Kalolo Steffany, Frieda also uses tapa boards to imprint the original geometric designs directly to dresses, shirts, blouses, lavalava, and napkins. Her other designs, some of the most creative in the South Pacific, feature flowers and leaves pressed directly onto the fabric. The shop shares space with Coffee 'n' Things down an alley running beside Gold Star Tours, off Beach Road in the block west of the Town Clock.

DAPHNE'S COFFEE SHOP, in John Williams Building, Beach Rd. Tel. 22-400.

If you can tear yourself away from Cable News Network while eating breakfast, you can look at Daphne's selection of wood carvings, baskets, mats, straw hats, some tapa, shell necklaces, and grass skirts. The coffee shop and handcrafts share the same space, so you won't have to leave your table to look around.

ISLAND STYLES, in the Wesley Arcade, Beach Rd. Tel. 21-850.

Island Styles is Apia's largest producer of South Pacific–style silk-screened and tie-dyed dresses, skirts, and lavalavas. In addition to this small shop near the Methodist church, it has a warehouse showroom on the cross-island highway in Vailima. If you want to bring home a little taste of Samoa, consider a bottle of **Talofa Wines** made from passion fruit, banana, mango, or papaya, or Talofa chocolate liqueur made from locally grown cacao; you can sample them at the Island Styles in Vailima.

JANES HANDICRAFTS, Leung Wai Arcade, Vaea St. Tel. 20-954.

Sharing space with Janes Tours, this shop has a wide array of handcrafts from Western Samoa, Tonga, and Fiji. Janes and Aggie's Gift Shop, in fact, are the two best places in Apia to look for tapa from Tonga and Fiji. Other items offered here include baskets, mats, handbags, carved wooden bowls, coconut ukuleles, spears and war clubs, and jewelry made of shell and black coral.

KAVA KAVINGS HANDICRAFT, Beach Rd. west of John Williams Building. Tel. 24-145.

Harry Paul's family has been collecting old tapa boards, some of which they now use to imprint lavalavas, shirts, and blouses. Harry also has been encouraging Western Samoans to resume making handcrafts, and he carries some of the resulting works: bone fishhooks, carved war clubs, spears, and orator's staffs of the type carried by high-talking chiefs; ukuleles made from coconut shells; grass skirts and dance costumes. He also has imported handcrafts from Tonga, Fiji, and other South Pacific islands; these are displayed in sections devoted to each country.

SOUTH PACIFIC DUTY FREE SHOPPERS LTD., in Aggie Grey's Hotel, Beach Rd. Tel. 22-880, ext. 4007.

Duty-free shopping is very limited in Western Samoa, but you can find a small selection of electronic gear, watches, perfumes, and name-brand liquors in this air-conditioned shop. Enter through the tour-desk office in the clapboard building beside Aggie's. The company also has an outlet in the departure lounge at Faleolo International Airport. The cigarettes available are produced by the Rothman's Tobacco Co. plant near Apia. (Although owned by the same company, the duty-free shop in American Samoa tends to have higher prices.)

SPORTS & RECREATION

SPORTS

The **Royal Samoan Golf Club** has a nine-hole course at Fagali'i, on the eastern side of Apia, and visitors are welcome to use the facilities. Call the club's secretary (tel. 20-120) for information and starting times. The Samoa Open Golf Championship tournament is played each year in August.

Public tennis courts were built in **Apia Park** prior to the 1983 South Pacific Games. They're open 7 days a week from 8am to 4pm and cost WS$1 (50¢) per player for each ½ hour. Just east of town (turn right past Aggie Grey's Hotel), 40-acre Apia Park originally was a racetrack built in German times. The property was confiscated from its German owner during World War I and is now used as a multipurpose recreation facility. Rugby and soccer games draw huge crowds on Saturday from May to September. An open-air gymnasium houses basketball and volleyball courts.

Channel College (tel. 21-821) in Moamoa and the **All Saints Anglican Church** (tel. 21-498) in Leififii both have private tennis courts, which can be reserved and used for a donation of WS$1 (50¢) per person. **Rainbow Springs Recreational Park** (see "Recreation," below) has tennis courts and a chip-and-putt golf course.

In addition to its tennis courts, Apia Park has a **public squash court** (tel. 22-571), also costing WS$1 (50¢) per person. The private **Apia Squash Centre,** opposite the main wharf on Beach Road (tel. 23-780), welcomes visitors. It's open from 8am to 10pm 7 days a week, and has gear for rent. Courts cost WS$5 ($2.50) an hour.

Apia Bowling Club has lawn-bowling greens (tel. 22-254) next to the Hotel Kitano Tusitala on the Mulinu'u Peninsula.

Scuba divers and deep-sea fishing enthusiasts should contact **Samoa Marine,** P.O. Box 4700, Matautu-Uta, Apia, Western Samoa (tel. 22-721, fax 20-087). Scuba-dive charters run about U.S. $40 per person for one-tank excursions, U.S. $50 for two tanks. Tank hires and refills also are available. Deep-sea fishing charters cost about U.S. $250 for ½ day, U.S. $500 for a full day, including boat, guide, equipment, and bait. Boat charters for sightseeing trips can be arranged. Samoa Marine requests at least 1 week's notice prior to fishing and sightseeing charters.

When I was in Apia recently, Australians Geoff and Barbara Hoddinott of **Cruising Samoa Ltd.** (tel. 21-550) were offering cruises of 1-, 2-, and 3-day duration on their 42-foot sailing ketch. Contact them for more information.

RECREATION

Just east of the main wharf in Apia is the **Palolo Deep Marine Reserve,** where canyons in the reef make for good snorkeling. The reserve, which has changing rooms, a bar, and snorkeling gear for hire, is open during the daylight hours every day. A contribution of WS$2 ($1) to the preservation fund and for maintenance of "Pleasure Island" (a shed built on a small rock islet on the reef) is required.

A short walk beyond Palolo Deep is **Vaiala Beach;** the swimming isn't as good there, but there are picnic tables in a grassy coconut grove between the road and the beach.

Some people think a trip to **Papase'a Sliding Rocks** is a highlight of a trip to Apia. You of strong bottom can slide down this waterfall into a dark pool. Take a taxi or the Se'ese'e village bus. The rocks are about 2km (1.2 miles) from the paved road; the bus driver may go out of his way to take you there, but you will have to walk back to the bus route. The villagers extract WS$1 (50¢) custom fee per person.

Another good outing, especially for children, is **Rainbow Springs Recreational Park** in the hills above Apia at the foot of Mount Vaea. A stream flows through this beautifully landscaped park, which has a chip-and-putt golf course, tennis courts, bowling greens, nature walks, shaded areas for barbecues and picnics, a children's playground, and a bar in a large fale. The park is open from 3pm to midnight Monday to Friday, from noon to midnight Saturday and Sunday. Admission costs WS$3 ($1.50) for adults, WS$1 (50¢) for children. To find it by car, go to the end of Vaea Street, turn right, then take the first left.

Other popular recreational outings away from Apia are to **Piula Cave Pool, Return to Paradise Beach,** and **Le Pupu-Pue National Park** and its adjoining **Togitogiga Recreational Reserve.** See "Touring Upolu," above, for details.

4. WHERE TO STAY

Western Samoa has two big hotels and a reasonably good selection of moderate and budget accommodations. While the establishments listed below are in Apia, three other properties were under construction in other parts of Upolu during my recent visit. They had been delayed by Cyclone Ofa in 1990, but they should be up and running by the time you plan your trip. Samoan Village Resorts, a luxurious bungalow complex at Cape Fatuosofia on Upolu's west end is one. Coconuts Beach Club, covered below under "Where to Dine," was planning very upscale bungalows to go with its beachside restaurant and bar. A third, the little village-owned resort at Vavau mentioned in "Touring Upolu," above, should have the best beach of all.

The devaluation of the Western Samoan tala has caused many of the country's hotels and guesthouses to set their rates in American dollars, and they are so quoted here unless otherwise indicated by the WS$ symbol.

EXPENSIVE

AGGIE GREY'S HOTEL, P.O. Box 67, Apia. Tel. 22-880, or toll free 800/448-8355 in the U.S. Fax 23-626. Telex 257. 169 rms. A/C TV TEL **Location:** Beach Rd., on the waterfront.

$ Rates (in U.S. dollars only): $70–$105 single; $80–$115 double. AE, DC, MC, V.

Half a dozen of us guests arrived at Aggie Grey's after midnight during my recent visit, having flown together on the evening flight from Tonga and withstood a grueling, bumpy, sweaty bus ride from Faleolo airport to Apia. Aggie's staff was up and waiting in the wee hours with fresh coffee, tea, and sandwiches. To me, that said it all about this grand hotel, perhaps the last bastion of the genteel old South Pacific.

Back in 1919, a young woman of British and Samoan descent named Aggie Grey started the Cosmopolitan Club on a point of land where the Vaisigano River flows into Apia Harbor. In 1943 she expanded the enterprise into a hotel housed in a three-story clapboard building, with a bar at ground level, a dining room on the next, and rooms to rent on the third. The thousands of U.S. servicemen who trained in Western Samoa for the Pacific campaigns against the Japanese took with them fond memories of Aggie Grey and her hotel. Although James A. Michener has denied it, it is widely believed that Aggie was the role model for Bloody Mary, the Tonkinese woman who provided U.S. servicemen with wine, song, and other diversions in his *Tales of the South Pacific.*

Like Robert Louis Stevenson before her, Aggie Grey was revered by the locals—they honored her by making her the only commoner to appear on a Western Samoan postage stamp. And Head of State Malietoa Tanufafili II and hundreds of other mourners escorted her to her final resting place in the hills above Apia when she died in 1988 at age 90.

Aggie's hotel made her famous outside Samoa, and it was well-warranted fame. Although it sprawled over the years to include more than 150 rooms, she always

FROMMER'S FAVORITE WESTERN SAMOA EXPERIENCES

Stevenson's Grave Anyone who has ever put words on paper will feel a sense of awe when reading Robert Louis Stevenson's requiem carved on his grave up on Mount Vaea overlooking Apia. The climb isn't easy, but it's worth it if you have a single literary bone in your body.

Return to Paradise Beach Although the beach at Vavau is more spectacular in most respects, a Sunday afternoon spent at this beautiful spot is a highlight of any trip to Western Samoa. This is what all beaches should be like: surf breaking around black rock outcrops, palm trees draped over white sand.

Fiafia Night at Aggie Grey's The dancing is more suggestive in French Polynesia and the Cook Islands, but there is a warmth and charm to Aggie's fiafia nights that no other establishment comes close to matching.

Visit the Market Being a poor country has one meritorious effect: The people of Western Samoa still grow an abundance of tropical fruits and vegetables, and they sell them at one of the South Pacific's busiest markets.

Walking in Apia A Hollywood set designer would be hard pressed to top Apia as an old South Seas town. I love to walk along the perfect half-moon curve of Beach Road and let the old churches and clapboard government buildings tell me how things used to be.

operated it like a family establishment. Circulating among her guests, she made them feel as welcome as if they were at home. Everyone sat down family-style when taking a meal in the old clapboard building on Beach Road, and afterward moseyed over for coffee in the lounge. Afternoon tea was a time of socializing and swapping gossip from places far away. And on *fiafia* nights, when the feasts were laid out, Aggie herself would dance the graceful Samoan *siva*.

Son Alan Grey, wife Marina, and granddaughter Aggie (the statuesque namesake everyone calls "Aggie Junior") are making sure that the warm, family feeling remains. Alan was forced to tear down the old clapboard hotel in 1988, but it has been replaced by a beautiful building now housing the reception area, an air-conditioned restaurant, an open-air bar facing the harbor, and two floors of modern rooms and suites with private verandas overlooking the water, the curve of Beach Road, and the town of Apia. Most impressively, the new building is a most appropriate replacement for its famous predecessor: siding that looks like clapboard, roof of corrugated tin, and verandas trimmed in gingerbread fretwork.

The new facility hasn't changed the relaxed atmosphere back in the large, exquisite fale beside the swimming pool with a palm tree growing in the middle. Guests can still take their meals under the great turtle-shaped roof or wander over to the bar for a cold Vailima beer and a chat with friendly strangers. A group of Samoans still strums guitars and sings in the bar after sundown. The efficient staff prepares feasts and barbecues in which the quantity of food dished out is, as always, astounding. And Alan, Marina, and Aggie Junior maintain the tradition of circulating among their guests. The most noticeable change since Aggie's passing is that Aggie Junior now dances the siva on fiafia nights.

The older rooms also have their charms. Most are in modern, stone-accented two-story buildings set in a garden so thick with tropical vegetation that it's easy to get lost trying to find your way from one room to another. Although not luxurious by today's standards, they are comfortable, well ventilated (with fans swinging from the ceiling or oscillating from a wall to help out the usual breeze) as well as air conditioned, and have special touches—like fold-down ironing boards, irons mounted in their own wooden holders, and comfy bent rattan furniture. Each has a veranda or balcony where guests can sip their morning tea or coffee made right in the rooms.

Individual "VIP fale suites" are scattered around the other buildings, each of enormous size and bearing the name of one of Aggie's famous past guests, such as actors Gary Cooper, William Holden, and Marlon Brando. Best of all, the rates are extraordinarily reasonable for a hotel of such fame and innate charm.

Dining/Entertainment: I can assure you that no one goes hungry at Aggie's. Hearty breakfasts—either continental or all the way with bacon and eggs—are served in the big fale from 7 to 9am, as are huge lunches from 12:30 to 2pm. Sandwiches, hamburgers, and other light items are available at the bar for lunch, but they can disappear by 1pm.

Fiafia nights (Wednesday when I was last there) feature an enormous buffet of European, Chinese, and Samoan selections (look the table over before going through the line, and watch for the Samoan dishes along the front). A similar spread, plus charbroiled steaks, chicken, and sausages is laid out on barbecue night (usually Sunday, when most private restaurants in Apia are closed). The all-you-can-eat fiafias and barbecues cost about WS$32 ($16). With Aggie Junior featured in the Samoan dancing, fiafia night should not be missed.

On other evenings, you can order either in the fashion of the old Aggie Grey's—that is, a complete dinner for WS$30 ($15)—or from the à la carte menu for about WS$18 ($9) per main course. Nonguests are welcomed at all meals, but men must wear long trousers and shirts with collars, women skirts or slacks, in the bar and dining areas after 6pm.

Services: Laundry, baby-sitting, free morning and afternoon tea.

Facilities: Swimming pool, tour desk.

HOTEL KITANO TUSITALA, P.O. Box 101, Apia, Western Samoa. Tel. 21-122, or toll free 800/624-3524 in the U.S. Fax 23-652. Telex 226. 96 rms. A/C TEL **Location:** Beach Rd., Mulinu'u Peninsula.

$ Rates: WS$191 ($95.50) single or double. AE, DC, MC, V.

Built in 1974 by the government and named the Tusitala Hotel in honor of Robert Louis Stevenson, this hotel was going downhill until purchased in 1991 by Kitano, the same Japanese construction company that took over the Mendana Hotel in Solomon Islands a year before. Renovations are sure to be taking place during the life of this book, so this description must be somewhat couched. The toll-free number given above also may change.

The modern structure is similar in appearance to the Rainmaker Hotel in Pago Pago in that its three main buildings are under huge turtle-shaped thatch roofs. They ring a tropical garden featuring a children's wading pool, from which water falls down two levels into a larger adult swimming pool. The rooms are all in five two-story buildings grouped beyond the swimming pools. They have typical Australian and New Zealand features: a double bed with a single bed serving as a settee, tropical-style lounge chairs, bath with shower, refrigerator, tea- and coffee-making facilities, and sliding glass door opening onto either a private patio or balcony. They are air conditioned, but there is no means of cross-ventilation without leaving the back door open.

Dining/Entertainment: A bar and lounge in an open-air Samoan fale stand next to the pool, as does the Apaula snack bar, open throughout the day. One of the three big common buildings houses Stevenson's Restaurant (with portraits of R. L. himself). Like Aggie's, the Tusitala has fiafia feast-and-dance nights (Thursday and Saturday during my recent visit) and a poolside barbecue night (Sunday). Prices are about the same as Aggie's.

Services: Laundry, baby-sitting.

Facilities: Two hard-surface tennis courts, swimming pool, children's wading pool, tour desk.

MODERATE

LE GODINET BEACHFRONT HOTEL, P.O. Box 9490, Apia, Western Samoa. Tel. 23-690. 10 rms. A/C **Location:** Beach Rd., Mulinu'u Peninsula.

$ Rates (in U.S. dollars only): $40 single; $60 double. AE, MC, V.

Derec Godinet returned to his native Apia after an entertainment career in Honolulu, Los Angeles, and Las Vegas to open this comfortable little establishment on the Mulinu'u Peninsula waterfront. Actually the white two-story building, which looks more like a home than a hotel, sits on the land side of Beach Road, but it has a tiny sliver of beach upon which lap the waters of Apia Harbour. The 10 long, rather narrow but very clean rooms are lined up along one side of the building's second story. (Their doors open to a covered balcony, as do a set of louvered windows in each). Some have one double bed and one single; others, two doubles. They all have desks and long, benchlike tables along one wall. Small baths have showers. There are no closets, so storage space is at a premium. The room at the front of the building has large windows facing the harbor; it is by far the choice here. A common area on the upstairs balcony has a fridge and tea- and coffee-making facilities.

A spacious restaurant with a small bar in one corner opens both to the harbor in front and to a carport along one side of the building. The food here is so good that I have included the restaurant separately in "Where to Dine," below. Local singers entertain during dinner. Derec sometimes gets visiting celebrities to perform; the place was packed recently when Mavis Rivers, another Samoan-born entertainer who made her mark in California, put on a cabaret show while in town.

VAIALA BEACH COTTAGES, P.O. Box 2025, Apia, Western Samoa. Tel. 22-202. Fax 22-713. Telex 2219. 7 bungalows. **Location:** On Vaiala Beach, about 1 mile from the main wharf.

$ Rates (in U.S. dollars only): $55 single; $65 double. V.

(S) If you want your own house in Apia, Helen Mihaljevich has seven comfortable, modern, and airy bungalows, which share a yard with plumeria, crotons, and other tropical plants and are across the street from Vaiala Beach, about a mile east of downtown Apia. Helen's sister, by the way, played Gary Cooper's daughter in the 1951 production of *Return to Paradise,* and her own daughter was a Miss Western Samoa.

Except for the tropical furnishings and decor, such as cane furniture and woven floor mats, the bungalows are all identical: a full kitchen with stainless-steel sink, a bedroom with either one double or two twin beds, a spacious bath with a shower and very hot water, and a narrow balcony off a bright living room. They were built in 1984 of New Zealand treated pine, including the varnished interior walls. The living rooms have ceiling fans hanging over the sitting area, but the large, screened louvered windows and sliding doors leading to the balconies usually allow the trade winds to cool the house without such assistance. Reservations are advised.

BUDGET

HARBOUR LIGHT HOTEL, P.O. Box 5214, Apia, Western Samoa. Tel. 21-103. 33 rms. A/C **Location:** Beach Rd., opposite the main wharf.

$ Rates (in U.S. dollars only): $25 single; $30 double. AE, MC.

If you arrive without a booking, try the shopworn but functional Harbour Light, which looks like a motel. The rooms are in an L-shaped building across from the main wharf on Beach Road, and have either one double or two twin beds, baths with showers, small refrigerators, tea- and coffee-making facilities, and unusually low ceilings. In the center of the complex is a common building with the reception area and an airy restaurant open for breakfast, lunch, and dinner; the accent is on local-style foods.

OLIVIA YANDALL ACCOMMODATION, P.O. Box 4089, Vaiala, Western Samoa. Tel. 22-110. Fax 22-110. 3 bungalows with bath, 1 fale with kitchen and bath, 3 communal units with shared facilities. **Location:** Matautu St. (east coast road), behind the BP service station 1km (.6 mile) from Aggie Grey's Hotel.

$ Rates: WS$44 ($22) bungalow single or double; WS$33 ($16.50) fale single or double; WS$15 ($7.50) share unit per person. No credit cards.

Friendly Olivia Yandall, whom I got to know on a low-budget trip back in the 1970s, has two motellike units with their own toilets and showers, one small Samoan-style fale with bath and kitchenette, and three two-bedroom bungalows in which the guests share baths and kitchen facilities.

SEASIDE INN, P.O. Box 3019, Apia, Western Samoa. Tel. 22-578. 9 rms (7 with bath). **Location:** Beach Rd., opposite the main wharf.

$ Rates (including breakfast): WS$28 ($14) single; WS$35 ($17.50) double. No credit cards.

Most convenient of Apia's guesthouses and most popular with the backpacking brigade, this one-story, clapboard establishment sits across Beach Road from the main wharf. The unpretentious rooms have electric fans, but try to get a corner room with a cross breeze. The guests share a common lounge area and front porch. Breakfast is the only meal served.

VALENTINE PARKER'S ACCOMMODATION, P.O. Box 395, Apia, Western Samoa. Tel. 22-158. 13 rms (none with bath). **Location:** Fugalei Street, 3 blocks inland from market.

$ Rates: WS$20 ($10) single; WS$30 ($15) couple (two persons of the same sex sharing a room each pay the single rate). No credit cards.

Grandson of an American from New Jersey, Valentine Parker in 1989 added four rooms to the nine he already had on the second floor of his house in a residential neighborhood about a 15-minute walk from the market. Unfortunately, Le LaLaga Bar opened not long afterward just two doors away, which created a ruckus into the wee hours of every night except Sunday. Thanks to the Parkers and their neighbors, the government then made all Apia bars close at midnight. It's still noisy until then. The rooms are plainly furnished but clean. Meals can be arranged.

5. WHERE TO DINE

If you tire of eating at Aggie Grey's and the Kitano Tusitala or slapping together a meal at your guesthouse, Apia offers a fairly broad range of eateries. New Zealand influence remains strong in Western Samoa, however, and the seasonings may not be the most exciting. At least once during your stay, you must try a traditional Samoan feast, even if it means a splurge.

Like other islanders, the Samoans gave up the use of pottery at least a thousand years before the Europeans arrived in the South Pacific. As did their fellow Polynesians in Tahiti, the Cook Islands, and Tonga, they cooked their foods in a pit of hot stones—Samoans call it an *umu*—over which they placed pig, fish, octopus, chicken, bananas, breadfruit, roots and leafy tops of taro, and other local foods, all wrapped in banana leaves and covered with the earth from the pit. When it had all steamed for several hours, they threw back the dirt, unwrapped the delicacies, and sat down to a ✪ **fiafia.** Favorite side dishes were fresh fruit and *ota* (fish marinated with lime juice and served with vegetables in coconut milk in a fashion similar to poisson cru in Tahiti).

If you happen to be in Samoa on the seventh day after the full moon in late October or early November (its date changes from year to year), the meal may include the coral worm known as palolo.

Aggie Grey's Hotel (tel. 22-880) and the **Hotel Kitano Tusitala** (tel. 21-122) each have at least one fiafia a week for about WS$30 ($15) per person. Guests pass a long buffet table loaded with European, Chinese, and Samoan dishes. After stuffing down the food, they watch a show of traditional Samoan dancing. Check with the hotels to find out when they have their fiafia nights.

EXPENSIVE

APIA INN, Beach Rd. at Ifi'ifi St. Tel. 21-010.

Cuisine: CONTINENTAL. **Reservations:** Recommended.

Location: Second floor of the John Williams Building.

$ **Prices:** Appetizers WS$9–WS$17 ($4.50–$8.50); main courses WS$20–WS$27 ($10–$13.50). V.

Open: Lunch Tues–Fri noon–2pm; dinner Mon–Sat 6–9pm.

When you enter Stefan Stedegi's restaurant, you'd swear that you just walked into an elegant restaurant in New York or Sydney, not a small South Seas outpost. Linen, crystal, and silverware grace the 15 tables, and the service is attentive and efficient (no "island time" here). Stefan's specialties are fish soup in a light, spicy broth with a hint of curry and red pepper; Swiss-style pork schnitzel with ham, tomato, and cheese; and beef médaillons Tyrol style with tomato, onion rings, and béarnaise sauce. He also offers steaks with a variety of sauces, such as hot tomato or cognac cream; pork filets in Bombay curry-cream sauce served with pineapple and baked banana; and local lobster thermidor, which is superb.

LE GODINET RESTAURANT, Beach Rd. Tel. 23-690.

Cuisine: SEAFOOD. **Reservations:** Recommended.

Location: On Mulinu'u Peninsula in Le Godinet Beachfront Hotel.

$ **Prices:** Appetizers WS$5–WS$11 ($2.50–$5.50); main courses WS$18–WS$25 ($9–$12.50). AE, MC, V.

Open: Breakfast daily 7–9am; lunch daily noon–2pm; dinner daily 6–11pm.

Derec Godinet's restaurant is worth a visit even if you don't stay in his house-cum-hotel. Occupying his spacious first floor, the dining room has stucco walls and heavy exposed beams of dark wood. The tables, each with a high-backed wicker chair at its head and frangipani in its center, are scattered among large potted plants. Fans hanging from the ceiling augment the breeze coming through large windows from the harbor just across the road. Although the menu features chicken, beef, and pork, go for the seafood, especially a combination of it mixed with homemade pasta. When available, local lobster is served either with Mornay, garlic butter, or spicy tomato sauce.

THE WATERFRONT RESTAURANT, Beach Rd. Tel. 20-977.

Cuisine: CONTINENTAL. **Reservations:** Advised.

Location: Beach Rd. opposite the main wharf.

$ **Prices:** Appetizers WS$6–WS$14 ($3–$7); main courses WS$22–WS$30 ($11–$15). AE, MC, V.

Open: Lunch Tues–Fri 11:30am–2pm; dinner Mon–Sat 6:30–10pm.

Adrienne Grey and Philip Postlethwaite—she of the Aggie Grey clan, he a chef from Wales—have Apia's best eatery. As its name states, their pleasant and well-appointed establishment occupies a converted house on Apia's waterfront a short walk east from Aggie Grey's Hotel; open to the water, the romantically lit main dining room is decorated with various nautical items, including large nets which form a false ceiling. Philip's kitchen offers a mixed bag of main courses, ranging from Italian pastas to curries to steaks with a variety of light, nouvelle cuisine–style sauces. Check the specials board for fresh fish of the day; if it features masimasi, order the filets of this moist, succulent local fish grilled in lime butter.

MODERATE

AMIGO'S RESTAURANT, Vaea St. Tel. 23-140.

Cuisine: STEAKS. **Reservations:** Not usually necessary.

Location: 3 blocks inland from the Town Clock on Vaea St.

$ **Prices:** Lunches WS$4.50–WS$10 ($2.25–$5); appetizers WS$6.50–WS$7.50 ($3.25–$3.75); main courses WS$10–WS$20 ($5–$10). MC, V.

Open: Lunch Mon–Fri 11:30am–2pm; dinner Mon–Sat 6:30–10pm.

Never mind the cheap, open-air cafeteria outside; go right in and you'll find three pleasant dining rooms frequented by local residents, especially at lunch. Amigo's has given up on Mexican fare and now sticks to steaks delightfully charbroiled over coconut husks. As appetizers, several Samoan dishes are featured, such as *faiai fe'e* (octopus baked in coconut cream), *palusami* (a modern Polynesian favorite of canned corn beef wrapped with taro leaves and baked in coconut cream), and, of course, *oka* (fish marinated in lime juice). There's a good selection of sandwiches, salads, and big, juicy burgers for lunch. By the way, the cafeteria outside isn't all that bad for inexpensive, local-style fare: Sandwiches, curries with rice, chicken-and-chips, and chow mein range from WS$1.50 to WS$2.50 (75¢ to $1.25). The same dishes served inside cost four times as much.

CANTON RESTAURANT, Matautu St. Tel. 22-818.

Cuisine: CHINESE. **Reservations:** Advised on weekends. **Location:** 50 yards inland from bridge adjacent to Aggie Grey's Hotel, on east coast road.

$ **Prices:** Appetizers WS$3–WS$8 ($1.50–$4); main courses WS$9–WS$16 ($4.50–$8); crabs WS$20–WS$35 ($10–$17.50). No credit cards.

Open: Lunch Mon–Sat 11:30am–2pm; dinner Mon–Sat 5:30–10pm, Sun 5:30–9pm.

S I'm sure glad one of your fellow readers, Genevieve Glass of Chicago, Illinois, found this gem because it's one of the best places east of Vanuatu to get those large crustaceans known in these parts as mud crabs. In fact, it's often difficult to hear yourself think in this plain but pleasant restaurant over the sound of shells being cracked. Harvested in the shallow, lakelike lagoon on Upolu's south shore, the creatures are best eaten here under black-bean sauce. Otherwise, the menu includes a variety of Cantonese with some spicy Szechuan dishes, all of them well prepared. Manager Ricky Wong, who attended university in San Francisco, serves up Samoan-sized portions.

COCONUTS BEACH CLUB, Maninoa, Siumu. Tel. 20-012.

Cuisine: REGIONAL. **Reservations:** Advised for dinner. **Location:** In Maninoa village, Siumu District, on Upolu's south coast, virtually at end of the cross-island road. Taxi fares aren't cheap: WS$60 ($30) round-trip.

$ **Prices:** Sandwiches and burgers WS$13–WS$17 ($6.50–$8.50); appetizers WS$8–WS$15 ($4–$7.50); main courses WS$14–WS$22 ($7–$11). MC, V.

Open: Mon–Thurs 11am–7pm, Fri 11am–10pm, Sat 9am–10pm, Sun 9am–7pm.

Los Angeles lawyers Barry and Jennifer Rose, who are developing this upscale resort, opened the restaurant before completing the accommodations, and a fine thatch-roofed, beachside pavilion it sits under. A comfy bar occupies most of the building; umbrella tables are set up on a wooden deck to one side. House specialty is fish cooked in coconut cream, sprinkled with toasted coconut, and served on a banana leaf. Sandwiches and hamburgers also are featured. There was no phone at the resort when I was there; the number above belongs to a travel agent in Apia. A WS$10 ($5) fee is charged to get into the resort, with the amount applied to purchases in the restaurant and bar. The club has changing rooms and showers for guests. Plan on taking lunch here during an island excursion; otherwise, make it an early dinner.

THE GODFATHER'S PIZZA, Clipper Arcade, Beach Rd. Tel. 22-221.

Cuisine: PIZZA/SNACKS. **Reservations:** Not accepted. **Location:** Same building as the Waterfront Restaurant, opposite main wharf.

$ **Prices:** Pizzas WS$22–WS$38 ($11–$19), sandwiches and burgers WS$4–WS$8 ($2–$4), salads WS$4 ($2). No credit cards.

Open: Mon–Sat 8am–9pm.

Clipper Arcade actually is a covered walkway alongside the Waterfront Restaurant. Order from The Godfather's fast-food counter and then either take your meal away or eat it at one of the tables in the covered walkway. The reasonably tasty pizzas come with a variety of toppings in both medium and large sizes. For something lighter, try a hot dog, burger, or sandwich. Something heavier? A plate of steak, french fries, and salad costs WS$12 ($6).

BUDGET

COFFEE 'N' THINGS, off Beach Rd., west of Town Clock. Tel. 21-038.

Cuisine: SNACK BAR. **Location:** Shares a shop with Carol 'n' Mark Boutique, down an alley off Beach Rd. in the block west of Town Clock.

$ **Prices:** WS$3–WS$5 ($1.50–$2.50). No credit cards.

Open: Mon–Fri 8am–4:30pm, Sat 8am–12:30pm.

Frieda Paul's snack bar shares space with her boutique. It's a fine place for a leisurely breakfast or snack during your shopping spree, but you'd better get there by noon for lunch: Apians eat promptly at midday, and all the good items will disappear within a few minutes after the stroke of 12. Freida serves light lunches, scones, cakes, juices, teas, and coffee, all at very reasonable prices. The tropical tables and chairs make for a very relaxing snack.

DAPHNE'S COFFEE SHOP, Beach Rd. at Ifi'ifi St. Tel. 22-400.

Cuisine: SNACK BAR. **Location:** First floor of John Williams Building.

$ **Prices:** Meals WS$3–WS$6 ($1.50–$3). No credit cards.

Open: Mon–Fri 7am–4pm, Sat 7am–12:30pm.

You'll find me at Daphne's pleasant if slightly cramped little place between 8:30 and 9am, scarfing down a hearty cooked breakfast while watching the world news on Cable News Network. The menu is posted on one wall; in addition to the full breakfasts, it features soups, New Zealand–style hot pies, burgers, sandwiches, tuna salads, and—if your sweet tooth can stand a piece—yummy coconut–passion fruit pie. The joint is a little cramped because it shares space with Daphne's array of clothing and handcrafts. Some of her tie-dyed lavalavas and straw mats turn up as table cloths and placemats, lending charm to the eatery side of the business.

RJ'S ICE CREAM PARLOUR AND COFFEE SHOP, Vaea St. Tel. 20-941.

Cuisine: SNACK BAR. **Location:** On Vaea St. just off Beach Rd. at Town Clock.

$ **Prices:** WS$2.50–WS$10 ($1.25–$5). No credit cards.

Open: Mon–Fri 8am–3pm, Sat 8am–1pm; sidewalk ice-cream take-out daily 8am–10pm (may offer food items in 1992).

Don't be fooled by the center-of-town storefront appearance, for RJ's air-conditioned interior has several tables pleasantly appointed with small flower bouquets. He also carries some very good food in addition to the cold stuff. Full cooked breakfasts will get you started, and huge, fresh sandwiches (the bread is baked on the premises) go well after a morning walking around Apia. For something hot, try the daily meat pie special.

6. EVENING ENTERTAINMENT

SAMOAN DANCE SHOWS

Western Samoa is no different from the other Polynesian countries in that watching a traditional dance show is a highlight of any visit. Samoan dance movements are graceful and emphasize the hands more than the hips; the costumes feature more tapa cloth and fine mats than flowers. While the dance shows are not as lively or as colorful as those in Tahiti and the Cook Islands, they are definitely worth seeing.

Other than the dance shows, nightlife in Apia centers on several pubs that attract local clientele. Most of these have live bands on Friday (the biggest night) and Saturday. Thanks largely to citizens outraged by bars opening in residential neighborhoods, pubs legally must close at midnight throughout the week (none are open on Sunday). As a practical matter, some of them keep right on going into the wee hours.

AGGIE GREY'S HOTEL, Beach Rd. Tel. 22-880.

The famous hotel puts on dance shows as part of its fiafia feast nights; check with them to find out when the shows are on. Even if you don't pay for the feast, you can wander into the bar under the big fale, order a cold Vailima, and watch the performance.

Prices: Dinner WS$32 ($16). Beers and drinks WS$3 ($1.50) and up.

Times: Usually 7pm (Wednesday during my recent visit).

HOTEL KITANO TUSITALA, Beach Rd., Mulinu'u Peninsula. Tel. 21-122.

Dance shows are also performed here as part of the fiafia nights; check with the hotel to find out when the shows are on. You don't have to pay for the feast, you can wander into the bar, order a drink, and watch the performance. On other evenings from 9pm to midnight, the Tusitala provides live music for dancing under its main fale, to the left of the reception area.

Prices: Dinner WS$32 ($16). Beers and drinks WS$3 ($1.50) and up.

Times: Usually 7pm (Thursday and Saturday during my recent visit).

MARGREY-TA'S LAGOON BEER GARDEN, Beach Rd., opposite main wharf. Tel. 23-440.

This beer garden actually is in a tropical garden setting, complete with thatch pavilions, near the main wharf, Aggie Grey's Hotel, and the Waterfront Restaurant. One night a week features a Samoan dance show staged by the owner's family and friends. Other nights, especially on Friday, bands play for dancing. This is a fun place to have a few beers with the locals. You shouldn't have to pay the cover charge if you get in by 7:30pm.

Prices: Cover WS$3 ($1.50) (performance nights only). Beer and drinks WS$3 ($1.50).

Times: Usually 9:30pm (on Friday during my recent visit).

PUB CRAWLING

The clubs listed below are those with live entertainment and dancing at least 1 night a week. In addition, there are several bars along the Beach Road waterfront that sell libations to the sounds of recorded tunes. Although you would never believe it by the slapped-together facade and worse-than-plain furniture on its sidewalk terrace, the most popular with local expatriate residents is **Otto's Reef** (tel. 22-691). Another favored watering hole is **The Loveboat** (tel. 24-065). Both are near the Catholic Cathedral and are open Monday to Saturday from 5pm to midnight.

BEACHCOMBER BAR AND NIGHT CLUB, Mulinu'u Rd. Tel. 20-248.

North of the Kitano Tusitala Hotel, this club has rock bands on Friday and Saturday nights, and recorded discotheque music Monday through Thursday nights. The clientele generally is older, more affluent, and well behaved than at some of the other clubs. Hours are 3pm to midnight Monday to Saturday.

Admission: WS$3 ($1.50) if live music. **Prices:** Drinks WS$3 ($1.50) and up.

LE LALAGA BAR, Fugalei St., 3 blocks inland from market. Tel. 20-673.

Francis Leelo, who lived in the United States for a number of years, started this bar in his backyard by selling a fine mat for a keg of beer; hence the name Le LaLaga ("The Fine Mat" in Samoan). He started out in a small fale, which now is the central bar of a much larger and very eclectic collection of roofs. Francis has had as many as 600 dancers on his floor on good nights. Hours are Monday to Saturday 3pm to midnight. Bands play rock and island tunes each night starting at 8pm.

Prices: Cover WS$3 ($1.50). Drinks and beers WS$3 ($1.50) and up.

MOUNT VAEA CLUB, corner Vaea and Vaitele Sts. Tel. 21-627.

This institution keeps rolling along as Apia's answer to the Banana Court Bar in Rarotonga and the late, much-lamented Quinn's Bar in Papeete. Don't expect much charm here, just loud music, much talk, a packed house of young Samoans, and an occasional fight around midnight on Friday and Saturday. Women should exercise caution if visiting this South Seas joint alone.

Admission: WS$3 ($1.50) weekends. **Prices:** Drinks WS$3 ($1.50).

7. AN EASY EXCURSION TO SAVAI'I

West of Upolu, the green mountains of Savai'i rise out of the sea and into the clouds across the 13-mile-wide Apolima Strait. The biggest Polynesian island outside Hawaii,

Savai'i is half again as large as Upolu, yet it has only a third as many people as its smaller and more prosperous neighbor, and they live in villages mainly along the east and south coasts. Elsewhere, Savai'i is made up of practically deserted lava fields and forests. It's chain of volcanic craters are considered to be dormant (the last major eruption occurred in 1911).

On Savai'i, rural Samoan life has changed less than on any other island, and travelers can visit picturesque villages sitting on the edge of the lagoon.

You can organize a trip to Savai'i yourself, but the easiest way is to contact one of the tour operators mentioned in the "Organized Tours" section under "What to See and Do" in this chapter. For example, **Oceania Tours** (tel. 24-443) has a 2-day, 1-night package starting at U.S. $75, including round-trip boat trip, transfers to the Safua Hotel, and a ½-day tour of Savai'i.

GETTING THERE

Polynesian Airlines (tel. 21-261 or 22-172) runs a shuttle between Faleolo International Airport and Maota airstrip, near Salelologa on the southeast coast of Savai'i. It also has several flights a day from Fagali'i airstrip, just east of Apia, to Maota. (An airstrip at Asau, the pretty town on the Savai'i's northwest coast, was destroyed by Cyclone Ofa in 1990; plans to rebuild had not been announced at press time.) Round-trip fares are WS$42 ($21) on the Faleolo-Maota shuttle; WS$55 ($27.50) from Fagali'i. If you want a reserved seat out of Fagali'i, add WS$15 ($7.50).

Passenger and automobile **ferries** operate between both Apia's main wharf and Mulifanua Wharf on the western end of Upolu, and Salelologa on Savai'i. The schedule calls for several departures daily, but it tends to change with the weather and condition of the ship. The fare is WS$8 ($4) each way between Apia and Salelologa; WS$6 ($3) each way between Mulifanua Wharf and Salelologa. Local buses leave regularly from the Apia market for Mulifanua Wharf. For more information, check the bulletin board in the visitors bureau or contact the **Western Samoa Shipping Corporation** (tel. 20-935) over the Ministry of Transport opposite the main wharf.

Off to the left during the ferry ride from Upolu to Savai'i, Manono and Apolima islands are visible. The latter is a volcanic crater, one side of which has fallen into the sea. On the shore where the collapsed side left a hole in the crater, you can see the village of Apolimatuai. Small boats shuttle between the two islands and Mulifanua Wharf, and it's possible to ride over to them for a look around. There are no hotels or restaurants on either island.

GETTING AROUND

A very limited number of **taxis** meet the planes and ferry; the fares are set by the government, and you can get a copy of the rate listings at the visitors bureau or at the Ministry of Transport before leaving Apia. The one-way fare from the Salelologa ferry wharf to Asau on the other end of the island, for example, is WS$60 ($30).

Local **buses** leave Salelologa shortly after the first ferry of the day arrives, and it's possible to take one of them as far as Asau, 55 miles and several hours away. The problem is that the buses make only one trip a day, which means that they don't turn around and come back (if at all) until around 3am the next morning. As a result, if you want to travel all 107 miles around Savai'i by bus, you'll have to remain at Asau for at least 1 night and travel a good part of the way in the dark.

Most visitors see the sights of the island on tours organized by the Savai'i hotels. An alternative would be to go to Salelologa by air or ferry and catch a bus to Asau. The road on the north shore, which crosses the lava fields, is paved only part of the way, and the remainder is rugged going. The south-coast road is paved all the way to Asau but misses the lava fields. Either way, the bus trip isn't easy or short, but you'll have an opportunity to meet your Samoan fellow passengers.

There are few vehicles to rent on Savai'i, and the rental-car companies in Apia frown on customers taking their vehicles on the ferries.

WHAT TO SEE & DO

The two hotels mentioned below offer tours of at least part of the island. Be smart. Take one rather than trying to find your way around this island with so little public transport. The guides will give you insights into Samoan culture—perhaps Savai'i's strongest selling point—that you won't get on your own.

Mount Matavanu was last active between 1905 and 1911, when it sent a long lava flow down to the northeast coast, burying villages and fields before backing up behind the reef and filling in a bay. It very nearly inundated the village of Mauga, which itself sits at the rim of an extinct volcano's cone. Thousands of people left Savai'i during the eruption and settled on Upolu. Today the lava field is populated primarily by wildflowers. Near Mauga there are long skinny caves known as lava tubes and an unusual rectangular indentation known as the **Virgin's Grave.**

On the south coast near Vailoa, especially on the Letolo Plantation, stand ancient **stone structures** similar to the ceremonial temples, or marae, in French Polynesia and the Cook Islands. These are so old, however, that the Samoans no longer have legends explaining their original function.

WHERE TO STAY & DINE

The hotels have the only restaurants on Savai'i.

VAISALA HOTEL, P.O. Box 570, Apia. Tel. 53-111 on Savai'i, or 22-557 in Apia. Fax 23-396. 27 rms (18 with bath). **Location:** On a white-sand beach at Vaisala.

$ Rates (in U.S. dollars only): $38.50 single; $44 double; $20 per person round-trip transfers. AE, MC, V.

This Samoan-owned hotel has a lovely location on a hill overlooking a white sandy beach and Vaisala Bay near Asau. Manager Papu Vaal has 18 rooms with their own kitchenettes, bathrooms, and tea- and coffee-making facilities and nine rooms that share common toilets and showers. One of the two bars stays open all day and evening. A restaurant on a long balcony overlooking the bay serves three meals a day. The Vaisala rents vans for tours of the island, with the cost depending on the number of persons going along.

SAFUA HOTEL, P.O. Box 5002, Salelologa, Savai'i. Tel. 24-262 or 24-202 in Apia. Fax 22-255. Telex 220. 9 fales (all with bath). **Location:** Lalomalava village, southeast coast, 4 miles north of wharf.

$ Rates (in U.S. dollars only): $48 single including three meals; $70 double including three meals; $10 per person dormitory including breakfast; $5 per person campground; $15 per person village accommodation including three meals. No credit cards.

This somewhat rustic hotel is known not so much for the quality of its accommodations as for its owner, Moelagi Jackson, who holds two chiefly titles in her own right. She prepares excellent and very large Samoan-style meals, and takes guests on highly informative sightseeing and cultural tours of the island, including picnic lunches and a swim. Her cultural tours visit villages for demonstrations of tapa making and other handcraft skills. Full-day sightseeing or cultural tours cost about U.S. $20 per person, but they won't go unless they have four people—or fewer willing to pay a total of U.S. $80. Half-day sightseeing tours are U.S. $10 per person, with a minimum of U.S. $40. Moelagi can arrange accommodation with local families if you want to stay in a Samoan village.

CHAPTER 9

AMERICAN SAMOA

The 7-mile ride into Pago Pago from the airport provides a fitting introduction to American Samoa. The road twists and turns along a gorgeous rocky coastline, at places rounding the cliffs of headlands that come down to the sea, at others curving along beaches in small bays backed by narrow valleys. All the way, the surf pounds on the reef. When you make the last turn at Blount's Point, there before you are the walls of fabled Pago Pago Harbor. The physical beauty of this little island, known as Tutuila, competes with the splendor of Moorea and Bora Bora in French Polynesia.

But you notice right away that this is an American place, for the roads—all paved with smooth asphalt—are crowded with automobiles and buses, and you may well hit a traffic jam before you get into Pago Pago. Big police cruisers, their drivers bedecked with revolvers, patrol the streets. Modern shopping centers, which could be in Honolulu or Los Angeles, are in marked contrast to the small shops and clapboard stores in other South Pacific countries, including next-door Western Samoa. The more you see, the more you realize that American Samoa is a blend of new Western wealth and old Samoan tradition.

1. INFORMATION, ENTRY REQUIREMENTS & MONEY

INFORMATION

The friendly staff of the **American Samoa Office of Tourism,** P.O. Box 1147, Pago Pago, AS 96799 (tel. 633-1091, fax 633-1094), have offices in the Harbor Wing of the Rainmaker Hotel. They are the ground floor offices nearest the street as you face the hotel. Staff members can provide information about the territory. They also act as booking agents for the *Fale, Fala Ma Ti* or homestay program (see "Where to Stay" in this chapter).

The Delegate from American Samoa to the U.S. Congress also dispenses some tourist information. The address: U.S. House of Representatives, Washington, DC 20515 (tel. 202/225-4906).

ENTRY REQUIREMENTS

Technically, U.S. citizens need only proof of citizenship (a birth certificate will do) to enter American Samoa. They will need valid passports to enter Western Samoa,

WHAT'S SPECIAL ABOUT AMERICAN SAMOA

Natural Spectacles

- ☐ Pago Pago: Sheer, green-shrouded walls drop almost into the South Pacific's most magnificent harbor.

Parks/Gardens

- ☐ National Park of American Samoa: Beautiful beaches, serrated mountain ridges, colorful reefs punctuate America's newest.

Literary Shrines

- ☐ Sadie's: An upscale restaurant now occupies the seedy boarding house where W. Somerset Maugham created Sadie Thompson in "Rain."
- ☐ Ta'u: Much of the new national park is on this Manu'a Group island where Margaret Mead came of age in Samoa.

however, and having them speeds reentry into the United States Citizens of other nations must have passports to enter American Samoa. Everyone must possess a ticket for onward passage. **Visas** are not required for stays of up to 30 days. Application for extensions of up to 90 days must be made at the Immigration Office in Fagatogo. For more information, contact the Chief Immigration Officer, American Samoa Government, Pago Pago, AS 96799 (tel. 633-4203).

Immunizations are required only if a person has been in an infected yellow fever or cholera area within 14 days of arrival at Pago Pago.

Customs: Visitors may bring 1 gallon of liquor or wine and either 200 cigarettes, 50 cigars, or 1 pound of tobacco into American Samoa without paying duty. Illegal drugs and firearms are prohibited, and pets will be quarantined.

Persons arriving in the United States are permitted to bring in two cartons of cigarettes, 1 gallon of alcoholic beverages, and $1,200 worth of other merchandise purchased in American Samoa, provided they have stayed in the territory at least 48 hours. A flat 10% duty is charged on the next $2,400 worth of merchandise purchased in American Samoa, and U.S. residents need declare only the total value of such purchases up to $3,200; over that amount, they must itemize their purchases. These limits, which are double those for goods purchased in other countries, apply only to items brought into the United States. The regular rules apply, for example, on goods purchased in American Samoa and brought into Australia and New Zealand.

MONEY

U.S. bank notes and coins are used in American Samoa. Western Samoan currency is not used, nor can it be exchanged in American Samoa. There is no bargaining over prices.

WHAT THINGS COST IN AMERICAN SAMOA	U.S. $
Taxi from airport to Pago Pago	10.00
Double room at Rainmaker Hotel (expensive)	85.00
Double room at Apiolegaga Inn (moderate)	50.00
Double room at Herb & Sia's Motel (budget)	38.00
Lunch for one at Soli & Mark's Family Restaurant (moderate)	10.00
Lunch for one at Paisano Pizza (budget)	5.50
Dinner for one, without wine, at Sadie's (expensive)	34.00
Dinner for one, without wine, at Soli & Mark's (moderate)	24.00
Dinner for one, without wine, at Paisano Pizza (budget)	9.00
Beer	2.25

	US$
Coca-Cola	1.00
Cup of coffee	.75
Roll of ASA 100 Kodacolor film, 36 exposures	6.00

2. GETTING THERE & GETTING AROUND

GETTING THERE

The runways at **Pago Pago International Airport** extend for half their length on landfills over the reef near the village of Tafuna, about 7 miles west of the Rainmaker Hotel. The open-air, island-style terminal complex has a snack bar, a duty-free shop with limited merchandise, and several small stores selling handcrafts, tropical clothing, and souvenirs.

The official taxi fares are $6 to the Rainmaker and about $8 to "downtown" Pago Pago, but they seldom are enforced. Expect to pay about $10 to the Rainmaker.

Local buses shuttle along the main road, which is about 1½ miles from the terminal. The bus fare to town is 50¢.

There is no departure tax on passengers leaving Pago Pago.

GETTING AROUND

The choices of transportation on Tutuila are rental cars, taxis, and "aiga buses," which, like *le truck* in Tahiti, have gaily painted passenger compartments built on the back of flatbed trucks. Daily air service and weekly boats go to the Manu'a Group, which is covered below as a side trip.

BY RENTAL CAR

American Samoa's rental-car firms have booths at the airport but staff them only when major international flights arrive unless passengers have made reservations.

Avis (tel. 699-4408, or toll free 800/331-1212 in the U.S.) rents air-conditioned cars for $40 a day, nonair-conditioned ones for $35, both with unlimited mileage, plus $7 for insurance. In addition, **Royal Samoan Car Rental** (tel. 633-2017 or 633-4545) and **Pavitt's U-Drive** (tel. 633-1456), both rent sedans and station wagons for that same price.

Driving Rules: Your valid home driver's license will be honored in American Samoa. Driving is on the right-hand side of the road, and traffic signs are the same as those used in the U.S. Speed limits are 15 m.p.h. in the built-up areas and 25 m.p.h. on the open road. Those may seem awfully slow, but there will be too much traffic in Pago Pago and too many curves in the road elsewhere to drive much faster.

BY BUS

It sometimes seems that every extended family on Tutuila owns an "aiga bus," since so many of these gaily painted vehicles prowl the roads from early in the morning until sunset every day except Sunday, when they are put to use to haul the family to church. Basically they run from the villages to the market in Pago Pago and back, picking up anyone who waves along the way. To get off, push the button for the bell as you approach your destination. Some buses leave the market and run to Fagasa on the north coast or to the east end of the island; others go from the market to the west.

IMPRESSIONS

A stout cop in full American fig—sun-glasses, dark uniform, badges, night-stick, revolver, cap, cigar—growled "Have a nice day" as I squelched over the ship's stern-ramp and was admitted to Uncle Sam's paradise in the South Seas.
—JOHN DYSON, 1982

None goes from one end of the island to the other, so you'll have to change at the market in order to do a stem-to-stern tour of Tutuila. The drivers are friendly and helpful, so just ask how far they go in each direction. Fares are between 50¢ and $1.50 a ride.

BY TAXI

There are **taxi stands** at the airport (tel. 699-1179) and at the Pago Pago market (no phone). The taxi companies are **Aeto Cab** (tel. 633-2366), **Black Ace** (tel. 633-5445), **Island Taxi** (tel. 633-5645), and **Samoa Cab Service** (tel. 633-5870 or 633-5871). None of the taxis has a meter, so be sure to negotiate the fare before driving off. As a starting point for your discussions, the fares should be about $1 a mile.

AMERICAN SAMOA

American Express There was no American Express representative operating in American Samoa during my recent visit. See the "Fast Facts: South Pacific" in Chapter 2 for information about reporting lost or stolen credit cards or traveler's checks.

Area Code The international country code is 684.

Baby-sitters The hotels can arrange for baby-sitters at reasonable rates.

Bookstores The Transpac Duty Free Shop under Sadie's Restaurant and 3U2 Dimension in the Rainmaker Hotel both carry a reasonably wide selection of paperback books and current U.S. magazines.

Business Hours Normal shopping hours are Mon–Fri 8:30am–5pm, Sat 8:30am–noon. Government offices are open Mon–Fri 7:30am–4pm. Some of the larger retail outlets stay open Fri until 9pm.

Car Rentals See "Getting Around" in this chapter.

Climate See "When to Go—Climate, Holidays and Events" in Chapter 7.

Clothing Lightweight, informal summer clothing is appropriate all year, with perhaps a light sweater or wrap for evenings June–Sept. I always carry a folding umbrella or plastic raincoat, since it can rain any time of the day or night in Pago Pago. Young American Samoans have adopted Western-style dress, including blue jeans and shorts of respectable length, although the traditional wraparound lavalava still is worn by many older men and women. In keeping with Samoan custom regarding modesty, visitors should not wear bathing suits or other skimpy clothing away from the hotels. This is not a French territory, so women must wear their bikini tops.

Credit Cards American Express, VISA, MasterCard, and Diners Club credit cards are accepted by the hotels, rental-car firms, and airlines. Otherwise, it's best to carry enough cash to cover your anticipated expenses.

IMPRESSIONS

It was only fair to declare that my spirits were in any case fairly mildewed by the solid dementing rain.
—JOHN DYSON, 1982

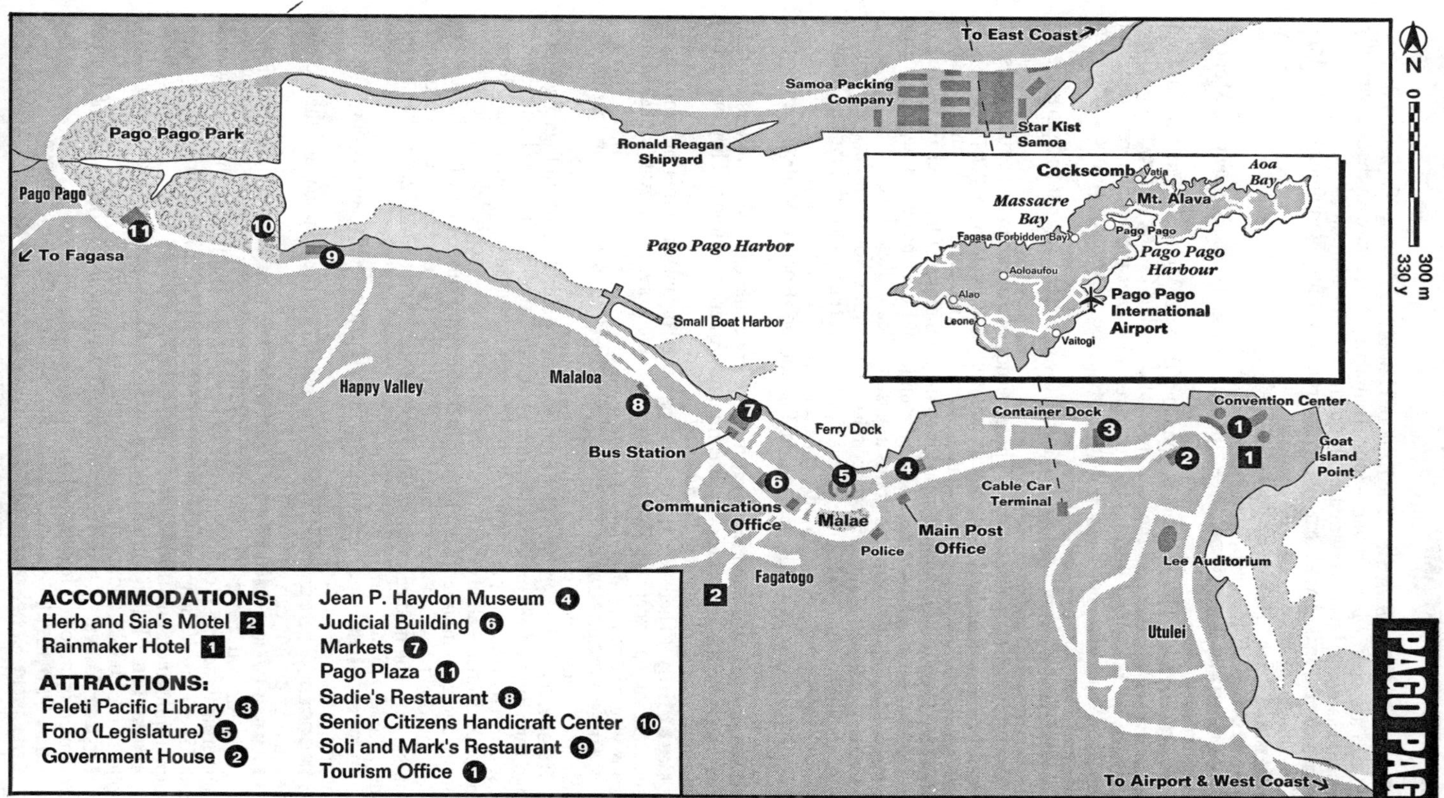
PAGO PAGO
N
0
300 m
330 y
To East Coast
Samoa Packing Company
Star Kist Samoa
Ronald Reagan Shipyard
Pago Pago Park
Pago Pago
To Fagasa
Pago Pago Harbor
Small Boat Harbor
Happy Valley
Malaloa
Bus Station
Ferry Dock
Communications Office
Malae
Police
Main Post Office
Fagatogo
Cable Car Terminal
Container Dock
Convention Center
Goat Island Point
Lee Auditorium
Utulei
To Airport & West Coast
Cockscomb
Vatia
Aoa Bay
Massacre Bay
Mt. Alava
Fagasa (Forbidden Bay)
Pago Pago
Pago Pago Harbour
Aoloaufou
Alao
Leone
Vaitogi
Pago Pago International Airport
ACCOMMODATIONS:
Herb and Sia's Motel 2
Rainmaker Hotel 1
ATTRACTIONS:
Feleti Pacific Library 3
Fono (Legislature) 5
Government House 2
Jean P. Haydon Museum 4
Judicial Building 6
Markets 7
Pago Plaza 11
Sadie's Restaurant 8
Senior Citizens Handicraft Center 10
Soli and Mark's Restaurant 9
Tourism Office 1

Currency Exchange The Bank of Hawaii and the Amerika Samoa Bank in Fagatogo are open Mon–Fri 9am–3pm. Transacting business with them is virtually the same as doing business with a bank on the U.S. mainland.

Customs/Immigration See "Information, Entry Requirements & Money" in this chapter.

Dentist See "Hospital," below.

Doctor See "Hospital," below.

Documents Required See "Information, Entry Requirements & Money" in this chapter.

Drugstores The Lyndon B. Johnson Tropical Medical Center in Faga'alu west of Pago Pago (turn off the main road at Tom Ho Chung's store) has the only pharmacy on the island (there are drugstores with over-the-counter remedies and cosmetics, but they don't fill prescriptions). The pharmacy is open Mon–Fri 8am–4pm, Sat–Sun 8–11am.

Electricity American Samoa uses 110-volt electric current and plugs identical to those in the U.S.

Embassies/Consulates The governor of American Samoa is a consular official of the U.S. federal government and can issue temporary passports to U.S. citizens and nationals who lose theirs, provided they have some other proof of citizenship. Applications should be made to the Immigration Office (tel. 633-4203), in the Department of Legal Affairs. The Republic of Korea has a consulate, and the Republic of China (Taiwan) maintains a liaison office in Pago Pago.

Emergencies The emergency telephone number for the police, fire department, and ambulance is 911. The emergency room at the Lyndon B. Johnson Tropical Medical Center (tel. 633-5555) in Faga'alu is open 24 hours a day.

Eyeglasses Go to the Lyndon B. Johnson Tropical Medical Center (see "Hospital," below).

Firearms Although the local police carry American-style revolvers on their belts, don't count on bringing a firearm into American Samoa. They are tightly controlled, and a permit will be required.

Gambling There are no casinos or other organized forms of gambling in American Samoa except for slot machines in some stores and private clubs. Money also is wagered at very popular bingo games.

Hairdressers/Barbers The Rainmaker Hotel has a beauty parlor, and there are several others in Pago Pago.

Hospital The Lyndon B. Johnson Tropical Medical Center in Faga'alu west of Pago Pago (turn off the main road at Tom Ho Chung's store) may be a classic example of socialized medicine, but it's one of the better hospitals in the South Pacific. To see a doctor or dentist—all of whom were trained in the U.S.—go to the front desk, fill out a form, and get a number that will be called when your turn comes. The visit will cost $2 if you don't have an appointment, $1 if you do. The outpatient clinic is open 24 hours a day. The medical center's main phone number is 633-1222. The "emergency line" is 633-5555.

Information See "Information, Entry Requirements, and Money" in this chapter.

Insects There are no dangerous insects in American Samoa, and the plentiful mosquitoes do not carry malaria.

Laundry/Dry Cleaning The hotels will take care of laundry and dry cleaning, or you can carry your dirty clothes to Mary's Home Style Self-Service Laundromat, next to Herb & Sia's Motel in Fagatogo. You'll need 50¢ to wash a load and 75¢ to dry it. Soap powder is extra. Mary's is open Mon–Fri 7am–9pm, Sat 7am–10pm, and Sun 10am–10pm.

Libraries Feleti Pacific Library, west of the Rainmaker Hotel, has a good collection of books about the South Pacific.

Liquor Laws There are no unusual laws to worry about. Most of the beer consumed is imported from the U.S.

Lost Property Contact the police. See "Emergencies," above.

Luggage Storage/Lockers There are no lockers in American Samoa. The hotels will keep your extra bags if necessary.

Maps The Office of Tourism in the Rainmaker Hotel distributes a one-sheet set of maps of the islands. The best commercial map available is *Islands of Samoa* by cartographer James A. Bier (University of Hawaii Press). Look for it in the 3U2 Dimension shop in the Rainmaker or at Transpac under Sadie's Restaurant.

Newspapers/Magazines American Samoa has two tabloid newspapers which carry local news, the weekly *Samoa Journal* and the daily *Samoa News*. Both papers' coverage of local events can be quite colorful. The 3U2 Dimension shop in the Rainmaker Hotel carries a reasonably wide selection of paperbook books and current U.S. magazines.

Photographic Needs A wide variety of film is available at reasonable prices. Samoa Photo Express, in the Pago Plaza mall at the head of the harbor (tel. 633-2374), has specialized, 1-hour film developing of color-print film.

Police See "Emergencies," above.

Post Office The United States Postal Service's main post office is in Fagatogo. U.S. postage rates apply, which means that your first-class letters will go to the U.S. via air for 29¢ (or 30¢, depending on whether the Postal Rate Commission has raised the rate by the time you read this). Unless you pay the first-class priority mail rate, parcel post is sent by ship and will take several weeks to reach the U.S. The main post office is open Mon–Fri 8am–4pm, Sat 8am–noon. The ZIP Code for American Samoa is 96799. United Parcel Service has a agency in the Pago Plaza mall at the head of the harbor.

Radio/TV Those transmitters atop Mount Alava are used during the day to send educational TV programs to the territory's public schools and to transmit the Cable News Network and live sporting events (Samoa is the one place in the South Pacific where you can keep up with what's happening worldwide at any time). At night they broadcast three channels of U.S. network entertainment programs which were taped a week earlier off the Honolulu stations and flown to Pago Pago (you may already have seen the same shows at home). The broadcasts can be seen 80 miles away in Western Samoa.

The territory has one FM and one AM radio station. The latter, WVUV, broadcasts around the clock and sounds very much like an American "Top 40" station with a little Samoan language thrown in for good measure. American network news broadcasts are transmitted on the hour. WVUV can often be heard at night as far away as Tonga.

Religious Services The Congregational Christian church, a Protestant denomination that grew from the London Missionary Society's early work in the islands, is the largest church in American Samoa. Others are the Assembly of God church, the Baha'i Faith, the Baptist church, the Roman Catholic church, the Church of Christ, the Church of God of Prophecy, Jehovah's Witnesses, the Seventh-Day Adventist church, the Methodist church, and the Church of Jesus Christ of Latter-Day Saints.

Rest Rooms You will have to rely on the restaurants, hotels, and bars.

Safety Street crime is not a serious problem in American Samoa except late at night around Pago Pago Harbor. Fa'a Samoa and its rules of communal ownership are still in effect, however, so it's wise not to leave cameras, watches, or other valuables lying around unattended. See the "Fast Facts: South Pacific" in Chapter 2 for more warnings.

Shoe Repairs Ask your hotel staff to recommend a cobbler.

Taxes The government of American Samoa imposes no sales tax; however, an import tax of 5% is imposed on most merchandise (it's much stiffer on tobacco and alcoholic beverages). There is no airport departure tax.

Taxis See "Getting Around" in this chapter.

Telegrams/Telex See "Telephone," below.

Telephone The telephone system in American Samoa is almost identical to that in the U.S., although service is not quite as sophisticated or as efficient. The pay telephones are the same type used in phone booths throughout the U.S. The number for **directory assistance** is 411. For **emergencies,** dial 911. For the time of day, dial 633-4949 (if you really care what time it is).

Local subscribers can dial their own international calls, and calls to American

Samoa can be dialed directly from areas of the U.S. where such service is available. The **country code is 684.**

Visitors can place overseas calls from the International Communications Office, which is diagonally across the Fagatogo *malae* (village green) from the Fono building. Station-to-station calls to the U.S. mainland cost $6.60 for the first 3 minutes and 90¢ for each additional minute. The office accepts credit cards issued by the American Bell telephone companies; you can also pay cash in advance or reverse the charges.

Time Local time in American Samoa is 3 hours behind Pacific standard time (4 hours behind during daylight saving time). In other words, if it's noon standard time in California and 3pm in New York, it's 9am in Pago Pago. If daylight saving time is in effect, it's 8am in American Samoa.

The islands are east of the international date line; therefore, they share the same date with North America and are one day behind Tonga, Fiji, Australia, and New Zealand. That's worth remembering if you're going on to those countries or will be arriving in Pago Pago from one of them.

Tipping Although this is an American territory, there is no tipping in American Samoa.

Weights/Measures American Samoa is the only country or territory in the South Pacific whose official system of weights and measures is the same as used in the U.S.—pounds and miles, not kilograms and kilometers.

3. WHAT TO SEE & DO

If you move fast enough, you can see American Samoa in one day as a **side trip from Western Samoa.** Here's how to do it:

Choose a clear day and an early-morning flight from Apia to Pago Pago. Head directly for the cable car and, if it's running, ride to the top of Mount Alava. Back down on solid ground, take the walking tour of Pago Pago described below, then stop for lunch. Afterwards, if you haven't rented a car, grab an aiga bus at the market for a ride out to the east end, followed by another bus ride to the west end. On the way back, you can get off and call a taxi or walk the 1½ miles from the main road to the airport for a late-afternoon return flight to Apia. You should be able to do all that for less than $100 per person, not counting lunch. Add another $60 for a rental car.

If you don't want to do the drive yourself, American Samoa's leading **tour operators** have booths to the left as you enter the Rainmaker Hotel. They are open from 8am to 4pm daily and offer sightseeing trips along the routes described below.

A CABLE-CAR RIDE

It has been an on-again, off-again operation during the past few years, but if it's running, a cable-car ride across Pago Pago Harbor to the top of 1,600-foot Mount Alava is an experience never to be forgotten.

Pago Pago Harbor was once a volcanic crater, and the land on the north shore rises from the water, almost like a wall, to heights in excess of 1,600 feet. When the then-governor H. Rex Lee decided to build a television transmitter back in the 1960s, the logical place to put it was on top of the highest point on the wall, Mount Alava. As building a permanent road to haul the equipment up there was impractical (as later fruitless attempts were to prove), he used helicopters to install one end of a cable on top of the mountain. The other end was emplaced more than a mile away on Solo Hill, which stands on the opposite side of the harbor above the Rainmaker Hotel.

The television transmitter has long since been installed, but the aerial tramway still carries maintenance personnel—and sometimes anyone else with a stout heart and $5 for the round-trip—on one of the most hair-raising rides in the entire South Pacific. Hanging below the cable, the car starts out slowly from Solo Hill and crosses the docks and harbor below before starting a steep ascent over the tuna canneries and climbing the clifflike wall of Mount Alava. The last part of the ride seems to go straight up. The view from Mount Alava, however, is worth it. There at your feet is the entirety of magnificent Pago Pago Harbor, bent like an arm and nearly cutting the island in two. To the east and west marches the skinny spine of Tutuila, and on a clear day you can see Western Samoa and the Manu'a Group off in the far distance. Go early in the morning, for clouds at midday usually fog the station in, and staring at a gray wall is no fun.

To reach the tramway terminal on Solo Hill, take the road that runs behind the Lee Auditorium near the Rainmaker Hotel. When the car operates, it runs from 7:30am to 4pm Monday through Saturday.

Near the terminal is a monument to six servicemen and two civilians who were killed on April 17, 1980, when a U.S. Navy plane ran into the cable while flying over the harbor and crashed next to one wing of the Rainmaker Hotel. That isn't likely to happen again, since the harbor is now off-limits to aircraft.

A WALKING TOUR OF PAGO PAGO

Although the actual village of Pago Pago sits at the head of the harbor, everyone refers to the built-up area on the south shore of the harbor, including Fagatogo, the government and business center, as Pago Pago. The harbor is also called the Bay Area. Despite development that has come with economic growth of the territory, Pago Pago still has much of the old South Seas atmosphere that captivated W. Somerset Maugham when he visited and wrote "Rain" in the 1920s.

We'll begin our tour at the **Rainmaker Hotel** at the east end of the inner harbor, actually in the village of Utulei. Just across the main road from the hotel is a set of concrete steps that climb to **Government House,** the clapboard mansion built in 1903 to house the governor of American Samoa. Except for those who have business with the governor, the mansion is not open to the public. There is a nice view, however, from the top of the steps looking back over the hotel and across harbor to Rainmaker Mountain.

Back on the main road heading west toward town, we pass the **Feleti Pacific Library,** which has a good collection of books on the South Pacific. Beyond the busy port terminal is the **Jean P. Haydon Museum,** featuring exhibits on Samoan history, sea life, canoes, kava making, and traditional tools and handcrafts, including the finely woven mats that have such great value in Samoa and Tonga. The old iron-roofed building housing the museum was once the U.S. Navy's commissary. The museum is open from 10am to 3pm Monday through Friday except on holidays, and admission is free.

Every Samoan village has a **malae,** or open field, and the area across from the museum is Fagatogo's. The chiefs of Tutuila met on this malae in 1900 to sign the treaty that officially established the United States in Samoa. The round modern building across the road beside the harbor is the **Fono,** American Samoa's legislature; the visitors' galleries are open to the public. The ramshackle stores along the narrow streets on the other side of the malae were for half a century Pago Pago's "downtown," although like any other place under the Stars and Stripes, much business now is conducted in suburban shopping centers.

The big white clapboard building with columns, which from its colonial style looks as if it should be in South Carolina rather than the South Pacific, is the **Judicial Building,** home of the High Court of American Samoa (everyone calls it the Court House). A little farther along, next to the harbor, are the **produce and fish markets,** which are usually poorly stocked, especially when compared with the large, perpetually active market in Apia over in Western Samoa. The market also serves as the bus terminal.

Continuing west, the large wooden building now housing Sadie's Restaurant and Transpac Duty Free was once the rooming house where W. Somerset Maugham was marooned during a measles epidemic early this century.

The stroll to the head of the harbor leads past the small-boat refuge on the right, the large **Burns Philp department store** and supermarket on the left, and the **Senior Citizens Handicraft Center,** just before the tennis courts in **Pago Pago Park** on the right again. Much of this flat area is reclaimed land.

The first road to the left past Burns Philp leads to **Happy Valley,** where the U.S. Navy built concrete bunkers as its local command center during World War II. Some of the old structures are now used as homes.

The Asian-style building across the playing fields at the head of the harbor may look like a Chinese restaurant but in reality it is **Korea House,** a hospitality center for the Korean sailors who man many of the boats that bring tuna to the canneries. The canneries are in the large, industrial buildings on the north side of the harbor at the base of Mount Alava.

TOURING TUTUILA

THE NORTH COAST

An unmarked paved road turns off the main highway at Spenser's Store in Pago Pago village and leads up **Vaipito Valley,** across a ridge, and down to Fagasa, a village huddled beside picturesque Fagasa, or **Forbidden Bay,** on Tutuila's north shore. The road is steep but paved all the way, and the view from atop the ridge is excellent. The track up Mount Alava begins on the saddle (see "The National Park," below). Legend says that porpoises long ago led a group of three men and three women to safety in Fagasa Bay, which is treated as a porpoise sanctuary today.

THE EAST SIDE

The 18-mile drive from Pago Pago to the east end of Tutuila is worth taking. The excellent blacktop road skirts along the harbor, past the canneries and their fishy odor, and then winds around one headland after another into small bays, many of them with sandy beaches and good swimming holes over the reef. Watch particularly for **Pyramid Rock** and the **Lion's Head,** where you can wade out to a small beach.

From Aua, at the foot of Rainmaker Mountain, a switchbacking road runs across Rainmaker Pass (great views from up there) to the lovely village of **Vatia** on a bay of the same name. World War II pillboxes still dot the beach here. Lands of the national park of American Samoa besiege the village, which eventually should give access to some of the park's features. At the north end of Vatia Bay sits the skinny, offshore rock formation known as **The Cockscomb,** one of Tutuila's trademarks.

Another paved road leaves Faga'itua village and climbs to a saddle in the ridge, where it divides. The left fork goes down to Masefau Bay; the right goes to Masausi and Sa'ilele villages. Near the east end, a road from Amouli village cuts across Lemafa Saddle to **Aoa Bay** on the north coast.

Aunu'u Island will be visible from the main road as you near the east end of Tutuila. Aunu'u is the top of a small volcanic crater and has a village near a famous quicksand pit. Motorboats leave for it from the small-boat harbor at Au'asi on the southeast coast.

Alao and **Tula** villages on the east end of Tutuila are the oldest settlements in American Samoa. They have long, gorgeous surf beaches, but be careful of the undertow from waves driven by the prevailing southeast trade winds.

THE WEST SIDE

You probably saw some of Tutuila's rugged coast on the drive in from the airport west of Pago Pago, including the **Flower Pot,** a tall rock with coconut palms growing on its top sitting in the lagoon. About halfway from the airport to the Rainmaker Hotel is a road inland (at Tom Ho Chung's store) leading to the **Lyndon B. Johnson**

Tropical Medical Center in the Faga'alu Valley. If you feel like a hike, take the left fork in the road past the medical center, and when the pavement ends, follow the track to **Virgin Falls.** It's not the easiest walk, but the falls have a nice pool beneath them. Give yourself several hours for this sweaty outing.

The **airport** sits on the island's only sizable parcel of relatively flat land, and the main road from there west cuts through rolling hills and shopping centers until emerging on the rugged west end.

At Pava'ia'i village a road goes to the right and climbs to the village of A'oloaufou, high on a central plateau. A hiking trail leads from the village down the ridges to the north coast; from there it drops to A'asutuai on **Massacre Bay,** where the La Pérouse expedition was attacked in 1787. The French have put a monument there to the members of the expedition slain by Samoan warriors.

Back on the main road, head west and watch for a big sign on the left marking the turn to the villages of Illi'ili and Vaitogi. Follow the signs to **Vaitogi,** and once in the village, bear right at the fork to the beach. Take the one-lane track to the right along the beach, past some graves and the stone remains of an old church, and up a rocky headland through pandanus groves. When you reach the first clearing on the left, stop the car and walk over to the cliff. According to legend, Vaitogi once experienced such a severe famine that a blind old woman and her granddaughter jumped off this cliff and were turned into a shark and a turtle. Today the villagers reputedly can chant their names and the turtle and the shark will appear. You may not be lucky enough to see them, but the view of the south coast from **Turtle and Shark Point,** with the surf pounding the rocks below you, is superb.

The picturesque village of **Leone,** which sits on a white-sand beach in a small bay, was chosen by the Rev. John Williams as his landing place on Tutuila in 1830, and it became the cradle of Christianity in what was to become American Samoa. There is a monument to Williams in the village. The road beside the Catholic church leads about 1½ miles to **Leone Falls,** which has a freshwater pool for swimming (but never on Sunday).

The road from Leone to the western end of the island is quite scenic, as it winds in and out of small bays with sandy beaches and then climbs spectacularly across a ridge to Poloa village on the northwest coast.

THE NATIONAL PARK

The National Park of American Samoa has been coming into existence slowly since being authorized by the U.S. Congress in 1988. When complete, the park will encompass some extraordinarily beautiful shoreline, magnificent beaches, cliffs dropping into the sea, colorful reefs, and rain forest reaching up to serrated, mist-shrouded mountain peaks. Of more than 9,000 total acres, most of the park is on Ta'u and Olosega islands in the Manu'a Group. Since development is ongoing, pick up an updated copy of the park's boundaries and facilities from the Office of Tourism in the Rainmaker Hotel.

On Tutuila, the park essentially starts along the ridge atop Mount Alava and drops down sharp ridges and steep valleys to the north coast. It includes The Cockscomb. The park is accessible on foot from atop Mount Alava. Take the cable car if it's running and hike down; if it's not, a track to the summit begins at the top of the pass separating Pago Pago from Fagasa (Forbidden) Bay on the north shore. Another track begins at the summit and leads down steeply to Vatia village on the north shore; this

---

IMPRESSIONS

The melancholy irony of this smug little island is that American Samoa epitomises the state of comfortable dependence on cash and Western goods to which so many aspire.

—John Dyson, 1982

one is not as well maintained. It's not easy hiking these slippery paths, and you must take water and provisions with you.

Unlike other U.S. national parks, in which the federal government buys the land outright, the National Park of American Samoa will be on land leased from the villages, thereby protecting both the natural environment and traditional Samoan ownership customs.

SPORTS & RECREATION

You'll find a number of sporting activities in American Samoa to keep the muscles moving.

DEEP-SEA FISHING & SCUBA DIVING

Mahi mahi, wahoo, sailfish, blue marlin, barracuda, and yellowfin, dogtooth, and skyjack tuna abound in Samoan waters. And if you know where to go, the fringing reefs beckon to serious scuba divers. Chuck Brugman of **Dive Samoa, Inc.,** P.O. Box 3927, Pago Pago, AS 96799 (tel. 633-2183), takes guests on fishing and diving expeditions on his 28-foot dive boat. He charges $30 for a one-tank dive, $50 for a two-tank dive, and $50 per person per day for fishing trips, with a minimum of three persons required (or you pay the full $150). He has special rates for frequent customers and likes to go night diving. He also takes divers on expeditions to Ofu in the Manu'a Group.

GOLF

The par-70 **Lava Lava Golf Course** has 18 holes rambling across the relatively flat land between the airport and village of Illi'ili. For a starting time, call 699-9366 or 633-1191. Equipment is available to rent at the clubhouse, which has a restaurant and bar. The course is open 7 days a week.

HIKING

Several exciting trails await adventurous hikers. One is the often slippery track to the Mount Alava summit, where another trail drops down to Vatia on the north shore (see "The National Park," above). If it's running, the cable car gives easy access to the top; from the terminal, turn left and go down the steps to the trail head. Also from the Pago Pago–Fagasa Pass, a difficult track leads to the summit of Matafao Peak, at 2,143 feet the highest point on Tutuila. Another, more often used track descends from A'asufou village high in the interior down to A'asutuai village and the French monument at Massacre Bay. Remember to take water and sunblock, and that you will be crossing someone else's land at all times, so be polite. Don't hesitate to ask directions, but don't pose questions that require a yes-or-no answer.

TENNIS

Hard-surface public tennis courts can be used on a first-come, first-served basis in **Pago Pago Park** at the head of the harbor, provided that American Samoa's avid tennis buffs don't have a tournament or classes going on. The courts are lit for night play. Tennis is known as *tenisi* in Samoan.

SHOPPING

Local artisans have their handcraft wares for sale on Monday through Saturday (except on holidays) in the **Handicrafts Fale,** between the Fono building and the Jean P. Haydon Museum in the Fagatogo area of Pago Pago. Frankly, the best buys in American Samoa are **Reebok shoes,** but only if you come from Australia, New

Zealand, or another country where they are exorbitantly expensive (they cost about the same in Pago Pago as in the United States). The sporting-goods shop in the Samoa News Building, between the Rainmaker Hotel and post office in Fagatogo, usually carries them. If they don't, they will know who does. See "Information, Entry Requirements, and Money" in this chapter for how much you can bring into the United States from American Samoa without paying duty.

LUANA'S SOUTH SEA CURIOS, Fagatogo. Tel. 633-1850.

Luana Brugman, wife of scuba-diver Chuck mentioned above, has a wide variety of handcrafts and tropical fabrics from many South Pacific countries. Her shop is in the Samoa News Building between the Rainmaker and post office. Look for Tongan baskets and black-coral jewelry, shell necklaces, wood carvings, and polished nautilus shells. Luana's hours are from 9am to 5pm Monday to Friday, 10am to 2pm Saturday.

SENIOR CITIZENS HANDICRAFT MARKET, Pago Pago. Tel. 633-1251.

Behind the Development Bank of American Samoa in Pago Pago Park, at the head of the harbor, this shop has a worthy goal (to keep alive the old arts and make some money for senior citizens while doing it), but it hardly is worth the effort unless you happen to be passing by or just want to contribute. Frankly, it almost always has a very small selection of locally produced mats, shell necklaces, mat place settings, and straw hats. It's open from 8am to 4pm Monday through Friday, except on holidays.

3U2 DIMENSION, in the Rainmaker Hotel. Tel. 633-5834.

Although she sells the usual gift-shop items such as toiletries, books, and magazines (the latest from the United States), Barbara Ueligitone also features the work of her husband, well-known local artist Sau Ueligitone. While the artisans in Western Samoa have turned to tapa boards for their inspiration, Sau uses Samoan tattoos as his. Himself tattooed from waist to knee in the traditional manner, Sau does pen-and-ink reproductions of the motifs on T-shirts, lavalavas, handbags, and other items. They are unusual and definitely worth a look.

SOUTH PACIFIC DUTY FREE SHOPPERS, Pago Plaza, Pago Pago. Tel. 633-5032.

A number of shops specialize in duty-free merchandise, such as watches, cameras, electronic equipment, and perfumes. This company, which has the best selection, also has outlets at Aggie Grey's Hotel in Apia and at the international airports in both Samoas. This one is in the Pago Plaza mall at the head of the harbor. As is the case with all duty-free shopping in the South Pacific, look around before leaving home so you'll know a good deal when you see one. American Samoa is technically a duty-free port, but the local government imposes up to 100% duty on tobacco products and alcoholic beverages. Cigarettes and liquor, therefore, are no bargain for those used to U.S. prices.

EVENING ENTERTAINMENT

RAINMAKER HOTEL, Utulei, at entrance to harbor. Tel. 633-4241.

The hotel has varying nightly entertainment, including an occasional Samoan dance show. Call the hotel or check the schedule posted on a chalkboard each day in the hotel lobby. The Sadie Thompson Bar has live music beginning at happy hour Monday to Saturday and continuing into Friday and Saturday evenings.

Admission: Free. **Prices:** Beers $2.50. Drinks $3.50.

SADIE'S NIGHTCLUB, west of market in Malaloa area. Tel. 633-5981.

Go up the steps to Sadie's Restaurant and turn left to find the upmarket nightclub under a peaked roof hung with nautical decor. Large doors open to a terrace overlooking the harbor. Monday to Thursday evenings hear recorded music, but a live band pumps out dance music from 9pm to 2am Friday and Saturday. The bar opens when someone shows up to buy a drink.

Admission: Free. **Prices:** Beers $2.50. Drinks $3.50.

4. WHERE TO STAY

Only three hotels exist on Tutuila—the Rainmaker Hotel and two small, pension-style establishments—and the Rainmaker has been in deplorable condition for years. Given this situation, the American Samoa Office of Tourism matches visitors seeking inexpensive accommodation with local families willing to take in paying guests. This **homestay program** is known as Fale, Fala Ma Ti. Prices vary from $25 to $40 a night, depending on the home. Some are Western-style houses, other are Samoan fales. All of them have modern toilets and showers. Some homes also have space for campers who bring their own tents. The Samoan hospitality will more than make up for the simple accommodation. Don't show up in Pago Pago and expect Emma Randall and her crew to work something out for you on the spot. Prior arrangements are required. Contact the Office of Tourism, P.O. Box 1147, Pago Pago, AS 96799 (tel. 633-1092, fax 633-1094, telex 782-500).

RAINMAKER HOTEL, P.O. Box 996, Pago Pago, AS 96799. Tel. 633-4241. Fax 633-5959. Telex 782-511. 184 rms (about 40 serviceable). A/C TEL **Location:** In Utulei at entrance to inner harbor.

$ Rates: $72 single, $85 double in Beach Wing. AE, DC, MC, V.

This establishment, now of infamous condition, was built with government backing in the 1960s and was operated for several years as an Inter-Continental Hotel when Pan American World Airways landed at Pago Pago on its way from the United States to New Zealand. When Pan Am stopped this service in the 1970s, the American Samoan government took over management of the hotel, and it steadily went downhill. Despite some fresh paint (which unfortunately covered up some of the hotel's best natural woodwork), in 1991 the Rainmaker still was sadly in need of serious renovation. It remains, nevertheless, the only hotel in American Samoa and for that reason is mentioned here.

If you stay at the Rainmaker, demand a room in the Beach Wing, a typical three-story hotel block that was rebuilt in 1980 after being partially destroyed when the U.S. Navy patrol plane hit the aerial tramway cable over the harbor and crashed next to the hotel. Avoid any attempt by the staff to put you in the Harbor Wing, which is in even more serious disrepair than the Beach Wing. Even in the Beach Wing, check the room out thoroughly (make sure the air conditioner works and works relatively quietly, the night latches engage properly, the plumbing actually does what it's supposed to do, and that the sheets and towels are clean). Do not hesitate to go back to the front desk and insist on another room until you get one that appears to be satisfactory (you won't be the first person they've heard make such a request, nor will you be the last). Leave absolutely no valuables in your room, and lock the safety latch when you're inside. A restaurant, snack bar, beauty salon, and tour desks are on the premises. The Sadie Thompson Bar is a popular hangout which has live music starting at happy hour most evenings.

APIOLEFAGA INN, P.O. Box 336, Pago Pago, AS 96799. Tel. 699-9124. 24 rms (all with bath). A/C TEL **Location:** From Pago Pago, go west past airport, take first right after American Samoa Community College, go to end of street.

$ Rates: $45 single; $50 double. MC, DC, V.

Despite its distance from town, this spotlessly maintained inn, which offers a glimpse of local life in a residential neighborhood about a 15-minute drive west of Pago Pago, is *the* place to stay in American Samoa. The modern, two-story house has 12 spacious, pension-style rooms, each with two twin beds, its own bathroom (including American-style tub and shower), and large louvered windows.

FROMMER'S FAVORITE AMERICAN SAMOA EXPERIENCES

Cable-Car Ride If it's running (which presumably means it's safe), I can think of no more stunning South Pacific experience than the cable-car ride to Mount Alava. The spectacular mountain-and-sea view from the top is almost secondary to the thrill of getting there.

Ride from the Airport As mundane as it sounds, the winding ride into Pago Pago along Tutuila's rugged coast is a scenic delight in its own right. And when you make that last turn into the harbor, it's an unforgettable sight.

Harborside Lunch Having lunch beside Pago Pago Harbor is almost on a scenic par with happy hour at the Club Bali Hai in Cook's Bay on Moorea. Both Sadie's Restaurant and Soli & Mark's have gorgeous views of the water and mountains.

The Turtle and the Shark I like to let the trade winds rustle my hair while standing on the volcanic shelf at Vaitogi village. I've never seen the blind old woman and her granddaughter who were turned into the turtle and the shark, but the waves breaking on the black rocks below have a mesmerizing effect.

The rooms are on the second story and open onto an inside balcony overlooking a breezy central lounge and kitchen area. A motel-style building next door has 12 comfortable rooms with balconies overlooking a swimming pool. The motel units have shower-only bathrooms. Home-cooked meals are available on request. Make your reservations as early as possible.

HERB AND SIA'S MOTEL, P.O. Box 430, Pago Pago, AS 96799. Tel. 633-5413. 9 rms (3 with showers, none with toilet). A/C **Location:** Fagatoga, up the street directly behind the communications office.

$ Rates: $33–$35 single; $38–$45 double. No credit cards.

Although a bit dark and set smack in Pago Pago's rain belt, this has been the island's long-standing budget establishment for years—by default if for no other reason. New Zealand–born Herb Scanlon and his American Samoan wife, Sia, built a bedroom for each of their nine children in their hillside house in Fagatogo. The children are grown now, so daughter Tina Scanlon rents the rooms to visitors. Six of them share two baths and don't have windows; the other three are on the outside of the building and have their own shower but share toilets. The rooms with showers are air conditioned and have small refrigerators. Tina provides coffee and juice in the mornings.

5. WHERE TO DINE

The three establishments listed below will keep you fed during your stay on Tutuila, and there are snack bars where you can get sandwiches or hamburgers. The most durable take-out joint is the **Icewich** on the harbor just west of the market; it has breakfasts, omelets, burgers, fish-and-chips, and other greasy fare and is open from 6am to 9pm daily. I haven't had time to try it, but local residents tell me **Pete's Diner** in Nu'uuli, on the main road just east of the airport turnoff, has fine breakfasts (perhaps a good stop after your early-morning flight from Apia).

SADIE'S RESTAURANT, Malaloa. Tel. 633-5981.

Cuisine: AMERICAN. **Reservations:** Recommended. **Location:** On south side of harbor, west of market in Malaloa area.

$ Prices: Appetizers $5–$9; main courses $14–$32.50. AE, MC, V.
Open: Mon–Sat 11am–11pm.

Appropriately located in the old building where W. Somerset Maugham stayed and set his short story "Rain," Sadie's during my recent visit was beginning to get that elegantly deteriorating look that Maugham would have loved. That is, it's seen just enough wear and tear to its cut glass-and-mauve style to look the South Seas outpost part. The best seats are on the refurbished front porch with a commanding view of the harbor, but reserve early or the local palagis and affluent American Samons will beat you to those tables.

The most popular item on Sadie's menu is the sashimi appetizer of raw fresh yellowfin tuna bought at the small-boat harbor virtually across the street. The yellowfin is known as *ahi* in Hawaiian and will be so identified on the menu. Daily specials feature such delicious items as "ahi mignon"—two chunks of tuna wrapped in bacon and charbroiled. The pasta dishes and steaks broiled over charcoal are also well prepared.

SOLI & MARK'S FAMILY RESTAURANT, Pago Pago. Tel. 633-4197.
Cuisine: AMERICAN/ITALIAN. **Reservations:** Recommended at dinner. **Location:** Waterside, near the head of the harbor.
$ Prices: Appetizers $2–$7.50; main courses $8–$19. AE, DC, MC, V.
Open: Mon–Sat 10am–10pm.

(S) This three-generation, family-owned establishment has been one of American Samoa's busiest eateries for years. Soli Aolaolagi (that's his chiefly last name; he was born Meredith) is the founding grandfather, Mark Meredith is the son, and Dino Meredith is the grandson (and chef, having been trained at the American Culinary Institute in New York City and experienced in Honolulu). Along with the help of wives, mothers, daughters, and sisters, the Merediths serve up a variety of well-prepared and interesting dishes, with an emphasis on seafood. The sashimi appetizer is Dino's best-known dish, but try some New Zealand mussels or oka, the Samoan-style marinated fish salad. He accents his pasta dishes with fresh local herbs. Dino draws a crowd at lunch when he offers sandwiches and hamburgers as well as his regular appetizers and some of his main courses. You'll have a grand view of the harbor and the mountains beyond from your table in this large air-conditioned perch at water's edge. A band plays during happy hour from 4:30 to 7pm Monday to Saturday.

PAISANO PIZZA, Pago Pago, in Pago Plaza. Tel. 633-2837.
Cuisine: ITALIAN. **Reservations:** Not accepted. **Location:** Street level in Pago Plaza mall near head of harbor.
$ Prices: Pizzas $12–$19; salads $2.50–$5; spaghetti $6–$7.50. No credit cards.
Open: Mon–Sat 7:30am–10pm.

(S) Red, green, and white are the colors of the day at Pago's local version of a shopping-mall Pizza Hut. Walk right up to the counter and order a pie, spaghetti, subs, salads, or Italian-style deli items, then eat in air-conditioned comfort inside or between showers at picnic tables on a terrace outside. All items are homemade and come out quite tasty.

6. AN EASY EXCURSION TO MANU'A

The three small, beautiful islands of the Manu'a Group—**Ofu, Olosega,** and **Ta'u**—lie about 80 miles east of Pago Pago and are unspoiled by commercialization.

All three islands offer outstanding scenery, as they are the remains of the northern rims of old volcanic craters, the walls of which fall steeply into the sea. Ofu and Olosega sit end-to-end and are joined by a causeway. A submerged volcano lies between them and Ta'u, about 7 miles away. There are no towns on either of the islands, only small villages. The beaches are more numerous on Ofu and Olosega than on Ta'u; in fact, the beach along Ofu's south coast is one of the most beautiful in the South Pacific.

The National Park of American Samoa has claimed some 5,000 pristine acres on Ta'u, including Mount Lata, at 3,170 feet the territory's highest peak. The mountain actually is the rim of an extinct volcanic crater whose walls drop sharply toward the island's south coast. Another park unit on the eastern end of Ofu includes another gorgeous beach.

Margaret Mead did the research for her *Coming of Age* in Samoa on Ta'u back in 1925. The high chief of the islands—Tui Manu'a—who took his title to the grave after signing the treaty with the United States in 1904, is buried on Ta'u.

GETTING THERE & GETTING AROUND

The Manu'a Group can be reached by daily air service—check with **Samoa Air** (tel. 699-9106 in Pago Pago or 22-321 or 22-901 in Apia)—or by weekly boat service from the main dock at Pago Pago. Samoa Air often has Manu'a packages that include airfare and accommodation at reasonable rates. Give them a call.

Get your feet in shape and limber up your hitchhiking thumb, for public transportation in the Manu'a Group is nonexistent. Furthermore, most of the scenic spots—the most spectacular views in a territory full of extraordinary sights—can be reached only on foot. Don't go without a copy of the excellent map, *Islands of Samoa,* by cartographer James A. Bier. It's available in Pago Pago at the Transpac store under Sadie's Restaurant and at 3U2 Dimension in the Rainmaker Hotel.

WHERE TO STAY & DINE

These lovely islands have yet to be discovered as tourist destinations, so the Manu'a Group's accommodations are very limited, and what there is of it falls just above the guesthouse category. You won't find an Aggie Grey's out here, but the rooms will be as clean as they are simple. The hotels are the only places to dine.

VAOTO LODGE, c/o Vili Malae, Ofu, Manu'a, AS 96799. Tel. 655-1120, 699-9628 in Pago Pago. 10 rms (all with bath). **Location:** Ofu, near the airport.
$ Rates: $35 single; $40 double. No credit cards.

Chuck Brugman puts his scuba divers up at this conveniently located little place; the airport is next door, and the beaches aren't far away. The rooms all have private baths and electric fans. The dining room serves breakfast, lunch, and home-cooked Samoan-style dinners.

FITIUTA LODGE, P.O. Box 1858, Pago Pago, AS 96799. Tel. 633-5841 or 677-3501. 8 rms (all with bath). **Location:** Fitiuta village, Ta'u Island.
$ Rates: $25 single; $30 double. No credit cards.

Although the island's main village of Ta'u lies on the northwest corner, its hotel is some 7 miles away in Fitiuta on the northeast corner near the airport. An unpaved road connects the two villages; it's up to you to find a ride. This unpretentious lodge has eight rooms with private baths and a dining room serving three home-cooked meals a day.

CHAPTER 10

TONGA

Thanks to a quirk of humankind and not of nature, the international date line swings eastward from its north-south path down the Pacific Ocean just enough to make the last Polynesian monarch the first sovereign to see the light of each new day.

When King Taufa'ahau Tupou IV of Tonga greets the morning and looks out on his realm from the veranda of his whitewashed Victorian palace, he sees a country of low but extremely fertile islands, of gorgeous sandy beaches, of colorful coral reefs waiting to be explored, and of Polynesian faces whose infectious smiles make it immediately obvious why Capt. James Cook named tiny Tonga "The Friendly Islands."

His is a nation protected but never ruled by a Western power. Like Western Samoa to the north, Tonga has managed to maintain its Polynesian culture in the face of modern change. As the Tonga Visitors Bureau says, the kingdom "still remains far away from it all; still different, still alone, and to the joy of those who find their way to her—essentially unspoiled."

1. GETTING TO KNOW TONGA

In other Polynesian languages, the word *tonga* means "south." It stands to reason that Tonga would be so named because the kingdom lies south of Samoa, the first islands permanently settled by Polynesians and presumably the launching site for the colonization of Tonga and the rest of Polynesia. But to the Tongans the name means "garden," and when you drive from the airport into **Nuku'alofa,** the nation's capital, you can see why. It seems that every square yard of the main island of **Tongatapu** ("Sacred Garden") not occupied by a building or by the road is either under cultivation or lying fallow but ready for the next planting of bananas, tapioca, taro, yams, watermelons, tomatoes, and a plethora of other fruits and vegetables. Crops grow in small plots under towering coconut palms so numerous that this flat island appears to be one huge copra plantation. The Tongans are generally poor in terms of material wealth, but they own some of the South Pacific's most fertile and productive land. There just isn't much of it.

The largest island in the kingdom, Tongatapu has about a third of Tonga's land

WHAT'S SPECIAL ABOUT TONGA

Beaches

- ☐ Vava'u: has tiny islets surrounded by white sand beaches and emerald lagoons.
- ☐ Oholei: Backed by limestone caves, this one hosts one of South Pacific's most authentic feasts and dance shows.

Natural Spectacles

- ☐ Vava'u: Unique in the South Pacific, this island actually is a collection of islands split apart by narrow, nearly landlocked waterways.

Cultures

- ☐ The King: Taufa'ahau Tupou and 33 Nobles of the Realm rule the last pure Polynesian chiefdom.

Ancient Monuments

- ☐ Ha'amonga Trilithon: Without wheels, the Tongans managed somehow to put the 35-ton stone on top in A.D. 1200.
- ☐ Graves: Ancient terraced tombs have given way to graves trimmed with beer bottles.

Great Towns/Villages

- ☐ Neiafu: Curving around Port of Refuge on Vava'u, this little gem evokes the South Seas of yesteryear.
- ☐ Nuku'alofa: Dusty or muddy, the nation's capital has rough-around-the-edges charm.

Sunday Selections

- ☐ The Sabbath is Sacred: Having a good time on Sunday is not as difficult as it may seem in this fundamentalist bastion.

Shopping

- ☐ Handcrafts: The South Pacific's great trove of tapa, anything woven of pandanus, and black coral.

Festivals

- ☐ *Heilala:* Tongans do just about everything they can think of to have a good time around the King's Birthday in July.

area and about two-thirds of its population. It's a flat, raised atoll about 40 miles across from east to west and 20 miles across from north to south at its longest and widest points. In the center is a sparkling lagoon now unfortunately void of most sea life.

The first Tui Tongas ruled from the village Niutoua on the northwest corner of the island. They moved to Lapaha on the shore of the interior lagoon about 800 years ago, apparently to take advantage of a safer anchorage for the large, double-hulled war canoes they used to extend their empire as far as Fiji and Samoa. At that time, a deep passage linked the lagoon to the sea; it has been slowly closing as geological forces raise the island and reduce the entrance to the present shallow bank.

Today the government and most businesses and tourist activities are in Nuku'alofa (pop. 22,000), but there is much to see on the island outside of town, including some of the South Pacific's most important and impressive archeological sites.

There are three major island groups in the country. Tongatapu and the smaller **'Eua** comprise the southernmost group. About 96 miles north are the islands of the **Ha'apai Group,** and about 67 miles beyond them is the beautiful **Vava'u Group.** Even farther north, and definitely off the beaten path, are the **Niuas Islands.** The most frequently visited islands are Tongatapu and the sailor's paradise of Vava'u.

HISTORY

Legend has it that the great Polynesian god Maui threw a fishhook into the sea from Samoa and brought up the islands of Tonga. He then stepped on some of his catch,

DATELINE

- **500 B.C.** Polynesians from Samoa settle in

(continues)

flattening them for gardens. Tofua and Kao in the Ha'apai Group and some of the Niuas were left standing as volcanic cones.

Polynesian settlers found and settled these gardens sometime around 500 B.C. on their long migration across the South Pacific. Around A.D. 950, according to another myth, the supreme god Tangaloa came down to Tongatapu and fathered a son by a lovely Tongan maiden named Va'epopua. The son, Aho'eitu, thus became the first Tui Tonga—King of Tonga—and launched one of the world's longest-running dynasties. Under subsequent Tuis, Tonga became a power in Polynesia, sending large war canoes loaded with fierce warriors who conquered and dominated the Samoas and the eastern islands of present-day Fiji.

Over time, however, the Tui became more of a figurehead, and his power was dispersed among several chiefs, all of them descendants of the original Tui. For centuries the rival chiefs seemed to stop warring among themselves only long enough to make war on Fiji and Samoa. One of the domestic wars was in full swing when missionaries from the London Missionary Society arrived in 1798 and landed on Lifuka in the Ha'apai Group. Two of the missionaries were killed. The rest fled to Sydney, leaving Tonga to the warring heathens.

EUROPEANS ARRIVE

Tongatapu and Ha'apai had been sighted by the Dutch explorers Schouten and Lemaire in 1616, and the Dutchman Abel Tasman had landed on them during his voyage of discovery in 1643. The missionaries knew of the islands, however, from the visits of British Captains Samuel Wallis, James Cook, and William Bligh in the late 1700s. During his third voyage in 1777, Captain Cook was feted lavishly on Lifuka by a powerful chief named Finau I. Cook was so impressed by this show of hospitality that he named the Ha'apai Group "The Friendly Islands." Unbeknownst to Cook, however, Finau I and his associates apparently plotted to murder him and his crew, but they couldn't agree among themselves how to do it before the great explorer sailed away. The name he gave the islands stuck, and today Tonga uses "The Friendly Islands" as its motto.

Captain Bligh and HMS *Bounty* visited Lifuka in 1789 after gathering breadfruit in Tahiti. Before he could leave Tongan waters, however, the famous mutiny took place near the island of Ha'afeva in the Ha'apai Group.

Some 20 years later Chief Finau II of Lifuka captured a British ship named the *Port au Prince*, brutally slaughtering all but one member of its crew, stealing all of its muskets and ammunition, and setting it on fire. The survivor was a 15-year-old Londoner named Will Mariner. He became a favorite of the chief, spent several years living among the Tongans, and was made a chief. Mariner later wrote an extensive account of his experiences, telling in one of the four volumes how the Tongans mistook 12,000 silver coins on the *Port au Prince* for gaming pieces they called pa'angas. The national currency today is known as the pa'anga.

DATELINE

what is now Tonga.

- **A.D. 950** By legend, supreme god Tangaloa comes to earth, fathers a son by beautiful virgin, thus founds Tui Tonga dynasty.
- **1616** Schouten and Lemaire are first Europeans to discover Tonga but do not land.
- **1642** Dutchman Abel Tasman is first European to set foot in Tonga.
- **1777** Captain Cook is feted by Finau I in Ha'apai, names them "The Friendly Islands," leaves just before Finau was planning to kill him.
- **1781** Spaniard Francisco Mourelle discovers Vava'u.
- **1789** Mutiny on the *Bounty* takes place off Ha'afeva in Ha'apai Group.
- **1798** First missionaries land in Ha'apai Group during Tongan wars; two are killed, the rest flee to Australia.
- **1806** Chief Finau II captures the *Port au Prince*, slays all its crew except young Will Mariner, who becomes the chief's favorite, later writes a book about his adventures.
- **1823** Wesleyan missionaries settle on Lifuka in Ha'apai Group; Chief Taufa'ahau

(continues)

The arrival of the Wesleyan missionaries on Lifuka in the 1820s coincided with the rise of Taufa'ahau, the powerful chief they converted to Christianity in 1831. With their help, he won a series of domestic wars and by 1845 had conquered all of Tonga. He made peace with Fiji, took a wife of the incumbent Tui Tonga as his own, and declared himself to be the new Tui Tonga. The deposed Tui, last of the direct descendants of the original Tui Tonga, lived on until 1865.

KING GEORGE I

Meanwhile, Taufa'ahau took the Christian name George and became King George I of Tonga. In 1862 he made his subordinate chiefs "nobles," but he also freed the commoners from forced labor on their estates and instituted the policy of granting each adult male a garden plot and house lot. He created a Privy Council of his own choosing and established a legislative assembly made up of representatives of both the nobles and commoners. This system was committed to writing in the Constitution of 1875, which still is in effect today, including its "Sabbath-is-sacred" clause. The legislative assembly is known now as Parliament.

King George I was dominated during his later years by the Rev. Shirley W. Baker, a missionary who came to Tonga from Sydney in 1860 under the auspices of the Wesleyan church. Over the next 30 years he held almost every important post in the king's government. When the British established their protectorate over Tonga according to the terms of the 1889 Berlin treaty, which also divided the Samoas between Germany and the United States, they found the kingdom's finances to be in a shambles. In cleaning up the mess, they arranged to have Baker deported to New Zealand, where he stayed for 10 years. Baker returned to Tonga in 1900 as a lay reader licensed by the Anglican church and died there in 1903. His children erected a large statue of his likeness at his grave on Lifuka, in the Ha'apai Group.

King George I died in 1893 at the age of 97, thus ending a reign of 48 years. His great-grandson, King George II, ruled for the next 25 years and is best remembered for signing a treaty with Great Britain in 1900. The agreement turned Tonga's foreign affairs over to the British and prevented any further encroachments on Tonga by the Western colonial powers. As a result, the Kingdom of Tonga is one of the few third world countries never to have been colonized.

King George II died in 1918 and was succeeded by his daughter, the 6-foot-2-inch Queen Salote (her name is the Tongan transliteration of "Charlotte"). For the next 47 years Queen Salote carefully protected her people from Western influence, even to the extent of not allowing a modern hotel to be built in the kingdom. She did, however, come to the world's attention in 1953, when she rode bareheaded in the cold, torrential rain that drenched the coronation parade of Queen Elizabeth II in London (she was merely following Tongan custom of showing respect to royalty by appearing uncovered in their presence).

DATELINE

begins his rise to power.

- **1831** Taufa'ahau converts to Christianity, names himself George and with missionary help launches wars against his rivals.
- **1845** Taufa'ahau conquers all of Tonga, proclaims himself King George I.
- **1860** Rev. Shirley Baker arrives, exercises influence over Tonga for next 30 years.
- **1862** King George I frees commoners, makes his chiefs "Nobles of the Realm," establishes Privy Council, gives land to every male.
- **1875** King George I adopts Constitution, including "Sabbath-is-sacred" clause, essentially shutting Tonga down on Sunday.
- **1890** Under Treaty of Berlin, Great Britain establishes protectorate over Tonga, kicks out Rev. Baker, straightens out kingdom's finances.
- **1893** King George I dies, ending reign of 48 years. King George II assumes throne.
- **1900** King George II turns Tonga's foreign affairs over to Great Britain, preventing further colonial encroachments.

(continues)

DATELINE

- **1918** King George II dies, Queen Salote begins 47-year reign during which Tonga remains a backwater.
- **1953** Queen Salote comes to world attention by going bareheaded during rainstorm at coronation of Queen Elizabeth II in London.
- **1965** Queen Salote dies, King Taufa'ahau Tupou IV begins opening Tonga to tourists.
- **1967** King Taufa'ahau Tupou IV coronated among pomp and circumstance; International Dateline Hotel opens.
- **1970** King ends treaty with Great Britain, Tonga resumes own foreign affairs.
- **1989** Commoner members of Parliament begin push for more accountability from king's government.
- **1991** Passport scandal rocks the government.

KING TAUFA'AHAU TUPOU

Queen Salote died in 1965 and was succeeded by her son, the present King Taufa'ahau Tupou IV. Trained in law at Sydney University in Australia, the new king—then 49 years old—set about bringing Tonga into the modern world. On the pretext of accommodating the important guests invited to his elaborate coronation scheduled for July 4, 1967, the modern International Dateline Hotel was built on Nuku'alofa's waterfront, and Fua'amotu Airport on Tongatapu was upgraded to handle jet aircraft. Tourism, albeit on a modest scale, had finally arrived in Tonga.

The king ended the treaty of protection with Great Britain, and in 1970 Tonga reassumed its small role on the world's stage. This enabled it to acquire aid from other countries with which to make further improvements.

Although not as tall as his mother, the king stands above 6 feet and once weighed on the order of 460 pounds (the large statue of him at Fua'amotu Airport is only a slight exaggeration of his former size). He has slimmed down in recent years to just over 300 pounds. You might see him strenuously rowing a skiff (especially equipped with rear-view mirrors so he can see where he's going) off the Nuku'alofa waterfront (late Wednesday afternoons at last report). On Monday and Friday he rides his mountain bike 30 times around Teufaiva rugby field, his bodyguards puffing along behind. He has been seen wearing ski goggles and a motorbike helmet when flying from island to island. Watching him arrive at an airport should not be missed.

GOVERNMENT, POLITICS & ECONOMY

GOVERNMENT

Although Tonga is a constitutional monarchy, the king is anything but a figurehead. He picks his own Privy Council of advisors and appoints seven cabinet members and the governors of Ha'apai and Vava'u. The cabinet members and the governors serve until they retire, and they hold 12 of the 30 seats in Parliament—in effect, for life. Of the 16 other members of the Parliament, the nobles choose nine from among their ranks, leaving nine to be elected by the taxpaying commoners.

The king's brother is prime minister. His son, Crown Prince Tupouto'a, is both minister of foreign affairs and minister of defense. It would be an understatement to say that the royal family has a hand in every important decision made in Tonga; in fact,

IMPRESSIONS

. . . the good natured old Chief interduced me to a woman and gave me to understand that I might retire with her, she was next offered to Captain Furneaux but met with a refusal from both, tho she was neither old nor ugly, our stay here was but short.

—CAPT. JAMES COOK, 1773.

very little gets done without its outright or tacit approval or involvement. Foreigners doing business in the country must have Tongan partners, and it's not surprising that many such partners are of royal or noble blood.

POLITICS

Thanks to more and more of his commoner subjects going overseas to work in the Western democracies, and to those at home becoming better educated and more aware of what's going on both in Tonga and in the world, the king and his government have had their problems in recent years. In the late 1980s a group of commoners founded *Kele'a*, a newspaper published without the king's input. The paper created a ruckus almost from its first issue by revealing that some government ministers had rung up excessive travel expenses on trips abroad.

Then came news that the government had stashed millions of dollars in U.S. banks, money earned from selling 426 Tongan passports to overseas nationals (most of them Hong Kong Chinese but including Imelda Marcos, wife of the deposed Philippine dictator). For $20,000 the buyers received a passport declaring them to be "Tongan protected persons." Since the documents didn't allow the person to live in Tonga, however, most other nations refused to recognize them. To compound the problem, the Tongan High Court ruled the sales to be unconstitutional. Rather than refund the money, Parliament held a special session in 1991 and amended the constitution—a document which had not been significantly changed since 1875. It also raised the price to $50,000. The new passports also allow the holders to live in Tonga (hence, the growing number of Chinese restaurants you will find in Nuku'alofa).

Incensed, some 350 to 1,000 (the estimates depending on who guessed—the police or the protesters) Tongans marched down Nuku'alofa's main street in a completely peaceful protest; nothing like that had ever happened before. Led by commoner parliamentarian 'Akilisi Pohiva and Catholic Bishop Patelisio Finau, and spurred on by the country's top Wesleyan minister, they presented a paper at the Royal Palace calling on the king to halt further sales and to fire the police commissioner, a noble who had jurisdiction. Rather than back down, however, the king signed the amendment and announced that sales would continue.

It was difficult at the time of writing to predict what course Tongan politics would take. Violence or a military coup are highly unlikely in Tonga, but the commoners are certain to continue their push for more accountability by the government. Many observers believe the monarchial system will stay intact as long as King Taufa'ahau Tupou is on the throne. What happens after he dies is very much up in the air.

ECONOMY

Tonga has few natural resources other than its fertile soil and the fish in the sea within its exclusive economic zone, and the world markets for its major exports—vanilla, kava, bananas, coconut oil, pineapples, watermelons, tomatoes, and other vegetables—have been unstable and even depressed at times in recent years. The country now imports more than it exports.

In addition, the kingdom has run out of land to apportion under the rule that gives each adult male 8¼ acres for growing crops. As a result, more and more Tongans—an estimated 30,000 of them—have left the country and now live overseas. Money sent home by them is a major source of foreign exchange for the country.

For the commoners who remain behind, labor unions are illegal, and the primary chance for economic advancement is in small businesses, which are flourishing when

---

IMPRESSIONS

Nature, assisted by a little art, no where appears in a more flourishing state than at this Isle.

—CAPT. JAMES COOK, 1773.

compared to other South Pacific island countries. Even there, however, the king can get involved when leases or permits are required from the government.

GEOGRAPHY

The Kingdom of Tonga consists of 170 islands, 36 of them inhabited, scattered over an area of about 100,000 square miles, south of the Samoas and southeast of Fiji. Although the country occupies an area about the size of Colorado, the amount of dry land is only 269 square miles—smaller than New York City.

Tonga lies roughly north-south along the edge of the Indo-Australian Plate. The Tonga Trench, one of the deepest parts of the Pacific Ocean, parallels the islands to the east where the Pacific Plate dips down and then under the Indo-Australian Plate. The resulting geological activity puts Tonga on the "Ring of Fire" that encircles the Pacific Ocean. One of Tonga's islands, Tofua, is an active volcano, and the entire country experiences frequent earth tremors. Legend says that earthquakes are caused when the Polynesian goddess Havea Hikule'o moves around under ground; consequently, Tongans customarily stomp the shaking ground to get her to stop whatever she's doing down there.

Most of the islands are raised coral atolls. The exceptions are the Niuas and, in the Ha'apai Group, the active volcano Tofua and its companion volcanic cone, Kao. Geologists say that the weight of the growing Ha'apai volcanoes has caused the Indo-Australian Plate to sag like a hammock, thereby raising Tongatapu and 'Eua on the south end of the Tongan chain and Vava'u on the north end. As a result, the sides of Tongatapu and Vava'u facing Ha'apai slope gently to the sea, while the sides facing away from Ha'apai end in cliffs that fall into the ocean.

THE INTERNATIONAL DATE LINE

One of our great contributions to the geography of the Pacific Ocean (and to the eternal confusion of travelers) is the international date line. Established by international agreement in 1884, this imaginary line marks the start of each calendar day. The date line *should* run for its entire length along the 180th meridian; that would put it exactly halfway around the world from the zero meridian, which passes through the Royal Observatory in Greenwich, England, the starting point for measuring international time. If it followed the 180th meridian precisely, however, most of the Aleutian Islands would be a day ahead of the rest of Alaska, and Fiji would be split into 2 days. To solve these problems, the date line swings west, leaving the Aleutians in the same day as Alaska, before returning to the 180th meridian. In the South Pacific, the line swings east between Fiji and the Samoas, leaving all of Fiji in one day and the Samoas in the previous day. Logically, it should then return to the 180th meridian, leaving Tonga in the same day as Samoa. But Tonga wanted to be in the same day as its major trading partners, Australia and New Zealand, so the line runs on the eastern side of Tonga before returning to the 180th meridian. It is for this reason that the king of Tonga is the first monarch to greet each new calendar day, even though his realm lies south of Samoa and entirely east of the 180th meridian.

As a traveler, you need to remember that when journeying from east to west you add a day when crossing the international date line, and when traveling from west to east you subtract a day.

Adding to the confusion is the fact that Tonga and Samoa are in the same time zone. When traveling from one to the other, therefore, only the date will change, not

---

IMPRESSIONS

We had come to see the island and the islanders had come to see us and both sides were having a fine time.

—John Dyson, 1982

NUKU'ALOFA

ACCOMMODATIONS:
- Beach House 3
- Friendly Islander Motel 1
- International Dateline Hotel 4
- Kahana Lagoon Resort 2
- Ramanlal Hotel 6
- Sela's Guest House 5

ATTRACTIONS:
- Basilica of St. Anthony 8
- Centenary Church 6
- Chapel Hill 4
- Royal Palace 3
- Royal Tombs 7
- Seaview Restaurant 5
- Tonga National Centre 9
- Visitors Bureau 1
- Vuna Wharf 2

the time of day. For example, if everyone is going to church at 10am on Sunday in Tonga, it's 10am on Saturday in Samoa.

PEOPLE & CULTURE

The population of Tonga is estimated at somewhere around 100,000 (no one knows for sure). Approximately 98% of the inhabitants are pure Polynesians, closely akin to the Samoans in physical appearance, language, and culture.

As in Samoa, the bedrock of the Tongan social structure is the traditional way of life—*faka Tonga*—and the extended family. Parents, grandparents, children, aunts, uncles, cousins, nieces, and nephews all have the same sense of obligation to each other as is felt in Western nuclear families. Although Tongans are poor by Western standards, the extended-family system makes sure that no one ever goes hungry or goes without a place to live. Little wonder, therefore, that they are an extremely friendly and hospitable people who are quick to smile, laugh, and welcome strangers to their country.

THE TONGAN SYSTEM

The extended family aside, however, some striking differences exist between Tonga and Samoa and the other Polynesian islands. Unlike the others, in which there is a certain degree of upward mobility, Tonga has a rigid two-tier caste system. The king and 33 "nobles of the realm"—plus their families—make up a privileged class at the top of society. Everyone else is a commoner, and although commoners can hold positions in the government, it's impossible for them to move up into the nobility even by marriage (the king once annulled the marriage of a niece rather than have a commoner in the family). Titles of the nobility are inherited, but the king can strip members of the nobility of their positions if they fail to live up to their obligations (presumably including loyalty to the royal family).

The king owns all the land in Tonga, which technically makes the country his feudal estate. Tonga isn't exactly like the old European feudal system, however, for although the nobles each rule over a section of the kingdom, they have an obligation to provide for the welfare of the "serfs" rather than the other way around. The nobles administer the villages, look after the people's welfare, and apportion the land among the commoners.

Under Tonga's constitution, each adult male is entitled to a garden plot of 8¼ acres and a site for a house in the village. Unfortunately, the population has outstripped the amount of available land, but this system is primarily responsible for the intensely cultivated condition of Tongatapu and the other islands and for the abundance of food in the country.

Foreigners are absolutely forbidden to own land in Tonga, and leases require approval of the Cabinet, which for all practical purposes means the king.

TONGAN DRESS

Even traditional Tongan dress reflects this social structure. Western-style clothes have made deep inroads in recent years, especially among young persons, but many Tongans still wear wraparound skirts known as *valas*. These come to well below the knee on men and to the ankles on women. To show their respect for the royal family and to each other, traditional men and women wear finely woven mats known as

---

IMPRESSIONS

Tonga's special quality came not from the island, but from the people themselves. They were hard-working, devoted to their Queen and passionate in their attachment to the Church, but their overwhelming characteristic was contentment.

—David Attenborough, 1960

ta'ovalas over their valas. Men hold these up with waistbands of coconut fiber; women wear decorative waistbands known as *kiekies*. Tongans have ta'ovalas for everyday wear, but on special occasions they will break out mats that are family heirlooms, some of them tattered and worn. The king owns ta'ovalas that have been in his family for more than 500 years.

Tongan custom is to wear black for months to mourn the death of a relative or close friend. Since Tongan extended families are large and friends numerous, the black of mourning is seen frequently in the kingdom.

In keeping with Tonga's conservatism, it's against the law for men as well as women to appear shirtless in public. While Western men can swim and sunbathe shirtless at the hotel swimming pools and beaches frequented by visitors, you will see most Tongans swimming in a full set of clothes.

RELIGION

Wesleyan missionaries gained a foothold in Tonga during the early 1820s and by 1831 had converted Taufa'ahau, the high chief of the Ha'apai Islands. As happened with the converted chief named Pomare in Tahiti, Taufa'ahau then used missionary support—and guns from other sources—to win a series of wars and become king of Tonga. Tonga quickly became a predominantly Christian nation—apparently an easy transition, as Tongan legend holds that their own king is a descendant of a supreme Polynesian god and a beautiful earthly virgin.

When Taufa'ahau instituted a constitution in 1862, a clause in that document declared, "The Sabbath Day shall be sacred in Tonga forever and it shall not be lawful to work, artifice, or play games, or trade on the Sabbath." The penalty for breaking this stricture is a T$10 ($8) fine or 3 months in the slammer at hard labor. Although there now is some flexibility that allows hotels to cater to their guests on Sunday, almost everything else comes to a screeching halt on the Sabbath. Most taxis don't run, airplanes don't fly, most restaurants other than those in the hotels don't open. Tongans by the thousands go to church, then enjoy family feasts and a day of lounging around in true Polynesian style. (See "What to See and Do," below, for how to survive a Sunday in Tonga.)

As was the case throughout Polynesia, the Tongans accepted most of the puritanical beliefs taught by the early missionaries but stopped short of adopting their strict sexual mores. Today Tongan society is very conservative in outlook and practice in almost every aspect of life except the sexual activities of unmarried young men and women.

In keeping with Polynesian custom described earlier in this book, Tongan families without enough female offspring will raise boys as they would girls. They are known in Tongan as *fakaleitis* ("like a woman") and live lives similar to those of the mahus in Tahiti and the fa'afafines in the Samoas. In Tonga they have a reputation for sexual promiscuousness and for persistently approaching Western male visitors in search of sexual liaisons.

About half of all Tongans belong to the Free Wesleyan Church of Tonga, founded by the early Methodist missionaries and headed by the king. The red national flag has a cross on a white field in its upper corner to signify the country's strong Christian foundation.

Seventh-Day Adventists, who celebrate the Sabbath on Saturday, have gained a foothold in Tonga. During the 1970s they complained about the international date line's "loop" around the kingdom. According to the "SDAs" (as they are known

---

IMPRESSIONS

What could the Tongan people do? "Not much," he reflected. "All we can do is resign ourselves to our lot, become very religious, and pray that there will be more land available in Heaven."

—John Dyson, 1982

throughout the South Pacific), since Tonga actually lies east of the 180th meridian, Sunday in Tonga is actually Saturday. The king wasn't about to change Sunday to Saturday, so the Tongan SDAs decided to observe their Saturday Sabbath on Sunday, which conveniently put them in compliance with the kingdom's tough blue laws.

The Mormon church has also made inroads in Tonga. Gleaming white Morman temples have popped up in many Tongan villages, along with modern schools that offer quality education and the chance for students to go on to Mormon colleges in Hawaii and Utah. Many Tongans have joined the church, reportedly for this very reason, and there are now sizable Tongan communities in Honolulu and around Salt Lake City, headquarters of the Mormon church. Unlike the Samoans and Cook Islanders, Tongans do not have unlimited access to a larger Western country such as the United States or New Zealand, and the promise of Mormon help in settling in America is an appealing prospect in light of the population pressures at home.

Tongans of all religions bury their dead in unique cemeteries set in groves of frangipani trees. The graves are sandy mounds decorated with flags, banners, artificial flowers, stones, and seashells. Many of them are bordered by brown beer bottles turned upside down.

LANGUAGE

The official language is Tongan, but English is taught in the schools and is widely spoken in the main towns.

Tongan is a Polynesian language similar to Samoan. One major difference between them is the enormous number of glottal stops (represented by an apostrophe in writing) in the Tongan tongue. These are short stops similar to the break between "Oh-oh" in English.

Every vowel is pronounced in the Latin fashion—*ah, ay, ee, oh,* and *oo* (as in kangaroo) instead of *ay, ee, eye, oh,* and *you* as in English. The consonants are sounded as they are in English.

An extensive knowledge of Tongan will not be necessary for English-speakers to get around and enjoy the kingdom, but to learn a few words, which you can use to elicit smiles from your hosts and to avoid the embarrassment of entering the wrong rest room, get a free copy of "Some Useful Tongan Words and Phrases" from the Tonga Visitors Bureau.

2. INFORMATION, ENTRY REQUIREMENTS & MONEY

INFORMATION

The friendly staff have many brochures, maps, and other materials available at the **Tonga Visitors Bureau,** P.O. Box 37, Nuku'alofa, Tonga (tel. 21-733, fax 22-129). The office is on Vuna Road near the International Dateline Hotel. Especially good are the bureau's brochures on Tongan dancing, handcrafts, archeology, construction skills, language, and a walking tour of central Nuku'alofa. A stop by the TVB is a must before setting out to see the country. Hours are 8:30am to 4:30pm weekdays and 9am to 1pm on Saturday.

Once you're in Tonga, be on the lookout for *'Eva: Your Holiday Guide to Tonga,* a slick bimonthly tabloid full of news about Tongan tourism and advertisements for the hotels, restaurants, and nightclubs. The *Times of Tonga* newspaper carries advertisements and announcements of special events, shows, and performances.

ENTRY REQUIREMENTS

Visas are not required to enter Tonga for bona-fide visitors, who are permitted to stay for up to 30 days provided they have a valid passport, an onward air or sea ticket, proof of adequate funds, and relevant health certificates. Applications for stays of longer than 30 days must be made to the principal immigration officer in Nuku'alofa.

Vaccinations are required only if a traveler has been in a yellow fever or cholera area within 2 weeks prior to arrival in Tonga.

Customs: Visitors are allowed to bring into Tonga the usual 200 cigarettes and 1 liter of alcoholic beverage, as well as personal belongings in use at the time of arrival. Pets, dangerous drugs, firearms, and ammunition are prohibited, and foodstuffs must be declared and inspected. Arriving visitors can buy duty-free merchandise at Fua'amotu Airport before clearing immigration and Customs.

MONEY

The Tongan unit of currency is the **pa'anga,** which is divided into 100 **seniti.** The pa'anga is abbreviated as **"T$."**

Although the pa'anga was pegged for several years to the Australian dollar, its value now is determined by a basket of currencies. At the time of writing, $1 U.S. was worth T$0.80. The equivalent U.S. dollar prices given in parentheses are based on this rate of exchange.

As a practical matter, most Tongans will refer to "dollars" and "cents" when doing business with visitors, meaning pa'angas and senitis. Tongan coins bear the likeness of the king on one side and such items as bananas, chickens, and pigs on the other.

WHAT THINGS COST IN TONGA	U.S. $
Taxi from airport to Nuku'alofa	9.50
Bus from airport to Nuku'alofa	5.00
Double room at International Dateline Hotel (expensive)	80.00
Double room at Ramanlal Hotel (moderate)	66.00
Double room at Sela's Guest House (budget)	24.00
Lunch for one at Davina's (moderate)	12.00

THE PA'ANGA & U.S. DOLLAR

At this writing, T$1 = approximately 80¢, the rate of exchange used to calculate the U.S. dollar prices given in this chapter. This rate has remained fairly stable during the past few years but may change by the time you visit. Accordingly, use the following table only as a guide.

$ T	$ U.S.	$ T	$ U.S.
.25	.20	15.00	12.00
.50	.40	20.00	16.00
.75	.60	25.00	20.00
1.00	.80	30.00	24.00
2.00	1.60	35.00	28.00
3.00	2.40	40.00	32.00
4.00	3.20	45.00	36.00
5.00	4.00	50.00	40.00
6.00	4.80	75.00	60.00
7.00	5.60	100.00	80.00
8.00	6.40	125.00	100.00
9.00	7.20	150.00	120.00
10.00	8.00	200.00	160.00

	US$
Lunch for one at Littlest Cafe (budget)	4.00
Dinner for one, without wine, at the Seaview (expensive)	22.50
Dinner for one, without wine, at Alisi & André (moderate)	14.50
Dinner for one, without wine, at Akiko's (budget)	6.50
Beer	2.00
Coca-Cola	.96
Cup of coffee	.80
Roll of ASA 100 Kodacolor film, 36 exposures	6.35
Movie ticket	2.40

3. WHEN TO GO — CLIMATE, HOLIDAYS & EVENTS

CLIMATE

Like Rarotonga in the Cook Islands to the east and New Caledonia to the west, Tongatapu is far enough south of the equator to have cool, dry, and quite pleasant weather during the austral winter months (June to September), when temperatures range between 60°F and 70°F. However, the ends of occasional cold fronts from the Antarctic and periods of stiff southeast trade winds can make it seem even cooler during this period. During the summer (December to March), the high temperatures can reach above 90°F, with evenings in the comfortable 70s. A sweater, jacket, or wrap will come in handy for evening wear at any time of the year.

The islands get about 70 inches of rainfall a year (compared to 200 inches in Pago Pago, American Samoa), the majority of it falling during the summer months. Vava'u to the north tends to be somewhat warmer and slightly wetter than Tongatapu.

Tonga is in the southwestern Pacific cyclone belt, and hurricanes are possible from November to April. Rest assured, however, that there will be ample warning if one bears down on the islands while you're there. The Tongans have seen enough hurricanes to ensure their guests' safety.

HOLIDAYS

Public holidays in Tonga are New Year's Day, Good Friday and Easter Monday, ANZAC (Memorial) Day (April 25), Crown Prince Tupouto'a's birthday (May 4), Emancipation Day (in honor of King George I, June 4), the King's Birthday (July 4), Constitution Day (November 4), King Tupou I Day (December 4), Christmas Day, and Boxing Day (December 26).

EVENTS

The largest annual festival is **Heilala,** which coincides with the King's Birthday on July 4. Nuku'alofa goes all out for a week of dance and beauty competitions, parades, sporting matches, band concerts, marching contests, yacht regattas, parties, and the lovely Night of Torches on the waterfront. Tongans living overseas like to come home for Heilala, so hotel reservations should be made well in advance. Vava'u stages its own version of Heilala early in May.

The Tongan version of a state fair is the Royal Agricultural Show. One show is held in each of the island groups during late August or early September. His Majesty visits them all and examines the best of the crops and handcrafts.

Other festivals are Red Cross Week in May, the opening of Parliament early in June, and the Music Festival early in December.

The Tonga Visitors Bureau keeps track of when the festivals will occur each year.

4. GETTING THERE & GETTING AROUND

GETTING TO TONGA

From North America, **Hawaiian Airlines** flies to Tonga at least once a week via Honolulu. **Air Pacific** connects Tonga to the international airport at Nadi in Fiji, which you can reach on **Air New Zealand, Qantas,** and **Canadian Airlines International. Air New Zealand** and **Polynesian Airlines** both fly to Tonga from Auckland and Sydney and go on to Western Samoa (Air New Zealand's weekly flight goes from Tonga to Apia but not the other way around). **Royal Tongan Airlines** was scheduled to begin Auckland-Tonga service after we went to press. **Samoa Air,** the small carrier based in American Samoa, flies its small planes between Pago Pago and Vava'u. The airstrip on Vava'u was scheduled to be upgraded in 1992, after which service may start between there and Nadi in Fiji.

For more information, see "Getting There" in Chapter 2.

Except for the few international flights destined for Vava'u, most land at **Fua'amotu Airport** on Tongatapu, 24km (14 miles) from Nuku'alofa. A new terminal had been completed but not opened during my recent visit; it was slated to have a bank and duty-free shop. International passengers will be able to purchase duty-free goods before going through immigration and Customs.

There are no flights into, out of, or within Tonga on Sunday, when the airport is closed.

The hotels send minibuses to the airport to meet flights arriving from overseas. Their representatives will be waiting just outside Customs to greet guests who have reservations. The bus ride to town costs T$6 ($5). Rental-car firms will also pick up their customers. Otherwise, the one-way taxi fare into Nuku'alofa is about T$12 ($9.50); the drivers will be happy to take U.S., New Zealand, or Australian currency.

A departure tax of T$10 ($8) is charged of all passengers leaving on international flights. (This amount may be increased in 1992.) You pay it in Tongan currency at the check-in counter. There is no departure tax for domestic flights.

GETTING AROUND TONGA

BY PLANE

Royal Tongan Airlines (tel. 23-414) has a monopoly on air travel within the Kingdom, providing at least two round-trip flights a day between Tongatapu and Vava'u on an 18-seat turboprop Twin Otter. Daily service is also provided between Tongatapu and 'Eua, with flights several times a week to Ha'apai. The one-way fare from Tongatapu to Vava'u is T$109 ($87); to 'Eua, T$23 ($18.50); and to Ha'apai, T$77 ($61.50). Round-trips are twice those amounts.

It's always a good idea to book your flights as far in advance as you can and a must to reconfirm your return flight as soon as possible after arriving on an outer island.

IMPRESSIONS

If I could repeat just one of my excursions in Polynesia, it would be that spent in a fast little jet-boat, exploring this maze of beaches, cliffs, caves, reefs, and lagoons—or at least, what small proportion of it could be fitted into a single day.

—Ron Hall, 1991

The airline's offices are in the Royco Building on Fatafehi Road at Wellington Road.

BY FERRY

It's not for everyone, but the **Shipping Corporation of Polynesia** (tel. 21-699) operates weekly ferry service from Nuku'alofa to Ha'apai and Vava'u using the MV *Olovaha,* a car-ferry with a few passenger cabins. It usually leaves Nuku'alofa 1 day a week at 6pm and takes about 16 hours to make the 163-mile trip to Vava'u, stopping at Lifuka in the Ha'apai Group on the way. The ship then turns around, reverses the trip, and arrives back in Nuku'alofa late the next afternoon. The schedule is subject to change according to the dictates of the weather and the mechanical condition of the ferry. One-way fares between Nuku'alofa and Vava'u are T$170 ($136) for a cabin, T$74 ($59) for "business class," and T$42 ($33.50) for deck passage. The cabin and business-class fares include meals. The Shipping Corporation's Nuku'alofa offices are in the tin-roof building opposite the Treasury Department on Railway Road near the waterfront; its mailing address is P.O. Box 453, Nuku'alofa, Tonga.

The Shipping Corporation also runs a boat between Nuku'alofa and nearby 'Eua Island. It departs Faua Jetty at 6:30am Tuesday through Saturday, returning to Nuku'alofa in the afternoon. Fares are T$6 ($5) one-way. Small, privately owned boats leave Faua Jetty for 'Eua around midday except on Sunday.

The **Warner Pacific Line,** P.O. Box 93, Nuku'alofa, Tonga (tel. 21-088), has freighter service between the Tongan islands and Fiji, the Samoas, Rarotonga, and other destinations. Its ships carry passengers around the South Pacific island ports, but comfort levels turn your trip on them into an adventure. The schedules vary.

GETTING AROUND TONGATAPU

BY RENTAL CAR

Vete Motors serves as the local licensee for **Budget** (tel. 23-510, or toll free 800/527-0700 in the U.S.). Rates range from T$40 ($32) a day for a small Toyota Starlet to T$65 ($52) for a Toyota with air conditioning and automatic transmission, all with unlimited mileage (you pay for the gasoline). Insurance is another T$8 ($6.50) per day. Budget offers a special weekend rate of 3 days for the price of 2 if you pick up the car by 5pm Friday and return it by 9am on Monday. Weekly rates are 7 days for the price of 6. Hours are 8am to 5pm Monday through Friday, until noon on Saturday. You can reach Vete Motors after hours by calling 22-390.

Avis (tel. 23-344, or toll free 800/331-1212 in the U.S.) has an office on Taufa'ahau Road in the Ramanlal Hotel. The rates are slightly less than Budget's, and the business hours are the same.

Gasoline (petrol) is readily available at stations only in Nuku'alofa, so fill up before leaving town. It cost about T92¢ (75¢) a liter during my recent visit.

Driving Rules: Before you can officially drive in Tonga you must obtain a local driver's license from the Traffic Department desk at the Central Police Station in Nuku'alofa. The duty officer will examine your valid home driver's license, fill out a form, and send you down the hall to the cashier. Fees are T$8 ($6.50) for rental cars, T$3 ($2.50) for private cars. Pay the cashier and take the receipt back to the traffic desk, where the officer will issue your license. The whole process takes about 10 minutes.

Driving in Tonga is on the left-hand side of the road. Speed limits are 65kmph (39 m.p.h.) on the open road and 40kmph (24 m.p.h.) in the towns and villages. Be alert for pigs, dogs, horses, chickens, and policemen on motorcycles escorting the king in his long black limousine bearing license plates with no numbers, only a crown.

BY TAXI

Taxis usually gather near Talamahu Market at the corner of Salote and Railway roads in Nuku'alofa. The largest firm is **Five Star Taxis** (tel. 21-595 or 21-429). Others are **Holiday Taxis** (tel. 21-858), **One-Way Taxis** (tel. 21-741), **Friendly Island Taxis** (tel. 21-023), **Malolala Taxis** (tel. 22-500), and **City Taxis** (tel. 22-734). Fares are T$1.30 ($1.05) for the first kilometer plus T30¢ (25¢) for each additional kilometer, but since the taxis have no meters, make sure you and the driver agree on just how much the fare will be. The fares are doubled on Sunday, when taxis officially are permitted only to take passengers to church and back (as a practical matter, some of them will carry tourists from their hotels or guesthouses to the wharf in order for them to get to the offshore islands).

BY BUS

Buses also use **Talamahu Market** as their terminal. Those going to the eastern end of Tongatapu line up on the east side of the market and vice versa for those going west. They fan out from there to all parts of Tongatapu, but there are no reliable schedules. Simply ask the bus drivers at the market where they are going. If you take one into the countryside, remember that they make their last runs back to Nuku'alofa at about 3pm daily, in time to pick up passengers who are getting off work. Once they make their last runs to the villages, they don't come back to town until the next morning. About T$1 (80¢) will take you to the end of the island in either direction.

BY BICYCLE

Tongatapu is virtually flat, making it an ideal island on which to ride a bicycle. "Push-bikes" can be rented beside the Pangaimotu Island Resort office on the west side of the International Dateline Hotel. One-speed models cost T$5 ($4) for ½ day and T$10 ($8) for a full day. Ten-speed bikes go for T$12 ($9.50) for a full day, T$6 ($5) for ½ day. Special long-term rentals are available.

TONGA

The following facts apply primarily to Nuku'alofa and Tongatapu, where you most likely will spend the majority of your time. See "An Easy Excursion to Vava'u" later in this chapter for facts specific to Vava'u.

American Express American Express has no representative in Tonga. See "Fast Facts: South Pacific" in Chapter 2 for information about reporting lost or stolen credit cards or traveler's checks.

Area Code The international country code is 676.

Baby-sitters The hotels can arrange for English-speaking baby-sitters.

Bookstores Friendly Islands Bookstore, on Taufa'ahau Rd. across from the Ramanlal Hotel, carries greeting cards made from tapa cloth, paperback books, postcards, international newsmagazines, week-old Australian newspapers, books about Tonga and the South Pacific, and maps of Tonga including the best available, *The Kingdom of Tonga,* published by Pacific Maps of Australia. Dateline Bookshop, in the second block of Wellington Rd. east of Taufa'ahau Rd., has a selection of novels and other paperback books.

Business Hours In general Tonga's shops are open Mon–Fri 8am–1pm and 2–5pm, Sat 8am–noon. Government offices are open Mon–Fri 8:30am–12:30pm and 1:30–4:30pm.

Climate See "When to Go—Climate, Holidays, and Events" in this chapter.

Clothing Summer clothing is in order during most of the year, but during the austral winter (June through September) the temperature can range from 60°F to 70°F, which can feel quite cool if the wind is blowing hard from the south. A sweater, jacket, or wrap should be taken for evening wear throughout the year. Tongans are very conservative, and visitors should not wear bathing suits or skimpy attire away from the hotel pools or beaches frequented by foreigners. In fact, appearing in public without a shirt is a punishable offense for both men and women, as is nudity of any degree.

Credit Cards The major hotels, rental-car firms, travel agencies, and Royal Tongan Airlines accept American Express, Diners Club, MasterCard, and VISA credit cards. Most restaurants and other businesses, however, do not. It's a good idea to ask first if you want to put your purchases on plastic.

Crime See "Safety," below.

Currency See "Information, Entry Requirements, and Money" in this chapter.

Currency Exchange The only bank in the country is the Bank of Tonga. The most convenient office is at the waterfront end of Taufa'ahau Rd., Nuku'alofa's main street; it is open Mon–Fri 9:30am–3:30pm. A small branch office in Tungi Arcade near the Ramanlal Hotel on Taufa'ahau Rd. is open during those same hours weekdays and Sat 9:30–11:30am. In addition, the bank has a new building and currency exchange on Railway Rd. in the block south of Wellington Rd. You will need your passport in order to exchange currency or traveler's checks. The International Dateline Hotel and the Ramanlal Hotel will change money at a rate slightly lower than you will get at the bank.

Customs See "Information, Entry Requirements, and Money" in this chapter.

Driving Rules See "Getting Around Tongatapu" in this chapter.

Drug Laws Don't even think about bringing illegal narcotics or dangerous drugs into Tonga. The dogs often seen on leashes at the airport are there to sniff for drugs.

Dentist Vaiola Hospital (tel. 21-200) provides dental service in Nuku'alofa; the outpatient clinics are open daily 8:30am–4:30pm.

Doctor German-trained Dr. Helga Schafer-Macdonald (tel. 22-736) practices on Wellington Rd. near Fatafehi Rd. Vaiola Hospital (tel. 21-200) provides medical, dental, and optical service, but it's not on a par with that of American Samoa or the Cook Islands and is considerably below Western standards. The outpatient clinics are open daily 8:30am–4:30pm.

Drugstores The Nuku'alofa Clinic and Pharmacy (tel. 21-007) is on Salote Rd. in the block west of Taufa'ahau Rd. Hours are Mon–Fri 9:30am–5pm, Sat 9am–noon. Frankly, if you take prescription drugs, bring an ample supply with you.

Electricity Electricity in Tonga is 240 volts, 50 cycles, and the plugs are the heavy, angled type used in Australia and New Zealand. You will need a converter and adapter plug to operate American and Canadian appliances.

Embassies/Consulates The nearest U.S. embassy is in Suva, Fiji. There is an office of the United States Peace Corps in Nuku'alofa (tel. 21-467). Consular offices in Tonga are the Australian High Commission (tel. 21-244), the British High Commission (tel. 21-021), the New Zealand High Commission (tel. 21-122), the Embassy of the Republic of China (Taiwan) (tel. 21-766), the Honorary Consulate of France (tel. 21-830), the Honorary Consulate of Germany (tel. 21-477), and the Honorary Consulate of Nauru (tel. 22-109).

Emergencies The emergency telephone number for the police, fire department, and hospital is 911.

Etiquette See the "People and Culture" section under "Getting to Know Tonga" in this chapter.

Eyeglasses Viola Hospital is the only place to get glasses fixed or replaced. See "Hospital," below.

Firearms Firearms are illegal in Tonga.

Gambling There is no casino or other form of organized gambling in Tonga.

Hitchhiking It's not against the law, but Tongans are not particularly accustomed to picking up strangers.

Information See "Information, Entry Requirements, and Money" in this chapter.

Insects There are no dangerous insects in Tonga, and the mosquitoes do not carry malaria. Vava'u, warmer and more humid than Tongatapu, tends to have more mosquitoes and has tropical centipedes that can inflict painful stings if touched; watch your step if walking around with bare feet.

Laundry The hotels can arrange to have your clothes washed and ironed, or you can take them to Iongi Laundry Services on Wellington Rd. just west of Taufa'ahau Rd. Hours are Mon–Fri 7am–5pm, Sat 7am–1pm.

Library 'Utue'a Public Library, on the ground floor of Basilica of St. Anthony of Padua on Taufa'ahau Rd. is open Mon–Fri 11am–1pm and 4–8pm, Sat 10am–1pm.

Liquor Laws Licensed hotels can sell alcoholic beverages to their guests 7 days a week; otherwise, sale is prohibited from midnight Sat to midnight Sun. The local beer is appropriately named Royal Lager.

Mail The Central Post Office is at the corner of Taufa'ahau and Salote roads in Nuku'alofa. It's open Mon–Fri 8:30am–4pm. Airmail letters to the U.S. cost T57¢ (50¢), post cards are T32¢ (30¢). Tongan stamps, some of which are in the shape of bananas and pineapples, are collectors' items. They are available at the post office or at the Philatelic Bureau, in the Treasury Building at the waterfront end of Taufa'ahau Rd. The Philatelic Bureau is open Mon–Fri 8:30am–12:30pm and 1:30–4:30pm.

Maps Free maps of Nuku'alofa, Tongatapu, and Vava'u are available at the Tonga Visitors Bureau. Friendly Islands Bookstore, on Taufa'ahau Rd. across from the Ramanlal Hotel in Nuku'alofa, carries maps of Tonga, including the best available, *The Kingdom of Tonga,* published by Pacific Maps of Australia.

Newspapers/Magazines The *Tonga Chronicle* is a government-owned weekly newspaper appearing on Fri. It carries world and local news in both Tongan and English, but there are so many stories about the king and his family that many locals facetiously call it the "Royal Diary." For a different view, look for *Kele'a* and *Times of Tonga,* two tabloid newspapers published by commoners. A fine local magazine, *Matangi Tonga,* edited by the noted Tongan writer and publisher Pesi Fonua, carries features about the kingdom and its people. For news of the world, you'll have to rely on the radio or the international newsmagazines.

Photographic Needs Color film and color-print film processing is available at a number of shops in Nuku'alofa, including the gift shop at the International Dateline Hotel.

Police The main station is on Salote Rd. at Railway Rd. The emergency phone number is 911.

Radio/TV The government-owned radio station, A3Z or "Radio Tonga," broadcasts on both the AM and FM bands. Most programming on the AM station is in Tongan, although the music played is mostly American, Australian, or British popular tunes. The news in English is relayed from the BBC or Radio Australia Mon–Sat at 7am, 1pm, and 8pm, Sun at 8pm. The news from the Voice of America is rebroadcast Mon–Sat at 1:15pm.

Tonga has a broadcast television station that is on the air daily 5–11pm. Like everywhere else in the South Pacific, videotapes are the rage. This is the South Pacific's "Bible Belt," and the sermons of American television evangelists are popular in Tonga. The king has his own satellite dish on the palace grounds.

Religious Services About half of all Tongans belong to the Free Wesleyan Church of Tonga, which was founded by the early Methodist missionaries. The Free Church of Tonga is another local Protestant denomination. There are also considerable numbers of Roman Catholics, Anglicans, Seventh-Day Adventists, and Mormons. Church services usually are held Sun at 10am, but very few of them are conducted in English. St. Paul's Anglican Church, corner of Fafatehi and Wellington roads, usually has communion in English at 8am Sun. When I was there recently, a nondenominational English-language service was held at 10am in the conference room of the Ramanlal Hotel. The royal family worships at 10am in the Free Wesleyan Church on Wellington Rd., a block behind the Royal Palace.

Rest Rooms You will have to rely on the hotels and restaurants.

Safety Although crimes against tourists are rare in Tonga, remember that the communal-property system still prevails in the kingdom. Items such as cameras and bags left unattended may disappear, so take the proper precautions. Street crime is not a problem, but it's a good idea to be on the alert if you walk down dark streets at night. Women should not wander alone on deserted beaches. See "Fast Facts: South Pacific" in Chapter 2 for more warnings.

Shoe Repairs Try Fale Su on Railway Rd. in the block south of Wellington Rd.

Taxes The government imposes a 5% sales tax on all items purchased in Tonga, including hotel rooms. The tax is added to the bill in the American fashion. All passengers on international flights pay a departure tax of T$10 ($8) at Fua'amotu Airport (an amount which may increase in 1992).

Telephone/Telex/Fax International calls, telegrams, and telex messages can be placed from your hotel or at the office of Cable and Wireless Ltd., on Salote Rd. at the corner of Takaunove Rd., which is open 24 hours a day, 7 days a week. Station-to-station phone calls to the U.S. cost T$10 ($8) for the first 3 minutes, T$13 ($10.50) for person-to-person. The rates to Australia and New Zealand are about half those amounts. Cable and Wireless accepts Bell System credit cards issued by the American telephone companies.

Public pay telephones are at the airport, post offices, and in red, English-style booths in a few villages. You lift the receiver, listen for a dial tone, deposit a Tongan 10-seniti coin, and dial the number. The number for **directory assistance** is 910 or 919; for **emergencies,** 911; and for the **international operator,** 913.

Calls from overseas to Tonga can be dialed directly. The international **country code is 676.**

Time Local time in Tonga is 13 hours ahead of Greenwich mean time. Translated, Tonga is 3 hours behind the U.S. West Coast during standard time (4 hours behind during daylight saving time)—and 1 day ahead. If it's noon on Tues in Tonga, it's 3pm Pacific standard time on Mon in Los Angeles and 6pm Eastern standard time on Mon in New York.

Remember when traveling in the South Pacific to add a day when crossing the international date line from east to west and to subtract a day when crossing it from west to east. I have had friends from Australia show up on my doorstep in the U.S. 24 hours earlier than planned simply because they forgot to subtract a day when adjusting their watches.

Tipping Although it has gained a foothold, tipping is officially discouraged in Tonga because it's considered contrary to the Polynesian tradition of hospitality to guests. One time it is encouraged is during Tongan dance shows, when members of the audience rush up to the female dancers and stick notes to their well-oiled bodies.

Tourist Offices See "Information, Entry Requirements, and Money" in this chapter.

Visas See "Information, Entry Requirements, and Money" in this chapter.

Water The tap water in Nuku'alofa is drinkable, but the same cannot be said about the rest of the kingdom. When outside of town, make sure to ask if the drinking water is from a rainwater catchment, in which case it's safe to imbibe.

Weights/Measures Tonga uses the metric system of weights and measures. See the appendix for methods of conversion.

5. WHAT TO SEE & DO

Since tourism is not as developed in Tonga as it is in some other South Pacific island countries, there are not as many activities here as you'll find elsewhere. That's not to say that you won't keep busy, however, for there are fine beaches to lie on, small islets to visit, and much to see of a historical nature in this quaint little kingdom.

Several travel agencies have daily tours of Nuku'alofa and Tongatapu. Most of them divide their trips into eastern and western tours, each taking between 2 and 3 hours. **Teta Tours** (tel. 21-688) has the best deal: T$21 ($17) for a full day doing the entire island, or T$10.50 ($8.50) for just one half. Other companies are **Union Travel** (tel. 21-645), **Jones Travel** (tel. 21-422), **Bonita Travel** (tel. 22-552), and **Moana Travel & Tours** (tel. 22-188). The activities desk at the International Dateline Hotel or the receptionists at the other hotels can make reservations.

Tonga closes on Sunday even tighter than the Cook Islands and Western Samoa. Only one restaurant outside the hotels serves food, and the national radio station doesn't come on until noon, when everyone is home from church. In other words, it takes a little planning if you want to do anything other than walk around the almost-deserted streets or hang around your hotel, which will be one of the few places in Tonga open for business. Here are some suggestions (also, see "Cruises," below).

Consider **going to church.** Nearly everyone else in Tonga does. Most hotels will arrange for you to attend a service of your choice and will scout around to find one in English (see the listing for "Religious Services" in "Fast Facts: Tonga," above). Even if you can't understand what's being said, you'll enjoy the beautiful harmony of the Tongans raising their voices in song. The royal family worships at 10am on Sunday at the Centenary Church, the large Free Wesleyan church we will see on our walking tour of Nuku'alofa. It's a good chance to get a look at His Majesty in person. The king and most other Tongan men wear neckties to church, but male tourists get by without one if they're neatly dressed. After church, most Tongans go home to a feast with their families and then enjoy lounging around the rest of the day.

A WALKING TOUR OF NUKU'ALOFA

Before you start out to see Nuku'alofa, drop by the Tonga Visitors Bureau office on Vuna Road near the International Dateline Hotel and pick up a copy of the excellent brochure, "Walking Tour of Central Nuku'alofa." A morning's stroll around this interesting town will be time well spent, for in many respects it's a throwback to times gone by in the South Pacific. Although there are no street-name posts, the visitors bureau has put up signs giving general directions to the main sights. In addition, Nuku'alofa more or less is laid out on a grid, so you shouldn't have trouble finding your way around. It's also flat, with no hills to climb.

The following is a truncated version of the visitors bureau tour that hits the highlights of Nuku'alofa. Let's start at the **visitors bureau** and walk west along Vuna Road toward the heart of town.

The park on the left as you leave the visitors bureau is known as **Fa'onelua Gardens.** You'll hear the tap-tap-tap of artisans working on the wood carvings they try to sell to us travelers. Other craftspeople gather on the water side of Vuna Road and display shell jewelry and interesting scrimshaw. The shack-looking buildings at the rear of the park are used by vendors selling various wares; it's a beehive of activity on Saturday morning, the traditional shopping time throughout the South Pacific.

The modern three-story building before Railway Road houses the government ministries of works, agriculture, health, education, lands and survey, and civil aviation. Every time I see this building, I—as a resident of the Washington, D.C., area—think of my own nation's capital, where it takes several huge buildings and hundreds of acres of land to house that many departments of the U.S. government.

Vuna Wharf, at the foot of Taufa'ahau Road, Nuku'alofa's main street, was built in 1906, and for some 60 years most visitors to Tonga debarked from ships that tied up here. It became less trafficked when Queen Salote Wharf was erected east of town in 1966 to handle large ships, and a major earthquake in 1977 damaged Vuna Wharf so extensively that it has been used since only in emergencies. A railroad once ran through town along Railway Road to transport copra and other crops to Vuna Wharf. Meat and some vegetables are sold at **Vuna Market** at the head of the wharf. Supplies of locally grown meat are irregular, and a sign on the market indicates which

---

IMPRESSIONS

The people of Tonga love their green islands and think anyone who lives elsewhere is unfortunate.

—Luis Marden, 1968

The people stay home on Sundays and entertain each other with good food, even if they have to semi-starve all week.

—John Dyson, 1982

types happen to be available each day. Crowds gather late in the afternoon to await the return of the fishermen, who quickly sell their catch at the adjacent fish market.

Directly across Vuna Road from the wharf is the low **Treasury Building.** Constructed in 1928, it's a fine example of South Pacific colonial architecture. Early in its life it housed the Tongan Customs service and the post office as well as the Treasury Department. The Philatelic Bureau is inside.

The field to the west of the wharf is the ✪ **Pangai,** where royal feasts, kava ceremonies, and parades are held. Overlooking the Pangai and surrounded by towering Norfolk pines is the **Royal Palace,** a white Victorian building with gingerbread fretwork and gables under a red roof. The palace was prefabricated in New Zealand, shipped to Tonga, and erected in 1867. The second-story veranda was added in 1882. You can get a good view over the low white fence built of coral blocks (the best spot for photographs is on the east side, so save some film until we get around there).

Now walk up Taufa'ahau Road past the modern Bank of Tonga on the right and the colonial-style **Prime Minister's Office** with its quaint tower on the left. **Parliament** meets from June to September in the old building behind the latter.

Turn right at the post office on Salote Road. The **Nuku'alofa Club** on the left, about halfway down the block, is another holdover from the old South Pacific: It's a private club where Tonga's elite males gather to relax over a game of snooker and a few Australian beers. The next block of Salote Road runs behind the Royal Palace; occasionally it's closed while the king rides his bicycle. Turn right on Vaha'akolo Road and walk along the east side of the palace toward the sea. The highest point on Tongatapu, **Chapel Hill** (or Zion Hill) to the left, part of the Royal Estate, was a Tongan fort during the 18th century and the site of a missionary school opened in 1830 and a large Wesleyan church built in 1865. The school is now located 4 miles west of Nuku'alofa and is known as **Sia'atoutai Theological College.** The church has long since been torn down.

When you get to the water, look back and take your photos of the palace framed by the Norfolk pines.

Picturesque **Vuna Road** runs west from the palace, with the sea and reef on one side and stately old colonial homes on the other. The house at the end of the first block was the home of a Tongan noble who on several occasions in the 1800s went to England, where he stayed with friends in Newcastle; accordingly, he named the house **Niukasa.** The British High Commissioner's residence, in the second block, sports a flagpole surrounded by four cannons from the *Port au Prince,* the ship captured and burned by the Tongans at Ha'apai in 1806 after they had clubbed to death all of its crew except the young Will Mariner. King George I had two wives—not concurrently—and both of them are buried in casuarina-ringed Mala'e'aloa Cemetery, whose name means "tragic field." The clapboard house in the next block is known as **Ovalau** because it was built in the 1800s at Levuka, the old capital of Fiji on the island of Ovalau, and was shipped to Tonga in the 1950s.

Turn inland at the corner, walk 2 blocks on 'Alipate Road, take a left on Wellington Road, and walk 2 blocks west to **Centenary Church.** The mansion just before the church was reputed to have been built about 1871 by the Rev. Shirley W. Baker, the missionary who had so much influence over King George I. Now it's the home of the president of the Free Wesleyan Church of Tonga. Centenary Church was built by the Free Wesleyan Church of Tonga between 1949 and 1952. Most of the construction materials and labor were donated by members of the church. While construction was going on, the town was divided into sections which fed the workers three meals a day on a rotating basis. The amount of money spent on the building was about T$80,000 ($72,000); the actual value of the materials and labor was many times that amount. The church seats about 2,000 persons, including the king and queen, who worship there on Sunday mornings.

Turn right past the church and proceed inland on Vaha'akolo Road. On the right behind the Centenary Church is the old **Free Wesleyan Church of Tonga,** built in 1888 and an example of early Tongan church architecture. Past the old church is **Queen Salote College,** a girls' school named for a wife of King George I and not for his great-great-granddaughter, the famous Queen Salote.

Turn left at the first street, known as Laifone Road, and walk along a large open space to your right. Since 1893 this area has been known as the ✪ **Royal Tombs,** and King George I, King George II, Queen Salote, and most of their various wives and husbands are buried at the center of the field. For many years the rest of the area was used as a golf course; today, however, the king's cattle keep the grass mowed.

Taufa'ahau Road runs along the far end of the Royal Tombs, and on the other side of it rises the modern, tent-shaped **Basilica of St. Anthony of Padua,** the first basilica built in the South Pacific islands. On the ground level are the **Loki Kai Cafeteria** (more commonly known as Akiko's Restaurant) and the **'Utue'a Public Library.** The **Maulua Women's Development Handicraft Center,** which carries a small selection of tapa cloth, baskets, wood carvings, and shell jewelry, is on the basilica grounds near the street.

Now follow **Taufa'ahau Road** toward the waterfront. This is Nuku'alofa's "main street," and you'll pass shop after shop, some of them carrying handcrafts and clothing. Between Wellington Road and Salote Road is an old house that now is the home of Teta Tours and the **Langa Fonua Women's Association Handicraft Center** (see "Shopping for Handcrafts," below). The clapboard house was built by William Cocker, a local merchant, for his five daughters, who lived in New Zealand but spent each winter in Nuku'alofa.

Turn right on the next street—Salote Road—and walk past the police station on the left to **Talamahu Market** in the second block. Inside the market's walls of concrete block are vendors selling a great variety of fresh produce ranging from huge taro roots and watermelons to string beans and bananas. Tongatapu's climate is just cool enough during the winter months that both European and tropical fruits and vegetables grow in great bounty. Several stalls along the interior walls carry handcraft items, such as tapa cloth and straw baskets and mats.

After looking around the market and perhaps munching on a banana or sipping a fresh young coconut, continue walking east. In the next block is the park known as Fa'onelua Gardens; walk through it to the Tonga Visitors Bureau, where we began our tour and where we end it.

TONGA NATIONAL CENTER

Anyone with the slightest interest in native cultures should make a point to visit the ✪ **Tonga National Centre** (tel. 23-022), one of the South Pacific's best exhibitions. Located on the lagoon shores across from Vaiola Hospital about a mile from Nuku'alofa on Taufa'ahau Road, the center's fale-style buildings house displays of Tongan history, geology, and handcrafts. In fact, artisans work daily on their crafts and sell their wares to visitors (no packing and shipping). In other words, you can see how Tonga's remarkable handcrafts are made, which should help as you later scour the local shops for good buys. The exhibition hall is open from 9am to noon Monday to Friday, and regular admission is T$2 ($1.60). Twice a week, usually on Tuesday and Thursday, a lunch of Tongan food is followed by special displays from 2 to 4pm featuring demonstrations of carving, weaving, tapa making, food preparation, a kava ceremony, and dance demonstration. The price is just T$5 ($4). A travel agent or hotel tour desk will make reservations for you.

History buffs will appreciate seeing the long robe Queen Salote wore at the coronation of Queen Elizabeth II in 1953 and the carcass of Tui Malila, the Galápagos tortoise Capt. James Cook reputedly gave the Tui Tonga in 1777. The beast lived until 1968.

TOURING TONGATAPU

THE EASTERN TOUR

Take Taufa'ahau Road out of Nuku'alofa, making sure to bear left on the paved road. If you want to see colorful tropical birds in captivity, watch for the signs on the right-hand side of the road directing you to the **Bird Exhibit,** and follow the dirt track about 3km (2 miles). There you will find a park with a small collection of birds from Tonga and other South Pacific islands kept in cages carefully planted with native vegetation. Admission is free, although donations are accepted. The exhibit is open from 10am to 5pm Wednesday to Sunday.

Now backtrack to the main road and turn right toward the airport. Keep left, especially at Malapo (where the road to the airport goes to the right), and follow the Tonga Visitors Bureau's excellent signs which will show you the way to **Mu'a.** When the road skirts the lagoon just before the village, watch for a grassy area beside the water where Capt. James Cook landed and rested under a large banyan tree in 1777. Cook came ashore to meet with Pau, the reigning Tui Tonga, and attended the traditional presentation of first fruits marking the beginning of the harvest season. The banyan tree is long gone; in its place is a stone-and-brass monument commemorating **Captain Cook's Landing Place.**

The next village is ✪ **Lapaha,** seat of the Tui Tonga for six centuries beginning about A.D. 1200. All that remains of the royal compound is a series of *langa,* or ancient terraced tombs, some of which are visible from the road. A large sign explains how the supreme Polynesian god, Tangaloa, came down from the sky about A.D. 950 and sired the first Tui Tonga. The last Tui Tonga, who died in 1865 after being deposed by King George I in 1862, is buried in one of the tombs. The 28 tombs around Lapaha and Mu'a are among the most important archeological sites in Polynesia, but none of them has been excavated. Walk down the dirt road near the sign to see more of the tombs.

From Lapaha, follow the scenic paved road along the coast until reaching the ✪ **Ha'amonga Trilithon,** near the village of Niutoua on the island's northeast point, 32km (19 miles) from Nuku'alofa. This huge archway, whose lintel stone is estimated to weigh 35 tons, is 16 feet high and 19 feet wide. Tradition says it was built by the 11th Tui Tonga about A.D. 1200, long before the wheel was introduced to Tonga, as the gateway to the royal compound. The present King Taufa'ahau Tupou IV advanced a theory that it was used not only as a gateway but also for measuring the seasons. He found a secret mark on top of the lintel stone and at dawn on June 21, 1967, proved his point. The mark pointed to the exact spot on the horizon from which the sun rose on the shortest day of the year. You can stand under this imposing archway and ponder just how the ancient Tongans got the lintel stone on top of its two supports; it's the same sense of mysterious wonderment you feel while looking at Stonehenge in England or contemplating the great long-nosed heads that were carved and somehow erected by those other Polynesians far to the east of Tonga on Easter Island.

The paved road ends at **Niutoua,** but a narrow dirt track proceeds down the east coast. **Anahulu** is a cave with limestone stalactites near the village of Haveluliku. A gorgeous sand beach begins here and runs to **Oholei Beach,** where the Kami family stages its Tongan feasts on Wednesday and Friday nights. 'Eua Island is visible on the horizon.

On the way back to Nuku'alofa you can take a detour to **Hufangalupe Beach** on the south coast for a look at a large natural bridge carved out of coral and limestone by the sea.

THE WESTERN TOUR

Proceed out of Nuku'alofa on Mateialona Road and follow the visitors bureau signs to the ✪ **blowholes** near the village of Houma on the southwest coast. At high tide the surf pounds under shelves, sending geysers of seawater through holes in the coral. These are the most impressive blowholes in the South Pacific, and on a windy day the coast for miles is shrouded in mist thrown into the air by hundreds of them working at once. They perform best on a day when the surf is medium—that is, just high enough to pound under the shelves and send water exploding up through holes in them. Lime sediments have built up terraces of circles, like rice paddies, around each hole, and the local women come just before dusk to gather clams in the shallow pools formed by the rings. There is a park with benches and a parking area at the end of the road near the blowholes, but you'll need shoes with good soles to walk across the sharp edges of the top shelf to get the best views. This area once was an underwater reef, and corals are still very much visible, all of them now more than 50 feet above sea level. (Look for what appears to be fossilized brains; they are appropriately named brain corals.) The blowholes are known in Tongan as Mapu'a a Vaea, "the chief's whistle."

From Houma, proceed west to the village of Kolovai and watch for the strange-looking trees across the road from the Loseli Art and Handicraft Center. The sounds you hear and the odors in the air are coming from what appear to be leaves on the trees. In reality, however, these are not leaves; they are the **Flying Foxes of Kolovai,** a type of bat with a foxlike head found on many islands in the Pacific. They are nocturnal creatures who spend their days hanging upside down from the branches of trees like a thousand little Draculas awaiting the dark, their wings like black capes pulled tightly around their bodies. They don't feed on blood but on fruit; hence they are known as fruit bats. On some islands they are considered a delicacy. In Tonga, however, where they live in trees throughout the villages of Kolovai and Ha'avakatolo, they are thought to be sacred, and only members of the royal family can shoot them. Legend says that the first bats were given to a Tongan navigator by a Samoan princess.

A road from Kolovai goes about a mile west of **Kolovai Beach** and the Good Samaritan Inn, a good place to sip a drink while watching the sun set or to enjoy a picnic on Sunday afternoons. Near the end of the island is **Ha'atafu Beach,** site of an offshore reef preserve.

The first missionaries to land in Tonga came ashore at the end of the peninsula on the northwest coast, and a sign now marks the spot at the end of the road. They obviously got their feet wet—if they were not inadvertently "baptized"—wading across the shallow bank just offshore.

You've now toured Tongatapu from one end to the other. Turn around and head back to town.

SPORTS & RECREATION

There is a reasonable selection of sporting activities available on Tongatapu, although the best water sports are on some of the small islets off Nuku'alofa.

SWIMMING & SNORKELING

Tongatapu has a number of lovely beaches—Oholei and Ha'atafu to name two—but the water off most of them is very shallow, especially at low tide, making snorkeling either impossible or precarious. Since there are no beaches near Nuku'alofa, you'll have to plan an outing, perhaps to one of the resorts on the small offshore islands. My own preference is to spend the day sunning and swimming at **Fafa Island Resort** (tel. 22-800) or **Pangaimotu Island Resort** (tel. 21-155 or 22-588). Both have boats leaving Faua Jetty at 11am returning in the late afternoon. You can also spend Sunday at **Royal Sunset Island Resort** (tel. 21-254). Day-trip prices are T$21 ($17) at Pangaimotu, T$23 ($18.50) at Fafa, and T$26 ($21) at Royal Sunset. (See "Where to Stay," below in this chapter, for more information about Fafa and Royal Sunset resorts.)

To reach the reefs offshore, **Coralhead Diving** (tel. 22-176) and **Tongan Fishing and Sea Tours** (tel. 23-777) both have snorkeling trips for T$15 ($12) per person, including equipment (see "Scuba Diving" and "Fishing," below, for their respective locations). You can rent snorkel, mask, and fins from Coralhead Diving for T$5 ($4) a day.

SCUBA DIVING

American Bob Holcomb of **Coralhead Diving** (tel. 22-176) takes divers to several interesting spots, including Hakaumama'o Reef Reserve and Malinoa Reef Reserve, both north of Nuku'alofa. Boat transportation is on the 27-foot *African Queen* or a 17-foot inflatable known as *White Knuckles*. Bob rents full scuba equipment and teaches certification courses. His prices range from T$40 ($32) to T$75 ($60) per dive, depending on how many people go along. Bob's headquarters are on the little side street that runs off Vuna Road opposite Faua Jetty (turn in at Davina's Restaurant). His address is P.O. Box 211, Nuku'alofa, Tonga.

Working in conjunction with Coralhead Diving, Colin Lynch of **South Seas Safaris** (tel. 22-176) has 6-day live-aboard cruises on a 47-foot sailboat to the Ha'apai Group, where divers can explore the rocks and coral reefs off hard-to-reach Tofua, Kao, Ofolanga, and Ha'ano islands. The hot seawater around Tofua's active volcano gives rise to very different sea life than found elsewhere in Tonga. Colin charges T$130 ($104) per person a day, plus T$25 ($20) for a dive guide and T$10 ($8) for gear hire.

The cruising yacht ***Anita*** (see "Cruises," below) also takes divers to various Tongan waters.

FISHING

Nonga Vea of **Tongan Fishing and Sea Tours** (tel. 23-777) keeps his fishing boat moored at the jetty opposite the International Dateline Hotel and will use it to take guests not only on fishing trips but on snorkeling expeditions and island-hopping tours as well. He even will drop you off on a small islet, where you can camp overnight. His bottom, reef, and deep-sea fishing trips cost T$30 ($24) per person a day. The boat is equipped with ship-to-shore radio and life jackets. You can find him at the jetty early mornings or late afternoons; if you call the phone number above, ask for Pauline.

Royal Sunset Sportfishing (tel. 21-254), based at Royal Sunset Island Resort on 'Atata Island, has two fully equipped boats that go in search of skipjack, yellowfin tuna, sailfish, blue marlin, and other deep-sea fish. Prices are NZ$400 ($240) per boat for ½ day.

CRUISES

Every time I'm in Tonga it seems that another New Zealander, Australian, or European has sailed a boat to the country and gone into the yacht-charter and cruise business. During my recent visit the new arrival was the ***Anita,*** a 57-foot, gaff-rigged trawling ketch built in Sweden in 1944. On Thursday and Sunday, it usually goes on day-trips from Nuku'alofa to uninhabited Malinoa Island, where guests can swim, snorkel, and enjoy a picnic on the beach. The price is T$30 ($24), including lunch. Reserve at Fasi-Moe-Afi Guest House (tel. 22-289) on Vuna Road before noon on Wednesday or Saturday.

In addition to the *Anita,* a popular way (for tourists) to spend Sunday, particularly if you don't attend church, is at either **Pangaimotu Island Resort** (tel. 21-155 or 22-588), **Royal Sunset Island Resort** (tel. 21-254), or at **Fafa Island Resort** (tel. 22-800), all just a few miles off Nuku'alofa. All three have boats leaving Faua Jetty about 11am and returning to Nuku'alofa about 5pm. Day-trip prices are T$21 ($17) at Pangaimotu, T$23 ($18.50) at Fafa, and T$26 ($21) at Royal Sunset. Bring your bathing suit, towel, sunscreen, and hat. The resorts have changing rooms, cold-water showers, toilets, and a bar. Some visitors go to the islands on Saturday and stay over until Sunday. See "Cruises," above, for information about the *Anita;* see "Where to Stay," below, for details on Royal Sunset and Fafa resorts.

When you get back to Nuku'alofa, plan on eating at one of the hotel restaurants or at the Phoenix Chinese Restaurant. It will be a very quiet evening in town.

IMPRESSIONS

Despite the lack of green fields and church spires, in the pearly dawn from the ship's bridge the Vava'u Group had the appearance of a lump of Cornwall or Brittany that had been dropped on a hard surface from a height just sufficient to scatter the thirty-four fragments and create deep channels, scarcely wider than rivers, between them. As the ship wandered among the scrub-covered limestone tableaux I thought it was the nearest thing in cruise-liner terms to cross-country driving.

—JOHN DYSON, 1982

GOLF

You won't be playing any golf on Sunday, but you can every other day at the flat, nine-hole **Manamo'ui Golf Course,** home of the Tonga Golf Club. The tour desk at the International Dateline Hotel (tel. 23-411) can arrange equipment rentals and tee-off times on this somewhat less than challenging course, which is on the main road between the airport and town.

SHOPPING FOR HANDCRAFTS

If you've shopped on Tahiti or most other South Pacific countries, you'll be shocked at the extraordinary quality, quantity, and value of Tongan tapa cloth, mats, carvings, shell jewelry, and other exquisite items. Indeed, Tonga is the place to shop for authentic handcrafts in Polynesia. Your large laundry basket may take a few months to get home via ship if you don't send it by air freight or check it as baggage on your return flight, but the quality of its craftmanship will be worth the wait.

Tapa cloth and mats are traditional items of clothing and gifts in Tonga, and the women of the kingdom have carried on the ancient skills, not only out of economic necessity (it is, after all, a poor kingdom) but also out of pride in their craft. Collectively they produce thousands of items a day, every one made by hand and no two exactly alike. The sounds of hammers beating tapa cloth from the bark of the paper mulberry tree is a familiar sound in many Tongan villages.

For an excellent description of how tapa cloth is made and the process by which the women weave baskets, mats, and other items from natural materials, pick up a copy of the Tonga Visitors Bureau's brochure "Tongan Handicrafts."

Individual artisans gather each evening along **Vuna Road** opposite the International Dateline Hotel and sell jewelry they have made from shells and black coral. The quality of some items is quite good, and contrary to the usual Polynesian practice, some vendors will bargain over the price. The more pieces you buy, the less each one will cost. Some vendors have scrimshawed tropical designs on the bones of humpback whales caught during Tonga's whaling season, from June to October. Some of them will tell you that the designs are on fish and not whale bones; believe them if you want, but remember that you cannot legally bring whale bones back to the United States or to most other Western countries (the same restriction applies to the varnished sea-turtle shells you may see at the handcraft shops).

There are handcraft stalls along the interior walls of the **Talamahu Market** on Salote Road, where occasionally you can find an excellent basket or other item. Wood-carvers are constantly at work in **Fa'onelua Gardens,** near the International Dateline Hotel, and they will hawk their products as you pass by on your way to or from town.

NOTE: The village women on Vava'u turn out some of Tonga's best handcrafts, and the prices there can be substantially less than what you will pay for their items after they are shipped to Nuku'alofa. If you're going to Vava'u, look around the shops in Nuku'alofa first but don't buy until you have seen what's available there. (See "An Easy Excursion to Vava'u," below, for details.)

Except for tobacco products and liquor, Tonga has little to offer in the way of duty-free shopping. Get your booze and smokes at the airport or order them at least 1 day prior to departure at the gift shop in the International Dateline Hotel.

IMPRESSIONS

The people were hospitable and, as you sailed in, local boats really did come alongside as they did in voyagers' tales, to invite you to their villages for a feast. Only when arrangements were finalised does the awful truth dawn: it is not natural hospitality being pressed so warmly upon you, but salesmanship.

—John Dyson, 1982

KALIA HAND CRAFTS, Fatafehi Rd. at Salote Rd. Tel. 23-155.

The retail outlet of the Friendly Islands Marketing Cooperative (FIMCO) is the place to start looking in Nuku'alofa, since this organization gets the best and largest supply of baskets, mats, tapa, shell jewelry, and other handcrafts. You can pay with American Express, Diners Club, and VISA credit cards, and the staff will pack and ship your purchases home. The shop is open 8:30am to 7:30pm Monday to Friday, 8am to 4pm Saturday.

LANGA FONUA WOMEN'S ASSOCIATION, Taufa'ahau Rd. Tel. 21-014.

Before FIMCO more or less cornered the market, this shop in the colonial house shared with Teta Tours, on the second block of Taufa'ahau Road from the waterfront, was the place to look. Queen Salote founded the association in 1953 in order to preserve the old crafts and provide a market. You may find an excellent piece or two at somewhat lower prices than you will pay elsewhere, but usually the selection is much narrower than at Kalia Hand Crafts.

EVENING ENTERTAINMENT

TONGAN DANCE SHOWS

Traditional **Tongan dancing** emphasizes fluid movements of the hands and feet instead of gyrating hips, as is the case in French Polynesia and the Cook Islands. There also is less emphasis on drums and more on the stamping, clapping, and singing of the participants. The dances most often performed for tourists are the *tau'olunga,* in which one young woman dances solo, her body glistening with coconut oil; the *ma'ulu'ulu,* performed sitting down by groups ranging from 20 members to as many as 900 for very important occasions; the *lakalaka,* in which rows of dancers sing and dance in unison; and the *kailao,* or war dance, in which men stamp the ground and wave war clubs at each other in mock battle.

FROMMER'S FAVORITE

TONGA EXPERIENCES

Seeing the King Being an American and therefore not particularly enamored of royalty, I nevertheless enjoy watching King Taufa'ahau Tupou being chauffeured around his kingdom—sometimes in the back seat of a stretched pickup truck—and being given the royal treatment whenever he arrives somewhere.

Sunday on an Islet I usually stay very busy revising this guide, but I am forced by law to put it aside and relax on Sunday in Tonga. I like to spend my day doing nothing at one of the little resorts off Nuku'alofa.

Oholei Beach Sometimes I think I've eaten every feast and seen every dance show in the South Pacific, but I never tire of the Kami family's at Oholei Beach. A new generation has taken over since I first met the Kamis, but it's still a joy to watch them prepare the meal, serve it, and then dance their hearts out.

Watching the Blowholes Having crossed the Pacific several times in U.S. Navy ships and sailed across it once in a small boat, I am acutely aware of the power of the sea. It's strangely comforting to watch it explode through the blowholes on Tongatapu's south coast. Maybe it's because I know those waves can't get me up there on dry land.

Exploring Vava'u There are a lot of South Pacific places where I would like to stay just a little longer, and beautiful Vava'u is at the top of the list. It's also one of the best lower-budget places I know to get away from it all.

A Wednesday or Friday evening in Tonga should be spent with the Kami family at its **Oholei Beach Feast** and traditional dance show. Also on Friday, Soeli Ofa and his family perform at **Keleti Beach Resort** (tel. 21-179) on Tongatapu's south shore. You'll have a chance to see Tongan dancing in Nuku'alofa at the **International Dateline Hotel** (tel. 23-411), usually on Thursday or Saturday evening, when floor shows start about 9pm after buffet-style dinners (the nights may change, so check with the hotel). See "Where to Dine," below, for information about prices, times, etc.

Don't hesitate to join the Tongans in sticking a few pa'anga notes to the dancers' shiny shoulders and arms.

PUB CRAWLING

Several nightclubs swing into action on Thursday, Friday, and Saturday nights, offering dancing to live bands or recorded rock music. They go until 2am or even 4am Friday and Saturday mornings but close on Saturday evenings when the stroke of midnight heralds the arrival of Sunday. Friday is the busiest night of the week.

AMBASSADOR NITE CLUB, Taufa'ahau Rd. on Fanga'uta Lagoon. Tel. 23-338.

This pleasant lagoonside pavilion south of the Tongan National Center covers a bar, dance floor, meeting areas, and a fast-food restaurant. A band plays Monday to Saturday from 8pm onward, and special performances frequently occur, especially if a successful Tongan singer or band is home from overseas. The club is open 5pm to midnight Monday to Wednesday, 5pm to 3:30am Thursday and Friday, noon to midnight Saturday. The fast-food bar (chicken- or fish-and-chips, chow mein, chicken curry, hot dogs, all in the T$2 to T$6 [$1.50 to $5] range) is open from 8am until closing time.

Admission: T$5 ($4). **Prices:** Drinks T$2 ($1.50) and up.

'OFA ATU NITE CLUB, Friendly Islander Motel, Vuna Rd. Tel. 21-900.

This pleasant nightclub at the rear of the Friendly Islander Motel features lively music from either a live band or disc jockey. The club is open only Friday from 8pm to 4am.

Admission: T$3 ($2.50) before 11pm, T$5 ($4) after 11pm. **Prices:** Beers T$2 ($1.50). Drinks T$1.50 ($1.20) and up.

SPACE WALKER NITE CLUB, Ramanlal Hotel, Taufa'ahau Rd. Tel. 21-344.

Guests here dance in blue light to the sounds of popular music handled by a deejay sitting in what looks like a space capsule. Except for the hotel's guests, it's first-come, first-served for the first 130 comers, who climb to the second-story room by a stairway that lifts up from the sidewalk. The club is open Thursday and Friday from 8pm until 4am the following morning. (Incidentally, the Ramanlal brothers spent a small fortune on soundproofing so the club wouldn't disturb their nearby hotel guests.)

Admission: T$5 ($4). **Prices:** Drinks T$3 ($2.50) and up.

TU'IMALIA DINING ROOM, International Dateline Hotel, Vuna Rd. Tel. 21-411.

Visiting diners at the International Dateline Hotel's Tu'imalia Dining Room can stay around on Thursday, Friday, and Saturday and dance to more tame live music, which cranks up about 9pm, than you'll hear at the other clubs.

Admission: You must have dinner at the hotel or be a guest in order to be admitted. **Prices:** Drinks T$3 ($2.50).

6. WHERE TO STAY

Although there has been a lot of talk during the past several years about an international hotel chain settling in Tonga, none of them operates in the kingdom at present. In fact, there are no large luxury resorts at all on Tongatapu, although there are comfortable—though far from deluxe—hotels and island hideaways to choose from.

Tonga offers us our first glimpse at a type of establishment we will see many of in Fiji: the **offshore resort.** By that I mean a hideaway resort sitting all by itself on a small island offshore from the main island. There may be a native village on the islet, but nothing else except the resort. You go there to rest, relax, sunbathe, swim, snorkel, dive, dine, get drunk, or do whatever comes naturally in a romantic South Seas bungalow. If you need some time away from civilization, then Royal Sunset Island Resort and Fafa Island Resort are remedies.

On the other hand, you do not spend your entire holiday at an offshore resort if you want to see much of the country or to sample exciting nightlife, since to get anywhere else requires a rather lengthy boat ride. If excitement is what you want, stay in Nuku'alofa.

The hotels and guesthouses in Nuku'alofa are listed first, then come the two offshore resorts.

HOTELS

FRIENDLY ISLANDER MOTEL, P.O. Box 142, Nuku'alofa. Tel. 23-810. Fax 24-199. Telex 66208. 26 units. A/C TEL **Location:** On Vuna Rd. waterfront 2 miles east of downtown Nuku'alofa. Local buses pass it.

$ Rates: T$42 ($33.50) single, T$55 ($40) double in room; T$65–T$85 ($52–$68) single or double in bungalow. No credit cards.

Papiloa Foliaki, once Tonga's only female member of Parliament, just keeps adding to her motel. Starting in 1980 with 12 comfortable, self-contained units, she has added a swimming pool, restaurant, nightclub, bar, and 14 bungalows. The older units are in a two-story building that faces the sea on one side and a courtyard full of tropical plants and swimming pool on the other. Those on the ocean side are small suites with separate bedrooms and sitting areas. All rooms have kitchenettes, tile baths, wall-mounted fans, radios, and sliding glass doors leading either to a patio on ground level or to a balcony on the second story. Built of modern materials but in the oval shape of Tongan fales, the new bungalows are across a side street or behind the main complex. Eight of them have one room; the others have a separate bedroom and are called "Family Fales." All bungalows have shower-only baths and both air conditioners and ceiling fans.

A dining room specializes in dishes featuring fresh local produce. The entrance to the restaurant is from the side street that runs off Vuna Road next to the motel. The establishment also is home to the 'Ofa Atu Nite Club, open only on Friday.

INTERNATIONAL DATELINE HOTEL, P.O. Box 39, Nuku'alofa. Tel. 23-411. Fax 23-410. Telex 66223. 76 rms. A/C TEL **Location:** Vuna Rd. at Tupoulahi Rd., on the waterfront.

$ Rates: T$74–T$88 ($59–$70.50) single; T$85–T$100 ($68–$80) double. AE, DC, MC, V.

Built prior to the king's coronation in 1967, this is Tonga's most widely known place to stay. It has been undergoing a slow and much-needed renovation since 1987, but until the full rehabilitation is completed, the Dateline will fall a bit short of the international status its name proclaims. Nevertheless, it still enjoys a choice location facing the harbor across Vuna Road on Nuku'alofa's waterfront a few blocks from downtown, and it's the only hotel on Tongatapu with spacious grounds featuring a riot of tropical plants surrounding a swimming pool.

The rooms are in an L-shaped, three-story building and are distinguished from typical American hotel accommodations only by the addition of the tea- and coffee-making facilities so popular in the South Pacific. That means a double bed or two single beds, a closet, and a bath (with stand-up shower). "Standard" rooms directly face the sea across the front of the building; "superior" rooms in a side wing are larger, but their angled windows have inferior water views.

In good weather, the Tu'imalia Dining Room has tables outside and some form of entertainment after dinner each evening, including traditional Tongan dance shows at least 2 nights a week. The food is plain but adequate. Even if you don't eat there, drop by for a drink at the bar and the dance show. The activities desk will tell you what's on during your stay.

Services include laundry and baby-sitting.

KAHANA LAGOON RESORT, P.O. Box 137, Nuku'alofa. Tel. 21-144. Fax 23-915. Telex 66217. 11 bungalows. TEL **Location:** Off Alaivahamama'o Rd. ("The By Pass"), on Fanga'uta Lagoon.

$ Rates: T$90–T$110 ($72–$88) single; T$110–T$130 ($88–$104) double. No credit cards.

You'll find Nuku'alofa's only waterside bungalows at this unusual property on the banks of Fanga'uta Lagoon. There's no beach here, but you can use special oversize steps built for the king to climb down a bulkhead for a swim in the lagoon. Without much land, the entire resort is couched virtually on the bulkhead, which curves at one point to make a pool in which tamed fish have been fenced. You can feed the fish from a short bridge leading to one of the fale-shaped bungalows sitting on its own little island. The others are waterside. Rustic-looking on the outside, their interiors have islandy charms, with reed walls and tapa-covered ceilings supported by coconut tree trunks. One of the units actually is fit for a king, having been specially outfitted to His Majesty's liking. Not that they are deluxe, however, for the lighting is unattractively fluorescent, and only the showers have hot water, not the hand basins.

A big airy fale holds a lagoonside bar, dining room, and so much dance space that the resort often hosts special public functions such as beauty contests. Diners choose from a blackboard menu featuring steaks, chicken, and lobster cooked in various European styles.

HOTEL NUKU'ALOFA, P.O. Box 32, Nuku'alofa. Tel. 24-244. Fax 23-154. 14 rms. A/C TEL **Location:** Taufa'ahau Rd., center of business district.

$ Rates: T$50 ($40) single; T$60 ($48) double. AE, DC, MC, V.

Opened in 1990, this modern version of the upstairs, business traveler's hotel shares a former cinema building with the Friendly Islands Bookshop, which is at street level. Steps lead from the sidewalk to a long and very pleasantly decorated second story reception-dining-bar area with huge windows overlooking busy Taufa'ahau Road. The hotel is owned primarily by the descendants of Ralph Sanft, a German who settled in Tonga early this century and made money as a trader. The family also owns a company which makes heavy, German-style furniture, and that's what you find in the lounge and throughout this establishment.

A hallway runs down the center of the building, the original peaked roof exposed high overhead. The rooms open off the hallway and have louvered windows to the outside. They have sitting areas and shower-only baths (which, like the Ramanlal's, have inadequate towel-hanging and toiletry-setting space). Otherwise, they are quite comfortable.

Although the dining area has only six tables, the chef serves excellent lobster and fish dishes. The bar and lounge area are very popular with Nuku'alofa's expatriate residents.

RAMANLAL HOTEL, P.O. Box 74, Nuku'alofa. Tel. 21-344. Fax 23-833. Telex 66205. 60 rms. A/C TEL **Location:** Taufa'ahau Rd., center of business district.

$ Rates: T$75 ($60) single; T$82 ($65.50) double; T$95 ($76) single, T$105 ($84) double executive suite for up to four; T$195 ($156) penthouse apartment for up to six. AE, DC, MC, V.

(S) The first time I saw the Ramanlal Hotel in the mid-1980s, I wondered if I had made a serious blunder in making a reservation there: The entrance was through a covered alley between two stores in the third block from the water on Taufa'ahau Road, and I had to look hard to find the name of the hotel written near the top of the building. Once through the dusty alley, however, I came upon a lush tropical garden surrounding a small swimming pool. Beyond stood two blocks of hotel rooms, all comfortable and modern and with balconies overlooking this surprising and quite incongruous sight in the middle of Nuku'alofa's busy shopping district.

Now Joe and Soane Ramanlal—sons of an Indian father from Fiji and a Tongan mother—have rebuilt the streetfront building to include a modern reception area paneled from floor to ceiling. To the rear, a small thatch-roofed bar sits at the edge of the garden. Beyond is another Tongan-style fale serving as a small dining room by the pool. They have converted the second and third stories of the streetfront commercial building into 30 spacious hotel rooms, including a two-bedroom executive suite and a penthouse apartment. Granted, the Ramanlal has the warranted air of an in-town commercial hotel rather than a resort, but it is perfectly comfortable and convenient as a base from which to tour the kingdom.

BUDGET GUESTHOUSES

Tonga is a bastion of the South Pacific guesthouse in which you share a simple house with other travelers on a low budget. In the case of Sela's Guest House, listed below, you also share it with a Tongan family. As for the others, their Tongan owners have developed an unfortunate pattern of hiring expatriate managers, who clean up the establishments and put them on the low-budget map only to be fired when they start making a profit. Accordingly, the conditions at the following properties may have changed since I was there. Though not as convenient, Sela should continue to offer a clean, friendly home. The others are within a block or two of each other on the waterfront, so it's easy to check them out before deciding on a place to stay.

THE BEACH HOUSE, P.O. Box 33, Nuku'alofa. Tel. 21-060. 8 rms. **Location:** Vuna Rd., on the waterfront 1 block east of International Dateline Hotel.

$ Rates (including breakfast): T$15 ($12) single; T$25 ($20) double. No credit cards.

This rambling old clapboard house has simple but adequate bedrooms flanking a central dining room and lounge. Guests share two bathrooms and a long, breezy verandalike sun porch facing the water. The rooms have screened doors to both the central lounge and side porches.

FASI-MOE-AFI GUEST HOUSE & CAFE GARDEN, P.O. Box 316, Nuku'alofa. Tel. 22-289. 5 rms (none with bath). **Location:** Vuna Rd. near International Dateline Hotel.

$ Rates (including breakfast): T$15 ($12) single; T$25 ($20) double. No credit cards.

This property was "in" when I was there recently, having been taken over by Boris and Heidi Stavenow, a young German couple whose family owns the Seaview Restaurant. They had given the place a good scrub and turned the outdoor café into a fine place for an inexpensive meal or snack. The house itself is nothing to write home about—five simple, clean, and basically furnished rooms sharing two toilets and showers—but the location virtually next door to the International Dateline Hotel is superb. The Stavenows do not accept reservations from overseas, so it's first-come, first-served.

KELETI BEACH RESORT, P.O. Box 192, Nuku'alofa. Tel. 21-179. 19 rms (7 with bath). **Location:** About 12 miles from Nuku'alofa on south shore of Tongatapu.

$ Rates: T$10–T$16 ($8–$13) single without bath, T$15–T$30 ($12–$24) single with bath; T$20 ($16) double without bath, T$40 ($32) double with bath; T$50 ($40) for families of four or five. No credit cards.

Although not strictly a guesthouse, Soeli Ofa's resort still falls into the low-budget category. Keleti Beach lies on the south coast of Tongatapu where the surf pounds on a rock ledge. Eight bungalows sit in a lawnlike coconut grove above the shore. A path leads down to a small sandy beach nestled in a break in the ledge, where guests and visitors can swim in a natural pool behind large rocks offshore. The bungalows are built of concrete blocks with tin roofs, and have baths with large showers (hot and cold water), screened windows on all four sides, covered porches on the front, and simple furniture. Four of the bungalows have one room; the other four have a bedroom on each side and a bath between them. For low-budget travelers, Soeli has four "economy rooms" that share two toilets and showers with hot water.

A central building housing a bar, lounge, and the 4Cs Restaurant ("Cleanliness, Cost, Cuisine, Comfort") is perched above the beach at the edge of a low cliff. The restaurant is notable primarily for its Friday-night traditional dance show and smörgåsbord, which costs T$12 ($9.50) for guests, T$15 ($12) for nonguests.

SELA'S GUEST HOUSE, P.O. Box 24, Nuku'alofa. Tel. 21-430. 14 rms (2 with bath). **Location:** Longoteme Lane, a narrow lane between Fatafehi and Tupoulahi roads, about 1 mile from waterfront.

$ Rates: T$12 ($9.50) single without bath; T$20 ($16) double without bath; T$30 ($27) single or double with bath. No credit cards.

In 1974 Sela launched her establishment by providing room and board for U.S. Peace Corps volunteers training in Nuku'alofa prior to serving on the outer islands. She now has 12 double and two single rooms in the main part of her house and in a wing that she subsequently added to the rear. Two of the rooms have their own baths; the others share four toilets and two showers (one with hot water). Home-cooked meals are available.

OFFSHORE RESORTS

The north shore of Tongatapu is for all practical purposes a huge lagoon, enclosed on two sides by reef and dotted with low, atoll-like islands encircled with white-sand beaches. Royal Sunset Island Resort and Fafa Island Resort, both mentioned previously as day-trips and Sunday escapes, are on two of these islands. They may not be luxurious when compared to Fiji's much more expensive versions, but they are fine get-away-from-it-all hideaways.

ROYAL SUNSET ISLAND RESORT, P.O. Box 960, Nuku'alofa. Tel. and fax 21-254. Telex 66284. 26 bungalows. **Location:** 'Atata Island, 7 miles off Nuku'alofa.

$ Rates: T$80 ($64) single; T$90 ($72) double. T$33 ($26.50) extra per person for three meals a day; transfers T$33 ($26.50) per person. AE, DC, MC, V.

(S) New Zealanders David and Terry Hunt have done a fine job developing this resort, which shares small A'tata Island with a native Tongan village. A gorgeous beach swings around their end of the island. A swimming pool sports a deck dotted with lawn tables and umbrellas, but the surrounding lagoon offers the real attraction for swimmers, snorkelers, scuba divers, and anyone who loves to fish (see "Fishing" under "What to See and Do," above, for information about Royal Sunset Sportfishing).

The Hunts have entertained several notable guests, including the actor Charles Haid, of "Hill Street Blues" fame, who took a break while filming a movie in New Zealand.

Each of the resort's one-bedroom bungalows sits behind privacy-providing foliage just off the beach. Of modern construction, they all have their own spacious baths with hot and cold water, kitchenettes, ceiling fans in both rooms, and large, fully screened windows. Three meals a day are offered to those who don't want to bring their own groceries.

FAFA ISLAND RESORT, P.O. Box 1444, Nuku'alofa. Tel. 22-800, or toll free 800/448-8355 in the U.S. Fax 23-592. Telex 66222. 12 units. **Location:** On Fafa Island, 6 miles off Nuku'alofa.

$ Rates (in U.S. dollars only): $39 single, $47 double for standard bungalow; $95 single or double for superior bungalows. Meal plans $42 per person per day; transfers $17 per person. AE, MC, V.

(S) German Rainer Urtel has stocked his little resort with bungalows made entirely of local materials: coconut timbers and shingles and lots of thatch. Although rustic and definitely not for anyone looking for all the comforts of home, they have Robinson Crusoe charm. He started out with eight very basic fales circling a central building, all set in the center of this 17-acre, atoll-like island studded with coconut palms. He has replaced his original central fale with a much improved version right on the beach and added four much larger guest bungalows, also on the beach. These new models have porches; over one of them is a romantic "honeymoon" sleeping loft with a lagoon view. An unusual feature has the toilets and lavatories on rear porches and showers actually sitting in the middle of fenced-enclosed courtyards. The push-out windows aren't screened, so each of the platform beds has its own mosquito net.

The beachside central building houses a bar and a restaurant that features excellent German and Tongan seafood specialties. Guests can use Windsurfers, Hobie Cat sailboats, and other nonmotorized toys. Transfers are by auxiliary sailboat.

7. WHERE TO DINE

Nuku'alofa is blessed with a few restaurants founded and operated by German expatriates; all of them serve continental cuisine of remarkably high quality for such a small and unsophisticated town. And like most other South Pacific capitals, there are also Chinese restaurants to choose from. But first, consider a Polynesian-style feast.

Like most Polynesians, the Tongans in the old days cooked their food over hot rocks in a pit—an *umu*—for several hours. Today they roast whole suckling pigs on a spit over coals for several hours (larger pigs still go into the umu). The dishes that emerge from the umu are similar to those found elsewhere in Polynesia: pig, chicken, lobster, fish, octopus, taro, taro leaves cooked with meat and onions, breadfruit, bananas, and a sweet breadfruit pudding known as *faikakai-lolo,* all of it cooked with ample amounts of coconut cream. Served on the side are fish (*ota ika*) and clams (*vasuva*), both marinated in lime juice.

For years the Oscar Kami family has been stuffing visitors with Tongan food at lovely ✪ **Oholei Beach,** on Tongatapu's east coast, and then entertaining them with a traditional dance show inside a torch-lit, sandy-bottom cave open to the stars through a hole in its roof. The setting alone is worth the trip out to Oholei Beach; the food and show make it one of the South Pacific's more memorable evenings. You arrive at Oholei Beach in time to see the finishing touches put on the spitted suckling pig, the earth removed from the umu, and the food placed on a *pola,* a long serving tray made of bamboo and covered with banana leaves. You and the other guests pass by the pola and are served buffet-style by Tongan girls who will gladly explain the ingredients of the feast laid before you. Silverware will be available but it's perfectly acceptable to eat Tongan fashion with your fingers.

If you're too full to stand after dinner, it's a short crawl into the cave for the dance show (see "Evening Entertainment" under "What to See and Do," above). The torch dance, during which young men toss around lighted torches in the darkened cave, is spectacular.

Now the really good part: The entire evening costs just T$21 ($17) per person, including transportation from and back to your hotel. Any of the hotels and travel agents in Nuku'alofa can make arrangements for Oholei feast night. The feasts are on Wednesday and Friday evenings, and the bus will pick you up at around 6pm.

READERS'S RECOMMEND

Keleti Beach Resort. *Tel. 21-179. "Owner Soeli Ofa, a choral director and composer of some renown in Tonga, puts his family (most of the staff are relatives) through their paces to the rhythm of homemade oil-can drums. . . . Couple this with the usual generous Tongan feast, the backdrop of sunset and blowhole activity on the reef below, and you've got an evening that rivals the* son et lumière *(sound and light show) at Versailles"*—Janet Dunbrack and Patrick Reid, Toronto, Canada. (*Author's Note:* The entire evening costs T$12 ($9.50) if you're staying there, T$15 ($12) if you're not, including transportation.)

EXPENSIVE

During my recent visit, Nuku'alofa's restaurants were fighting it out in what local residents facetiously called "lunch wars" to see which could offer meals at the most attractive prices. Ask around. If the war is still on, it means fine midday meals at a bargain. I've given their lunch-special prices in the listings which follow.

FRED'S RESTAURANT, Salote Rd. Tel. 22-100.

Cuisine: CONTINENTAL. **Reservations:** Recommended at dinner. **Location:** 9 blocks east of Taufa'ahau Rd. near Cable & Wireless.

$ Prices: Lunch specials T$4.50 ($3.50); appetizers T$3–T$7 ($2.50–$5.50); main courses T$10–T$15 ($9–$13.50). No credit cards.

Open: Lunch Mon–Sat noon–2pm; dinner Mon–Sat 7–10pm.

Like the Seaview, Fred's also is owned by a German chef and occupies an old house, this one about 50 yards east of the Cable and Wireless office. Fred offers a variety of delicious main courses. Some of them, like wienerschnitzel, reflect his German origins. My advice is to stick with the fresh spiny lobster, of which Tonga is one of the last South Pacific storehouses; try it cooked Polynesia-style with tomatoes, papaya, and garlic. Also on the menu is roast beef in red wine. Seating at Fred's is inside the old home's living room, on a screened porch across the front, or under a Tongan fale sitting in the yard.

SEAVIEW RESTAURANT, Vuna Rd. Tel. 23-709.

Cuisine: CONTINENTAL. **Reservations:** Essential. **Location:** On Vuna Rd. waterfront, 3 blocks west of Royal Palace.

$ Prices: Appetizers T$3–T$5.50 ($2.50–$4.50); main courses T$11.50–T$18 ($9–$14.50). AE, DC, MC, V.

Open: Dinner Mon–Fri 6–10pm; coffee garden opens 2:30pm.

Originally from Hamburg, Germany, the Stavenow family now runs this extremely pleasant establishment in an old colonial clapboard house tastefully decorated inside with tapa cloth and mats to give the dining room an appropriately tropical atmosphere. Daily specials depend on the availability of fresh lobster and quality meats imported from New Zealand. Some items that might appear are filet mignon wrapped in bacon and grilled, pepper steak, fresh lobster, or fish "Polynesia." Try a lobster cocktail as an "entree" (that's an "appetizer" in American English) and homemade German pastries for dessert. Try to get a table on the breezy front porch. The Stavenows serve the pastries and coffee outdoors beginning at 2:30pm Monday to Friday.

MODERATE

CHEZ ALISI & ANDRE ("THE FRENCH RESTAURANT"), Wellington Rd. Tel. 21-087.

Cuisine: FRENCH. **Reservations:** Recommended at dinner. **Location:** Wellington Rd. 2 blocks west of Taufa'ahau Rd.

$ Prices: Lunch special T$4.50 ($3.50); appetizers T$4–T$10 ($3–$6); main courses T$8.50–T$14 ($7–$11). V.

Open: Lunch Mon–Sat noon–2:30pm; dinner Mon–Sat 6:30–10pm.

Nuku'alofa's French restaurant doesn't look like much from the outside, but once you get past the entrance you'll find a clean and comfortable dining room. The cuisine can best be described as good French home-cooking, but that's satisfactory in a little outpost like Tonga. Look for steaks or fresh lobster in béarnaise, mushroom, cream, or forestière sauces. My own favorite is lobster provençal.

DAVINA'S RESTAURANT AND BAR, Vuna Rd. Tel. 23-385.

Cuisine: EUROPEAN. **Reservations:** Recommended at dinner. **Location:** On Vuna Rd. waterfront opposite Faua Jetty.

$ Prices: Lunch specials T$4.50 ($3.50); appetizers T$2.50–T$5.50 ($2–$4.50); main courses T$9.50–T$14 ($7.50–$11). MC, V.

Open: Mon–Sat 10am–11pm (breakfast 10am–noon, lunch noon–3pm, snacks 3–6pm, dinner 6–11pm).

The name Davina is derived from David Foy and Gina Greguhn, who with silent partner Princess Pilolevu own this pleasant establishment in a pink stucco-over-cinderblock house opposite the small-boat harbor at Faua Jetty. David is English; Gina is Tongan. Together they keep the place open all day for breakfast, lunch, afternoon snacks, and dinners. You can take your afternoon tea on the front porch or under a small Tongan fale in the front yard. Other meals are eaten in a dining room attractively furnished with cane. Ceiling fans whirring overhead add to the tropical atmosphere. Most main courses feature fish, chicken, and steaks and are moderately priced; however, giant lobsters cost T$20 ($16).

BUDGET

The food at the **snack bar** in the Burns Philp department store, on Salote Road across from Talamahu Market, is ordinary, but I mention it because the menu is an interesting lesson in Tongan-English transliteration. For example, *sanuisi* means sandwich; *sekoni,* scones; *keke,* cake; *pateta,* potato; *sitiu,* stew; *salati,* salad; *sosisi,* sausage; and *hamipeka,* hamburger. Sosisi and pateta, therefore, are sausage and french fries.

AKIKO'S RESTAURANT (LOKI KAI CAFETERIA), Taufa'ahau Rd. No phone.

Cuisine: EUROPEAN/CHINESE/JAPANESE. **Reservations:** Not accepted. **Location:** Ground floor of Basilica of St. Anthony of Padua.

$ Prices: Lunch specials T$2.50 ($2); appetizers T$1.20–T$1.50 ($1–$1.20); main courses T$4.50–T$8 ($3.50–$6.50). No credit cards.

Open: Lunch Mon–Fri 11:30am–1:45pm; dinner Mon–Fri 6:30–8pm.

Although a sign may still say "Loki Kai Cafeteria" on the ground floor of the basilica, this extraordinarily popular eatery is known locally as Akiko's, in honor of its Japanese owner. Her plain but spotlessly clean establishment provides a selection of European, Chinese, and—yes—Japanese selections that are marvelous bargains. Local expatriates flock here for dinner when they don't want to dress up. No alcoholic beverages are served.

THE HUA HUA, Vuna Rd. Tel. 21-780.

Cuisine: CANTONESE. **Reservations:** Not necessary. **Location:** Vuna Rd. two doors west of International Dateline Hotel.

$ Prices: Soups T$2–T$5 ($1.50–$4); main courses T$2.50–T$10 ($2–$8). V.

Open: Lunch Mon–Sat 11am–2pm; dinner Mon–Sat 5–10pm.

Of Nuku'alofa's Chinese restaurants, this has the most pleasant setting: an old colonial residence on the waterfront. The original wide-plank walls of the former residence are accented with just enough red woodwork to give you a hint this is a Chinese restaurant. A variety of dishes feature chicken, pork, beef, fish, and lobster with seasonal vegetables (more carrots than bamboo shoots) in light sauces. The portions were rather small when I ate there recently, but that may change as the owners—recent immigrants from mainland China—learn of Tongan-size appetites.

JOHN'S TAKEAWAY, Taufa'ahau Rd. Tel. 21-246.

Cuisine: SNACK BAR. **Reservations:** Not accepted. **Location:** Taufa'ahau Rd. opposite Ramanlal Hotel.

$ Prices: Sandwiches and burgers T$1.50–T$3.50 ($1.20–$3); chow mein, fish- or chicken-and-chips T$3.50 ($3).

Open: Mon–Thurs 8am–midnight, Fri 8am–Sat midnight.

It doesn't look like much, but of several snack bars and local *fale kai* (literally, "house eat" in Tongan), John's consistently has the best fish-and-chips and chicken-and-chips. You also can get sandwiches, burgers, and simple Cantonese dishes such as chow mein. Order at the counters at the front or side, eat at the picnic tables under the shed.

THE LITTLEST CAFE, Taufa'ahau Rd. Tel. 23-435.

Cuisine: BARBECUE. **Reservations:** Not accepted. **Location:** East side of Taufa'ahau Rd. opposite Ramanlal Hotel.

$ **Prices:** Salads T$2.50–T$3.50 ($2–$3); sandwiches or plates T$4.50–T$6 ($3.50–$5). No credit cards.
Open: Mon–Sat 10am–10pm.

Place your order at the counter and then eat your delicious charbroiled beef or chicken at one of a few wooden tables in this tiny and very clean place. The sandwiches on French bread are large enough to feed two persons—or save half for another meal later. In addition to sandwiches, the barbecue is served on platters with rice and salad.

PHOENIX RESTAURANT, Fatafehi Rd. Tel. 21-834.
Cuisine: CANTONESE. **Reservations:** Recommended Sun. **Location:** Fatafehi Rd. 3 blocks inland next to large Shell service station.
$ **Prices:** Appetizers T$2–T$4 ($1.50–$3), main courses T$2–T$15 ($1.50–$12). No credit cards.
Open: Lunch Mon–Sat 11:30am–2pm; dinner daily 5:30–10pm.

A very popular place to eat on Sunday evening, when everything else outside the hotels is closed, the Phoenix offers a wide variety of Cantonese dishes, the best of the lot being served in black bean or sweet-and-sour sauces.

8. AN EASY EXCURSION TO VAVA'U

Approximately 163 miles north of Tongatapu lies enchanting Vava'u, the second most-visited group of islands in the kingdom and one of the South Pacific's most unusual destinations.

Often pronounced "Va-vow," the group consists of one large, hilly island shaped like a horseshoe around the magnificent fjordlike harbor known as **Port of Refuge,** one of the finest anchorages and most popular destinations for cruising yachts in the South Pacific. From its picturesque perch above the harbor, the main village of **Neiafu** (pop. 5,000) evokes scenes from the South Pacific of yesteryear.

The first European visitor was Spanish explorer Francisco Antonio Mourelle, who happened upon Vava'u in 1781 on his way to the Philippines from Mexico. He gave Port of Refuge its name. At the time, Vava'u was the seat of one of three chiefdoms fighting for control of Tonga. Finau II, who captured the *Port au Prince* in 1806, built a fortress at Neiafu and kept Will Mariner captive there until the young Englishman became one of his favorites. Two years later the brutal Finau won a major victory by faking a peace agreement with rival chiefs. He then tied them up and let them slowly sink to their deaths in a leaky canoe.

Finau II's successor, Finau 'Ulukalala III, converted to Christianity but died before his successor was old enough to rule. Before dying he asked George Taufa'ahau, who was then chief of Ha'apai, to look after the throne until the young boy was old enough. George did more than that; he took over Vava'u in 1833. Twelve years later he conquered Tongatapu and became King George I, ruler of Tonga.

To the south of town, the reef is speckled with 33 other small islands, 21 of them inhabited. The others are spectacularly beautiful little dots of land that fall into the Robinson Crusoe category of places to escape from it all for a day. The white beaches and emerald surrounding lagoon are unsurpassed in their beauty.

Vava'u is heaven for water-sports enthusiasts and sailors. Getting out on the water for a day is easy, and if you want to make a week of it, The Moorings yacht charter company has one of its two South Pacific operations based in Port of Refuge (the other is on Raiatea in French Polynesia). When you see these protected waterways, you'll know why cruising sailors love Vava'u. If you like walking on unspoiled white sandy beaches on uninhabited islands, swimming in crystal-clear water, and taking boat rides into mysterious caves cut into cliffs, you'll like Vava'u too.

I recommend that side trips to Vava'u be made early in a visit to Tonga in order to allow a day or two leeway in case you can't (or don't want to) get back to Nuku'alofa on the day planned.

GETTING THERE

The airport is on the north side of Vaua'u, about 7km (4 miles) from Neiafu. The strip was scheduled to be paved and upgraded as we went to press. It should have a new terminal building by the time you arrive.

The hotels and guesthouses provide airport transfers, or you can take one of the island's few taxis to Neiafu for about T$7 ($6).

Don't forget that it's imperative to reconfirm your return flight to Tongatapu as soon as possible after arriving on Vava'u. The staff at your hotel can take care of this for you, or you can visit the office of Royal Tongan Airlines, next to the Burns Philp store on the main road in Neiafu.

The ferry from Nuku'alofa lands at *Uafu Lahi,* the Big Wharf, in Neiafu. From there you can walk or take a taxi ride to your hotel or guesthouse. If on foot, turn right on the main street to reach the center of town and the accommodations.

The road from the airport dead-ends at a T intersection atop the hill above the wharf. The main street runs from there in both directions along the water, with most of the town's stores and government offices flanking it. The government used convicted adulteresses to help build this road. They sang as they worked; hence, its Tongan name is Hale Lupe (Road of the Doves). There are no street signs, but the Tonga Visitors Bureau's helpful signs point the way to most establishments and points of interest.

GETTING AROUND

Public transportation on Vava'u is limited. If you book an excursion, ask about the availability of transportation to and from the event. **Taxis** are not metered, so be sure you determine the fare before getting in. Leopote Taxis (tel. 70-136), Paradise Taxis (tel. 70-083), and Ikahihifo Taxi (tel. 70-129) are available for about T$10 ($8) per hour or T$25 ($20) a day, but be sure to negotiate a fare in advance. **Buses** and pickup trucks fan out from the market in Neiafu to various villages, but they have no fixed schedule. If you take one, make sure you know when and if it's coming back to town.

VAVA'U

If you don't see an item here, check the "Fast Facts: Tonga" earlier in this chapter, or just ask around. Vava'u is a very small place where nearly everyone knows everything.

Currency Exchange The Bank of Tonga office, on the main road in Neiafu, is open Mon–Fri 9:30am–3:30pm. When it's closed, traveler's checks can be exchanged at the Paradise Hotel.

Dentist See "Hospital," below.

Doctor Dr. Alfredo Carafa (no phone), a young Italian, has a private practice in Neiafu. You'll see a sign on his house near The Moorings. Also see "Hospital," below.

Hospital The government has a 60-bed hospital in Neiafu. It's staffed with volunteer doctors and dentists from overseas, but with the equipment on hand, they are able to tend to only relatively minor illnesses and injuries.

Market Sailoame Market in Neiafu is open Mon–Fri 7am–5pm, but its busiest time is Sat from 7am until everything is sold.

Police The telephone number for the police is 70-234.

Post Office/Telephone/Telegrams The post office is open Mon–Fri 8:30am–12:30pm and 1:30–3:30pm. Local calls can be made at the post office, which has the island's only public telephone.

Telephone Tonga Telecom next to the post office is open 24 hours a day, 7 days a week for domestic and international long-distance calls.

Tourist Information The Tonga Visitors Bureau (tel. 70-115) has an office on the main road in Neiafu, under the able direction of Sione Manu. Check there for lists of local activities while you're in town. The staff can also help arrange road tours of the island and boat tours of the lagoon. The office is open Mon–Fri 8:30am–4:30pm. The address is P.O. Box 18, Neiafu, Vava'u.

WHAT TO SEE & DO

TOURING NEIAFU

You can take a **walking tour** of Neiafu, the picturesque little town curving along the banks of Port of Refuge, with the help of *Walking Tours of Neiafu* by Pesi and Mary Fonua. It's available at the gift shop in the Paradise Hotel and at the Friendly Islands Bookshop in Nuku'alofa. The Tonga Visitors Bureau (tel. 70-115) might also be able to organize a walking tour for a small group.

Be sure to make the walk from the Paradise Hotel/Vava'u Guest House into town, a stroll of about 15 minutes.

The flattop mountain across the harbor is **Mo'unga Talau,** at 204 meters (675 ft.) the tallest point on Vava'u. A hike to the top takes about 2 hours round-trip. To get there, turn inland a block past the Bank of Tonga on the airport road, then left at Sailoame Market. This street continues through the residential area and then becomes a track. The turnoff to the summit starts as the track begins to head downhill. It's a steep climb and can be slippery in wet weather.

Both the Paradise Hotel (tel. 70-211) and the Tonga Visitors Bureau (tel. 70-115) will arrange **sightseeing tours** of the island if enough persons are interested. You will see lovely scenery of the fingerlike bays cutting into the island, visit some beautiful beaches, and take in the sweet smell of vanilla—the principal cash crop on Vava'u—drying in sheds or in the sun.

SPORTS & RECREATION

Water Tours/Water Sports

The thing to do on Vava'u is to get out on the fabulous fjords for some swimming, snorkeling, and exploring of the caves and uninhabited islands.

The typical boat tour follows Port of Refuge to Swallows Cave on Kapa Island and then to Mariner's Cave (named for Will Mariner, the young Englishman captured with the *Port au Prince* in 1806) on Nuapapu Island. Both of these have been carved out of cliffs by erosion. Boats can go right into Swallows Cave for a look at the swallows flying in and out of a hole in its top. Swimmers with snorkeling gear and a guide can dive into Mariner's Cave. Both caves face west and are best visited in the afternoon, when the maximum amount of natural light gets into them. Most trips also include a stop at one of the small islands for some time at a sparkling beach and a swim over the reefs in crystal-clear water.

Soki Island Tours hits the high spots and includes lunch and a swim at an uninhabited islet. The trip costs T$48 ($38.50) if up to three persons go, T$17 ($13.50) per person if more than three go along. Inquire at the reception desk of the Paradise Hotel (tel. 70-211).

Vava'u Watersports (tel. 70-193), the scuba-diving specialists (see below), offers speedy jetboat trips through the islands for T$49 ($39) per person. They also will rent you a Hobie Cat or Windsurfer for T$20 ($16) per hour, and take you waterskiing for T$15 ($12) per 10 minutes. Check in with Peter Goldstern and crew at waterside near The Moorings to see what they have going.

Sione Fo'i'akau of **Sione's Tours** was just starting out in business during my recent visit. He charges T$50 ($40) per trip regardless of how many people come along, but bring your own lunch and something to drink. Book Sione through the Tonga Visitors Bureau (tel. 70-115).

Scuba Diving

The clear, sheltered waters of Vava'u are excellent for scuba diving, particularly since divers don't have to ride on a boat for several hours just to get to a spot with colorful coral and bountiful sea life. In Port of Refuge, divers can explore the wreck of the copra schooner *Clan McWilliam,* sunk in 1906.

New Zealand–born and American-raised Peter Goldstern of **Vava'u Watersports,** Private Bag, Neiafu, Vava'u (tel. and fax 70-193), charges T$75 ($63) per dive and teaches PADI open-water courses for T$315 ($252) per diver (based on groups of three or more divers).

Sailboat Cruising

The Moorings, the Florida-based company that helped pioneer charter sailboats in the Caribbean, has sailboats ranging in length from 37 feet to 51 feet based at Neiafu. They range in price from U.S. $2,200 to U.S. $3,650 a week per boat for bareboat charters (that is, you hire the "bare" boat and provide your own skipper and crew). The Moorings requires that its clients be qualified to handle sailboats of the size it charters, and the staff will check out your skills before turning you loose. A skipper or guide is available for U.S. $45 and U.S. $40 a day, respectively, not including their food. For another U.S. $23 a day, the Moorings will do your shopping and have the boat provisioned with food and drink when you arrive. For more information, contact The Moorings, 19345 U.S. 19 North, Suite 402, Clearwater, FL 34624 (tel. 813/535-1446, or toll free 800/535-7289).

SHOPPING FOR HANDCRAFTS

If you depart Vava'u directly for Pago Pago on Samoa Air, you can buy some ✪ **duty-free** merchandise at the Tonga Visitors Bureau office on the main street.

As noted earlier in this chapter, Vava'u produces some of the finest handcrafts in Tonga. The establishments listed below will pack and ship your purchases home.

THE DOUBLE DOLPHIN, Main St., opposite The Moorings. Tel. 70-327.

This carries an excellent and broad-ranging selection personally chosen by David McLean, a Canadian who has lived and created black-coral jewelry on Vava'u since 1973. Hours are 8am to 4pm Monday through Saturday, dark June through November.

FRIENDLY ISLANDS MARKETING COOPERATIVE, Main St. Tel. 70-242.

The shop between the Double Dolphin and the Paradise Hotel is the Vava'u branch of FIMCO, whose main shop is in Nuku'alofa. Since most of the good stuff is shipped to Tongatapu for sale, the selection here is not as wide as at the Double Dolphin. Open Monday to Friday from 8:30am to 4:30pm (to 5pm June through November), Saturday 8:30am to noon.

LANGA FONUA HANDICRAFTS, Main St., in Tonga Visitors Bureau. Tel. 70-356.

The Vava'u branch of Langa Fonua, the women's handcraft association founded by Queen Salote, has a shop in a Tongan fale adjacent to the Tonga Visitors Bureau. It has a good variety of baskets, mats, wood carvings, and other items at reasonable prices. Open Monday to Saturday 8:30am to 4pm.

LEONATI'S GIFT SHOP, in the Paradise Hotel. Tel. 70-211.

As with FIMCO's branch, you might find an unusual or high-quality piece here, although chances are you will be more successful at the Double Dolphin or Langa Fonua. Since you likely will either stay at the Paradise or visit it, stop in and have a look.

WHERE TO STAY

Although the government does not encourage **camping,** it is possible to take a tent, sleeping gear, supplies, *and water* to one of the little uninhabited islands and spend some time there. You will need permission, however, from the villagers who own the island or the island council. Contact the Tonga Visitors Bureau.

PARADISE HOTEL, P.O. Box 11, Neiafu, Vava'u, Tonga. Tel. 70-211 or 70-094. Fax 70184. 43 rms. A/C TEL **Location:** East end of Neiafu town, overlooking Port of Refuge.

$ Rates: T$24 ($19) economy single, T$31 ($25) economy double; T$65 ($52) gardenview single, T$75 ($60) gardenview double; T$80 ($64) harborview single, T$90 ($72) harborview double. AE, DC, MC, V.

Perched on a grassy ridge overlooking Port of Refuge and a short walk from Neiafu, this is the most luxurious hotel in Tonga. Kentuckian Carter Johnson, who made his fortune in building pipelines in the United States and Australia, bought the Paradise at an auction in 1981 as "something to do" during an early retirement. What he has done is create an unusual property whose blocks of humongous rooms are joined by covered walkways sided with white pipe railings (a testament to his abilities with a welding torch). A large central building houses the reception area, a gift shop, bar, restaurant, and dance area. Next to it on a grassy lawn is a swimming pool with a panoramic view of the harbor below. A path leads down to the water's edge, where the hotel has its own pier, a popular spot for "yachties" from June to November.

The large, American-size rooms are in one- and two-story buildings. Each has a queen or two double beds, a ceiling fan, a spacious bath with shower and tub, and enough room left over for a sitting area facing the glass doors opening onto a balcony. The few older "economy" rooms have ceiling fans but no air conditioners, tea- and coffee-making facilities, refrigerators, hot water, or harbor views.

Yachties and other travelers congregate in the bar during happy hour from 6 to 7pm nightly and contribute to a very friendly, informal atmosphere that gives the Paradise the feel of a comfortable inn rather than a South Seas resort. Incidentally, the airplane engine hanging near the bar once was part of the hotel's aircraft that Carter crash-landed in 1985. Fortunately, no one was seriously injured.

Germans Bert and Ev Filke-Vince, who gave up their own restaurant in Nuku'alofa, have done wonders since taking over the Paradise's dining room in 1991. Their lunch menu changes weekly to feature Italian, Mexican, and other offerings. Dinners feature lobster, fish, steaks, and pork chops in German and other European sauces. For breakfast, try Bert's hearty farmer's breakfast; it'll hold you during a morning on the water.

The hotel has a games room in which video movies are shown in the evenings, and a local musical group plays in the dance area off the bar beginning at 9pm Monday through Saturday during the sailing season from June to November. The reception staff can tell you what's happening while you're there and also arrange tours and boat trips.

VAVA'U GUEST HOUSE, P.O. Box 148, Neiafu, Vava'u, Tonga. Tel. 70-300. 10 rms (none with bath), 4 bungalows (all with bath). **Location:** East end of Neiafu, directly across from Paradise Hotel.

$ Rates: T$25 ($20) single bungalow, T$35 ($28) double bungalow; T$12 ($10) single room, T$20 ($16) double room. No credit cards.

You can get a room or stay in your own bungalow—and eat excellent home-cooked, family-style meals—at this convenient establishment. After operating it successfully for many years (during which it became famous for its family-style dinners), Mikio Filitonga and his family turned management over to a young Swedish couple in 1991. The four Tongan-fale bungalows are quite comfortable (albeit with cold-water showers). A European-style house on the property contains 10 rooms sharing two baths.

The price for family-style meals—very popular with cruising yachties and other visitors to Vava'u—is just T$8.50 ($7), and that includes very nearly all the European-style food you can eat. Guests should book by 4pm for the 7:30pm sitting each night. It's a fine way to meet fellow travelers.

HILL TOP MOTEL, c/o General Delivery, Neiafu, Vava'u. Tel. 70-209. 7

rms (none with bath), 1 apartment, 5 bunks. **Location:** On Holopeka Hill overlooking Port of Refuge. Go inland at the Bank of Tonga, follow TVB signs.

$ Rates: T$6 ($5) dorm bunk per person; T$10 ($8) single, T$12 ($9.50) double room with no view; T$18 ($14.50) single or double "veranda" room with harbor view; T$30 ($24) 2-bedroom apartment. No credit cards.

Low-budget travelers can get a bit of everything at this guesthouse, which overlooks Port of Refuge. Two "veranda" rooms provide a vista unparalleled for the money. Guests share toilets, showers, and a full kitchen complete with dishware stored in cubbyholes marked for each room. A two-bedroom apartment on the ground level is available, but unfortunately I found it a bit musty. Otherwise, the rooms and facilities were immaculately clean and comfortable despite their simplicity.

WHERE TO DINE

If you missed a Tongan feast in Nuku'alofa, or just liked it so much you want to try it again, **Isiah's Tongan Feast** takes place at Lisa Beach, and **Matato's Feast** at lovely Ano Beach, usually on Saturday if demand warrants. Both cost about T$15 ($12) per person. Inquire at the Paradise Hotel or your guesthouse.

For groceries, go to the Morris Hedstrom and Burns Philp stores on the main street in town. Morris Hedstrom (known as "MH" in these parts) has a snack bar that is reasonably clean. Fresh local vegetables and fruits are sold at Sailoame Market.

THE DOUBLE DOLPHIN, Main St. Tel. 70-327.

Cuisine: BURGERS/SANDWICHES. **Reservations:** Not accepted. **Location:** On Main St. opposite The Moorings.

$ Prices: Burgers and sandwiches T$3–T$7 ($2.50–$5.50). No credit cards.

Open: Mon–Sat 8am–4pm, 8am–dark June–Nov.

This is the place to have lunch while strolling around Neiafu. Operated by Canadian David McLean, this small establishment offers burgers and sandwiches from tables on a porch overlooking the harbor. The top price is T$7 ($5.50) for a "lobster burger" (actually lobster salad garnished with crispy cucumbers and green peppers). Also on the premises: a shop with some of the finest handcrafts to be found in Tonga.

GUENTER'S BELLEVUE RESTAURANT, Main St. Tel. 70-514.

Cuisine: EUROPEAN. **Reservations:** Essential. **Location:** Main road, walking distance east of Paradise Hotel.

$ Prices: Appetizers T$3.50–T$4 ($3–$3.50); main courses T$13–T$16.50 ($10.50–$13); three-course menu of the day T$10.50 ($8.50). V.

Open: Nov–Mar Mon–Sat 6–10pm; Apr–Oct sittings at 6 and 8pm.

German-born Guenter Haak, a professional hotel chef for 36 years before settling in Vava'u, now serves his guests in what amounts to a sun-room addition to his house overlooking Port of Refuge. In fact, his view of the harbor is about as good as you will find without trespassing. He does all the cooking, and his menu has varied items—Vienna schnitzel, *vakaviti* (a curried fish dish we shall enjoy in Fiji), fresh snapper in aspic. The three-course daily menu including salad, fish, vegetables, and cake is a bargain.

OCEAN BREEZE RESTAURANT, Old Harbour. Tel. 70-582.

Cuisine: REGIONAL. **Reservations:** Essential. **Location:** On the Old Harbour. Take a cab for T$2 ($1.60).

$ Prices: Appetizers T$1.50–T$4.50 ($1.20–$3.50), main courses T$8.50–T$22.50 ($7–$18).

Open: Lunch Mon–Sat noon–3pm; dinner Mon–Sat 6–10pm.

Born in Tonga, Amelia Dale lived for 15 years in England, where she met and married husband John. Now back in Vava'u, she and John have converted their living room into a restaurant, where she cooks up her curry specialties (I had her lobster in curry sauce, and it was right up there with any I've had in Fiji). In fine weather guests dine on the veranda, where they have a view of Neiafu Tahi, or the Old Harbour. You can walk across the peninsula from Port of Refuge and the Paradise Hotel, but the trail is narrow and can be muddy.

CHAPTER 11

GETTING TO KNOW FIJI

If charm, beauty, and variety were the criteria for arranging the chapters of this book instead of the east-to-west dictates of geography, Fiji would be first.

You'll experience the immense charm of the Fijian people as soon as you get off the plane, clear Customs and immigration, and are greeted by a procession of smiling faces, all of them exclaiming an enthusiastic *"Bula!"* Technically, bula means "health" in Fijian. As a practical matter, it expresses the warmest and most heartfelt welcome you'll receive anywhere.

Fiji's great variety is evident even sooner, for the drivers who whisk you to your hotel are not Fijians of Melanesian heritage but are Indians whose ancestors immigrated to Fiji as agricultural workers to escape the shackles of poverty in places like Calcutta and Madras. Today slightly less than half the population of the country is of Indian descent. The "Fiji Indians" have played major roles in making Fiji the most developed of the independent South Pacific island countries.

The great variety continues to impress as you get around the islands, for in addition to Fiji's cultural mix, you'll find gorgeous white-sand beaches bordered by curving coconut palms, azure lagoons and colorful reefs waiting to be explored, green mountains sweeping to the sea, and a warm climate in which to enjoy it all.

For budget-conscious travelers, Fiji is an affordable paradise. Its wide variety of accommodations ranges from deluxe resorts nestled in tropical gardens beside the beach to down-to-basics hostels catering to the young and the young-at-heart. It has a number of charming and inexpensive small hotels and the largest and finest collection of remote, Robinson Crusoe–like offshore resorts in the entire South Pacific—if not the world. Regardless of where you stay, you are in for a memorable time. The Fijians will see to that.

WHAT'S SPECIAL ABOUT FIJI

Beaches/Natural Spectacles
- ☐ More than 300 tropcial islands: equals thousands of beaches.
- ☐ Rainbow Reef: scuba-divers' heaven.

Great Towns/Villages
- ☐ Levuka: looks much the same as it did a century ago.
- ☐ Savusavu: evokes memories of South Seas copra-trading days.
- ☐ Suva: still has touches of the British Empire.

DATELINE

- **1500 B.C.** Polynesians arrive from the west.
- **500 B.C.** Melanesians settle in Fiji, push Polynesians eastward.
- **A.D. 1300–1600** Polynesians, especially Tongans, invade from the east.
- **1643** Abel Tasman sights some islands in Fiji.
- **1774** Capt. James Cook visits Vatoa.
- **1789** After mutiny on the *Bounty*, Capt. William Bligh navigates his longboat through Fiji, is nearly captured by a war canoe.
- **1804** Sandalwood rush begins on Vanua Levu.
- **1808** Swedish mercenary Charlie Savage arrives at Bau, supplies guns to Chief Tanoa in successful wars to conquer western Fiji.
- **1812** Cakobau, future king of Fiji, is born.
- **1813** Charlie Savage is killed; sandalwood era ends.

(continues)

1. HISTORY

Although the Dutch navigator Abel Tasman sighted some of the Fiji Islands during his voyage of discovery in 1642 and 1643, and Capt. James Cook visited Vatoa, one of the southernmost islands, in 1774, Capt. William Bligh was the first European to sail through and plot the group. After the mutiny on the *Bounty* in April 1789, Bligh and his loyal crew sailed their longboat through Fiji on their way to safety in Indonesia. They passed Ovalau and between Viti Levu and Vanua Levu. Large Fijian *druas* (speedy war canoes) gave chase near the Yasawas, but with some furious paddling, the help of a fortuitous squall, and the good luck to pass through a break in the Great Sea Reef, they made it to the open ocean. The druas turned back.

Bligh's rough, handmade charts were amazingly accurate and shed the first European light on Fiji. For a while, Fiji was known as the Bligh Islands, and the passage between Viti Levu and Vanua Levu still is named Bligh Water.

Like Bligh, the Europeans who later made their way west across the South Pacific were warned by the Tongans of Fiji's ferocious cannibals, and the reports by Bligh and others of reef-strewn waters only added to the dangerous reputation of the islands. Consequently, European penetration into Fiji was limited for many years to beachbums and convicts who escaped from the British penal colonies in Australia. There was a sandalwood rush between 1804 and 1813. Other traders arrived in the 1820s in search of bêche-de-mer (sea cucumber). This trade continued until the 1850s and had a lasting impact on Fiji, since along with the traders came guns and whisky.

RISE OF CAKOBAU

The traders and settlers established the first European-style town in Fiji at Levuka on Ovalau in the early 1820s, but for many years the real power lay on Bau, a tiny island just off the east coast of Viti Levu. With the help of Swedish mercenary Charlie Savage, who supplied the guns, High Chief Tanoa of Bau defeated several much larger confederations and extended his control over most of western Fiji.

Bau's influence grew even more under Tanoa's son and successor, Cakobau. Monopolizing the bêche-de-mer trade and waging almost constant war against his rivals, this devious chief rose to the height of power during the 1840s. He never did control all of the islands, however, for Enele Ma'afu, a member of the Tongan royal family, moved to the Lau Group in 1848 and quickly exerted Tongan control over eastern Fiji. Ma'afu brought along Wesleyan missionaries from Tonga and gave them a foothold in Fiji.

Even though Cakobau ruled much of western Fiji as a virtual despot, the chiefs under him continued to be powerful enough at the local level to make his control tenuous. The lesser chiefs, especially those in the mountains, also saw the Wesleyan missionaries as a threat to their power, and most of them refused to convert or even to allow the missionaries to establish outposts in their villages. (During an attempt to convert the Viti Levu highlanders in 1867, the Rev. Thomas Baker was killed and eaten.)

FALL OF CAKOBAU

Cakobau's slide from power is usually dated from the Fourth of July 1849, when John Brown Williams, the American consul at Levuka, celebrated the birth of his own nation. A cannon went off and started a fire that burned Williams's house. The Fijians retrieved his belongings from the burning building and kept them. Williams blamed Cakobau and demanded $5,000 in damages. Within 2 years an American warship showed up and demanded that Cakobau pay up. Other incidents followed, and American claims against the chief totaled more than $40,000 by 1855. Another American man-of-war arrived that year and claimed several islands in lieu of payment; the United States never followed up, but the ship forced Cakobau to sign a promissory note due in 2 years. In the late 1850s, with Ma'afu and his confederation of chiefs gaining power, and disorder growing in western Fiji, Cakobau offered to cede the islands to Great Britain if Queen Victoria would pay the Americans. The British pondered the offer for 4 years, then turned him down.

Cakobau worked a better deal when the Polynesia Company, an Australian planting and commercial enterprise, came to Fiji looking for suitable land after the price of cotton suddenly skyrocketed on world markets during the American Civil War. Instead of offering his entire kingdom, Cakobau this time tendered only 200,000 acres of it. The Polynesia Company accepted, paid off the American claims, and in 1870 landed Australian settlers on 23,000 acres of its land on Viti Levu near a Fijian village known as Suva. The land was unsuitable for cotton and the climate too wet for sugar, but Suva grew up to be Fiji's bustling capital.

FIJI BECOMES A COLONY

The Polynesia Company's settlers were just a few of the several thousands of European planters who came to Fiji in the 1860s and early 1870s. They bought land for plantations from the Fijians, sometimes fraudulently and often for whisky and guns. Claims and counterclaims to landowner-

DATELINE

- **1822** European settlement begins at Levuka.
- **1835** Methodist missionaries settle on Lekeba in Lau Group.
- **1840** United States Exploring Expedition under Capt. John Wilkes explores Fiji and charts waters.
- **1846** John Brown Williams becomes U.S. consul in Fiji.
- **1848** Prince Enele Ma'afu exerts Tongan control over eastern Fiji from outpost in Lau Group.
- **1849** John Brown Williams's home burned and looted during July 4th celebrations; he blames Cakobau.
- **1851** American warship arrives, demands Cakobau pay $5,000 for Williams's losses.
- **1853** Cakobau installed as high chief of Bau, highest post in Fiji.
- **1854** Cakobau converts to Christianity.
- **1855** American claims against Cakobau grow to $40,000; U.S. warship arrives, claims some islands as mortgage.
- **1858** Cakobau offers to cede Fiji to Britain for $40,000.
- **1860** John Brown Williams dies, his claims still unsettled.

(continues)

ship followed, and with no legal mechanism to settle the disputes, Fiji was swept to the brink of race war. Some Europeans living in Levuka clamored for a national government; others advocated turning the islands over to a colonial power. Things came to a head in 1870, when the bottom fell out of cotton prices, hurricanes destroyed the crops, and anarchy threatened. Within a year the Europeans established a national government at Levuka and named Cakobau king of Fiji. The situation continued to deteriorate, however, and 3 years later Cakobau was forced to cede the islands to Great Britain. This time there was no price tag attached, and the British accepted. The deed of cession was signed on October 10, 1874.

Britain sent Sir Arthur Gordon as the new colony's first governor. As the Americans were later to do in their part of Samoa, he allowed the Fijian chiefs to govern their villages and districts as they had done before (they were not, however, allowed to engage in tribal warfare) and to advise him through a Great Council of Chiefs. He declared that native Fijian lands could not be sold, only leased. That decision has to this day helped to protect the Fijians, their land, and their customs, but it has led to bitter animosity on the part of the land-deprived Indians.

In order to protect the native Fijians from being exploited, Gordon prohibited their being used as laborers (not that many of them had the slightest inclination to work for someone else). When the planters decided in the early 1870s to switch from profitless cotton to sugarcane, he convinced them to import indentured servants from India. The first 463 of them arrived on May 14, 1879 (see "The Indians" under "People" below).

TWENTIETH CENTURY

Following Gordon's example, the British governed "Fiji for the Fijians"—and the European planters, of course—leaving the Indians to struggle for their civil rights. The government exercised jurisdiction over all Europeans in the colony and assigned district officers (the "D.O.s" of British colonial lore) to administer various geographic areas.

As usual there was a large gulf between the appointed civil servants sent from Britain and the locals. In 1917 when Count Felix von Luckner arrived at Wakaya Island off eastern Viti Levu in search of a replacement for his infamous World War I German raider, the *Seeadler,* a local constable became suspicious of the armed foreigners and notified the district police inspector, who in turn was forbidden to arm his Fijian constables. Only Europeans—not Fijians or Indians—could use firearms. As it turned out, the inspector took his band of unarmed Fijians to Wakaya in a small cattle trading boat anyway. Thinking he was up against a much larger armed force, von Luckner unwittingly surrendered.

The British continued to rely on the Fijian chiefs at the village level. One of the highest-ranking, Ratu Sir Lala Sukuna, rose to prominence after World War I. (Like *tui* in Polynesian, *ratu* means "high chief" in Fijian.) Born of the chiefly lineage of both Bau and the Lau Islands in eastern Fiji, Ratu Sukuna was educated at Oxford, served in World

DATELINE

- **1862** Britain rejects Cakobau's offer.
- **1867** Unrest grows; Europeans crown Cakobau as King of Bau; Rev. Thomas Baker eaten.
- **1868** Polynesia Company buys Suva in exchange for paying Cakobau's debts.
- **1870** Hurricanes destroy cotton crop as prices fall.
- **1871** Europeans form central government at Levuka, make Cakobau king of Fiji.
- **1874** Cakobau's government collapses, he and other chiefs cede Fiji to Britain without price tag.
- **1875** Measles kills one-fourth of all Fijians; Sir Arthur Gordon becomes first colonial governor.
- **1879** First Indians arrive as indentured laborers.
- **1882** Capital moved from Levuka to Suva.
- **1916** Recruitment of indentured Indians ends.
- **1917** Count Felix von Luckner captured at Wakaya.
- **1917–18** Fijian soldiers support Allies in World War I.
- **1942–45** Fijians serve as scouts with Allied units in World War II; failure of Indians to fight angers Fijians.

(continues)

War I, and worked his way up through the colonial bureaucracy to the post of chairman of the Native Land Trust Board. Although dealing in that position primarily with disputes over land and chiefly titles, he used it as a platform to educate his people and to lay the foundation for the independent state of Fiji. As much as anyone, he was the father of modern, independent Fiji.

After Pearl Harbor began the Pacific war in 1941, the Allies first rushed to Fiji's defense in the face of the Japanese advance across the Pacific, then turned the islands into a vast training base. The airstrip at Nadi was built during this period, and several coastal gun emplacements can still be seen. The steel-girdered Rewa River bridge between Suva and Nausori Airport is another leftover.

Heeding Ratu Sukuna's call to arms (and more than a little prodding from their village chiefs), thousands of Fijians volunteered to fight and did so with great distinction as scouts and infantrymen in the Solomon Islands campaigns. Their knowledge of tropical jungles and their skill at the ambush made them much feared by the Japanese. The Fijians were, said one war correspondent, "death with velvet gloves."

The war also had an unfortunate side: Although many Indians at first volunteered to join, they also demanded pay equal to the European members of the Fiji Military Forces. When the colonial administrators refused, the Indians disbanded their platoon. Their military contribution was one officer and 70 enlisted men of a reserve transport section, and they were promised they would not have to leave Fiji. Many Fijians to this day begrudge the Indians for not doing more to aid the war effort.

INDEPENDENCE

Ratu Sukuna continued to push the colony toward independence until his death in 1958, and although Fiji made halting steps in that direction during the 1960s, the road was rocky. The Indians by then were highly organized, in both political parties and trade unions, and they objected to a constitution that would institutionalize Fijian control of the government and Fijian ownership of most of the new nation's land. Key compromises were made in 1969, however, and on October 10, 1970—exactly 96 years after Cakobau signed the deed of cession—the Dominion of Fiji became an independent member of the British Commonwealth of Nations.

DATELINE

- **1956** First Legislative Council established with Ratu Sir Lala Sukuna as speaker.
- **1966** Fijian-dominated Alliance Party wins first elections.
- **1969** Key compromises pave way for constitution and independence. Provisions guarantee Fijian land ownership.
- **1970** Fiji becomes independent; Alliance party leader Ratu Sir Kamisese Mara chosen first prime minister.
- **1987** Fijian-Indian coalition wins majority, names Dr. Timoci Bavadra as prime minister with Indian-majority cabinet; Col. Sitiveni Rabuka leads two bloodless military coups, installs interim government.
- **1991** New constitution guaranteeing Fijian majority is promulgated; elections scheduled for 1992.

Under the 1970 constitution, Fiji had a Westminster-style Parliament consisting of an elected House of Representatives and a Senate composed of Fijian chiefs. For the first 17 years of independence, the Fijians maintained a majority—albeit a tenuous one—in the House of Representatives and control of the government under the leadership of Ratu Sir Kamisese Mara, the country's first prime minister.

Then, in a general election held in April 1987, a coalition of Indians and liberal Fijians voted Ratu Mara and his Alliance party out of power. Dr. Timoci Bavadra, a Fijian, took over as prime minister, but his cabinet was composed of more Indians than Fijians. Hard feelings immediately flared between some Fijians and Indians.

THE MILITARY COUPS

Within little more than a month of the election, members of the predominantly Fijian army stormed into Parliament and arrested Dr. Bavadra and his cabinet. It was the

South Pacific's first military coup, and although peaceful, it took nearly everyone by complete surprise.

Then-Col. Sitiveni Rabuka (Ram*bu*ka), the coup leader, was a 38-year-old Sandhurst-trained career soldier who at the time was third in command of Fiji's army. A Fijian of nonchiefly lineage and a lay preacher in the Methodist church, Rabuka immediately became a hero to his "commoner" fellow Fijians, who saw him as saving them from the Indians and preserving their land rights from a government dominated by Indians, who at the time slightly outnumbered the Fijians.

Rabuka at first installed a caretaker government, retaining Ratu Sir Penaia Ganilau as governor-general and Ratu Mara as prime minister. In September 1987, after the British Commonwealth suspended Fiji's membership, he staged another bloodless coup. A few weeks later he abrogated the 1970 constitution, declared Fiji to be an independent republic, and set up a new interim government with Ganilau as president, Ratu Mara as prime minister, and himself as minister of home affairs and army commander.

The government instituted pay cuts and price hikes in 1987 after the Fijian dollar fell sharply on world currency markets. Coupled with the coups, the economic problems led to thousands of Indians—especially professionals, such as doctors, lawyers, accountants, and schoolteachers—fleeing the country.

Dr. Bavadra was released shortly after the coups. He died of natural causes in 1989.

2. GOVERNMENT, POLITICS & ECONOMY

GOVERNMENT

As we went to press, Fiji was still under the interim government imposed after the second military coup. In 1990 it promulgated a new constitution under which Fiji is to have a Fijian president and another Westminster-style Parliament. Fijians will always hold 37 of the 70 total seats, Indians will have 27 seats, one will be reserved for Rotuma (a Polynesian island that is part of Fiji), and five will be held by general electors (that is, Europeans, Chinese, or persons of mixed race). General elections have been scheduled for July 1992.

POLITICS

In general, politics in Fiji can be expected to follow a Fijian-Indian breakdown. "Fijians generally perceive Indians as mean and stingy, crafty and demanding to the extent of being considered greedy, inconsiderate and grasping, uncooperative, egotistic, and calculating," writes Prof. Asesela Ravuvu of the University of the South Pacific. On the other hand, he says, Indians see Fijians as "jungalis," still living on the land which they will not sell, poor, backward, naive, and foolish. Given that these attitudes are not likely to disappear, a result satisfactory to all in Fiji will not come easily.

In my view, the result will be determined as much by what happens within each community—especially on the Fijian side—as what occurs between them. Much of Dr. Bavadra's support came from more educated, affluent Fijians who have ongoing differences with the country's system of chiefs and the conservative, village-oriented way of life they represent. This trend is seen throughout the South Pacific: Many islanders who move to the cities and towns and become exposed to Western ways and affluence do not want to return to the communal village style of life, as represented in Fiji by General Rabuka and the Great Council of Chiefs. Robert Keith-Reid, publisher of *Islands Business Pacific* magazine, predicts if these younger, more liberal Fijians win enough of the 37 seats reserved for their race, Fiji may see a "series of short-lived, shaky, inefficient coalition administrations of misadventure." As we went to press, the picture was not at all clear.

ECONOMY

Fiji is the most self-sufficient of the South Pacific island countries covered in this book. Sugar and tourism are its two major industries. Most sugar is grown by Indian farmers and milled by the Fiji Sugar Company, a government-owned corporation that bought out the private Colonial Sugar Refining Company in 1973 (you still see the initials CSR on much of the company's equipment).

Copra is still important, as are gold, timber, garments, and other consumer goods produced by small manufacturers (the Colgate toothpaste you buy in Fiji will have been made there). Fiji also is a major transshipment point for goods destined for other South Pacific island countries.

The economy nosedived into recession after the 1987 coups. Tourism dropped to a relative trickle, and unemployment became even more of a problem than it was before. The Fiji dollar lost nearly 25% of its value against the U.S. and Australian dollars (in most respects a boon to budget-conscious travelers, except that the higher-priced resorts promptly increased their room rates to make up the difference).

Although the Fiji dollar still is depressed against the major foreign currencies, tourism and the overall economy quickly returned to levels experienced before the first coup. In fact, so much foreign capital had flowed into the country by 1990 that the costs of housing and real estate have skyrocketed.

Despite its relative prosperity, unemployment still is a problem. More than half the population is under the age of 25, and there just aren't enough jobs being created for the youngsters coming into the work force. A marked increase in burglaries and other property crimes has been linked to high unemployment.

3. GEOGRAPHY

The Fiji Islands lie in the southwestern Pacific some 3,200 miles southwest of Honolulu and 1,960 miles northeast of Sydney. This strategic position has made Fiji the transportation hub of the South Pacific islands. **Nadi International Airport** is the main connection point for flights going to the other island countries, and Fiji's capital city, **Suva,** is one of the region's prime shipping ports.

The archipelago forms a horseshoe around the reef-strewn **Koro Sea,** a body of water shallow enough for much of it to have been dry land during the last Ice Age some 18,000 years ago. There are more than 300 bits of land ranging in size from **Viti Levu** ("Big Fiji"), one of the largest South Pacific islands, to tiny atolls that barely break the surface of the sea. With a total land area of 7,022 square miles, Fiji is slightly smaller than the state of New Jersey. Viti Levu has 4,171 of those square miles, giving it more dry land than all the islands of French Polynesia put together (it's almost 10 times the size of Tahiti).

Viti Levu and **Vanua Levu,** the second-largest island, lie on the western edge of Fiji. The **Great Sea Reef** arches offshore between them and encloses a huge lagoon dotted with beautiful islands. Many scuba divers think of the coral reefs in this lagoon, the Astrolabe Reef south of Viti Levu, and the Rainbow Reef between Vanua Levu and Taveuni as the closest thing on earth—or below it—to paradise.

THE REGIONS IN BRIEF

From a tourist's standpoint, Fiji is divided into several regions, each with its own special characteristics and appeal.

NADI

Most visitors arrive at Nadi International Airport, a modern facility located among sugarcane fields on Viti Levu's dry western side. Known collectively as **Nadi,** this area is the focal point of much of Fiji's tourism industry. There are a variety of hotels between the airport and the small farming and tourism community of **Nadi Town,** and several things to see and do in the area, but most visitors sooner or later fan out from Nadi to other destinations.

Beckoning offshore, the **Mamanuca Islands** offer day cruises and several small, relatively isolated offshore resorts that appeal to a broad spectrum from young, swinging singles to quieter couples and families. They all have lovely beach settings and modern facilities, and without exception they are excellent places to "get away from it all." The major drawback of any offshore resort, however, is that you've done just that. You won't see much of Fiji while you're basking in the sun on a tiny rock some 25 miles offshore. Consider them for what they have to offer, but not as bases from which to explore the country.

Other visitors join up with **Blue Lagoon Cruises** at its base in nearby **Lautoka,** Fiji's second-largest city and its prime sugar milling center. The cruises spend several days or a week in the **Yasawas,** a chain of gorgeous and unspoiled islands shooting off north of the Mamanucas. Like Moorea and Bora Bora in French Polynesia, the Yasawas are often used as movie sets. *The Blue Lagoon,* a film starring Brooke Shields as a castaway schoolgirl, was filmed there.

THE CORAL COAST

The paved **Queen's Road** runs around the south coast of Viti Levu through the **Coral Coast,** an area of beaches, comfortable hotels, luxury resorts, and fire-walking Fijians. For those who want on-the-beach resort living along with the convenience of being able to get around and see the country, the Coral Coast offers an excellent choice. Offshore lie the islands of **Vatulele** and **Beqa.** The former already has an upscale resort hosted by Fiji's most entertaining manager, and Beqa was slated to have one up and running by 1992. Farther south, **Kadavu** and its Astrolabe Reef already are meccas for scuba divers.

SUVA

The Queen's Road goes on to **Suva** (pop. 85,000), Fiji's busy capital and one of the South Pacific's most cosmopolitan cities. Steamy Suva houses a fascinating mix of atmospheres and cultures. Remnants of Fiji's century as a British possession and the presence of so many Indians give the town a certain air of the colonial "Raj"—as if this were Agra or Bombay, not the edge of Melanesia. On the other hand, Suva has modern high-rise buildings and lives at as fast a pace as will be found in the South Pacific—no surprise since in many respects it's the bustling economic center of the region. The streets are filled with a melting-pot blend of Indians, Chinese, Fijians, other South Pacific islanders, "Europeans" (a term used in Fiji to mean persons of white skin regardless of geographic origin), and individuals of mixed race.

OVALAU & LEVUKA

From Suva, it's an easy side trip to **Toberua Island** and **Wakaya Club,** two of the South Pacific's finest small offshore resorts, or to the picturesque island of **Ovalau** and its historic town of **Levuka,** which has changed little in appearance since its days as a boisterous whaling port and the first capital of a united Fiji in the 1800s. Few places in the South Pacific have retained their frontier facade as has this living museum.

THE NORTH

Vanua Levu, Taveuni, and their nearby islands are known locally as The North since they comprise Fiji's Northern Province. Over on Vanua Levu, a little town with the exotic name **Savusavu** lies nestled in one of the region's most gorgeous bays. It and

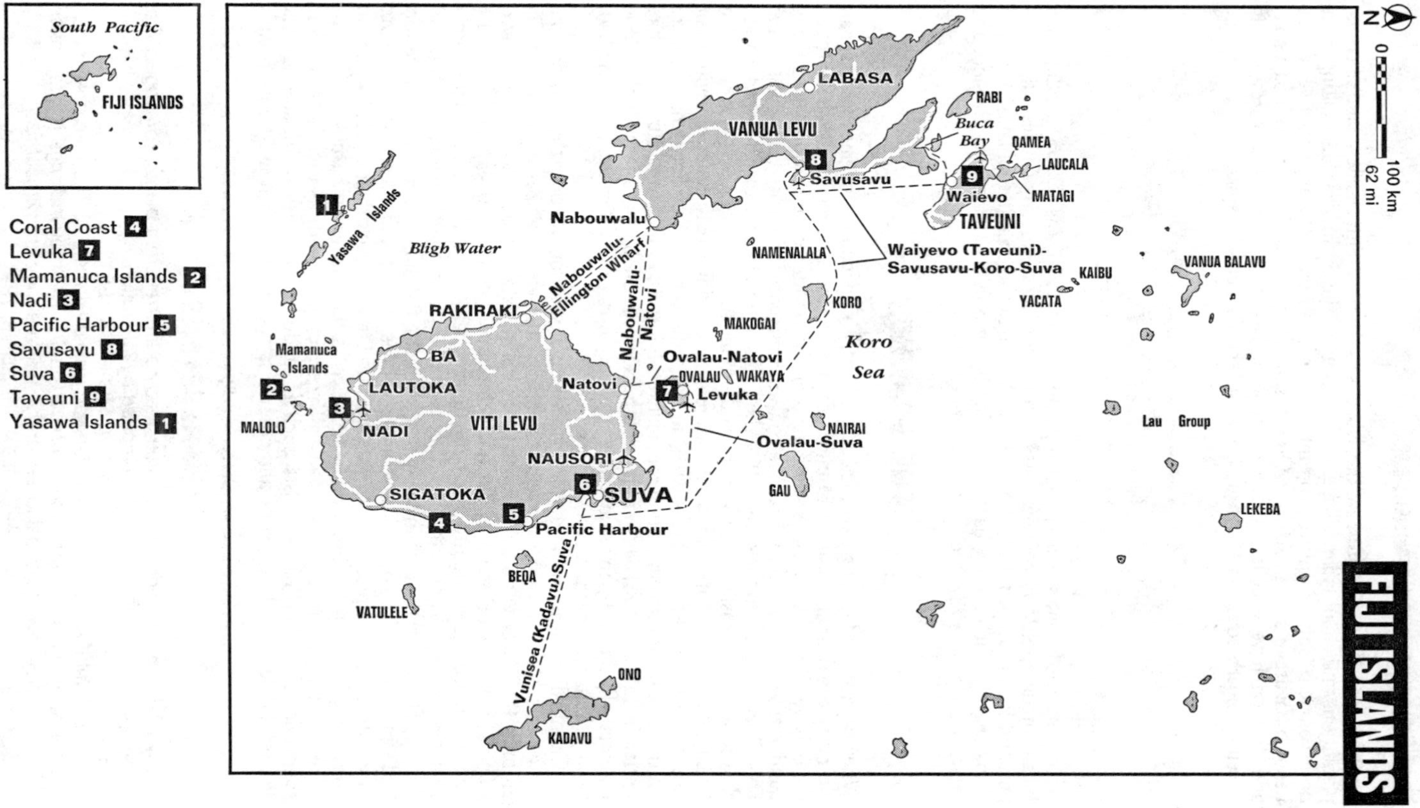

FIJI ISLANDS

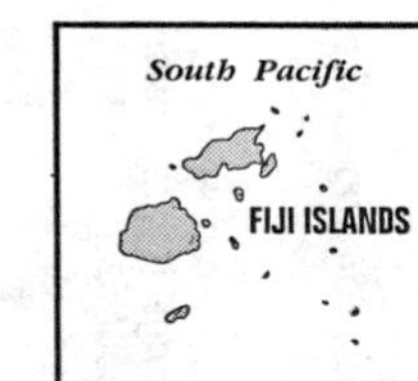

Coral Coast 4
Levuka 7
Mamanuca Islands 2
Nadi 3
Pacific Harbour 5
Savusavu 8
Suva 6
Taveuni 9
Yasawa Islands 1

the "Garden Isle" of **Taveuni** are throwbacks to the old South Pacific, a land of copra plantations and small Fijian villages tucked away in the bush. Travelers looking for a do-it-yourself "soft adventure" trip into the past can take a local bus across Vanua Levu to Savusavu and an *African Queen*–style ferry on to Taveuni. Both Savusavu and Taveuni have excellent places to stay, and there are fine luxury resorts off Taveuni's north coast on **Matagi, Qamea,** and **Laucala** islands.

4. PEOPLE

According to the latest census, Fiji's population in 1990 was 735,985. Indigenous Fijians made up 49.9%, Indians 46.2%, and other races—mostly Chinese, Polynesians, and Europeans—the remaining 3.9%. Although the overall population has been rising slightly, the country has been losing about 5,000 Indians annually since the military coups of 1987 (see "History," above).

THE FIJIANS

When meeting and talking to the friendly Fijians, it's difficult to imagine that less than a century ago their ancestors were among the world's most ferocious cannibals. Today the only vestiges of this past are the four-pronged wooden cannibal forks sold in any handcraft shop (they make interesting conversation pieces when used at home to serve hors d'oeuvres). Yet in the early 1800s, the Fijians were so fierce that Europeans were slow to settle in the islands for fear of literally being turned into a meal—perhaps even being eaten alive. More than a few white-skinned individuals ended up with their skulls smashed and their bodies baked in an earth oven. William Speiden, the purser on the U.S. exploring expedition that charted Fiji in 1840 long after Europeans had settled in Tahiti and elsewhere in the South Pacific, wrote home to his wife that "one man actually stood by my side and ate the very eyes out of a roasted skull he had, saying, 'Venaca, venaca,' that is, 'very good.' "

Cannibalism was an important ritualistic institution among the Fijians, the indigenous Melanesian people who came from the west and began settling in Fiji around 500 B.C. Over time they replaced the Polynesians, whose ancestors had arrived some 1,000 years beforehand, but not before adopting much of Polynesian culture and intermarrying enough to give many Fijians lighter skin than that of most other Melanesians, especially in the islands of eastern Fiji near the Polynesian Kingdom of Tonga. (This is less the case in the west and among the hill dwellers, whose ancestors had less contact with Polynesians in ancient times.) Similar differences occur in terms of culture. For example, while Melanesians traditionally pick their chiefs by popular consensus, Fijian chiefs hold title by heredity, in the Polynesian fashion.

Ancient Fijian society was organized by tribes, each with its own language, and subdivided into clans of specialists, such as canoe builders, fishermen, and farmers. Powerful chiefs ruled each tribe and constantly warred with their neighbors, usually

IMPRESSIONS

Many of the missionaries were eaten, leading an irreverent planter to suggest that they triumphed by infiltration.

—JAMES A. MICHENER, 1951

It is doubtful if anyone but an Indian can dislike Fijians. . . . They are one of the happiest peoples on earth and laugh constantly. Their joy in things is infectious; they love practical jokes, and in warfare they are without fear.

—JAMES A. MICHENER, 1951

with brutal vengeance. Captured enemy children were hung by the feet from the rigging of the winners' canoes, and new buildings sometimes were consecrated by burying live adult prisoners in holes dug for the support posts. The ultimate insult, however, was to eat the enemy's flesh. Victorious chiefs were even said to cook and nibble on the fingers or tongues of the vanquished, relishing each bite while the victims watched in agony.

Fijians wouldn't dream of doing anything like that today, of course, but they have managed to retain much of their old life-style and customs, including their hereditary system of chiefs and social status. Most Fijians still live in small villages along the coast and riverbanks or in the hills, and you will see many traditional thatch *bures,* or houses, scattered in the countryside away from the main roads. Members of each tribe cultivate and grow food crops on small plots of communally owned native land that are assigned to them as individuals, not as groups. More than 80% of the land in Fiji is owned by Fijians.

A majority of Fijians are Methodists today, their forebears having been converted by puritanical Wesleyan missionaries who came to the islands in the 19th century.

FIJIAN CULTURE

Kava

Kava, or *yaqona* (yong-gona) in Fijian, rivals the potent Fiji Bitter beer as the national drink. You likely will have half a coconut shell full of "grog" offered—if not shoved in your face—beginning at your hotel's reception desk. Fiji has more "grog shops" than bars.

In addition to its widespread recreational use, yaqona still plays an important ceremonial role in Fijian life. No important occasion takes place without a yaqona ceremony. Mats are placed on the floor, the participants gather around in a circle, and the yaqona is mixed in a large carved wooden bowl called a *tanoa* during an elaborate ritual. The ranking chief sits next to the tanoa. During the welcoming ceremony, he extends in the direction of the guest of honor a cowrie shell attached to one leg of the bowl by a cord of woven coconut fiber. It's extremely impolite to cross the plane of the cord once it has been extended. The guest of honor offers a gift to the village and makes a speech explaining the purpose of his visit. The chief then passes the first cup of yaqona to the guest, who claps once, takes the cup in both hands, and gulps down the contents in one swallow (to gag is gauche). Everyone else then claps three times. Next, the chiefs each drink a cup, clapping once before bolting it down. Again, everyone else claps three times after each cup is drained. Except for the clapping and formal speeches, everyone remains silent throughout the ceremony.

The Tabua

The highest symbol of respect among Fijians is the tooth of the sperm whale known as a *tabua* (tam*bu*a). Like large mother-of-pearl shells used in other parts of Melanesia, tabuas in ancient times played a role similar to money in modern society and still have various ceremonial uses. They are presented to chiefs as a sign of respect, given as gifts to arrange marriages, offered to friends to show sympathy after the death of a family

---

IMPRESSIONS

Societies that do not eat people are fascinated by those that do (or did).
—Ronald Wright, 1986

There is no part of Fiji which is not civilized, although bush natives prefer a more naked kind of life.
—James A. Michener, 1951

member, and used as a means to seal a contract or other agreement. The value of each tabua is judged by its thickness and length, and some of the older ones are smooth with wear. It is illegal to export a tabua out of Fiji, and even if you did, the international conventions on endangered species make it illegal to bring them into the United States and most other Western countries.

Fire Walking

Legend says that a Fijian god once repaid a favor to a warrior on Beqa island by giving him the ability to walk unharmed on fire. His descendants, all members of the Sawau tribe on Beqa, still walk across stones heated to white-hot by a bonfire—but usually for the entertainment of tourists at the hotels rather than for a particular religious purpose.

Traditionally, the participants—all male—had to abstain from women and coconuts for 2 weeks before the ceremony. If they partook of either, they would suffer burns to their feet. Naturally a priest (some would call him a "witch doctor") would recite certain incantations to make sure the coals were hot and the gods were at bay and not angry enough to scorch the soles.

Today's fire walking is a bit touristy but still worth seeing. If you don't believe the stones are hot, go ahead and touch one of them—but do it gingerly.

Some Indians in Fiji engage in fire walking, but it's strictly for religious purposes.

Etiquette

Fijian villages are easy to visit, but remember that to the people who live in them, the entire village is home, not just the individual bures. In your native land, you wouldn't walk into a stranger's living room without being invited, so find someone and ask permission before traipsing into a Fijian village. The Fijians are highly accommodating people, and it's unlikely they will say no; in fact, they may ask you to stay for a meal or perhaps stage a small yaqona ceremony in your honor. They are very tied to tradition, however, so do your part and ask first.

If you are invited to stay or eat in the village, a small gift to the chief is appropriate. A pound or two of yaqona roots will do just fine. The gift should be given to the chief or highest-ranking person present to accept it. Sometimes it helps to explain that it is a gift to the village and not payment for services rendered, especially if it's money you're giving.

Only chiefs are allowed to wear hats in Fijian villages, so it's good manners for visitors to take theirs off. Fijians go barefoot and walk slightly stooped in their bures. Men sit cross-legged on the floor; women sit with their legs to the side. They don't point at one another with hands, fingers, or feet, nor do they touch each other's heads or hair. They greet each other and strangers with a big smile and a sincere "Bula."

THE INDIANS

The Fiji Indians' version of America's *Mayflower* was the *Leonidas,* a labor transport ship that arrived at Levuka from Calcutta on May 14, 1879, and landed 463 indentured servants destined to work the sugarcane fields.

As more than 60,000 Indians would do over the next 37 years, these first immigrants signed agreements (*girmits,* they called them) requiring that they work in Fiji for 5 years; they would be free to return to India after 5 more years. Most of them labored in the cane fields for the initial term of their girmits, living in "coolie lines" of squalid shacks hardly better than the poverty-stricken conditions most left behind in India. After the initial 5 years, however, they were free to seek work on their own. Many leased small plots of land from the Fijians and began planting sugarcane or raising cattle on their own. To this day most of Fiji's sugar crop, the country's most important agricultural export, is produced on small leased plots rather than on large plantations. Other Indians went into business in the growing cities and towns and,

IMPRESSIONS

The question of what to do with these clever Indians of Fiji is the most acute problem in the Pacific today. Within ten years it will become a world concern.
—JAMES A. MICHENER, 1951

joined in the early 1900s by an influx of business-oriented Indians, thereby founded Fiji's modern merchant and professional classes.

Of the immigrants who came from India between 1879 and 1916, when the indenturing system ended, some 85% were Hindus, 14% were Muslims, and the remaining 1% were Sikhs and Christians. Fiji offered these adventurers far more opportunities than they would have had in caste-controlled India. In fact, the caste system was scrapped very quickly by the Hindus in Fiji, and, for the most part, the violent relations between Hindus and Muslims that wracked India were put aside on the islands.

Life for the Indians was so much better in Fiji than it would have been in India that only a small minority of them went home after their girmits expired. They tended then—as now—to live in the towns and villages and in the sugar-growing areas on the north and west coasts of Viti Levu and Vanua Levu; Hindu and Sikh temples and Muslim mosques abound in these areas. Elsewhere the population is overwhelmingly Fijian.

5. LANGUAGE

Fiji has three official languages. To greatly oversimplify the situation, the Fijians speak Fijian, the Indians speak Hindi, and when they speak to each other they use English. Schoolchildren are taught in their native language until they are proficient in English, which thereafter is the medium of instruction. This means that English-speaking visitors will have little trouble getting around and enjoying the country.

There is one problem for the uninitiated, however: the unusual pronunciation of Fijian names. For instance, Cakobau is pronounced "Thak-*om*-bau." There are many other names of people and places that are equally or even more confusing.

FIJIAN

As is the case throughout Melanesia, many native languages are spoken in the islands of Fiji, some of them similar, others quite different. Fijians still speak a variety of dialects in their villages, but the official form of Fijian—and the version taught in the schools—is based on the language of Bau, the small island that came to dominate western Fiji during the 19th century.

Fijian is similar to the Polynesian languages spoken in Tahiti, the Cook Islands, Samoa, and Tonga in that it uses vowel sounds similar to those in Latin, French, Italian, and Spanish: *a* as in b*a*d, *e* as in s*a*y, *i* as in b*ee*, *o* as in g*o*, and *u* as in kangar*oo*.

IMPRESSIONS

A hundred years of prodding by the British have failed to make the Fijians see why they should work for money.
—JAMES A. MICHENER, 1951

Some Fijian consonants, however, sound very different from their counterparts in English, Latin, or any other language. In devising a written form of Fijian, the early Wesleyan missionaries decided to use some familiar Roman consonants in unfamiliar ways. It would have been easier for English speakers to read Fijian had the missionaries used a combination of consonants—*th,* for example—for the Fijian sounds. Their main purpose, however, was to teach Fijians to read and write their own language. Since the Fijians separate all consonant sounds with vowels, writing two consonants together only confused them.

Accordingly, the missionaries came up with the following usages: **b** sounds like *mb* (as in reme*mb*er), **c** sounds like *th* (as in *th*at), **d** sounds like *nd* (as in Su*nd*ay), **g** sounds like *ng* (as in si*ng*er), and **q** sounds like *ng* + *g* (as in fi*ng*er).

Here are some Fijian names followed by their unusual pronunciations:

Ba mBah
Bau mBau
Beqa m*Beng*-ga
Buca *mBu*-tha
Cakobau Thak-*om*-bau
Korotogo Ko-ro-*tong*-o
Labasa Lam-*ba*-sa
Mamanuca Ma-ma-*nu*-tha
Nadi *Nan*-di
Tabua Tam-*boo*-a
Toberua Tom-bay-*roo*-a
Tubakula Toom-ba-*ku*-la

You are likely to hear these Fijian terms used during your stay:

ENGLISH	**FIJIAN**	**PRONUNCIATION**
Hello	**bula**	***boo*-lah**
Hello (formal)	**ni sa bula**	**nee sahm *boo*-lah**
Good morning	**ni sa yadra**	**nee sah *yan*-drah**
Good night	**ni sa moce**	**nee sah *mo*-thay**
Thank you	**vinaka**	**vee-*nah*-kah**
Thank you very much	**vinaka vaka levu**	**vee-*nah*-kah *vah*-ka *lay*-voo**
House/bungalow	**bure**	***boo*-ray**
tapa cloth	**masi**	***mah*-see**
sarong	**sulu**	***sue*-loo**

If you want to know more Fijian, look for A. J. Schütz's little book, *Say It in Fijian* (Pacific Publications, Sydney), available at most bookstores and hotel boutiques. An American, Dr. Schütz is a professor of linguistics at the University of Hawaii.

FIJI HINDI

The common everyday language spoken among the Indians is known as Hindi or Hindustani. Although it is based on Hindustani, in fact it is very different from that language as spoken in India. The Indians of Fiji, in fact, refer to it as *Fiji Bat,* or "Fiji talk," because it grew out of the need for a common language among the immigrants who came from various parts of the subcontinent and spoke some of the many languages and dialects found in India and Pakistan. Thus it includes words from Urdu, a variety of Indian dialects, and even English and Fijian.

Unlike the Fijians, who are likely to greet you with a "Bula," the Indians invariably address visitors in English. If you want to impress them, here are the greetings in Fiji Hindi:

ENGLISH	**HINDI**	**PRONUNCIATION**
Hello and good-bye	**namaste**	**na-*mas*-tay**
How are you?	**kaise?**	**ka-*ee*-say**
Good	**accha**	***ach*-cha**

I'm okay	**Thik hai**	**teak high**
Right or okay	**rait**	**right**

Jeff Siegel's slim handbook, *Say It in Fiji Hindi* (Pacific Publications, Sydney), is available at most bookstores and hotel boutiques in Fiji.

6. INFORMATION, ENTRY REQUIREMENTS & MONEY

INFORMATION

The outstanding staff at the **Fiji Visitors Bureau** provides maps, brochures, and other materials at the bureau's head office in a restored colonial house at the corner of Thomson and Scott streets in the heart of Suva (tel. 302433, fax 300970) and at its small office in the international arrivals concourse at Nadi International Airport (tel. 722433). A stop at one or both of these offices is a must. The FVB's mailing address is G.P.O. Box 92, Suva, Fiji Islands.

The Fiji Visitors Bureau has an office in **North America** at 5777 West Century Boulevard, Suite 220, Los Angeles, CA 90045 (tel. 213/568-1616, fax 213/670-2318), which will provide brochures about Fiji and a list of hotels with their rates (and approximate taxi fares to them) compiled by the Fiji Hotel Association. Other FVB offices are:

Australia: 225 Clarence St., 9th Floor, Sydney, NSW 2000 (tel. 02/262-3630, fax 02/262-3636).

New Zealand: 48 High St., 5th Floor, P.O. Box 2279, Auckland (tel. 09/732-134, fax 09/394-720).

Residents of Tokyo, Japan; Kuala Lumpur, Malaysia; and London, England, may contact the Fiji diplomatic missions in their cities.

Before you leave Nadi International Airport, drop in at the Fiji Visitors Bureau office and pick up a copy of ***Spotlight on Fiji, Fiji Beach Press,*** or ***Fiji Magic,*** all informative publications aimed at the tourist market. They will tell you what is going on during your visit.

ENTRY REQUIREMENTS

Tourist **visas** good for stays of up to 30 days are issued upon arrival to visitors who have valid passports, onward or return airline tickets, and enough money or proof of finances to support them during their stay. Persons wishing to remain longer must apply for extensions from the Immigration Department, whose primary offices are at the Nadi International Airport terminal (tel. 722454) and in the Labour Department building on Victoria Parade in downtown Suva (tel. 211775).

Vaccinations are not required unless you have been in a yellow fever or cholera area shortly before arriving in Fiji.

Customs allowances are 200 cigarettes, 1 liter of liquor or 2 liters of beer or wine, and F$50 ($34) worth of other goods (including film) in addition to personal belongings. Pornography is prohibited. Firearms and nonprescription narcotic drugs are strictly prohibited and subject to heavy fines and jail terms. Pets will be quarantined. Any fresh fruits and vegetables must be declared and are subject to inspection and fumigation.

For more information, contact the **Embassy of Fiji,** 2233 Wisconsin Avenue NW, Washington, DC 20007 (tel. 202/337-8320, fax 202/337-1996), or the **Permanent Mission of Fiji to the United Nations,** One UN Plaza, 26th Floor, New York, NY 10017 (tel. 202/355-7316, fax 202/319-1896). Fiji also has diplomatic missions in London, England; Canberra and Sydney, Australia; Wellington and

Auckland, New Zealand; Brussels, Belgium; Tokyo, Japan; and Kuala Lumpur, Malaysia. Check your local phone book.

MONEY

The national currency is the Fiji dollar, which is divided into 100 cents and trades independently on the foreign-exchange markets. At the time of writing it was worth about 70¢ U.S. The exchange rate is not published in American newspapers, but someone at the Fiji Visitors Bureau offices (See "Information," above) usually knows the approximate value. The Fiji dollar is abbreviated FID by the banks and airlines, but I use **F$** in this chapter. A few establishments quote their rates in U.S. dollars, indicated here by U.S. $.

Like their islander counterparts elsewhere in the South Pacific, Fijians may take offense if you try to haggle over a price. On the other hand, most Fiji Indian merchants will expect you to do just that (see "Shopping" under Nadi in Chapter 12).

The Fiji government instituted currency-export controls in the wake of many Indians' fleeing the country after the 1987 coups. As a practical matter, however, the controls do not affect visitors from overseas as long as they do not try to smuggle large sums of money out of the country. If someone approaches you with such a proposition, turn and walk away.

WHAT THINGS COST IN FIJI	U.S. $
Taxi from airport to Nadi Town	4.20
Bus from airport to Nadi Town	.25
All-inclusive double room at Wakaya Club (very expensive)	875.00
Double room at Regent of Fiji (expensive)	161.00
Double room at Tokatoka Resort Hotel (moderate)	88.00
Double room at Sandalwood Inn (budget)	32.00
Lunch for one at Pizza King (moderate)	6.30
Lunch for one at Coffee Lounge (budget)	3.20
Dinner for one, without wine, at Tiko's (expensive)	18.20
Dinner for one, without wine, at Maharaja's (moderate)	8.40
Dinner for one, without wine, at Chopsticks (budget)	4.35
Beer	1.40
Coca-Cola	.63
Cup of coffee	.53
Roll of ASA 100 Kodacolor film, 36 exposures	3.85
Movie ticket	1.12

7. WHEN TO GO — CLIMATE, HOLIDAYS & EVENTS

CLIMATE

During most of the year, the prevailing southeast trade winds temper Fiji's warm, humid, tropical climate. Average high temperatures range from 83°F during the austral winter (June to September) to 88°F during the summer months (December to March). Evenings are in the warm and comfortable 70s throughout the year.

The islands receive the most rain during the summer, but the amount depends on

THE FIJI & U.S. DOLLARS

At this writing, F$1 = approximately 70¢, the rate of exchange used to calculate the U.S. dollar prices given in this chapter. This rate has remained fairly stable during the past few years but may change by the time you visit. Accordingly, use the following table only as a guide.

$ F	$ U.S.	$ F	$ U.S.
.25	.18	15	12.60
.50	.35	20	14.00
.75	.53	25	17.50
1.00	.70	30	21.00
2.00	1.40	35	24.50
3.00	2.10	40	28.00
4.00	2.80	45	31.50
5.00	3.50	50	35.00
6.00	4.20	75	52.50
7.00	4.90	100	70.00
8.00	5.60	125	87.50
9.00	6.30	150	105.00
10.00	7.00	200	140.00

which side of each island the measurement is taken. The north and west coasts tend to be drier; the east and south coasts, wetter. Nadi, on the west side of Viti Levu, gets considerably less rain than does Suva, on the southeast side (some 200″ a year). Consequently, most of Fiji's resorts are on the western end of Viti Levu. Even during the wetter months, however, periods of intense tropical sunshine usually follow the rain showers.

Fiji is in the heart of the South Pacific cyclone belt and receives its share of hurricanes between November and April. Fiji's Meteorological Service is excellent at tracking hurricanes and issuing timely warnings, and the local travel industry is very adept at preparing for them. I've been through the excitement of a few Fiji cyclones and I never let the thought of one keep me from returning every chance I get.

HOLIDAYS

Banks, government offices, and most private businesses are closed for New Year's Day, Good Friday, Easter Saturday and Easter Monday, the Monday closest to June 14 (in honor of Queen Elizabeth's Birthday), the Monday closest to October 10 (for Fiji Day, in honor of the country's independence), the Monday closest to November 14 (in honor of Prince Charles's Birthday), November 25 (for the Prophet Mohammad's Birthday), Christmas Day, and December 26 (for Boxing Day). Some businesses may also close for various Hindu and Muslim holy days. Banks take an additional holiday on the first Monday in August.

Occasionally the government will announce a holiday on short notice. For example, Fiji has developed a habit of winning the world seven-man rugby championships in Hong Kong during April each year, and a public holiday is sure to follow a victory.

SUNDAY IN FIJI

Prior to the 1987 coups, Fiji was relatively open on Sunday. One of the first things the deeply Methodist Colonel Rabuka did, however, was to promulgate a tough Sunday decree. The hotels and other tourist facilities were permitted to operate as usual, but the country was shut down as tight as Tonga from midnight Saturday to midnight

Sunday. Needless to say, the Non-Christian Indians didn't like it, nor did the many Fijians who had difficulty getting to church on time with no buses or taxis running on Sunday morning.

The Sunday decree has since been relaxed so that most taxis can haul passengers. The buses in Nadi still don't run, but those in Suva operate a truncated schedule. The airlines have full schedules of flights. Hotel restaurants and bars have been open all along; now restaurants licensed to sell alcoholic beverages can be open from noon to 2pm and from 7 to 10pm.

Things still move slowly on Sunday, and you should think of making it a time to stay around the hotel, take an excursion to an offshore resort, or be "in transit." During my recent visits, I have made it a practice to drive from Nadi to Suva one Sunday and back the next.

EVENTS

The annual **Hibiscus Festival,** held in Suva during the first week of August, features a plethora of events, including traditional dance shows, parades, and the Hibiscus Ball. A similar **Bula Festival** is held in Nadi during the middle of July.

A colorful military ceremony marks the **changing of the guard** at Government House in Suva during the first week of each month.

Hindus celebrate the **Diwali,** or "Festival of Lights," in late October or early November, when they light their houses with oil lamps and candles.

SUGGESTED ITINERARIES

These are *suggested* itineraries. Since Fiji is a relatively large country with much to see and do, your actual itinerary obviously will depend on your particular interests—water sports or cultural tours, lounging on a beach or sightseeing.

Many people stop in Fiji for a few days on their way to or from Australia or New Zealand. If you're one of them, don't cut your visit too short. Give yourself at least enough time to learn something about the islands and their peoples. I have designed the following itineraries with that goal in mind.

If your ambition is to rest on a tropical beach and not do much else, choose an offshore resort rather than staying on the "mainland" of Viti Levu. Frankly, their beaches are better than what you will find on the big island.

The usual "circuit" goes something like this: Nadi; Coral Coast; Suva; day-trip to Levuka; Taveuni or Savusavu; return to Nadi. An option in the dry season (May to September) is to drive from Nadi to Suva on the King's Road around northern Viti Levu, overnighting in Rakiraki, then return to Nadi via the Queen's Road.

IF YOU HAVE 1 DAY

Visit your hotel desk early to see what's happening. If nothing out of the ordinary catches your eye, spend the morning touring the Mamanuca Islands on the *Island Express*. Have lunch in Nadi Town, quickly shop for handcrafts, then take the open-air local bus to Lautoka. The bus stops at the market, so look there first for handcrafts. Stroll around the business district, including the duty-free shops (Lautoka's merchants are more low-key than Nadi's). During the evening, take in a *meke,* the traditional Fijian feast and dance, at one of the Nadi hotels.

IF YOU HAVE 3 DAYS

Unless you can afford a room at the Regent or Sheraton, which are on Denaru Beach (see "Where to Stay in Nadi" in Chapter 12), consider staying 1 night in Nadi and then moving to the Coral Coast. You'll be on the beach and closer to Suva.

Day 1 Do what I recommend above for a 1-day visit.

Day 2 Move to the Coral Coast, doing some sightseeing on the way (including a stop at the Ka Levu Cultural Centre for a look at how the Fijians lived in the old days). Enjoy an afternoon at the beach.

Day 3 Take a day-trip to Suva (don't miss the Fiji Museum).

IF YOU HAVE 7 DAYS (BLUE LAGOON CRUISE)

Days 1–4 Take a Blue Lagoon Cruise through the Yasawa Islands. You will see a meke and eat Fijian food, so on night 4 (back in Nadi), eat curry at Maharaja's.

Day 5 Now that you're rested up, drive to Suva, stopping at either the Ka Levu Cultural Centre, Pacific Harbour Cultural Centre and Marketplace, or Orchid Island on the way. Tour the town, including the Fiji Museum. Do your handcraft shopping.

Day 6 Take a day-trip to Levuka, Fiji's first capital. Set it up with Fiji Air, which will arrange a tour of the old town.

Day 7 Morning flight back to Nadi, followed by a day of rest or one of the tours described in "What to See and Do" in Chapter 12.

IF YOU HAVE 7 DAYS (NO CRUISE)

Day 1 Do what I recommend above for a 1-day visit. Overnight in Nadi.

Day 2 Make your way by bus, taxi, or rental car to the Coral Coast. Stop at Ka Levu Cultural Centre on the way. Overnight in vicinity of the Reef Resort.

Day 3 Proceed on to Suva, tour the town. Overnight in Suva.

Day 4 Take a day-trip to Levuka, Fiji's first capital. Set it up with Fiji Air, which will arrange a tour of the old town.

Day 5 Return to Nadi in the morning, then go to one of the resorts in the Mamanucas.

Day 6 Enjoy a day of relaxation and water sports.

Day 7 Return to Nadi, take one of the tours mentioned under "What to See and Do" in Chapter 12.

IF YOU HAVE 7 DAYS (WHIRLWIND)

I actually did this quick swing around Fiji once, so I know it can be done. You won't have much time to do much other than sightsee.

Day 1 Catch an early morning flight from Nadi to Savusavu. Tour the town in the morning, spend the afternoon swimming and relaxing. Overnight at Savusavu.

Day 2 Morning flight to Taveuni (about 20 min.). Tour the island and have lunch, then overnight on Taveuni or at one of the resorts on Matagi, Qamea, or Laucala (see Chapter 14).

Day 3 Morning flight to Suva. Tour the city. Overnight at Suva.

Day 4 Day-trip to Levuka. Overnight at Suva.

Day 5 Drive the Coral Coast, stopping off at Pacific Harbour Cultural Centre and Marketplace. Overnight on Coral Coast.

Day 6 Spend the morning resting on the Coral Coast, then drive to Nadi.

Day 7 Take the *Island Express* tour of the Mamanucas during the morning. Shop in Nadi Town or Lautoka during the afternoon.

IF YOU HAVE 14 DAYS

Days 1–4 Take one of Blue Lagoon Cruises' short trips through the Yasawa Islands. You will see a meke and eat Fijian food, so on night 4 (back in Nadi), eat curry at Maharaja's.

Day 5 Drive the Coral Coast, stopping off at Ka Levu Cultural Centre. Overnight on Coral Coast.

Day 6 Spend the morning resting on the Coral Coast, then drive to Suva (plan to arrive before dark).

Day 7 Tour Suva, including the Fiji Museum. Do your handcraft shopping.
Day 8 Take a day-trip to Levuka, Fiji's first capital. Set it up with Fiji Air, which will arrange a tour of the old town.
Day 9 Fly to Taveuni on the morning Fiji Air flight. Tour the island and overnight there or at Matagi, Qamea, or Laucala offshore resorts.
Day 10 Spend the day at leisure.
Day 11 Take Sunflower Airlines' morning flight to Savusavu. Tour the town and overnight there.
Day 12 Spend the day at leisure.
Day 13 Fly to Nadi and overnight there.
Day 14 Take one of the tours mentioned in Chapter 12 and complete any unfinished handcraft shopping.

IF YOU ARE A BACKPACKER

Of all the South Pacific island countries, Fiji is best equipped to offer a low-budget experience. Backpackers will have lots of company—Australians and New Zealanders on break, Europeans making a shoestring world tour, Canadians going to or coming from work Down Under. After 1 night in a Nadi hostel, you will have no trouble picking up the scent of the trail. In general, here's how it goes:

Side trips from Nadi include Beachcomber Island Resort or longer excursions to backpacker-style hostels in the Yasawas.

From Nadi, the circuit usually swings around the north side of Viti Levu to Nananu-I-Ra, an island off Rakiraki which is equipped with basic accommodation (take your own food) and occasionally a shortage of water. After a few days on the lovely beaches there, proceed by bus to Suva. The city is interesting, but it pales in comparison to Levuka on Ovalau as a backpacker's paradise. There are no beaches on Ovalau, but you can stay in very basic huts on Leleuvia, a tiny islet between Ovalau and Viti Levu.

If you can pry yourself away from Levuka, you can take the ferry-bus ride from

FROMMER'S FAVORITE FIJI EXPERIENCES

Cruising One of my more pleasant tasks is to visit the offshore resorts in the lovely Mamanuca Islands; the best part is getting there on one of the cruise boats operating out of Nadi. Once I had the flu on a Blue Lagoon Cruise and still loved it.

Meeting the People The Fijians are justly renowned for their friendliness to strangers, and the Indians are as well educated and informed as anyone in the South Pacific. Together, these two peoples make for fascinating conversations at every turn.

Touring Levuka Having grown up in Edenton, which still looks very much like it did as North Carolina's colonial capital in the 1700s, I feel almost nostalgic in Levuka, which hasn't changed much since it played the same role in Fiji.

The North The old South Pacific of copra plantation and trading boat days still lives in Savusavu and Taveuni. True, it rains more up there in Fiji's "North," but that makes the steep hills greener and the acrid smoke from the copra dryers seem sweet.

Offshore Resorts Nothing relaxes me more than running sand between my toes at one of Fiji's small get-away-from-it-all resorts.

there to Labasa on Vanua Levu, where buses connect across the mountains to Savusavu. From there another bus-ferry combination goes to popular Taveuni. From Taveuni, it's back to Suva and the Coral Coast. A popular side trip from Suva leads to unspoiled Kadavu, which during my recent visit still had only basic accommodation for low-budget travelers and divers who needed no frills.

8. GETTING THERE & GETTING AROUND

GETTING THERE

Most international flights arrive at and depart from Nadi International Airport, about 7 miles north of Nadi Town. A few flights arrive from Auckland, Western Samoa, and Tonga at Nausori Airport, some 12 miles from Suva on the opposite side of the island. Both airports are used for domestic flights.

Arriving passengers may purchase duty-free items before clearing Customs (imported liquor is expensive in Fiji, so if you drink, don't hesitate to buy a bottle).

If you don't have a room reserved, a large sign on the wall behind the immigration counters lists all the hotels in the Nadi area, their present room rates, and the taxi fares to get to them.

After clearing Customs, you emerge to an open-air concourse lined on both sides by airline offices, travel and tour companies, rental-car firms, and a 24-hour branch of the **ANZ Bank** (you will pay F$2 [$1.40] per transaction more than at banks with regular hours).

The **Fiji Visitors Bureau** has an office just to the left, and the friendly staff will give advice, supply information, and even make a hotel reservation for the cost of the phone call. Ask them for a map of Fiji, a copy of *Spotlight on Fiji, Fiji Magic,* and *Fiji Beach Press,* and, if you don't have a reservation, a list of hotels and approximate taxi fares to them. Brochures from every hotel and activity in Fiji are on display. The bureau's airport office is open during regular business hours (see "Fast Facts: Fiji" in this chapter) and for at least an hour after the arrival of all major international flights.

Touts for the inexpensive hotels will be milling about, offering free transportation to their establishments. The larger hotels will also have transportation available for their guests.

Taxis will be lined up to the right outside the concourse (see "Getting Around," below, for fares to the hotels).

Local buses to Nadi and Lautoka pass the airport on the main road Monday through Saturday; walk straight out of the concourse, across the parking lot, and through the gate in the chain-link fence to the road. Driving in Fiji is on the left, so buses heading for Nadi and its hotels stop on the opposite side, next to Raffles Gateway Hotel; those going to Lautoka stop on the airport side of the road. You will see the covered bus stands.

The Nadi domestic terminal and the international check-in counters are to the right of the arrivals concourse as you exit Customs (or to the left if you are arriving from the main road). A good and inexpensive **snack bar** can be found between the two terminals. There also are baggage lockers, but I have never found one with an operable lock. The hotels all have baggage-storage rooms and will keep your extra stuff for free.

A **post office,** in a separate building across the entry road from the main terminal, is open from 8am to 4pm Monday to Friday.

Departing

Passengers leaving the country must pay a **departure tax** of F$10 ($7)—in Fiji currency—to the ticketing agent at the check-in counter. There is no departure tax for domestic flights.

Once you have checked in and cleared immigration, the modern, air-conditioned international departure lounge has a bar, showers, and the largest duty-free shop in the South Pacific. Duty-free prices, however, are higher than you'll pay elsewhere in the country, and there is no bargaining.

NAUSORI AIRPORT (SUVA)

Suva, the capital city, is served by **Nausori Airport,** on the flat plains of the Rewa River delta about 12 miles from downtown. The small terminal has a snack bar but few other amenities. Taxis between Nausori and Suva cost about F$15 ($10.50) each way. Nausori Taxi & Bus Service (tel. 477583 at the airport or 312185 in Suva) has regularly scheduled bus service between the airport and the city for F$2 ($1.40) per person each way. Look for the buses at the curb across from the baggage-claim platform. The company's Suva terminal is behind the Air Pacific office in the Colonial Mutual Life Association (CML) building on Victoria Parade. Passengers departing on international flights must pay F$10 ($7) departure tax. There is no tax on domestic flights.

GETTING AROUND

Fiji has an extensive and reliable transportation network of airlines, rental cars, taxis, ferries, and both long-distance and local buses. This section deals primarily with getting from one island or major area to another; see the "Getting Around" sections in Chapters 12, 13, and 14 for details on transportation within the local areas.

BY PLANE

Since the Fiji government divides up landing rights to avoid competition among the country's three major domestic air carriers (and then tightly controls their fares), the choice of airline depends on where you want to go within Fiji.

Air Pacific, the government-owned carrier whose international service is covered in the "Getting There" section of Chapter 2, provides flights between Nadi and Suva. The one-way fare is F$52 ($36.50). Air Pacific has an office in the international arrivals concourse at Nadi International Airport (tel. 722648 in Nadi, or toll free 722499 from anywhere in Fiji). Its main ticketing office is in the CML Building on Victoria Parade in downtown Suva (tel. 304388).

Air Pacific has a small sales-promotion office at 6151 West Century Boulevard, Suite 524, Los Angeles, CA 90045 (tel. 213/417-2236).

Fiji Air flies between Suva and almost everywhere else in the country except Nadi. There is one morning and one afternoon flight between Suva and Levuka, making possible a day-trip to the old capital, for F$57 ($40) round-trip. At least one flight a day is scheduled between Suva and Labasa and the popular tourist destinations of Savusavu and Taveuni; one-way fares are F$61 ($43) to Labasa, F$56 ($39) to Savusavu, and F$73 ($51) to Taveuni. Fiji Air's main office is at 219 Victoria Parade, Suva, next to Lucky Eddie's and Rockefeller's nightclubs (tel. 313666). It also has an office in the international concourse at Nadi International Airport (tel. 722521).

FROMMER'S SMART TRAVELER: AIRFARES

Ask about Fiji Air's "Discover Fiji" pass if you're going to Suva and are planning to fly from there to Kadavu, Levuka, Savusavu, and Taveuni. For F$150 ($105) you get unlimited travel on those routes within 30 days of the first flight taken. The main drawback is that Fiji Air flies "spoke" routes from Suva to its other destinations. For example, you won't be able to fly from Taveuni to Savusavu (a flight of 20 minutes) without backtracking to Suva.

Sunflower Airlines (tel. 723016 in Nadi, 315755 in Suva), serves the tourist market with flights from Nadi to Pacific Harbour for F$46 ($32), to Savusavu for F$82 ($57), to Taveuni for F$98 ($69), to Labasa for F$82 ($57), or the Plantation Island and Musket Cove resorts on Malololailai for F$25 ($17.50); prices cited are for one-way fares from Nadi. Sunflower's flights from Nadi to Taveuni stop in Savusavu going and coming, so don't let your travel agent book you back to Nadi in order to get between Taveuni to Savusavu (it has been known to happen).

Turtle Airways (tel. 722988) flies small seaplanes from Nadi Bay to the offshore resorts all over Fiji, usually on a charter basis. One-way fares to Mana Island are F$64 ($45) per person, but otherwise you hire the entire plane. For example, Moody's Namenalala in the Koro Sea hires the entire plane and charges F$660 ($462) per trip regardless of how many guests fly in it (like many resorts, the Moodys schedule the transfers so their guests can share the cost).

Baggage allowances may be 10kg (22 lb.) instead of the 20kg (44 lb.) allowed on international flights. Check with the airlines to avoid showing up with too much luggage.

Remember, too, to **reconfirm** both your international and domestic return flights as soon as possible after arriving at your destination.

BY RENTAL CAR

Budget Rent-A-Car (tel. 722735, or toll free 800/527-0700 in the U.S.) has an office in the international arrivals concourse at Nadi airport. It's open 24 hours a day, 7 days a week. The headquarters office, at 123 Foster Road, Walu Bay, Suva (tel. 315899), is open from 7:30am to 5pm daily. Other offices are on Victoria Parade in Suva (tel. 303506), in Lautoka (tel. 661733), in Sigatoka (tel. 500986), and in Labasa on Vanua Levu (tel. 811199).

Budget's cars start at F$52 ($36.50) for a tiny Suzuki Alto. That includes 150 kilometers per day and comprehensive insurance. Each kilometer in excess of 150 costs F15¢ (10¢). Larger, more comfortable cars cost F$85 ($59.50) and up. Full insurance coverage, including third-party liability and injuries to the driver, is an additional F$17 to F$19 ($12 to $13.50) a day. The company has weekend rates covering Thursday or Friday to Sunday, and special hourly, weekly, and monthly rates. You can save 33% if you book and pay for your car at least 30 days in advance.

Avis at Nadi airport (tel. 722233, or toll free 800/331-1212 in the U.S. for reservations) is open during regular business hours and when international flights arrive. Other Avis offices are in Suva (tel. 313833), Korolevu Airport on the Coral Coast (tel. 500176), Nausori Airport (tel. 478936), and in Savusavu (tel. 850184). It also has desks at Hideaway Resort, the Warwick Fiji, Reef Resort, Regent of Fiji, Sheraton Fiji, and The Fijian. Its prices are approximately the same as Budget's.

The Budget and Avis agencies don't charge a "drop" fee for one-way rentals. In other words, you can pick up a car in Nadi and leave it on the Coral Coast or in Suva (or vice versa) without paying extra. Other firms charge up to F$30 ($21) for this privilege.

Thrifty Car Rental (tel. 722607 in Nadi, or toll free 800/367-2277 in the U.S.) is handled in Fiji by Rosie The Travel Service. I have found its cars to be in excellent condition each time I have rented one. Thrifty's all-inclusive rates (car, unlimited kilometers, insurance, government tax) start at F$95 ($66.50) a day.

Other firms at Nadi airport are **Hertz** (tel. 722146, 383677 in Suva, or toll free 800/654-3001 in the U.S.), **UTC** (tel. 722811), **Roxy Rentals** (tel. 722763), and **Central Rent-A-Car** (tel. 722711). **Sharmas Rent-A-Car** (tel. 701055) and **Khan's Rental Cars** (tel. 701009) have their offices in Nadi Town.

All of the companies accept American Express, VISA, Diners Club, and MasterCard.

Driving Rules

Your valid home driver's license will be honored in Fiji.

Driving is on the **left-hand side** of the road, not on the right as in North America and Europe, so remember to get into the "wrong" side of the car. **Seat belts are mandatory.**

Speed limits are 80kmph (48 m.p.h.) on the open road and 50kmph (30 m.p.h.) in the towns and built-up areas.

Driving under the influence of alcohol or other drugs is a criminal offense in Fiji, and Breathalyzer tests can be required of anyone suspected of doing so. You must **stop for pedestrians** in all marked crosswalks.

The **roads** in Fiji are narrow, poorly maintained, and often crooked. Not all drivers are well trained, experienced, or skilled, and some of them (including bus drivers) go much too fast for the conditions. Consequently, **drive defensively at all times.**

Always be alert for potholes, landslides, hairpin curves, and various stray animals including cows and horses.

Also watch out for speed bumps known in Fiji as **road humps;** many villages have them, and most are poorly marked with small black and white roadside posts. You will be upon them before you see them. They are large enough to do serious damage to the bottom of your car.

The Queen's Road is paved between Suva and Lautoka, and the King's Road has been sealed from Lautoka to Rakiraki. Most other roads, including the King's Road east of Rakiraki on the north side of Viti Levu, can be impassable during periods of heavy rain. Be very careful when coming down a hill on an unpaved road, as cars can easily skid on the dirt and gravel.

Gasoline (petrol) is readily available except on Sunday at Shell, Mobil, and BP service stations in all the main towns and near the resort hotels. When I was there it was selling for F75¢ (55¢) a liter, or about U.S. $2 for an American-size gallon.

See "Maps" in "Fast Facts: Fiji," below, for information about road maps. I highly recommend that anyone planning to see Fiji by car buy a copy of *The Fiji Explorer's Handbook* by Kim Gravelle from a hotel gift shop or bookstore. Its maps alone are worth the F$6.50 ($4.50) price.

DISTANCES

From Nadi International Airport to:	Km	Miles
Fiji Mocambo and Travelodge hotels	1.3	.8
Skylodge Hotel	3.3	2.0
Dominion International, Sandalwood Inn, New Westgate	5.2	3.1
Turnoff to Regent of Fiji and Sheraton	8.7	5.2
Nadi Town	9.0	5.4
The Fijian Resort	60.0	36.0
Sigatoka	70.0	42.0
Crow's Nest Hotel	76.6	46.0
Casablanca and Vakaviti hotels	77.0	46.2
Reef Resort	78.0	46.8
Tambua Sands	88.8	53.2
Hideaway Resort	92.0	55.2
The Naviti	97.0	58.2
Korolevu Airport	102.0	61.2
The Warwick Fiji	104.0	62.4
Pacific Harbour	148.0	88.8
Orchid Island	182.0	109.2
Suva	197.0	118.2

BY BUS

Coral Coach Express (tel. 722177 in Nadi, 312287 in Suva) operates an air-conditioned express bus between Nadi and Suva, with stops at the hotels in

IMPRESSIONS

The buses in Fiji are like mobile balconies, with no glass in their windows.
—JOHN DYSON, 1982

between. The coach leaves Suva daily at 7am and arrives in Nadi at noon. It then turns around, leaving Nadi at 1:30pm and arriving back in Suva at 5:30pm. Maximum fare is F$25 ($17.50).

Fiji Express Coach Services/UTC (tel. 722821 in Nadi, 312287 in Suva) operates between Lautoka Wharf and the Warwick Fiji on the Coral Coast, stopping at Nadi airport in both directions. It leaves the Warwick at 6:30am and arrives at Lautoka at 9:15am. The return trip leaves Lautoka at 5:15pm and arrives back at the Warwick at 8pm. Fares run up to F$15 ($10.50), depending on how far you go.

Pacific Transport Ltd. (tel. 700044 in Nadi, 304366 in Suva) has several express buses, none of them air conditioned, which travel between Lautoka and Suva with stops at Nadi airport. These cater primarily to local residents. The Nadi-to-Suva fare is about F$8 ($5.50), depending on where you get on.

Fume-belching **local buses** ply regularly between Lautoka and Suva, stopping at Nadi airport and every village between the two, and less frequently on the King's Road and other highways. They take about 6 hours to travel between Nadi and Suva by the Queen's Road, compared to 4 hours for the express buses, but they stop wherever you want to get off, not just at the major hotels. Fares vary according to the length of the trip but are low; about F35¢ (25¢) will get you around the Nadi area, and the full Nadi-to-Suva trip costs only about F$7 ($5). Pay the driver when you board the bus.

As is true throughout the South Pacific islands, local buses use the produce markets as their terminals, but they'll stop anywhere if you signal the driver from the side of the road. Instead of glass, most have side windows made of canvas panels that are rolled down during inclement weather (they usually fly out the sides and flap in the wind like great skirts).

Buses run every few minutes along the road between Lautoka and Nadi Town, passing most of the hotels and restaurants along the way.

FROMMER'S SMART TRAVELER: TAXI FARES

Since Nadi's taxis don't have meters, here are the unofficial fares to some key locations. Use this table only as a guide. If in doubt, ask the persons at the hotel reception desks how much a ride should cost.

Nadi International Airport to:	**F $**	**U.S. $**
Fiji Mocambo and Travelodge hotels	2.00	1.40
Sandalwood Inn, New Westgate Hotel	5.00	3.50
Nadi Town	6.00	4.20
Regent of Fiji, Sheraton Fiji	15.00	10.50
Lautoka	14.00	9.80
The Fijian Resort	40.00	28.00
The Crow's Nest, Tambua Sands, Reef Resort	42.00	29.50
Pacific Harbour	80.00	56.00
Suva	120.00	84.00

BY TAXI

Taxis are as abundant in Fiji as taxi meters are scarce outside of Suva. Although the government refused to raise the official fares, the Nadi cab drivers took it upon themselves in 1991 to charge more. Make sure, therefore, that you settle on a fare to your destination before setting out. In Suva, make sure the meter is turned on. See "Frommer's Smart Traveler: Taxi Fares," above, for more tips.

In Nadi and on the Coral Coast, you will see the same taxi drivers stationed outside your hotel every day. Usually they are paid a salary rather than on a fare basis, so they may be willing to spend more time than usual showing you around.

BY FERRY

As an alternative to flying, you can ride one of several ferries between Viti Levu and Ovalau, Vanua Levu, and Taveuni. They take a lot longer, but the "deck" fares are about a third less than airfare over the same routes. Just don't count on the vessels being spotlessly clean or necessarily on time. If you are on a tight schedule, fly.

The *Spirit of Free Enterprise* plies between Suva, Koro, Savusavu, and Taveuni. A large vehicle-passenger ferry formerly used between the North and South islands in New Zealand, it has airline-type chairs in air-conditioned quarters for its deck passengers and cabins for those who want to go first-class. Snack bars are available for all passengers around the clock. It normally leaves Suva at 5am on Wednesday and Saturday for 2-day runs out to Savusavu, stopping at Koro Island on the way. Once a week it goes on to Taveuni. It turns around at Savusavu or Taveuni and repeats the same stops in reverse order back to Suva. One-way deck-class fares from Suva are F$23 ($16) to Koro, F$27 ($19) to Savusavu, and F$31 ($22) to Taveuni. Double the fares for round-trips, and add F$20 ($14) to each for a first-class cabin. For reservations and tickets, contact **Consort Shipping Lines** (tel. 302877 in Suva). The company's main ticketing office is in the Dominion Arcade behind the Fiji Visitors Bureau in downtown Suva.

Patterson Brothers Shipping Co. Ltd., Suite ½, Epworth House, Nina Street, Suva (tel. 315644 in Suva, 661173 in Lautoka), operates three ships, as follows:

The *Princess Ashika* usually leaves Suva at midnight Monday for Gau, Koro, Savusavu, and Taveuni, arriving back in Suva at 2pm Thursday. It then leaves midnight Thursday for Vunisea on Kadavu, returning to Suva at 2pm the next day. Fares range from F$25 ($17.50) for Suva-Gau to F$33 ($23) for Suva-Taveuni.

The *Jubilee* begins Monday-to-Saturday runs from Ovalau at 4am (a bus leaves Levuka at 3:30am for the wharf), lands at Natovi on Viti Levu's east coast at 6:30am for about 15 minutes, then goes on to Nabouwalu on Vanua Levu, arriving there at 10am. The ferry then turns around and repeats the route. Buses connect between Suva and Navoti on Viti Levu and between Nabouwalu and Labasa on Vanua Levu. The Suva-Levuka fare is F$16 ($11) one-way; Suva-Labasa is F$30 ($21), including the 3-hour bus ride from Nabouwalu to Labasa.

The *Ovalau II* operates between Ellington Wharf on Viti Levu's north shore and Nabouwalu. Buses leave Nadi at 3:45am Monday to Saturday for Ellington Wharf. The Nadi-Labasa fare is F$30 ($21).

Emosi's Express Shipping (tel. 44057 in Levuka) provides Monday-to-Saturday service between Suva and Levuka. A bus leaves Suva's General Post Office (GPO) at 11am for the Bau Landing in the Rewa Delta. A boat departs there at noon for Levuka, stopping at Leleuvia Island on the way. (That's actually the return journey, for the boat leaves Levuka at 8am, stops at Leleuvia at 9:30am, arrives at Bau Landing at 11:30am.) The Suva-Levuka fare is F$17 ($12) one-way.

FAST FACTS: FIJI

The following facts apply to Fiji generally. For more specific information, see the "Fast Facts" in the chapters that follow.

American Express The full-service representative, Tapa International Ltd., has offices in Nadi and Suva. See the "Fast Facts" for Nadi (Chapter 12) and Suva (Chapter 13) for details.

Area Code The international country code is 679.

Baby-sitters The major hotels can arrange for baby-sitters. You may have to pay your sitter's taxi fare home from the hotel.

Bookstores Sigatoka Bookshops and Desai Bookshops, Fiji's largest chains of bookstores, have outlets in all the main towns. See the "Fast Facts" in Chapters 12 and 13 for specific locations.

Business Hours Stores generally are open Mon–Fri 8am–4:30pm, although many close for lunch 1–2pm. Sat hours are 8:30am–noon. Shops in many hotels stay open until 9pm. Government office hours are Mon–Thurs 8am–1pm and 2–4:30pm, Fri 8am–1pm and 2–4pm. Other than tourist-related establishments and nonhotel licensed restaurants, which can open noon–2pm and 7–10pm, no business is open Sun.

Climate See "When to Go—Climate, Holidays, and Events" in this chapter.

Clothing Modest dress is the order of the day, particularly in the villages. As a rule, don't leave the hotel swimming pool or the beach in a bathing suit or other skimpy attire. If you want to run around half naked, go to Tahiti or New Caledonia where the French think it's all right. The Fijians do not. Do not enter a Fijian village wearing a hat or with your shoulders uncovered.

For their part, Fijian men and women wear *sulus,* the same wraparound skirts known as pareus in Tahiti and the Cook Islands and lavalavas in the Samoas. Fijian women wear *chambas,* or hip-length blouses, over their sulus. Many Indian women prefer to wear colorful saris, 6-foot lengths of cloth wrapped and pleated around the body.

Credit Cards American Express, VISA, Diners Club, and MasterCard are accepted by the larger hotels, rental-car firms, travel and tour companies, duty-free shops, and some restaurants.

Crime See "Safety," below.

Currency See "Information, Entry Requirements, and Money" in this chapter.

Currency Exchange ANZ Bank, Westpac Bank, National Bank of Fiji, and Bank of Baroda all have offices throughout the country where currency and traveler's checks can be exchanged. Banking hours are Mon–Thurs 9:30am–3pm, Fri 9:30am–4pm. Thomas Cook Travel Service, 21 Thomson St., Suva, will cash traveler's checks from 8:30am to noon on Saturday.

The ANZ Bank branch on the international arrivals concourse at Nadi International Airport is open 24 hours a day, 7 days a week. It charges a F$2 ($1.40) fee for each transaction; neither ANZ's other branches nor any other bank charges such a fee.

ANZ and Westpac will make cash advances against MasterCard and VISA credit cards. All the banks can arrange international transfers of funds.

Customs See "Information, Entry Requirements, and Money" in this chapter.

Doctor Medical and dental care in Fiji is not up to the standards common in the industrialized world. The hospitals tend to be overcrowded and understaffed. Most hotels have private physicians on call or can refer one. Doctors are listed at the beginning of the white pages section for each town or area in the Fiji telephone directory under the heading "Medical Practitioners." See the "Fast Facts" in Chapters 12, 13, and 14 for specific doctors.

The acquired immune deficiency syndrome (AIDS) virus is present in Fiji, and visitors should therefore exercise the same degree of caution in their choice of sexual partner and in practicing safe sex as they would at home.

Documents Required See "Information, Entry Requirements, and Money" in this chapter.

Driving Rules See "Getting Around" in this chapter.

Drug Laws One drive past the Suva jail will convince you not to smuggle narcotics or dangerous drugs into the Fiji.

Drugstores The main towns have reasonably well stocked drugstores. Their medicines are likely to be from Australia or New Zealand. See the "Fast Facts" in Chapters 12, 13, and 14 for specific locations.

Electricity Electric current in Fiji is 240 volts, 50 cycles, so converters are necessary in order to use 110-volt American or Canadian appliances. Many hotels have converters for 110-volt shavers, but these are not suitable for hairdryers. The plugs are the angled two-prong types used in Australia and New Zealand, so an adapter will be necessary. Most outlets have separate on-off switches mounted next to them.

Embassies/Consulates The **U.S. Embassy** is at 31 Loftus St., Suva (tel. 314466). Other diplomatic missions in Suva are: **Canada,** c/o Canadian Airlines International, Honson Arcade, Thomson St. (tel. 311844); **Australia,** 8th Floor, Dominion House, Thomson St. (tel. 312844); **New Zealand,** 10th Floor, Reserve Bank of Fiji Bldg., Pratt St. (tel. 311244); **Great Britain,** 47 Gladstone Rd. (tel. 311033); **Japan,** 2nd Floor, Dominion House, Thomson St. (tel. 302-122); **Papua New Guinea,** Macarthur St. (tel. 304244); **France,** Thomson St. (tel. 312925); **People's Republic of China,** 147 Queen Elizabeth Drive (tel. 311836).

Emergencies The emergency telephone number for police, fire, and ambulance is 000 throughout Fiji.

Etiquette See "Etiquette" under the "People" section in this chapter.

Firearms They are illegal in Fiji, and persons found with them may be fined severely and sentenced to jail.

Gambling There are no casinos in Fiji, and except for off-track betting on Australian and New Zealand horse races and a newspaper numbers game known as "Fiji Sixes," gambling is illegal in the country.

Hairdressers/Barbers See the "Fast Facts" in Chapters 12 and 13 for specific locations.

Hitchhiking Local residents seldom hitchhike, so the custom is not widespread. Women traveling alone should not hitchhike.

Holidays See "When to Go—Climate, Holidays, and Events" in this chapter.

Information See "Information, Entry Requirements, and Money" in this chapter.

Insects Fiji has no dangerous insects, and its plentiful mosquitoes do not carry malaria. The only dangerous creature is the bolo, a venomous snake that is docile and rarely seen.

Language See "Language" in this chapter.

Laundry Except for a few hotels which provide Laundromat facilities for their guests, laundry must be done by hand or sent to a professional laundry. See the "Fast Facts" in Chapters 12 and 13 for specific laundries.

Liquor Laws Except in the hotels and licensed restaurants, alcoholic beverages may not be sold on Sun. Both beer and spirits are produced locally and are considerably less expensive than imported brands, which are taxed heavily. If you drink quality brands of liquor, bring a bottle with you. Fiji Bitter, the local beer, is sold both in bottles and on draft; the bottles are known as "Stubbies."

Mail All the main towns have post offices, and there is a branch at Nadi International Airport across the entry road from the terminal. Airmail connections between Fiji and North America are fairly rapid but allow at least a week for delivery. Surface mail can take 2 months or more to reach the U.S. mainland. Airmail rates are F30¢ (25¢) for postcards and airgrams and F50¢ (35¢) for letters. Post offices are open Mon–Fri 8am–4pm. Mail will move faster if you use the country's official name—Fiji Islands—on all envelopes and packages sent there.

Maps The Sigatoka Bookshops chain publishes one of the best road maps of Fiji; it has stores in Sigatoka, Nadi, Laukoka, and Ba. The free brochure published by the Fiji Hotel Association contains an excellent map of the country; ask for it at the Fiji Visitors Bureau. The *Fiji Explorer's Handbook* by Kim Gravelle, an outstanding guide for anyone planning to see Fiji by road, contains very good maps. Other maps are available from the Department of Land and Surveys, in the Government Buildings, Suva. Desai Bookshops carry the department's excellent map, *Suva and Lami Town,* which shows the bus routes in the Suva area.

Newspapers/Magazines Two national newspapers are published in English, the *Fiji Times* and the *Fiji Post.* Both are tabloids and appear every morning except Sun. They carry the latest major stories from overseas. The international editions of *Time* and *Newsweek* (the latter in the rear of *The Bulletin*, an Australian newsmagazine), and the leading Australian and New Zealand daily newspapers are available at some bookstores and hotel shops. The latter usually are several days old before they reach Fiji. Two magazines cover South Pacific regional news: the excellent *Islands Business Pacific* and *Pacific Islands Monthly*, both published in Suva.

Pets You will need advance permission to bring any animal into Fiji; if not, your pet will be quarantined.

Photographic Needs Caines Photofast, the largest processor of Kodak films, has shops in the main towns.

Police The emergency phone number is 000 throughout Fiji. See "Safety," below.

Radio/TV The Fijian government operates three nationwide radio networks whose frequencies depend on the location of the relay transmitters. Radio Fiji 1 carries programming in Fijian and English. Radio Fiji 2 is primarily in Hindi. Radio Fiji 3 has mostly English programs and relays the world news from Radio Australia at 7 and 9am, and from the BBC at 8am and 11pm, both followed by the local news and weather. Radio Fiji 2 and 3 both carry a full world, regional, and local news report at 7pm daily. Two English-language FM stations can be heard in Suva on 90.6 and 96.0.

Fiji has been discussing broadcast TV for several years, but as we went to press it had not been installed. There are plenty of television sets used to play videotapes, which are rented in every town and village.

Religious Services Anglican, Roman Catholic, Congregational, Methodist, Seventh-Day Adventist, Assembly of God, Baptist, and Mormon churches can be found throughout Fiji. Services may be in English, Fijian, or even Hindi. Ask at your hotel for the church of your choice, its schedule of services, and the language it uses. In addition to Christianity, a wide range of Asian-based religions are represented in Fiji, with Hindu, Muslim, and Sikh sects predominating.

Rest Rooms Red signs point in the general direction of a few "Public Conveniences" in downtown Suva. While these will do in an emergency, the hotels and restaurants offer a much higher degree of cleanliness. Most hotels have public rest rooms in their lobby areas, usually close to the bar. The Fiji Visitors Bureau has rest rooms in its old house at the corner of Scott and Thomson streets in downtown Suva.

Safety By and large, Fiji is a safe country in which to travel, although it has experienced an increase in property crime in recent years. A tourist's chances of being robbed or assaulted in Fiji are lower than in most large American cities, but caution is advised. Stick to the main streets after dark and take a taxi back to your hotel if you're out late at night. Some of the smaller hotels in Suva lock their front doors at 11pm, and the large resorts have checkpoints to monitor who comes and who goes. Do not leave valuables unattended or in your hotel room or rental car.

As noted in "For Women Traveling Alone" under "Tips for the Disabled, Seniors, Singles, and Families" in Chapter 2, women should not wander alone on deserted beaches and should be extremely cautious about accepting an offer to have a few beers outside a bar or to be given a late-night lift back to their hotel or hostel. See "Fast Facts: South Pacific" in Chapter 2 for more warnings.

Taxes All hotel, restaurant, rental-car, and bar bills will have a 10% government sales tax added to them. The government had proposed a 10% value-added tax, but as we went to press it had not been approved. As noted above, visitors leaving the country by air must pay a departure tax of F$10 ($7) in Fiji currency to the ticketing agent at the airport check-in counter.

Telephone/Telex/Fax Fiji has been upgrading its telephone system so that every number will have international access. When complete, every phone in the country will have a six-digit number. Accordingly, numbers in this book with five digits are likely to change. If you can't get through, consult the international operator from overseas or directory assistance from within Fiji. The number for **directory assistance** in Fiji is 011.

Calls to Fiji may be dialed directly from areas in the U.S. or other countries where this service is available. The country code for Fiji is 679.

Pay phones are located at most post offices. They come in two types. One is an older rotary model: To make a local call from one of these, lift the handset, listen for a dial tone, deposit a Fijian 20-cent coin, and dial the number; for long distance, dial 010, and deposit the money when the operator tells you to. The second type of phone is orange and has push buttons and digital readout; you can call local, domestic long distance ("trunk calls"), or international without operator assistance—just deposit enough money to cover the cost and dial away.

International phone calls, telegrams, and telex service is provided by Fiji International Telecommunications Ltd. (FINTEL). They may be placed at your hotel, any post office, or at FINTEL's colonial-style building on Victoria Parade in downtown Suva (it's open 24 hours a day, 7 days a week). If placing a call at the FINTEL office in Suva, you may reverse the charges or put the call on a credit card issued by an American Bell System telephone company (the card *must* have an international number on it). Otherwise, you must deposit enough cash in advance to cover the cost of the call. Stand by for a short wait, for the operator will place your call and ring you when the connection is made. A typical station-to-station call from Fiji to the U.S. will cost F$8.50 ($6) for the first 3 minutes. Person-to-person calls cost an additional F$5.50 ($3.85).

Time Local time in Fiji is 12 hours ahead of Greenwich mean time. The country sits just west of the international date line, so it's 1 day ahead of the U.S. and shares the same day with Australia and New Zealand. Translated: When it's 5am on Tues in Fiji during standard time in the U.S., it's noon on Mon in New York and 9am on Mon in Los Angeles. (During daylight saving time it's 1 hour earlier in the U.S.; thus it would be 11am on Monday in New York and 8am on Monday in Los Angeles.)

Tipping Tipping is discouraged throughout Fiji unless truly exceptional service has been rendered. That's not to say, however, you won't get that where's-my-money look once they figure out you're from America.

Tourist Offices See "Information, Entry Requirements, and Money" earlier in this chapter.

Visas See "Information, Entry Requirements, and Money" earlier in this chapter.

Water Except during periods of continuous heavy rain, the tap water in the main towns and at the resorts is safe to drink.

Weights/Measures Fiji is on the metric system. See the appendix for methods of conversion.

CHAPTER 12

NADI & THE CORAL COAST

No other South Pacific island has as many organized tours, cruises, and other attractions designed for travelers as does Fiji, and many of the activities take place or begin in the Nadi area. Whether it's a leisurely day cruise over calm blue waters to a deserted island or rafting down a wild river, Nadi has something for almost everyone.

The airport (see "Getting There" in Chapter 11) lies midway on Viti Levu's west coast. Most of the area's hotels are along the Queen's Road, which runs through sugarcane fields between the airport and Nadi Town (pop. 9,000), some 9km (5.4 miles) to the south.

Nadi Town is little more than a 5-block-long strip of the Queen's Road lined on either side by a few restaurants and a plethora of duty-free, handcraft, and other retail shops. Unlike **Lautoka,** Fiji's second-largest city (pop. 30,000), 33km (20 miles) to the north, Nadi Town has tourism as its major reason for being.

1. GETTING AROUND NADI

Budget, Avis, Thrifty, Hertz, Roxy, UTC, and Central car-rental firms have offices on the international arrivals concourse of Nadi International Airport. Sharmas and Khan's have offices in Nadi Town.

Taxis gather outside the arrival concourse at the airport and are stationed at the larger hotels. Ask the reception desk to call you one.

Local buses ply between the markets in Nadi Town and Lautoka, leaving each on the hour and on the half hour between 6am and 8pm Monday to Saturday. Fares vary according to the length of trip, but F35¢ (25¢) will get you around the Nadi area. Tell the driver where you're going; he'll tell you how much to pay.

See "Getting Around" and "Frommer's Smart Traveler: Taxi Fares" in Chapter 11.

NADI

The following facts apply specifically to Nadi and Lautoka. For more information, see "Fast Facts: Fiji" in Chapter 11.

American Express Tapa International Ltd. (tel. 722325), the Fiji representative, has an office on the arrivals concourse of Nadi International Airport. The

WHAT'S SPECIAL ABOUT NADI & THE CORAL COAST

Natural Spectacles

- ☐ Great Sea Reef: Makes a water playground by enclosing a huge lagoon dotted with islands.

TV & Film Locations

- ☐ The Yasawas: Three versions of *The Blue Lagoon* were made there.

Activities

- ☐ Cruising: Protected waters and beautiful islands abound offshore.
- ☐ Tours: Train and boat rides, sightseeing, orchids, cultural experiences equal South Pacific's widest variety.

address is P.O. Box 9240, Nadi Airport, Fiji Islands. Personal checks are first endorsed at the airport office, then you go to the ANZ Bank in Nadi Town to get the traveler's checks. Tapa's hours are Mon–Fri 8:30am–4:30pm, Sat 8:30am–noon.

Bookstores Sigatoka Bookshops is on Sahu Kahan St. between Clay St. and Hospital Rd. in Nadi Town. To find it, go east on Clay St. off the Queen's Rd. and turn right on Sahu Kahan St.

Currency Exchange ANZ Bank, Westpac Bank, National Bank of Fiji, and Baroda Bank all have offices on the Queen's Rd. in Nadi Town and in Lautoka. ANZ Bank's branch at Nadi International Airport is open 24 hours a day.

Dentist Ask your hotel staff to recommend a dentist in private practice. The government runs a dental clinic (tel. 700370).

Doctor Many Nadi-area expatriates go to Dr. Ram Raju, 36 Clay St., Nadi Town (tel. 700240 or 701769 after hours).

Drugstores There are three drugstores on Queen's Rd. in Nadi Town.

Emergencies The emergency telephone number is 000.

Eyeglasses Opticare, 54 Naviti St. (near Vakabale St.), Lautoka (tel. 663337).

Hairdressers/Barbers Tokatoka Resort Hotel (tel. 790222) opposite the airport has a full-service beauty salon.

Hospitals The main Western Province hospital is in Lautoka (tel. 662399). There is a medical clinic in Nadi Town (tel. 701108).

Information The Fiji Visitors Bureau (tel. 722433) has an office on the arrivals concourse of Nadi International Airport.

Laundry/Dry Cleaning Northern Press Ltd. (722787) on Northern Press Road between the airport and Nadi Town has 1-day laundry and dry-cleaning service.

Libraries Nadi Town Council Library is in the town council shopping arcade, east side of the Queen's Rd. about midway through Nadi Town. It's open Mon–Fri 9am–5pm, Sat 9am–1pm.

Photographic Needs Caines Photofast has a film and 1-hour processing shop on Queen's Rd. in Nadi Town. Most of the hotel gift shops also sell film and 1-day processing.

Police The Royal Fiji Police has stations at Nadi Town (tel. 700222) and at the airport terminal (tel. 722222).

Post Office The Nadi Town post office is on Queen's Rd. near the south end of town. There is a small airport branch across the main entry road from the terminal (go through the gates and turn left).

Safety See "Fast Facts: Fiji" in Chapter 11.

Shoe Repairs Narayan & Sons, Clay St., Nadi Town (tel. 700908).

VITI LEVU & OVALAU

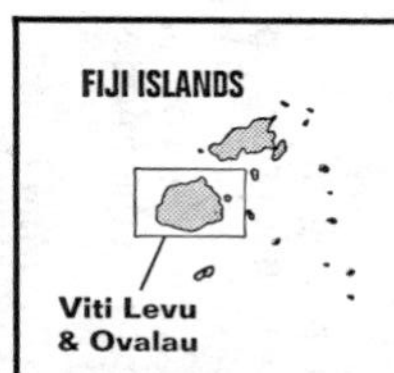

- Coral Coast 9
- Garden of Sleeping Giant 2
- Lautoka 1
- Levuka 13
- Mamanuca Group Resorts 3
- Momi Guns 5
- Nadi Town 4
- Natadola Beach 6
- Orchid Island 11
- Pacific Harbour 10
- Sigatoka River Valley 8
- Sigatoka 7
- Toberua Island Resort 12

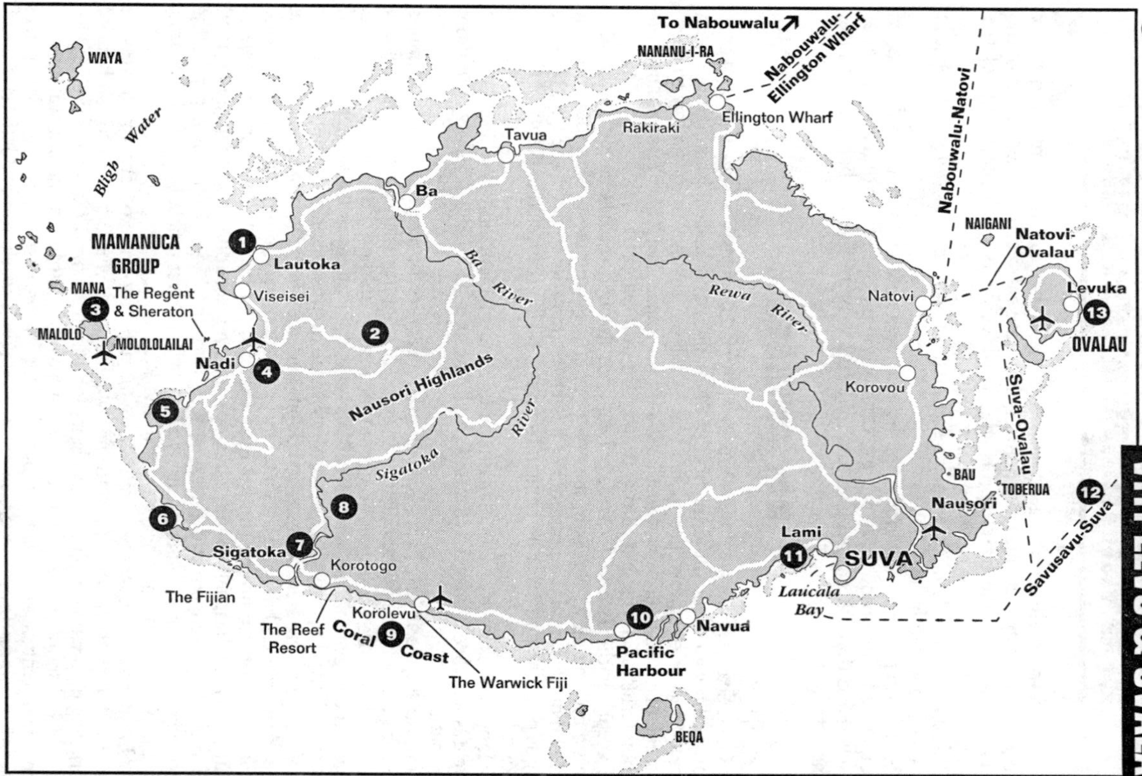

2. WHAT TO SEE & DO IN NADI

All but a few hotels have at least one tour desk that can make reservations or arrangements for the activities mentioned below, and the reception-desk staffs of the others will do so. Like travel agents, the activities desks get a percentage of the proceeds; their services cost you nothing extra.

Pick up copies of *Spotlight on Fiji, Fiji Beach Press,* and *Fiji Magic,* which give up-to-date, detailed information.

Round-trip bus transportation from the Nadi area hotels is included in the price of the organized cruises and outings; a bus usually will pick you up within 30 minutes of the scheduled departure time. Children under 12 years of age pay half fare on most of the activities.

DAY CRUISES

The Great Sea Reef off northwest Viti Levu in effect encloses a huge lagoon whose usually calm waters surround the nearby Mamanuca and Yasawa island groups with speckled shades of yellow, green, and blue as the sea changes from shallow to deep. It's a fine place to go cruising for at least a day or longer. See "The Yasawas and Blue Lagoon Cruises" at the end of this chapter for more information.

Except for the *Island Express,* which goes through the Mamanucas every day unless a cyclone blows through, the other day cruises (and most other tours, for that matter) require a minimum number of passengers in order to make the trip. Book as early as possible, and insist on being informed if a trip is canceled in plenty of time to make other plans.

Many cruises go to Malololailai Island, home of Plantation Island and Musket Cove resorts. See "Easy Excursions" and "Resorts Off Nadi," below, for more information.

Island Express (tel. 700144), a 300-passenger diesel-powered catamaran, makes two trips a day through the hilly, picturesque Mamanuca Islands and is the primary means of transport for visitors heading to the resorts on those little offshore jewels. It departs the Regent at 9am for Mana Island and stops briefly at Castaway Island, and Plantation Island resorts (see "Resorts Off Nadi" in this chapter) on the way back. It usually departs the Regent again at 1:30pm and goes over the same route in reverse order. Day-trippers have two options. One, you can spend 4 hours sightseeing through the islands on the morning run for F$25 ($17.50) per person. You won't be able to luxuriate on any beaches, as the boat stops at each resort only long enough to put off and pick up passengers and their luggage. Two, for F$54 ($39) you can take the morning trip, get off at Mana Island Resort, have a buffet lunch, swim and sunbathe, and catch the afternoon voyage back to the Regent.

Mamanutha Explorer (tel. 722696), a 39-foot motor cruiser, leaves the Sheraton Fiji at 10am for cruises to tiny Magic Island, where it stops for an hour of snorkeling before proceeding on to Plantation Island Resort. Cost is F$39 ($27.50) for the ride and snorkeling at Magic Island; you pay for your lunch and any water-sports equipment rentals at Plantation Island. The *Mamanutha Explorer* also makes **sunset cruises** from the Sheraton 3 evenings a week for F$30 ($21) a head, including a complimentary drink. Rum, beer, wine, and soft drinks are available on board. Call 722696 for details.

Seaspray (tel. 700144), an 86-foot sailing schooner, sails from the Regent at 9am daily for Plantation Island Resort. The F$54 ($39) per-person fare includes transfers from the Nadi hotels, snorkeling gear, and coral viewing on a glass-bottom boat. You pay for the bar service provided on board and at Plantation Island, plus the cost of water-sports equipment rental at the resort. You return to the Regent on the midday voyage of the *Island Express.*

Beachcomber Day Cruises (tel. 661500) sail aboard the *Tui Tai* from Lautoka to youth-oriented Beachcomber Island Resort (see "Resorts Off Nadi" in this

IMPRESSIONS

The air smelled of blossoms and moistened earth; the hotel maids, who looked and dressed rather like Africans, were singing in the corridors. Most surprising of all, the neatness and tranquillity extended to the town outside the front door, and the countryside at the back. The hotel did not seem to be an island built for foreigners in a sea of squalor.

—RONALD WRIGHT, 1986

---

chapter). Adults pay F$50 ($35) for bus transportation from Nadi to Lautoka, the cruise, and an all-you-can-eat buffet lunch on Beachcomber Island. Snorkeling gear costs F$2 ($1.40) for 2 hours, plus a refundable F$40 ($28) deposit. It's a fine way to join the young folks frolicking in the sun without having to stay overnight. A few tops have been known to drop at Beachcomber, so if the sight of a woman's unclothed breasts offends, think twice before signing up for this one.

Daydream Cruises (tel. 723314) takes its guests on the 115-foot, diesel-powered *Adi Litia* for a full day's visit to tiny Malamala Island—a flat, 6-acre atoll studded with palm trees and circled with white-sand beaches. The island's only inhabitants will be you and your fellow passengers, who will use its only building, a thatch bure built by Daydream Cruises. The boat leaves Newtown Beach at 10am daily for the 1-hour cruise to Malamala. The F$59 ($41.50) price includes lunch on the island and round-trip bus transportation to the beach.

Ra Marama (tel. 701823), is a 110-foot square-rigged brigantine (that is, a "tall ship") built in Singapore during the 1950s and used as the official yacht for Fiji's colonial governors-general. Now fully restored, it leaves at 10am daily for a cruise through the Mamanuca Islands, including a stop at Magic Island. The day-trip costs F$59 ($41.50) per person. The ship also is used for **sunset cruises** at F$35 ($24.50) a head, and for all-evening bashes known as "Hot Summer Nights" at F$59 ($41.50) per person. It also is used for 4-day, 3-night voyages between Nadi and Kadavu Island (see "Sailboat Charters," below).

Whale's Tale (tel. 722455 or 790134), a luxury, 100-foot auxiliary sailboat, takes no more than 12 guests on day cruises from the Regent through the Mamanucas. The F$125 ($87.50) per person cost may seem steep, but it includes a continental breakfast with champagne on departure; a buffet lunch prepared on board; all beverages including beer, wine, and liquor; and sunset cocktails. The boat also makes 3-day, 2-night cruises to the Yasawas and is available for charter (see "Sailboat Charters," below).

SIGHTSEEING TOURS

Several companies operate tours on air-conditioned buses to various destinations near Nadi, on the Coral Coast, and to Suva. Their rates are about the same, but some shopping around could pay off. Talk to more than one hotel activities desk; since most desks are operated by the tour companies, they understandably will steer you to their trips. Following are some of the more popular excursions:

Nadi Area: Optional Tours of Fiji (tel. 722666) uses an air-conditioned bus for a morning tour of the Nadi area, including the Nadi Town market, an Indian sugarcane farm, a Fijian village, a Muslim mosque and Hindu temple, historical Viseisei village, and the orchid range at Garden of the Sleeping Giant. Cost is F$35 ($24.50) for adults, F$17 ($12) for children. Another version of this tour, for the same price, goes to Lautoka instead of Nadi Town, with a stop at the Garden of the Sleeping Giant on the way.

Garden of the Sleeping Giant: Most of the tour companies have ½-day guided tours of the Garden of the Sleeping Giant, an orchid range started in 1977 by actor Raymond Burr of "Perry Mason" and "Ironsides" fame to house his private collection of tropical orchids (he once also owned a small island in Fiji). The tours cost about F$35 ($24.50). You can visit the collection on your own by rental car or taxi. Look for the sign at Wailoko Road off the Queen's Road between Nadi and Lautoka. It's open from 9am to 5pm Monday to Saturday. Entrance fees are F$8.50 ($6) for one adult, F$16 ($11) for a couple, F$20 ($14) for a family. A guide and a fruit drink are included. A tour of Burr's former home in the hills overlooking Saweni Bay north of Nadi costs F$5 ($3.50) per person. It's now owned by Don and Aileen Burness (tel. 662206), who have a collection of Fijian artifacts on display.

Coral Coast Railway/Ka Levu Cultural Centre: Sun Tours (tel. 722666) has a day-trip to a Coral Coast feature: the *Fijian Princess*, a restored sugarcane locomotive that takes passengers from The Fijian Resort to lovely Natadola Beach, where they swim and have lunch (bring your own towel), then a visit to the Ka Levu Cultural Centre (see "Cultural Tours," below). Cost is F$49 ($34.50) per person from the Nadi hotels, slightly less from those on the Coral Coast.

Sigatoka Valley/Kula Bird Park: Road Tours of Fiji (tel. 722935) offers this full-day tour to the town of Sigatoka on the Coral Coast and the meandering river and flat valley of the same name. The land is so fertile that Sigatoka Valley is known as "Fiji's Salad Bowl." The tour usually includes a stop at Nadroga, a small village in the valley where Fijians still make pottery in the traditional way of their ancestors. There also will be time for lunch and some shopping in Sigatoka. Kula Bird Park on the Coral Coast has a collection of tropical birds, whose collective feathers have the colors of a rainbow, and an aquarium stocked with examples of local sea life. Price: F$35 ($24.50), excluding lunch. You can visit Kula Bird Park (tel. 500505) on your own. It's opposite the Reef Resort on the Coral Coast. Admission is F$10 ($7) for adults, F$5 ($3.50) for children. Hours are 8am to 5pm Monday to Saturday.

Highland Tour: For a variation of the Sigatoka Valley trip, Highland Tours (tel. 520285 in Sigatoka) uses a 25-seat four-wheel-drive rough-terrain bus to go up the valley and then on forestry roads across the steep hills of the scenic Nausori Highlands to Nadi. The full-day trip includes information about Fiji's Pre-European days. Price is F$60 ($42), including lunch in a Fijian village.

Suva Guided Day Tour: United Touring Fiji (UTC) (tel. 722811), Road Tours of Fiji (tel. 722935), and Optional Tours of Fiji (tel. 722666) all have buses that leave Nadi about 8am Monday through Saturday for the 4-hour drive to Suva, picking up passengers at the Coral Coast hotels along the way. Guests have lunch on their own in Suva and then are escorted on a guided tour of the city. The buses leave Suva about 4pm for the return trip. You'll pay about F$50 ($35) per person from Nadi, less from the Coral Coast hotels. Optional Tours (tel. 722666) has a variation of this tour which includes an escorted visit to Orchid Island, the Fijian cultural center west of Suva. Prices are F$49 ($34.50) from Nadi, F$24.50 ($17) for children under 16. For more information about Suva and Orchid Island, see Chapter 13.

CULTURAL TOURS

Not everyone has time to strike out into the hills and hunt for a village where they might be offered accommodation and a chance to learn firsthand about Fijian culture. Accordingly, here are some tours that will give you a glimpse of Fijian life.

Three Nights in a Village: Not for anyone who needs lots of comforts, this 4-day, 3-night tour goes to the highland village of Korolevu in the hills above the Coral Coast (there is another Korolevu village of the same tribe down on the coast). Guests stay in a large, simple Fijian-style bure with its own toilets and cold-water showers. In addition to learning about Fijian village life, guests go riding, rafting, hiking, and swimming in a pool under a waterfall. Cost is F$120 ($84) for the entire trip, including transfers, meals, accommodation, and activities. The bus usually leaves Nadi on Monday and Thursday mornings. For information and reservations, contact "Momma Violet" at the Nadi Sunseekers hostel (tel. 700400 or 701655).

Ka Levu Cultural Centre: Optional Tours of Fiji (tel. 722666) runs ½-day trips to Ka Levu Cultural Centre, a re-creation of an ancient Fijian village—complete with a towering *bure kalou*, or temple. Fijian women make and sell handcrafts on the spot, and guides explain various facets of ancient Fijian life. A cultural show was presented at 10:30am Thursday during my recent visit; see when it's on, for that will be the best day to visit. The day tour costs F$30 ($21) per person from the Nadi hotels, F$25 ($17.50) from those on the Coral Coast. Note that Ka Levu Cultural Centre sits across the Queen's Road from The Fijian Resort on the Coral Coast, so you can visit it on your own if you're going that way. Entrance fees are F$10 ($7) for adults, F$5 ($3.50) for children between 5 and 12 years old. Admission to the tour and Thursday cultural show is F$15 ($10.50) for adults, F$7.50 ($5) for children. *Note:* Ka Levu Cultural Centre is included in the Coral Coast Railway tour mentioned above.

Namuamua Inland Tour: Optional Tours (tel. 722666) runs this full-day trip by bus to the Navua River, then by boat past waterfalls and through forests to a Fijian village, where guests participate in a yaqona ceremony and watch traditional entertainment during a lunch of local-style foods. Price is F$65 ($45.50) from the Nadi hotels, F$51 to F$55 ($35.50 to $38.50) from those on the Coral Coast.

Pacific Harbour: Optional Tours (tel. 722666), UTC (tel. 722811), and Road Tours of Fiji (tel. 722935) all have full-day tours to this planned resort development 30 miles west of Suva to visit the Cultural Centre and Marketplace and see what Fijian life was like before the Europeans came. The trips include time for shopping at the Marketplace. Prices are about F$65 ($45.50) from the Nadi hotels, slightly less from those on the Coral Coast.

EASY EXCURSIONS

PLANTATION ISLAND

Rather than take one of the day cruises, you can go over to Plantation Island Resort for the day on your own via Sunflower Airlines (tel. 723016), which has frequent flights from Nadi airport to the little gravel strip separating Plantation Island and Musket Cove resorts on Malololailai Island some 9 miles offshore. Sunflower's special excursion round-trip fare is F$38 ($26.50). Its flights leave at 8:30 or 10:30am and return at 2:30 or 5:30pm. The trip includes free use of the facilities at Plantation Island Resort.

Once on Malololailai, you can hang out at either resort, shop at Louis and Georgie Czukelter's Art Gallery on the hill above Musket Cove (see "Shopping," below), and dine at Anandas Restaurant and Bar (tel. 722333) by the airstrip. Anandas' specialties are barbecues on a beachside patio for F$14 ($10) a person. See "Resorts Off Nadi" in this chapter for more information about Plantation Island and Musket Cove resorts.

LAUTOKA

Towering royal palms march in a long, orderly row down the middle of Vitogo Parade, the broad main street that runs from the harbor into the heart of Lautoka, Fiji's second-largest town (pop. 30,000). A major seaport in its own right, Lautoka serves as the jumping-off point for Blue Lagoon Cruises (see "The Yasawas and Blue Lagoon Cruises," below, in this chapter) and the boats heading to the resorts on Beachcomber and Treasure islands.

Few visitors stay in Lautoka. Most make their base in Nadi and come to Lautoka to spend a few hours looking around the pleasant town and doing some shopping.

Local buses leave the market in Nadi Town every half hour for the Lautoka Market between 6am and 8pm Monday to Saturday. The fare is no more than F$1 (70¢) depending on where you get on. The taxi fare from Nadi airport to Lautoka is F$14 ($10).

If you're driving yourself, you will come to two traffic circles on the outskirts of Lautoka. Take the second exit off the first one, the first exit off the second. That will take you directly to the post office and the southern end of Vitogo Parade, the main drag with stores on one side, a row of royal palms down the center, and a park on the other.

The duty-free shops and other stores along Vitogo Parade mark the boundary of Lautoka's business district; behind them are several blocks of stores and a busy market, which doubles as the local bus station. Shady residential streets trail off beyond Churchill Park on the other side of Vitogo Parade. The Hare Krishnas have their most important temple in the South Pacific on Tavewa Avenue; it's open every day until 8:30pm and has a restaurant serving excellent and very reasonably priced vegetarian curries.

Tourism may be important to Lautoka, but sugar is king. The **Fiji Sugar Corporation**'s huge mill, one of the largest crushing operations in the southern hemisphere, was built by the Colonial Sugar Refining Company in 1903. Free guided tours can be arranged by calling 660800 in Lautoka.

Other than the Hare Krishna temple on Tavewa Avenue, you won't have much choice of places to have lunch. Best of a poor selection is the **Seacoast Restaurant,** corner of Naviti and Nede streets (tel. 660675), a clean, air-conditioned establishment that serves Chinese fare. Dishes range from F$4.50 to F$7 ($3 to $5). Open 8:30am to 8:30pm Monday to Saturday. To find it, head toward the harbor from the post office, turn right on Naviti Street, walk 2 blocks. It's on the left.

SPORTS/RECREATION

GOLF

The hotel tour desks can arrange for you to play at the 18-hole **Nadi Airport Golf Club** near Newtown Beach behind the airport. The course isn't particularly challenging, but the setting, on the shores of Nadi Bay, is attractive. Greens fees are F$10 ($7). The Fiji Mocambo Hotel has a short course for its guests, and an 18-hole course was under construction on Denaru Island for the Regent and Sheraton hotels during my recent visit. The South Pacific's best course is at **Pacific Harbour** near Suva, some 89 miles from Nadi. Greens fees there are F$30 ($21).

TENNIS

As the hotel descriptions below indicate, many Fiji accommodations have tennis courts for their guests' use. In addition, **Denaru Tennis Club** (tel. 780000), located adjacent to the Regent, has four all-weather courts, six Wimbledon-standard grass courts, a pro shop, and a snack bar. Use of the courts costs F$16 ($11) an hour (free to guests of the Regent and Sheraton). The club is open from 7am to 10pm daily.

SAILBOAT CHARTERS

Fiji's reef-strewn waters will not permit strictly "bareboat" yacht charters, but you can rent both boat and skipper for extended cruises through the islands.

The 100-foot schooner ***Whale's Tale,*** P.O. Box 9625, Nadi Airport (tel. 722455 or 790134, fax 790441), is available for charters ranging from 1 day in the Mamanucas to 3 days and 2 nights in the Yasawas. Rates depend on the length of trip, starting at F$125 ($87.50) per person for a day cruise to F$3,700 ($2,590) for six people on a 3-day, 2-night Yasawas cruise.

Stardust Cruises, Private Mail Bag, Nadi Airport (tel. 662215, 662878, or 722077, fax 662633 or 790378), operates the 103-foot schooner ***La Violante*** out of Musket Cove Resort on Malololailai Island in the Mamanucas (which means you have to fly over on Sunflower Airlines or take the *Island Express*). The boat can accommodate up to six persons in three private cabins. Rates are F$150 ($113) per person a day, with a F$600 ($420) per-day minimum.

Captain Cook Cruises (tel. 701823, fax 780045) has regularly scheduled 4-day, 3-night cruises on the ***Ra Marama,*** the 110-foot square-rigged brigantine mentioned under "Day Cruises," above, to Kadavu Island and its Astrolabe Reef. Prices are F$600 ($420) per person.

SCUBA DIVING

Fiji has some of the best diving spots in the South Pacific, if not the world. Most popular are those off Beqa and Kadavu (see Chapter 13) and Taveuni (see Chapter 14).

There also are dive operations on the Coral Coast (see below) Suva (see Chapter 13), and Savusavu (see Chapter 14). In the Nadi area, **Tropical Divers Fiji** (tel. 701777, ext. 189) at the Sheraton Fiji Resort and **South Sea Divers** (tel. 701445) both have dive guides and teach PADI courses. On the offshore islands, **Mamanutha Divers** (tel. 722077) is based at Musket Cove Resort and **Aqua-Trek Ocean Sports Adventures Ltd.** (tel. 661455, or 415/398-8990 in the U.S.) has its headquarters at Mana Island Resort. Prices are about F$50 ($35) for a one-tank dive, F$300 ($210) for courses.

SPORT FISHING

The Islander, a 28-foot motor cruiser, and ***The Duke,*** a speedy 21-foot catamaran, both go in search of marlin, sailfish, tuna, mackerel, barracuda, wahoo, and other game fish in the Mamanuca Islands from the Sheraton at Denaru Beach. For times and prices, contact Bay Cruises (tel. 722696).

Natawa Princess (tel. 723161), a 23-foot twin-engine cabin cruiser takes guests fishing both day and night. Rates are F$200 ($140) for 4 hours, F$380 ($266) for 8.

Pleasure Marine (tel. 701445) has a fleet of fishing boats, including *Bill Collector II* and *The Fishing Machine,* based at the Regent of Fiji and at Mana Island Resort.

HIKING

New Frontiers, an arm of Rosie The Travel Service (tel. 722755), takes trekkers (as hikers are known in these parts) on walks through Viti Levu's central highlands during Fiji's dry season from May to October. The trips vary from 6 to 10 days and generally proceed from Tavua on Viti Levu's north coast across the highlands to Nalawa on the King's Road. Freshwater streams provides baths, latrines serve as toilets, and villagers provide each night's dinner and accommodation. Prices range from F$70 to F$80 ($49 to $56), depending on the size of the trekking party.

RIVER RAFTING

Wilderness (Fiji) Tours (tel. 780026 in Nadi, 386498 in Suva) and **Roaring Thunder** (tel. 780029) operate rafting trips down the Ba River, the stream that flows swiftly through the Naloto Range and crosses a delta to Ba, a predominantly Indian town on Viti Levu's north coast. The amount of "white water" will depend on the amount of rain the area has received. The first 2 hours of the all-day trip are spent in a bus winding through the countryside and up into the hills. Wilderness (Fiji) Tours charges F$69 ($48.50) per person; Roaring Thunder's price is F$70 ($49). Both include a riverside lunch. The trips are restricted to visitors between 15 and 45 years of age, unless they are "perfectly fit" and willing to sign a form releasing the company of liability. Bring bathing suit or shorts, lace-up athletic shoes, plenty of sunscreen, and insect repellent.

SHOPPING

Fiji is noted primarily for its duty-free and handcraft shops, and Nadi Town has ample numbers of both.

When dealing with Fijians—at a local market, for example—bargaining is usually not considered polite. When dealing with Indian merchants, however, the opposite is true. They will start high, you will start low, and somewhere in between will be found a mutually agreeable price. I usually knock 40% off the asking price as an initial counteroffer and then suffer the merchants' indignant snickers, secure in the knowledge that they aren't about to kick me out of the store. After all, the fun has just begun.

Caution: Fijians normally are extremely friendly people, but beware of so-called **sword sellers.** These men carry bags under their arms and approach you on the street and ask, "Where you from, the States?" followed quickly by "What's your name?" More often than not they will try to sell you the sloppily carved wooden sword they pull from the bag and quickly inscribe with your name. They are especially numerous in Suva, but they may come up to you in Nadi, too. The Fiji government discourages this practice but has had only limited success in stopping it.

Duty-Free Shopping

Fiji has the most developed duty-free shopping industry in the South Pacific, as will be very obvious when you walk along the main thoroughfare in Nadi Town. One tout after another will beseech you in Hindi-accented English to "Come in, take a look" at his store's offerings of brand-name perfume, jewelry, watches, electronic equipment, cameras, liquor, cigarettes, and a plethora of other items. Before you dash in and start spending money, go back to the "What to Buy" section in Chapter 2 for some advice from the Fiji National Duty Free Merchants Association. It could save you some regrets later.

By the way, the Fiji government charges a flat 10% import tax on merchandise brought into the country, so the stores aren't exactly "duty free." If you end up with a complaint, the mailing address of the Fiji National Duty Free Merchants Association is P.O. Box 2068, Suva, Fiji Islands (tel. 314129). Members of the association display a yellow, black, and brown sticker in the windows of their shops. Take their advice and be sure to keep your receipts.

Inasmuch as the merchants constantly try to woo customers, it's virtually impossible to miss the duty-free establishments along Queen's Road in Nadi Town. To avoid the hassle, visit the two largest and most reputable merchants: **Proud's** and **Tappoo.** They have well-stocked shops on Queen's Road in Nadi Town as well as in the shopping arcades of the larger hotels in Nadi and on the Coral Coast, and in downtown Suva. Tappoo carries a broad range of merchandise, including electronics, cameras, and sporting goods. Proud's concentrates more on jewelry, perfumes, and watches.

The duty-free merchants along Vitogo Parade, the main drag in Lautoka (see "Lautoka," above), tend to be less pushy than their Nadi colleages, as do those in Sigatoka (see "Shopping" under the "The Coral Coast," below). Consider looking there if the bustle of Nadi Town gets to you.

If you missed anything, you'll get one last chance at the huge shop in the departure lounge at Nadi airport.

HANDCRAFTS

Fijians produce a wide variety of handcrafts, such as carved tanoa (kava) bowls, war clubs, and cannibal forks, woven baskets and mats, pottery, and masi (tapa cloth). Although generally not of the quality of those produced in Tonga, the quantity is prolific. Be careful when buying some wood carvings, however, for many of today's items are machine-made. On the other hand, virtually every shop now sells some very fine face masks and *nguzunguzus* (*noo*-zoo *noo*-zoos), the inlaid canoe prows carved in Solomon Islands (see Chapter 17), and some primitive art from Papua New Guinea. (Although you will see plenty hanging in the shops, the Fijians never carved masks in the old days.)

If you're going to Suva, wait until you've visited the **Government Handicraft Centre** there before making purchases elsewhere. You'll see some of the best items and get a firm idea of the going prices.

Local artisans operate small handcraft stalls near the market and bus station in the center of town. Look there for baskets and other woven goods.

Two shops on Queen's Road in Nadi Town have wide selections of Fijian and imported handcrafts: **Jack's Handicrafts** (tel. 700417) and **Nadi Handicraft Center** (tel. 780357). They are in the same block, middle of the shopping strip near the big Morris Hedstrom department store. Both are open from 7:30am to 6pm Monday to Friday, 7:30am to 1pm Saturday. Both shops will pack and ship your purchases.

Jack's Handicrafts also has a shop in the arcade of the Sheraton Fiji Resort (tel. 701777) and in Sigatoka. Also in the Sheraton arcade, the **General Store** has a small but excellent selection. The Sheraton's shops are open daily 9am to 9pm.

If you're going that way, check out the handcraft stalls in the **Lautoka Market** for shells and shell jewelry, mats, straw hats and purses, grass skirts, and tapa cloth. The wood carvings tend to be a bit touristy, since the stalls do most of their business on days when cruise ships put into Lautoka.

Out at Malololailai Island, Louis and Georgie Czukelter have their **Art Gallery** (tel. 790250) in an old house on a ridge overlooking Musket Cove Resort. Louis is Hungarian, Georgie is French; they settled in Fiji in 1983 after sailing a yacht to the South Pacific. They've been making shell jewelry and tie-dyed tropical clothing ever since. Their quality is excellent, their prices are fair.

TROPICAL CLOTHING

Although not of the quality of other South Pacific countries, you will see colorful tie-dyed clothing and sulus at most of the hotel boutiques and in the shops along Queen's Road in Nadi Town. For the most unusual, pay a visit to the shopping arcade of the Sheraton Fiji Resort. There you will find **Michoutouchkine Creations** (tel. 700158), the major outlet for Nicolai Michoutouchkine's squiggly swirls. Each shirt, blouse, pants suit, towel, and other item is individually painted by the artist and his colleagues in Port Vila, Vanuatu (see Chapter 15 for more information).

EVENING ENTERTAINMENT

The large hotels usually have something going on every night. As noted in the "Where to Dine" section, below, this may be a special meal followed by a Fijian meke dance show. They also frequently have live entertainment in their bars during the cocktail hour. Check the *Fiji Magic* tourist publication for what's happening.

3. WHERE TO STAY IN NADI

Except for a few inexpensive establishments in Nadi Town, the hotels are located among the patchwork cane fields along the Queen's Road between the airport and Nadi Town.

EXPENSIVE

THE REGENT OF FIJI, P.O. Box 441, Nadi, Fiji Islands. Tel. 700700, or toll free 800/545-4000 in the U.S. Fax 700850. Telex 5214. 291 rms, 9 suites. A/C MINIBAR TEL **Location:** On Denaru Island, 7 miles west of Nadi Town.

$ Rates: F$230 ($161) single or double with garden view; F$285 ($200) single or double with ocean view; F$570 ($400) suite. AE, DC, MC, V.

The Nadi area's long-standing deluxe resort, this is generally conceded—along with the Sheraton Fiji next door and the Fijian Resort on the Coral Coast—to be one of the finest hotels in the South Pacific. It's located on a gray-sand beach on Denaru Island, about 7 miles across a mangrove swamp east of Nadi Town (the poorly marked turnoff is just north of the Nadi River bridge). The Regent's main entrance leads to jungly potted palms that wave in the breeze sweeping through a magnificent grand foyer covered by a peaked roof.

The rooms are in a series of two-story motel-style blocks that flank a central building and are surrounded by tropical gardens; they are equipped with twin or double beds, large baths and wardrobes, dressing areas with twin vanities, refrigerators, radios, tea- and coffee-making facilities, and private patios or balconies, depending on whether they're on the first or second floor. The furnishings are made of rattan or bamboo and are accented with tapa cloth and exposed timbers.

Dining/Entertainment: The Regent boasts that the choices at its three restaurants are so extensive that guests can remain on the premises for a month without eating the same dish twice. The Regent has barbecue buffets several nights a week and a Fijian meke feast once a week. The barbecues and mekes cost about F$40 ($28) per person.

Services: Laundry, baby-sitting, 24-hour room service, business services.

Facilities: Shopping arcade with several boutiques; bank; beauty salon; swimming pool with sunken bar; beach; sailboats; Windsurfers; paddleboats; private island across the lagoon where guests can swim, snorkel, and sunbathe; tennis club; tour desk.

SHERATON FIJI RESORT, P.O. Box 9761, Nadi, Fiji Islands. Tel. 701777, or toll free 800/325-3535 in the U.S. and Canada. Fax 701818. Telex 5303. 300 rms. A/C MINIBAR TV TEL **Location:** On Denaru Island, 7 miles west of Nadi Town.

$ Rates: F$350–F$450 ($245–$315) single or double. AE, DC, MC, V.

Sharing Denaru Island's gray-sand beach and sunset views with the Regent, this 1987-vintage resort is more luxurious than its older neighbor but does not have as much Fijian physical charm. A fountain flows through a series of pools (each stocked with fish of a size to match) running down the center of its airy, off-white grand foyer, which opens to a large rectangular swimming pool and the beach beyond. With the lawn-type umbrella tables of a café on one side and a series of glass-enclosed boutiques and shops on the other, the Sheraton's is strongly reminiscent of a shopping mall back home (it does indeed have some very fine shops) and contrasts sharply with the dark-wood, handcraft-accented public areas of the Regent. In other words, the Sheraton could be put down in any tropical resort location, not necessarily in the South Seas.

Nevertheless, its spacious rooms each have an ocean view, private terrace or balcony, two queen-size beds or one king-size bed, in-house video movies, ceiling fans for days when the air conditioning is unnecessary, and the usual fridge and tea- and coffee-making facilities.

Dining/Entertainment: Three bars and four restaurants offer some of the finest cuisine in Fiji (none of it inexpensive). A group of Fijians strum their guitars and sing island songs every evening. In case you need a dimly lit pub with disco dancing after 9pm, Planters Bar provides it every night.

Services: Laundry, baby-sitting, 24-hour room service, business services.

Facilities: Shopping arcade with several boutiques; swimming pool; beach; sailboats; Windsurfers; paddleboats; private island across the lagoon where guests can swim, snorkel, and sunbathe; tennis club; activities desk.

MODERATE

DOMINION INTERNATIONAL HOTEL, P.O. Box 9178, Nadi Airport, Fiji Islands. Tel. 722255, or toll free 800/448-8355 in the U.S. Fax 790187. Telex 5176. 85 rms. A/C TEL **Location:** Queen's Rd., 3.1 miles south of airport.

$ Rates: F$77 ($54) single; F$82 ($57.50) double. AE, DC, MC, V.

The Dominion is more like a motel than any other property in Fiji. In fact, it's one of the few at which you can park a car right next to your door or the stairs leading to your room. Two white, three-story buildings flank a central garden with swimming pool. A central building with restaurant and bar sits at the Queen's Road end, completing the hotel's U-shape. The rooms are very much motel-style, with tub-shower bathrooms at the entrance on one end and glass doors sliding to patios or bougainvillea-draped balconies on the other. Carpets and drapes carry out a blue theme. All rooms have a queen and twin bed plus two chairs and a table in a small sitting area. A few are equipped for disabled guests. The bar charges near-exorbitant prices for soft drinks and other libations, but the dining room extracts a reasonable price for rather plain fare. Also on the premises are a tour desk and hard-sell gift shop. Built in 1973, the property is reasonably maintained. As a 1-night layover when tropical charm doesn't matter, it's good value for the price.

FIJI MOCAMBO, P.O. Box 9195, Nadi Airport, Fiji Islands. Tel. 722000, or toll free 800/942-5050 in the U.S. Fax 790324. Telex 5147. 124 rms. A/C MINIBAR TEL **Location:** Votualevu Rd., 1 mile south of airport.

$ Rates: F$140–F$145 ($98–$102) single; F$145–F$150 ($102–$105) double. AE, DC, MC, V.

At this pick of the hotels near the airport, each of the rooms has its own patio or balcony overlooking the hotel grounds, the surrounding cane fields, and the sea or mountains beyond. The standard rooms are older and somewhat smaller than the deluxe versions, but those on the end of the buildings have plantation-style fretwork verandas that wrap around them—you can sit out there and pretend you're overseeing your own sugar plantation. The newer rooms on the top floor have peaked ceilings that give them the feel of individual bungalows.

The Mocambo's open-air Coffee Garden Restaurant, off the large swimming pool, is open 24 hours a day for snacks and full meals. The hotel's Vale ni Kuro Restaurant is one of Nadi's finest in terms of both cuisine and elegant decor; it's open only from 6:30 to 11pm daily. Evening entertainment features traditional Fijian dance shows, including fire walking, at least 1 night a week. The main lounge has live music and is a popular spot for dancing on Friday and Saturday evenings (the music can be heard in some rooms; don't hesitate to ask for another if it bothers you).

The Mocambo also has lighted tennis courts and a short, nine-hole golf course, plus a beauty salon. Room service is available 24 hours a day, and there's a full-service business center.

NADI TRAVELODGE, P.O. Box 9203, Nadi Airport, Fiji Islands. Tel. 722277, or toll free 800/835-7742 in the U.S. Fax 790191. Telex 5186. 114 rms. A/C MINIBAR TEL **Location:** Votualevu Rd., 1 mile south of airport.

$ Rates: F$120 ($84) single or double. AE, DC, MC, V.

This has Australian-style hotel rooms—which is no surprise since Australians built and operate the Travelodge chain. The Travelodge differs from the Mocambo by its emphasis on things Fijian, from the *lali* (drum) that announces the arrival of cocktail hour to Aparosa, a Fijian chief who conducts and explains yaqona ceremonies in the lobby every afternoon from 3:30 to 6:30pm. The rooms here are in two-story buildings that spread away from a central area with pool and activities area featuring a trampoline.

Penny's Restaurant features European-style dishes and is open every day from 6am to 11pm. One evening a week features a Fijian earth-oven *lovo* feast for F$20 ($14) per person. The meal is followed by a traditional dance show. A special Travelodge facility: a guest Laundromat.

NEW WESTGATE HOTEL, P.O. Box 10097, Nadi Airport, Fiji Islands. Tel. 790044. Fax 790132 or 790092. 62 rms. A/C MINIBAR TEL **Location:** Queen's Rd., 3.2 miles south of airport.

$ Rates: F$40–F$50 ($28–$35) single; F$50–F$60 ($35–$42) double. AE, DC, MC, V.

Mel and Yvonne Bloom left their respective barrister and real estate careers in Sydney, Australia, in 1989 and commenced to completely refurbish the former Westgate Hotel, which had been closed for many years. Located a short walk from the Dominion International, Sandalwood Inn, and the Bloom's other property, the budget Nadi Bay Motel, the New Westgate has charms of the old and new. They retained the unusual swimming pool, which wraps partially around an ancient mango tree. The pool, tree, and pleasant patio are nearly surrounded by a white, two-story, U-shaped building. The first floor of one wing is open from front entrance to patio; the Blooms refinished that area and used lots of blond Fiji pine and potted tropical plants to accent their bar, dining area, and coffee shop. The higher priced "deluxe" rooms have air conditioners, minibars, tile floors, wooden louvered windows, and small baths. "Standard" rooms are similar but have ceiling fans instead of air conditioning.

Jessica's, a full-fledged discotheque, had just opened during my recent trip. It has various bridges—Sydney Harbour, Golden Gate, Rewa River—as its theme. It's open 9pm to 2am Monday to Friday, 9pm to midnight Saturday. Admission is F$7 ($5).

RAFFLES GATEWAY HOTEL, P.O. Box 9891, Nadi Airport, Fiji Islands. Tel. 722444. Fax 790163. Telex 5177. 93 rms. A/C TEL **Location:** Queen's Rd., directly opposite airport.

$ Rates: F$83 ($58) single; F$91 ($64) double; F$120 ($84) suite. AE, DC, MC, V.

Along with the Tokatoka Resort Hotel next door, the Gateway (Raffles is a relatively new addition to the name; everyone in Nadi still calls it simply the Gateway) is Nadi's most convenient place to wait for a flight at the airport just across Queen's Road. A plantation theme dominates the property, with the main building somewhat reminiscent of a colonial planter's home. Medium-size rooms are in two-story buildings on either side of a courtyard and swimming pool with its own bar. The rooms are nicely appointed with tropical furniture, drapes, and spreads. The suites have separate sitting areas. All units have shower-only baths.

The roadside main building houses a 24-hour coffee shop (room service is available around the clock, too), a more formal restaurant, and large bar-lounge upstairs that has the ambience of a colonial social club.

SKYLODGE HOTEL, P.O. Box 9222, Nadi Airport, Fiji Islands. Tel. 722200, or toll free 800/448-8355 in the U.S. Fax 790212. Telex 5148. 60 rms. A/C TEL **Location:** Queen's Rd., 2 miles south of airport.

$ Rates: F$70 ($49) single; F$80 ($56) double. AE, DC, MC, V.

(S) This was built as a crew base for Qantas Airways in the early 1960s, shortly after big jets started arriving at Nadi airport 2 miles away, and it has been well maintained and still has South Pacific atmosphere. The preferable rooms are in four-unit bungalows scattered through 11 acres of tropical gardens. The other, smaller rooms are in the original wooden lodge, which resembles one of those "temporary" structures built by the U.S. armed forces during World War II; most of them are long and narrow and have rather small bathrooms. Some are next to the bar and swimming pool, where a band plays dance music every evening until midnight.

The restaurant and bar are in a low, thatch-accented central building adjacent to the swimming pool. The restaurant offers well-prepared European, Fijian, and Indian dishes at moderate prices. Dining is inside or al fresco at the side of the pool. You can also enjoy the tennis court and the "pitch 'n' putt" golf course.

TOKATOKA RESORT HOTEL, P.O. Box 9305, Nadi Airport, Fiji Islands. Tel. 790222. Fax 790400. 70 units. A/C TV TEL **Location:** Queen's Rd. opposite airport.

$ Rates (all single or double): F$85 ($59.50) villa studio; F$90 ($63) studio apartment; F$110 ($77) villa apartment; F$115 ($80.50) apartment; F$125 ($87.50) executive studio; F$175 ($122.50) villa. AE, DC, MC, V.

Opened in 1990, Nadi's newest hotel has its most unusual mix of accommodations. A main building and a two-story wing with rooms face Queen's Road. Larger "executive studios" in that wing have double beds, sitting areas, and full kitchens. Adjoining "studio apartments" have Pullman kitchens and small baths. When rented as one, the two units become an "apartment." Behind the two front buildings sit spacious three-room bungalows known as "villas." The living rooms and one of the two bedrooms rented together are "villa apartments." The second bedroom can be rented alone as a "villa studio." The latter have tiny baths which share a sink with the units' Pullman kitchens. The entire complex is equipped with pleasant, if somewhat utilitarian, tropical-style furniture. When I was there, only the units in the two-story block were air conditioned, but management had promised to cool the villas as well. Facilities include a beauty salon and guests' Laundromat.

The highlight of the Tokatoka is its swimming pool–restaurant-bar complex at the rear of the property. An S-shaped water slide, flanked by a waterfall, streams down into an angular pool that is partially under the same steel-beam and brick supported roof that covers the restaurant and bar. It's a very popular spot for local families to spend lazy Sunday afternoons. Open 24 hours a day, the Harvesters' Restaurant serves snacks all the time and goes heavy on barbecues and buffets for lunches and dinners. Evening entertainment is provided; when I was there, Fiji's top jazz guitarist played and sang every evening from an island in the pool.

BUDGET

NADI BAY MOTEL, Private Bag, Nadi Airport, Fiji Islands. Tel. 723599. Fax 790092. 26 bunks, 21 rms (all with bath). A/C (11 rooms) **Location:** Newtown Beach Rd., about 100 yards west of Queen's Rd., 3.2 miles south of airport.

$ Rates: F$10 ($7) bunk per person, F$8 ($5.50) bunk for YHA members with cards; F$25–F$55 ($17.50–$38.50) single; F$35–F$65 ($24.50–$45.50) double. AE, DC, MC, V.

The rooms in this two-story concrete-block building are clean, spacious, and well if basically furnished, and have sliding glass doors opening onto a balcony or a patio. Eleven "deluxe" rooms have kitchens, separate sitting areas, and air conditioners; the other 10 rooms have no kitchens and are cooled by electric fans instead of air-conditioning units. Two dormitory rooms have 13 bunks each. The motel has a bar, a dining room specializing in Indian curries, a swimming pool, and a laundry room with coin-operated washing machines. Be prepared for roosters crowing outside your window early in the morning.

NADI SUNSEEKERS HOTEL, P.O. Box 100, Nadi, Fiji Islands. Tel. 700400 or 701655. Fax 780047. 32 bunks, 19 rms (4 with bath). A/C (4 rooms). **Location:** Narewa Rd., Nadi Town. North of Nadi River bridge, follow signs to Regent of Fiji.

$ Rates: F$8 ($5.50) bunk; F$25 ($17.50) single, F$30 ($21) double with fan; F$30 ($21) single, F$35 ($24.50) double with air conditioning and private bath. V.

One of the more popular and convenient of the hotel-hostels that cater to low-budget travelers, the Sunseekers has been in business at least since I weathered a cyclone there in 1978, as has its friendly Fijian manager, "Momma Violet." The dorm rooms have screened windows and fans, and a coffee shop serves snacks and simple, inexpensive meals. Momma Violet, a wealth of information about Fiji, will book tours for her guests, including the Highland Tour mentioned under "Cultural Tours" above and to the backpacker's retreat of Nananu-I-Ra Island off northern Viti Levu.

SANDALWOOD INN, P.O. Box 445, Nadi, Fiji Islands. Tel. 722553, or toll free 800/223-9868 in the U.S. Fax 700103. Telex 5312. 25 rms (20 with bath). A/C TEL **Location:** Queen's Rd., 3.1 miles south of airport.

$ Rates: F$20 ($14) single, F$26 ($12) double without bath; F$26–F$40 ($18–$28) single, F$32–F$46 ($22.50–$32) double with bath. AE, DC, MC, V.

John and Ana Birch's inn is a small but comfortable establishment. The top floor of the two-story, concrete main building houses spacious, air-conditioned rooms with telephones and large windows opening to balconies. The ground level holds a restaurant, small bar, and lounge. An older, one-story building on the opposite side of the swimming pool has smaller, nonair-conditioned rooms, some with their own private bathrooms, others sharing two toilets and two showers. The furniture isn't fancy, but the entire place is kept immaculately clean.

TRAVELER'S BEACH RESORT, P.O. Box 700, Nadi, Fiji Islands. Tel. 723322. Fax 790026. 20 rms (all with bath). **Location:** Newtown Beach, 1 mile west of Queen's Rd. between airport and Nadi Town. Follow Turtle Airways signs off Queen's Rd.

$ Rates: F$10 ($7) bunk per person; F$30 ($21) single, F$40 ($28) beachfront single; F$35 ($24.50) double, F$45 ($31.50) beachfront double. AE, DC, MC, V.

Other than the luxury Regent and Sheraton resorts, this is the only accommodation near Nadi located right on a beach. The small establishment, opened in 1986 and managed now by Tilly Karan, who did a stint as a journalist in

Australia, feels more like a pension than a hotel. Eight of the rooms are in a motel-style wing added to the Karans' home in the Nadi Bay Beach Estates housing development, on Newtown Beach. The others are in a two-story building across the street. Two rooms are on the beachfront, and each room has at least two beds, a fan, and a kitchenette. A swimming pool sits between the building and the beach, and a restaurant and bar provide reasonably priced meals and poolside libations.

4. WHERE TO DINE IN NADI

Nadi's finer restaurants are all in the hotels described above, especially the Sheraton Fiji and the Fiji Mocambo.

Most of the larger hotels devote at least 1 night a week to special meals, usually a poolside barbecue, a buffet of Indian curries, or a Fijian feast followed by traditional dancing. The *Fiji Beach Press* and the *Fiji Magic* list the schedules and prices, or you can phone the hotels to find out when.

THE FIJIAN MEKE

Like most South Pacific islanders, the Fijians in pre-European days steamed their food in an earth oven, known here as a *lovo*. They would eat with their fingers the huge feasts (mekes) that emerged with their fingers and then settle down to watch traditional dancing and perhaps polish off a few cups of yaqona.

The ingredients of a lovo meal are *buaka* (pig), *doa* (chicken), *ika* (fish), *mana* (lobster), *moci* (river shrimp), *kai* (freshwater mussels), and various vegetables, such as dense *dalo* (taro root), spinachlike *rourou* (taro leaves), and *lumi* (seaweed). Most dishes are cooked in sweet *lolo* (coconut milk). The most plentiful fish is the *walu*, or Spanish mackerel.

Several Nadi hotels have mekes on their schedule of weekly events. The foods are cooked in a lovo on the hotel grounds and served buffet-style, often beside the swimming pool if weather permits. Prices range from F$25 to F$40 ($17.50 to $28) per person depending on the hotel. The Regent of Fiji and Sheraton Fiji are the most expensive; the Nadi TraveLodge usually has the best value. Traditional Fijian dance shows follow the meals.

CURRY ETIQUETTE

While you will see Fijian-style dishes on many menus, invariably they will have at least one Indian curry. Most curries in Fiji are prepared on the mild side, but you can ask for it extra spicy and get it so hot you can't eat it. Curries are easy to figure out from the menu: lamb, goat, beef, chicken, vegetarian. If in doubt, ask the waiter or waitress.

What's not so easy to figure out is how to eat curry, since it may not be put before you in the way we Westerners serve our meals. The entire meal may come on a round steel plate, the curries, condiments, and rice in their own dishes arranged on the larger plate. It's perfectly all right to pick at the various small dishes with your fork as you would a European meal. The authentic method, however, is to dump the rice in the middle of the plate, add the smaller portions to it, then mix them all together. Sometimes you will see Indians eating their meals by picking up the curry with small pieces of bread held by their fingers, but forks are more common in Fiji.

The key words to know are the names of those delicious Indian breads. *Roti* is the round, heavy bread normally used to pick up food. *Puri* is a soft, puffy bread. *Pappadum* (an appetizer) is round, crispy, and chiplike.

CHOPSTICKS, Queen's Rd., Nadi Town. Tel. 700178.

Cuisine: CANTONESE. **Reservations:** Not required. **Location:** Queen's Rd. midway in Nadi Town.

$ Prices: Dishes F$2–F$7 ($1.50–$5). No credit cards.

Open: Mon–Sat 9am–10pm, Sun 10am–10pm.

Colin Chan serves up reasonably good and certainly inexpensive Cantonese fare at both his restaurants—one a second-floor establishment on the east side of Queen's Road in Nadi Town, the other in a storefront on Queen's Road in Namaka (tel. 723008), a shopping strip between the Skylodge Hotel and the airport. You can also get morning or afternoon tea if you're not hungry enough for a full meal.

COFFEE LOUNGE RESTAURANT, Queen's Rd., Nadi Town. Tel. 701240.
Cuisine: INDIAN. **Reservations:** Not accepted. **Location:** Queen's Rd., Nadi Town, opposite Jack's Handicrafts.
$ Prices: Snacks 50¢–F$1.50 (35¢–$1.05); curries F$1–F$2.50 (70¢–$1.75). No credit cards.
Open: Mon–Sat 8am–6pm.

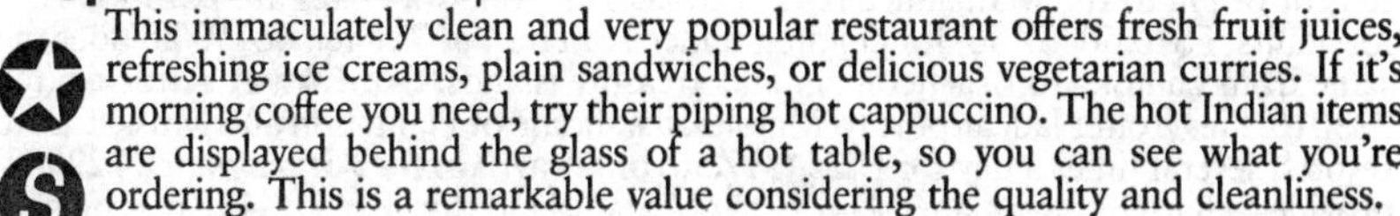

This immaculately clean and very popular restaurant offers fresh fruit juices, refreshing ice creams, plain sandwiches, or delicious vegetarian curries. If it's morning coffee you need, try their piping hot cappuccino. The hot Indian items are displayed behind the glass of a hot table, so you can see what you're ordering. This is a remarkable value considering the quality and cleanliness.

MAMA'S PIZZA INN, Queen's Rd., Nadi Town. Tel. 701221.
Cuisine: ITALIAN. **Reservations:** Not accepted. **Location:** Opposite Mobil station and Morris Hedstrom, Queen's Rd., north end of Nadi Town.
$ Prices: Appetizers F$2–F$3.50 ($1.50–$2.50); pizzas F$4–F$18 ($3–$12.50); pastas F$5 ($3.50). No credit cards.
Open: Mon–Sat 10am–11pm, Sun 7–10pm.

Travelers in need of a tomato-sauce fix can follow the aroma of garlic along Queen's Road and find it here. Pizzas range from a small plain model to a large deluxe version with all the toppings. Mama's also has spaghetti, lasagne, and fresh salads. Order at what looks like a bar in a drinking establishment, take your meal at one of the picnic-style tables.

MAHARAJA RESTAURANT, Queen's Rd. Tel. 722962.
Cuisine: INTERNATIONAL. **Reservations:** Not accepted. **Location:** In K. Nataly & Sons Building, 2 miles south of airport near Skylodge Hotel.
$ Prices: Main courses F$4.50–F$11 ($3–$7.50). No credit cards (foreign currency accepted).
Open: Mon–Sat noon–10pm.

Airline flight crews laying over at Nadi have made an institution of Kishore Nand's storefront establishment. The menu has Chinese and European selections, but the Indian dishes, including spicy curries of beef, lamb, goat, chicken, and vegetables, are the main attractions for the pilots and cabin attendants. They are as well seasoned as you will find in Fiji and clearly reflect Kishore's motto: "Good food at a good price." The European dishes lean toward plain but hearty grilled steaks, fish, and pork and lamb chops. The Chinese selections are prepared in the Cantonese style.

5. RESORTS OFF NADI

Although I am placing Fiji's offshore resorts in the sections devoted to their jumping-off points, I suggest you review each of them carefully before making a

IMPRESSIONS

Every resort seemed to have a platoon of insanely friendly Fijians.
—Scott L. Malcolmson, 1990

choice. As I have pointed out previously in this book, offshore resorts are great places to relax or engage in water sports, but they are not in themselves bases from which to explore the country. Just because a resort is situated close to Nadi, therefore, doesn't necessarily mean it will have the features that will appeal to you. I recommend that you review all of Fiji's offshore resorts carefully before making a decision.

As previously indicated in "What to See and Do in Nadi," above, and in "Getting Around" in Chapter 11, there are several ways of **getting to the resorts** from Nadi. The resorts will make the arrangements when you reserve, but here's a brief recap.

The ***Island Express*** (tel. 700144) essentially provides ferry service from the Regent of Fiji to the Mamanuca resorts twice daily; one-way fares are F$21 ($14.50) for adults, F$10.50 ($7.50) for children under 16. The ***Tui Tai*** (tel. 6615000) does the same from Lautoka to Beachcomber and Treasure islands. **Sunflower Airlines** (tel. 723016) flies from Nadi airport to Malololailai, home of Plantation and Musket Cove resorts, several times a day for F$25 ($17.50) one-way. **Turtle Airways** (tel. 722988) provides chartered seaplane service to Mana Island for F$64 ($45) per person; passengers connect by boat from there to Matamanoa and Tokoriki for another F$16 ($11) one-way. **Pleasure Marine** (tel. 700144) provides water-taxi service to the islands for about F$150 ($105) per boatload. The resorts on Matamanoa and Tokoriki both have helipads and can arrange helicopter transportation from Nadi.

VERY EXPENSIVE

VATULELE ISLAND RESORT, P.O. Box 9936, Nadi Airport, Fiji Islands. Tel. 790300, or toll free 800/828-9146 in the U.S. Fax 790062. Telex 5136. 12 bungalows. MINIBAR **Location:** Vatulele Island, 30 miles south of Viti Levu, a 40-minute charter-seaplane flight from Nadi.

$ **Rates** (in U.S. dollars only, including room, food, bar, and all activities): $495 single; $660 double. Round-trip transfers $250 per person. AE, DC, MC, V.

When Australian TV producer Henry Crawford ("A Town Like Alice") and Fiji-born hotel manager Martin Livingston both turned 40 in the late 1980s, they decided to build the ultimate hideaway resort. They chose a ½-mile-long beach on Vatulele, a relatively flat island off the Coral Coast—but listed here because you get there from Nadi—known for its unique red prawns (that is, shrimp that are red while alive, not just after being cooked). With an eye on the environment, they cleared just enough thick native brush to build 12 spacious bures and a central dining room–bar-lounge complex. Each bure faces the beach but is separated from its companions by lots of privacy-providing foilage and distance. In a fascinating blend of New Mexico and Fijian native architectural styles, the bures and main building have thick adobe walls supporting tall Fijian thatch roofs. Each L-shaped bure has a lounge and raised sleeping area under one roof, plus another roof covering an enormous bath that can be entered both from the bed/dressing area and from a private, hammock-swung patio. Each unit has a king-size bed with mosquito net suspended from the rafters. Although benchlike seats in the lounge can double as beds for children, kids under 12 are allowed only during certain weeks, usually coinciding with Australian school holidays.

Dining/Entertainment: Before they opened in 1990, Henry and Martin hired a gourmet chef away from the Regent, so the food is top-notch. Weather permitting, guests dine on a patio beside the central building. They can dine anytime and anyplace they want, but most meals are taken dinner party–fashion with Martin acting as host (Henry spends most of his time in Australia). Frankly, dining at the same table with Martin Livingston is one reason to visit Vatulele, providing you can hold your own in razor-sharp conversation and don't mind a bit of raunchy humor. Although staff members play guitars and sing island songs, the nightly dinner parties *are* the entertainment at Vatulele, and they can go into the wee hours.

Services: Laundry, evening turn-down.

Facilities: Library with 2,000 volumes; wide array of nonmotorized water-sports equipment; tiny private island for picnics; all-weather tennis court.

EXPENSIVE

CASTAWAY ISLAND RESORT, Private Mail Bag, Nadi Airport, Fiji Islands. Tel. 661233. Fax 723699. Telex 5330. 66 bungalows. **Location:** Qalito Island, 13 miles off Nadi.

$ Rates: F$248 ($174) single or double beach bungalow; F$216 ($151) garden bungalow. AE, DC, MC, V.

Built in the mid-1960s of logs and thatch without the use of heavy equipment,with many improvements over the years, Castaway has not been robbed of its rustic, Fijian-style charm. The central activities building, perched on a point with white beaches on either side, still has a thatch roof, and the ceilings of the bures are still lined with genuine tapa cloth. In fact, the sounds of mallets can be heard as women pound new tapa in the adjacent village the staff calls home. Fijian staff members mingle freely with guests in what manager Robert Walker calls an "integrated community of 100 permanent residents and 100 temporary residents." The staff even has its own church, which guests—the "temporary residents"—can attend. Although the guest bures sit relatively close together in a coconut grove, their roofs sweep low enough to provide privacy. Each unit has a queen-size bed, two settees which can double as beds for children, and rattan tables and chairs. In addition to the central lounge-dining-bar building, a beachside water-sports shack has a "Sundowner Bar" upstairs appropriately facing west toward the Great Sea Reef.

Dining/Entertainment: Guests dine in the central building, usually at umbrella tables on a stone beachside patio. The food is adequate but not gourmet, with an emphasis on midday buffet lunches and evening curry nights and Fijian lovos. Staff members entertain with Fijian songs. For children, the staff provides a wide range of activities, from learning Fijian to sack races.

Services: Laundry, baby-sitting.

Facilities: Swimming pool, tennis court, games room, water sports, medical center with nurse, well-stocked boutique, children's playroom and nursery.

MATAMANOA ISLAND RESORT, P.O. Box 9729, Nadi Airport, Fiji Islands. Tel. 723620. Fax 790282. Telex 5240. 6 rms, 20 bungalows. A/C MINIBAR **Location:** Matamanoa Island, 21 miles off Nadi.

$ Rates: F$260 ($182) single or double bungalow; F$150 ($105) single or double room. AE, DC, MC, V.

Owned and managed jointly with nearby Tokoriki Island Resort (see below), this complex sits on Matamanoa, a small island consisting of one steep hill surrounded by a white-sand beach. The bungalows, one motellike block of rooms, and central building occupy a small flat shelf on one end of the island. The shelf falls away steeply to the beach, which lacks shade but has great snorkeling over a reef drop-off near the shore. Each of the spacious, rectangular bungalows faces the beach; they have sleeping areas separated from lounges by dividers. The lounge areas have wet bars in one corner. Sliding doors open to covered porches. The six rooms sit at the base of the hill; much smaller than the bungalows, they are air conditioned (the bures have ceiling fans) and are reserved for couples. All units have tile floors, clock radios, and tiled, shower-only baths.

Dining/Entertainment: Meals are served in a beachside central building with high peaked roof. A gourmet chef oversees the kitchen both here and at Tokoriki. Entertainment consists of the Fijian staff playing guitars and singing during cocktails and the evening meal. A meke buffet is followed by traditional Fijian dancing one night a week.

Services: Laundry, baby-sitting. Guests can visit Tokoriki and even overnight there if room is available.

Facilities: Swimming pool; water sports including scuba diving; tennis court; boutique.

TOKORIKI ISLAND RESORT, P.O. Box 9729, Nadi Airport, Fiji Islands. Tel. 723620. Fax 790282. Telex 5240. 19 bungalows. MINIBAR **Location:** Tokoriki Island, 20 miles off Nadi.

$ Rates: F$260 ($182) single or double. AE, DC, MC, V.

The neighbor of Matamanoa (see above), this property opened in 1990 on a flat shelf of land on the west side of hilly Tokoriki. A wide, ½-mile-long beach runs the length of the resort, but the relatively dry location means a scarcity of tall palm trees and other sources of beachside shade. Virtually identical to Matamanoa's, the rectangular bungalows all face the beach from a forest of low native trees.

Dining/Entertainment: A large, open central building under a soaring roof is long enough to house two dining areas (one for breakfast and lunch, another for dinner). When weather permits, guests dine al fresco on a poolside patio. Evening entertainment consists of Fijian staff members playing guitars and singing island songs, with a traditional meke dance show once a week.

Services: Laundry, baby-sitting. Guests can visit Matamanoa and even overnight there if room is available.

Facilities: Swimming pool; water sports including scuba diving, sport fishing, and a semisubmersible craft for coral viewing; tennis court.

MODERATE

MANA ISLAND RESORT, P.O. Box 610, Lautoka, Fiji Islands. Tel. 661333. Fax 662713. Telex 5216. 132 bungalows. A/C TEL **Location:** Mana Island, 20 miles off Nadi.

$ Rates: F$175 ($123) single or double. AE, DC, MC, V.

The largest resort off Nadi, this Japanese-owned property attracts Japanese couples (30% to 50% of its clientele) and Australian and New Zealand couples and families. Since it has the only pier big enough to land the *Island Express,* Mana is a popular day-trip destination from Nadi (see "What to See and Do in Nadi," above). Seaplanes land here, and Pleasure Marine has its water-taxi base at Mana, so the island sees quite a bit of business other than from its guests. The complex sits on a flat saddle between two hills and two beaches, which gives guests a calm place to swim and snorkel whichever way the wind blows. Accommodation is in bungalows of European construction with Fijian-shaped tile roofs. The management does not advertise that 10 bungalows are air conditioned; you have to insist on one if that's what you want. Otherwise, the units have ceiling fans but still can be quite warm at midday.

Guests can dine on European-style fare in a large central building, which also has a bar, lounge, and nightclub, at a Japanese restaurant, or a small daytime cafeteria. There's a wide range of water-sports activities, most of it on a pay-extra basis. Aqua Trek Ocean Sports Adventures, an American firm, has its scuba-diving operation here.

MUSKET COVE RESORT, Private Mail Bag, Nadi Airport, Fiji Islands. Tel. 722371. Fax 790378. Telex 5230. 26 bungalows, 6 villas. **Location:** Malololailai Island, 9 miles off Nadi.

$ Rates: F$165 ($116) single or double bungalow; F$225 ($158) single or double villa. AE, DC, MC, V.

Old Fiji hands will remember Musket Cove as Dick's Place. One of three Australians who own Malololailai Island, Dick Smith founded this little retreat in 1977. A few luxury villas have been added, a marina was under construction during my recent visit, and a golf course is planned. The older bures and modern villas are bargains for offshore resorts, since they have kitchen facilities, and there are two stores stocked with groceries on the island. The older bures, all built of native materials and decorated accordingly with rattan and tapa cloth, sit in a row across a coconut grove from the beach and come in two sizes. Smaller bures have one room and an appendage to one side with the bath and kitchenette. Larger, "deluxe family bures" have separate bedrooms, much larger bathrooms, and more complete kitchens. The new, luxury villas have a living room and master bedroom downstairs and two bedrooms upstairs; each bedroom has its own private bath.

Dick's Place has been retained as the name of Musket Cove's pleasant, open-air bar and restaurant next to the swimming pool and a large flame tree (poinciana) that bursts into bloom around Christmas. Cruising yachts call at Musket Cove from June to September, and the names of the boats and their skippers are posted on a wall in the bar. You can get into fascinating conversations about some really remote places when the yachties congregate around the bar. The marina will make boating and water sports easier, for a broad mudbank appears here at low tide, forcing guests over to Plantation Island to find water deep enough for swimming and snorkeling.

PLANTATION ISLAND RESORT, P.O. Box 9176, Nadi Airport, Fiji Islands. Tel. 722333. Fax 790163. Telex 5177. 40 rms, 43 bungalows. **Location:** Malololailai Island, 9 miles off Nadi.

$ Rates: F$180 ($135) single or double duplex bure; F$210 ($158) "Sunlodge" bure a day for up to 10 persons. AE, DC, MC, V.

One of the largest and most diverse of the offshore resorts, Plantation attracts couples, families, and day-trippers from Nadi, giving it a Club Med–style atmosphere of nonstop activity. The resort has four types of accommodations: duplex bures suitable for singles or couples, large "Sunlodge" bures that can sleep as many as 10 persons, and hotel rooms in a two-story building. My personal choice is one of the spacious duplex bures with two ceiling fans. A large central building beside the beach has a bar, dance floor, lounge area, coffee shop, and restaurant. Facilities include a freshwater swimming pool; tennis courts; beach; free nonpowered water sports; waterskiing; parasailing; scuba diving; and coral viewing in a semisubmersible craft for a fee. There's also a children's playroom with a full-time baby-sitter.

TREASURE ISLAND, P.O. Box 364, Lautoka, Fiji Islands. Tel. 661500, or toll free 800/521-7242 in the U.S and Canada. Fax 664496. Telex 5189. 66 rms. **Location:** About 12 miles off Lautoka.

$ Rates: F$160 ($112) single; F$186 ($130) double. AE, DC, MC, V.

Treasure Island, which occupies a tiny atoll that barely breaks the surface of the vast lagoon, is about an hour's boat ride from the port town of Lautoka. It's geared to couples and families rather than to the sometimes-raucous singles who frequent its nearby neighbor, Beachcomber Island Resort. Treasure's 33 duplex bungalows hold 66 rooms. They have wood-paneled walls, rattan furniture, built-in vanities, private baths with showers, and three single beds, one of which serves as a settee. Each bungalow has a porch facing the emerald lagoon and white beach that encircles the island (a sandy stroll of 20 minutes or less brings you back to your starting point). A series of pathways wandering through tropical shrubs joins the bures, several playgrounds for both adults and children, and a swimming pool set off by a row of red hibiscus from an airy central activities building. Three tasty meals a day are served in Treasure Island's pleasant dining room.

BUDGET

BEACHCOMBER ISLAND RESORT, P.O. Box 364, Lautoka, Fiji Islands. Tel. 661500, or toll free 800/521-7242 in the U.S. and Canada. Fax 664496. Telex 5189. 40 bunks, 8 "lodge" rms (none with bath), 19 bures (all with bath). **Location:** Tai Island, about 12 miles off Lautoka.

$ Rates (including three all-you-can-eat meals a day): F$57 ($40) bunk; F$121 ($85) single lodge, F$154 ($108) double lodge; F$144 ($101) single bure, F$190 ($133) double bure. AE, DC, MC, V.

(S) Definitely not for everyone, this famous little resort attracts those who like the roaring singles life. In fact, it's one of the hottest spots in the South Pacific. Back in the early 1960s, Fiji-born Dan Costello bought an old Colonial Sugar Refining Company tugboat, converted it into a day cruiser, and started carrying tourists on day-trips out to a little atoll known then as Tai Island. The visitors liked it so much that some of them didn't want to leave. Recognizing the market, Costello built a few rustic bures, a dining area and bar, and gave the little dot of sand and palm trees a new name: Beachcomber Island.

Today it still packs in the young and young-at-heart on a "deserted" island—deserted, that is, except for other like-minded souls, the majority of them Australians, in search of fun, members of the opposite sex, and a relatively inexpensive vacation. The youngest-at-heart cram into two 20-bunk, coed dormitories. If you want more room, you can have or share a small lodge room (they have communal toilets and showers) with two or three beds. And if you want your own bure with private bath, you can have that, too—just don't expect luxury. The buffet-style, all-you-can-eat meals are included in the rates, which puts Beachcomber in the budget category. Rates also include snorkeling gear, coral viewing in glass-bottom boats, volleyball, and mini-golf; you pay extra for sailboats, canoes, windsurfing, scuba diving, waterskiing, and fishing trips.

6. THE YASAWAS & BLUE LAGOON CRUISES

Off the coast from Nadi and Lautoka lie the magical line of small, rugged islands known as the Yasawas. Lt. Charles Wilkes, commander of the U.S. exploring expedition that charted Fiji in 1840, said they reminded him of "a string of blue beads lying along the horizon," and they haven't changed much over the intervening century and a half. Fijians still live in small villages huddled among the curving coconut palms beside some of the South Pacific's most awesomely beautiful beaches.

BLUE LAGOON CRUISES

Started with a converted American crash vessel in the 1950s by the late Capt. Trevor Withers, Blue Lagoon Cruises has grown into a six-ship operation. Its cruises are so popular with Australians, New Zealanders, and a growing number of Americans and Canadians that they're usually booked solid more than 2 months in advance of each daily departure from Lautoka.

Four of Blue Lagoon's vessels are identical, 126-foot-long ships capable of carrying 54 passengers in 22 air-conditioned cabins. Two others, the 181-foot-long *Yasawa Princess* and the 155-foot-long *Nanuya Princess*, carry up to 66 passengers in 33 staterooms and look as if they should belong to a Greek shipping magnate. Their accommodations may not be up to tycoon standards, but they are comfortable enough for cruises oriented toward going ashore and getting in the water.

All the smaller ships and one of the larger ones make 4-day, 3-night cruises through the islands. The other big boat leaves Lautoka once a week and takes 7 days and 6 nights for a more extensive circuit. All the vessels leave Lautoka at 3pm and arrive in the Yasawas in time for a welcoming cocktail party and dinner on board. They then proceed to explore the islands, including the intriguing, grottolike Sawa-i-Lau caves. They stop in little bays for snorkeling, picnics or lovo feasts on sandy beaches, and visits with the Yasawans in their villages. The ships anchor in peaceful coves at night, and even when they cruise from island to island, the water is usually so calm that only incurable landlubbers get seasick.

There are three cruises to choose from: a short "Popular Cruise" in one of the older boats, a short "Club Cruise" in one of the larger ships, and the 1-week cruise. In addition to being on the newer ships, guests on the Club Cruises are treated to a free captain's cocktail party and get wine with a meal and a souvenir T-shirt.

For a Popular cruise, lower-deck staterooms cost F$500 ($350) per person, double occupancy; those on the upper deck cost F$590 ($413). Single-occupancy rates are F$850 ($595) and F$1,000 ($700), respectively.

On the short Club Cruises, lower-deck cabins cost F$610 ($427), those on the main deck go for F$700 ($490), and those on the bridge deck cost F$750 ($525). Single-occupancy rates are F$1,045 (F$728), F$1,190 ($833), and F$1,270 ($889), respectively.

On the 1-week cruises, lower-deck cabins cost F$1,150 ($805), those on the main deck go for F$1,320 ($924), and those on the bridge deck cost F$1,380 ($966). Single-occupancy rates are F$1,960 ($1,372), F$2,240 ($1,568), and F$2,340 ($1638), respectively.

The rates include all meals and transfers.

For reservations or information, contact a travel agent or **Blue Lagoon Cruises,** P.O. Box 54, Lautoka, Fiji Islands (tel. 661622 or 661268, fax 664098, telex 5285).

WHERE TO STAY IN THE YASAWAS

TURTLE ISLAND LODGE, P.O. Box 9317, Nadi Airport, Fiji Islands. Tel. 722921, or toll free 800/826-3083 in the U.S., 800/447-9222 in Canada. Fax 790007. Telex 5197. 14 bungalows. MINIBAR **Location:** Nanuya Levu Island, about 55 miles off Lautoka (transfers are by chartered seaplane only).

$ Rates (in U.S. dollars only, including everything, even liquor): $640 per couple per night. Round-trip transfers $520 per couple. Payable 45 days prior to arrival. AE, DC, MC, V.

San Franciscan Richard Evanson graduated from Harvard Business School, married into a prominent Seattle, Washington, family, made a bundle in cable television, and then, he admits, ran into alcoholism and divorce. In 1972 he bought hilly, 500-acre Nanuya Levu, one of the few privately owned islands in the Yasawas, and shortly thereafter founded this retreat for the rich and famous. Until the resorts on Vatulele, Wakaya, and Kaibu opened in 1990, he had the top-of-the-line market in Fiji all to himself (competition is tough now; some regular clients have followed Turtle's former manager, the highly entertaining Martin Livingston, to Vatulele). Turtle's guests have included such luminaries as ex-Beatle Ringo Starr and U.S. Senator John McCain of Arizona, the former Vietnam war prisoner.

Turtle's 14 spacious, thatch-roofed bures sit next to two of the island's 12 picturesque beaches, some of which were used as settings for *The Blue Lagoon,* the movie starring Brooke Shields. The other beaches on Nanuya Levu are deserted, as are four of the seven smaller islands nearby (one of which is owned by Blue Lagoon Cruises, which anchors its boats there and lets its guests play ashore; another is home of David Doughty's backpacker paradise—see below). According to its brochure, Turtle Island will accommodate 14 "mixed adult couples" (translated: no children and no same-sex couples welcome; you don't have to be married, but you do need to be straight).

Dining/Entertainment: Excellent quality meals are served in the thatch-roofed, beachside dining room, with Richard acting as dinner host most evenings. Staff members strum guitars and sing island songs during cocktail hour and after the meals. Fijian mekes are staged some evenings.

Services: Laundry; guests' names are carved on wooden plaques attached to their bures.

Facilities: Wide range of water-sports activities and equipment.

DAVID'S PLACE, c/o Lautoka Hotel, P.O. Box 51, Lautoka, Fiji Islands. Tel. 660388. Telex 5378. 5 bungalows. **Location:** Tavewa Island, about 60 miles off Lautoka.

$ Rates (including cooking facilities): F$9 ($6.30) single bungalow; F$20 ($14) double bungalow; F$6 ($3.50) per person campsite. Rates are F$1 (70¢) less without cooking facilities. Round-trip boat transfers F$80 ($56) per person. No credit cards.

This little retreat in a coconut grove on Tavewa Island (you can see Turtle Island Lodge from there) is about as basic as you can get, but a magnificent beach makes this a popular hideaway for low-budget travelers. Owner David Doughty, great-grandson of an English planter and his Fijian wife, has five thatch bures just like those in Fijian villages: no electricity, no screens, mats on sand floors, platform beds (he provides the linen, you bring a towel). Thatch roofs cover a rustic kitchen, communal toilets and cold-water showers. Three Fijian-style meals a day cost F$8 ($5.50). If you're going to do your own cooking, bring ample provisions from Lautoka. Boat trips to the Sawa-i-Lau caves go for F$23 ($16). Getting to David's Place is a slight challenge, since there is no phone on the island. Brother Jim Doughty usually takes a boat to Lautoka on Monday morning, where he checks in at the Lautoka Hotel. If there are guests to pick up, he returns to Tavewa on Tuesday; if not, on Wednesday. He makes another trip to Lautoka on Thursday, returning to Tavewa on Saturday. In other words, ask for the David's Place boat at the Lautoka Hotel on Tuesday and Friday. The open-boat ride takes about 3½ hours each way; bring plenty of sunscreen, a hat, and something to drink.

READERS RECOMMEND

Dive Expeditions. *Tel. 664422, fax 664681, telex 5249. "The highlight of my trip to Fiji was my island stay at the Dive Expeditions beach camp on Waya Island in the Yasawa Island chain. Yalobia village on Waya Island reminds me of perhaps a primitive version of a Club Med, but without all the pressures of participation. They simply leave you alone. The reefs there are excellent and can be enjoyed by scuba divers and snorkelers. The food is plentiful and varied. The bures were interesting. They are on a share basis. The mattresses are firm and come with a mosquito net. This is truly a South Pacific retreat for the budget traveler."*—John Cross, Atlanta, Ga. (*Author's Note:* Rates are F$18 [$12.50] per person for bunk, F$25 [$17.50] for meals, F$50 [$35] round-trip boat transfer, F$45 [$31.50] per dive.)

7. THE CORAL COAST

Long before big jets began bringing loads of visitors to Fiji, many affluent local residents—most of them Europeans—built cottages on the dry southwestern shore of Viti Levu as sunny retreats from the frequent rain and high humidity of Suva. When visitors started arriving in big numbers during the early 1960s, resorts sprang up among the cottages almost overnight, and promoters gave a new, more appealing name to the 50km (30-mile) stretch of beaches and reef on either side of the town of Sigatoka: the Coral Coast.

The appellation was apt, for coral reefs jut out like wide shelves from the white beaches that run between mountain ridges all along this picturesque coastline. In most spots the lagoon just reaches snorkeling depth at high tide, and when the water retreats, you can put on a pair of old running shoes and walk out nearly to the surf pounding on the outer edge of the shelf.

GETTING THERE: THE QUEEN'S ROAD

Most visitors reach the Coral Coast from Nadi International Airport by way of the Queen's Road. After a sharp right turn at the south end of Nadi Town, the highway runs well inland, first through sugarcane fields undulating in the wind and then past acre after acre of pine trees planted in orderly rows, part of Fiji's national forestry program. The blue-green mountains lie off to the left; the deep-blue sea occasionally comes into view off to the right.

MOMI BAY & NATADOLA BEACH

The old Queen's Road branches off toward the coast and Momi Bay 16km (10 miles) south of Nadi Town. This graded dirt road leads to the **Momi gun emplacements,** the World War II naval batteries now maintained as a historical park by the National Trust of Fiji. To make this side trip, turn at the Momi intersection and follow the dirt road for 5km (3 miles) through the cane fields to a school, then turn right and drive another 4km (2½ miles) to the concrete bunkers. They command a splendid view over the water to the west. The park has toilets and drinking water and is open until dark; it's closed Sunday.

Maro Road branches off the Queen's Road 35km (21 miles) south of Nadi and runs down to **Natadola,** site of one of the prettiest, most unspoiled beaches in the South Pacific. A sign pointing to the village of Bairi marks the Maro Road intersection. Turn right on Maro Road and right again at the first intersection almost immediately after leaving the Queen's Road. This dirt track leads another 8km (5 miles) to a T intersection. Turn left and look for sand pathways leading to the beach. There are snakes in this South Seas Garden of Eden: Thefts have occurred at Natadola Beach, so be careful with your valuables. The *Fijian Princess,* a refurbished train, makes daily trips to Natadola Beach from The Fijian Resort (see "What to See and Do in Nadi," above).

SIGATOKA

The pine forests on either side of the Queen's Road soon give way to rolling fields of mission grass before the sea suddenly emerges at a viewpoint above The Fijian Resort on Yanuca Island. Watch on the right about 8km (5 miles) past this posh institution for a series of **desertlike dunes of fine white sand.** They extend for several miles, separating the fields from the crashing—and dangerous—surf. Pieces of ancient pottery have been found among the dunes, but be warned: Removing them is against the law.

The Queen's Road leaves the coast for a few miles and then enters Sigatoka (pop. 2,000), a quiet, predominantly Indian town perched along the west bank of the **Sigatoka River,** Fiji's longest waterway. The broad, muddy river lies on one side of the main street; on the other is a row of duty-free and other shops.

The stoplight—one of the few in Fiji outside Suva—controls traffic across the long one-lane bridge that spans the river. Drivers who cheat at the light run the risk of being met halfway across by a vehicle coming in the opposite direction. Wait your turn, for the resulting impasses have been known to turn into heated mid-river fistfights.

For an inexpensive daytime meal, try the tearoom on the third floor of the large Tappoo store at the stoplight.

SIGATOKA RIVER VALLEY

The Queen's Road turns right at the stoplight and crosses the bridge. The road straight ahead follows the west bank of the river as it meanders inland, flanked on both sides by a patchwork of flat green fields of vegetables that give the Sigatoka Valley its nickname: "Fiji's Salad Bowl." The pavement ends about 1km (½ mile) from the town; after that, the road surface is poorly graded and covered with loose stones.

The residents of **Lawai** village at 1.6km (1 mile) from town offer Fijian handcrafts for sale. Two kilometers (1.2 miles) farther, a small dirt track branches off to the left and runs down a hill to **Nakabuta,** the "Pottery Village," where the residents make and sell authentic Fijian pottery. Tour buses from Nadi and the Coral Coast stop there most days.

If you're not subject to vertigo, you can look forward to driving past Nakabuta: The road climbs steeply along a narrow ridge commanding panoramic views across the large Sigatoka Valley with its quiltlike fields to the right and much smaller, more rugged ravine to the left. It then winds its way down to the valley floor and the **Sigatoka Agricultural Research Station,** on whose shady grounds some tour groups stop for picnic lunches. The road climbs into the interior and eventually to Ba on the northwest coast; it intersects the **Nausori Highlands** road leading back to Nadi, but it can be rough or even washed out during periods of heavy rain. Unless they have a four-wheel-drive vehicle or are on an organized tour with a guide, most visitors turn around at the research station and head back to Sigatoka.

THE CORAL COAST

The Queen's Road reaches the sea 5km (3 miles) east of Sigatoka and hugs the shoreline for the next 50km (30 miles) in a fashion reminiscent of the round-island road on Tahiti. You will cross rivers leading up into picturesque valleys, pass through Fijian villages still possessing a few thatch bures nestled among the more prevalent tin roofs, and skirt half-moon beaches of amber sand. Fijians will be wading offshore on the reef, fishing with spears or prying clams off the rocks with knives. One modern hotel and resort after another, all of them tucked among coconut palms on the narrow shelf of land between the hills and the beach, attest to your officially being on the Coral Coast.

The side road running parallel to the airstrip at Korolevu goes inland to a hot spring and the tall, impressive **Savu-na-matelaya waterfall.** Some of the larger hotels have horseback outings to the falls, or you can drive up the side road about a kilometer (½ mile) to Baiusevu village. The residents guide visitors to the springs and falls for F$1 (70¢) per person. Wear canvas shoes, since you will wade across seven streams during the 20-minute walk.

GETTING AROUND

The larger hotels have car-rental desks as well as taxis hanging around their main entrances. Express buses between Nadi and Suva stop at The Fijian, The Reef Resort, The Naviti, and The Warwick Fiji hotels. Local buses ply the Queen's Road and will stop for anyone who flags them down. See "Getting Around" in Chapter 11 for more information.

FAST FACTS: THE CORAL COAST

The following information applies to Sigatoka and the Coral Coast. If you don't see an item here, see the "Fast Facts" for Nadi earlier in this chapter and for Fiji in Chapter 11.

Bookstores Sigatoka Bookshops (tel. 500166) has an outlet at the market in Sigatoka. Boutiques in the larger hotels carry paperback novels and some Australian magazines.

Currency Exchange Fiji's major banks all have branches on Queen's Rd. in Sigatoka. Otherwise, the hotel desks will cash traveler's checks.

Doctor Dr. Ram Raju (tel. 599765), who also has a practice in Nadi, maintains an office in Sigatoka.

Drugstores Patel Pharmacy (tel. 500213) is on Market Rd. in Sigatoka; Sigatoka Pharmacy (tel. 500305) is on Vunasalu St.

Emergencies The emergency phone number for police, fire, and ambulance is 000.

Hospital Government-run Sigatoka Hospital (tel. 500455) can handle minor problems.

Photographic Needs Caines Photofast has a shop in Sigatoka. Most hotel boutiques sell color-print film and provide 1-day processing.

Police The emergency number is 000. The Royal Fiji Police has posts at Sigatoka (tel. 500222) and at Korolevu (500322).

Post Office Post offices are in Sigatoka and Korolevu.

Telephone/Telegrams/Telex See "Post Office," above. Coral Coast telephone numbers are listed under Sigatoka in the Fiji directory.

WHAT TO SEE & DO ON THE CORAL COAST

EXCURSIONS

The hotel reception or tour desks can make reservations for many of the activities mentioned under "What to See and Do in Nadi," above, in this chapter. These include tours of the Sigatoka Valley and day-trips to Pacific Harbour and Suva. You may have to pay more for such Nadi-area activities as cruises on the *Island Express* than if you were staying on the west coast. On the other hand, you are closer to Suva and can more easily take advantage of the sights and activities near the capital city. See details in "What to See and Do" in Chapter 13.

On the Coral Coast itself, the hotels will arrange horseback excursions to **Savu-na-matelaya waterfall** and the hot spring near the Korolevu airstrip. The walk from the road to the waterfall takes about 20 minutes and fords seven streams. Bring canvas shoes for the hike and a bathing suit and wraparound sulu if you want to take a dip in the cascade.

You can make your way to the Fijian Resort for a visit to Ka Levu Centre or a ride on the *Fijian Princess,* both described in the Nadi sections, above.

SPORTS & RECREATION

Most hotels have abundant sports facilities for their guests (see "Where to Stay on the Coral Coast," below). If yours doesn't, **The Reef Resort** (tel. 500044) rents its equipment to nonguests for reasonable fees: F$5 ($3.50) will cover greens fees at the resort's nine-hole golf course, an hour of tennis, an hour's bicycle hire, an hour in a kayak, or an hour's use of snorkeling gear. F$4 ($3) gets you an hour's horseback riding.

Seasports Ltd., based at The Fijian Resort, serves all the Coral Coast hotels. One tank dives cost F$38 ($26.50), F$72 ($50.50) with full equipment rental. You can take an introductory lesson for F$75 ($52.50) or a NAUI certification course for F$395 ($277). Book at any hotel activities desk.

EVENING ENTERTAINMENT

Nightlife centers around the hotels and whatever Fiji meke shows they are sponsoring. Check the *Fiji Beach Press* or the *Fiji Magic* for fire-walking exhibitions on tap while you're there. The famous **Fijian fire walkers** from Beqa parade across the steaming stones to the incantations of "witch doctors" at various hotels on the Coral Coast and at Nadi. The Naviti (tel. 520444) usually sponsors a performance at 7pm on Wednesday. Admission there is F$8 ($5.50) per person.

SHOPPING

Although the larger hotels have shopping arcades with duty-free shops and clothing and handcraft boutiques, most visitors do their serious shopping in the town of Sigatoka, where the merchants generally put less pressure on shoppers than those in Nadi Town do.

For handcrafts, **Jack's Handicrafts** (tel. 500810) and **Sigatoka Handicraft Centre** (tel. 500914), both on Queen's Road in Sigatoka, are well stocked and worth a look. **Korotongo Souvenir Centre** (tel. 520188), opposite the Reef Resort, has fixed prices on its merchandise, as does **Baravi Handicrafts** (tel. 500432) at Vatukarasa village 13km (8 miles) east of Sigatoka.

WHERE TO STAY ON THE CORAL COAST

The Coral Coast is anchored on either end by two of Fiji's big deluxe resorts, The Fijian to the west and The Warwick Fiji 44km (26 miles) away to the east. Most of the area's moderate and less expensive hotels are nestled in between near the Fijian village of Korotogo, about 5 miles east of Sigatoka.

Although the Hideaway Resort is listed below in the moderate category, its dormitory is popular with young low-budget travelers who can afford meals in the dining room (the Hideaway does not have kitchen facilities).

EXPENSIVE

THE FIJIAN RESORT, Private Mail Bag, Nadi Airport, Fiji Islands. Tel. 50155, or toll free 800/942-5050 in the U.S. Fax 500155. Telex 4241. 436 rms, 4 bungalows. A/C MINIBAR TEL **Location:** Yanuca Island, 36 miles from Nadi Airport, 6 miles west of Sigatoka.

$ Rates: F$220–F$275 ($154–$193) single or double; F$600 ($420) bungalow. AE, DC, MC, V.

Fiji's largest hotel, this resort occupies all 105 acres of flat Yanuca Island, which is joined to the mainland by a one-lane causeway. The spacious rooms, all equipped with comfortable wicker lounge furniture and colorful flower-print spreads, occupy 13 three-story buildings. All of them are on the shore of the island so that each room has a view of the lagoon and sea from its own private balcony (if upstairs) or patio (if at ground level). Each has a refrigerator, tea- and coffee-making facilities, a radio, and piped-in music.

Covered walkways wander through thick tropical foilage to link the hotel blocks to two main restaurant-and-bar buildings, both adjacent to swimming pools, shady lawns, and beaches (blue road-signs point the way, for it's easy to miss a turn in this sprawling complex). Fijian artisans weave baskets and mats, carve war clubs, and string shell jewelry in a handcraft demonstration area near the hotel's entrance, a large bure set in a lush grove of banana and breadfruit trees. Near the reception desk, a wooden wall carved in bas-relief depicts scenes of Fijian village life.

Dining/Entertainment: The Fijian's four restaurants have a little something for everyone's taste, if not necessarily for everyone's pocketbook. In case you get thirsty. The Fijian has five bars. Evening entertainment features buffet dinners followed by various Fijian dance demonstrations and fire walking.

Services: Laundry, baby-sitting, business services.

Facilities: Two swimming pools; six tennis courts; water sports; a "Quiet Room" for reading or just getting away from your fellow tourists; games room for children; scuba diving and deep-sea fishing, for a fee; a nine-hole golf course, which nonguests can use for F$20 ($14) per person for greens fees, including a motorized buggy—call extension 760 for a starting time (call a day early if you want to reserve a buggy).

THE NAVITI, P.O. Box 29, Korolevu, Fiji Islands. Tel. 520444. Fax 500444. Telex 3236. 144 rms. A/C MINIBAR TEL **Location:** Queen's Rd., Korolevu, 58 miles from Nadi airport, 16 miles east of Sigatoka.

$ Rates: F$155 ($109) single; F$165 ($116) double. AE, DC, MC, V.

(S) The Warwick hotel chain took over this property (along with The Warwick Fiji, listed below) in 1989 and proceeded to renovate it throughout. The Naviti already had some of Fiji's largest rooms for the price; now it has some of the most tastefully decorated. They have bright floral print drapes and spreads to compliment blond tropical furniture and varnished natural wood doors and trim. The site is spacious, too: 40 acres of coconut palms waving in the trade winds beside a lovely beach. That's plenty of room for a nine-hole golf course, five lighted tennis courts, and playgrounds for kids, which means the Naviti will continue to attract golf and tennis buffs who want to vacation with the children (translated: lots of active Australian families). Three-story concrete block buildings hold the rooms and are joined to a central facility by double-deck covered walkways.

Dining/Entertainment: The central complex under several Fijian-shaped shingle roofs holds a coffee shop, an intimate, candle-lit restaurant for evening dining, and a large lounge where a band plays for dancing every evening. In addition, The Naviti hosts a Fijian fire-walking show, usually on Wednesday (see "Evening Entertainment," above).

Services: Laundry, baby-sitting. Guests can share facilities at The Warwick Fiji (see below).

Facilities: Swimming pool, golf course, tennis courts (F$10 [$7] per hour for night play), children's playground, games room, water sports (including scuba diving), deep-sea fishing, coral viewing, horseback and donkey riding, Laundromat, tour and car-rental desks.

THE WARWICK FIJI, P.O. Box 100, Korolevu, Fiji Islands. Tel. 520555. Fax 520010. Telex 3237. 250 rms. A/C MINIBAR TEL **Location:** Queen's Rd., Korolevu, 62 miles from Nadi airport, 20 miles east of Sigatoka.

$ Rates: F$185 ($130) single or double ocean view; F$165 ($116) single or double garden view. AE, DC, MC, V.

The Coral Coast's other deluxe resort, the former Hyatt Regency Fiji was taken over by the Warwick hotel chain in 1989 and was undergoing an extensive renovation when I was there recently. It sits on a lovely palm-fringed beach. The complex appears to be little different from other tropical resorts when seen from the road, but the interior of the central building clearly reflects the unusual architecture that is a legacy from its days as a Hyatt hotel. A sweeping roof supported by natural wood beams covers a wide reception and lobby area bordered on either end by huge carved murals depicting Capt. James Cook's discovery of Fiji in 1779. Tall windows across the rear look out on the towering palms, the white beach, the speckled reef, and the azure sea beyond. In the center of the room a curving staircase descends into a large square well, giving access to the dining and recreation areas on the beach level. A lounge and café open to the multiangled swimming pool bordered by palms and a sprawling poinciana tree; a wooden footbridge spans the pool to a swim-up-and-have-a-drink bar. Hammocks swing between the trunks of the palm trees that fringe the beach.

The Warwick's comfortable but not overly large rooms (for more space, stay at The Naviti) are in two- and three-story blocks that flank the central building. Each room has its own balcony or patio with a view of the sea or the tropical gardens surrounding the complex. There are standard rooms and somewhat better-appointed "Warwick Club" models.

Dining/Entertainment: With its elegant, linen-and-crystal decor and excellent continental cuisine, the Fine Dining Restaurant could grace a hotel in New York or Sydney. The Wicked Walu, under a thatch roof on a tiny island offshore, features seafood selections. The Cafe Korolevu, on the other hand, appeals to the masses by offering a wide variety of cuisine, from Indonesian nasi goreng (spicy fried rice) to plain fish-and-chips, Polynesian buffet nights to Fijian-style lovo feasts.

Services: Laundry, baby-sitting, business services. Guests can share facilities at The Naviti.

Facilities: Swimming pool with bar, water sports, tennis courts, volleyball, jogging paths, horseback riding along the beach, sports and fitness center, tour desks, beauty salon, boutique, drugstore.

MODERATE

THE CROW'S NEST, P.O. Box 270, Sigatoka, Fiji Islands. Tel. 500230.
Fax 500354. Telex 4262. 18 units. **Location:** Queen's Rd., 46 miles from Nadi Airport, 4 miles east of Sigatoka.
$ Rates: F$75–F$90 ($52.50–$63) single or double. AE, DC, MC, V.

(S) As the name implies, the Crow's Nest has a nautical theme throughout. Each of its 18 apartments bears not a number but the name of a ship that sailed the waters of Fiji in the 19th century (one wall of each unit sports a chart of Fiji showing the namesake ship's course through the islands). Situated in duplex buildings that have the look of a contemporary condominium complex, the split-level units are like small apartments. Each has a double bed in a sleeping loft upstairs and a full kitchen, two single beds, a table, and comfortable chairs in a lounge downstairs. The living areas open onto private verandas overlooking the sea. Steering wheels, brass clocks, and other nautical items decorate the Crow's Nest Restaurant, but they hardly distract the eye from its magnificent view over the reef from the hill above the rooms. The ship's lanterns are kept low at night, not just to create a romantic atmosphere but to preserve the effect of the moonlit lagoon sparkling at your feet. Owner Julie Doyle alters the menu according to what's being caught by the local fishermen, but it always features Fijian and Indian specialties of such good quality that the restaurant consistently is rated one of the top places to eat—not just on the Coral Coast but in all of Fiji.

HIDEAWAY RESORT, P.O. Box 233, Sigatoka, Fiji Islands. Tel. 500177.
Fax 500025. Telex 4264. 42 units, 52 dorm bunks. **Location:** Queen's Rd., 55 miles from Nadi airport, 13 miles east of Sigatoka.
$ Rates: F$13–F$15 ($9–$10.50) bunk; F$85 ($59.50) single or double bungalow; F$125 ($87.50) family unit. AE, DC, MC, V.

Although this establishment has bungalow-style accommodation suitable for couples and families, it is a mecca for young backpackers, surfers, and divers drawn by its large dormitory and lengthy list of activities. The complex lies in a narrow strip of land between the Queen's Road and the beach. Buildings of various vintages give the place a somewhat slapped-together, hodge-podge look, as if there were no master plan.

Older bungalows have high ceilings lined with bamboo, bedrooms separated from the lounge by 8-foot-high dividers, and small baths with tiled showers. The larger family units can sleep up to five persons. Newer units are in duplex bungalows; they have rather plain furnishings but sport toiletries and hairdryers. A two-story A-frame dormitory sits by its own beach at a far end of the property; downstairs is somewhat crowded with 42 over-and-under bunk beds, while upstairs has 10 beds which cost F$2 ($1.40) more than those downstairs. The main building with dining, bar, and entertainment areas is somewhat dark. Meals are plain European, Fijian, and Indian fare and feature buffets or Fijian lovos several nights a week. In the absence of cooking facilities, low-budget travelers are offered a complete meal for F$8 ($5.50). A band plays every evening for dancing in the main lounge. Activities include tennis, horseback tours, trips to the mountains and waterfalls, snorkeling, scuba diving, and a host of on-site games such as crab races.

THE REEF RESORT, P.O. Box 173, Sigatoka, Fiji Islands. Tel. 500044, or toll free 800/624-3524 in the U.S. Fax 500056. Telex 4242. 72 rms. A/C TEL **Location:** Queen's Rd., 47 miles from Nadi Airport, 5 miles east of Sigatoka.

$ Rates: F$110 ($77) single or double. AE, DC, MC, V.

Even if you don't stay here, this venerable if uninspired hotel is a good bet for a meal or some entertainment. Newer properties have stripped The Reef of its position as the Coral Coast's leading resort, but it's well maintained and provides all the facilities found at its larger and more expensive competitors. It also is well promoted in Australia as a reasonably priced destination, so it usually stays full. The complex snuggles on a narrow strip of land between the Queen's Road and the shore, putting the main building and its restaurant, bar, lounge, and patio right on what used to be a beach but because of erosion is now sand piled behind a breakwater.

Of The Reef's spacious rooms, 48 are in a three-story concrete-block building set perpendicular to the beach and separated from the activities building by the larger of two swimming pools. My personal choice, however, would be one of the 24 rooms in the older, two-story Korotogo Wing, which is a short, grassy crawl from the beach. These rooms are somewhat smaller than those in the newer building and don't have bathtubs under their showers, but their private balconies or patios directly face the lagoon. Three somewhat larger rooms on the beach end of the newer wing cost slightly more than the other rooms.

The cuisine in the pleasant, air-conditioned Village Restaurant features a few interesting local specialties, but basically its fare is pitched to Australian tastes. The pleasant Palm Court Bar & Brasserie is open 24 hours a day for meals and snacks. A band plays every evening for dancing, and various Fijian-style shows are staged several nights a week. The hotel has a full range of water-sports equipment, a nine-hole golf course, tennis courts, and horses to ride.

TAMBUA SANDS BEACH RESORT, P.O. Box 177, Sigatoka, Fiji Islands. Tel. 500399. Telex 4247. 31 units. **Location:** Queen's Rd., 53 miles from Nadi airport, 11 miles east of Sigatoka.

$ Rates: F$80 ($56) single; F$90 ($63) double. AE, DC, MC, V.

Barry and Kath Brenton's little resort appeals to those of us who prefer to stay in our own bungalow set in a grove of coconut palms beside a beach. The bungalows have high peaked ceilings lined with tapa cloth, wooden louvered windows that let in as much or as little light and breeze as you want, ceiling fans to augment the trade winds, large baths with showers, queen-size beds and two single beds (which also serve as settees), comfortable lounge chairs and coffee tables, refrigerators, and coffee- and tea-making facilities. They are placed in a narrow palm grove between the Queen's Road and part of a 3-mile-long stretch of truly gorgeous beach.

A wooden footbridge crosses a stream flowing through the Tambua's grounds and connects the bungalows with a swimming pool and plantation-style bar-dining-lounge building. The open-air restaurant concentrates on dishes made from fresh local produce. There are curry nights, fish nights, and barbecue nights. Usually Tuesday is meke night, and on Wednesday residents of a nearby village come over, prepare a Fijian-style meal in a lovo, and then perform traditional Fijian dances.

BUDGET

TUBAKULA BEACH RESORT, P.O. Box 2, Sigatoka, Fiji Islands. Tel. 500097 or 500201. Fax 393056. 24 bunks, 23 bungalows (all with bath). **Location:** Queen's Rd., 49 miles from Nadi airport, 7 miles east of Sigatoka.

$ Rates: F$8 ($5.50) bunk; F$33 ($23) single or double bungalow. AE, DC, MC, V.

Pronounced "Toomb-a-koola," this establishment in a beachside coconut grove appeals to anyone who wants a dorm bunk or a comfortable, clean bungalow with kitchen but none of the usual hotel facilities. The bungalows are A-frame cottages with basic furnishings. Downstairs has a lounge, kitchen, bath, and bedroom; upstairs is a sleeping loft. Each unit can sleep six persons, so sharing one represents good value. The dorm units are in European-style houses. No more than eight bunks are in any one room, and guests share communal kitchens, showers, and toilets. The beach is not the best on the Coral Coast, but there is a swimming pool.

VAKAVITI HOTEL, P.O. Box 5, Sigatoka, Fiji Islands. Tel. 500526. Fax 520319. 4 rms, 2 cottages (all with bath). **Location:** Queen's Rd., 46 miles from Nadi airport, 4 miles east of Sigatoka.

$ Rates: F$45 ($31.50) single; F$55 ($38.50) double; F$60 ($42) cottage for up to four. MC, V.

This basic but very clean establishment right next to the Crow's Nest offers one of the Coral Coast's best values for the money. You drive up a winding concrete driveway through towering coconut palms and other tropical foliage. On the right as you ascend the hill is a concrete-block structure housing the Vakaviti's four motel-style rooms. Two of them sport a double bed; the others, two single beds. They all have small kitchenettes with refrigerators and two-burner hotplates, ample baths with showers, tile floors, ceiling fans, and louvered windows and doors looking out over a long patio and small swimming pool. Of the two cottages hidden down the hill, one has a double bed, two single beds, a kitchen, and a bath.

WARATAH LODGE, P.O. Box 86, Sigatoka, Fiji Islands. Tel. 500278. Fax 520219. 5 units. **Location:** Queen's Rd., 46 miles from Nadi airport, 4 miles east of Sigatoka.

$ Rates: F$30 ($21) single; F$40 ($28) double. No credit cards.

A short walk from The Reef Resort, The Crow's Nest, and two of the restaurants mentioned below, this little property on the mountain side of Queen's Road lacks charm but is very convenient. Accommodation is in A-frame buildings almost identical to those at the Tubakula; each has a lounge, kitchen, bedroom, and bath downstairs, a sleeping loft–like bedroom upstairs. The units flank a swimming pool.

WHERE TO DINE ON THE CORAL COAST

As previously noted, most of the restaurants on the Coral Coast are located in the hotels and are included above in the descriptions of those establishments. Many hotels have special nights, such as meke feasts of Fijian foods cooked in a lovo, served buffet-style, and followed by traditional dancing. The specifics, including prices, are given in the two tourist publications, the *Fiji Beach Press* and *Fiji Magic.*

ANGIE'S RESTAURANT AND TAKEAWAYS, Queen's Rd. opposite the Reef Resort. Tel. 500194.

Cuisine: CHINESE/EUROPEAN. **Reservations:** Not accepted.

$ Prices: Appetizers F$3–F$4 ($2–$3); main courses F$3.50–F$15 ($2.50–$10.50). No credit cards.

Open: Mon–Sat 8am–10pm, Sun 5–10pm.

This very clean storefront establishment dishes up large portions of Chinese cuisine—chow mein, chop suey, a variety of dishes with duck, chicken, pork, beef, and seafood—plus some plain European fare such as roast chicken. The decor also is plain, except for woven placemats and a flower on each of the wooden tables.

CASABLANCA PIZZA HOUSE, Queen's Rd. between the Reef and the Crow's Nest. Tel. 500766.

Cuisine: ITALIAN/INDIAN. **Reservations:** Not accepted.

$ Prices (including tax): Pizzas F$7–F$18 ($5–$12.50); pastas and curries F$10.50–F$12.50 ($7.50–$9). No credit cards.
Open: Daily 9am–9pm.

Lester and Lois Stock make spicy pizzas in this establishment in a Mediterranean-look building with arches. Order at the counter and either take the pies away or chow down at one of the heavy tables and chairs that share the shop with shelves full of grocery items (the place doubles as a small general store).

VILISITE'S SEAFOOD RESTAURANT, Queen's Rd. between the Warwick and the Naviti. Tel. 500395.
Cuisine: SEAFOOD. **Reservations:** Required.
$ Prices: Full meals F$18–F$29 ($12.50–$20.50). MC, V.
Open: Lunch daily 10am–3pm; dinner daily 6–10:30pm.

Vilisite, a friendly Fijian, operates this little restaurant in two rooms of her seaside home. It's nothing fancy but tastefully decorated with woven placemats on tapa-print table cloths, louvered windows and old-fashioned screen doors to let in the breeze, and oscillating fans hanging from the walls to give it a boost. She has a bar set up in the front yard. The food is strictly fresh local seafood—fish, shrimp, lobster, octopus—fried, broiled, or cooked in coconut milk the Fijian way. All meals are three courses, with a fruit plate and tea or coffee to finish.

CHAPTER 13

SUVA

Neither the likelihood of frequent showers nor the chance of an occasional deluge should discourage anyone from visiting Suva, Fiji's vibrant capital city. Grab your umbrella and hit the sidewalks. Wander through narrow streets crowded with Fijians, Indians, Chinese, Europeans, Solomon Islanders, Rotumans, Tongans, Samoans, and people of various other ancestries. Stroll among grand public buildings, broad avenues, and orderly parks and parade grounds—souvenirs of an age when the British ruled these islands as a Crown Colony.

1. GETTING TO KNOW SUVA

Suva sprawls over a hilly, 10-square-mile peninsula that juts out like a thumb from the southeastern coast of Viti Levu. To the east lies windswept Laucala Bay; to the west, Suva's busy harbor and the suburbs of Lami Town and Walu Bay. Jungle-draped mountains rise to heights of 4,000 or more feet on the "mainland" to the north, high enough to condense moisture from the prevailing southeast trade winds and create the damp climate that cloaks the city in lush green foliage all year round.

Modern Suva began in 1870, when the Polynesia Company, having bought the land in exchange for paying Chief Cakobau's foreign debts, sent a group of Australian settlers to the area. They established a camp on the flat, swampy, mosquito-infested banks of Nubukalou Creek, on the western shore of the peninsula. When the settlers failed to grow first cotton and then sugar, speculators obtained the land and in 1875 convinced the new British colonial administration to move the capital from Levuka. The move was approved in 1877, and the government shifted to Suva in 1882.

The business heart of the city still sits near Nubukalou Creek, but roads and streets now trail off haphazardly into the hills, changing name every time they change direction. Compounding the confusion is a system of one-way streets in downtown Suva. Visitors can see most of Suva's sights and find most of its shops, interesting restaurants, and lively nightspots within a 10-block area of downtown. (See the walking tour under "What to See and Do," below.)

IMPRESSIONS

The English, with a mania for wrong decisions in Fiji, built their capital at Suva, smack in the middle of the heaviest rainfall. . . . Yet Suva is a superb tropical city.
—JAMES A. MICHENER, 1951

2. GETTING THERE & GETTING AROUND

GETTING THERE

By Air: Suva is served by **Nausori Airport** 12 miles east of downtown. Taxis between there and Suva cost F$15 ($10.50) each way. Nausori Taxi & Bus Service (tel. 477583 in Nausori, or 312185 in Suva) has regularly scheduled bus service between the airport and the city for F$2 ($1.40) per person each way. Look for the buses at the curb across from the baggage-claim platform. The company's Suva terminal is behind the Air Pacific office in the Colonial Mutual Life Association (CML) building on Victoria Parade. Buses leave there for the airport at 6, 9, 10, and 11:15am and 1:45pm daily.

By Road: If you are driving to Suva, plan to arrive during the daylight hours, and don't leave Nadi or Lautoka without a good map of Suva. Desai Bookshops in Nadi Town and Lautoka sell the best map, *Suva and Lami Town* (No. FSM-1), published by the Fiji Department of Lands and Surveys.

GETTING AROUND

Hundreds of **taxis** prowl the streets of Suva. Licensed taxis have meters, but occasionally a driver without one will claim to be a "private car" or "limousine." Official fares are F50¢ (35¢) at the flag fall, F40¢ (30¢) for each kilometer, but you will have to negotiate anything over 5km (3½ miles). Make sure the driver drops the flag. I have been very satisfied with **Black Arrow Taxis** (tel. 300139 or 300541 in Suva, 477071 in Nausori). The main **taxi stand** is on Central Street behind the Air Pacific office in the CML Building on Victoria Parade (tel. 312266). Other taxis gather at the Suva Municipal Market.

Big, fume-belching local **buses** fan out from the municipal market from before daybreak to midnight Monday to Saturday (they have limited schedules on Sunday). The fares vary but should be no more than F50¢ (35¢) to most destinations in and around Suva. The excellent *Suva and Lami Town* map mentioned above shows the bus routes by color-coding the streets.

See "Getting Around" in Chapter 11 for the phone numbers of the major **rental-car firms.**

SUVA

The following facts apply to Suva. If an item isn't here, see "Fast Facts: Fiji" in Chapter 11.

American Express Tapa International Ltd. (tel. 302333) has an office in the ANZ Building, 25 Victoria Parade. Hours are Mon–Thurs 8:30am–5pm, Sat 9am–noon. Personal-check cashing is available only weekdays 10am–3pm. The mailing address is P.O. Box 654, G.P.O., Suva.

Bookstores Dominion Book Centre (tel. 304334), in the Dominion Arcade, Thomson St. (behind the Fiji Visitors Bureau), has the latest newsmagazines, local and Australian newspapers, and books on the South Pacific. Desai Bookshops (tel. 314088) is at the corner of Thomson and Pier streets, opposite the Fiji Visitors Bureau. The *Fiji Times,* 177 Victoria Parade, sells maps and books, including A. J. Schütz's *Suva: A History and Guide* (Sydney, Pacific Publications, 1978), to which I am indebted for much of the walking tour in this chapter. Go upstairs to the circulation department.

Currency Exchange Westpac, ANZ, National Bank of Fiji, and Bank of Baroda have offices on Victoria Parade south of the Fiji Visitors Bureau.

Dentist Ask your hotel staff for a recommendation.

Doctor The Suva Travelodge sends its guests to the private Gordon Street Medical Centre, 98-100 Gordon St. (tel. 313355).

Drugstores Gordon Street Medical Centre (see "Doctor," above) has a pharmacy.

Embassies/Consulates See "Fast Facts: Fiji" in Chapter 11.

Emergencies Phone 000.

Eyeglasses Jekishan & Jekishan, Epworth House, Victoria Parade (tel. 311002). Asgar & Co. Ltd., Queensland Insurance Centre, Victoria Parade (tel. 300433).

Hairdressers/Barbers Cut Above Salon, Honson Arcade, Thomson St., next to Canadian International Airlines (tel. 304533).

Hospital Colonial War Memorial Hospital, end of Ratu Mara Rd. at Brown St., is the public hospital, but see "Doctor," above, for a private clinic.

Information The Fiji Visitors Bureau (tel. 302433) has its headquarters in a restored colonial house at the corner of Thomson and Scott streets in the heart of Suva. *Fiji Magic* and *Fiji Beach Press,* the tourist publications, have up-to-date information about what's going on.

Laundry/Dry Cleaning The hotels will send your laundry out, or you can take it to Flagstaff Laundry & Drycleaners, 62 Bau St. (tel. 301214), or War Hing Laundry on Amy St. (tel. 301575).

Libraries Suva City Library on Victoria Parade (tel. 313433) has a small collection of books on the South Pacific. It's open Mon–Tues and Thurs–Fri 9:30am–6pm, Wed noon–6pm, and Sat 9am–1pm. The library at the University of the South Pacific (tel. 313900) has one of the largest collections in the South Pacific. The University is on Laucala Bay Rd.

Maps Desai Bookshops, corner of Thomson and Pier streets opposite the Fiji Visitors Bureau, carries the excellent *Suva and Lami Town* map. The Department of Lands and Surveys' main map sales office is in the Government Buildings on Victoria Parade. The *Fiji Times,* 177 Victoria Parade, sells maps, and the Fiji Visitors Bureau gives them away (see "Information," above).

Photographic Needs Caines Photofast, corner of Victoria Parade and Pratt St. (tel. 313211).

Police Central Police Station (tel. 311222) is on Joske St. between Pratt and Gordon streets.

Post Office The General Post Office is on Thomson St. opposite the Fiji Visitors Bureau. It's open Mon–Fri 8am–4pm.

Radio/TV AM stations are Radio Fiji 1 (Fijian) at 558, Radio Fiji 2 (Hindi) at 774, and Radio Fiji 3 (English) at 1089. In the FM band, two stations—at 90.6 and 96.0—broadcast in English.

Rest Rooms The Fiji Visitors Bureau has a clean rest room in its old house on Thomson St. Otherwise, use the hotels and restaurants or look for signs pointing to "public conveniences."

Safety The downtown area around Victoria Parade is relatively safe during the evenings, but many areas of town are not. Don't take chances anywhere in Suva. Stick to the main, well-lit streets after dark and take taxis if you're out late at night. Burglary and theft are problems: Keep an eye on your belongings. See "Safety" in the "Fast Facts: Fiji" in Chapter 11.

Shoe Repairs Meanger Ltd., 179 Victoria Parade (tel. 301071).

Telephone/Telegrams/Telex Overseas communication is handled by FINTEL in its colonial-style building on Victoria Parade. It's open 24 hours a day, 7 days a week. See "Fast Facts: Fiji" in Chapter 11 for details.

3. WHAT TO SEE & DO

Too many visitors spend only a day in Suva, which is hardly enough time to do justice to this fascinating city. Two or 3 days can easily be spent walking through its streets, seeing its sights, and poking your head into its multitude of duty-free and handcraft shops.

WALKING TOUR — Suva

Start: The Triangle.
Finish: Government House.
Time: 2½ hours.
Best Time: Early morning or late afternoon.
Worst Time: Midday, or Saturday afternoon and Sunday, when the shops are closed.

Begin at the four-way intersection of Victoria Parade, Renwick Road, and Thomson and Central streets. This little island in the middle of heavy traffic is:

1. **The Triangle.** Now the center of Suva, in the late 1800s this spot was a lagoon fed by a stream that flowed along what is now Pratt Street. A marker in the park commemorates Suva's becoming the capital, the arrival of Fiji's first missionaries, the first public land sales, and Fiji's becoming a colony. Three of the four dates are slightly wrong. From the Triangle, head north on Thomson Street, bearing right between the Fiji Visitors Bureau and the old Garrick Hotel (now the Sichuan Pavilion Restaurant), whose wrought-iron balconies recall a more genteel but nonair-conditioned era. Continue on Thomson Street past the Morris Hedstrom department store to:
2. **Nubukalou Creek.** The Polynesia Company's settlers made camp beside this stream and presumably drank from it. A sign on the bridge warns against eating fish from it today—with good reason, as you will see and smell. Morris Hedstrom's picturesque covered walkway along the south bank gives the creek its nickname: The Venice of Fiji. Across the bridge, smiling Fijian women wait under a flame tree in a shady little park to offer grass skirts and other handcraft items for sale. Pass to the left of them for now and head down crooked, narrow:
3. **Cumming Street.** This area, also on reclaimed land, was home of the Suva market until the 1940s. Cumming Street was lined with saloons, yaqona "grog" shops, and curry houses known as "lodges." It became a tourist-oriented shopping mecca when World War II Allied servicemen created a market for curios. When import taxes were lifted from electronic equipment and cameras in the 1960s, Cumming Street merchants quickly added the plethora of duty-free items you'll find there today. When you've finished browsing, return to Thomson Street, turn right and then left on Usher Street, which takes you past the intersection at Rodwell Road and Scott Street to:
4. **Suva Municipal Market,** the largest and most lively produce market in the South Pacific and Suva's main supply of food. A vast array of tropical produce is offered for sale. The market teems on Saturday morning, when, it seems, the entire population of Suva shows up to shop and select television programs for the weekend's viewing. Few sights say as much about urban life in the modern South Pacific as does a Fijian carrying home in one hand a bunch of taro roots tied together with pandanus and in the other, a collection of rented videocassettes stuffed into a plastic bag. Big ships from overseas and small boats from the other islands dock at Princes Wharf and Kings Wharf beyond the market on Usher

WALKING TOUR—SUVA

1. The Triangle
2. Nubukalou Creek
3. Cumming Street
4. Suva Municipal Market
5. Municipal Curio and Handicraft Centre
6. Sukuna Park
7. Suva Town Hall
8. Suva City Library
9. Native Land Trust Board
10. Government Buildings
11. Albert Park
12. Grand Pacific Hotel
13. Thurston Gardens
14. Fiji Museum
15. Gates to Government House

Street, but we will follow wide Stinson Parade back across Nubukalou Creek and along the edge of Suva's waterfront to the large parking garage on the left. Downstairs is the:

5. **Municipal Curio and Handicraft Centre.** In yet another bit of cultural diversity, you can haggle over the price of handcrafts at stalls run by Indians, but not at those operated by Fijians. Wait until you have visited the Government Handicraft Centre, however, before making a purchase. Continue on Stinson Parade past Central Street. The gray concrete building on the corner is the YWCA. When you get there, cut diagonally under the palms and flame trees across:
6. **Sukuna Park,** named for Ratu Sir Lala Sukuna, founding father of independent Fiji. This shady waterfront park is a favorite brown-bag lunch spot for Suva's office workers. On the west side is the harbor; on the east, Victoria Parade. For many years only a row of flame trees separated this broad avenue from the harbor, but the shallows have been filled and the land extended by the width of a city block. The nondescript modern building standing south of the park is the Suva Civic Centre. Head south on the seaward side of Victoria Parade, pass the cream-colored colonial-style headquarters of FINTEL, the country's electronic link to the world, to:
7. **Suva Town Hall,** a picturesque old building with an intricate, ornamental wrought-iron portico and a sign proclaiming it now to be the Ming Palace Restaurant. Built as an auditorium in the early 1900s and named Queen Victoria Memorial Hall, this lovely structure later was used as the Suva Town Hall. The stage still stands at the rear of the restaurant. At this point you can take a shopping break at the Government Handicraft Centre, in the rear of Ratu Sukuna House, the tall office building across Victoria Parade at the corner of Macarthur Street (see "Shopping," below). Afterward, continue south on Victoria Parade until you come to the:
8. **Suva City Library.** The American industrialist and philanthropist Andrew Carnegie gave Fiji £1,500 sterling to build this structure. The central portion of the colonnaded building opened in 1909 with an initial collection of 4,200 books. The wings were added in 1929. Books on Fiji and the South Pacific are shelved to the left of the main entrance. (See "Fast Facts: Suva," above, for the library's hours.) Keep going along Victoria Parade past Loftus Street to the corner of Gladstone Road, where sits the:
9. **Native Land Trust Board Building.** This site is known locally as Naiqaqi (The Crusher) because a sugar-crushing mill sat here during Suva's brief and unsuccessful career as a cane-growing area in the 1870s. A small statue of Ratu Sukuna stands in front of the modern office building that now occupies the site. Ratu Sukuna served as chairman of the Native Land Trust Board, whose main job is to collect and distribute rents on the more than 80% of the country that is owned by the Fijians. Across Gladstone Road you can't miss the imposing gray edifice and clock tower of:
10. **Government Buildings.** Erected between 1935 and 1939 (they look much older), these stone buildings house the High Court, the prime minister's office, and several government ministries. Parliament met here until 1987, when Colonel Rabuka and gang marched in and arrested its leaders (if and when it resumes, parliament will meet in a new complex on Ratu Sukuna Road in the Muanikau suburb). The clock tower is known as "Fiji's Big Ben." When it works, it chimes every 15 minutes from 6am to midnight. Before the Government Buildings were erected, this area was swampy and populated with shacks, some of them houses of ill-repute. According to Albert J. Schütz's history, local residents tell of a sailor who left Suva in 1931. Upon returning in 1939 and seeing the great new structures, he exclaimed, "My God, the old girl's done well!" Stop laughing and walk past the large open field on the south side of the building, which is:
11. **Albert Park,** named for Queen Victoria's consort, Prince Albert. The pavilion opposite the Government Buildings, however, is named for Charles Kingsford

Smith, the Australian aviator and first person to fly across the Pacific. When Smith took off from Hawaii on the second leg of his historic flight, he was unaware that a row of palm trees stretched across the middle of Albert Park, his intended landing place. A local radio operator figured out Smith's predicament, and the colonial governor ordered the trees cut down immediately. The resulting "runway" across Albert Park was barely long enough, but Smith managed to stop his plane within a few feet of its end on June 6, 1928. Opposite the park on Victoria Parade stands a perfect refueling stop, the

12. **Grand Pacific Hotel.** The Union Steamship Company built this white colonial-style hotel on the shore of the harbor in 1914 to house its transpacific passengers during their stopovers in Fiji. The idea was to make them think they had never gone ashore, for rooms in the GPH were designed like first-class staterooms, complete with saltwater baths and plumbing fixtures identical to those on an ocean liner. All rooms were on the second floor, and guests could step outside on a 15-foot wide veranda overlooking the harbor and walk completely around the building—as if they were walking on the "deck." When members of the British royal family visited Fiji, they stood atop the wrought-iron portico, the "bow" of the Grand Pacific, and addressed their subjects massed across Victoria Parade in Albert Park. Have a drink at the harborside bar. When you've rested, continue south on Victoria Parade to the corner of Ratu Cakobau Road and enter:
13. **Thurston Gardens.** Originally known as the Botanical Gardens, this cool, English-like park was renamed in 1976 for its founder, the amateur botanist Sir John Bates Thurston. He started the gardens at another location in 1881; they were moved to this site in 1912. Henry Marks, scion of a local trading company, presented the drinking fountain in 1914. After G. J. Marks, a relative and lord mayor of Suva, was drowned that same year in the sinking of the SS *Empress* in the St. Lawrence River in Canada, the Marks family erected the bandstand in his memory. Children can climb aboard the stationary *Thurston Express,* a narrow-gauge locomotive once used to pull harvested cane to the crushing mill. Walk to the southeast corner of the gardens, where you will find the fascinating:
14. **Fiji Museum,** one of the South Pacific's finest. Although some of the museum's artifacts were damaged by Suva's humidity while they were hidden away during World War II, a marvelous collection of war clubs, cannibal forks, tanoa bowls, shell jewelry, and other Fijian relics remains. Exhibits in the rear of the building explain Fiji's history. The rudder and other relics of HMS *Bounty*—burned and sunk at Pitcairn Island by Fletcher Christian and the other mutineers in 1789 but recovered in the 1950s—are on display. The museum is open Monday through Saturday from 8:30am to 4:30pm. Admission is F$2 ($1.40) for tourists, F$1 (70¢) for locals, free for school-age children. It's well worth a visit. When you've had a good look, backtrack to Victoria Parade and head south again until, just past the manicured greens of the Suva Bowling Club on the harbor, you arrive at the big iron gates of:
15. **Government House,** the home of Fiji's president, guarded like Buckingham Palace—this one by two spit-and-polish, sulu-clad Fijian soldiers. The original house, built in 1882 as the residence of the colonial governor, was struck by lightning and burned to the ground in 1921. The present rambling mansion was completed in 1928 and opened with great fanfare. It is closed to the public, but a colorful military ceremony marks the changing of the guard during the first week of each month. Ask the Fiji Visitors Bureau if a ceremony will take place while you're there. From this point, Victoria Parade becomes Queen Elizabeth Drive, which skirts the peninsula to Laucala Bay. With homes and gardens on one side and the lagoon on the other, it's a lovely walk or drive. The manicured residential area in the rolling hills behind Government House is known as The Domain; an enclave of British civil servants in colonial times, it now is home to Fiji government officials and affluent private citizens.

A GUIDED TOUR OF SUVA

The easiest way to see the residential suburbs as well as downtown Suva is on a guided tour. **United Touring Fiji,** which has a tour desk in the lobby of the Suva Travelodge (tel. 312287), charges F$15 ($10.50) per person for the 3-hour tour. **Livai Fiji Ethnic Tours** (tel. 394692) has a similar tour with a longer stop at the Fiji Museum for F$20 ($14) per adult, F$10 ($7) per child.

EXCURSIONS FROM SUVA

Set aside a day to get out of Suva, perhaps to visit one of the two nearby replicas of pre-European native villages, take a canoe trip down a tropical river, or walk peacefully through a refreshingly cool, misty rain forest.

ORCHID ISLAND

A self-described "living museum" 7km (4 miles) west of Suva on the Queen's Road, Orchid Island (tel. 361128) gives a glimpse into Fijian life in the days before Europeans arrived on the islands. The world's largest drua (war canoe) and a 50-foot-high "spirit house"—the first such thatch temple constructed since Christianity conquered Fiji more than a century ago—dominate the replica of a traditional village, which was built on a small island in the crook of a river with help from the Fiji Museum. Fijians go about the routines of life as did their forebears: preparing food, building fires, plaiting rope from coconut fibers, making handcrafts for everyday use. They don't war with their neighbors or cook their prisoners, but they do perform the spear-waving war dance during the "folks spectacular" staged for visitors each day. A "mini museum" explains the country's history, and a small zoo houses turtles, mongooses, vivid parrots, monkeys, and the rare crested iguana, a species found only in Fiji. The village and surrounding area are made lush—and educational—by examples of all the various plants found in the islands. After a tour through Orchid Island, you'll know more about Fiji than your friends back home will ever want to hear.

Two-hour guided tours, including demonstrations of Fijian skills and handcrafts and a dance show, begin Monday through Saturday at 10:30am. Admission is F$7 ($5) for adults, F$3.50 ($2.50) for children. Taxi fares are about F$12 ($8.50) each way. United Touring (UTC) charges F$18 ($12.50) per person for round-trip transportation and admission; book at its desk in the Suva Travelodge (tel. 312287).

PACIFIC HARBOUR

A meticulously planned, recreation-oriented residential community with luxury villas nestled on manicured lawns beside artificial lakes and fairways (translated: a real-estate development), Pacific Harbour is noted primarily for its excellent golf course (see "Sports & Recreation," below) and the Cultural Centre and Marketplace of Fiji.

On the Queen's Road, 30 miles west of Suva, the **Marketplace** is a shopping center of colonial-style clapboard buildings joined by covered walkways. You can wander through its boutiques and handcraft shops (open Monday through Saturday from 9am to 5pm), have a light meal at one of three restaurants, poke through a small museum, and examine two thatch-roofed Fijian bures (one for a chief, one for the commoners). You don't have to pay for anything so far except the meal—about F$4.50 ($3) for a hamburger, omelet, fish-and-chips, sandwich, or a plate of curry.

It will cost, however, to visit the **Culture Centre** on "Sacred Island," across a lake behind the Marketplace. Boats paddled by muscular young Fijian men dressed in traditional costumes leave a wharf at the end of a covered walkway for tours of the island with its replica of an ancient Fijian village. As on Orchid Island, a tall "spirit house" dominates the other thatch-roofed buildings in the village, and Fijians demonstrate age-old skills, such as fire walking and handcraft making. The boats leave

IMPRESSIONS

The balcony I recognized from Derek's reminiscences on many a Canadian winter night. When it was thirty or forty below zero outside, we would open a bottle of brandy, watch his Fiji slides, and talk quietly of warm tropical evenings. But here in Suva it was still rush hour, and we had to shout above the roar of Leyland buses. One of the things I always forget about the Third World is the noise.
—RONALD WRIGHT, 1986

---

for hour-long guided tours of the island every 15 minutes between 9:30am and 2pm from Monday to Saturday.

If you missed them on the Coral Coast, Beqa Islanders perform their **fire-walking ceremony** here at 3:30pm on Tuesday, Friday, and Saturday. An announcer explains what's going on—which may not happen during performances at the hotels.

The **Dance Theatre of Fiji,** dedicated to preserving ancient dances and rituals, performs at 3:30pm on Monday, Wednesday, and Thursday. You're not likely to see more authentic Fijian dancing.

Tickets for either the guided tour, fire-walking ceremony, or dance show cost F$10 ($7) for adults, F$5 ($3.50) for children between 5 and 15 years old. A combination ticket for any two events costs F$18 ($12.50) for adults and F$9 ($6.50) for children.

The telephone number at the Marketplace and Cultural Centre was 45011 at the time of writing, but this is sure to change. If you get no answer, call 011 for directory assistance.

Wilderness (Fiji) Tours (tel. 386498) has an all-day tour which includes a stop at the Suva Municipal Market, Orchid Island, and Pacific Harbour. Cost is F$55 ($38.50) adults, F$30 ($21) children.

COLO-I-SUVA FOREST PARK

At a 400- to 600-foot altitude in the upper drainage area of Waisila Creek, the Fiji Forestry Department's Colo-I-Suva Forest Park provides a cool, refreshing respite from the heat, if not the humidity, of the city below. Picnic at tables in thatch pavilions with fire grates, or hike the well-marked system of trails through the heavy indigenous forests and stands of mahogany to one of several lovely waterfalls that cascade into swimming holes. Bring walking shoes with good traction because the trails are covered with gravel or slippery soapstone. The park is best visited on a clear day, since Colo-I-Suva gets twice as much rain as Suva, and even under the best of conditions the thick overhanging foliage blocks out as much as 90% of the sunlight that does reach the treetops (holding the high temperature to 70°F on most days).

Colo-I-Suva is open every day until 5:30pm. The entrance is just beyond Tamavua village on the Princes Road, about 11km (6.6 miles) from Suva. Signs at intersections in the area show the way to the park. It's a long walk from the bus stop at the Colo-I-Suva Forest Station to the pools, but you can get there on the Sawani bus—one leaves Suva Municipal Market every hour. The fare is about F50¢ (35¢).

The creeks can flood quickly during periods of heavy rains, so be careful in the park. And don't dive into the swimming holes unless you know how deep they are.

RIVER TRIPS

★ **Wilderness (Fiji) Tours** (tel. 386498), operates a popular, full-day trip on the Navua River west of Suva. A bus or car picks you up at 8am for a 2-hour drive through fields, forests, and villages to the upper reaches of the river. You then spend the rest of day canoeing down the river, navigating over cascades in the hills, and then meandering through rice paddies in the flat valley below. A bus or car brings you back to Suva from the river's mouth 39km (23 miles) west of the city on the Queen's Road. Cost for the full day, including lunch beside the river, is F$49 ($34.50) per person.

Wilderness Adventures (same firm as Wilderness Tours) runs similar bus-and-boat ½-day trips to roaring Wairoro Falls, up the Rewa River east of Suva. The Rewa begins high in the mountains of eastern Viti Levu and twists and turns through a broad, flat delta before reaching the sea. These popular tours include a visit to a Fijian village for a cup of yaqona. Cost is F$25 ($17.50) per person.

LEVUKA

Fiji Air (tel. 313666) has a full-day outing to Levuka, Fiji's first capital, for F$45 ($31.50) per person, including round-trip airfare, ground transfers, morning and afternoon tea, and a light lunch. Hotel pickup is at 7:30am Monday to Friday, with return about 5:45pm. See Chapter 14 for details about Levuka.

SPORTS & RECREATION

GOLF

Pacific Harbour Golf and Country Club (tel. has been 45048 in Deuba, but it will change) is the centerpiece of the planned resort community. The club brags that its 18-hole, par-72 course, designed by Robert Trent Jones, Jr., is the South Pacific's finest. Some of the fairways cross lakes; others cut their way through narrow valleys surrounded by jungle-clad hills. Visitors are welcome to use the links: Greens fees are F$30 ($21). A full range of equipment can be rented at the pro shop. There is a restaurant and bar in the clubhouse.

Closer to town, the less challenging 18-hole course of the **Fiji Golf Club** (tel. 382872) lies along Rifle Range Road, on the eastern side of the peninsula. Contact the club's secretary to get more information or to arrange a tee-off time. Green fees are F$10 ($7).

TENNIS

Suva has lighted, hard-surface **public tennis courts** in Albert Park on Victoria Parade and in Victoria Park on Disraeli Road. Telephone 313428 to make a reservation.

SWIMMING/SNORKELING

Beaches are scarce in the Suva area, but **Coral Sea Cruises** (tel. 321570) goes daily to Nukulau Island, a tiny atoll on the reef where you can swim and snorkel. Fresh fruit and morning tea are served on the way out, and Fijian divers hand-feed the fish beneath glass observation panels in the hull. The boats leave at 9:30am and return at 3:30pm. The fare is F$40 ($28) per person, including hotel transfers and lunch on the island. Nukulau once was a quarantine station, and many of Fiji's indentured laborers spent their first few weeks in Fiji on this tiny isolated outpost.

To the rear of the Old Town Hall on Victoria Parade, the **Suva Olympic Pool** is open to all comers from 10am to 6pm Monday through Friday and from 8am to 6pm on Saturday during the winter months (April to September); in summer (October to March), it's open from 9am to 7pm Monday through Friday and from 6am to 7pm on Saturday. Admission is F40¢ (28¢) for adults and F10¢ (7¢) for children. Lockers rent for F20¢ (14¢) plus a refundable F$1 (70¢) key deposit.

SCUBA DIVING

Beqa Divers (tel. 361088) takes snorkelers along on a variety of scuba-diving expeditions from its base at the marina of the former Tradewinds Hotel, about 4 miles west of town on the Bay of Islands. Most dives on the reefs in the immediate Suva area take ½ day, but the company also has full-day trips to the gorgeous, unspoiled Beqa lagoon from an auxiliary base at Pacific Harbour, 30 miles west of town. Two-tank Beqa dives cost F$115 ($80.50); snorkelers pay F$55 ($38.50), including equipment and lunch. Beqa Divers does not take snorkelers on its night-dive trips.

Ocean Pacific Divers (tel. 303252) also has dive expeditions to Beqa Lagoon from its base at Ocean Pacific Club, about 15 miles west of Suva.

FISHING

The waters off southern Viti Levu are renowned for their big game fish, and **Ocean Pacific Club,** P.O. Box 3229, Lami Town (tel. 303252, fax 300732), caters to anyone who is serious about fishing. Located on a peninsula about 15 miles west of Suva, the Club has a fleet of boats, comfortable accommodations, a restaurant, and bar.

SHOPPING

If you took the walking tour of Suva, you already have a good idea of where to shop for handcrafts and duty-free merchandise. Suva is crawling with the **sword sellers** I warned you about in the Nadi shopping section of Chapter 12. Avoid them!

Stamp collectors will find colorful first-day covers from Fiji and other South Pacific island countries at the **Philatelic Bureau,** Edward Street, on the first floor of the new wing of the General Post Office. It's open from 8am to 1pm and 2 to 4pm Monday through Thursday, to 3:30pm on Friday. American Express, Diners Club, MasterCard, and VISA cards are accepted.

Bargaining is the order of the day in most of Suva's duty-free shops. Before you put your money down or whip out your credit card, however, read the discussion of duty-free shopping under "What to Buy" in Chapter 2. And stick to stores that have the Fiji National Duty Free Merchants Association's emblem posted on their windows.

You will see most of Suva's shops during a stroll down **Cumming Street.** The two largest and most-reliable merchants are **Proud's,** at The Triangle, corner of Thomson Street and Renwick Road (tel. 312495), and at the corner of Thomson and Cumming streets (tel. 312656); and **Tappoo,** which has a large store at the corner of Thomson and Usher streets (tel. 315422).

HANDCRAFTS

GOVERNMENT HANDICRAFT CENTRE, rear of Ratu Sukuna House, corner of Victoria Parade and Macarthur St. Tel. 211306.

Before buying Fijian handcrafts elsewhere, you should browse through the merchandise here. Operated by the Ministry of Trade and Commerce, the center was founded in 1974 to continue and promote Fiji's handcrafts. Special attention is given to rural artisans who cannot easily market their works. Although Wolfe's Boutique (see below) generally has the highest-quality merchandise, you will see fine wood carvings, woven goods, and tapa cloth here, and you will learn from the fixed prices just how much the really good items are worth. The staff is friendly and helpful. It's open from 8am to 4:30pm Monday to Thursday, 8am to 4pm Friday, 9am to noon Saturday.

MUNICIPAL CURIO AND HANDICRAFT CENTRE, Municipal Car Park, Stinson Parade, on the waterfront. Tel. 313433.

Having checked out the government center, you can visit these stalls and bargain (with the Indian merchants, not with the Fijians) from a position of knowledge, if not strength. Be careful, however, for some of the work here is mass-produced and aimed at cruise-ship passengers who have only a few hours in Fiji to do their shopping.

WOLFE'S BOUTIQUE, Thomson St., opposite Fiji Visitors Bureau. Tel. 302320.

This little store consistently has the highest-quality handcrafts, not only from Fiji but from other South Pacific island countries as well. For example, Wolfe's may charge twice what you would pay in Honiara, but it has some nguzunguzus (inlaid canoe prows) that are better than most you will see in Solomon Islands. Prices for Fijian-carved war clubs and figurines, on the other hand, are very reasonable for the excellent quality. Look also for straw hats, baskets, and mats; tapa cloth; shell jewelry; and drawings and paintings by local artists.

EVENING ENTERTAINMENT

Fijian-style meke feast-and-dance nights are scarce in Suva. The Suva Travelodge, Victoria Parade (tel. 301600), usually has one a week. It was on Wednesday during my recent visit and cost F$22 ($15.50) for a buffet of Fijian-style foods followed by traditional dancing. Otherwise, nocturnal activities in Suva revolve around "polishing the floors" (dancing).

LUCKY EDDIE'S AND ROCKEFELLER'S, 215 Victoria Parade. Tel. 312968.

These two clubs, joined by a door, share a building with the Red Lion Restaurant and the Pizza Hut. Entrance to both is up a stairwell next to the Pizza Hut, posted "ONLY SOBER AND WELL-BEHAVED PEOPLE ADMITTED." Lucky Eddie's side of the establishment appeals to a younger set who like ear-shattering rock and disco music. Rockefeller's features softer rock music, plush lounge furniture, and wood-paneled walls. Diners at the Red Lion can enter Rockefeller's free. Open 7pm to 1am Monday through Friday, and 7:30 to 11:30pm on Saturday.

Admission (includes both clubs): F$3 ($2) Thurs and Sat, F$4–F$6 ($3–$4) Fri. **Prices:** Drinks F$2.50–F$5 ($1.75–$3.50), slightly higher in Rockefeller's.

O'REILLY'S, Macarthur St., off Victoria Parade. Tel. 312968.

Opened in 1991 by the owners of Lucky Eddie's and Rockefeller's (in the same building but around the corner on Macarthur Street), O'Reilly's is Suva's sole Irish-style pub. Semicircular booths line the walls, separated by a white rail fence from a sunken area with a large square bar and plenty of room for standing—but not for dancing, despite some rather loud music. Hors d'oeuvres are served until 9pm. Open 11:30am to 2:30pm and 6pm to 1am Monday through Friday, to 11:30pm Saturday.

Admission: F$1 (70¢). **Prices:** Drinks F$2.50–F$5 ($1.75–$3.50).

TINGLE'S BAR, in Tiko's Floating Restaurant, Stinson Parade at Sukuna Park. Tel. 313626.

In the former engine room of Tiko's (see "Where to Dine," below), this pleasant establishment has lots of nautical touches. There's enough room here to dance to recorded music after 9pm, provided the well-behaved clientele isn't singing along to music videos (an activity that was sweeping across the antipodes during my recent visit). Open noon to 1am Monday through Friday, noon to 11:30pm Saturday.

Admission: Free. **Prices:** Drinks F$3–F$3.50 ($2–$2.50).

4. WHERE TO STAY

Suva has good first-class hotels but no deluxe properties. The best bets for moderately priced accommodations are "apartment hotels." These establishments have efficiency apartments that are rented on a daily rather than a monthly basis. None of them is the least bit luxurious, but all are quite comfortable, and maids give the apartments a good cleaning each morning.

EXPENSIVE

SUVA COURTESY INN, P.O. Box 112, Suva, Fiji Islands. Tel. 312300, or toll free 800/223-9868 in the U.S. Fax 301300. Telex 2272. 50 rms. A/C MINIBAR TV TEL **Location:** Corner of Gordon and Malcolm Sts.

$ Rates: F$115 ($80.50) single or double. AE, DC, MC, V.

Even sans balcony, you will have a commanding view over Suva, the harbor, and the south coast of Viti Levu from this curving, eight-story building. All of the rooms face the harbor; even though the rates for the rooms are the same for each floor, the rooms on the sixth, seventh, and eighth floors have the best views. The neighborhood is quiet and residential, and the hotel is a mere 3-block walk from the shops on Victoria Parade.

Dining/Entertainment: A Malaysian restaurant shares a room on the building's second floor with a bar that features quiet jazz music on weekend nights. Lobby has 24-hour coffee shop with patio seating.

Services: Laundry, baby-sitting.

Facilities: Swimming pool, beauty salon, tour desk.

SUVA TRAVELODGE, P.O. Box 1357, Suva, Fiji Islands. Tel. 301600, or toll free 800/835-7742 in the U.S. Fax 300251. Telex 2159. 134 rms. A/C MINIBAR TEL **Location:** Victoria Parade, opposite Government Buildings.

$ Rates: F$155 ($109) single or double. AE, DC, MC, V.

This hotel's waterfront location couldn't be better: Suva Harbour laps one side, the stately Government Buildings sit across Victoria Parade on the other, and the business district is a 3-block walk away. The balconies or patios of the Australian-style rooms look out from two-story buildings onto a tropical garden and a boomerang-shaped swimming pool by the water's edge.

Dining/Entertainment: Central building has a coffee shop, a more formal restaurant, and a bar. Poolside barbecues on Sunday afternoons for about F$9 ($6.50) per person are popular with locals.

Services: Laundry, baby-sitting, business services.

Facilities: Swimming pool, tour desk, conference rooms.

MODERATE

CAPRICORN APARTMENT HOTEL, 7 St. Fort St., P.O. Box 1261, Suva, Fiji Islands. Tel. 314799. Fax 303069. Telex 2443. 34 rms. A/C TEL **Location:** End of St. Fort St. Go up Stewart St. past the large Centenary Church and bear left on St. Fort St.

$ Rates: F$55 ($38.50) single; F$65 ($45.50) double. AE, DC, MC, V.

(S) The establishment just 2 blocks from Cumming Street is popular with Australians and New Zealanders who like to do their own cooking. Owner Mulchand Patel's furniture might be a little on the plain side, but he keeps his roomy efficiencies spotless. The three-story L-shaped building looks out on Suva Harbour and down the mountainous coast. Private balconies off each apartment share the view, as does a pear-shaped swimming pool on the Capricorn's grounds. Each unit has an air conditioner, although windows on both sides of the building let the cooling trade winds blow through.

There's no restaurant, but the reception staff will sell you some canned goods from its small on-premises store or have the Lantern Palace Chinese restaurant bring a meal to your room. The maids will do your laundry in the Capricorn's washers for F$2 ($1.50) per load.

GRAND PACIFIC HOTEL, P.O. Box 2086, Government Buildings, Suva, Fiji Islands. Tel. 301011. Fax 302967. Telex 2270. 74 rms. A/C TEL **Location:** Victoria Parade opposite Albert Park.

$ Rates: F$35 ($24.50) single, F$40 ($28) double without air conditioning or bath; F$60–F$70 ($42–$49) single, F$70–F$80 ($49–$56) double with air conditioning and bath. AE, DC, MC, V.

This stately hotel, which we saw on our walking tour of Suva, has lost its title as "the" place to stay in the South Pacific, but if sleeping in a museum with the ghosts of Fiji's colonial past appeals to you, it still has its well-worn charms. All of the old shiplike fixtures are long gone, but the balcony still circles the grand salon, double windows still reach to tall ceilings, and you can still sip your cold Fiji Bitter out by the swimming pool at harbor's edge—and imagine how grand this hotel must have been in the old days. Sooner or later, someone is going to do a major Raffles-style renovation and bring it back.

Rooms in the original building—the "Colonial Wing"—are less expensive than those in a somewhat more modern "South Wing." For the budget-conscious, seven less expensive rooms without air conditioners (they do have ceiling fans) share baths and showers in a third wing. The dining room has a great harbor view through two walls of windows; it charges very reasonable prices for rather plain fare (cooked breakfasts are about half what you pay at the Suva Travelodge).

SUNSET APARTMENT MOTEL, P.O. Box 485, Suva, Fiji Islands. Tel. 301799. Fax 301578. Telex 2141. 12 units. A/C **Location:** Corner of Gordon and Murray Sts.

$ Rates: F$36 ($25) single or double room without kitchen; F$38 ($26.50) single or double room with kitchen; F$48 ($33.50) single or double apartment. AE, DC, MC, V.

Manager Violet Matalau keeps a tight rein at this clean and quiet hotel. Nine larger units have two bedrooms each—one with a double bed, one with two single beds—and full kitchens off their living rooms. Of six other one-room units, two have kitchens and four don't. Each unit has a sliding glass door leading to a private balcony. The furniture is dated but adequate. The location, just 2 blocks off Victoria Parade, is very convenient.

BUDGET

COCONUT INN, P.O. Box 12539, Suva, Fiji Islands. Tel. 312904. Fax 701169. 4 rms (none with bath), 20 bunks, 1 apartment. **Location:** 8 Kimberley St., off Gordon St.

$ Rates (including tax): F$4.50 ($3) bunk; F$9.50 ($6.50) bunk with breakfast; F$25 ($17.50) single or double room; F$38.50 ($27) air-conditioned apartment. No credit cards.

Many members of the backpack brigade flock to this house, which has rock-bottom, dormitory-style accommodations, rooms without baths, and one fully self-contained, one-bedroom, air-conditioned apartment. There's a communal kitchen and a comfortable lounge with TV and videocassette player.

SOUTH SEAS PRIVATE HOTEL, P.O. Box 157, Suva, Fiji Islands. Tel. 312296. 34 rms (none with bath), 42 bunks. **Location:** 6 Williamson Rd., off Ratu Cakobau Rd. (behind Albert Park).

$ Rates: F$4 ($3) dorm bunk; F$7 ($5) single, F$11 ($7.50) double room. No credit cards.

This large barrackslike wooden structure with a long sun room across the front has dormitories, basic rooms, a rudimentary communal kitchen, and laundry facilities. Linen is provided, but bring your own towel or pay F$1 (70¢) to rent one. Showers have both hot and cold water.

SUVA APARTMENTS, P.O. Box 12488, Suva, Fiji Islands. Tel. 304280. Fax 302294. 11 units. **Location:** 17 Bau St., 15-minute walk from Victoria Parade (follow Gordon St. and MacGregor Rd., which becomes Bau St.).

$ Rates: F$23 ($16) single, F$28 ($19.50) double. No credit cards.

This basic but clean establishment is owned by the Fiji Amateur Sports Association and the National Olympic Committee, which share the profits. It's very popular, especially when sporting events are on, so reserve early. The top two floors of this three-story building have studio apartments; the ground floor has larger units for families. Each unit has a kitchen, private bath (in which the noncurtained shower and toilet share a space), and heavy bars on the entry door and across a balcony (it's on the fringes of one of Suva's burglary districts).

5. WHERE TO DINE

No one will allege that dining out in Suva matches the excitement of exploring the French restaurants in Tahiti or New Caledonia, but in recent years the city has made great culinary strides across a broad spectrum of cuisines. A growing number of restaurants now offer more than curry, chow mein, and the bland roast-and-potato legacy of the British and Australian colonists.

RESTAURANTS BY CUISINE

EUROPEAN RESTAURANTS

SWISS TAVERN, 16 Kimberley St. Tel. 303233.

Cuisine: EUROPEAN. **Reservations:** Required.

$ Prices: Lunches F$7–F$19 ($5–$13.50); appetizers F$4.50–$110 ($3–$77); main courses F$14.50–F$30 ($10–$21). AE, DC, MC, V.

Open: Lunch Mon–Fri noon–2pm; dinner Mon–Sat 6–10pm.

Hans Kehrli, former chief chef at The Fijian Resort, specializes in the cuisine of his native Switzerland at this house which he remodeled into a restaurant. Both a downstairs bar and upstairs dining room are completely paneled in blond Fiji pine. The F$110 ($77) price of an appetizer given above is no mistake: It's caviar.

TIKO'S FLOATING RESTAURANT, Stinson Parade at Sukuna Park. Tel. 313626.

Cuisine: EUROPEAN. **Reservations:** Recommended.

$ Prices: Appetizers F$4–F$10 ($3–$7); main courses F$15–F$20 ($10.50–$14). AE, DC, MC, V.

Open: Lunch Mon–Sat noon–2pm; dinner Mon–Sat 6–10pm.

Founder-owner-manager Tiko Eastgate describes himself as a fourth-generation English-Fijian, since two of his ancestors were Fiji's first English magistrate and the Fijian woman he married in the 1870s. After nearly 20 years with The Fijian Resort, Tiko bought this ship for scrap-metal prices, replaced everything below deck, and opened the restaurant and bar in 1985. He keeps making improvements, to both ship and cuisine. The menu features nicely prepared fresh local seafoods, such as *walu* (Spanish mackerel) or *pakapaka* (snapper). The service is attentive, and someone always provides dinner music. The engine room–level bar is a popular spot for after-work drinks (see "Evening Entertainment," above).

RED LION RESTAURANT, 215 Victoria Parade. Tel. 312968.

Cuisine: EUROPEAN. **Reservations:** Not accepted for lunch, recommended for dinner.

$ Prices: Appetizers F$3–F$10 ($2–$7); main courses F$12.50–F$18 ($9–$12.50). AE, DC, MC, V.

Open: Lunch Mon–Sat noon–2:30pm; dinner Mon–Sat 6–11:30pm.

Tudor England is the theme here: French horns, antique china, brass lanterns, and copper pots and kettles hang from the exposed-beam ceiling of this dimly lit "Olde English" pub. The Red Lion shares a building with Luckie Eddie's and Rockefeller's nightclubs, but the clubs' disco beat doesn't come close to overpowering the recorded flutes and harpsichords that add to the restaurant's Shakespearean atmosphere. The menu offers delicious freshwater shrimp in garlic or chili sauces, fish under peppercorns, some refined Indian dishes, and Czechoslovakian steak (guess where the chef's from).

INDIAN RESTAURANTS

HARE KRISHNA RESTAURANT, 16 Pratt St. Tel. 314154.

Cuisine: INDIAN. **Reservations:** Not accepted.

$ Prices: Curries F$1–F$6 (70¢–$4.50). No credit cards.

Open: Mon–Sat 11am–2:30pm; downstairs yogurt, ice-cream, and curry snack bar Mon–Thurs 9am–8pm, Fri 9am–9pm, Sat 9am–5pm.

Operated by the religious sect of the same name, this popular restaurant specializes in a wide range of vegetarian curries—eggplant, cabbage, potatoes and peas, okra, and papaya to name a few—each seasoned delicately and differently from the others. Interesting pastries, breads, side dishes, and salads (such as cucumbers and carrots in yogurt) cool off the fire set by some of the curries. If you can't decide what to order, check the items on display in a cafeterialike steam table near the entrance to the second-floor dining rooms or get the *thali* sampler and try a little of everything—it's the most expensive item on the menu and will tingle your taste buds. A branch at 37 Cumming Street (tel. 312259) serves lunch Monday to

Friday from 11am to 2:30pm and dinner Friday from 6 to 9pm; reservations are not accepted. Both branches have excellent yogurt and ice-cream bars downstairs; climb the spiral stairs at the back of the yogurt bars to reach the dining rooms. The Hare Krishnas allow no alcoholic beverages or smoking in the establishments.

CURRY PLACE, 16 Pratt St. Tel. 313885.
Cuisine: INDIAN. **Reservations:** Not accepted.
$ Prices: Main courses F$2–F$5.50 ($1.50–$4). No credit cards.
Open: Mon–Sat 9am–9pm, Sun 10am–4pm.

If you want meat curry, make your choice from the selections displayed in the steam-heated cabinet at the entrance. Meat curries (goat is the best) include rice, dal soup, and two pieces of roti. If you don't want meat, you can choose from two vegetarian curries. Alcoholic beverages are not served, but you can bring your own wine or beer after 6pm.

CURRY HOUSE, 255 Victoria Parade. Tel. 313000.
Cuisine: INDIAN. **Reservations:** Not accepted.
$ Prices: Main courses F$2–F$5.50 ($1.50–$4). No credit cards.
Open: Mon–Wed 9am–9pm, Thurs–Sat 9am–9:30pm, Sun 5–8pm.

This clean eatery is very similar to the Curry Place, above, in that it displays its curries cafeteria-style at the front of the building and has booths and Formica-top tables inside. All curry meals are served with dal soup, potato and eggplant curry, chutney, and choice of two rotis or rice.

CHINESE RESTAURANTS

GREAT WOK OF CHINA, Bau St. at Laucala Bay Rd., Flagstaff Tel. 301285.
Cuisine: SZECHUAN. **Reservations:** Recommended.
$ Prices: Appetizers F$3–F$8 ($2–$5.50); main courses F$9–F$27 ($6.50–$19). AE, DC, MC, V.
Open: Lunch Mon–Fri noon–2pm; dinner Mon–Sat 6:15–10:45pm.

Get to Suva's most elegant Chinese restaurant early enough to order a cold beer and a serving of *kwai me far sing;* you'll need the beer to wash down these mouth-watering, spicy roasted peanuts. Otherwise, you won't go wrong ordering any of the Szechuan offerings, especially the whole crispy fish big enough to feed at least two persons.

MING PALACE, Victoria Parade in Old Town Hall. Tel. 315111.
Cuisine: CANTONESE. **Reservations:** Recommended.
$ Prices: Appetizers F$1.50–F$3 ($1–$2); main courses F$5.50–F$12.50 ($4–$9). AE, DC, MC, V.
Open: Lunch Mon–Sat noon–2pm; dinner Mon–Sat 6–10pm.

The owners here completely refurbished the Old Town Hall, which we passed during our walking tour of Suva. A huge Chinese dragon and bird now hang above the stage, and lanterns dangle from long poles reaching down from the high, arch-supported ceiling. Screens separate the tables to keep you from feeling as if you're dining in an auditorium, and the service is attentive and efficient. The menu includes Cantonese-style dishes of beef, chicken, pork, prawns, and crayfish lobster.

LANTERN PALACE, 10 Pratt St. Tel. 314633.
Cuisine: CANTONESE. **Reservations:** Recommended.
$ Prices: Appetizers F$1.20–F$4.50 (85¢–$3); main courses F$4.50–F$9 ($3–$6.60). AE, DC, MC, V.
Open: Lunch Mon–Sat 11:30am–2:30pm; dinner Mon–Sat 5–10pm.

Another pleasant establishment, this occupies a storefront on the same block of Pratt Street as the Hare Krishna Restaurant and the Curry Place. It has the usual assortment of Chinese letters on the wall and lanterns hanging overhead, but the tables are draped with white linen cloths that contribute to a quiet, upscale atmosphere. You can choose from a wide range of excellent Cantonese dishes. Those with lobster cost F$18 ($12.50).

WAN-Q RESTAURANT, 25 Cumming St. Tel. 313314.
Cuisine: CANTONESE. **Reservations:** Recommended at dinner Sun.
$ Prices: Appetizers F$1.50–F$4 ($1–$3); main courses F$3–F$9 ($2–$6.50). AE, DC, MC, V.
Open: Mon–Sat 10am–9:30pm; lunch Sun noon–2pm; dinner Sun 7–9:30pm.

This popular local haunt is on the second floor of a building in the heart of Suva's duty-free shopping district, so consider it for a lunch. Although the chow is ordinary mein, it's worth the money you will have saved during your nearby haggling sessions. And the pleasantly appointed dining room is air conditioned, a real plus in the midday heat and humidity. Sunday evenings here can be packed.

ITALIAN RESTAURANTS

PIZZA HUT, 207 Victoria Parade. Tel. 311825.
Cuisine: PIZZA/ITALIAN. **Reservations:** Recommended on weekends.
$ Prices: Pizzas F$4–F$12 ($3–$8.50); appetizers F$1.50–F$2.50 ($1–$2); pasta dishes F$4.50–F$5 ($3–$3.50). AE, DC, MC, V.
Open: Mon–Fri 9:30am–11pm, Sat 9:30am–10:30pm, Sun 7–10pm.

This is not related to the American chain by either ownership or quality, but it still has good pizza and pasta. Pies range from small and plain ones to large ones with prawns. Also on the menu: salads, spaghetti, rigatoni, lasagne, cannelloni. The bar draws a crowd of young people on Friday and Saturday nights.

PIZZA KING, Scott St., in the Harbour Center Arcade. Tel. 315726.
Cuisine: PIZZA. **Reservations:** Not accepted.
$ Prices: Pizzas F$4.50–F$12 ($3–$8.50); salads F$1.50 ($1); spaghetti F$4.50 ($3). AE, DC, MC, V.
Open: Mon–Sat 9am–11pm; lunch Sun noon–2pm; dinner Sun 7–10pm.

One of my favorite Suva eateries, this cozy little establishment sports brick archways, booths as well as tables, and a bar in the rear. Pizzas range from small ones with nothing but cheese to large "Pizza King Specials" loaded with everything. Other items are limited to fresh salads and spaghetti under a very sweet bolognese sauce.

SNACK BARS

PALM COURT BISTRO, Victoria Parade, in the Palm Court Arcade, Queensland Insurance Centre. Tel. 304662.
Cuisine: SNACK BAR. **Reservations:** Not accepted.
$ Prices: Breakfasts F$4–F$7.50 ($3–$5); sandwiches, meat pies, burgers, and fish-and-chips F$1–F$3 (70¢–$2). No credit cards.
Open: Mon–Fri 7am–6pm, Sat 7am–3pm.

You can enjoy excellent cooked breakfasts and a variety of other snacks and light meals at this walk-up take-out in the open-air center of the Palm Court Arcade. Order at the counter and then eat at umbrella tables under cover, or go sit in the shade of the namesake palm in the middle of the arcade.

WISHBONE FRIED CHICKEN, Scott St., beside Nubukalou Creek. Tel. 315677.
Cuisine: FRIED CHICKEN. **Reservations:** Not accepted.
$ Prices: F$1.50–F$3 ($1–$2). No credit cards.
Open: Mon–Sat 11am–8pm.

If you miss Colonel Sander's Kentucky Fried Chicken, you'll enjoy Fiji's version of it. Walk up the counter and order by the piece or in combination with chips (french fries) just like you would at a Colonel's anywhere else in the world.

JUDE'S, Victoria Parade, in Vanua Arcade, behind Zenon Bookshop. Tel. 315461.
Cuisine: SNACK BAR. **Reservations:** Not accepted.
$ Prices: F$1–F$2.50 (70¢–$2). No credit cards.
Open: Mon–Fri 8am–4:30pm, Sat 8am–noon.

Get hot Australian meat pies and thick, made-to-order cold sandwiches at the counter in this clean and tastefully decorated little establishment. If you like corned beef or pastrami on rye, this is the place to eat it.

MORRIS HEDSTROM CAFETERIA, Thomson St., at Nubukalou Creek. Tel. 311811.

Cuisine: FIJIAN/INDIAN/CHINESE. **Reservations:** Not accepted.

$ Prices: 65¢–F$3 (50¢–$2). No credit cards.

Open: Mon–Sat 9am–5pm.

Like most Morris Hedstrom department stores in the South Pacific, this one has a very clean cafeteria (just inside the Thomson Street entrance to the Food Hall) with reasonable prices. Don't expect gourmet quality, of course, but for cheap meals you can't beat the fried rice, fish-and-chips, and curries. Sandwiches also are offered. You can see the food while waiting in line.

6. RESORTS OFF SUVA

Although guests can get there from Nadi, Suva is the usual jumping-off point to three small offshore resorts, including the two most expensive in Fiji. One is on Toberua, a tiny atoll off Viti Levu's east coast. Another is on Wakaya, in the Lomaiviti (Central Fiji) group of islands, where Count Felix von Luckner was captured in 1917. The third is on Kaibu (*Kaimbu*) in the Lau Group, Fiji's easternmost islands.

KAIMBU ISLAND RESORT, P.O. Box 7, Suva, Fiji Islands. Tel. 880333, or toll free 800/473-0332 in the U.S. Fax 880333 (same as tel.) or 714/730-0827 in the U.S. 3 units. MINIBAR **Location:** Kaibu Island, Lau Group, eastern Fiji, 50 minutes by chartered airplane from Nausori Airport.

$ Rates (in U.S. dollars only, including bungalow, food, bar, all activities, chartered flight from Nausori, and round-trip limousine from guests' home to their local airport): $995 per couple per day; $2,500 per day for whole island. AE, DC, MC, V.

Americans Jay and Margie Johnson's little hideout is about as far away from the madding crowd as rich and famous people like actors Goldie Hawn and Kurt Russell can get. The Johnsons were living on Kaibu, which they own, but apparently got bored being by themselves; hence, they built three deluxe, 1,000-square-foot bungalows and a cliff-top central building to entertain guests. The 800-acre island is a relatively flat uplifted coral atoll with several gorgeous beaches (each bungalow has its own). A 14-mile-long barrier reef encloses both Kaibu and its neighbor island, hat-shaped Yacata, thus creating a water-sports playground, including coral viewing on a unique solar-powered raft. There's even a little islet for private "Adam and Eve" champagne picnics (only adult couples are allowed as Kaimbu guests unless they rent the entire resort).

Dining/Entertainment: Guests can choose when and where to dine; the excellent cuisine features fresh seafood and homegrown vegetables and fruits.

Services: Laundry; anything else you need that's within the realm of the possible.

Facilities: Sailing, waterskiing, Windsurfers, sport fishing, golf driving range.

WAKAYA CLUB, P.O. Box 15424, Suva, Fiji Islands. Tel. 302630, or 212/644-7100 in the U.S. Fax 302714, or 212/644-7916 in the U.S. 8 units. MINIBAR **Location:** Wakaya Island, Lomaiviti Group, 20-minute flight from Nausori Airport, 50 minutes from Nadi.

$ Rates (in U.S. dollars only, including bungalow, food, bar, all activities, and transfers from Nausori or Nadi): $675 single; $875 double. AE, DC, MC, V.

This superdeluxe facility and the resorts on Kaimbu (above) and Vatulele (see "Resorts Off Nadi" in Chapter 12) set new standards of price and comfort for Fiji when they all opened in 1990. This one belongs to Canadian entrepreneur David Gilmore, who acquired the island in the 1970s. He had an interest in the Pacific

Harbour development back then; as he did there, Gilmore is selling off pieces of Wakaya for deluxe get-away homes (his own Japanese-influenced mansion—the largest private residence in Fiji—sits high on a ridge overlooking the resort). Wakaya is an uplifted, tilted coral atoll with cliffs falling into the sea on its western side and beaches along the north and east. There are still relics of a Fijian fort atop the cliffs; a chief and all his men once leapt to their deaths from there rather than be eaten by a rival tribe. The spot is known as Chieftain's Leap. More recent famous events have included visits by actress Cheryl Ladd (who poses—without being identified—on Wakaya's brochure) and supermodel Christie Brinkley, who brought along her son and nanny—but not husband Billy Joel.

People like that will feel right at home in Wakaya's 1,500-square-foot, deluxe rectangular bungalows. On one end they have large living rooms with wet bars. Separate entrances off spacious decks lead to bedrooms with built-in desks and enough closets to satisfy a pack rat like Imelda Marcos. Baths on the far end have oversize tubs, separate shower stalls, three sinks each, toilets, and bidets. Crabtree and Evelyn toiletries are imported from England.

Dining/Entertainment: The food is of gourmet quality and outstandingly presented. Guests dine in a huge thatch-roofed beachside building or outside, either on a patio or under two gazebolike shelters on a deck surrounding a swimming pool with its own waterfall.

Services: Laundry, anything else you need. Management leaves most guest contact to a highly efficient, unobtrusive Fijian staff.

Facilities: Nine-hole golf course, tennis and croquet courts, sailing, fishing.

TOBERUA ISLAND RESORT, P.O. Box 567, Suva, Fiji Islands. Tel. 479177 or 302356 in Suva, or toll free 800/426-3610 in the U.S. Fax 302215. Telex 2350. 14 bungalows. MINIBAR **Location:** Toberua Island, 12 miles off Viti Levu. Reached by 45-minute taxi-and-boat trip from Nausori Airport or Suva.

$ Rates: F$230–F$270 ($161–$189) single; F$252–F$297 ($176–$208) double. AE, DC, MC, V.

Michael Dennis's resort is one of the oldest in Fiji but still going strong. He has comfortable bures and a main building on his tiny palm-dotted and beach-encircled atoll. The island is too flat to draw moisture from the sky; therefore, it isn't in the "rain belt" created by the mountains behind Suva and the rest of eastern Viti Levu. In fact, Toberua gets so much sunshine and so little rain that fresh water is brought by barge over from the "mainland." Guests enjoy such an easygoing life-style that they are warned to take at least 4 days to slow down and grow accustomed to the pace. They can sunbathe, swim, snorkel, collect shells, sail, windsurf, visit nearby uninhabited islands for picnics, fish in the lagoon for their evening's meal, or play a round of "reef golf" (which is exactly what it sounds like: holes and fairways out on the reef at low tide). The Toberua's large, Fijian-style bures are constructed of native materials. Each has its own modern bath with indoor and outdoor entrances.

Anyone who gets "bure fever" after a few days on the small atoll can charter the *Adi Toberua*, a cross between a cabin cruiser and a comfortable houseboat, for trips to nearby destinations such as the old capital of Levuka on Ovalau Island. Overnight-charter rates are F$400 ($280) per night for two persons, F$80 ($56) for each additional person, including all meals, a captain, and a cook.

Dining/Entertainment: Three excellent meals a day at Toberua cost F$55 ($38.50) per person.

Services: Laundry.

Facilities: Snorkeling equipment, sailboats, Windsurfers, fishing equipment for free; fishing trips for F$60 ($42) per hour, scuba tanks refilled for a small charge (bring your own equipment).

CHAPTER 14

LEVUKA, SAVUSAVU & TAVEUNI

Compared to populated and developed Viti Levu, the islands of eastern and northern Fiji look and feel more like those we saw in Polynesia. The rolling plains of northern Vanua Levu, the country's second-largest island, are devoted to sugarcane, but elsewhere rugged mountains drop to lagoonside coconut plantations, and smiling people go about life at the ageless pace of tropical islands everywhere.

1. LEVUKA

In Levuka, Fiji's first capital, the past is unusually well preserved. Towns like Avarua in the Cook Islands, Apia in Western Samoa, and Nuku'alofa in Tonga have retained an air of the slow, easygoing days of the old South Pacific, but few have changed as little as this sleepy village on the ruggedly beautiful island of Ovalau, off eastern Viti Levu.

Indeed, you may think you've slipped into the "Twilight Zone" as you stroll along historic Beach Street on Levuka's curving waterfront—everything seems to be from a century earlier: ramshackle dry-goods stores with false fronts, clapboard houses with tin roofs to keep them dry and shaded verandas to keep them cool, and round clocks in the baroque tower of Sacred Heart Catholic Church. Where the regular streets end, "step streets" climb to more houses up near the base of the jagged cliffs towering over the town.

Not that Levuka hasn't changed at all since its 19th-century days as one of the South Pacific's most notorious seaports. All but one of the 50 or more hotels and saloons that dispensed rum and other pleasures disappeared long ago. The sole survivor—the Royal Hotel—is now a quiet, family-run establishment. The fist-fighting whalers and drifting beachbums went the way of the square-rigged ships that once crowded the blue-green harbor beyond the row of glistening ficus trees and freshly painted park benches along Beach Street. Gone, too, are the pioneering merchants and copra planters who established Levuka as Fiji's first European-style town in the 1830s and who for years carried guns to protect themselves from its ruffians.

But Levuka still looks much the same as it did in 1882, when the colonial administration pulled up stakes and moved to Suva. The 1,200-foot-tall walls of basalt, which caused the demise of Levuka by preventing expansion, create a soaring backdrop that puts Ovalau in the big leagues of dramatic tropical beauty.

Despite its history, beauty, and extremely hospitable residents, Levuka is relatively off the beaten tourist track. The volcano that created Ovalau has eroded into such rugged formations that it has very little flat land and only one decent beach; therefore, the island has not attracted resort or hotel development. All of Levuka's accommodations are basic and fall in the budget category. Couple that with low-cost tours and activities, and you have a backpacker's heaven. Unless you're willing to put up with very little in the way of comforts and amenities, make Levuka a day-trip (see "Levuka" under "What to See and Do" in Chapter 13).

GETTING THERE

Fiji Air has morning and afternoon flights from Nausori to Ovalau's unpaved airstrip, which is at Bureta, on the island's west coast. Levuka is halfway around Ovalau on the east coast. An unpaved road circles the island along its shoreline and makes the bus ride from airport to town a sightseeing excursion in its own right. (*Note:* Airport transfers cost F$4 [$3] each way.)

More adventurous souls can watch Ovalau's jagged green peaks go by from one of the **ferries** that run between Viti Levu and Levuka. Most boats land on the northwest coast, a 30-minute bus or taxi ride from Levuka.

For the details, see "Getting Around" in Chapter 11.

GETTING AROUND

Levuka is a small town, and your feet can get you to most places in 10 minutes.

For **taxis,** call **Vuniba Taxis** (tel. 44322) or **B. Murgan Transport Co.** (tel. 44180). Fares are F$1 (70¢) in town plus F50¢ (40¢) per kilometer thereafter; F$15 ($10.50) to the airport; F$20 ($14) to Lovoni; F$40 ($28) around Ovalau. Be sure you and the driver agree on a fare before departing.

For **rental cars,** contact Mary Yee at the Old Capitol Inn (tel. 44045). She charges F$72 ($50.50) a day. To rent a Mini Moke (a small, canvas-topped vehicle), contact Ovalau Holiday Resort (tel. 44329). Mokes cost F$30 ($21).

Local **buses** depart for the outlying villages from Beach Street about four times a day. They don't run after dark, so make sure you find out from the driver when—and if—he returns to Levuka at the end of the day. Fares should be no more than F$1.50 ($1). Buses to **Lovoni,** a Fijian village up in the old volcanic crater, leave at 7:30am, noon, and 5pm. They leave Lovoni for Levuka at 6:30am, 8:30am, and 5pm. **Mesake's Carriers** leave town for Rukuruku village and Ovalau's only sand beach Monday to Saturday 6:30am and 1:30pm; they depart Rukuruku for town at 7:30am, 11am, 4pm and 5pm. Fares to Lovoni or Rukuruku are F$1.20 (85¢).

FAST FACTS LEVUKA

The following facts apply to Levuka and Ovalau. If you don't see an item here, look in the "Fast Facts for Fiji (Chapter 11), Nadi (Chapter 12), and Suva (Chapter 13).

Currency Exchange Westpac Bank has an agency opposite the Levuka Community Centre (old Morris Hedstrom store). Hours are Mon–Thurs 9:30am–3pm, Fri 9:30am–4pm.

Dentist See "Hospital," below.

Doctor See "Hospital," below.

Emergencies The emergency phone number is 000.

Hospital The government maintains a small hospital in Levuka (tel. 44105).

Information The best source is Kathy Hoare, proprietor of Café Levuka (see "Where to Dine," below). The staff at the Levuka Community Centre (tel. 44356) can provide information. The center is open Mon–Fri 9am–1pm and 2–5pm, Sat 9am–1pm.

Libraries The community center has a small library. You pay F$3 ($2) registration fee to use the library and make a refundable F$10 ($7) deposit to check out books.

Police The Royal Fiji Police station is opposite the Masonic Lodge (tel. 44222).

Post Office The post office is behind the Café Levuka.

Safety See "Police," above.

Telephone/Telegrams/Telex Public phones are scarce on Ovalau. Place long distance and international calls at the post office. **The local numbers on Ovalau will change** to six digits as Fiji upgrades its telephone system. If you call a number listed in this chapter and don't get an answer, call 011 for directory assistance.

WHAT TO SEE & DO

AROUND LEVUKA

A walking tour of Levuka should take about 1 hour. Begin at the **Levuka Community Centre,** across the street from the Fiji Air office, in the quaint old **Morris Hedstrom** store, which Levukans Percy Morris and Maynard Hedstrom built in 1878. The trading company they founded, now one of the South Pacific's largest department store chains, pulled out of Levuka entirely a century later. After the company donated the dilapidated structure to the National Trust of Fiji, the Levuka Historical and Cultural Society raised money throughout the country to restore the structure and install a small branch of the Fiji Museum, a public library, a meeting hall, a crafts and recreational center, and a small garden. The furniture is made of timbers salvaged from the rotting floor. Mrs. Dora Patterson, matriarch of the Patterson Brothers Shipping Company family, donated the museum's waterside garden; she could oversee the project from her colonial-style mansion on the hill above Levuka. From the community center, head south.

The post office stands at the entrance to the **Queens Wharf** on the south side of the museum. The drinking fountain in front marks the site of a carrier-pigeon service that linked Suva and Levuka in the late 1800s. The Queens Wharf is one of Fiji's three ports of entry (Suva and Lautoka are the others), but along with domestic cargo, it now primarily handles exports from the Pacific Fishing Company's **tuna cannery,** established by a Japanese firm in 1964. You can follow your nose to the cannery in the industrial buildings south of the pier.

Keep going south to **Nasova,** a village on the shore of the little bay about ½ mile south of the cannery. Chief Cakobau signed the deed that ceded Fiji to Great Britain here. The site is now marked by three stones in the center of a grassy park at the water's edge. Plaques commemorate the signing ceremony on October 10, 1874; Fiji's gaining independence exactly 96 years later; and the 1974 centennial celebration of the deed of cession. A Fijian-style thatch meetinghouse stands across the road.

South of Nasova, the **Old Levuka Cemetery** is tended to perfection by prison inmates.

Backtrack to the weathered storefronts of Levuka's 2-block-long business district along **Beach Street.** Saloons no longer line this promenade; instead, the Indian- and Chinese-owned stores now dispense a variety of dry goods and groceries. On the horizon beyond the ficus trees and park benches lie the smoky-blue outlines of Wakaya, Makogai, and other members of the Lomaiviti (Central Fiji) group of islands. The green cliffs still reach skyward behind the stores, hemming in Levuka and its narrow valley. Walk along the waterfront, and don't hesitate to stick your head into the dry-goods stores.

After the last store stands the **Church of the Sacred Heart,** a wooden building fronted by a baroque stone tower. It was built by the Marist Fathers who came to Levuka in 1858. In case you missed the number of chimes marking the time, the clock in the tower strikes once on the hour—and again, for good measure, 1 minute later. Across Beach Street stands a **World War I monument** to the Fijian members of the Fiji Labour Corps who were killed assisting the British in Europe.

Walk on across Totoga Creek to low **Niukaubi Hill,** on top of which is another

NORTHERN FIJI

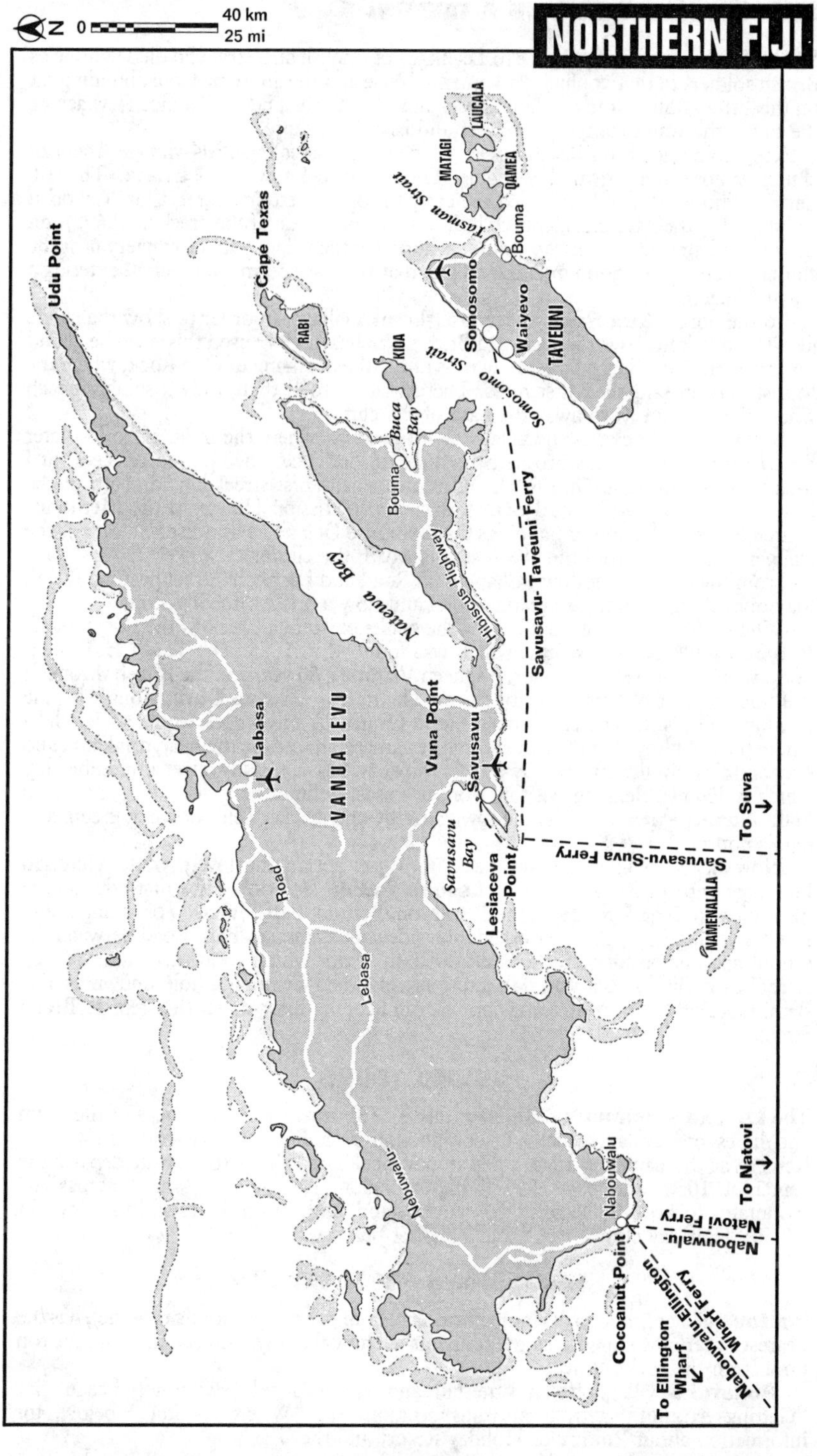

N
0 40 km
25 mi

Udu Point
Cape Texas
RABI
Labasa
Road
VANUA LEVU
Lebasa
Natewa Bay
Bouma
Buca Bay
KIOA
Nebuwalu-
Vuna Point
Hibiscus Highway
Savusavu Bay
Savusavu
Lesiaceva Point
Somosomo Strait
Tasman Strait
MATAGI
LAUCALA
QAMEA
Somosomo
Waiyevo
Bouma
TAVEUNI
Savusavu- Taveuni Ferry
Savusavu-Suva Ferry
Cocoanut Point
Nabouwalu
To Ellington Wharf
Nabouwalu-Ellington Wharf Ferry
Nabouwalu-Natovi Ferry
To Natovi
NAMENALALA
To Suva

World War I monument, this one to Levukans of English ancestry who died fighting as British soldiers in that conflict. Parliament House and the Supreme Court building sat on this little knoll before the capital was moved to Suva. They had a nice view across the town, the waterfront, and the reef and islands offshore.

Keep going north on Beach Street, which soon passes the 1904-vintage Anglican church before arriving in the original Fijian village known as **Levuka.** The Tui Levuka who lived here befriended the early European settlers. Later, Chief Cakobau worshiped in the Methodist church built on the south side of the creek in 1869. John Brown Williams, the American consul, is buried in the village's Old Cemetery near the church. (Remember, good manners dictate that you have permission before entering a Fijian village.)

To the north, **Gun Rock** towers over Levuka village. In order to show the chiefs just how much firepower it packed, a British warship in 1849 used this steep headland for target practice. Beach Street now runs under the overhang of Gun Rock, where the Marist Fathers said their first mass. There was no road then, only a shingly beach where the sea had worn away the base of the cliff.

Beyond Gun Rock lies the village of **Vagadaci,** where the duke of York—later King George V—and his brother, the duke of Clarence, once played cricket, but I usually turn around at Gun Rock and return to the first street inland south of the hospital. It leads to the **199 steps** that climb Mission Hill from the Methodist church to the collection of buildings that comprise Delana Methodist School. For the energetic, the view from the 199th step is worth the climb.

From the church, cut down Chapel Hill Road and Langham Street past the Royal, the South Pacific's oldest operating hotel and now a good refueling stop.

When refreshed, stroll south along the banks of Totoga Creek to the Roman-style **Polynesia Masonic Lodge,** which was founded in 1875. The **Town Hall,** next door, was built in 1898 in honor of Queen Victoria's 50 years on the British throne; it still houses most of Levuka's city offices. The nearby **Ovalau Club,** along with the bowling club, is the center of social life in Ovalau. A throwback to the social clubs where the "old boys" of the British Empire gathered to escape the heat, drink gin, and play snooker (billiards), the Ovalau Club today has a racially diverse membership which welcomes clean-cut visitors from overseas. Behind the lodge, club, and Town Hall, **Nasau Park** serves as the town's rugby and cricket field, bowling green, and tennis courts.

Now head uphill along the creek until you get to the lovely white Victorian buildings with broad verandas of **Levuka Public School,** Fiji's first educational institution (opened in 1879) and still one of its best. A row of mango and sweet-smelling frangipani trees shade the sidewalk known as Bath Road between the school and the rushing creek. Walk up Bath Road, which soon turns into a "step street" as it climbs to a waterfall and concrete-lined swimming hole known as The Bath. Cool off at this refreshing spot before heading back down the steps to Beach Street.

GUIDED TOURS

The **Levuka Community Centre** (tel. 44356) provides guided tours of the town and hikes on Ovalau, usually in conjunction with Fiji Air's day-trips from Suva. Reserve at the center at least a day in advance. The 2-hour town tour departs the center at 10am and costs F$4 ($3) per person. All-day bush walks across the mountains to Lovoni village in the center island, with return by local bus, cost F$5 ($3.50). Half-day climbs to Ovalau's highest peak cost F$3 ($2).

EXCURSIONS FROM LEVUKA

Waitovu village, about a 30-minute walk north of town (look for its mosque), has the nearest waterfall to town. Ask the residents to show the way. You can dive into the top pool from the rocks above.

Rukuruku village has a waterfall and Ovalau's sole swimming beach. See "Getting Around," above, for transportation. See "Where to Stay," below, for information about Rukuruku Holiday Resort and the beach.

Lovoni, the picturesque Fijian village in the crater of Ovalau's extinct volcano, is a popular day-trip by guided hike or via local bus. In precolonial days, Lovoni was the home of ferocious warriors who stormed down to the coast and attacked Levuka on several occasions. Chief Cakobau settled that problem by luring them into town to talk peace; instead, he captured them all and deported them to other parts of Fiji. Today's Lovonians have seen so many travelers wandering around their village that most are adept at pleasantly smiling while ignoring you. The houses are of wood with corrugated iron roofs. See "Getting Around" and "Guided Tours," above, for more information.

Leleuvia Island, a tiny atoll between Viti Levu and Ovalau with gorgeous beaches, is a popular retreat for backpackers and anyone else who wants to camp or stay in primitive thatch bures. Guests can sunbathe (topless if desired) and swim and snorkel over some lovely reefs. A small shop sells beer and some groceries, and the staff prepares basic meals. Rates, including three meals, are F$17 ($12) for a dorm bunk, F$20 ($14) per person in bures, and F$15 ($10.50) per person for campsite (bring your own tent). Transportation is by Emosi's Express Shipping, which leaves Levuka at 8am Monday to Saturday. The boat ride costs F$10 ($7) each way, but you can go from Leleuvia to Viti Levu. Book at the Old Capitol Inn (tel. 44057) in Levuka.

Caqeli Island (Than-*kay*-lee) also has camping and primitive bures. Run by the local Methodist church, who provide simple meals, it is more peaceful and gets fewer visitors than nearby Leleuvia. Rates are slightly less than at Leleuvia. Book at Paak Kum Loong Restaurant (no phone) on Beach Street.

Lost Island, or Yanuca Taitai, is large enough for bush walks ("hikes" in American English) by guests who go for the day. It's run by villagers who prepare lovo-style lunches on a beach, provided five or more guests attend. Inquire at the Levuka Community Centre (tel. 44356) at least a day in advance.

WHERE TO STAY

ROYAL HOTEL, P.O. Box 47, Levuka, Ovalau, Fiji Islands. Tel. 44024. 14 rms (none with bath), 3 cottages. **Location:** On Totoga Creek, just off Beach St.

$ Rates: F$14 ($10) single; F$19 ($13.50) double; F$50 ($35) cottage. No credit cards.

Even if you don't stay at the South Pacific's oldest operating hotel, have a look at its public rooms. It was built about 1852 and "modernized" in the 1890s. Little imagination is required to picture W. Somerset Maugham or Robert Louis Stevenson relaxing in the comfortable rattan chairs of the Royal's lounge, slowly sipping gin and tonics at its polished bar, or playing a game of snooker at its antique billiard table.

One of Levuka's fine old families, the Ashleys, has run the Royal for more than half a century with such attentive care that it seems more like a pension full of antiques than a hotel. In contrast to the ancient and very basic rooms, the three modern cottages are the pick of Levuka's lodgings. The Ashleys serve three meals a day in the dining room.

MAVIDA LODGE, P.O. Box 91, Levuka, Ovalau, Fiji Islands. Tel. 44051. 5 rms (none with bath). **Location:** Beach St., on the waterfront, north end of Levuka.

$ Rates (including continental breakfast and tax): F$6.60 ($4.50) bed; F$16 ($11) single or double. No credit cards.

This clapboard cottage has all the trappings of a turn-of-the-century Levukan home, including antique beds with mosquito nets sweeping down from their 7-foot-tall headboards. As with many such high-ceilinged colonial houses, an enclosed veranda–living room across the front funnels the trade winds into a hallway down the center of the cottage. Guests share two baths and a communal kitchen. Only breakfast is served.

OLD CAPITOL INN, P.O. Box 50, Levuka, Ovalau, Fiji Islands. Tel. 44057. 3 rms (none with bath), 4 bunks. **Location:** Convent Rd., off Beach St. in center of town.

$ Rates (including breakfast and tax): F$7 ($5) bunk; F$10 ($7) single; F$17 ($12) double. No credit cards.

Emosi and Mary Yee (he runs Emosi's Express Shipping) have simple but clean rooms (one of them dormitory-style) on the second floor of their storefront building. Their downstairs dining room offers home-cooked roast chicken or Chinese-style dishes with chicken, fish, or beef.

OLD CAPITOL INN II, P.O. Box 5, Levuka, Ovalau, Fiji Islands. Tel. 44013. 12 rms (none with bath), 15 bunks. **Location:** Beach St., north end of town.

$ Rates (including breakfast and tax): F$7 ($5) bunk; F$10 ($7) single; F$17 ($12) double. No credit cards.

Clara and Ned Fisher refurbished this colonial-style waterfront house and opened it in competition with her parents, Emosi and Mary Yee of the original Old Capitol Inn. The house has a sun room across the front. The basically furnished rooms flank a central hallway which leads to a communal kitchen and washing machine.

RUKURUKU HOLIDAY RESORT, P.O. Box 112, Levuka, Ovalau, Fiji Islands. Tel. 312507 in Suva. 15 bunks, 4 cottages (all with bath). **Location:** Rukuruku village, 17km (10 miles) from Levuka. Local bus stops 1km (.6 mile) from the resort.

$ Rates: F$7 ($5) dorm bunk; F$5 ($3.50) per person campground; F$15 ($10.50) per person in cottage; F$60 ($42) cottage. No credit cards.

A river separates this low-budget retreat from the Fijian village of the same name. The bungalows are of modern construction and have electricity and cold-water showers. A small restaurant offers meals, and a bar provides libation. The nearby black-sand beach is the best on Ovalau, although that's not saying much. Snorkeling offshore, however, is excellent.

WHERE TO DINE

CAFE LEVUKA, Beach St., next to Levuka Community Centre. No phone.

Cuisine: REGIONAL. **Reservations:** Not accepted.

$ Prices: Sandwiches and burgers F$2–F$3 ($1.50–$2), meals F$3–F$6 ($2–$4). No credit cards.

Open: Mon–Sat 9am–6pm, Sun 9am–2pm.

★ Kathy Hoare, an American from New Jersey by way of San Francisco, settled in Levuka, opened this storefront café, and quickly cornered the traveler's market. Guests show up not just for her cappuccino, espresso coffee, fresh fruit juices, cooked breakfasts, sandwiches, burgers, and meals such as fish in lolo, but also to have a look at her information book, which has the latest on Levuka and Ovalau. It should be your first stop.

PAAK KUM LOONG RESTAURANT, Beach St., next to the Catholic church. No phone.

Cuisine: CHINESE/INDIAN. **Reservations:** Not accepted.

$ Prices: Main courses F$2.50–F$5 ($2–$3.50). No credit cards.

Open: Breakfast and lunch Mon–Sat 8am–2pm; dinner Mon–Sat 6–9pm.

There's nothing fancy about this basic but clean establishment with a take-out counter in the storefront, a dining room, and a "Fishermen's Lounge" to one side. The food is simple curries or Cantonese dishes such as chow mein, chop suey, and meat and poultry in sweet-and-sour or black-bean sauce.

2. SAVUSAVU

Except for a long peninsula jutting out toward the east from its south coast, most of Vanua Levu's 2,140 square miles lie in a southwest-northeast configuration. A

IMPRESSIONS

They passed the kava cups around and drank deep of the milky, slightly stupefying grog. They chatted quietly under the starlight. They laughed, one would propose a song, and then they would break into chorus after chorus, in perfect harmony, of some of the great Fijian folk songs, songs that told of sagas of long ago and far away, and always of war and peace, of love, and of triumph over disaster.

—Simon Winchester, 1990

spine of volcanic mountains runs lengthwise down the center of the island, trapping moisture from the prevailing southeast trade winds and giving the rolling hills and deltas of the north shore an ideal climate for growing sugarcane. Consequently, the flat area around the main town of **Labasa** is one of Fiji's prime sugar-producing regions, but it holds little interest for most travelers except as a starting point for a spectacular bus ride across Vanua Levu (see below).

On the south coast, however, the usually cloud-topped mountains quickly give way to narrow, well-watered coastal plains, ideal for copra plantations. In fact, until the Great Depression of the 1930s, copra production made picturesque **Savusavu** a thriving European settlement. Once again fast developing because of tourism, Savusavu is Vanua Levu's major attraction, primarily because of its volcanic hot springs and magnificent scenic harbor—a bay so large and well protected by the steep surrounding mountains that the U.S. Navy chose it as a possible "hurricane hole" during World War II. They never had to use it, but much of the Pacific Fleet could have used it to escape a passing cyclone.

The town sits snugly behind a small island in the southeastern corner of Savusavu Bay. The road from Labasa runs along the eastern shore, through town, and out to Lesiaceva Point at the end of a peninsula that forms the southern side of the bay and protects it from the Koro Sea. The Hibiscus Highway starts at Savusavu and cuts across the hilly peninsula to the airport before continuing along the south shore to Buca Bay.

GETTING THERE

Most visitors to Savusavu arrive at the grass-strip airport on Vanua Levu's south coast. The hotels send buses to meet guests who have reservations. Taxi fare into town is F$2 ($1.50).

Ferries land at Savusavu's main wharf, which is on the west end of town. See "Getting Around" in Chapter 11 for details.

BY BUS ACROSS VANUA LEVU TO TAVEUNI

Adventurous travelers can make a 2-day trip all the way from Viti Levu to Taveuni without flying. First comes a bus-ferry trip from Suva or Nadi to Nabouwalu on Vanua Levu, then a 3-hour bus trip along Vanua Levu's north coast to Labasa, then another 3 hours by bus across Vanua Levu to Savusavu (where you must overnight), and from there by bus to Buca Bay, where a boat leaves for Taveuni Monday to Saturday. An alternative to the Viti Levu–Nabouwalu ferry is a morning Fiji Air flight from Suva to Labasa and an afternoon bus ride across the mountains to Savusavu.

Labasa to Savusavu

Local buses to Savusavu leave the market by the river bridge in Labasa at 7am, 9am, 12:30pm, and 3:15pm. The trip is best taken in the dry season, from April to October. The Labasa-Savusavu bus fare is F$6 ($4).

The road runs through the silvery cane fields on the flat Labasa River delta, then up through valleys with patches of cane trailing off to either side. To the south, mountain peaks stick up like points in the icing of a cake; to the north, the blue sea recedes into the distance. As the road twists into higher altitudes, pine forests take over, then thick native bush. The air streaming through the open windows becomes refreshingly cool at the high altitudes. The bus rounds a curve and there to the side is a Fijian village of thatch bures, one of many in the highlands surrounded by bush gardens of bananas, tapioca, and taro. Carrying baskets plaited of green pandanus especially for the trip, Fijian women with their grandchildren climb on the bus at one village and jump off at the next. For an hour the road twists and turns from village to village along slender ridges that separate deep valleys to either side. Then it rounds a bend and below you in the distance lies the blue splendor of Savusavu Bay. Down you go, ears popping, until the valley floor flattens into plains ending at the bay.

Savusavu to Taveuni

At the Savusavu market you can connect with the daily 10:30am bus to Buca Bay, a ride of 47 miles along the Hibiscus Highway on Vanua Levu's eastern peninsula. Despite its name, the road is neither lined with hibiscus nor is it a highway. It's not just another unpaved Fiji road, however, for it runs through a series of copra plantations on a narrow coastal plain. The palms arch overhead, the azure lagoon lies to one side, and the mountains rise slowly on the other. Cattle graze lazily beneath the palms, and occasionally you catch a whiff of acrid smoke drifting from copra dryers back among the trees. After an hour the road begins to climb through rolling hills, up through Fijian villages and gardens to the crest of a range. From the top comes a sudden view of round, nearly landlocked Buca Bay.

The bus will continue on to Napuka, an old Catholic mission station at the end of the peninsula, but first it stops at a Buca Bay copra plantation. There awaits a small ferry that could have played the title role in *The African Queen*. As soon as its passengers are brought out on skiffs from a black-sand beach, this putt-putting old craft gets under way for the rocking, rolling 2-hour trip across the Somosomo Strait to Taveuni.

The ferry doesn't wait around once the bus arrives, and there are no rest rooms, stores, or snack bars between Savusavu and Taveuni. In other words, take care of your needs as best you can and bring along something to eat and drink. The boat cruises over calm waters behind the reef for the first ½ hour, so a cruising picnic might be in order then.

The bus from Savusavu to Buca Bay and the ferry over to Taveuni cost F$10 ($7). The entire trip requires about 5 hours.

GETTING AROUND

Some 30 **taxis**—an incredible number for such a small place—gather by the market in Savusavu when not hauling passengers. Fares from Savusavu are F$2 ($1.50) to the airport, F$5 ($3.50) to Namale Plantation Resort, F$10 ($4) to Kon Tiki Resort, and F$5 ($3.50) to Lesiaceva Point Beach Apartments and Na Koro Resort.

Avis (tel. 850184), next to the Shell station on the main street, rents air-conditioned sedans and four-wheel-drive vehicles. Rates start at F$35 ($24.50) a day plus 35¢ (25¢) per kilometer, or F$79 ($55.50) with unlimited kilometers. Insurance in either case is F$15 ($10.50) a day. If you rent a car, remember that few roads are paved on Vanua Levu, that the mountain roads can be washed out during heavy rains, and that finding gasoline outside Labasa or Savusavu is a challenge.

Local buses fan out from the Savusavu market to various points on the island. Most of them make three or four runs a day to outlying destinations, but ask the drivers when they will return to town. The longest runs should cost no more than F$6 ($4), with local routes in the F55¢ to F$1 (40¢ to 70¢) range.

Buses to Na Koro Resort on Lesiaceva Point and the closest beach to town, leave the market at 6am, 7am, 10am, noon, 2:15pm, 4pm, and 5:15pm Monday to Saturday. The fare is F45¢ (35¢).

SAVUSAVU

The following facts apply to Savusavu. If an item isn't here, check the "Fast Facts" in Chapters 11, 12, and 13.

Currency Exchange Westpac Bank, ANZ Bank, and National Bank of Fiji have offices on the main street.

Dentist See "Hospital," below.

Doctor Dr. Joeli Taoi (tel. 850346 or 850186 at home) has an office over the Anderson Fong store on the east end of Savusavu. A Fijian, he was trained in New Zealand and is much admired by the local expatriate residents.

Drugstores See "Hospital," below.

Emergencies Phone 000.

Hospitals The government hospital (tel. 850800) is east of town in the government compound.

Police The police station (tel. 850222) is east of town.

Post Office The post office is east of town.

Safety Savusavu generally is a safe place to visit, but don't tempt the mortals. Keep an eye on your personal property.

Shoe Repairs Savusavu Footwear (tel. 850239) is on the main street.

Telephone/Telegrams/Telex Go to the post office.

WHAT TO SEE & DO

STROLLING AROUND SAVUSAVU

For practical purposes, there is only one street in Savusavu, and that runs along the shore for about a mile. Highlights of a stroll along this bay-hugging avenue are the gorgeous scenery, the busy waterfront market, and a stop at the volcanic **hot springs.** Steam from underground rises eerily from the rocky shore on the west end of town, and you can see more white clouds floating up from the ground beyond the sports field behind the Shell station. To reach the springs, go inland at the Shell station, then bear left at the oil storage tanks. A concrete pot has been built to make a natural stove in which local residents place meals to slowly cook.

SCUBA DIVING

Diving in Fiji's North, which includes Savusavu and Taveuni, is among the world's best. Most of the resorts have complete diving facilities.

H2O Sportz welcomes nonguests to join it at Na Koro Resort (tel. 850156 or 850188). It has beach dives for F$20 ($14), two-tank boat dives for F$85 ($59.50), and teaches PADI open-water certification courses for F$350 ($245).

Curly Carswell of **Sea Fiji Travel,** Post Office, Savusavu (tel. 850345, fax 850344), specializes in diving vacations. Curly's office is in the Copra Shed on Savusavu's waterfront.

SWIMMING & SNORKELING

The nearest beach is on Lesiaceva Point about 3 miles west of town. Take the frequent bus (see "Getting Around," above). There's a wonderful beach partially shaded by a huge tree just outside Na Koro Resort, which is the end of the line.

YACHT CHARTERS

Emerald Yacht Charters, P.O. Box 225, Savusavu (tel. 850441), takes guests on all-day sailboat cruises of Savusavu Bay for F$50 ($35) per person, including lunch, and on sunset cruises for F$30 ($21) per person. The sailboats range in length from 36 to 45 feet and are available for extended cruises. Fiji's reef-infested waters are too dangerous for "bareboat" chartering, so the owners of the boats go along as captain and crew.

SHOPPING

Pickings are slim in Savusavu, but the **Copra Shed,** a shopping center in a converted copra storage shed, has two small boutiques with a few handcraft items and colorful tie-dyed sarongs. The shed is a green-roofed building on the water, about midway through town where the main street curves around a point.

EVENING ENTERTAINMENT

The expensive resorts provide nightly entertainment for their guests. Otherwise, there's not much going on in town after dark. Visitors are welcome at the **Planter's Club** (tel. 850233) in a low-slung building near the west end of town. This holdover from the colonial era has a "snooker" pool table and a pleasant bar. It's open from 10am to 10pm Monday to Saturday. Closed Christmas and Good Friday. Admission is free (bona-fide visitors are asked to sign in). Drinks and beers cost from F85¢ to F$2 (60¢ to $1.50). **Savusavu Yacht Club** (no phone), upstairs in the Copra Shed overlooking the harbor, also welcomes visitors. It's open noon to 8pm Monday to Friday, 10am to 9pm Saturday.

WHERE TO STAY

Savusavu has two properties that you will hear about. **Namale Plantation Resort** was being sold for the second time in 2 years during my recent visit, and **Kontiki Resort** was in receivership. Both were operating, and I am sure they will reappear in future editions. But for now, here are your choices.

NA KORO RESORT, Post Office, Savusavu, Fiji Islands. Tel. Savusavu 850118, or toll free 800/624-3524 in the U.S. Fax 850340. Telex 8297. 20 bungalows. MINIBAR **Location:** Lesiaceva Point, 3 miles west of town.

$ Rates: F$190 ($133) single; F$220 ($154) double. AE, DC, MC, V.

This entire complex looks like an old-time Fijian village, with the bures built around two central buildings. Reception and the resort's bar are under a large roof built like a chief's bure; the dining room sits under a taller and more impressive roof constructed to resemble a priest's bure. These central buildings are joined for the convenience of guests, and they sit next to a deck-surrounded swimming pool just steps from one of the best beaches in the area. Snacks are available at the Bikini Bar during the day. Spacious bures of modern materials under natural thatch roofs have ceiling fans to augment the natural breeze flowing through floor-to-ceiling louvered windows that make up the front and rear walls. Water sports except scuba diving are included in the rates, as are trips into Savusavu some 5km (3 miles) away.

LESIACEVA POINT BEACH APARTMENTS, P.O. Box 57, Savusavu, Fiji Islands. Tel. 850250. Fax 850350. 2 apartments. **Location:** Lesiaceva Point, 3 miles west of town.

$ Rates: F$35 ($24.50) single, F$45 ($31.50) double; F$210 ($147) single weekly, F$270 ($189) double weekly. AE, DC, MC, V.

Australians Glenn and Rhonda Mulligan moved to Fiji in 1984, bought a house on the side of a hill on Lesiaceva Point, and turned the first floor of their new home into apartments. The living area of each has lounge furniture, a fully equipped kitchen, and metal over-and-under bunk beds for children. The Mulligans do not prepare meals, but Na Koro Resort is just 400 yards away. They will pick you up at the airport and take you to town to shop each day without additional charge, and they'll rent you a boat for coral viewing or exploring for F$20 ($14) per hour plus fuel. They will also organize tours of Vanua Levu, and they have access to a small island to which you can walk at low tide and where you can even camp overnight if you pay the local chief F$1.50 ($1) per person per night.

SAVUSAVU HOLIDAY HOUSE, P.O. Box 65, Savusavu, Fiji Islands. Tel. 850216 or 850149. 6 rms (none with bath). **Location:** In town behind Shell station's storage tanks.

$ Rates (including breakfast): F$11 ($7.50) single; F$16.50 ($11.50) double. No credit cards.

For guesthouse living, David Lal has clean and totally unpretentious rooms. Each has a table fan, two nightstands, and a coffee table, and guests can share the communal kitchen. David will do your laundry for free if you stay for long periods.

SAVUSAVU BAY ACCOMMODATION, P.O. Box 290, Labasa, Fiji Islands. Tel. 850100. 11 rms (all with bath). A/C (4 rooms) **Location:** Main street, west end of town.

$ Rates: F$11 ($7.50) single; F$16 ($11) double; F$22 ($15.50) single, F$25.50 ($18) double with air conditioning. No credit cards.

For less communal living, Lal Chand's establishment is upstairs in the storefront building housing the Patterson Brothers ferry agency on the main street in Savusavu. The rooms are small but clean, and a communal kitchen on an outside balcony is available for preparing light meals.

WHERE TO DINE

As the number of its visitors grows, Savusavu may get some fine eating establishments. The **Flying Fish Cafe** in the Copra Shed was in the process of opening during my recent visit and should be in business by the time you get there. Otherwise, the choices are two simple but clean Chinese restaurants on the main street in town. Neither takes credit cards.

Dishes at **Da Chang Restaurant,** in the block east of Westpac Bank (tel. 850420), range from F$2.50 to F$6.50 ($2 to $4.50). It's open Monday to Saturday from 9am to 3pm and 6 to 9pm.

Most meals at **Wing Yuen,** next to the National Bank of Fiji (tel. 850108), cost from F$2.50 to F$7 ($2 to $5), but for a treat, try the tasty prawn special at F$9 ($6.50). Hours are 8am to 2pm and 6 to 9pm daily.

3. A RESORT OFF SAVUSAVU

A question put to me frequently is, "Where can I go to a small island and completely get away from it all?" In answering, I mention several places where you can find a Robinson Crusoe–like existence; that is, without much in the way of amenities. Vava'u in Tonga and the Western Province of Solomon Islands leap to mind. But if you really want to get away from it all yet still have most of the comforts of home at a reasonable price—plus a charming host couple to keep you entertained in a low-key, engaging manner—I suggest you consider joining the Moodys.

Tom and Joan Moody (she pronounces her name "Joanne") left western Pennsylvania in the 1960s to work at various resorts in the Florida Keys and the Caribbean. They scraped together some capital and in 1974 opened a small, isolated resort in Panama's San Blas Islands, catering to serious scuba divers and others who just wanted a total escape. Terrorists attacked their peaceful outpost in 1981, however, shooting and nearly killing Tom and tying Joan up. Fortunately, Tom survived. They soon sold out and left Panama.

After searching the South Pacific, they settled on Namenalala and in 1984 started slowly building their very unusual little hideaway.

Dragon-shaped Namenalala is little more than a rocky ridge protruding from the sea and covered with dense native forest and bush. A huge barrier reef sweeps down from Vanua Levu and creates a gorgeous lagoon in which Tom can indulge his passion for diving. The Moodys have designated most of Namenalala as a nature preserve in order to protect a large colony of boobies that nest on the island, and sea turtles that climb onto the beaches to lay their eggs from November through February. In other words, the setting is remote and interesting. So is their little resort:

MOODY'S NAMENALALA, Private Mail Bag, Savusavu, Fiji Islands. Tel. 813764. 5 bungalows. **Location:** Namenalala Island, Koro Sea, 1 hour by chartered seaplane from Nadi, 3 hours by boat from Savusavu.

$ **Rates** (including meals and fishing and snorkeling trips): F$176 ($123) single or double; F$70 ($49) per person per day for meals, including wine at dinner. AE, MC, V. **Closed:** Mid-Mar to mid-May.

The Moodys perched all but one of their comfortable bungalows up on the ridge so that each has a commanding view of the ocean but not of one another. Each of the hexagonal structures resembles a tree house; in fact, the huge trunk of a tree grows right through the balcony surrounding one of the bures. Surely this was how Robinson Crusoe would have preferred to live.

A lack of fresh ground water and electricity adds to the effect. The "his and her" toilets in each bungalow are flushed with seawater, and rainwater takes care of drinking and bathing. Propane provides both lights and refrigeration (you will find a cigarette lighter in your room to ignite the gaslights at dusk). The entire walls of the bungalows slide back to render both views and cooling breezes, so you will sleep under a mosquito net. Instead of treading sandy paths among palm trees, you climb rocky pathways along the wooded ridge to the central building, where the Moodys provide excellent meals and ice upon which to pour the booze you bought at the duty-free store (they do not have a liquor license). After 1 day in their care, these "hardships" matter not at all.

Scuba diving among the colorful reefs and sea turtles costs extra. Tom does not teach scuba diving, so you must be certified in advance. Pathways down to four idyllic beaches have OCCUPIED/UNOCCUPIED signs to protect guests' privacy.

If you don't want to take the long boat trip from Savusavu, the Moodys will arrange to charter Turtle Island Airways' four-passenger seaplane. That costs F$660 ($462) round-trip, but Tom and Joan try to schedule their guests' arrivals and departures to limit the cost per person to about F$165 ($115).

4. TAVEUNI

Cigar-shaped Taveuni, Fiji's third-largest island, lies just 4 miles from Vanua Levu's eastern peninsula across the Somosomo Strait, one of the world's most famous scuba-diving spots. Although the island is only 6 miles wide, a volcanic ridge down Taveuni's 25-mile length soars to more than 4,000 feet, blocking the southeast trade winds and pouring as much as 30 feet of rain a year on the mountaintops and the island's rugged eastern side. Consequently, Taveuni's 9,000 residents (three-quarters of them Fijians) live in a string of villages along the gently sloping, less rainy but still lush western side. They own some of the country's most fertile and well-watered soil; hence Taveuni's nickname: "The Garden Isle."

Fiji's incumbent president and one of the nation's highest-ranking chiefs, Ratu Sir Penaia Ganilau, calls Taveuni's **Somosomo** village his home. A big new meeting-house was built there for the 1986 gathering of Fiji's Great Council of Chiefs.

Lake Tagimaucia, home of the rare tagimaucia flower that bears red blooms with white centers, is Taveuni's most famous sight. A shallow lake whose sides are ringed with mud flats and thick vegetation, it sits among the clouds in a volcanic crater at an altitude of more than 2,700 feet. Only hikers who are in shape should make the full-day trek to see the lake and back, and then only with a guide.

On the other hand, one of Fiji's finest waterfalls is easily accessible near the village of **Bouma,** on the northeast coast some 11 miles from the airport and 23 miles from the main village of **Waiyevo,** which sits halfway down the west coast. The falls plunge about 60 feet straight down into a cool, refreshing pool. Bouma's residents have built a very pleasant park around the falls and charge each person F$5 ($3.50) admission.

Half a mile south of Waiyevo, a brass plaque marks the 180th meridian of longitude. This would have been the international date line were it not for its slicing the Aleutians and Fiji in two and for Tonga's wish to be in Australia's day. The village of Waikiki sports a "Meridian Cinema."

GETTING THERE

See "Getting Around" in Chapter 11 and "By Bus Across Vanua Levu to Taveuni" in the Savusavu section, above.

Taveuni's airport is at its northern tip. The hotels send buses or hire taxis to pick up their guests. Taxis are available (see "Getting Around," below). The ferries land—and most commerce takes place—at Waiyevo.

GETTING AROUND

Taxis are reasonably plentiful, but they don't regularly ply the roads. Your hotel staff can hail one within a few minutes or you can phone 880424. Negotiate for a round-trip price if you're going out into the villages and have the driver wait for you. None of the taxis has a meter, but the fare from the airport to Navacoca (Qamea Landing) should be about F$10 ($7); to Dive Taveuni, F$2 ($1.50); to Waiyevo, F$12 ($8.50); to Bouma, F$15 ($10.50). Taxis will take you anywhere and back for about F$10 ($7) an hour.

Local **buses** fan out from Waiyevo to the outlying villages about three times a day. For example, one of them leaves Waiyevo for Bouma at 7am, 11am, and 3pm, returning shortly after they get there. The one-way fare to Bouma is F$2 ($1.50).

Kaba's Rentals (tel. 880233) in Nagara, the village next to Somosomo north of Waiyevo, rents Jeeps and sedans starting at F$30 ($21) a day plus F45¢ (35¢) a kilometer and F$10 ($7) for insurance. Fuel is included. **Caution:** Taveuni's roads are rough, winding, and narrow, and many local drivers—including bus drivers—seem to roar along at top speed. There can be very little room to get off the road when you meet a speeding vehicle, so drive at your own risk.

FAST FACTS: TAVEUNI

The following facts apply to Taveuni. If an item isn't here, see the "Fast Facts" in Chapters 11, 12, and 13.

Currency Exchange The *only* banking facility is a Westpac Bank agency at Waiyevo, and it's open just 2 days a week: Tues 1–4pm, Thurs 7:30–8:30am and 1–4:30pm. The hotels will cash traveler's checks.

Doctor There are no doctors on the island. See "Hospital," below.

Emergencies Phone 000.

Hospital The government hospital (tel. 880284) is in the government compound in the hills above Waiyevo, but it has only nurses on its staff. To get there, go uphill on the road opposite the Garden Island Resort, then take the right fork.

Police The police station (tel. 880222) is in the government compound. Go up the road opposite the Garden Island Resort, then take the left fork.

Post Office It's in the government compound (see "Police," above).

Safety Taveuni is relatively safe, but exercise caution if out late at night.

Telegrams/Telex See "Post Office," above.

WHAT TO SEE & DO

See "Getting Around," above, for information about how to get to the **Bouma waterfall** park. It's Taveuni's most popular outing.

SCUBA DIVING

The swift currents of the Somosomo Strait feed the soft corals on the Rainbow Reef and the White Wall between Taveuni and Vanua Levu, making them two of the world's most colorful and famous scuba-diving sites. In addition to the operators mentioned here, Matagi and Qamea resorts off Taveuni (see below) specialize in diving these great locations.

New Zealanders Ric and Do Cammick can accommodate up to 10 experienced divers at their **Dive Taveuni,** Post Office, Matei, Taveuni (tel. 880441, fax 880466). Their six bures surround their own home, which commands a magnificent view of the strait from a bluff 1 mile south of the airport and directly across the road from Maravu Plantation Resort. They charge U.S. $114 per person a day for a bed in one of the bungalows and three meals. Ric runs two dives a day to the Rainbow Reef, White Wall, and other spots around Taveuni at a cost of U.S. $75 a day. Bring your own regulators, wet suits, masks, fins, and snorkels. He supplies the weight belts, backpacks, and tanks. They limit the diving to persons both qualified and experienced.

Prices at the **Garden Island Resort** dive shop (tel. 880286) start at F$90 ($63) for a two-dive excursion. PADI learn-to-dive courses cost F$400 ($280).

Rainbow Divers (tel. 880125) specialize in the Vuna Lagoon off its base at Susie's Plantation Resort on Taveuni's south end. One-tank boat dives cost F$40 ($28); two tanks, F$70 ($49); dives off the beach, F$10 ($7); NAUI open-water courses, F$380 ($266), including accommodation at Susie's.

YACHT CHARTERS

Warwick and Diane Bain base their 45-foot steel-hull ketch *Seax of Legra* in Taveuni and take charter parties through the colorful waters around the island and nearby Vanua Levu. For a full week's worth of sailing, count on U.S. $3,800 for two persons, U.S. $4,200 for four, including meals. The Bains will pick you up at Savusavu. For more information, write them at P.O. Box 69, Waiyevo, Taveuni. They have no phone on board.

MOUNTAIN HIKES

Both **Maravu Plantation Resort** (tel. 880555) and **Garden Island Resort** (tel. 880286) organize bush walks that go through villages and up rivers to waterfalls to Desveoux Peak for a view down over Lake Tagimaucia, weather permitting. The knowledgeable local guides explain the wild orchids, exotic ferns, and bird life you will see. Prices range from F$40 to F$60 ($28 to $42) per person.

WHERE TO STAY

Campers who like to sleep by the sea can find an incredibly beautiful site at **Beverly Campground,** on the beach about a mile south of the airport (no phone). Large trees completely shade the sites and hang over portions of the lagoon-lapped shore. The ground has two rustic bures (they are little more than thatch tents with double beds), flush toilets, and a rudimentary beachside kitchen. Per person rates are F$10 ($7) in the bures, F$5 ($3.50) for a tent site, F$8 ($5.50) for a site and rental tent. **Tom Valentine Camping** (no phone) nearby has sites in the large lawn surrounding Tom's home, in which campers can share the toilets, cold-water showers, and kitchen with the Valentine family. Rates there are F$3 ($2) for one person, F$5 ($3.50) for two. Bring your own tent.

I haven't been there, but several backpackers have told me they enjoyed their time at **Susie's Plantation Resort** (tel. 880125), home of Rainbow Divers (see "What to See and Do," above). It's on Taveuni's southern end.

There are no restaurants on Taveuni, so you will have to dine or make your own meals at Maravu Plantation Resort or the Garden Island Resort.

MARAVU PLANTATION RESORT, Post Office, Matei, Taveuni, Fiji Islands. Tel. 880555. Fax 880600. Telex 8291. 10 bungalows (all with bath). **Location:** 1km (½-mile) south of airport.
$ Rates: F$150 ($105) single; F$180 ($126) double. AE, DC, MC, V.

$ A flight steward for Qantas Airways for 14 years, Ormond Eyre returned to his native Fiji in 1984, took over the family plantation, and began work on the resort. His great-great-grandfather came to Fiji from England with Sir Arthur Gordon, the first colonial governor, and was secretary to the lands commission until he married a Fijian chief's daughter from Beqa Island; banished from the Colonial Service, he became a successful planter and merchant. Maravu Plantation, however, came to Ormond through his mother's Swedish-Fijian side of the family.

Ormond has created an unusual retreat. His 10 bures, central building, and swimming pool exist among the palms of a working copra plantation (with some cocoa, coffee, and vanilla thrown in for diversification). The bures—three of which have outdoor showers—sit among grounds Ormond has carefully planted with bananas, papayas, and a plethora of ginger plants and wild orchids brought down from the mountains. Except for the main building, which has a thatch roof, the other buildings are constructed like planters' cabins. Tongue-in-groove boards and shady porches give them a decidedly colonial look. Very fine meals cost F$64 ($45) per person a day. Nonguests should call ahead for reservations.

GARDEN ISLAND RESORT, P.O. Box 1, Waiyevo, Taveuni, Fiji Islands. Tel. 880286, or toll free 800/521-7242 in U.S. and Canada. Fax 880288. Telex 8277. 30 rms. A/C TEL **Location:** Waiyevo village, 12km (7 miles) south of airport.

$ Rates: F$40 ($28) single; F$60 ($42) double. AE, DC, MC, V.

Built as a Travelodge in the 1960s, this hotel has been spiffed up with some new paint by owner Daniella Prym Waga, an American who married a Fijian. There's a swimming pool on the shores of Somosomo Strait, but no beach; much of the clientele are divers looking for less expensive accommodation than elsewhere on Taveuni and its nearby resorts. The motel-style rooms have the original furniture made brighter with white paint. Ten rooms are air conditioned; the others have ceiling fans. Some have telephones. A dining room serves plain meals at reasonable prices. As noted above, there is a dive shop.

KABA'S MOTEL AND GUEST HOUSE, P.O. Box 4, Waiyevo, Taveuni, Fiji Islands. Tel. 880233. Fax 880202. 5 rms (none with bath), 6 motel units. TV TEL **Location:** Nagara village, north of Waiyevo.

$ Rates: F$12 ($8.50) single room, F$20 ($14) double room; F$25 ($17.50) single unit, F$30 ($21) double unit. AE, MC, V.

Rates can be negotiable from November through April at this motel in Nagara, a predominantly Indian village next to Somosomo on the west coast. Opened in 1987, the six modern, comfortable, and airy motel units have kitchens, tiled floors, ceiling fans, radios, and even video movies at night. Rooms in the clean guesthouse next door are also negotiable from November through April or other slack times. The little complex is owned by the Kaba family, who run Kaba's Market nearby, the island's largest trading store. There is no dining room.

KOOL'S ACCOMMODATION, P.O. Box 10, Waiyevo, Taveuni, Fiji Islands. Tel. 880395. 6 rms (none with bath). **Location:** Nagara village, north of Waiyevo.

$ Rates: F$8 ($5.50) single, F$12 ($8.50) double. No credit cards.

This has small, rock-bottom rooms in a plywood-and-tin building behind a home a short walk south of Kaba's. The roof covers a picnic and communal kitchen area between the rooms and the shacklike toilets and cold-water showers. The electricity goes off at 9:30pm. You can buy beer on the premises.

5. RESORTS OFF TAVEUNI

The northern end of Taveuni gives way to a chain of small, rugged islands that are as beautiful as any in Fiji. Their steep, jungle-clad hills drop to rocky shorelines in most places, but here and there little shelves of land and narrow valleys are bordered by beautiful beaches. The sheltered waters between the islands cover colorful reefs, making the area a hotbed of scuba diving and snorkeling. Except for a few Fijian villages and the three resorts that follow, these little gems are undeveloped and unspoiled.

FORBES' LAUCALA ISLAND, P.O. Box 9952, Nadi Airport, Fiji Islands. Tel. 880077, or 719/379-3263 in the U.S. Fax 880099. Telex 4976112 in the U.S. 6 units. A/C (bedrooms only) MINIBAR TEL **Location:** Laucala Island, 20 minutes by boat from Taveuni or 1 hour by private plane from Nadi or Suva.

$ Rates (in U.S. dollars only, including room, food, bar, all activities, and local transfers): $2,400 per person per week. No credit cards on island; must be prepaid. AE, DC, MC, V.

The late publisher Malcolm S. Forbes, Sr., bought 3,000-acre Laucala Island in 1974 and grew to love it so much that his ashes are buried there. Guests are not allowed to visit the crypt, but they can use the swimming pool outside his hilltop home and enjoy the stunning, 360° view of Laucala and surrounding islands and reefs. Laucala is a plantation worked by Fijians who live in a modern village Forbes built for them. In fact, the ambience here is more like being a houseguest than a customer at a resort. The 1920s clapboard planter's home serves as gathering place for guests, who live in comfortable but not overly luxurious one- or two-bedroom bungalows scattered in a coconut grove beside a beach. There are no planned activities; guests are on their own to use a wide range of playthings, such as fishing boats and canoes.

Dining/Entertainment: Staff members prepare breakfasts in the bungalows' own kitchens, lunches are served picnic-style at various points (such as a ridge-top retreat overlooking the islands or a unique tree house perched above its own private beach), and dinners are taken in the planter's home.

Services: Laundry, baby-sitting.

Facilities: Swimming pool, wide range of water sports.

QAMEA BEACH CLUB, P.O. Matei, Taveuni, Fiji Islands. Tel. 880220, or toll free 800/447-8999 in the U.S. Fax 880092. Telex 8277. 10 bungalows. **Location:** Qamea Island, 15 minutes by boat from Taveuni.

$ Rates: F$270 ($189) single; F$300 ($210) double; add F$65 ($45.50) per person per day for three meals. AE, DC, MC, V.

American Jo Kloss and ex-husband Frank created this resort after selling their business interests in San Francisco and moving in 1982 to a 43-acre parcel of beachfront property on hilly Qamea Island, 2 miles east of Taveuni. Enlisting the aid of nearby villagers, they proceeded to build a little resort that shows remarkable attention to American-style comfort and Fijian detail. Qamea's centerpiece is a soaring, 52-foot-high bure supported by two huge tree trunks. Rope made of coconut fiber and some well-disguised nuts and bolts hold the poles and sweeping thatch roof together. Orange light from kerosene lanterns hung high under the roof lends a soft, romantic charm at twilight when guests gather to sip cocktails and dine on well-prepared local delicacies.

Guests relive the old South Seas days and nights in my favorite of all bures. If you were to build a set for a World War II South Pacific movie, the star (perhaps Cary Grant in *Father Goose*) would live in one of these thatch bungalows. The spacious, rectangular houses have old-fashioned screen doors leading out to porches complete with hammocks strung between two posts. Inside, they are large enough to swallow the king-size beds, lounge chairs, tables, and several other pieces of island-style furniture, most of them handcrafted by Frank and his Fijian helpers.

Dining/Entertainment: Excellent meals are served in the big central bure. The staff entertains several nights a week.

Services: Laundry.

Facilities: You can do as much as you want—snorkel, swim, scuba dive, windsurf, sail, paddle an outrigger canoe, visit the village across the bay, or go to Taveuni (2 miles away by boat) for a tour. On the other hand, you can swing slowly in your hammock all day. Your peace won't be disturbed by children under 13 years old, since they aren't permitted as guests.

MATAGI ISLAND RESORT, P.O. Box 83, Waiyevo, Taveuni, Fiji Islands. Tel. 880260. Fax 880274. Telex 8287. 10 units. MINIBAR **Location:** Matagi Island, 20 minutes by boat from Taveuni.

$ Rates (in U.S. dollars only): $80–$108 single; $103–$135 double; add $42 per person per day for meals. AE, DC, V.

It's unfortunate that geography places this resort last in my coverage of Fiji, for Matagi is one of the best values in Fiji—which is one reason it's also one of the most popular (book early, for it's usually full). Another reason is owners Nigel and Flo Douglas and their sons, Nigel and Frederick. Of English descent, Flo's family owns all of hilly, 260-acre Matagi. After managing Forbes' Laucala for a number of years, the Douglases built their own resort in a beachside coconut grove on Matagi's western side (gorgeous sunset views of Qamea and Taveuni). Their first bungalows were rectangular, but they have since added round bures in the Polynesian-influenced style of eastern Fiji: Reed-lined conical roofs are supported by umbrellalike spokes radiating from hand-hewn central poles. All of the units are spacious and furnished in island styles. One is equipped for disabled guests.

Dining/Entertainment: Guests dine in a somewhat small but comfortable central building with bar and lounge area. The menus are limited, but the staff will cater to all tastes on request. Staff members entertain at night.

Services: Laundry, baby-sitting.

Facilities: World-famous scuba diving; wide range of water-sports equipment; private beach in a lovely bay can be reserved for whatever couples can think of to do.

CHAPTER 15
VANUATU

Contrasts leap forth at every turn in the fascinating islands once known as the New Hebrides but now officially the Republic of Vanuatu, the South Pacific's youngest nation.

Port Vila (or simply Vila to local residents), the cosmopolitan little capital, boasts modern resorts of concrete and steel, yet on islands not far away people live in huts of bamboo and grass. While European and Australian expatriates discuss world affairs in Port Vila's fine French restaurants, elsewhere villagers observe ancient and often exotic Melanesian customs. Port Vila's chic shops stock Parisian fashions, but in places like Maewo and Malekula women wear only grass skirts and men only *nambas* (penis sheaths). Protestant ministers wield enormous clout in the national government, but in the jungle whole villages throw Christianity aside like so much colonial baggage, and a "cargo cult" worships a mythical American named John Frum.

Physically, Vanuatu's lush tropical islands offer their own contrasts. Visitors stroll on peaceful, pristine beaches or hike to the edge of Mount Yasur's crater on Tanna and look directly into the flaming bowels of the earth.

This varied country charmed novelist James Michener, who set his *Tales of the South Pacific* there. It will do the same to you.

1. GETTING TO KNOW VANUATU

You will arrive at **Vila** on **Efate,** the central island. Vila (pop. 15,000) began life in the 1870s as a small trading center. Today it's the governmental, commercial, and tourist center of the country and the only town other than Luganville on Espíritu Santo (or simply **Santo**). It sits on a narrow shelf of land between the picturesque harbor and Erakor Lagoon, a skinny, L-shaped body of water slicing deep into the island. Although Erakor Lagoon has a narrow opening to the sea, it seems more like a tranquil lake than a typical lagoon.

European settlers picked Efate because of its central location in the Y-shaped New Hebrides chain and the excellent natural harbor at Vila. To the south of Efate lie the **Tafea Islands** of Erromango, Tanna, Anatom, Aniwa, and Futuna. To the north, past the **Shepard Islands** and **Epi,** the Y splits. **Ambrym, Pentecost, Maewo,** and **Aoba** branch off to the east, and **Malekula** and Santo to the west. Farther north and definitely off the beaten track are the **Banks** and **Torres** groups.

Other than Efate, only Tanna and Santo are equipped to handle tourists. Elsewhere

WHAT'S SPECIAL ABOUT VANUATU

Natural Spectacles
- ☐ Mount Yasur: Roaring volcano is one of the world's most accessible.

Beaches
- ☐ Champagne Beach: Long and magnificent, it's totally undeveloped.

Literary Shrines
- ☐ Santo: James A. Michener set *Tales of the South Pacific* here.
- ☐ Aoba Island: On the hazy horizon, it inspired Michener's "Bali Ha'i."

Museums
- ☐ Michoutouchkine-Pilioki Art Gallery: some 19,000 artifacts from around the South Pacific.
- ☐ Cultural Centre: sculpted skulls and pig-killing clubs.

Offbeat Oddities
- ☐ John Frum Cult: believes a mysterious American will bring lots of cargo.
- ☐ Land Diving: Men of Pentecost were the original "bungee jumpers."

you'll be on your own to round up transportation, lodging, and meals from the local residents, usually in very primitive conditions.

HISTORY

Pedro Ferdández de Quirós discovered Santo in 1606 and tried unsuccessfully to establish a Spanish colony there. His discovery went virtually unnoticed, and 162 years passed before Louis Antoine de Bougainville happened upon Santo in 1767 after visiting Tahiti. Capt. James Cook charted the entire island group and named them the New Hebrides in 1774. The French explorer Jean La Pérouse sailed through the islands in 1788, then mysteriously disappeared. His ship, the *Astrolabe,* was found in 1828 lying in the lagoon at Vanikoro in Solomon Islands.

In the early 1800s, sandalwood and bêche-de-mer traders dealt with the indigenous people harshly and unscrupulously, and introduced Western diseases that decimated the populations of some islands. "Blackbirders" took away an estimated 40,000 islanders between 1840 and 1904 to work the sugar plantations of Australia and Fiji.

In the 1860s, when the American Civil War drove up the price of cotton, British and French planters purchased large tracts of land for plantations; within a few years they owned much of the best property. The islanders held property communally in the Melanesian custom, and when it dawned on them what they had done by selling the land, they took vengeance by killing a number of European traders, missionaries, and planters, including the Rev. John

DATELINE

- **2000 B.C.** Melanesians settle on Malo near Santo, spread to other islands.
- **A.D. 1606** De Quirós discovers Santo, fails to establish Spanish colony.
- **1767** Bougainville spends a week in the islands.
- **1774** James Cook names the New Hebrides.
- **1788** La Pérouse visits the islands, then disappears.
- **1825** Sandalwood traders arrive at Erromango.

(continues)

Williams of the London Missionary Society (Vanuatu holds the South Pacific record in this respect).

Anglican and Presbyterian missionaries nevertheless gained footholds in the islands during the mid-1800s. When Catholic priests arrived in 1887, a pattern developed: Protestant missions (and the English language) on one side of an island, Catholic missions (and French) on the other. That arrangement continues on many islands today.

Despite the missionaries' success, sporadic violence continued in the islands. British and French warships responded by shelling some of the coastal villages. A leading trader, Irish-born French citizen John Higginson, proposed in 1877 that the French annex the New Hebrides to their colony in New Caledonia. At the urging of Australians, who didn't want another French colony in the neighborhood, Britain and France agreed not to colonize the New Hebrides without consulting each other. In 1887 the two countries set up a joint naval commission to enforce law and order. When Germany expressed an interest in claiming the New Hebrides at the turn of the new century, Britain and France soon appointed resident commissioners in Vila and in 1906 formalized the arrangement as a joint government.

Under this cumbersome Condominium, which quickly became known as the "Pandemonium," the British and French maintained duplicate administrations, police forces, courts, schools, and hospitals. Both French and English were official languages. The French relied on civil servants sent from France (a system they continue to follow with much controversy in New Caledonia and Tahiti), while the British trained a cadre of Melanesians to fill the lower-level administrative jobs. The Catholic priests came from overseas; the Protestants trained Melanesian ministers and missionaries.

Somehow law and order were maintained, but the basic infrastructure went lacking until 1942, when the Japanese advanced into the neighboring Solomon Islands. Almost overnight more than 100,000 Americans arrived in the New Hebrides and proceeded to establish huge forward bases. They unloaded such enormous amounts of matériel at Vila and Santo that it gave rise to religious "cargo cults" among some of the recruited Melanesian laborers (see "Tanna" in "Easy Excursions," below).

James A. Michener was among the Americans who spent time on Santo. After the war, the New Hebrides reverted to the quiet, backwater land of French planters he described in his fiction. Then, in the early 1970s, a Melanesian movement formed under the leadership of Father Walter Lini, an Anglican priest, demanded not only the return of all land to its custom (Melanesian) owners, but also immediate independence from Britain and France. Although the French were reluctant, a national assembly was established in 1977, and independence was scheduled for July 30, 1980. The British-trained, English-speaking local civil servants and church leaders won the 1977 elections and, as we went to press, were still in power.

Meanwhile, another movement demanded separate independence for Santo, and a so-called Coconut War broke out there on the dawn of independence in 1980. Although

DATELINE

- **1839** Rev. John Williams killed and eaten on Erromango.
- **1840** Blackbirders begin slave trade, take away 40,000 ni-Vanuatu over next 44 years.
- **1848** First Presbyterian missionaries arrive.
- **1857** John and Ellen Gordon of London Missionary Society settle on Erromango.
- **1861** The Gordons are murdered.
- **1860s** Planters arrive, buy up large tracts of land; many are murdered.
- **1877** Britain and France agree not to colonize New Hebrides.
- **1887** Britain and France set up joint naval commission to enforce law and order; Catholic missionaries arrive from France.
- **1906** Britain and France establish joint Condominium government at Port Vila.
- **1923** French allow importation of Vietnamese laborers.
- **1942** Americans build huge bases to support Solomon Islands campaign against the Japanese; cargo cults spring up.
- **1977** Condominium government establishes a National Assembly;

(continues)

France and Britain sent troops, they couldn't agree what to do. Much of Luganville, Santo's only town, was looted, and the island's large coconut-oil mill was destroyed. Despite talk of a delay, independence was granted as scheduled. At the request of the new prime minister, Father Lini, Papua New Guinea forces put a quick end to the rebellion. A simultaneous movement advocating independence for Tanna fizzled when its leader was mysteriously assassinated.

DATELINE

Anglophiles win majority of seats under Father Walter Lini.

- **1980** Vanuatu becomes independent; Father Lini chosen first prime minister; Papua New Guinea soldiers crush Jimmy Stevens' revolt in the "Coconut War" on Santo; resistance on Tanna ends when rebel leader is mysteriously assassinated.
- **1987** Father Lini suffers stroke in Washington, D.C.
- **1988** Pres. George Sokomanu dissolves parliament, names his nephew head of interim government; Lini offers big raise to police, who topple interim government; Sokomanu and nephew jailed but released on appeal.

GOVERNMENT, POLITICS & ECONOMY

Under its constitution of 1980, Vanuatu has a Westminster-style Parliament of 46 members, all of them elected for 4-year terms. Parliament and the heads of 11 Regional Councils choose a figurehead president, who serves for 5 years. A National Council of Chiefs advises the government on matters of Melanesian custom, and regional and local councils handle matters at their levels. The official name of the country is Republik Blong Vanuatu ("Republic of Our Land" in the local pidgin).

In a general sense, politics in Vanuatu is divided along English- and French-speaking lines. The Vanuaaku party, dominated by Father Walter Lini and his fellow English-speaking Protestants, still controlled a majority in Parliament as we went to press. They were opposed by the Union of Moderate Parties, whose members primarily are Catholic French-speakers.

Vanuatu is a "tax haven" for capitalists. There are no personal or corporate income taxes, capital-gains taxes, estate or gift taxes, or exchange controls, and the banking laws provide for strict financial secrecy. The huge plantations and all other foreign-owned lands were repossessed by the government after independence in 1980, but many were then leased from the "custom" owners and continued on as before. Copra, cacao, beef (the fine Hereford and Charolais steaks you eat in Vila will have been raised in Vanuatu), and fish canned on Santo are the chief exports. The country earns substantial foreign exchange from tourism. Nevertheless, Vanuatu has a huge negative trade balance and is officially recognized by the United Nations as one of the world's poorest countries. Accordingly, foreign aid makes up a large portion of the government's revenues each year.

GEOGRAPHY

This 450-mile-long, Y-shaped chain of 82 islands lies along the edge of the Indo-Australian Plate some 500 miles west of Fiji, between New Caledonia and

IMPRESSIONS

The business of having two governments—called the Condominium and universally burlesqued as the Pandemonium—is one of the most fantastic phenomena in the Pacific. . . . The comic opera confusions are so hilarious they practically justify the exorbitant expense.

—James A. Michener, 1951

Solomon Islands. The New Hebrides Trench to the east dives to a depth of more than 25,000 feet where the Pacific and Indo-Australian plates meet.

Volcanoes caused by the resulting geological turmoil are building the islands on Vanuatu's eastern side, while those on the western edge are being slowly pushed up as the Pacific Plate rises up over the Indo-Australian Plate. The country has six active volcanoes, one each on Tanna (**Mount Yasur**), Lopevi, Ambrym, Aoba, and Santa Maria, and one off Tangoa that boils below the surface of the sea. The uplifting has caused a series of limestone (originally coral) plateaus on some of the islands and occasionally sends earthquakes and tremors rumbling through the archipelago.

PEOPLE

Of Vanuatu's 130,000 or so residents, about 93% are Melanesian, or **ni-Vanuatu,** as they prefer to be called. About 80% of all ni-Vanuatu still live in small settlements of thatch buildings and raise yams, tapioca, and taro in small gardens—virtually in the same way as their Melanesian ancestors who migrated down from Southeast Asia, possibly 3,000 years ago.

The traditional Melanesian way of life continues on most of the islands (see "People & Culture" in Chapter 1). The "Big Nambas" and "Little Nambas" tribes on Malakula are among the world's most primitive peoples and derive their names from the nambas worn by the men. One of the few traditions not practiced today is cannibalism, although there was plenty of that right into the early 20th century.

The old ways are known today as **"custom"**—a word you will hear frequently, not only in Vanuatu but in Solomon Islands. Custom not only lives, it is very strong in these countries where many people couldn't care less about Western ways.

The other 7% of the population is an assortment of French, British, Europeans, Australians, Chinese, New Caledonians, Pacific islanders, and Vietnamese (the Tonkinese of Michener's fiction, who were imported as laborers in the 1920s). Most of the Non-Melanesians live in Vila or elsewhere on Efate.

LANGUAGE

English and French are official languages, and although entire villages will speak one or the other depending on which colonial power set up the local school, English-speaking visitors will have little trouble getting around most of Vanuatu.

The ni-Vanuatu still speak some 115 distinct Melanesian tongues, some of them with several dialects. The common language is **Bislama,** a form of Pidgin English originated by the early traders who came to the islands for bêche-de-mer (from which the name is derived). The broken English they used eventually grew into the organized, structured pidgin languages spoken in Vanuatu, Solomon Islands, and Papua New Guinea.

Bislama is predominantly English with Melanesian grammar. The spelling is phonetic. Prince Charles, for example, is the *Nambawan pikinini blong Kwin.* In English, that's "Number one pickaninny belong queen," or the queen's son. (Sensitive American ears should not take offense at "pikinini," a perfectly acceptable term in Vanuatu and Solomon Islands.)

Here are some common phrases (*save* is pronounced "savvy"):

Goodmorning Gudmoning
Good night Gudnaet
Good-bye Tata
See you later Lukim yu
How are you? Yu orait?
Just fine I gud nomo
Thank you very much Tangkyu tumas
My name is . . . Nem blong me . . .
I want some (beer) Mi wantem sam (bia)
I don't understand (Bislama) Mi no save (Bislama)

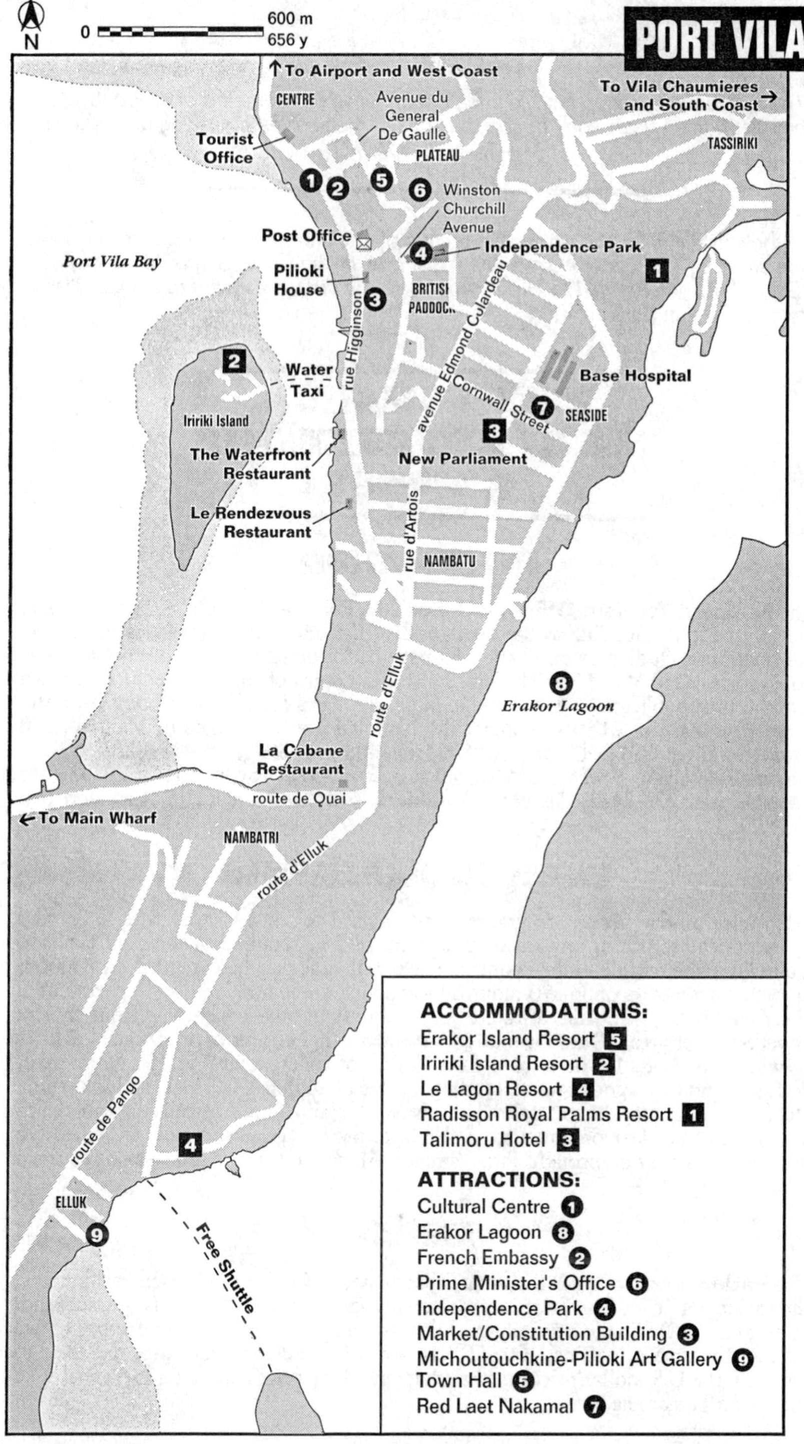
PORT VILA
0
600 m
656 y
N
To Airport and West Coast
To Vila Chaumieres and South Coast
CENTRE
Avenue du General De Gaulle
Tourist Office
PLATEAU
TASSIRIKI
Winston Churchill Avenue
Post Office
Independence Park
Port Vila Bay
Pilioki House
BRITISH PADDOCK
avenue Edmond Colardeau
rue Higginson
Water Taxi
Cornwall Street
Base Hospital
SEASIDE
Iririki Island
The Waterfront Restaurant
New Parliament
Le Rendezvous Restaurant
rue d'Artois
NAMBATU
route d'Elluk
Erakor Lagoon
La Cabane Restaurant
route de Quai
To Main Wharf
NAMBATRI
route d'Elluk
route de Pango
ELLUK
Free Shuttle
ACCOMMODATIONS:
Erakor Island Resort 5
Iririki Island Resort 2
Le Lagon Resort 4
Radisson Royal Palms Resort 1
Talimoru Hotel 3
ATTRACTIONS:
Cultural Centre 1
Erakor Lagoon 8
French Embassy 2
Prime Minister's Office 6
Independence Park 4
Market/Constitution Building 3
Michoutouchkine-Pilioki Art Gallery 9
Town Hall 5
Red Laet Nakamal 7

IMPRESSIONS

They gave us to understand in such a manner which admitted of no doubt that they eat human flesh, they began the subject themselves by asking us if we did.
—JAMES COOK, 1774

Look in the Vila bookstores for a copy of the entertaining little cartoon book, *Evri samting yu wantem save long Bislama be yu fraet tumas blong askem* (*Everything you wanted to know about Bislama but were afraid to ask)*, by Darrel Tryon and Allan Langoulant.

2. INFORMATION, ENTRY REQUIREMENTS & MONEY

INFORMATION

The **National Tourism Office,** P.O. Box 209, Port Vila (tel. 22685, fax 23889), in the International Building at the north end of the main street, provides up-to-date information, including an excellent, 189-page background guide to the country. The book costs 1,250 VT ($11). The office also has copies of the latest editions of two useful tourist publications, *What to Do in Vanuatu* and *Hapi Tumas Long Vanuatu.*

In the United States, contact the National Tourism Office of Vanuatu, 520 Monterey Drive, Rio Del Mar, CA 95003 (tel. 408/685-8901, fax 408/685-8903). **In Australia,** call Air Vanuatu in Melbourne (tel. 417-3977), Sydney (tel. 223-8333), or Brisbane (tel. 233-2452). **In New Zealand,** call Air Vanuatu in Auckland (tel. 733435).

ENTRY REQUIREMENTS

Temporary 30-day **visas** are granted upon arrival to most visitors who have valid passports and return or onward tickets. Proof may be required of sufficient funds to maintain oneself while in the country. The initial visas may be extended, in 1-month increments, for stays of up to 3 months by applying to the Immigration Department in Vila (tel. 22222). **Vaccinations** are required only of travelers coming from cholera or yellow fever areas. **Customs allowances** are 200 cigarettes or 50 cigars, 2 liters of wine and up to 1.5 liters of liquor, ¼ liter of toilet water and 10 centiliters of perfume, and other goods not exceeding a value of 20,000 VT ($180), including film. Dogs and cats may be brought from New Zealand and Australia provided import permits are first obtained from the Ministry of Agriculture and Fisheries. No other animals may be brought into Vanuatu. All agricultural products also require a permit.

MONEY

The **national currency** is the **vatu,** abbreviated **VT.** Like the French Pacific franc, the vatu is not divided, so prices are quoted in even numbers. The exchange rate is not quoted in the U.S. daily newspapers, but travel agents can give you the approximate rate. At the time of writing, 100 VT was worth U.S. 90¢, the exchange rate used to compute the U.S. dollar prices in this chapter. Many prices are fixed in Vanuatu, so there's no bargaining.

THE VATU & THE DOLLAR

At this writing, 100 VT = approximately U.S. 90¢, the rate of exchange used to calculate the U.S. dollar prices given in this chapter. This rate may not be the same when you visit. Accordingly, use the following table only as a guide.

VT	$ U.S.	VT	$ U.S.
100	.90	1,000	9.00
150	1.35	1,500	13.50
200	1.80	2,000	18.00
300	2.70	3,000	27.00
400	3.60	4,000	36.00
500	4.50	5,000	45.00
600	5.40	6,000	54.00
700	6.30	7,000	63.00
800	7.20	8,000	72.00
900	8.10	9,000	81.00
1,000	9.00	10,000	90.00

WHAT THINGS COST IN VANUATU	U.S. $
Taxi from airport into Vila	3.60
Double room at Le Lagon Resort (expensive)	160.00
Double room at Iririki Island Resort (moderate)	102.00
Double room at Talimoru Hotel (budget)	26.00
Lunch for one at The Waterfront Bar & Grill (moderate)	6.50
Lunch for one at Le Café (budget)	4.50
Dinner for one, without wine, at Le Rendez-Vous (expensive)	32.50
Dinner for one, without wine, at La Cabane (moderate)	19.00
Dinner for one, without wine, at Bloody Mary's (budget)	5.85
Beer	1.80
Coca-Cola	1.35
Cup of coffee	1.08
Roll of ASA 100 Kodacolor film, 36 exposures	4.50
Movie ticket	2.70

3. WHEN TO GO — CLIMATE, HOLIDAYS & EVENTS

Vanuatu has a tropical climate in its northernmost islands, subtropical in those to the south. Overall, high temperatures average about 84°F during the drier and cooler months from May to October and about 87°F during the warmer and humid season from November to April. Evenings usually are in the comfortable 70s year round, although they can seem relatively cool from June to September, especially on Tanna. Tropical showers may occur at any time of the year. The South Pacific cyclone belt encompasses the southern half of Vanuatu, and hurricanes can roar through from November to April. They are much less frequent—though not unknown—in the northern islands.

Holidays are: New Year's Day, Custom Chief's Day (March 5), Good Friday and Easter Monday, May Day (May 1), Ascension Day (40 days after Easter Sunday), Independence Day (July 30), Assumption Day (August 15), Constitution Day (October 5), National Unity Day (November 29), Christmas Day, and Family Day (December 26).

The following **events** are worth noting. **February 15:** Members of the John Frum cargo cult stage dances, parades, and feasts in anticipation of the return of the mysterious American of that name (see "Tanna" and "Santo" in "Easy Excursions," below). **April-May:** The land divers of Pentecost Island do their thing on Saturday from mid-April to mid-May. **Late August:** Other villagers on Tanna stage celebrations in honor of the custom chiefs at which multitudes dance the stomping *Toka*. They kill hundreds of pigs and feast and drink kava for several days. **September-October:** Agricultural shows featuring large "custom" dance performances are held on Tanna in September and at Vila in October.

4. GETTING THERE & GETTING AROUND

GETTING THERE

From North America, the most direct route is to Fiji on one of the major carriers, then on to Vila on **Air Pacific, Solomon Airlines,** or **Air Vanuatu,** the national carrier. Air Vanuatu also connects the country with Melbourne, Sydney, Brisbane, and Auckland. **Air Calédonie International** flies there from Australia and New Zealand through Nouméa. Solomon Airlines connects Vila to Honiara. See "Getting There" in Chapter 2 for more information.

Visitors arrive at **Bauer Field Airport,** the country's only international airport, 6km (4 miles) north of Vila. The field is named for Lt. Col. Harold M. Bauer, a U.S. Marine fighter pilot who was shot down in 1942 fighting the Japanese in the Battle of Guadalcanal. The new international terminal, opened in 1991, was built with Japanese money; hence, Col. Bauer's name is not on it. Westpac Bank, rental-car firms, tour operators, and the National Tourism Office all have booths in the terminal, as does a small snack bar.

Taxis and an airport tour bus provide transport into Vila; both cost about 400 VT ($3.60) to the center of town. Local buses also pass the terminal (see "Getting Around," below).

A **departure tax** of 1,500 VT ($13.50) for international flights and 200 VT ($1.80) for domestic flights must be paid in vatu to the clerk at the check-in counter. The departure lounge has a duty-free shop and a drugstore which carries some handcraft and curio items. Domestic flights leave from the old terminal.

GETTING AROUND

BY PLANE

Vanair (tel. 22643) flies to most of the islands, including two flights a day from Vila to both Santo and Tanna. One-way fares are approximately 8,000 VT ($72) to Santo and

7,000 VT ($63) to Tanna; double them for round-trip. Both islands are about an hour's flying time from Vila. Vanair's main ticketing office is north of the post office on Vila's main street. Baggage allowance is 10kg (22 lb.).

Don't forget to reconfirm your return flight as soon as you arrive on an outer island.

BY SHIP

There is no ferry system in Vanuatu. **David Edson & Co. Ltd.** (tel. 22569), and **Pacific Shipping Ltd.** (tel. 23097) both operate very basic—repeat: very basic—freighters between Vila and Santo by way of Malakula, Epi, Paama, Ambrym, Pentecost, Maewo, and Aoba. A trip from Vila to Santo takes 2 to 3 days, maybe longer. **Burns Philp** (tel. 22456) sends several trading boats through the islands. All shipping schedules are highly irregular.

BY CAR

Daily rates at **Budget Rent-A-Car,** in the Nissan dealership on the main street (tel. 23170, or toll free 800/527-0700 in the U.S.), start at 5,000 VT ($45) a day, including unlimited kilometers. Full insurance costs 1,100 VT ($10).

Avis (tel. 22570, or toll free 800/331-1212 in the U.S.) has both unlimited-kilometer and daily-plus-kilometer rates. It has a desk at the Radisson Royal Palms Resort. **Hertz** (tel. 22244, or toll free 800/654-3001 in the U.S.) has offices on Vila's main street and at the Radisson Royal Palms and Le Lagon resorts.

A local firm is **Discount Rentals** (tel. 23242), which also calls itself **No Frills Car Rentals Ltd.**

Although **gasoline** is available at the cooperative stores in the villages on Efate, don't drive away from Vila without a full tank. At this writing, gasoline cost about 90 VT (80¢) a liter or about $3 for an American-size gallon.

BY MOPED

The hotel tour desks can arrange moped rentals, or contact **IS Rentals** (tel. 22470) opposite La Cabane Restaurant south of town. Mopeds cost approximately half the rental-car rates.

Driving Rules

Your home driver's license will be honored in Vanuatu. Driving is on the right-hand side of the road, American fashion. Very few roads are paved outside the vicinity of Vila, and even in town, be careful of potholes and serious ruts as well as the usual South Pacific assortment of pigs, chickens, dogs, and people.

BY BUS

A reliable minibus system operates in Vila daily from sunrise to about 8pm. **Route 1** runs along the main street from the airport to the Vila market on the waterfront. **Route 2** goes from the market south to Le Lagon and Erakor Island resorts. **Route 3** runs from the waterfront east to the Radisson Royal Palms Resort. That having been said, tell the driver where you want to go, and he will take you anywhere within a reasonable distance of these routes. Fares are 50 VT (45¢) around town, 60 VT (54¢) to the airport or main wharf. Bus stops are clearly marked, although the buses themselves are not. Merely wait at the bus stop and ask the driver where he's going.

BY TAXI

Metered taxis gather at the **Taxi Depot** (tel. 22870) next to the Cultural Centre on the waterfront. Fares are about 100 VT (90¢) per kilometer. Here are some distances in kilometers from the airport: Downtown taxi stand (4km); Hideaway Island (8km); Radisson Royal Palms Resort (5km); Le Lagon Resort (7km); Vila Chaumières (8km); Teouma Village (6km).

FAST FACTS: VANUATU

The following facts apply to Vila and Efate. Tanna and Santo are so small that you have merely to ask for details on those islands.

American Express There is no representative in Vanuatu. See the "Fast Facts" in Chapter 2 for how to report stolen or missing credit cards and traveler's checks.

Area Code The international country code is 678.

Baby-sitters Most hotels will arrange for English-speaking baby-sitters.

Bookstores Vanuatu Stationery and Books, on the main street opposite the French Embassy, has a good selection of books. In addition to regular business hours (see below), the store is open Sun 8:30–11:30am. Vila Book Market, on the street in front of ANZ Bank, has used books at a fraction of the original price and sells the Bislama language book I recommend above for 700 VT ($6.50), the lowest price in town.

Business Hours Businesses, shops, and government offices are open Mon–Fri 7:30–11:30am, then they close for a 2-hour siesta. Private businesses and shops are open again 1:30–5pm, while government offices are open 1:30–4:30pm. Only the shops are open on Sat, most of them 8am–noon. Some grocery stores open Sun 6:30am–10pm.

Climate See "When to Go—Climate, Holidays & Events" in this chapter.

Clothing Informal cottons or cotton blends are appropriate during the day all year, but a sweater or light wrap will come in handy in the evenings, especially during the cooler and drier months (May to October). You'll definitely need a sweater or windbreaker on top of Mount Yasur on Tanna. A few French and Australian women sunbathe topless at the resorts, but modest attire is in order away from the beaches. If you're going to climb Mount Yasur or trek to see the land divers on Pentecost, take along a pair of good walking shoes with excellent tred.

Credit Cards Most hotels, restaurants, rental-car firms, and major shops accept American Express, VISA, Diners Club, and MasterCard credit cards—but only in Vila.

Crime See "Safety," below.

Currency See "Information, Entry Requirements & Money" in this chapter.

Currency Exchange Goodie's Treasure Box (tel. 23445) in the Olympic Hotel building on the main street, changes currency at slightly better rates than the banks. ANZ Bank, Westpac Bank, and Banque Indosuez Vanuatu—all on the main street—are open Mon–Fri, as follows: ANZ 8am–3pm; Westpac 8:30am–8pm; and Banque Indosuez 8–11am and 1:30–3pm. ANZ and Westpac banks have offices in Luganville on Santo; otherwise, there are no other branches in the country. Accordingly, take enough cash with you if you go to Tanna or elsewhere.

Customs See "Information, Entry Requirements & Money" in this chapter.

Doctor Dr. Ernest Finberg runs the Vila Medical Centre above The Drug Store on main street (tel. 22826 or 22565 at home).

Documents Required See "Information, Entry Requirements & Money" in this chapter.

Driving Rules See "Getting Around" in this chapter.

Drug Laws Narcotics and dangerous drugs are illegal and the penalties are severe.

Drugstores Two well-stocked drugstores are located on Vila's main street in the heart of town. In keeping with Vanuatu's split personality, the French-owned store is called the pharmacie; the English version is the drugstore.

Electricity Standard electrical current is 220 volts, 50 cycles. Vanuatu uses the angled two-prong plugs found in Australia and New Zealand, so both converter and adapter will be necessary to operate American and Canadian appliances. Some but not all hotels have 110-volt converters for electric shavers.

Embassies/Consulates Although the U.S. and Vanuatu established diplomatic relations in 1986, there is no American embassy in Vanuatu. The country comes under the jurisdiction of the U.S. embassy in Honiara, Solomon Islands. Diplomatic missions present in Vila are the British High Commission (tel. 3100), the Australian High Commission (tel. 2777), New Zealand High Commission (tel. 2933), and the French Embassy (tel. 2353).

Emergencies The Vila telephone number for the police is 22222; for fire, 22333; for Central Hospital and its ambulance service, 22100.

Etiquette See "People" under "Getting to Know Vanuatu" in this chapter.

Eyeglasses Vanuatu Optical Boutique (tel. 23564) next to Hotel Rossi, Vila's main street.

Firearms They are illegal.

Gambling The Radisson Royal Palms Resort has a gambling casino (see "Where to Stay" in this chapter).

Hairdressers/Barbers Gisele Coiffure (tel. 22746) is in Pilioko House on Vila's main street. The Radisson Royal Palms Resort (tel. 22040) has a beauty salon.

Hitchhiking It's not illegal for either sex, but for safety's sake, women should not hitchhike without a male companion.

Holidays See "When to Go—Climate, Holidays & Events" in this chapter.

Hospital Medical care at the Central Hospital in Vila is extremely basic by Western standards. See "Doctor," above.

Information See "Information, Entry Requirements & Money" in this chapter.

Insects Mosquitoes carry malaria in many parts of the country, especially in the northern islands. Antimalarial medication should be taken prior to arrival, while in Vanuatu, and for a month after leaving. See "Health & Insurance" in Chapter 2.

Language See "Language" in this chapter.

Laundry Ezy Wash Laundromat (tel. 24386) is in the Olympic Hotel building, Vila's main street. A load costs 300 VT ($2.70) to wash or dry. Tebakor Pressing (tel. 22072) on the airport road is the country's professional laundry and dry cleaners.

Liquor Laws There are no arcane laws. Tusker is the local beer; it's about 100 VT (90¢) a bottle cheaper than imported beer. Kava is the national drink (see "Evening Entertainment" under "What to See & Do," below).

Luggage/Storage Lockers The hotels have free storage rooms.

Mail The Central Post Office, on Vila's main street, is open Mon–Fri 7:30am–3:30pm. Airmail letters to the U.S. cost 65 VT (60¢); postcards, 60 VT (55¢). The service is reliable.

Maps *Hapi Tumas Long Vanautu,* the free tourist publication available at the National Tourism Office, has a map inside. Vanuatu Stationery and Books (see "Bookstores," above) carries *Instant Vanuatu,* a fine map of Vila and Efate with lots of background and historical information printed on it. The government's Survey Department behind the Court House sells excellent topographical maps of the country.

Newspapers/Magazines The government-controlled *Vanuatu Weekly*, the only newspaper, carries local news and a few international stories in English, French, and Bislama; frankly, it's useful primarily as a souvenir. Vanuatu Stationery and Books (see "Bookstores," above) carries the international newsmagazines and recent Australian and New Zealand newspapers.

Passports See "Information, Entry Requirements & Money" in this chapter.

Pets You can bring them from Australia and New Zealand but not from any other country.

Photographic Needs A wide range of color-print film and processing is available at the shops along Vila's main street. Fung Kuei and Photo Express, both just north of ANZ Bank, provide overnight developing of Kodak print film.

Police The police station (tel. 22222) is on the main street opposite the French Embassy.

Radio/TV Radio Vanuatu, the country's only radio station, carries programs—some in English or French but most in Bislama—throughout the day in the AM and FM bands. The world news is rebroadcast from Radio Australia every day at 7am. Wire-service news in English is read after the news in Bislama at noon and at 8pm. Vanuatu does not have broadcast television, though videotapes are popular.

Religious Services There are numerous Anglican, Presbyterian, and Roman Catholic churches in Vanuatu. There also are Seventh-Day Adventists, Churches of Christ, Apostolic churches, Assemblies of God, Reformed churches, Jehovah's Witnesses, Baha'is, and Independent churches.

Rest Rooms Go to the hotels, restaurants, and bars.

Safety Street crimes, such as robbery, are rare. There may be some sticky fingers, however, so you shouldn't leave valuables unattended. Women should not swim alone at isolated beaches or visit remote villages without a male companion. See "Health & Insurance" and the "Fast Facts" in Chapter 2 for more warnings.

Shoe Repair Go up the street by Ma Barker's Restaurant to a white apartment building on the left. The shop is on the ground floor but has no name. You will smell it before you see it.

Taxes In addition to the airport departure taxes mentioned above, the government imposes a 10% sales tax on all hotel, liquor-licensed restaurant, and rental-car bills.

Telephone/Telex/Fax The post offices have pay telephones operated like those in the U.S. Lift the receiver, listen for the dial tone, deposit a 20 VT (20¢) coin, and dial the number. Dial 91 for directory assistance, 00 for international calls. Make overseas calls and send faxes at the Vanuatu International Telecommunications Ltd. (VANITEL) office next to the large Hebrida store on the main street. VANITEL is open 7am–10pm 7 days a week, including holidays. Credit cards are not accepted; pay with vatu after completing your call. Station-to-station calls to the U.S. cost 1,500 VT ($13.50) for the first 3 minutes. The country was being wired for international service when I was there recently, so you should be able to dial Vanuatu directly from the U.S. and elsewhere. The country code is 678.

Time Vanuatu is the only South Pacific island country with daylight saving time (it goes on and off when Australia does).

From the third Sun in Mar to the third Sun in Sept, local time is 11 hours ahead of Greenwich mean time. (Translated: When it's 4am on Tues in Vanuatu during standard time in the U.S., it's noon on Mon in New York and 9am on Mon in Los Angeles. During U.S. daylight saving time, it's 11am on Mon in New York and 8am on Mon in Los Angeles.)

From the third Sun in Sept to the third Sun in Mar, Vanuatu time is 12 hours ahead of Greenwich mean time. During that period, subtract 1 hour from the times given in the translation above.

Tipping Tipping is discouraged.

Tourist Offices See "Information, Entry Requirements & Money" in this chapter.

Visas See "Information, Entry Requirements & Money" in this chapter.

Water Tap water in Vila is safe to drink, though the same cannot be said elsewhere. Bottled water is available at the department stores in Vila.

Weights/Measures Vanuatu is on the metric system of weights and measures. See the appendix for methods of conversion.

5. WHAT TO SEE & DO

Three stops are in order before choosing among Vila's myriad activities, and you can accomplish them all while ambling down the main street. First, drop in on the

IMPRESSIONS

Throughout the day I spent there with a friend I saw no one until the late afternoon, when a man in a loincloth with a spear and two boys with bows and arrows crossed the beach and disappeared into the jungle. They were followed by a man with a radio playing "Hey, Mister Tambourine Man."

—FRANCES FITZGERALD, 1986

National Tourism Office and grab the latest brochures, maps, and tourist publications. See the "Fast Facts," above.

Second, stop by **Frank King Tours** (tel. 22808), beside the Constitution Building on the main street. A burly, red-headed Australian who gave up a coat-and-tie career as an IBM salesman in Sydney back in the 1970s for life as a shorts-and-sandals tour operator in Vila, Frank King produces a brochure that is worth collecting just for its maps of Vila and Efate.

Third, drop in at **Tour Vanuatu** (tel. 22745), the ni-Vanuatu-managed tour company that can have the inside track on certain activities. Tour Vanuatu's office is on the main street in the middle of town next to Vanair. It also has tour desks at Le Lagon and the Radisson Royal Palms resorts.

Since most tours and events don't take place every day, schedule your activities early.

SIGHTSEEING

THE CULTURAL CENTRE

Another early visit should be paid to the **museum** at the Cultural Centre on the main street. Your interest surely will be piqued by the Ambrym slit drums, made by hollowing out tree trunks and carving stylized heads on one end; shell necklaces used as money to purchase brides; *rambaramp* effigies from Malekula, complete with the deceaseds' skulls overmodeled with paste to resemble them in life; ritual clubs for killing pigs with one swift blow to the head; arrow points made from human forearm bones and dipped in a decaying corpse to transfer infection to the target; male and female figures carved from tree-fern trunks on Ambrym and Malekula; double-circled pigs' tusks used for ceremonial purposes, including the one presented to Queen Elizabeth II during her visit to Vanuatu in 1974, now on permanent loan to the museum; various objects carved in the likeness of young boys about to be

FROMMER'S FAVORITE VANUATU EXPERIENCES

Tanna I've seen few more awe-inspiring sights than looking down into fiery Mount Yasur at night from its narrow volcanic lip. The next day I visited the "custom people" of Yaohnanen village. Later it occurred to me that on Tanna, I had seen both nature and human beings in their most primitive states.

Santo Once I spent a day driving around Santo with Frank Taylor, an Australian who was there during World War II. As we examined the ghostly remains of the great Allied base, tingles ran up my spine at the thought of what my father's generation had accomplished in the year I was born.

Nakamals Root-tasting kava doesn't particularly agree with my stomach, but I met an extraordinarily interesting group of ni-Vanuatu and expatriates during a nighttime tour of Vila's *nakamal* grog parlors. Needless to say, the conversations were mellow.

circumcised; and, of a more mundane nature, wooden taro- and breadfruit-pounding bowls carved to represent turtles and fish. The anchor recovered from La Pérouse's *Astrolabe* is on display. If nothing else, a tour through the museum will provide the education necessary to shop at **Handikraf Blong Vanuatu,** the center's handcraft shop (see "Shopping," below).

The museum is open from 9am to 11:30am and from 2 to 5:30pm Monday through Friday and from 9 to 11:30am on Saturday. An adjacent **library** stocked with a good collection of books in both English and French is open from 9 to 11:30am and from 2 to 6pm Monday through Friday, from 8:30 to 11:30am on Saturday. The library is free but admission to the museum is 200 VT ($1.80) for adults, 50 VT (45¢) for children.

A WALKING TOUR OF VILA

The waterfront area on Port Vila Bay remains the heart of town, since most of the businesses and shops straddle the main street along the shoreline. Side streets snake off into the hills above the bay where the British and the French settled in different neighborhoods. The streets, accordingly, were given either English or French names. Some streets share a name: The main street is both Kumul Highway and rue Higginson. Few signs tell which streets are which, so as a practical matter, street names are virtually useless to the visitor. You'll learn right away to look for landmarks instead of street signs.

Start at the Cultural Centre and walk south along the main street business district, past the French Embassy's iron fence on the left. Streets with shops and offices run off at right angles up the hill. On your left, **Pilioko House,** an office and retail building, is named for Alio Pilioko, the noted artist from Wallis Island who now lives in Vila. His colleague and fellow artist, Nicolai Michoutouchkine, has a clothing shop in the building (see "Shopping," below). A brass plaque on the side of Pilioko House marks the spot where the Anglo-French Condominium was proclaimed in 1906.

Alio Pilioko designed and decorated the facade of the **post office,** a few blocks farther along. On the harbor side of the street, the **open-air market** attracts a crowd of ni-Vanuatu women in their ankle-length "Mother Hubbard" dresses early on Wednesday, Friday, and Saturday mornings. They sell a variety of tropical fruits and vegetables, and even bundles of live crabs strapped together with pandanus strips.

Across the street stands the **Constitution Building,** once the Condominium headquarters and now home of many government offices. The mural on the front, depicting scenes of everyday Melanesian village life, was drawn by students from the Technical Institute.

Another block south, a launch leaves a jetty every few minutes for **Iririki Island.** This rock across the channel is now dotted with the bungalows of Iririki Island Resort, but during the Condominium, it was where the British resident commissioners lived and dined. The launch ride is free and the view from the restaurant worth the trouble.

Now backtrack to the post office and head up the hill past the power plant. At the top, just before the BESA Club, turn right and walk a block to **Independence Park.** This village green–like setting is now used for ceremonies, parades, and cricket and rugby matches. In the days of the Condominium, it was known as the British Paddock, and lower-level British administrators lived in the white clapboard houses on the far side of the field. The long, tin-roofed former **British Residency** building, now occupied by Vanuatu government ministries, overlooks the park.

Return to the street you came in on, known here as Winston Churchill Avenue, and turn right at the BESA Club. The street now becomes avenue du Général-de-Gaulle and takes you up to the **Plateau,** the old French compound.

The first right turn off avenue de Gaulle leads past the **Town Hall** to the entrance to the former **French Residency,** now the prime minister's office. Ever with an eye for beauty, the French built this lovely colonial structure so that it commands a panoramic view of the town and Port Vila Bay. The president of Vanuatu now lives in the former home of the French resident commissioner behind the prime minister's office.

ERAKOR ISLAND

Now find your way back down the hill to the main street and take a taxi or a Route 2 bus south to Le Lagon Resort. Take a refueling stop here or walk down the hill and catch a launch to Erakor Island Resort, which has a restaurant on the beach.

When finished resting, stroll around tiny **Erakor Island,** which sits astride the shallow entrance to Erakor Lagoon and was once home to a thriving village and an early missionary settlement. Pathways through the bush go by missionary graves from the late 19th century, and to judge from the moldy headstones, life was tough in those days. Erakor village was moved to the other side of the lagoon after a devasting cyclone in 1959, but the white-sand beach remains a pleasant place to sunbathe and swim, although the aquamarine water almost disappears at low tide.

MICHOUTOUCHKINE-PILIOKI ART GALLERY

Take the launch to the mainland and head back to town. If you have a car, turn left at the top of the hill on the road to Pango Point. Look on the left side for **Michoutouchkine-Pilioki Art Gallery.** That's where Nicolai Michoutouchkine and Alio Pilioko display their paintings, silk-screened prints, and sculptures, and a massive collection of some 19,000 pieces of artwork and handcrafts from throughout the South Pacific. The two men live and work in the little compound nestled beside the sea in a grove of coconut palms, but their gallery—formally known as Michoutouchkine-Pilioko Foundation Permanent Oceanic Art Display (tel. 23367)—is open to the public from 10am to 5pm daily. They do not charge admission.

TOURING EFATE

Except for a distance of about 5 miles in either direction from Vila, the 159km (95-mile) road around Efate is not paved; in fact, in many places it has barely been maintained since U.S. Navy Seabees built it during World War II. Nevertheless, you can drive all the way around the island in about 5 hours. Having done it, I can honestly say that a bus tour, with a Melanesian-style lunch at Nagar Restaurant on the north shore and a stop for a swim at sandy Eton Beach included, is a more comfortable and informative way to see the island. You will see waterfalls, caves, and other sights that you simply won't be able to find by yourself. Both **Frank King Tours** and **Tour Vanuatu** have all-day, round-island trips for about 4,500 VT ($40.50) per person.

If you do decide to drive yourself around, don't go without a map, a copy of the Vanuatu Visitors Bureau's *Guide to Vanuatu*, and a full tank of gas.

SPORTS & RECREATION

GOLF

Guests can tee off on **Le Lagon Resort**'s nine-hole golf course, and both guests and outsiders can play the 18-hole course at the **Radisson Royal Palms Resort.** On

---

IMPRESSIONS

The tribe, I read later, had belonged to another cargo cult. They were naked because they preferred it that way, having considered the alternatives.

—Frances FitzGerald, 1986

Efate's south shore some 19km (11½ miles) from Vila, **Whitesands Resort and Country Club** (tel. 22090) has 18 holes open for play. Greens fees are 1,000 VT ($9). The Golfer's Grill in the open-air clubhouse serves light lunches. **Vila Golf and Country Club** (tel. 22564) has a flat nine holes, but the setting, in an old coconut grove behind Mele Beach north of Vila, makes up for the lack of challenge. Greens fees here are 1,000 VT ($9). Bags, clubs, and carts (they call them trollies) can be rented at all four courses.

HORSEBACK RIDING

Frank King Tours (tel. 22808) uses the Club Hippique's horses and charges 2,500 VT ($22.50) for 1 hour's riding, 3,500 VT ($31.50) for 2 hours, including bus transportation.

DAY CRUISES

The most popular cruise is on the 74-foot-long sailing ketch ***Coongoola*** (tel. 23244), which takes guests to Havannah Harbor (where a sizable Allied fleet was moored during World War II) and Lelepa Island off Efate's northwest coast. The cruise includes morning and afternoon teas, swimming and snorkeling among vast numbers of tropical fish over extraordinarily colorful reefs, and a barbecue luncheon on a magnificent beach on Moso Island. Cost is about 5,600 VT ($50.50) per person. The *Coongoola* also is available for longer cruises and scuba-diving expeditions.

The 42-foot trimaran sailboat **Golden Wing** (tel. 22743) wanders from island to island, reef to reef for snorkeling and picnics. Cost is 4,800 VT ($43).

The glass-bottom ***L'Espadon 2*** (tel. 22808) and ***Neptune II*** (tel. 22272) cruise to Hideaway Island, stopping for snorkeling expeditions along the way. They charge 4,000 VT ($36) per person for the full-day excursion, including a buffet lunch at the island's little resort. Both boats have ½-day coral viewing and snorkeling trips for about 2,000 VT ($18) per person.

SAILING, CRUISING & FISHING

Yachting World (tel. 23273), rents catamarans, sailboards, outboard runabouts, outrigger canoes, and yachts up to 40 feet in length from its dock next to the Waterfront Bar & Grill. The yachts can be chartered either "bareboat" or with a skipper and crew. Smaller catamaran sailboats and dinghies rent for 1,000 VT ($9) an hour, plus a 2,000 VT ($18) deposit.

For deep-sea fishing, contact Peter Gawlter of **Phantom Charters** (tel. 23285). His trawler-style motor cruiser goes offshore in search of the big game; it's docked at the Waterfront Bar & Grill.

SCUBA-DIVING

Vanuatu's incredibly clear water, the colorful reefs, and the wrecks of the *Star of Russia,* the *Kathleen,* the *President Coolidge* (the latter is at Santo) and other unfortunate ships attract scuba divers from all over the world. **Nautilus Scuba** (tel. 2398), next door to the Waterfront Bar & Grill, and **Scuba Holidays** (tel. 22963), at the Hideaway Island Resort, are the operators. Rates range from about 3,300 VT ($30) for a single dive to 35,000 VT ($315) for a full PADI instruction course.

IMPRESSIONS

The lifestyle was French on the surface but the bias was British.
—JOHN DYSON, 1982

SWIMMING & SNORKELING

The crystal-clear waters, colorful reefs, and abundant fish life off Vila are prime attractions. Unless you're hopelessly landbound, plan to get there and have a look for yourself. It will be time rewarded and money well spent.

Iririki Island Resort, Le Lagon Resort, and **Radisson Royal Palms Resort** all rent their snorkel gear and other water-sports equipment to nonguests. See "Where to Stay," below, for details. Iririki Island is nearest to town; take the water taxi to the island and turn left when you get off the boat.

Hideaway Island, one of the more popular spots, is nearly surrounded by Mele Reef, now a marine reserve where you can watch the sea life—but can't remove it from the water. The tiny, flat island is home to **Hideaway Island Resort** (tel. 22936), which invites the public to swim, snorkel, lie on its white beach, and partake of a buffet lunch in its restaurant—complete with crushed coral floor. Lunches are served at 12:30pm and cost 1,200 VT ($11) per person. To reach Hideaway Island by car, go north out of town on the main road, bear left at the airport traffic circle, pass the Vila Golf and Country Club, and then take the first left after the next one-lane bridge (at the Hideaway sign). You can walk across the sandbar at low tide. A ferry runs to the island on the hour. The glass-bottom ***L'Espadon 2*** (tel. 22808) and ***Neptune II*** (tel. 22272) cruise to Hideaway Island, stopping for snorkeling expeditions along the way.

TENNIS & SQUASH

Guests can use the hard-surface tennis courts at **Le Lagon** and **Radisson Royal Palms** resorts. Others can play both tennis and squash at the **Port Vila Tennis Club** (tel. 22437) for 350 VT ($3) each an hour, 250 VT ($2) each if there are four players using a court. Squash players can use the BESA Club's courts (tel. 22615).

SHOPPING

You can very easily spend a fortune in the handcraft, perfume, apparel, and duty-free shops along Vila's main street. I suggest you stroll all the way up one side of the street and down the other, poking your head into the various establishments before making your selections. And watch out for a few items bearing trademarks that really don't belong on them (that supercheap, allegedly genuine LaCoste shirt may quickly shrink to an extra-small size).

A number of **duty-free shops** populate the main street, offering perfumes, electronic appliances, cameras, French clothing and shoes, cigarettes, liquor, and a wide range of other imported goods. See "What to Buy" in Chapter 2 for some advice about duty-free shopping; it applies to Vila. In Vanuatu, you take possession of your duty-free purchases at the shop, but your airline ticket (which you must have with you during your shopping spree) will be stamped "Duty Free Goods in Possession." Make sure you have the duty-free items and your receipt with you when you check in for your departing flight.

Stamp collectors can examine the colorful Vanuatu sets at the post office's Philatelic Bureau from 7:30 to 11:30am and from 1:15 to 4:30pm Monday through Friday.

HANDIKRAF BLONG VANUATU, in the Cultural Centre. Tel. 23228.

This is the best place to purchase authentic handcrafts produced in the country. You will have a chance to buy replicas of many of the artifacts you saw in the museum: slit drums (some 8 feet tall); straw hats, mats, and baskets; carved masks and clubs used in war or to ceremonially kill pigs; carved stone tikis; grass skirts; and rounded pigs' tusks.

GOODIE'S TREASURE BOX, Main Street in the Olympic Hotel Building. Tel. 23445.

This shop has many of the handcraft items we saw at Handikraf Blong Vanuatu plus some excellent finds from Solomon Islands and Papua New Guinea. There's also an assortment of pink-, ivory-, and black-coral jewelry, books on Bislama and Vanuatu, original paintings by local artist Olwyn Hirsch, coconut and sandalwood soaps, postcards, and curios. There's a branch at Le Lagon Resort.

MICHOUTOUCHKINE CREATIONS, Main Street in Pilioki House. Tel. 23367.

We've already seen Russian-born Nicolai Michoutouchkine's art gallery and museum south of Vila and one of his shops at the Sheraton Fiji (see Chapter 12). This one is home base, where he and Alio Pilioki sell their tropical clothing covered in squiggly swirls. Each item is signed by the artist.

VILA HANDPRINTS, Main Street opposite post office. Tel. 23687.

For tropical clothing along the tie-dyed lines we have seen in other countries, look in this shop or the branch at the Radisson Royal Palms Resort. They have a good selection of pareus, dresses, shopping bags, and other items, some produced in the company's factory (at the Y-intersection south of Le Rendez-Vous Restaurant), others by local artisans.

LA CABANE BOUTIQUE, main road, south of town at turnoff to wharf. Tel. 22763.

Annie Tehei, wife of Tahitian Felix Tehei, sells hand-printed clothing and shell-jewelry creations in her boutique, which is part of Félix's La Cabane Restaurant. See "Where to Dine," below.

EVENING ENTERTAINMENT

Much of Vila's evening entertainment takes place at **Le Lagon Resort** (tel. 22313), **Radisson Royal Palms Resort** (tel. 22040), and **Iririki Island Resort** (tel. 23388). See "Where to Stay," below, for more information. **Tour Vanuatu** (tel. 22745) has a "Vila by Night" tour which essentially bar-hops through town; the price is 6,000 VT ($54), including dinner and drinks.

ISLAND NIGHTS

The "custom" dance styles of the ni-Vanuatu differ considerably from those in Polynesia. Instead of the gyrating hips in Tahiti and the Cook Islands or the graceful hand-and-feet movements in Samoa and Tonga, the Melanesians stamp their feet while moving about and singing. In the villages, hundreds of men, women, and children often dance in unison, depending on the occasion. Although they vary from one village to the next, some typical dances are those that welcome strangers to the village or celebrate circumcision or pig-slaughtering rituals. During the latter, pigs are slaughtered by the dozens—but don't worry, you won't see a young boy put to pain, or a pig knocked dead with a skillfully carved club. Both Le Lagon and the Radisson have island-night buffet dinners followed by traditional Melanesian dancing. Call them to find out when.

Friendly Bob Kalfabun usually hangs out at Goodie's Treasure Box on the main

---

IMPRESSIONS

Multiplicity seems to be in the nature of the country, and although most educated ni-Vanuatu are committed Christians—and many of the missionaries are ni-Vanuatu—there remains a certain amount of work to be done.

—FRANCES FITZGERALD, 1986

street selling tickets to his weekly **Melanesian Village Feast** (tel. 24484). The village residents spend all day cooking a huge meal in a *laplap* (earth oven). You enjoy a bowl of kava or fruit juice (no alcoholic beverages are served) while the oven is opened and the meal set out on a buffet table under a thatch pavilion. After the meal, the villagers put on a short dance show, then everyone dances under the stars to a string band. The entire evening costs 2,000 VT ($18) per person.

Frank King Tours (tel. 22808) has an island night—usually Friday—at Hideaway Island Resort for the same price.

KAVA DRINKING

Vanuatu produces very potent kava, which has become the national drink. In the villages, men gather in the central, banyan-shaded *nakamal* to drink theirs. Today the term applies as well to rustic kava bars, which have sprung up in backyards all over Vila. Expatriate residents frequent the **Red Laet Nakamal** (no phone). To find it, take the street going east off the traffic circle behind Independence Park and look for the red light. It's in the block beyond the Talimoru Hotel. Admission is free. Cups of kava cost 50 VT and 100 VT (45¢ and 90¢). The Red Laet opens at 4pm Monday to Saturday and closes around midnight. Take along some hard candy to suppress the rooty kava taste.

If you want an escort, **Frank King Tours** (tel. 22808) has a "kava appreciation" tour for 2,000 VT ($18).

GAMBLING

The **Palms Casino,** Vanuatu's only gambling establishment, is in the Radisson Royal Palms Resort (tel. 22040). It opens at 11:30am every day and closes at 3am the next morning. Admission is free. It has slot machines and blackjack and baccarat tables.

6. WHERE TO STAY

EXPENSIVE

LE LAGON RESORT, P.O. Box 86, Port Vila. Tel. 22313, or toll free 800/663-1515 in North America. Fax 23817. Telex 1032. 113 rms, 32 bungalows. A/C MINIBAR TV TEL **Location:** 2 miles from Vila on Erakor Lagoon. Route 2 bus.

$ Rates (in U.S. dollars only): $120–$160 single or double room; $160–$200 bungalow; $240–$500 suite. AE, DC, MC, V.

Sprawled through a coconut grove at the mouth of Erakor Lagoon, this Pan Pacific resort has a wide range of luxurious accommodations in both standard hotel rooms

---

IMPRESSIONS

On some islands there are women's nakamals; *on other islands, until recently, women could be killed for entering a* nakamal.

—SCOTT L. MALCOLMSON, 1990

At the precious best, a nakamal *evening acquires a fragile intimacy, everyone whispering and laughing softly with no particular awareness of time.*

—SCOTT L. MALCOLMSON, 1990

and thatch-roofed bungalows. Seven one-story buildings hold the least expensive motel-style rooms, each with its own private balcony or patio. The bungalows sit in the gardens or along the beach, with four of them perched by themselves on a tiny, casuarina-shrouded island. The two-bedroom suites, the most expensive, are beside the beach.

Dining/Entertainment: Two separate buildings hold a ballroom, an upmarket French restaurant, an all-day coffee shop, and the Tam Tam Night Club, a piano bar-type lounge with nightly entertainment. Melanesian feasts and dance shows are held 1 night a week.

Services: Baby-sitting, laundry.

Facilities: Boutiques; adult and children's swimming pools; poolside bar; beach; tennis courts; nine-hole golf course; on-premises sports center. Nonguests can purchase coupons at the reception desk to rent the equipment on an hourly or ½-day basis at rates ranging from 500 VT ($4.50) an hour for snorkeling gear, canoes, and paddleboats to 1,000 VT ($9) for greens fees or 1 hour's use of a catamaran.

RADISSON ROYAL PALMS RESORT AND CASINO, P.O. Box 215, Port Vila. Tel. 22040, or toll free 800/333-3333 in the U.S. and Canada. Fax 23340. Telex 1042. 156 rooms. A/C MINIBAR TV TEL **Location:** East side of Vila on inner lagoon. Route 3 bus.

$ Rates: 13,500 VT ($121.50) single or double garden view; 18,000 VT ($162) single or double lagoon view; 25,000 VT–35,000 VT ($225–$315) suite. AE, DC, MC, V.

Formerly an American-owned property known as the Intercontinental Island Inn, this hotel situated on the east side of town along the banks of the inner lagoon was given a thorough face-lift in 1990–91. Old, worn carpets in the public areas were replaced by ceramic tiles so bright they look like water. The hotel-style rooms, which open off hallways in two, double-storied wings flanking a central building, were repainted and refurnished. "The Radisson" now is popular with Australians, including families, who take advantage of reasonably priced packages to have a beachside holiday punctuated by gambling in the hotel's casino.

If you are a snorkeling addict, the water in the inner lagoon is not as clear as that off Le Lagon and Erakor Island resorts.

Dining/Entertainment: Restaurant, open-air coffee shop, poolside bar with snacks. Beachside Melanesian feast and dance show 1 night a week. A discotheque was under construction during my recent visit. Children's movies are shown on the in-house cable system in the afternoons, adult films at night. The Palms Casino, Vanuatu's only gambling establishment, is on the premises.

Services: Baby-sitting; laundry; business center; beauty salon.

Facilities: Shops; adult and children's swimming pools; beach; tennis courts; childrens' games room; 18-hole golf course; water-sports equipment. Nonguests can play golf and tennis; fees are 1,000 VT ($9) per person for golf and 1,000 VT ($9) for each hour of court time. They also can rent the water-sports equipment at hourly rates ranging from 400 VT ($3.50) for canoes to 1,000 VT ($9) for catamarans.

MODERATE

ERAKOR ISLAND RESORT, P.O. Box 24, Port Vila. Tel. 22983. Fax 22899. Telex 1069. 13 bungalows. **Location:** Erakor Island, south end of town on Erakor Lagoon. Route 2 bus.

$ Rates: 7,500 VT ($67.50) single; 9,500 VT ($85.50) double. AE, DC, MC, V.

Although slightly on the basic side for the money, the bungalows at this little resort we visited on our walking tour of Vila (see "What to See & Do," above) have their charms. Most have little gardens behind bamboo fences, which offer privacy while you dash between a separate toilet-shower building and the bungalow itself. You can walk directly from beach to shower through a break in the bamboo. Others have sleeping lofts in addition to beds downstairs. Meals are served in a large, airy building on a beach-sided point where a shuttle launch from the mainland lands. Day-trippers are not allowed to bring their own food, but they can rent snorkeling gear and outrigger canoes if the guests aren't using them for free.

IRIRIKI ISLAND RESORT, Central Post Office, Port Vila. Tel. 23388. Fax 23880. Telex 1080. 72 bungalows. A/C TV TEL **Location:** Iririki Island in Port Vila Harbor. 24-hour free water taxi from Vila's waterfront.

$ Rates: 9,000 VT ($81) single or double island bungalow; 110,500 VT ($100) single or double bungalow on stilts over a beach. AE, MC, V.

A free water taxi gives easy access to Vila's shops and restaurants by constantly crossing the narrow channel separating the island resort and town (the dock is just south of the market). Each of the rectangular bungalows has a double bed and settee, video movies piped to a television set, and a breezy covered porch. The more expensive bungalows stand on steel stilts over a small beach and have unobstructed views of the harbor and town. Not all of the hillside units have views, so the extra cost of a beach bungalow is well spent if you want a guaranteed vista. Above the resort sits the colonial-style, Condominium-era home of the British resident commissioner.

Iririki's central building's restaurant and bar command vistas of Port Vila and its gorgeous harbor. An island band usually plays in the bar from 6:30 to 10pm nightly. The resort stages a poolside barbecue lunch on Sunday and a Melanesian-style feast 1 night a week. Snacks and light meals are available all day Monday through Saturday. Facilities include a boutique, swimming pool, beach, and water-sports equipment shed. Nonguests can rent catamarans, surf skis, paddleboats, and snorkeling gear for prices ranging from 250 VT to 1,500 VT ($2.25 to $13.50) an hour (turn left when you get off the water taxi).

VILA CHAUMIERES, P.O. Box 400, Port Vila. Tel. 22866. Fax 24238. 4 bungalows. A/C **Location:** 3km (2 miles) east of Vila on the Forari road, between the lagoons.

$ Rates: 6,000 VT ($54) single or double. AE, MC, V.

Australians Bea Harmshaw and Colin Newman have four bungalows at their establishment on the banks of the narrow, riverlike passage between the two lagoons. *Chaumière* in French means a thatch hut, and that's exactly what the bungalows had on top until Cyclone Uma ripped away the straw in 1987. Now they have regular roofs, but inside they still boast tile floors and baths, ceiling fans, and full kitchens, plus a bedroom separated from the living area by a partial wall. No children under 16 need apply here.

The restaurant with outdoor dining areas on the water is a comfortable spot for a cold beer in an icy mug and congenial conversation with the local expatriates who hang out here and munch on Bea's assortment of sandwiches, cold plates, and seafood specials such as coconut crab and lobster.

BUDGET

TALIMORU HOTEL, P.O. Box 110, Port Vila. Tel. 22656. Fax 22700. 42 rms (none with bath). **Location:** Street running east off traffic circle behind Independence Park. Ask Route 3 bus to take you there.

$ Rates: 1,700 VT ($15.50) single, 2,650 VT ($24) double without balcony; 1,850 VT ($16.50) single, 2,850 VT ($25.50) double with balcony. Less 10% with valid student ID card. No credit cards.

Rightfully advertised as "Port Vila's First Budget Hotel," this former apartment building was completely refurbished and opened in 1989. There's absolutely nothing fancy here, but it's very clean. The rooms are small and simply furnished; some are barely large enough for one person. They all have table fans. Three or four rooms on each floor share two toilets and cold-water showers. Guests also share a small laundry area. Plans call for a restaurant and nakamal kava bar.

7. WHERE TO DINE

One local delicacy shows up on many menus: the **coconut crab.** Although the preparation varies from one restaurant to another, the beast itself is a terrestrial crab with claws so strong it can climb up a palm and snap a coconut loose; hence, its name. They may lack the natural seafood flavor of their saltwater cousins, but those powerful claws make a delicious meal when boiled or steamed and served under a tasty sauce, be it garlic or chili in a French restaurant or black bean in a Chinese establishment. Another local specialty is the **flying fox,** the same fruit bat that looks like a fox and is considered sacred in Tonga. Frankly, having seen thousands of them hanging upside down in the treetops, I've never had the courage to order one for dinner.

FRENCH RESTAURANTS

LE RENDEZ-VOUS RESTAURANT, main street, uphill south of downtown. Tel. 23045.

Cuisine: FRENCH. **Reservations:** Recommended.

$ Prices: Appetizers 650 VT–1,400 VT ($6–$12.50); main courses 1,450 VT–2,800 VT ($13–$25). AE, DC, MC, V.

Open: Lunch Mon–Fri 11am–2pm; dinner Mon–Sat 6–10:30pm, or later, depending on demand.

Arrive early enough for a drink and a look at the view from this gorgeous building hanging on the edge of a bluff and open on its backside to the harbor and the yachts anchored in the sparkling channel behind Iririki Island. Start with a "millionaire's salad" of fresh hearts of palm (in copra planting days, only millionaires could afford to waste palms in salads). Go on to the house specialty, coconut crab *out* of its shell, either au gratin or with a touch of garlic. Local lobster is prepared the same way if crab isn't available. Save room for another specialty, a mouth-watering Grand Marnier soufflé for dessert.

CHEZ GILLES ET BRIGITTE, uphill from ANZ Bank, first street to left. Tel. 23797.

Cuisine: FRENCH. **Reservations:** Recommended.

$ Prices: Appetizers 600 VT ($5.50); main courses 1,200 VT–2,100 VT ($11–$19). AE, V.

Open: Lunch Mon–Fri 11am–1:30pm; dinner daily 6:30–9:30pm.

This couple from Réunion Island in the Indian Ocean serve up delicious traditional French fare at this pleasantly decorated house on the hill above the heart of town. You can dine inside or outside on the veranda with view of the harbor. Daily specials feature coconut crab and lobster.

L'HOUSTELET RESTAURANT, main street, south of town beyond the Y-intersection. Tel. 22303.

Cuisine: FRENCH/ITALIAN. **Reservations:** Recommended.

$ Prices: Appetizers 500 VT–1,000 VT ($4.50–$9); main courses 600 VT–1,600 VT ($5.50–$14.50). AE, DC, MC, V.

Open: Lunch daily 11am–2pm; dinner daily 6–11pm.

Frenchman Clément Martinez offers "local curiosities," such as a flying-fox terrine and coconut crab either in a soup or as a main course, with garlic butter. Other main courses include steaks, fish, and chicken in excellent piquant-style sauces. The garlic prawns are delicious. He also prepares excellent pizza and spaghetti.

MA BARKER'S RESTAURANT, main street, opposite Cultural Centre. Tel. 22399.

Cuisine: STEAKS. **Reservations:** Not accepted.

$ Prices (including tax): Appetizers 400 VT–600 VT ($3.50–$5.50); main courses 850 VT–1,300 VT ($7.50–$11.50). AE.

Open: Daily 7:30am–10:30pm.

Australian Rosie Barker offers breakfasts, sandwiches, burgers, and a variety of steaks, fish, and poultry in French sauces at her storefront restaurant. The decor here is turn-of-the-century with large copper pots and pans sitting on shelves or hanging from exposed joices. A popular bar also is done in Old-English style.

STEAKS & GRILLS

THE WATERFRONT BAR & GRILL, south end of main street, on waterfront. Tel. 23490.

Cuisine: STEAKS. **Reservations:** Not accepted.

$ **Prices:** Salads 500 VT ($4.50); sandwiches 450 VT ($4); steaks 1,200 VT ($11). No credit cards.

Open: Lunch daily 11:30am–2:30pm; dinner daily 6–10pm; bar daily 11am–11pm, or later if anyone wants to keep on drinking.

This stunning thatch-roofed pavilion is a popular eatery and drinking hole for local expatriate residents and the "yachties" who pass through Vila and moor alongside the restaurant or in the channel between it and Iririki Island. Some of the sailors have hung pennants and spinnakers from the high peaked ceiling. After you have selected the steak, fish, kebab, or hamburger that will be slapped on the outside grill for you, take a pass by the salad bar. As a regular bar, the Waterfront can't be beaten in Vila.

TERRACE RESTAURANT, in Hotel Rossi, main street. Tel. 22528.

Cuisine: STEAKS/SANDWICHES. **Reservations:** Not accepted.

$ **Prices:** Appetizers 550 VT–1,300 VT ($5–$11.50); main courses 800 VT–1,300 VT ($7–$11.50). AE, DC, MC, V.

Open: Mon–Fri 10am–6pm, Sat–Sun 10am–3pm.

The Rossi is a popular lunch spot and after-work drinking hole, sitting pleasantly as it does right on the waterfront. On Friday, Saturday, and Sunday, the hotel stages well-attended harborside barbecues of steaks, chicken, and sausage. You also can order from the snack menu, which features sandwiches and hamburgers, or more substantial fare from the hotel's dining room, such as grilled steaks or lobster and coconut crab. The sweet coconut sauce served with the charbroiled chicken is absolutely mouth-watering. (There's even a little waterside playground, with a baby-sitter on duty during the Sunday brunches.)

ASIAN & POLYNESIAN RESTAURANTS

LA CABANE [CHEZ FELIX], main road, south of town at turnoff to wharf. Tel. 22763.

Cuisine: TAHITIAN. **Reservations:** Recommended for dinner.

$ **Prices:** Lunch specials 600 VT ($5.50); appetizers 500 VT–900 VT ($4.50–$8); main courses 1,000 VT–1,200 VT ($9–$11). AE, MC, V.

Open: Breakfast daily 8–11am; lunch daily 11am–2pm; dinner daily 6–10:30pm.

Also known as Chez Félix in honor of gregarious owner, Tahitian Félix Tehei, La Cabane is indeed a thatch cabin. Félix's Australian-born wife, Annie, scours the market every morning, and if she has found a reef fish known as picot (or *pauwara* in Tahitian), try it. Félix fries it plain to preserve the succulent taste of the white flaky meat and serves it with taro, vegetables, a salad of pawpaw (papaya) with grated coconut, and a slice of pamplemousse (a thick-skinned grapefruit) to clear the palate. Tahitian-style poisson cru is a house specialty. A string band usually strums Melanesian and Tahitian tunes during dinner, and be on the lookout for notices of a Tahitian night with hip-grinding dancers.

THE HARBOUR VIEW, main street, uphill south of Le Rendez-Vous. Tel. 23668.

Cuisine: CHINESE. **Reservations:** Recommended.

$ **Prices:** Appetizers 300 VT–500 VT ($2.50–$4.50); main courses 750 VT–2,000 VT ($7–$18). AE, MC, V.

Open: Lunch Tues–Sun 11:30am–2pm; dinner daily 6:30–10pm.

The best and certainly the most picturesque of several Chinese restaurants in Vila, this one can be found in a lovely house, complete with swimming pool, on a bluff overlooking the passage behind Iririki Island. You can swim in the pool and then have lunch or watch the sun set over the harbor and then have dinner. The selection of dishes ranges from vegetable chow mein to lobster or coconut crab in black-bean sauce. Most beef, pork, and chicken dishes cost about 800 VT ($7.20).

CHENG'S CHINESE SNACK AND TAKE-AWAY FOOD, main street opposite market. Tel. 24344.
Cuisine: CHINESE. **Reservations:** Not accepted.
$ Prices: Main courses 220 VT–600 VT ($2–$5.50). No credit cards.
Open: Mon–Sat 7am–9pm.

This little storefront shop has a hot table displaying the day's mass-produced Cantonese dishes, or you can choose from the main menu (and pay more) for meals prepared to order. Diners can eat at four tables and watch customers order at the take-out bar.

SNACKS & LIGHT MEALS

LA TENTATION PATISSERIE, main street opposite post office. Tel. 22261.
Cuisine: CAFE/PATISSERIE. **Reservations:** Not accepted.
$ Prices: Meals 250 VT–650 VT ($2–$6). No credit cards.
Open: Mon–Fri 7am–7pm, Sat–Sun 7am–1pm.

This pleasant outdoor eatery has umbrella tables on a shady patio, at which you can sample a wide array of fancy continental pastries or just plain doughnuts. You can also order breakfasts of eggs or omelets, sandwiches, and hamburgers with "the lot" (meaning Aussie-style with cheese, a slice of beet, and a fried egg).

LA TERRASSE, main street opposite French Embassy. Tel. 22244.
Cuisine: BISTRO CAFE. **Reservations:** Not accepted.
$ Prices: Meals and plats du jour 750 VT–950 VT ($7–$8.50); sandwiches and burgers 400 VT–600 VT ($3.50–$5.50). No credit cards.
Open: Mon–Sat 7am–8pm.

Take your pick of where to eat your fine food at this genuine French-style, French-owned bistro: at umbrella tables under the canvas right at curbside, inside by the bar, or on a covered patio with harbor view. In addition to pastries and light meals, a daily three-course plat du jour is good value.

LE CAFE, main street near the post office. Tel. 22226.
Cuisine: CAFE/PIZZA. **Reservations:** Not accepted.
$ Prices: Sandwiches and salads 350 VT–600 VT ($3–$5.50); breakfasts 500 VT ($4.50); pizzas 700 VT–2,350 VT ($6.50–$21). No credit cards.
Open: Mon–Fri 6:30am–9:30pm, Sat–Sun 6:30am–1:30pm; pizza bar Wed–Sun 5:30–9pm.

This little snack bar has outdoor seating in an alley along one side of its storefront location. In addition to an assortment of French pastries, it has some unusual sandwiches such as tropical salad, avocado and chicken, curried egg with watercress, and banana with bacon and cream cheese. The pizza bar justifiably calls its pies the "largest in Vanuatu."

BLOODY MARY'S, main street at the market. Tel. 22669.
Cuisine: BURGERS/FISH-AND-CHIPS. **Reservations:** Not accepted.
$ Prices: Burgers 200 VT ($1.80); fish-and-chips 500 VT ($4.50). No credit cards.
Open: Daily 8am–11:30pm.

One of the more famous (if also a bit seedy) take-out establishments in the South Pacific, this has become a landmark on Port Vila's waterfront. In fact, you can't help photographing its gaudy red-and-white building surrounded by a red picket fence as you look through the market next door. Hamburgers are served Australian style.

8. EASY EXCURSIONS

TANNA

Tanna is one of the most fascinating islands in the South Pacific, and a trip there should not be missed. The island is primitive, however, and the government will not let anyone off the plane who is neither on a day tour nor booked into one of the island's two hotels. Accordingly, consider a day trip (see below) or an overnight. Mount Yasur is best seen at dusk, which requires staying overnight.

GETTING THERE & GETTING AROUND

You must book your trip in advance through your hometown travel agent or, in Vila, **Tour Vanuatu** (tel. 22745) or **Frank King Tours** (tel. 22808). Tour Vanuatu sends most of its overnight guests to Tanna Beach Resort; Frank King sends his to White Grass Bungalows (see "Where to Stay," below). In other words, if you're going to stay over, pick your hotel first, then your agent.

Tour Vanuatu's day-trips cost about 30,000 VT ($270), which is about what Frank King charges for an overnight excursion.

There is no public transportation system whatsoever on Tanna, so once there, you're at the mercy of a tour group or your hotel.

WHAT TO SEE & DO

The tours, either booked in advance or arranged by the two hotels after you get to Tanna, take in the key sights. Here's what you will see.

The John Frum Cult

The villages around Sulfur Bay, at the base of Mount Yasur, are hotbeds of the John Frum cargo cult, one of the world's most unusual "religions." No one is quite sure of the cult's origins. It's known to have sprung up during World War II, when Americans unloaded huge amounts of cargo in the islands. The cultists believe that one of the airmen—John "from" America—will return one February 15 with great riches and that thereupon they can kill all their pigs, stop working, and run all white persons off the island (they've already done a good job of the latter, since only some 20 of Tanna's 20,000 residents are now white).

In the meantime, John Frum sends messages to his adherents through radio waves received by imitation antennae strung with tin cans. His followers hold a large celebration with much dancing, feasting, and kava drinking every February 15 at Sulfur Bay in anticipation of his arrival. The symbol of the cult is the red cross, apparently taken from the insignia worn by American Red Cross workers who visited the island during the war. Village greens in the area have carefully tended red crosses enclosed in picket fences (you can photograph the crosses but not touch them). A John Frum "church" in a thatch building in Yaneumakel village has a picture of American astronauts mounted over an altar consisting of a red cross with a picture postcard of Jesus attached to it.

At first the cult was considered subversive and its leaders imprisoned, but now it's considered a fact of life on Tanna. However, during the disorders in 1980, when Tanna had its own independence movement, the government in Port Vila sent policemen to remove the American flags flown by the cult on February 15.

The "Custom People"

Another group of Tannese made a conscious decision in the 1960s to throw off Western ways entirely and return to the customary life-style of their ancient ancestors, growing crops in small gardens, raising pigs for their value, and wearing nothing but grass skirts or nambas. Today a number of villages in the hills subscribe to custom, but

---

IMPRESSIONS

Tanna was one of the oddest places I have ever been, which is saying a great deal. It is proof that even on the smallest island all sorts of differing life-styles can flourish simultaneously.

—Paul Theroux, 1991

most tourists visit **Yaohnanen,** home of the high chief of the "custom people." Women do the work while the men hang out in the nakamal under a sprawling banyan.

When tour groups arrive, the villagers perform a custom dance and sell grass skirts dyed bright red, yellow, and green. Afterward, visitors are free to wander around the primitive village, where pigs run free and the only metal to be found is in the axes and cooking pots (which are never washed, only hung out of reach of the pigs until the next meal). It's slightly touristy, but if you don't have time to get thoroughly off the beaten path, the "custom village" is an easy way to see what life was like in the old days—and still is in many parts of Melanesia. It will make you appreciate the little things in life, like electricity and running water.

Tanna has five distinct languages, 27 dialects, myriad cultures, and rival clans who no longer go to war but shun each other and demand payments of pigs and money for real or supposed wrongs committed by one against another. Every year or so, when the high chiefs feel wealthy enough, the people all come together for the **Nekowiar,** a huge festival noted for the Toka, a dance performed by hundreds of stomping, waving participants in custom dress. Nekowiars are never announced until the last minute, so it's impossible to plan to attend—you just have to be lucky. Local custom dances and John Frum celebrations, however, are held every weekend.

Mount Yasur

Capt. James Cook saw the top of Mount Yasur glowing red and pink from far out at sea when he approached Tanna in 1774. Although the Melanesians wouldn't let him cross the surrounding ash plain to climb the sacred 1,190-foot-high cone, they now have cut a road most of the way up the volcano and allow tour groups to climb the rest of the way across loose stones and sandlike ash to the narrow rim of the crater. It's not a hike for the fainthearted, for once on top you look almost straight down through nose-burning sulfur fumes and fine, eye-watering volcanic dust into three calderas. The jagged rocks deep in the hole nearest you glow bright red; every few minutes the fissure erupts with a thundering explosion that reverberates through the crater. Red-hot lava shoots hundreds of feet into the air in an awesome display of pyrotechnics.

This most accessible of volcano craters is at its impressive best in the waning light of dusk, when the boiling belly of the sulfur cloud turns pink over the red fires of the caldera.

Be sure to bring walking shoes with good traction and a windbreaker or sweater from which the fine volcanic dust can be washed.

WHERE TO STAY

TANNA BEACH RESORT, P.O. Box 27, Tanna. Tel. 68610, or toll free 800/443-0799 in the U.S. Fax same as phone. 11 bungalows. **Location:** 3km (2 miles) from airstrip on west coast.

$ Rates: 7,000 VT ($63) single; 9,000 VT ($81) double. No credit cards.

Most of Tour Vanuatu's clients stay at this charming collection of clean and comfortable thatch bungalows operated by the McGeough brothers from Ireland. You can take a dip in the swimming pool or in the surf pounding on the nearby beach, relax with a cold drink on the veranda, and eat home-cooked local produce in a pleasant dining room overlooking the pool.

WHITE GRASS BUNGALOWS, P.O. Box 5, Tanna. Tel. 6868888, or 22808 in Vila (Frank King Tours). 4 bungalows. **Location:** 10km (6 miles) north of airstrip on west coast.

$ Rates: 3,500 VT ($31.50) single; 4,000 VT ($36) double. No credit cards.

Chief Tom Numake, one of the paramount chiefs on Tanna, runs this establishment and doubles as tour guide. The thatch bungalows sit in a lawn on a bluff above the rocky shore. They're basic but clean, and they do have screens on the louvered windows. Electricity and hot water are supplied by solar panels. The restaurant overlooks the sea from the edge of the bluff and serves very plain but filling local-style meals.

SANTO

After de Quirós's abortive attempt to establish a Spanish colony named New Jerusalem on Santo in 1606, this largest of all Vanuatu islands virtually disappeared from the pages of world history. French and British planters moved in during the late 1800s and established large copra plantations along the coast of the island's eastern half, but the rugged, jungle-clad mountain range running down its western side was so impenetrable that to this day Melanesian culture is better preserved there than anywhere else in Vanuatu. The planters lived their genteel lives along the flat coastal plains of the east and were hardly noticed by the primitive peoples of the interior.

Santo suddenly came to the world's attention again when the Allies arrived in 1942 to build a huge support base for the battles against the Japanese in Solomon Islands to the north. Within a matter of months they constructed five airfields, 43 cinemas, a sophisticated telephone system, four large hospitals, a huge steam laundry, a radio station, monstrous "market gardens" to grow fresh vegetables, an extensive network of roads and bridges, wharves capable of handling the largest ships afloat, and a complete naval repair facility. The base soon had a population of some 100,000 American and New Zealand servicemen and even some women nurses, who inspired James A. Michener to create Nurse Nellie Forbush, the Arkansas belle who fell head over heels for the dashing and mysterious French planter named Emile De Becque in *Tales of the South Pacific.*

After the war ended in 1945, the Americans offered to sell much of the surplus matériel to the local government and planters at scrap-metal prices. When the offer was refused (the locals believing the Yanks would give the stuff away), the Americans built a ramp into the water and proceeded methodically to push everything from Jeeps to Coca-Cola bottles into the lagoon. The rusting, coral-encrusted litter still covers the beach and floor of the lagoon at **Million Dollar Point.**

Elsewhere the jungle has reclaimed much of the old base, but Quonset huts have been turned into houses and shops in sleepy **Luganville.** This wide-avenued town was built on land reclaimed by the Americans in order to construct a seaport on Segond Canal, the magnificent anchorage between Santo and Aore Island. Leftover Marston matting, once used to build airstrips, has been turned into fences to restrain the herds of cattle that now graze under the palms of the old plantations. Concrete foundations in Luganville's Unity Park are all that's left of the PT boat nest where John F. Kennedy and PT-109 were based before leaving for combat—and a sunken boat—in Solomon Islands. Up on a plateau, the jungle has reclaimed most of its apron, but "Bomber 3" airstrip still cuts a ghostly 4,000-foot pathway through the growth; it almost seems as though a Flying Fortress could take off this afternoon with a load of bombs destined for Guadalcanal. Ammunition bunkers and gun emplacements are used to dry copra and coffee beans, and occasionally a planter will drive his Land Rover along the crushed-coral roads that separated thousands of tents pitched among the palms. Carcasses of warplanes, left where they crashed, rest deep in the undergrowth. Indeed, the haunting remains of the war effort lie virtually everywhere on Santo.

The problem is that nothing is marked, not even the little trail that leads just a few yards off a main road to Million Dollar Point. Except for a monument to the memory of Capt. Elwood J. Euart, the only life lost when the luxury-liner-turned-troop-

---

IMPRESSIONS

Of all the islands in the Pacific, Santo has made the most profound impression on me.

—James A. Michener, 1951

transport *President Coolidge* struck a mine and sank on October 26, 1942, there simply has been little effort to preserve the past.

For this reason, I recommend a guided tour of Santo: You'll get a reasonably knowledgeable escort to the remains of the war effort, and someone who'll help you find places like **Champagne Beach** (one of the most magnificent beaches in all of the South Pacific), the eerie airstrip known as "Bomber 3," the incredibly translucent **Blue Holes,** and the old nurses' compound at little **Saraundu Beach,** where surely Nurse Nellie Forbush must have cavorted with Emile De Becque while Aoba—Michener's mythical "Bali-hai"—loomed through the haze on the horizon.

GETTING THERE & GETTING AROUND

See "Getting Around" earlier in this chapter for information about Vanair's twice-daily flights between Vila and Santo.

Tour Vanuatu (tel. 22745) offers a weekend trip leaving Vila every Friday and returning on Sunday. It costs 32,400 VT ($292), including airfare and hotel.

Hotel Santo (tel. 36250) rents cars. If you do travel around Santo on your own, take along a copy of the visitors bureau's *Guide to Vanuatu,* which has an excellent chapter on Santo.

WHAT TO SEE & DO

Tour Vanuatu (tel. 22745 in Vila, 36343 in Santo) works with Fred Kleckham of **Driftravel** on Santo to offer several excursions once you get there. One all-day tour includes Champagne Beach and the Blue Holes, and Big Bay where de Quirós landed. It costs 6,000 VT ($54). An overnight version, with accommodation in a village, costs 10,500 VT ($94.50). Another day-trip goes by boat to the beautifully rugged—and very primitive—west coast for 6,600 VT ($59.50).

Allan Power of **Santo Dive Tours,** P.O. Box 233, Santo, (tel. 36822), has been going down to the *President Coolidge* since 1969 and still hasn't seen it all. The 32,000-ton ship rests just offshore, in 80 to 240 feet of water, making it the most accessible large wreck in the world.

WHERE TO STAY & EAT

The economy of Santo was slow to recover after the "Coconut War" in 1980, and even though things have picked up considerably in recent years, accommodations are still scarce; restaurants, even more so.

BOKISSA ISLAND RESORT, P.O. Box 261, Luganville, Santo. Tel. 36855. Telex 1099. 12 bungalows. **Location:** Bokissa Island, 40 minutes by boat from Luganville.

$ Rates: 7,500 VT ($67.50) single; 8,500 VT ($76.50) double. AE, MC, V.

Australians Carmel Hanson and Robin McLare operate this little offshore resort on Bokissa, a small island off Luganville (stay here for relaxation, not to run around Santo looking for World War II relics). The bungalows are comfortably appointed and have ceiling fans. A central building houses a dining room and bar. Water-sports equipment is provided on the beach.

HOTEL SANTO, P.O. Box 178, Luganville, Santo. Tel. 36250. Fax 36749. Telex 1086. 22 rms (all with bath). A/C TEL **Location:** Luganville, west end of town.

$ Rates: 6,000 VT ($54) single; 7,000 VT ($63) double. AE, MC, V.

The Australian-style rooms in this modern hotel have balconies overlooking the main street or a courtyard surrounding a swimming pool and thatch-roofed games room. The dining room serves breakfast, lunch, and dinner. The bar is decorated with photographs of the *President Coolidge* and various objects brought up from the wreck by Allan Power, who has his Santo Dive Tours operation across the street (see Santo's "What to See & Do," above).

NEW LOOK HOTEL, P.O. Box 114, Luganville, Santo. Tel. 36440. 6 rms (all with bath). A/C **Location:** Wong Building, main street, Luganville.

$ Rates: 2,500 VT ($22.50) single; 3,500 VT ($31.50) double. AE, MC, V.
Don't expect any frills at this establishment over Wong's Store. It's much like Chinese-run, in-town hotels in other countries: a bit sterile in terms of atmosphere but clean. Guests can share cooking facilities.

ASIA MOTEL, P.O. Box 78, Luganville Santo. Tel. 36323. 8 rms (all with bath). **Location:** Luganville, opposite Burns Philp store.
$ Rates: 1,650 VT ($15) single; 2,200 VT ($20) double. No credit cards.
This establishment has basic accommodations with simple furniture on the second floor above a Chinese-owned grocery store. It's suitable for backpackers looking for inexpensive lodging.

PENTECOST

The South Pacific's most spectacular ritual takes place during April and May each year on **Pentecost,** the skinny but rugged island east of Santo: the famous **"land diving,"** or "Pentecost Jump" as it's sometimes called. You've seen it in *National Geographic* or on The Discovery Channel.

According to the most widely accepted "custom story," a woman once ran away from her harsh husband and took refuge in the top of a tall tree. Her husband found her and began climbing the tree to bring her down. Just before he reached the top, she called him a coward and dared him to follow her. She then leaped head-first toward the ground. Seeing her land unhurt, he accepted the dare and jumped after her. Unbeknownst to him, the wife had tied vines to her ankles to break her fall. He didn't and was killed. The other men of the village were humiliated that a woman could so trick one of their number, so they proceeded to build a tower taller than the highest tree, strap vines to their ankles, and leap off to prove their manhood.

Whether or not the story is true, men and boys from the villages on Pentecost gather at the end of the yam harvest in April and May, select sites on the edge of hills overlooking the sea, and build towers of tree limbs lashed together, some of them reaching 85 feet. Each man or boy builds his own "diving board" on the tower and installs a carefully measured set of liana vines that will break his fall. One by one, beginning with boys as young as 8 years old and working up to the strongest men, they climb the tower to their individual platforms. After an assistant ties the vines to his ankles, each jumper signals for quiet from the other villagers, all dressed in grass skirts or nambas, who dance and sing below. He then makes a short speech (perhaps confessing his wrongs), closes his hands to his chest, and plunges gracefully toward the muddy earth below. If the vines are measured just right, they tighten with a loud crack like a gunshot just before the jumpers hit the mud, popping them upright, unharmed. If they are too short, the jumpers are thrown into the tower. If they are too long, necks are broken and skulls crushed.

The late 20th century has arrived on Pentecost, of course, and the villages now stagger their jumps to occur on a series of Saturdays from mid-April to mid-May, and tour groups are invited to attend. It's a somewhat arduous day-trip from Port Vila: The plane leaves for the 1-hour flight to Pentecost's grass strip early in the morning and guests are ferried by open truck or coastal boat to the village staging the jump; then everyone climbs a steep, slippery path of mud to the hilltop where the tower stands. Sunscreen, a hat, an umbrella or raincoat, and comfortable shoes with excellent tred are all absolute musts.

Tour Vanuatu, P.O. Box 409, Port Vila (tel. 22745 in Port Vila), sponsors a complete day-trip, including a picnic lunch and admission to the jump. Dates—as well as prices—vary from year to year, but the jumps generally take place on Saturday. Tour Vanuatu publishes a brochure well in advance listing the dates and the contents of its Pentecost-jump tour packages.

Adventure Express Travel, 650 Fifth Street, San Francisco, CA 94107 (tel. 415/442-0799, or toll free 800/442-0799), arranges package tours to the jumps each year (and will know when they are scheduled).

CHAPTER 16

NEW CALEDONIA

New Caledonia's busy capital, Nouméa, is commonly dubbed "The Paris of the Pacific." It might better be compared to Saint-Tropez, so reminiscent of the French Riviera are the white and pastel buildings that climb its hills and overlook its golden beaches. Its fine French restaurants, its chic shops loaded with merchandise straight from Paris, even its Cannes-like casino, could just as well be in a Mediterranean resort and not half a world away in the South Pacific.

Drive a few miles from Nouméa or visit one of the territory's smaller islands, however, and suddenly you're in Melanesia. Like their counterparts in Vanuatu and Solomon Islands, the indigenous Melanesians of New Caledonia live a land-oriented, custom-dictated life-style more akin to that of their ancestors of a thousand years ago than to the modern, sophisticated French down the road.

This contrast of French and Pacific islander cultures is even more pronounced than the dichotomies of French Polynesia and Vanuatu, and it makes New Caledonia so unlike its South Pacific neighbors that the local tourist promotion authority is entirely correct when it says, *"Vive la différence!"*

1. GETTING TO KNOW NEW CALEDONIA

The largest South Pacific island covered in this book and the main island of New Caledonia, ***Grande Terre*** stretches for some 240 miles along the Melanesian archipelago, halfway between Fiji and Australia. The hauntingly beautiful **Isle of Pines (Ile des Pins)** and the less-visited **Belep Islands** lie within the world's second-longest barrier reef, which nearly encloses Grande Terre. The territory also includes a chain of raised-atoll islands known as the **Loyalty Group:** Lifou, Ouvéa, Tiga, and Maré. They lie in a line about 60 miles off Grande Terre's east coast.

Most visitors with a week or two spend the majority of their time in **Nouméa** (pop. 60,000), on the relatively dry southeastern corner of Grand Terre, and make short excursions to the lovely Isle of Pines or to Lifou in the Loyalty Islands. Nouméa is built on a hilly peninsula indented along its shores by half-moon bays. The downtown area, near the head of the peninsula, has as its center a rectangular park known as **place des Cocotiers** (Coconut Palms Square). On the south end, about 3 miles from downtown, are the gorgeous beaches of **Anse Vata** and **Baie des Citrons.** Most of Nouméa's hotels and other tourist facilities are on or near these two adjacent beaches. They are linked to downtown by the inland route de l'Anse Vata and a series of streets which hug Baie des Citrons, **Baie de l'Orphelinat,** and **Baie de la Moselle.**

WHAT'S SPECIAL ABOUT NEW CALEDONIA

Beaches
- ☐ Anse Vata and Baie des Citrons: two great half-moons right in town.
- ☐ Isle of Pines: Talcumlike sands almost join at Kuto and Kanuméra.

Great Towns/Villages
- ☐ Nouméa: The French Riviera lives in the South Pacific.

Natural Spectacles
- ☐ World's third-longest barrier reef: encloses a vast aquatic playground.

Cultures
- ☐ Melanesian and French: *Vive la différence!*

DATELINE

- **1000 B.C.** Melanesians settle New Caledonia.
- **1774** Capt. James Cook discovers the islands, names them for Scotland (*Caledonia* in Latin).
- **1788** Jean La Pérouse explores the west coast of Grande Terre before *Astrolabe* disappears.
- **1791–93** French expedition fails to find La Pérouse; Huon de Kermadec is first Frenchman to die in New Caledonia.
- **1830s** Cannibals eat some sandalwood traders.
- **1841** London Missionary Society establishes base in Loyalty Islands.
- **1843** Catholic priests arrive at Balade on Grande Terre.
- **1845** English seaman John Padden sets up

(continues)

HISTORY

Capt. James Cook discovered Grande Terre in 1774. Its mountains so reminded him of the Scottish Highlands that he named the island New Caledonia (*Caledonia* was the Roman name for Scotland). Jean La Pérouse explored the west coast in 1788 before he and the *Astrolabe* disappeared.

Cannibalism took its toll on a succession of sandalwood and bêche-de-mer traders who roamed the islands in the 1830s. In 1841, Protestant missionaries of the London Missionary Society obtained a toehold in the Loyalty Group, and in 1845 an English seaman established a small post on Ile Nou, near the present town of Nouméa.

France's long involvement began in 1843, when Catholic priests arrived at Balade. Four years later, starving kanaks raided their mission, beheaded and ate a priest. The Catholics immediately withdrew. French warships sent from Tahiti to support the reestablishment of the mission bombarded recalcitrant villages along the coasts. It was the beginning of a long and sometimes violent French-kanak relationship.

In 1850, kanaks massacred 17 members of a French raiding party. The Paris government used the incident as a pretext to establish a new penal colony. Emperor Napoléon III declared New Caledonia to be a French possession in 1853, and Admiral Febvrier-Despointes planted the tricolor at Pouébo on September 24 of that year. The French soon bought Ile Nou, and the English presence disappeared from the territory, except for family names, such as Johnston, Williams, and Wright.

France established penal compounds at Ile Nou, the Ducos Peninsula, and the Isle of Pines. Thousands of convicts arrived between 1864 and 1898. Nearly 4,000 Communards—most of them artisans and working-class citizens seized after their Paris Commune revolt failed in 1871—were confined on the Isle of Pines until granted amnesty in 1880. The old prison infirmary on Ile Nou now houses the territorial mental-health hospital, and a few decaying ruins of fortress walls and cellblocks can be seen on the Isle of Pines. Although the guillotine flourished on hardened criminals, most convicts roamed freely, distinguished from free settlers by their white uniforms and straw hats (they were known as *les chapeaux de paille,* "the straw hats"). They were used for public-works projects, such as construction of some of Nouméa's finest buildings.

In 1864, a French mining engineer named Jules Garnier explored Grande Terre and discovered one of the world's largest reserves of a high-grade nickel ore that now bears his name: garnierite. John Higginson (the same Irish-born French citizen who campaigned unsuccessfully to incorporate the New Hebrides into New Caledonia) founded *Société Le Nickel* to mine the ore and smelt it using a new process developed by Garnier. Employing free convict labor at first and later indentured workers imported mostly from Indonesia and Vietnam, "Le Nickel" soon became one of the world's largest producers of the metal. It has dominated New Caledonia's economy to the present.

In 1868, the government herded most of the Melanesians onto reservations and opened the rest of Grande Terre to mining claims and cattle raising. French miners and settlers soon claimed all the best land. This didn't sit well with the kanaks, and in 1878 the high chief of La Foa district launched a revolt, in which some 200 Frenchmen and 1,000 kanaks died. The fight ended when he was assassinated. The French put down another brief kanak revolt in 1917. Although some is now being redistributed, most of the prime land still is concentrated in large, predominantly French-owned estates.

New Caledonia was virtually a mining company town from 1853 until 1940, when France fell to the Germans. A Pro-Vichy government took over in Nouméa, but Henri Sautot, the French resident commissioner in the New Hebrides, soon slipped onto Grande Terre and ousted that regime. New Caledonia then joined Free France under Gen. Charles de Gaulle. When the Japanese advanced into the Solomons, Free France offered Nouméa as an Allied base. In March 1942 an American task force arrived in the sleepy port, which became the U.S. Navy's main South Pacific support base. Adm. William F. ("Bull") Halsey directed fleet operations from Anse Vata Beach. The stately building that served as his headquarters now houses the South Pacific Commission, a research and advisory organization, at the corner of route de l'Anse Vata and promenade Roger Laroque. The valley nearby is known to this day as Motor Pool.

In 1946, France granted citizenship to the kanaks and for the first time since 1868 allowed them to leave their native reservations without police permission. Their general discontent with French rule remained submerged until 1969, when a group of Melanesians on Maré in the Loyalty Group demanded independence from France. Today the independence movement consists of several groups advocating various forms of freedom (a small splinter group, *Les Amis des Etats-Unis* [Friends of the United States], reportedly would like to see an alliance with the U.S.). Some groups established a coalition, the *Front de la Libération National Kanake Socialiste* (Kanak Socialist Liberation

DATELINE

sandalwood trading post at Ile Nou.

- **1847** Catholics withdraw after kanaks raid their mission, behead and eat a priest; French warships retaliate by shelling coastal villages.
- **1850** Kanaks massacre 17 French raiders.
- **1853** Napoléon III declares New Caledonia to be French; Admiral Febvrier-Despointes hoists tricolor at Pouébo.
- **1864** First convicts arrive, begin building penal colony; Jules Garnier discovers high-grade nickel ore.
- **1868** Government herds Melanesians into reservations, opens land for mining and ranching.
- **1871** Arabs captured in Algerian insurrection arrive.
- **1871–80** After Paris Commune revolt fails, 4,000 Communards are confined at Isle of Pines.
- **1874** Communard editor and parlimentarian Henri de Rochefort escapes to Australia; John Higginson founds *Société Le Nickel*, large-scale mining begins.
- **1878** Melanesian revolt is crushed, 1,000 kanaks and 200 Frenchmen die.

(continues)

Front, or FLNKS), which is working for an independent New Caledonia controlled by its native-born minority. They are opposed by a reactionary segment of French settlers, including some who were forced out of Vanuatu after the abortive uprising there in 1980. Thousands of other French, Pacific islanders, Indonesian, Vietnamese, and others favor retaining ties to France.

Violence broke out between the competing factions in 1981 with the unsolved murder of a pro-independence politician. It continued sproadically until April 1988, when a kanak faction killed four French gendarmes on Ouvéa and a few weeks later captured 27 others, holding them captive in a cave. French troops stormed the cave and killed nine Melanesians. Both sides quickly reached a settlement and signed an accord in Paris during August 1988.

The accords seem to be working. Peace ruled during my recent visit. Many private and public construction projects were underway not only in the South but in the other provinces as well, and visitors were once again exploring the territory and finding some of the world's most wonderful beaches.

GOVERNMENT, POLITICS & ECONOMY

Under the 1988 accords, New Caledonia is divided into three largely autonomous provinces—South around Nouméa, North on the rest of Grande Terre, and Loyalty in the Loyalty Group. The French and their Polynesian allies control Nouméa and the South, while Melanesians have a majority in the other two. A federal government based in Nouméa is in charge of territorial affairs as a whole. The metropolitan French government is providing $300 million in economic aid, most of it for the undeveloped North and Loyalty provinces.

New Caledonians will hold a referendum in 1998 on whether to become independent. Only persons who lived in the territory in 1988, and their children, will be eligible to vote.

Nickel still dominates the economy—as evidenced by the huge smelter you will pass on your way into Nouméa. Only Canada and the Soviet Union produce more nickel than New Caledonia. The money it brings, coupled with the same duty-based tax system we found in French Polynesia, results is a high standard—and high cost—of living.

Cattle raising is New Caledonia's second-largest industry, but the domestic demand is so great that much beef—along with other foodstuffs—is imported. Food costs, accordingly, are relatively high. A limited quantity of excellent coffee is produced, so pick up a bag to take home.

DATELINE

- **1880** All political prisoners except Arabs are freed, some remain as settlers.
- **1897** Last convicts arrive.
- **1917** French crush brief Melanesian uprising.
- **1918** Penal colony comes to an end.
- **1940** New Caledonia joins Free French side in World War II.
- **1942** Americans under Admiral Halsey set up war headquarters in Nouméa.
- **1946** France grants citizenship to kanaks, lets them leave reservations; independence movement begins.
- **1981** Violence erupts between pro-independence Melanesians and right-wing French settlers.
- **1984** Ten kanaks die in minibus ambush near Hienghène.
- **1988** Hostage incident spurs both sides to sign Paris accord bringing new government, peace.

IMPRESSIONS

The U.S. occupied the country from 1942 to 1945, leaving one lasting caldoche *perception: that the U.S. knows how to take care of business and France doesn't.*

—Scott L. Malcolmson, 1990

IMPRESSIONS

Noumea is a blown-away French provincial town. . . . Its character is coconut Provencal.

—JOHN DYSON, 1982

Tourism did not come into its own as an industry until a nickel bust in the 1970s forced the territory to find new ways of making money. It now is reasonably developed, especially in the Japanese market. In fact, New Caledonia gets more Japanese visitors than any other South Pacific island country or territory. The Japanese kept the tourism industry afloat during the troubled 1980s.

GEOGRAPHY

Grande Terre was lifted upward as the Indo-Australian Plate crawled up over the adjacent Pacific Plate to the east. In the distant past, it may even have been joined to Australia. The bending and folding accompanying this movement created the rugged mountains of the Chaîne Centrale, the towering range that runs like a backbone the length of the 30-mile-wide landmass. It also exposed one of the world's largest reserves of nickel, as well as lesser but still substantial amounts of copper, gold, zinc, silver, lead, chrome, cobalt, and iron. Scientists say the uplifting is over and that Grande Terre is slowly sinking back into the sea. The shallow waters left behind are now nearly enclosed by the world's third-longest barrier reef, which makes Nouméa a water-sports heaven.

About two-thirds of New Caledonia's some 3,000 species of plants are unique to the islands. The white-barked *niaouli* tree, a cousin of the Australian eucalyptus, covers much of Grande Terre's western half. The Isle of Pines gets its name from the tall, skinny pines that in 1774 impressed Capt. James Cook into giving the island this name. Land fauna, on the other hand, were scarce until Europeans introduced a variety of animals. Before they came, the only native mammals were the rat and the fruit bat known elsewhere as the "flying fox." Bird life, on the other hand, was more abundant. New Caledonia's unique and unusual territorial bird, the **cagou,** is a flightless creature whose squawk sounds like the bark of a dog. About the size of a rooster, the cagou is so slow afoot that it has been chased almost into extinction by the territory's real dogs. The beautiful Ouvéa parakeet also is threatened with extinction.

PEOPLE

When Captain Cook discovered New Caledonia in 1774, he estimated that it was inhabited by about 50,000 Melanesians who lived a late Stone Age existence in small villages. The descendants of Melanesians who had migrated down from Southeast Asia more than 3,000 years ago, they built windowless, conical-roofed houses of thatch, fished in the lagoon, and grew crops of taro and other root plants, often in irrigated terraces cut into the hillsides. They used pottery, as evidenced by the modern finds at Lapita. Tribal groups had their own distinct cultures, languages, and religions based on the worship of ancestral spirits. Altogether they spoke more than 20 languages, none of which was understood outside the tribal group. They were governed by a system of chiefs, and in times of war they could be ferocious fighters.

IMPRESSIONS

The skirts of this isle is wholy covered with trees so often mention on which account it obtained the name of Isle of Pines.

—JAMES COOK, 1774

Cannibalism often was practiced, usually on the vanquished—and on European sandalwood traders in the early 1800s.

Western ways have made their inroads, but *coutume* (custom) continues to be a strong force. Today most of New Caledonia's Melanesians, or kanaks as they are called (from the Hawaiian word *kanaka* for "person"), still live in tribal villages, mainly on the east coast of Grande Terre and on the outlying islands. The system of chiefs is intact. As in all Melanesian countries, it's customary if you enter a kanak village to speak to the highest chief and to present a small gift. This is especially true if you are camping.

The territory's 74,000 or so Melanesians are a minority in their own islands, for Europeans—mostly French—number about 55,000; Wallis islanders and Tahitians, about 19,000; and Indonesians, Vietnamese, and others, about 17,000. The overwhelming majority of Non-Melanesians live in or around Nouméa.

LANGUAGE

French is the official language and is spoken by everyone. English is becoming increasingly common in the hotels and many shops and restaurants of Nouméa, especially around the Anse Vata and Baie des Citrons tourist areas. Even the taxi drivers have been boning up. Although the Melanesian languages spoken on the Isle of Pines and in the Loyalty Group contain many words contributed by the early English and Australian missionaries and traders, you may have trouble being understood outside Nouméa and on the other islands unless you can speak some French.

2. INFORMATION, ENTRY REQUIREMENTS & MONEY

INFORMATION

Destination Nouvelle-Calédonie, B.P. 688, Nouméa (tel. 27-26-32, fax 27-46-23), primarily is responsible for promoting the territory, but its friendly, English-speaking staff will respond to inquiries from overseas. It has foreign offices in: **Australia:** 410 Collins St., 7th Floor, Melbourne, VIC 3000 (tel. 6420949, fax 642095); and 39 York St., 11th Floor, Sydney, NSW 2000 (tel. 292573, fax 2902242). **New Zealand:** 57 Fort St., 3rd Floor, P.O. Box 4300, Auckland (tel. 375257, fax 793874). **France:** Maison de la Nouvelle-Calédonie, 7, rue du Général Bertrand, 75007 Paris (tel. 42-73-24-14).

Once you're in Nouméa, some brochures are available in the main lobby of the **Hôtel de Ville** (Town Hall) on the west end of place des Cocotiers. Plans were afoot during my recent visit to open a tourist information office in the new Marchés Municipaux (Municipal Markets) on Baie de la Moselle waterfront in downtown Nouméa; it may be open when you get there. **Center Voyages,** 27 av. du Maréchal-Foch, 4th Floor (tel. 28.47.37 or 28.40.40), the local American Express agent, publishes a handy brochure, "Welcome to New Caledonia," which has the

IMPRESSIONS

Many of New Caledonia's older caldoche *families are descended from convicts, a subject rarely broached among the local French, though the Kanaks like to remind them of it from time to time.*

—SOTT L. MALCOLMSON, 1990

names and addresses of just about every hotel, restaurant, night club, and merchant in Nouméa.

For information about the Isle of Pines, go to **La Maison de Kunie,** 26 rue de l'Alma (tel. 28.27.74). For Lifou, go to **La Maison de Lifou** (tel. 27.47.81), on rue Anatole France just above the place des Cocotiers.

Also check in with **AMAC Tours** (tel. 26.38.38), next to the Palm Beach shopping mall on Anse Vata Beach for maps and brochures. As noted in "What to See & Do," below, AMAC Tours is a full-service travel agency whose English-speaking, expatriate staff I have found to be quite helpful. Hours are Monday to Friday 8am to 5:30pm and Saturday 8am to noon and 3 to 6pm.

ENTRY REQUIREMENTS

Visitors with valid passports and onward or return tickets are granted visas good for 30 days upon arrival at Tontouta International Airport. Extensions for up to 3 months may be granted upon application to the Immigration Department in Nouméa. French embassies or consulates overseas can grant 3-month visas in advance. In the United States, France has consulates in Boston, Chicago, Detroit, Houston, Los Angeles, New York, San Francisco, New Orleans, and Honolulu. Residents in or near those cities are required to apply there. The French Embassy is at 4102 Reservoir Road NW, Washington, DC 20007 (tel. 202/944-6000).

Vaccinations are required only if you are coming from a yellow fever or cholera area.

Customs allowances are 200 cigarettes, 100 cigarillos, or 250 grams of tobacco; 2 liters of wine and 1 liter of spirits; and 50 grams of perfume or ¼ liter of toilet water. Drug-related products and counterfeit books are prohibited, and weapons, ammunition, animals, and animal or vegetable products require special permits. Currency in the amount of 50,000 CFP ($500) must be declared. You cannot export cagou birds or objects of ethnographic interest from New Caledonia.

MONEY

Along with French Polynesia, New Caledonia uses the French Pacific franc **(CFP).** You get 5.5 CFP for every regular French franc. To find out how many CFP you will get for a U.S. dollar, look in the financial section of your hometown newspaper, locate the number of French francs per U.S. dollar, and multiply that number of francs by 18.18. At the time of writing, the exchange rate was approximately 100 CFP per U.S. $1. No decimals are used in dealing with French Pacific francs, so prices are quoted in even numbers. Bargaining over prices is not an accepted practice in New Caledonia. The franc notes and coins used in French Polynesia are interchangeable with those in New Caledonia.

WHAT THINGS COST IN NEW CALEDONIA	U.S. $
Taxi from Tontouta Airport to Nouméa	50.00
Bus from Tontouta Airport to Nouméa	15.00
Double room at Le Surf Novotel Hôtel (expensive)	160.00
Double room at Hôtel Ibis Nouméa (moderate)	86.00
Double room at Môtel Le Bambou (budget)	42.00
Lunch for one at Peter's Grill (moderate)	11.00
Lunch for one at Snack Julius (budget)	5.00
Dinner for one, without wine, at La Coupole (expensive)	50.00
Dinner for one, without wine, at San Rémo Pizzeria (moderate)	22.00
Dinner for one, without wine, at Snack Bambino Vata (budget)	7.50
Beer	3.50
Coca-Cola	2.00

THE FRANC & THE DOLLAR

At this writing, $1 = approximately 100 CFP, the rate of exchange used to calculate the U.S. dollar prices given in this chapter. This rate has fluctuated widely and may not be the same when you visit. Accordingly, use the following table only as a guide.

CFP	$ U.S.	CFP	$ U.S.
100	1.00	1,000	10.00
150	1.50	1,500	15.00
200	2.00	2,000	20.00
300	3.00	3,000	30.00
400	4.00	4,000	40.00
500	5.00	5,000	50.00
600	6.00	6,000	60.00
700	7.00	7,000	70.00
800	8.00	8,000	80.00
900	9.00	9,000	90.00
1,000	10.00	10,000	100.00

	US$
Cup of coffee	2.00
Roll of ASA 100 Kodacolor film, 36 exposures	12.00
Movie ticket	6.00

3. WHEN TO GO — CLIMATE, HOLIDAYS & EVENTS

The **climate** is semitropical with two distinct seasons: a relatively humid summer from December to April and a drier austral winter from June to September. Daily high temperatures average 81°F during the summer but drop to 70°F during the winter, when the evenings and even some days can be cool. The waters are relatively warm, however, and visitors play in the sea all year. Hurricanes are possible from November to April. The high mountain range down the center of Grande Terre creates two rainfall patterns on the big island. The peaks water the rugged east coast by trapping moisture from the prevailing trade winds. However, the west coast, including Nouméa, has a drier climate that is perfect for cattle ranching and, during the winter months, reminiscent of summers along the coast of Southern California.

Public **holidays** are New Year's Day (January 1), Easter Monday, Labor Day (May 1), Armistice Day (May 8), Ascension Day (40 days after Easter Sunday), Whitmonday, Bastille Day (July 14), New Caledonia Day (September 24, the anniversary of Admiral Despointes' taking possession of the territory for France), All Saints Day (November 1), Armistice Day (November 11), and Christmas.

Some **events** are worth noting. **February or March:** During Mardi Gras, Nouméa's children put on costumes and gather in the place des Cocotiers. **May:** The Museum of New Caledonia holds an arts festival during the first week. **July:** Bastille

Day on July 14 sees the usual French verve, with parades and a grand ball. **December:** On Père Noël Day, just before Christmas, Father Christmas arrives at an annual parade by some unusual and unannounced mode of transportation.

4. GETTING THERE & GETTING AROUND

GETTING THERE

There are two more or less direct ways to get there from North America. One is to fly to Nadi on one of the major international carriers, then switch to **Air Calédonie International** from there to Nouméa. Another is to fly on **UTA French Airlines** or **Air France** to Tahiti, then on Air Calédonie International to Nouméa via Wallis Island and Fiji. Ask about a combined fare on this second option. In addition to its Fiji and Tahiti routes, Air Calédonie International also links the territory to Sydney, Melbourne, Auckland, and Port Vila. **Air New Zealand** flies to Nouméa from Auckland. **Qantas Airways** goes there from Sydney. See "Getting There" in Chapter 2 for more information.

All international flights arrive 47km (28 miles) northwest of Nouméa at **Tontouta Airport.** After clearing Customs, returning resident New Caledonians are directed to the left, while visitors are herded out a door to the right and toward a shelter housing desks for the airport bus companies, tour operators, and Club Med. Follow the residents to find the bank, rental-car desks, and other facilities. The modern glass-and-steel terminal building has a restaurant and bar upstairs and a duty-free shop in its comfortable departure lounge. New Caledonia does not charge an airport departure tax.

The major rental-car companies have desks in the terminal's concourse. Tontouta is linked to Nouméa by the *péage*, a **toll road** costing 140 CFP ($1.40) each way for automobiles—it even has exact-change lanes—and the old highway that runs through several villages before reaching the city. **Taxi** fare into Nouméa is approximately 5,000 CFP ($50). At least two airport **express buses** will be waiting to take passengers to the hotels; they charge 1,500 CFP ($15) per person. You also can catch one of the blue **interurban buses** that stop once an hour between 6am and 6pm at the left end of the terminal (as you exit) on their way to Nouméa from Bourail. Their fare to Nouméa is about 400 CFP ($4). For express-bus service back to the airport, telephone 28.61.00 in Nouméa.

GETTING AROUND

BY PLANE

Air Calédonie, 38–41 rue de Verdun (tel. 25.21.77), the domestic airline, uses **Magenta Airport,** about 5km (3 miles) from downtown Nouméa, for all its flights. **City bus 7** goes right to the terminal from the downtown bus depot. **Taxi** fares from downtown to Magenta are about 600 CFP ($5.50).

From a visitor's standpoint, Air Calédonie's most popular flights go to and from the Isle of Pines twice a day—once in the morning and once in the afternoon—thereby making possible a comfortable day-trip to this enchanting island. The round-trip fare from Magenta to the Isle of Pines is 8,600 CFP ($86).

IMPRESSIONS

The mountains of New Caledonia, great glowing red hills rising from green valleys, were brilliantly beautiful.
—JAMES A. MICHENER, 1951

Other one-way fares for well-traveled routes from Magenta are 6,400 CFP ($64) to Lifou, Maré, Ouvéa, or Tiga in the Loyalty Group; 5,300 CFP ($53) to Koumac; and 4,800 CFP ($48) to Touhou.

The **baggage allowance** on domestic Air Calédonie flights is 10kg (22 lb.) of baggage.

BY CAR

Many roads in the countryside are not paved, so be on the lookout for potholes and loose surfaces that make traction difficult to come by. See "Maps" in "Fast Facts," below, for the best road maps. **Gasoline** is available in Nouméa and in the main towns and villages elsewhere. It was selling for 96 CFP ($1) a liter during my recent visit, or about $3.65 for a U.S.-size gallon.

Rentals

Daily rates at **Budget Rent-a-Car** (tel. 26.20.69, or toll free 800/527-0700 in the U.S.), in the AMAC Tours office on Anse Vata Beach, start at 2,600 CFP ($26) plus 28 CFP (30¢) a kilometer and 1,100 ($11) for insurance. The unlimited-kilometer rate is 10,000 ($100) for one day, 7,500 CFP ($75) for 2 to 4 days, plus insurance. You pay the gas.

The least expensive rental-car company is **AB Rent a Car** (tel. 28.12.12). Others are **Avis** (tel. 27.54.84, or toll free 800/331-1212 in the U.S.); **Hertz** (tel. 26.18.22, or toll free 800/654-3001 in the U.S.); and **Pacific Car** (tel. 27-60-60).

All the rental-car companies will deliver their vehicles to your hotel if you call in advance. You must be at least 25 years old to rent a car from any of these companies.

Driving Rules

Your home-state driver's license will be honored in New Caledonia. New Caledonians drive "American-style," on the right-hand side of the road. Unless you're on a main road in the countryside or an intersection is marked with stop signs, traffic coming from your right has the unhindered right-of-way. In other words, cars entering the intersection from your right can and will barrel through without stopping. Some of these tricky intersections are marked with signs that say *priorité à droite* ("priority to the right," or give way to traffic coming from the right). To park on the street or in a municipal lot in downtown Nouméa, buy a ticket from one of the electronic parking meters you will see on most corners. Rates are 50 CFP (50¢) for each 30 minutes. Put the ticket on your dash board.

BY BUS

Blue minibuses with white tops and "Transport du Commun" stenciled on their sides provide excellent service in Nouméa from 5:30am to 6:15pm daily. They don't have regular schedules, but they fan out on their routes every 15 minutes or so from place de Bus alongside Baie de la Moselle on avenue de la Victoire. The fares are listed on a card posted by the driver, but 100 CFP ($1) will take you around most of Nouméa during the week, 120 CFP ($1.20) after noon on Saturday and all day Sunday.

The routes are posted on a sign at place de Bus. Most tourist maps (see "Maps" in the "Fast Facts," below) show the bus routes in detail. With one of these in one hand and a wad of francs in the other, you can see much of Nouméa in an afternoon. The following are the major bus routes.

Bus 3: To Anse Vata Beach and Val Plaisance via Motor Pool and route de l'Anse Vata.

Bus 6: To Anse Vata Beach via Baie de l'Orphelinat, Baie des Citrons, and the aquarium (a scenic tour in its own right).

Bus 7: To Magenta Airport via route Territorial 13. The bus stops at the airport going out but not coming back to downtown.

Bus 13: To Ile Nou and Nouville, going on to Kuendu Beach at 7:45am, 10:45am, 1:45pm, and 5:30pm.

Buses to the other towns on Grande Terre also leave from place de Bus, on the other side of the terminal building from the domestic buses. Ask at the terminal for the latest schedules and fares. A bus to La Foa and Bourail via Tontouta Airport leaves every hour on the half hour from 5:30am to 5:30pm Monday through Saturday and every 2 hours on the half hour from 6:30am to 5:30pm on Sunday and holidays. The fare to Tontouta is 400 CFP ($4).

BY TAXI

You can find metered taxis gathered in the place des Cocotiers in the heart of town. Minimum fare is 350 CFP ($3.50) during daylight hours, 450 CFP ($4.50) after dark, after noon on Saturday, and all day on Sunday and holidays. Fares will be about 800 CFP ($8) around town, about 1,200 CFP ($12) from Anse Vata Beach to Magenta Airport. Radio-dispatched taxis may be hailed by calling 28.53.70 or 28.35.12.

BY BICYCLE/MOTORBIKE

AMAC Tours, on Anse Vata Beach (tel. 26.38.38), and **Moto Vélo,** on route de la Baie des Citrons (tel. 26.23.78), both rent bicycles for 1,600 CFP ($16) a day plus a refundable 2,000 CFP ($20) deposit.

Moto Vélo also rents motorbikes for 3,000 CFP ($30) for ½ day, 4,000 CFP ($40) a day, including gasoline and insurance. A deposit of 10,000 CFP ($100) or 30,000 CFP ($300) is required (cash or credit card), depending on the size of the bike.

NOUMEA

Most of the following information is about Nouméa. You should have little trouble outside of town or on the outer islands. Just muster up your best French and ask someone.

American Express Center Voyages, 27 av. du Maréchal-Foch, 4th Floor (tel. 28.47.37 or 28.40.40), provides full card-member services and will cash American Express traveler's checks at the bank rate without charging the 500 CFP ($5) fee extracted by the banks (see "Currency Exchange," below). As noted above, the company also publishes a brochure that has the names and addresses of most hotels, restaurants, and merchants in Nouméa. Take the elevators beside the spiral staircase to the fourth floor; don't go into the travel agency on the street level. Hours are Mon–Fri 7:30–11:30am and 1:30–5:30pm, Sat 8–11am. The mailing address is Center Voyages, B.P. 50, Nouméa.

Area Code The international country code is 687.

Baby-Sitters The hotels will arrange for English-speaking baby-sitters.

Bookstores Owner Phillida Stephens of The English Bookshop, 11 route du Port Despointes (tel. 27.23.25), has Nouméa's only sizable collection of English books and rental videotapes. Her little store is 2 blocks downhill from the big cross at the corner of route du Port Despointes and bd. Extérieur (Bus 3 passes the intersection). Librairie Pentecost, 37 rue de l'Alma, is the best-stocked French bookshop in town; it carries a few English-language magazines, novels, and books on New Caledonia and the South Pacific as well as the two best maps of the area.

Business Hours Although the times may vary by 30 minutes or so, most of Nouméa's offices and shops are open Mon–Fri 7:30–11:30am and 2–5:30pm, Sat 7:30–11am. Banks, many duty-free shops, the large department stores, and some smaller retail establishments around place de Bus in downtown Nouméa stay open all day Mon–Fri, and a few downtown duty-free shops remain open until 5:30pm on Sat. Except for the post office (see below), government bureaus keep hours Mon–Fri 7:30am–3:30pm.

Car Rentals See "Getting Around," above.

Climate See "When to Go—Climate, Holidays & Events," above.

Clothing Light and informal clothing is worn throughout the year, but bathing suits and other skimpy attire should stay at the beach. Although men seldom wear jackets, neckties are often worn in offices. Evening dress, especially for women, tends to be more chic than in most other South Pacific destinations. A windbreaker, sweater, or light wrap will come in handy during the cooler months (June to September) or at any time in the mountains. The beaches at Anse Vata, Baie des Citrons, and Kuendu are topless for both men and women. Anyone offended by a woman's bare breasts should avoid these areas at all costs. Women should keep their tops on in predominantly Melanesian areas such as the Loyalty islands and on the Isle of Pines. Although the string bikini bottoms (and nothing else) worn by some young New Caledonian women are so skimpy as to leave little to the imagination, nude sunbathing is illegal.

Credit Cards American Express, VISA, MasterCard, Diners Club, and the Japanese card JCB are accepted by the airlines and rental-car firms and by most hotels, restaurants, and duty-free shops in Nouméa. If traveling outside the city, particularly to the Isle of Pines, carry enough traveler's checks and cash to see you through.

Crime See "Safety," below.

Currency See "Information, Entry Requirements & Money" above.

Currency Exchange Banque Nationale de Paris, Westpac Bank, Banque de Paris et des Pays-Bas (PARIBAS), Société Générale, and Banque de Nouvelle-Calédonie Crédit Lyonnais have offices in Nouméa, most of them on the north side of the place des Cocotiers or on rue de l'Alma. Anse Vata has two branches, one beside the Lantana Beach Hotel, the other in the Palm Beach shopping center. Nearest branch to Baie des Citrons is in the Port Plaisance shopping center in Baie des Pêcheurs.

All banks charge a 500 CFP ($5) fee for each foreign-currency transaction, so you may want to change more money than usual each time. If you're carrying American Express checks, Center Voyages (see "American Express," above) will cash them without a commission.

Banking hours are Mon–Fri 7:30am–3:30pm. Center Voyages is also open on Sat 8–11am. The banks close on Good Friday.

There is no bank on the Isle of Pines.

Customs See "Information, Entry Requirements & Money" above.

Dentist If you don't speak French, ask someone at the two English bastions—AMAC Tours (tel. 26.38.38) or the Squash Club (tel. 26.22.18)—to recommend one who speaks English.

Doctor Polyclinique de l'Anse Vata (26.14.22), a block inland from Anse Vata Beach on route de la Corniche, treats a number of visitors.

Documents Required See "Information, Entry Requirements & Money" above.

Driving Rules See "Getting Around," earlier in this chapter.

Drug Laws Dangerous drugs and narcotics are illegal and the penalties for their use are severe.

Drugstores Nouméa has a number of pharmacies in which French products predominate, so if you take prescription medications, carry enough with you. Look for the green cross marking each shop. The nearest to Anse Vata Beach is a short walk inland on rue Gabriel Laroque in Val Plaisance. The nearest to Baie des Citrons is over the hill on route Jules Garnier in Baie des Pêcheurs. In the small villages and outer islands, go to the local infirmary.

Electricity Electricity is 220 volts, 50 cycles, and the plugs are the French kind with two round, skinny prongs. Few hotels have 110-volt outlets for shavers, so you'll need a converter with French plugs for American and Canadian appliances.

Embassies/Consulates The U.S. does not maintain a diplomatic post in New Caledonia. The nearest U.S. embassy is in Suva, Fiji; consulates in Sydney, Australia, and Auckland, New Zealand. Nations that do have consulates in Nouméa are Australia, 19-21 av. du Maréchal-Foch (tel. 27.24.14); New Zealand, 4 bd. Vauban (tel. 27.25.43); Belgium, 13 rue Jules Ferry (tel. 28.46.44); Italy, 10 rue Auguste Bourgine, Trianon (tel. 28.21.82); Indonesia, 2 rue Lamartine, Baie de l'Orphelinat (tel. 28.25.74); and Japan, 45 rue du 5 Mai, Haut Magenta (tel. 25.37.29).

Emergencies The emergency telephone number for the police is 17, and for an ambulance, 27.21.21.

Etiquette Unlike the Parisian French, who have a reputation for snobbishness and brusqueness, New Caledonians tend to be relaxed, soft-spoken, even a bit shy. Good manners and a friendly smile nearly always are returned with the same, even if your French stinks. Like their counterparts described elsewhere in this book, most Melanesians and Polynesians also are modest and shy but will openly warm to you when approached with respect and a genuine smile. See "Clothing," above, for proper attire, especially at the beaches in Melanesian areas.

Eyeglasses There are a number of optical shops in Nouméa. Optique Betrancourt, corner of rue de Sébastopol and rue de Verdun (tel. 27.58.53), has its own equipment and duty-free prices.

Firearms Special permits are required to bring in firearms and ammunition.

Gambling You can try your luck at Casino Royale in Le Surf Novotel Hôtel, one of the South Pacific's two gambling casinos, or at the big bingo hall, 7 rue Jules Ferry on the downtown Nouméa waterfront. Details are in "What to See & Do," below.

Hairdressers/Barbers Isle de France Appartements, rue Boulari in Anse Vata Beach (tel. 26.24.22), has a beauty salon with English-speaking staff.

Hitchhiking It's possible but not advisable on Grande Terre.

Holidays See "When to Go—Climate, Holidays & Events" above.

Hospitals The main government hospital on av. Paul Doumer (tel. 27.21.21) accepts visitors to the territory on an emergency basis only. For anything else, you'll have to rely on private practitioners or clinics (see "Doctor," above).

Information See "Information, Entry Requirements & Money" above.

Insects New Caledonia has no harmful insects, and although it has its share of mosquitoes, they do not carry malaria. If you forgot to bring insect repellent, look for Dolmix Pic, a French brand, at the pharmacies.

Language See "Language" under "Getting to Know New Caledonia," above.

Laundry Most of the hotels have 1-day laundry and dry-cleaning service, but the prices are relatively high. For laundry, expect to spend 400 CFP ($4) for a shirt or blouse and 1,900 CFP ($19) for a dress. The least expensive Laundromat is Répassvit (tel. 28.68.86), at rues Jean Jaurès and Sébastopol just off place des Cocotiers. The staff there will wash and dry a 5kg load (11 lb.) for 700 CFP ($7), but they do not speak English. You will want them to *laver et sécher* ("lavay ay sayshay"—wash and dry).

Libraries Bibliothèque Berheim, rue de la Somme at av. du Maréchal-Foch (tel. 27.23.83), has few books in English. It's open Mon–Tues 1:30–6:30pm, Wed and Fri 1:30–7pm, and Sat 9–11am and 2–5:30pm.

Liquor Laws There are no arcane laws. Although you cannot purchase from bottle shops on Sun, the bars are open.

Lost Property Contact the Town Hall (tel. 27.31.15) at the west end of place des Cocotiers.

Mail The main post office, known as Postes et Télécommunications (P.T.T.), is at the corner of av. du Maréchal-Foch and rue Eugène Porcheron and is open Mon–Fri 7:45–11:15am and 12:15–3:30pm. Airmail letters to the U.S. cost 80 CFP (80¢); postcards, 64 CFP (65¢). Stamps are available at most *tabac* (tobacco) and hotel gift shops. Although most businesses have street addresses, they receive their mail through a *boîte postale* (post office box), or "B.P." for short.

Maps Librairie Pentecost, 37 rue de l'Alma, carries the two best maps of the territory: the *Carte Touristique Nouvelle Calédonie,* published by the Institut Géographique National, an excellent road map of the islands, which also shows the major topographical features; and *Plan de Nouméa/Nouméa Map.* Buy maps of the Isle of Pines and Lifou if you're going there. Another very good road and street map is available free from the Town Hall tourist information desk and AMAC Tours, and La Maison de Lifou gives away maps of Lifou. (See "Information, Entry Requirements & Money" above.)

Newspapers/Magazines The territory's one daily newspaper, *Les Nouvelles Calédoniennes,* is published entirely in French. Librairie Pentecost, 37 rue de l'Alma, carries a few English-language newsmagazines.

Passports See "Information, Entry Requirements & Money" above.

Pets Animals require special permission. Forget it.

Photographic Needs A wide range of film and film processing is available at shops in downtown Nouméa and on Anse Vata Beach, although the price will be about twice what you'd pay at home.

Police The Commissariart Central (central police station) is on av. de la Victoire between rue de Sébastopol and av. Maréchal-Foch. The emergency police number is 17.

Radio/TV The government-owned radio and TV stations broadcast French programs throughout the day and evening. It's highly unlikely that you will hear English on radio or TV other than in the lyrics of popular records.

Religious Services Most residents are Roman Catholic or Protestant, and most worship at the Cathédrale St-Joseph on rue Frédéric-Surleau or at the Temple Protestant on the hill above bd. Vauban, respectively. Services are in French.

Rest Rooms There are public toilets in place des Cocotiers, at the corner of rue Anatole France and rue d'Austerlitz (opposite the big Prisunic store), and beside the Fun Beach Grille & Brasserie opposite Le Surf Novotel Hôtel. Otherwise, public facilities are few and far between, so you'll have to rely on the hotels and restaurants.

Safety The areas around Anse Vata and Baie des Citrons are relatively free of street crime, but the same cannot be said about downtown Nouméa after dark. Do not leave valuables unattended or in your hotel room or rental car. See "Health & Insurance" and "Fast Facts: South Pacific" in Chapter 2 for more warnings. Some sea life, such as stonefish, demon stingers, and snakes, can be venomous, and some reef fish can cause a deadly form of food poisoning (menus will feature deep-sea species rather than those caught close to shore). The hospital has serum for the most dangerous poisons.

Shoe Repair *Cordonniers* (shoemakers) are in the Ballande department store, rue de l'Alma at rue d'Austerlitz, and in the Centralma mall, rue Clemenceau north of rue de l'Alma.

Taxes A room tax, which varies from 70 CFP to 300 CFP (70¢ to $3) per night, depending on the cost of the room, is added to all hotel bills. The more expensive the room, the higher the tax. That's the tax you will see; invisible but certainly felt are the large duties charged on most items imported into New Caledonia.

Telephone/Telex/Fax Pay phones are located at all post offices and in phone booths elsewhere. Local calls cost 50 CFP (50¢). For directory assistance (*service des renseignements*), dial 12. There are three types of pay phones. On one of them, you lift the receiver, listen for the dial tone, deposit your money in the slots across the top of the phone that match the size of the coins, watch them stack up behind the glass window under each slot, dial the number, and start talking when the party answers. The coins drop from sight at the beginning of each time period, and a light in the upper left-hand front of the phone will start flashing 12 seconds before the last coin drops. A second type of pay phone has a digital readout; put your money in and keep an eye on the screen, which will tell how much money you have left. A third type takes only a *télécarte,* which you must buy at a post office.

International calls can be placed through your hotel, but usually at a surcharge, which can double the fee. It's cheaper to make them from a post office or even a pay phone, especially those that accept a télécarte purchased from the post office. If using one of the télécarte phones, dial 00 first, then the international country code, area code, and local number. On coin phones, dial 19 for the international operator. The minimum charge for calls to the U.S. is about 700 CFP ($7) for each minute. The telephone, telegraph, and telex desk in the main Nouméa post office is open Mon–Fri 7:15am–6pm. There you can reverse the charges or pay by cash.

Direct international dialing is available into New Caledonia. The country code is 687.

Time Local time in New Caledonia is 11 hours ahead of Greenwich mean time. Translated: When it's 4am on Tues in Nouméa during standard time in the U.S., it's noon on Mon in New York and 9am on Mon in Los Angeles (during daylight saving time, it's 11am in New York and 8am in Los Angeles).

Tipping You don't tip in New Caledonia.

Tourist Offices See "Information, Entry Requirements & Money," above.

Visas See "Information, Entry Requirements & Money," above.

Water Tap water is safe to drink throughout New Caledonia. Most grocery stores carry bottles of French mineral water.

Weights/Measures New Caledonia is on the metric system of weights and measures. See the appendix for methods of conversion.

5. WHAT TO SEE & DO

THE BEACHES

The first item of relaxation on almost everyone's mind—resident and visitor alike—is to hit one of Nouméa's beaches, which are without doubt some of the finest any town has to boast. The sand at Anse Vata and Baie des Citrons stretches so far in each direction that some sections draw different types of sunworshipers. Here's a brief rundown so that you can find your own crowd.

At one end of Anse Vata, the Club Med and nearby Pointe Mangin usually draw a younger set of both tourists and local French residents, most of them single. Although the Club Med is off-limits for nonguests, the beach is public and can be reached either from Pointe Magnin or by rock stairs on the Nouméa side. Anse Vata itself—meaning the area in front of the Nouvàta Beach and Lantana Beach hotels—is a popular sunbathing and swimming area for guests from those two establishments and, especially during the long lunch break, young French women who drive down to the beach for some time lying topless in the sun. In addition to its hotel guests, Baie des Citrons and its calmer waters tend to get French families and military personnel, which usually means lots of single men in addition to the children.

As noted elsewhere in this chapter, both Anse Vata and Baie des Citrons are topless beaches for women, and French men tend to wear very skimpy attire themselves. Except for the area around the Club Med, however, both beaches are so long that you can easily find a spot where such visions are barely in sight.

SIGHTSEEING

You can see most of the other major sights in and around Nouméa on foot or by taking the local blue-and-white buses for short rides (see "Getting Around," above). Remember that during the week Nouméa gets going at 7:30am and stops abruptly at 11am for its leisurely 3-hour lunch break.

WALKING TOUR OF NOUMEA

The sights of downtown Nouméa can be seen in a leisurely stroll of about 1½ hours. The best times are early morning or afternoon; worst is during the long lunch break when most stores are closed. We'll finish at the Municipal Markets, but let's begin at the Hôtel de Ville (Town Hall) on rue du Général Mangin at the west end of:

IMPRESSIONS

The beach was covered with Causasian bodies, very close to naked. Women went topless and had painted toenails. On the street at our backs people wore socks and shoes and even blazers. Everyone looked tanned, fit, and stylish. Was this the Riviera? Had someone in the projection room changed reels when I wasn't watching?

—Scott L. Malcolmson, 1990

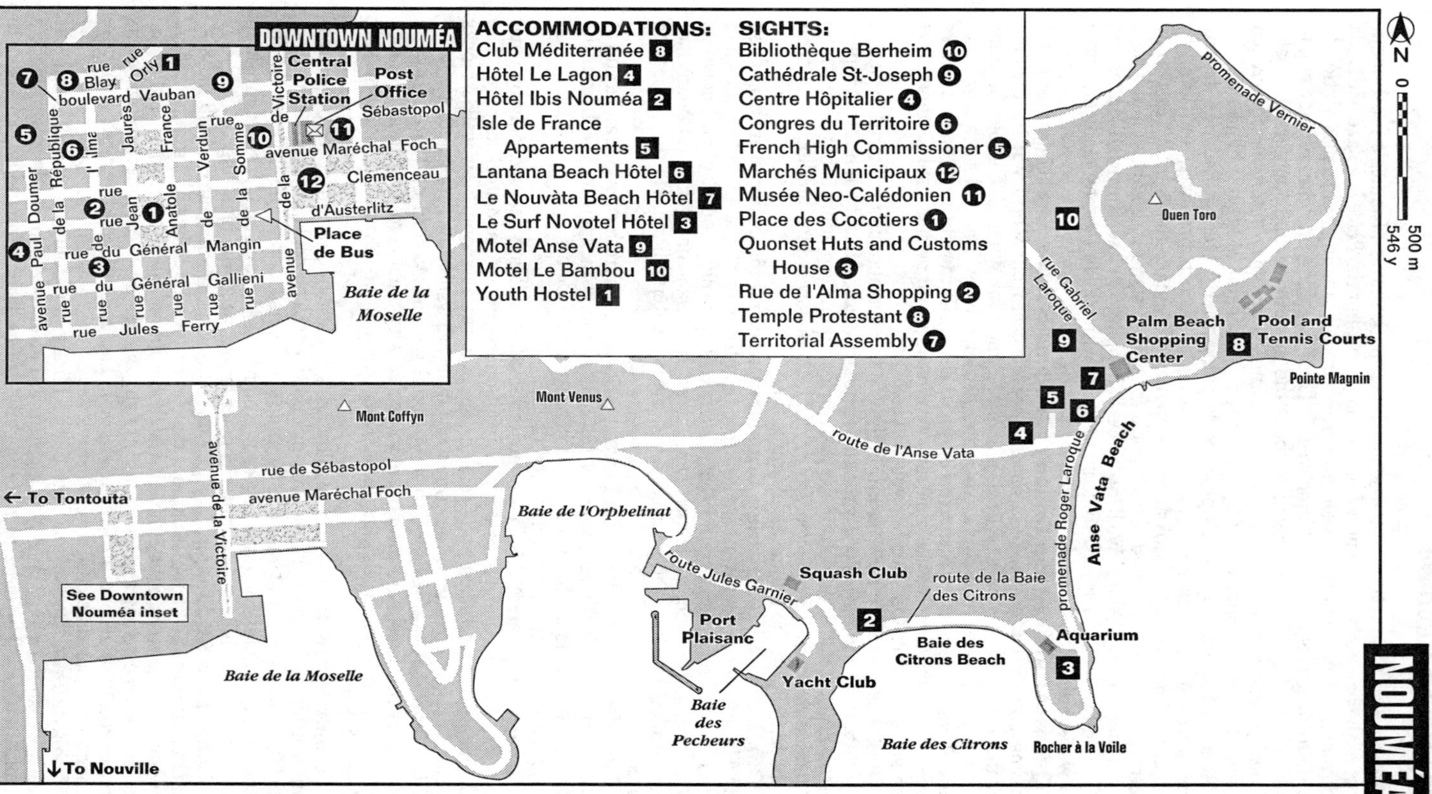
NOUMÉA
500 m
546 y
ACCOMMODATIONS:
Club Méditerranée 8
Hôtel Le Lagon 4
Hôtel Ibis Nouméa 2
Isle de France Appartements 5
Lantana Beach Hôtel 6
Le Nouvàta Beach Hôtel 7
Le Surf Novotel Hôtel 3
Motel Anse Vata 9
Motel Le Bambou 10
Youth Hostel 1
SIGHTS:
Bibliothèque Berheim 10
Cathédrale St-Joseph 9
Centre Hôpitalier 4
Congres du Territoire 6
French High Commissioner 5
Marchés Municipaux 12
Musée Neo-Calédonien 11
Place des Cocotiers 1
Quonset Huts and Customs House 3
Rue de l'Alma Shopping 2
Temple Protestant 8
Territorial Assembly 7
DOWNTOWN NOUMÉA
Central Police Station
Post Office
Place de Bus
Baie de la Moselle
rue Blay
rue Orly
boulevard Vauban
République
Paul Doumer
Jaurès
France
Verdun
Somme
Anatole
Jean
rue du Général Mangin
rue du Général Gallieni
rue Jules Ferry
avenue Maréchal Foch
Sébastopol
Clemenceau
d'Austerlitz
Victoire
promenade Vernier
Ouen Toro
Pool and Tennis Courts
Pointe Magnin
Palm Beach Shopping Center
rue Gabriel Laroque
Anse Vata Beach
promenade Roger Laroque
route de l'Anse Vata
Mont Venus
Mont Coffyn
rue de Sébastopol
avenue Maréchal Foch
avenue de la Victoire
To Tontouta
Baie de l'Orphelinat
route Jules Garnier
Squash Club
route de la Baie des Citrons
Aquarium
Baie des Citrons Beach
Port Plaisanc
Yacht Club
Baie des Pecheurs
Baie des Citrons
Rocher à la Voile
Baie de la Moselle
See Downtown Nouméa inset
To Nouville

Place des Cocotiers, the 4-square-block park that is Nouméa's focal point. Most of the namesake coconut palms are long gone, but the Place is ablaze with reds and oranges in November and December, when its blooming poincianas gloriously live up to their reputation as "flame trees." Their sprawling branches provide ample shade for local residents who gather about the monuments and fountains to make political speeches (especially on Saturday mornings) and play *pétanque,* the French version of bowls or boccie. Walk west on rue du Général Mangin 2 blocks to:

Rue de l'Alma, Nouméa's primary shopping artery. The big Ballande department store on the corner carries a wide array of French products, and Librairie Pentecost—the city's best bookstore—is up rue de l'Alma to the right. It's easy to be sidetracked at this point, and if your pocketbook can stand it, go ahead and have a look along rue de l'Alma. We'll do more "Shopping" below. Turn left on rue de l'Alma and walk 1 block west to its intersection with rue du Général Gallieni. There you will see signs of Nouméa's history:

Quonset huts and the Douane (Customs House). The semiround metal buildings, now used for private businesses, are left over from World War II, when the Americans turned this part of town into the "American Wharf." The old Customs House is a brick-and-stone relic from penal colony times. You will see a few other colonial warehouses and other structures in this area. Turn right here, walk 2 blocks north on rue du Général Gallieni, take another right on avenue Paul Doumer, and keep going straight. On your left you will see:

Centre Hôpitalier Territorial. Built with convict labor as a military hospital in the 1880s, this institution is today the city's primary medical facility. It houses Hôpital Gaston-Bourret and a branch of the Pasteur Institute. Keep going 3 blocks past the hospital to the end of avenue Paul Doumer. The impressive white building surrounded by shade trees on the hill ahead of you is the:

Office of the French High Commissioner and the center of metropolitan France's presence in New Caledonia. More than likely you'll see a number of men in uniform standing guard around the residence. Their spiffy round caps, known as *képis,* distinguish them as French gendarmes. Turn right on avenue du Maréchal-Foch, walk a block to the intersection of rue de la République. On the corner is a perfect:

Refueling stop: Pop into **La Terrasse Snack** for a fresh croissant and a cup of strong coffee; or, if it's lunchtime, a full and relatively inexpensive meal from the cafeteria-style table in the rear. See "Where to Dine," below.

Across the street on the corner stands the:

Congrès du Territoire in a nondescript office building denoted only by what looks like Melanesian-style columns painted on its concrete-and-steel supports. The federal congress meets here and decides issues of territorial scope. Now walk 2 blocks up rue de la République to the corner of boulevard Vauban, where stands the:

Territorial Assembly, or so it was until the Paris accord of 1988. Now the South Province legislature meets here to decide what's going to happen in Nouméa and the rest of southern Grande Terre. Walk south on boulevard Vauban, observing on your left the:

Temple Protestant. Most of Nouméa's Protestants, regardless of denomination, worship in this lovely church, another product of convict labor which dates from 1893. Continue on until you reach the dead-end intersection of rue Jean Jaurès. The steps there lead uphill for a fine view over Nouméa. If you aren't up for the climb, keep going for 5 short blocks to another convict masterpiece, the imposing:

Cathédrale St-Joseph, the city's main Roman Catholic church, built in 1894. An unusual open-air chapel is cut into the cliff behind the cathedral. From here, head downhill via the steps beside the Air Calédonie International office (they lead to the Hickson City cinema) and continue straight on rue de la Somme 1 block to its intersection with avenue du Maréchal Foch. The colonial building with distinctive wrought-iron balconies you'll see there is the:

Bibliothèque Berheim. This public library was founded in 1907 and was greatly expanded a year later with a gift from Lucien Berheim, a miner who made a fortune in nickel. The older part of the building was dismantled and brought back to

IMPRESSIONS

We went and ate lunch on the beach, a flawless strip of pale sand bordering calm water. . . . The sheer weight and expanse of undressed white bodies were overwhelming.

—Scott L. Malcolmson, 1990

Nouméa after being used as the New Caledonia pavilion at the Paris Universal Exposition in 1900. Now walk due south on avenue du Maréchal Foch across the broad avenue de la Victoire and past the post office, until you're in front of the:

Musée Neo-Calédonien, an excellent museum devoted to the life-style, arts, and traditions of New Caledonia's kanak population. Exhibits include full-size houses and canoes built entirely of native materials, as well as examples of ancient Lapita pottery, stone and shell objects, and petroglyphs uncovered during archeological expeditions in the islands. The descriptions are all in French, but a brochure giving some information in English is available at the entry desk. The museum is open Wednesday through Monday, except holidays, from 9 to 11:30am and from 12:15 to 4:30pm. Admission is free. When finished at the museum, walk across the park in front to the blue roofs of the:

Marchés Municipaux, the new municipal markets on the shores of Baie de la Moselle. These modern buildings replaced the colorful old market, which stood at the corner of rues Clemenceau and Anatole France on the place des Cocotiers. Each holds a different type of produce: Take a look at the tropical fruits, vegetables, and seafood offered for sale.

Across avenue de la Victoire is the place de Bus, where you can catch a ride back to the beach. Take Bus 6 for the scenic route home.

OTHER ATTRACTIONS

Bus 6 will take you from the city terminal to the ✪ **Nouméa Aquarium** (tel. 26-27-31), on the point between Baie des Citrons and Anse Vata behind Le Surf Novotel Hôtel. This fascinating institution was founded in 1956 by Dr. René Catala, who discovered that living corals give off brilliant colors when exposed to fluorescent light. Accordingly, he has devoted one of the aquarium's rooms to a tank full of corals lighted only by fluorescent tubes. If you've seen coral on the reef, you'll be astounded at the colors given off under "black light." The aquarium's other tanks are illuminated entirely by natural light, so the specimens are best observed on a sunny afternoon (flash photography is not allowed). Fresh seawater is pumped continuously through all the tanks, no artificial "props" are used, and all species on display are indigenous to New Caledonia's waters. A park behind the building goes up to the edge of the cliff overlooking Baie des Citrons. Admission is 500 CFP ($5) for adults, 200 CFP ($2) for students, and 100 CFP ($1) for children under 12. The aquarium is open Tuesday through Sunday from 1:30 to 4:30pm.

Bus 13 will take you a few hundred yards beyond the Gare Maritime (main wharf) and across an artificial isthmus to **Ile Nou,** or **Nouville** as it's also called. John Padden, an English seaman and sandalwood trader, bought Ile Nou from the local kanaks in 1845, established a trading station there, and even brought settlers over from Australia. When the French took possession of New Caledonia in 1853, however, they bought the island from him and soon turned it into a penal colony that housed about 3,000 prisoners. The bus usually ends at the stone walls of the territorial

IMPRESSIONS

The Alsatian emphasized that New Caledonia was a land of opportunity where one didn't have to work very hard and could go to the beach any time.

—Scott L. Malcolmson, 1990

mental-health hospital, originally a cellblock built with convict labor, but four times a day it goes on to arid **Kuendu Beach,** a popular (and topless) hangout for local residents on the weekends. A beachside restaurant serves buffet lunches on weekends and holidays.

Nouméa's **botanical gardens and zoo** are known as the *Parc Forestier* (Forestry Park), an 85-acre preserve in the hills 5km (3 miles) northeast of downtown, near Montravel. The botanical gardens consist primarily of one of the last indigenous forests left in the Nouméa area, but the collection of birds makes it worth a visit. Included are the cagou and the increasingly rare and beautiful Ouvéa parakeet. A pathway leads to the top of Montravel, which, at 548 feet, renders a panoramic view up and down Grande Terre's southwest coast and over the reef as far as Amadée Lighthouse, some 11 miles offshore. You can drive to the park, take Bus 12 to Montravel, and walk uphill 1½km (1 mile) to the entrance (ask the driver to tell you when to get off), or book a trip with one of the tour operators mentioned below. Admission is 200 CFP ($2) for adults and 50 CFP (50¢) for children 3 to 11. The main gate is open daily from 1:30 to 5:30pm from September to April and from 1:30 to 4pm from May to August.

ORGANIZED TOURS

If you aren't up to finding your own way to Nouméa's sights, you can take an escorted bus tour of the city organized by the helpful and English-speaking staffs at **AMAC Tours** (tel. 26-38-38), located in the Palm Beach shopping center on Anse Vata Beach, and at **South Pacific Tours** (tel. 26-23-20), which has a desk in Isle de France Appartements in Anse Vata. A ½-day trip around town costs 3,000 CFP ($30) per person. The two companies also have shopping tours and excursions outside Nouméa to Mont Dore, Mont Koghis, and Yaté. The frequency of the tours depends on the volume of business during any particular week, so check early to make sure about availability.

For a bird's-eye view of Nouméa, southern Grande Terre, and the reefs and islands offshore, go by helicopter with **Héliocean** (tel. 25-39-49). Prices start at 3,000 CFP ($30) per person for a 10-minute flight to 17,000 CFP ($170) for an hour.

LAGOON EXCURSIONS

Small islands off Nouméa beckon anyone who wants to escape for a day—or longer—to remote specks of land, casuarinas, and palms surrounded by one of the world's largest lagoons.

The most popular day-trip is to ✪ **Phare Amadée,** the tall lighthouse that soars above tiny Amadée atoll some 11 miles offshore. Made of metal in France and reassembled on Amadée in 1865, the lighthouse guides ships through a narrow break in the reef to safety in the lagoon. The flat little atoll is surrounded by an excellent swimming beach of powdery white sand.

American Patrick Helmy and Tahitian-born wife Minerva take their luxury catamaran ***Mary D Princess*** to Amadée each day. The Helmys serve a picnic lunch under Amadée's banyan trees. You can book at the Helmys' office (tel. 26-31-31) in the Palm Beach shopping center on Anse Vata Beach. The cost is 3,850 CFP ($38.50) per person Tuesday to Friday, 4,850 CFP ($48.50) Saturday to Monday. Snorkeling gear can be rented for 750 CFP ($7.50). On Sundays they drop passengers at Signal Island, a deserted atoll, for 2,000 CFP ($20); bring your own lunch and something to drink. They also have **sunset cruises** for 1,750 CFP ($17.50) per person. The boat has a bar on board.

Starship Genesis (tel. 26-24-40), another large catamaran, also has Amadée trips. Transportation alone costs 2,750 CFP ($27.50); with lunch and Tahitian dancing, 5,000 CFP ($50). It also goes to Ile Ouen Turtle Club, a popular weekend retreat for local residents. That trip costs 2,000 CFP ($20) for transport alone, 5,800 CFP ($58) with lunch.

Escapade Resort (tel. 28-53-20) has three boats—two in the morning and one in the afternoon—between Nouméa and its home on Ilot Maître (Wing Island), a small atoll directly off Anse Vata Beach. Guests can ride out on the morning launch and spend the day windsurfing, swimming in the lagoon or in the resort's pool, sunbathing on the white-sand beach, and having lunch in its fine restaurant.

COUNTRYSIDE EXCURSIONS

With the coming of peace in 1988, more and more visitors are finding their way to other parts of 240-mile long Grande Terre, New Caledonia's main island. Unfortunately, I have not been one of them, but I have heard great things about the lush, tropical beauty of the east coast around Hienghène (*Yang*-gane) and the rugged hinterlands of the Chaîne Centrale. Good roads run up and down the coasts, and the territory has several small, comfortable hotels (with their own French restaurants) and less expensive *gîtes,* or Melanesian-owned accommodations, sometimes called tribal lodging in English.

AMAC Tours (tel. 26-38-38), in the Palm Beach shopping center on Anse Vata Beach, can quickly organize trips throughout New Caledonia, including popular day-trips by four-wheel-drive safaris with **Pacific Raid,** a local tour company, to such places as Thio, Canala, and Yaté on the east coast.

SPORTS & RECREATION

New Caledonia's most popular local sport is an unusual, fun-filled form of **cricket** played by Melanesian women of all ages dressed in matching ankle-length "Mother Hubbard" dresses. Rather than being stiffly formal as you might expect from the players' garb, the matches tend to be wild, with lots of shouting, laughing, and bending of the rules. Matches are played on Saturday afternoons from March to November at various sites around town, including the big Terrain de Cricket on route de l'Anse Vata about 5 blocks from the beach.

If you prefer to swim in freshwater, the Olympic-size **Piscine Municipal** (Municipal Swimming Pool), next to the Club Med, is open from 7:30am to 5pm Monday through Friday, from 1 to 5pm on Saturday, and from 9:30am to noon and from 1 to 4:15pm on Sunday. Admission fees are 150 CFP ($1.50) for adults, half that for children under 14.

For tennis addicts, the **municipal tennis courts** next to the swimming pool have all-weather surfaces and are lighted for night play. Phone 27-65-32 to reserve a court.

Golfers can play the **Dumbea Golf Club** nine-hole course in the Dumbea district, about a 15-minute drive north of downtown (take the old road, not the toll expressway). For a starting time, call 36-83-03.

The Australian-owned and -operated **Squash Club** (tel. 26-22-18), in Baie des Pêcheurs on route Jules Garnier opposite the Port Plaisance mall, has courts and equipment for rent to visitors. It's a hotbed of English-speakers, as is the nearby yacht club, and has some of the least expensive drink prices in town.

There's a very active scuba-diving club in Nouméa, but visitors will have to journey to **Amadée Diving Club** (tel. 26-40-29), out at the lighthouse of the same name (see "Lagoon Excursions," above). One dive costs 6,000 CFP ($60), but you can dive twice for 8,000 CFP ($80), plus 2,200 CFP ($22) to get out there and back on the *Starship Genesis.*

Pacific Charter (tel. 26.10.55) takes guests sport fishing in fully equipped boats. Prices start at 20,000 CFP ($200) for ½ day.

For "bareboat" sailboat yachts, contact **Nouméa Yacht Charters,** B.P. 848, Nouméa (tel. 27-58-48). The company rents French-built Bénéteau sloops ranging in size from 35 feet to 43 feet and capable of accommodating between six and eight people each. The 35-footers cost 23,000 CFP ($230) a day; the 39- to 43-footers go for 38,000 CFP ($380) a day. Skippers can be hired for 8,000 CFP ($80) a day. When its boats aren't rented, Nouméa Yacht Charters uses them for day-trips and sunset sails.

SHOPPING

Several **curio shops** around Le Nouvàta Beach Hôtel on Anse Vata Beach and in downtown Nouméa on the place des Cocotiers sell handcrafts produced locally and imported from other South Pacific islands. Kanak-made handcrafts tend to be carved war clubs and bowls and in general lack the quality found elsewhere in the region.

The **Philatelic Bureau** in the main post office sells colorful stamps issued by New Caledonia, French Polynesia, and the French protectorates of Wallis and Futuna islands. It's open Monday through Friday from 7:45am to 11:15am and on Saturday from noon to 2:30pm.

Although prices are high, best buys in Nouméa are **French goods,** such as perfumes, cosmetics, clothes, and lingerie, and leather bags and shoes. Visitors can take advantage of 20% to 30% savings on purchases of 2,000 CFP ($20) or more by shopping at the more than 50 **duty-free shops** that display red, white, and blue stickers in their front windows. You'll need your passport and airline ticket. Save your receipt in order to clear the purchases at Tontouta Airport on your way home. Center Voyages, the American Express agent (see "Fast Facts: Nouméa," above) publishes a handy booklet with the names and addresses of Noumeá's key shops. Any store with a *soldes* (sale) sign in the window is worth stepping into, for many items can be marked down as much as 50%—to which you may or may not be able to add the duty-free discount, depending on the merchant. You aren't likely to find many bargains, however, on electronic goods and cameras.

There are too many quality stores to mention them all here. Instead, here's a walk through downtown Nouméa that will take you past the best:

Begin at the intersection of rues de la Somme and Sébastopol south of place des Cocotiers. Go 5 short blocks north on rue de Sébastopol until you have reached the northwest corner of the square. Turn left on rue Jean Jaurès and walk 3 blocks downhill along the square to rue d'Austerlitz. A right turn here will take you to the large **Océánie** department store, the least expensive place in town to buy *claquettes* (shower sandals). The next street is rue de l'Alma, the heart of the shopping district; take a left to **Ballande** in the first block; it's another department store stocked with French goods and a grocery supermarket.

Now backtrack to rue d'Austerlitz and take a left toward the hospital. On the left in the first block are some fine examples of colonial warehouses. Opposite them, go through the parking lot and into **Centralma,** a covered shopping mall. You could spend hours in these upscale shops, or having a refueling stop at **Snack Centralma,** which has beers from all over the world (see "Where to Dine," below).

Go out the opposite end of the mall from which you entered, turn right on rue Clemenceau, return the ½ block to rue de l'Alma, and turn left (heading uphill). Take your time in these next 2 blocks of rue de l'Alma, which are filled with boutiques and

FROMMER'S FAVORITE
NEW CALEDONIA EXPERIENCES

On the Beach My personal hell will be to spend eternity on Anse Vata Beach surrounded by beautiful, nearly unclothed French women sunning themselves on this expanse of palm-draped sand. The hell of it will be that they don't speak English—and I don't speak French.

Ride the Bus Nouméa is a wonderful town for taking in the views of its pastel houses and surrounding bays from a local minibus as it comes to the top of one hill after another. Bus 7 goes to Hôtel Le Stanley on Pointe aux Longs cous; it's too far out to recommend as a place to stay, but it has fine fixed-price lunches and a marvelous view of Mont Dore across the aqua lagoon.

Isle of Pines The South Pacific has few more hauntingly beautiful strolls than along the great white beaches of Kuto and Kanuméra bays. The ruins of the old French penal colony and a modern hotel stand testimony to people's failure to despoil this unique paradise.

duty-free emporia. At avenue Maréchal-Foch, take a right and follow it across place des Cocotiers. On the south side, you can go up rue Anatole France a block for another refueling stop at the square-side **Brasserie St-Hubert,** one of Nouméa's most popular watering holes (see "Where to Dine," below).

Now backtrack to avenue Maréchal-Foch, turn left, and walk south to **Le Village,** a collection of shops in a renovated mansion. Highlight here is **Produits Nouvelle-Calédonie,** which carries local coffee, cagou dolls, chocolates, honey, soaps, books, and even venison and prawns. It's owned by Mike Hosken, a New Zealand photographer who settled in Nouméa. Look for his colorful book, *new Caledonia,* which makes a nice souvenir.

If you have any money left, you can burn it at the Chinese shops between Le Village and the bus terminal.

EVENING ENTERTAINMENT

Nouméa has a number of fashionable discotheques, but as in any other sophisticated city, they tend to go up and down in popularity rather quickly. In fact, several of those I recommended in the previous edition of this book had folded by the time I got back to prepare this one. Accordingly, ask at your hotel which ones are up.

Many of the better nightspots are *clubs privés,* which means they are technically private clubs. As a practical matter, visitors from overseas have little trouble gaining admission, either at the door by paying a membership fee (translated: cover charge) or through their hotel staff.

Unfortunately, downtown Nouméa has seen its share of after-dark crime in recent years. For this reason, I suggest you confine your nocturnal activity to Anse Vata and Baie des Citrons. The Anse Vata Beach area around Le Nouvàta Hôtel and the nearby Palm Beach shopping center is very popular with local residents, who go there for dinner. Join them for a moonlit stroll along the promenade.

Overseas performers occasionally visit. For concerts and appearances on tap, check the daily editions of *Les Nouvelles Calédoniennes* and look for *Le Cagou futé* (tel. 27-81-82), a little free monthly magazine with a calendar of events inside. Both are published in French.

CASINO ROYALE, in Le Surf Novotel Hôtel, Roche à la voile. Tel. 28-66-88.

One thing visitors find in every hotel room is a coupon for 1,000 CFP ($10) free gambling at this, one of two casinos between Las Vegas and Australia. From all appearances it should be in Cannes, since the women croupiers have on long evening dresses and the men staffers don traditional black tie. For the gamblers, smart casual is the rule. The casino has blackjack, roulette, baccarat, punto y banco, an American-style craps table, and enough slot machines to build up a hefty bicep. The gaming tables are open from 6pm to 1am Monday through Thursday, to 2am on Friday and Saturday, and from 3 to 9pm on Sunday. You can get at the "one-armed bandits" ("poker machines" to you Australians) from noon to midnight Monday through Thursday, to 1am on Friday and Saturday, and from 1 to 10pm on Sunday. The slot machines are open to the public, but you must show your passport to be admitted to all but one of the gaming tables.

Admission: Slots free; tables 400 CFP ($4) per person except Le Surf guests, who get in free. **Prices:** Drinks 350 CFP–500 CFP ($3.50–$5).

CLUB MED DISCO, in Club Méditerranée, Anse Vata Beach. Tel. 26-12-00.

The staff puts on a cabaret show every night at the Club Med, and you don't have to be a member to attend. The stage is just inside the main entrance to the club. There's a stage with stall-like seating, which is pushed away for dancing after the show. Dinner begins at 7pm, followed by performance and dancing.

Admission: 2,300 CFP ($23) for men, including 1,800 CFP ($18) for drinks; 1,400 CFP ($14) for women, including 900 CFP ($9) for drinks; 5,400 CFP ($54) for men or women, including dinner with wine. **Prices:** Drinks 250 CFP–500 CFP ($2.50–$5).

LE SURF NOVOTEL HOTEL, Roche à la voile. Tel. 28-66-88.

Depending on the number of tourists in town, this hotel may have traditional Tahitian or Melanesian dance shows when you are visiting. For some quiet jazz piano, try the Piano Bar in the downstairs lobby. Blown-up posters for old Humphrey Bogart movies set an appropriate atmosphere.

Admission: Free. **Prices:** Shows about 3,500 CFP ($35) including dinner; drinks 450 CFP ($4.50).

LE LAGON HOTEL, 143 route de l'Anse Vata, Anse Vata Beach. Tel. 26-12-55.

This hotel just off Anse Vata Beach also may have traditional Tahitian or Melanesian dance shows or performances by visiting musicians, singers, and dancers; check with them to see if any are scheduled when you're in the area.

Admission: Depends on performer. **Prices:** Drinks 350 CFP ($3.50).

6. WHERE TO STAY

Some tourists and business people stay in the downtown commercial hotels some 3km (2 miles) away, but most visitors opt for the sands of Anse Vata or Baie des Citrons and their wide range of accommodations, restaurants, and water-sports activities. There has been much talk in recent years about a large Sheraton hotel being built at Anse Vata and a new Club Méditerranée going up, so there might be some additions by the time you plan your trip.

EXPENSIVE

LE SURF NOVOTEL HOTEL, B.P. 4230, Nouméa. Tel. 28-66-88, or toll free 800/221-4542 in the U.S. Fax 28-52-23. Telex 3118. 253 rms. A/C MINIBAR TV TEL **Location:** Roche à la voile, between Anse Vata and Baie des Citrons. Bus 6.

$ Rates: 12,300 CFP–14,500 CFP ($123–145) single; 14,300 CFP–16,500 CFP ($143–$165) double. AE, DC, MC, V.

Nouméa's best digs for the time being, Le Surf commands a panoramic view of the lagoon from its perch on Roche à la voile, the rocky point separating Anse Vata and Baie des Citrons (rooms with a garden view are less expensive than those with a sea view). Three- and four-story buildings hold the guest rooms, all brightly accented in a lime-green-and-white theme with bold printed drapes and spreads and floral arrangements of hibiscus and roses. A small cove across the street sports a shady beach.

Dining/Entertainment: Poolside Le Grille coffee shop serves snacks and meals all day. Beachside Fun Beach Grille & Brasserie is a delightful spot for a meal or sunset cocktail. La Coupole French restaurant and Le Samourai Japanese restaurant are among Nouméa's finest eateries.

Services: Laundry, baby-sitting, business services. Overall service is among best in South Pacific.

Facilities: Swimming pool; boutiques; casino; bank; tour desks; Gymstyle Fitness Center with bodybuilding equipment, saunas, spa pools, massages, beauty treatments, and a "super shower" costs 1,200 CFP ($12) per hour, 5,000 CFP ($50) per week.

CLUB MEDITERRANEE, B.P. 115, Nouméa. Tel. 26-12-00, or toll free 800/528-3100 in the U.S. Fax 26-70-71. 280 rms. A/C **Location:** Pointe Magnin, south end of Anse Vata Beach.

$ Rates (all inclusive): 13,000 CFP ($130) double per person. AE, DC, MC, V.

This eight-story landmark was formerly known as the Hôtel Château Royale. The rooms are a bit Spartan, with no telephones or televisions to detract from a wide range of nonstop activities. The only extras are drinks at the bar, and you pay for those with beads purchased in advance. Persons traveling alone will be assigned a roommate of the same sex. From an economic standpoint, Club Med vacations are best purchased as part of a package including substantially reduced airfare.

Dining/Entertainment: Room rates include three whopping meals a day, including wine at lunch and dinner. Staff puts on cabaret shows nightly (see "Evening Entertainment," above).

Services: Laundry, baby-sitting.

Facilities: Tennis courts, Windsurfers, swimming pool, tour desk.

ISLE DE FRANCE APPARTEMENTS, B.P. 1604, Nouméa. Tel. 26-24-22. Fax 26-17-20. Telex 3143. 113 apartments. A/C TV TEL **Location:** Rue Boulari, a small street off route de l'Anse Vata 1 block inland from beach. Bus 3.

$ Rates: 12,000 CFP–23,000 CFP ($120–$230). AE, DC, MC, V.

This five-story former Travelodge hotel was completely refurbished and reopened in 1988, and a 13-story circular structure was added next door in 1989 (apartments near the top have spectacular views of the lagoon and offshore islands). This is a "serviced apartment" complex, which means you get your own fully equipped apartment as well as chamber and other services provided by a hotel. The rates depend on the size of the apartment and the view it commands; it makes no difference if you have one person or five staying in the apartment. Units in the old wing are less expensive than those in the high-rise.

Dining/Entertainment: The area between the two buildings contains a swimming pool and restaurant. Guests have free access to Le Privilège, a quiet and dimly lit nightclub.

Services: Chiropractor on the premises offers massage and beauty treatments; laundry/valet.

Facilities: Swimming pool, hairdresser, boutique, tour desk, coin-operated laundry with ironing boards.

AN OFFSHORE RESORT

ESCAPADE ISLAND RESORT, B.P. 4918, Nouméa. Tel. 28-53-20. Fax same as tel. 44 rms. **Location:** Ilot Maître, 30 minutes by boat off Nouméa.

$ Rates: 129,000 CFP ($120) single or double. AE, DC, MC, V.

It was entirely appropriate for Corsican-born Australian Robert Maestracci to bring a few burly Fijians with him when he came to New Caledonia from Fiji to manage the territory's first offshore hideaway. Located on tiny, atoll-like Ilot Maître, the Escapade has four guest rooms in each of 11 bungalows around a central building housing its bar and primarily French restaurant. Count on spending 6,000 CFP ($60) or so per person a day for meals, since you won't be able to walk to a nearby snack bar. Day trips to the Escapade are popular with visitors staying in town (see "What to See & Do," above, for more details). There's a beachside swimming pool.

MODERATE

HOTEL LE LAGON, B.P. 440, Nouméa. Tel. 26-12-55. Fax 26-12-44. Telex 3017. 24 rms, 30 apartments. A/C TV TEL **Location:** 143 route de l'Anse Vata, 2 blocks from beach. Bus 3.

$ Rates: 9,200 CFP ($92) single room, 10,200 CFP ($102) double room; 13,200 CFP ($132) studio apartment; 15,200 CFP ($152) 1-bedroom apartment; 17,200 CFP ($172) 2-bedroom apartment. AE, DC, MC, V.

$ Vivianne Cardin and son Patrick recently renovated their hotel, turning most of their rooms into airy apartments. They apparently raised the money by rounding up lots of Japanese guests—so many, in fact, that advance reservations are a must between December and April. The apartments have Japanese touches, such as paper walls dividing bedroom from lounge. On the higher floors they have balconies overlooking the Anse Vata area. The older rooms have modern furnishings and ceiling fans as well as window-type air-conditioning units. You can wink at the fish swimming in the huge aquariums in L'Amiral Bar and Restaurant just beyond the reception desk.

LE NOUVATA BEACH HOTEL, B.P. 137, Nouméa. Tel. 26-22-00. Fax 41-60-70. Telex 3145. 50 rms, 36 bungalows. A/C TV TEL **Location:** 123 promenade Roger Laroque, on Anse Vata Beach. Bus 3 and Bus 6.

$ Rates: 4,500 CFP ($45) single bungalow, 5,400 CFP ($54) double bungalow; 9,000 CFP ($90) single room, 10,000 CFP ($100) double room. AE, DC, MC, V.

I mention this hotel with some caution because developers have owned it since 1988 and plan eventually to rebuild it into a large luxury resort. In the meantime, the main three-story building has 50 spacious rooms and 36 bungalows. The latter, situated to the rear, present somewhat basic accommodations that are popular with rural New Caledonians who come into Nouméa. Although the property is not as well maintained as under its previous owners, the older bungalows offer one of Nouméa's better accommodation bargains. They make worthwhile an inquiry as to the status of this hotel. A ground-floor restaurant has fine seafood offerings, and a next-door bar is a popular local watering hole. There's a swimming pool behind the main building. The location is in the middle of Anse Vata's tourist area; the beach is right across the street.

HOTEL IBIS NOUMEA, B.P. 819, Nouméa. Tel. 26-20-55, or toll free 800/221-4542 in the U.S. Fax 26-20-44. Telex 3152. 60 rms. A/C TV TEL **Location:** 8 route de la Baie des Citrons. Bus 6.

$ Rates: 8,000 CFP ($80) single; 9,000 CFP ($90) double. AE, DC, MC, V.

Although I personally prefer to stay at Anse Vata, the tree-shaded beach of Baie des Citrons lies just across the promenade from this hotel, which makes it a viable option if you want sand just a few steps away. Although somewhat small, the clean, comfortable rooms here have French video programming and small refrigerators. Those on the upper floors facing the beach have sliding glass doors opening onto narrow balconies. All are pleasantly decorated in the same lime-green-and-white motif used at Le Surf.

On the ground level, the Ibis sports an open-air bar, the Tappanyaki Japanese restaurant, and a second restaurant specializing in Basque-style sauces.

LANTANA BEACH HOTEL, B.P. 4075, Nouméa. Tel. 26-22-12. Fax 26-16-12. 37 rms. A/C TV TEL **Location:** Promenade Roger Laroque, Anse Vata Beach. Bus 3 and Bus 6.

$ Rates: 7,000 CFP ($70) single; 8,000 CFP ($80) double. AE, DC, MC, V.

If you like to be in the middle of things and don't need a lot of frills in your room, this hotel is it. The four-story building stands a few doors from the Le Nouvàta Beach Hôtel and right in the middle of Anse Vata's collection of snack bars and restaurants. The rooms aren't spacious but are reasonably comfortable for the price. Ask for a room on one of the top two floors, since they have balconies overlooking the beach.

BUDGET

MOTEL ANSE VATA, B.P. 4453, Nouméa. Tel. 26-26-12. Fax 28-44-53. Telex 3178. 22 apartments (all with bath). A/C TV TEL **Location:** 19 rue Gabriel Laroque, 2 blocks from Anse Vata Beach. Bus 3.

$ Rates: 4,500 CFP ($45) single; 5,000 CFP ($50) double; 500 CFP ($5) extra per day for air conditioning. AE, MC, V.

Pierre Ciry has efficiency apartments at this three-story, walk-up building a 5-minute walk from Anse Vata Beach. Each apartment has a complete kitchen and a bath with shower and bidet. The furniture is basic and dated and the flowery wallpaper a bit on the gaudy side, but the building is well maintained, and the apartments are serviced Monday through Saturday and kept immaculately clean. Videocassette players are supplied free of charge.

MOTEL LE BAMBOU, 44 rue Edouard-Spahr, Nouméa. Tel. 26-12-90. Fax 28-44-53. 22 rms (all with bath). TV TEL **Location:** In Val Plaisance, 15-minute walk from Anse Vata Beach. Bus 3.

$ Rates: 3,900 CFP ($39) single; 4,200 CFP ($42) double. AE, MC, V.

The rooms are quite small but nevertheless pleasant at Mme Renée Pessina's motel, a two-story building almost hidden in a residential neighborhood of Val Plaisance, near Anse Vata. The rooms have Pullman kitchens, French television programming, and balconies or patios. Each room has an electric fan, and you can throw open the kitchen windows to let in a refreshing cross breeze. To find Le Bambou, follow its signs up rue Gabriel Laroque from Anse Vata Beach. Bus 3 runs along rue Gabriel Laroque.

AUBERGE DE JEUNESSE (YOUTH HOSTEL), B.P. 767, Nouméa. Tel. 27-58-79. 56 bunks, 10 rms (none with bath). **Location:** Rue Orly. Go up rue Jean Jaurès, right on rue Orly, right at Municipal Centre on top of hill.

$ Rates: 900 CFP ($9) for Youth Hostel Association members; 1,000 CFP ($10) for others.

The young backpack brigade frequents the South Pacific's only official youth hostel, which is located on the hill behind Cathédrale St-Joseph. As in all YHA hostels, you'll have to do a housekeeping chore; unlike many, however, the auberge is open all day. It's informal and very well managed. The bulletin board is a wealth of information about traveling on the cheap in New Caledonia.

7. WHERE TO DINE

Nouméa has more than 100 restaurants, enough to satisfy its residents' seemingly insatiable appetites for good food and more than enough to keep a visitor well fed. It's difficult to find a bad meal in Nouméa. Almost any restaurant you pass is likely to serve delicious if not outright gourmet meals. The prices won't be cheap, since many ingredients are shipped in from New Zealand or Australia, and the service may move at a tropical pace, but you're in for a treat. I'll mention a few establishments to keep you from going hungry with indecision, but don't hesitate to pick up a complete list of restaurants from the Center Voyages (see "American Express" in "Fast Facts," above) and strike out on your own.

There are no McDonald's or other American-style fast-food establishments, but you won't have trouble finding a snack bar for a croissant and a cup of strong coffee for breakfast or a take-out lunch, perhaps a **casse-croûte**—one of those long sandwiches made of a loaf of crusty French bread and such ingredients as *jambon et fromage* (ham and cheese) with a touch of lettuce. Another option is to pick up a baguette of bread, a block of French cheese, and some other "fixin's" plus a bottle of *vin ordinaire* for a make-it-yourself picnic. The beaches at Anse Vata and Baie des Citrons are perfect; so is place des Cocotiers if you're downtown.

There are two well-stocked grocery stores 2 blocks up route de l'Anse Vata from the beach: **Océanie** is open Monday to Friday 6:30am to 12:30pm and from 3 to 7pm, Saturday and Sunday from 7:30am to noon. **Ballandette** is open Monday to Saturday from 7am to noon, Sunday from 7:30am to noon. In downtown, the big **Prisunic** department store, corner of rues Anatole France and d'Austerlitz on place des Cocotiers, has a well-stocked grocery supermarket with a good wine selection, as does **Ballande,** on rue de l'Alma at rue d'Austerlitz. Both are open over the lunch break on weekdays.

During the day, you can relieve the heat of Anse Vata Beach at two ice-cream stands just across the promenade. One of these, **Caprice Ice Cream Shop,** in front of Le Nauticus curio shop, makes its own waffle cones in front of you.

FRENCH CUISINE

LA COUPOLE, in Le Surf Novotel, Roche à la voile. Tel. 28-66-88.
Cuisine: FRENCH. **Reservations:** Recommended.

$ Prices: Appetizers 1,300 CFP–2,950 CFP ($13–$29.50); main courses 1,850 CFP–2,800 CFP ($18.50–$28.50); fixed-price lunch 2,000 CFP ($20). AE, DC, MC, V.

Open: Lunch daily 11am–2pm; dinner Mon–Sat 7:30–11pm.

If you're staying at Le Surf Novotel, you don't even have to go out to find one of Nouméa's finest and most elegant French restaurants, located on the Anse Vata side of the hotel. Some specialties of the chef are roast fresh tuna and young leeks in a Spanish mackerel sauce, filet of parrot fish in a light orange sauce, and enough prime rib in red wine sauce to feed two hungry travelers. At lunchtime, a special "menu express" offers a choice of mouth-watering main courses, plats du jour, and desserts.

LE BERTHELOT, 13 route du Port Despointes, near downtown Nouméa. Tel. 28-32-70.

Cuisine: FRENCH. **Reservations:** Recommended.

$ Prices: Appetizers 850 CFP–2,100 CFP ($8.50–$21); main courses 1,400 CFP–2,600 CFP ($14–$26). AE, DC, MC, V.

Open: Lunch daily 11am–2pm; dinner Mon–Sat 7:30–11:30pm.

Local residents have good reason to rave about the nouvelle cuisine offerings of Le Berthelot, in a converted house in the Faubourg-Blanchot neighborhood next to the English Bookshop (it's 2 blocks downhill from the big cross at the intersection of boulevard Extérieur and route de l'Anse Vata). The seafood dishes are exquisite. For a splurge, try the lobster flambéed with whisky and fresh cream.

LE PETIT TRAIN and MAEVA SNACK BAR, 22 route de la Baie des Citrons. Tel. 26-28-11.

Cuisine: FRENCH. **Reservations:** Recommended for dinner.

$ Prices: Appetizers 750 CFP–1,400 CFP ($7.50–$14); main courses 1,450 CFP–1,750 CFP ($14.50–$17.50). AE, DC, MC, V.

Open: Breakfast and lunch Wed–Mon 9am–2pm; dinner Wed–Mon 6–10pm.

Speaking of views, it's hard to beat Le Petit Train, whose big picture windows look across the water and down the beach from its perch on the rocks at the north end of Baie des Citrons. That's a fine place to partake of Paul Bocuse-inspired nouvelle-cuisine specialties such as fresh salmon in a light sorrel sauce and shrimp with fine-cut vegetables in an Armagnac-tinged sauce. Le Petit Train is open only for dinner; the downstairs, beachside Maeva Snack Bar serves during the day.

LE SYDNEY, 47 rue Jules Garnier, Baie des Citrons. Tel. 26-16-99.

Cuisine: FRENCH. **Reservations:** Recommended.

$ Prices: Appetizers 1,000 CFP–1,400 CFP ($10–$14); main courses 1,500 CFP–2,500 CFP ($15–$25). AE, MC.

Open: Dinner Wed–Mon 7–11pm.

This bistro-style restaurant 2 blocks north of Le Petit Train, on the hill between Baie des Citrons and Baie des Pêcheurs, has steaks and prime rib designed to appeal to the Australians who hail from its namesake city as well as seafood dishes prepared in the light, nouvelle-cuisine style.

LE BILBOQUET, in Le Village shops, 35 av. du Maréchal Foch, downtown Nouméa. Tel. 28-43-30.

Cuisine: FRENCH. **Reservations:** Not accepted.

$ Prices: Appetizers 550 CFP–1,650 CFP ($5.50–$16.50); main courses 900 CFP–1,950 CFP ($9–$19.50). AE, DC, MC, V.

Open: Mon–Sat 7am–midnight.

For less-expensive French cuisine, the best bets are Nouméa's many bistro-style establishments. Le Bilboquet, among Le Village shops in the second block south of the place des Cocotiers, is a trendy spot, with tables both inside the restaurant and outside in the brick-lined, foliage-accented shopping mall. The menu features soups, sandwiches, and tasty specials that vary from day to day.

PALM BEACH BRASSERIE, in Palm Beach shopping center, promenade Roger Laroque, Anse Vata Beach. Tel. 26-46-60.

Cuisine: FRENCH. **Reservations:** Recommended on weekends.

$ Prices: Appetizers 350 CFP–1,100 CFP; main courses 850 CFP–1,700 CFP ($8.50–$17). AE, MC, V.

Open: Daily 11am–midnight.

At Anse Vata Beach, don't miss a meal at the Palm Beach Brasserie, located in the plantation-style shopping center of the same name. One of Nouméa's largest restaurants, this second-floor establishment peeks out toward the beach

FROMMER'S SMART TRAVELER: RESTAURANTS

1. Take advantage of *plats du jour* (daily specials), especially at lunch. These three-course offerings usually are made from fresh produce direct from the market and represent a significant savings over ordering from the menu.
2. Look for *prix-fixe* (fixed-priced) menus. These three-course meals usually are much less expensive than if you order *à la carte*.
3. Order *vin ordinaire* (table wine) served in a carafe. The chef buys good quality wine in bulk; you get the savings.

from under a light green peaked ceiling—from which are suspended dark green ceiling fans and various vines. The white-tile floor and lawn tables and chairs add to a very distinct impression of outside dining, while the staff creates a fun atmosphere in which to enjoy a variety of tasty offerings.

FUN BEACH GRILLE & BRASSERIE, promenade Roger Laroque, opposite Le Surf Novotel, Anse Vata Beach. Tel. 26-31-32.
Cuisine: FRENCH. **Reservations:** Not required.
$ **Prices:** Appetizers 350 CFP–550 CFP ($3.50–$5.50); main courses 1,050 CFP–2,800 CFP ($10.50–$28); pizzas 1,300 CFP ($13). AE, MC, V.
Open: Lunch daily 9:30am–2pm; dinner Mon–Thurs 6:30–10pm, Fri–Sat 6:30–11:30pm, Sun 6:30–10:30pm.

Visit this establishment perched above the end of Anse Vata Beach if for no other reason than to sip a cool drink while the setting sun paints the sky orange, pink, and purple. Plus, you can do that on an open deck above the beach. The dining room under a soaring conical roof enjoys almost as good a view, which may distract you from various salads (the only appetizers offered) as well as grilled steaks, veal, and local fish, such as tuna and grouper. If there's no table available when you show up, have a drink on the deck and let the trade wind run its fingers through your hair.

ITALIAN CUISINE

BRASSERIE ST-HUBERT, 12 rue de Sébastopol, at southeast corner of place des Cocotiers. Tel. 27-21-42.
Cuisine: ITALIAN. **Reservations:** Not required.
$ **Prices:** Appetizers 450 CFP–1,850 CFP ($4.50–$18.50); pizzas and pastas 1,150 CFP–1,400 CFP ($11.50–$14). AE, MC, V.
Open: Lunch Mon–Sat 11am–2pm; dinner Mon–Sat 6:30–10:30pm; bar with snacks Mon–Sat 10am–10:30pm.

One of the city's institutions, this restaurant and civilized drinking establishment occupies a choice location in a low tin-roofed colonial building. A wrought-iron railing runs along the edge of the open-air dining area and bar, separating patrons from the populace strolling under the poincianas of the park. Omelets, hamburgers, steaks, salads, and other selections—including Tahitian-style *poisson cru* (marinated fish) and, on Saturday nights, couscous—are available in the bar area. One end of the building has been turned into a fine, reasonably priced Italian restaurant, which offers individual-size pizzas and various pasta dishes. Even if you don't eat at Brasserie St-Hubert, it's fun to sit by the railing, sip a drink or beer, and watch Nouméa pass by. If you understand French, you're also likely to catch the gist of some heated political discussions at the nearby tables.

SAN REMO PIZZERIA, promenade Roger Laroque, Anse Vata Beach. Tel. 26-18-02.
Cuisine: ITALIAN. **Reservations:** Not required.
$ **Prices:** Appetizers 900 CFP–1,600 CFP ($9–$16); main courses 1,000 CFP–

1,400 CFP ($10–$14); pizzas 900 CFP–1,400 CFP ($9–$14). AE, MC, V.
Open: Lunch daily 11am–1:30pm; dinner Sun–Thurs 6:30–10:30pm, Fri–Sat 6:30pm–4am.

This is extremely popular with visitors and locals alike, and not just for its location—right on Anse Vata Beach between Le Nouvàta and Lantana Beach hotels. It serves a spicy but delicate tomato sauce on a variety of thin-crust, wood-oven pizzas and homemade pasta dishes, such as spaghetti, gnocchi, ravioli, cannelloni, and lasagne. Small pizzas are just big enough to satisfy one person. Pizza légumes is just that, absolutely loaded with vegetables—not the kind your mother forced you to eat, though, but peppers, onions, mushrooms, and artichoke hearts. Daily specials usually feature seafood.

PIZZA PINO, 5 route de la Baie des Citrons, next to Ibis Nouméa Hôtel. Tel. 26-21-33.
Cuisine: ITALIAN. **Reservations:** Not required.
$ Prices: Appetizers 800 CFP–1,400 CFP ($8–$14); main courses 1,000 CFP–1,500 CFP ($10–$15); pizzas 950 CFP–1,400 CFP ($9.50–$14). AE, V.
Open: Lunch Thurs–Tues 10:45am–noon; dinner Thurs–Tues 6:30–11pm.

You can eat good-quality pizzas or lasagne inside or on the shady veranda just across the route de la Baie des Citrons from the beach, or try the house specialty, spaghetti marinara (complete with squid). If you're lying on the sand and suddenly need something sweet and refreshing, stroll to the snack bar next door for an ice-cream sundae.

JAPANESE CUISINE

LE SAMOURAI, in Le Surf Novotel Hôtel, Roche à la voile. Tel. 28-66-88.
Cuisine: JAPANESE. **Reservations:** Not required.
$ Prices: Lunch menu 1,600 CFP ($16); appetizers 350 CFP–950 CFP ($3.50–$9.50); main courses 1,150 CFP–2,000 CFP ($11.50–$20). AE, DC, MC, V.
Open: Lunch daily 11am–2pm; dinner daily 6:30–10pm.

Local residents now concede the top spot in Japanese cuisine to this excellent establishment in Le Surf Novotel Hôtel. House specialties are teppanyaki-style sautées of meats and vegetables; diners watch the chef prepare the dishes at their table. Sashimi is offered as an appetizer.

TAPPANYAKI RESTAURANT, in Hôtel Ibis Nouméa, 8 route de la Baie des Citrons. Tel. 26-20-55.
Cuisine: JAPANESE. **Reservations:** Recommended.
$ Prices: Appetizers 350 CFP–600 CFP ($3.50–$6); main courses 1,400 CFP–1,650 CFP ($14–$16.50); full dinners 2,500 CFP–3,000 CFP ($25–$30). AE, DC, MC, V.
Open: Lunch daily 11am–2pm; dinner daily 7–10pm.

You can leave your shoes outside at this pleasantly and appropriately decorated restaurant, whose varnished wood floor is recessed under the tables, thereby giving the impression you're sitting on the floor in the Japanese fashion when in fact you're not. The food is cooked at your table, hibachi-style. Full dinners include sashimi, a meat course, fried rice, and a choice of dessert.

DAISHIN SUSHI-BAR, in Port Plaisance shopping center, route Jules Garnier, Baie des Pêcheurs. Tel. 26-23-10.
Cuisine: JAPANESE. **Reservations:** Not required.
$ Prices: Sushi 300 CFP–800 CFP ($3–$8); main courses 800 CFP–1,300 CFP ($8–$13). AE, V.
Open: Lunch Mon–Sat 11am–2pm; dinner Fri–Wed 6–11pm.

This blond-wood establishment actually has a little Japanese-style garden outside its big windows at the rear of the Port Plaisance shopping center (it's within walking distance over the hill from Baie des Citrons). That's a proper setting for fresh sushi and "burned food," as the management calls cooked fish and steak, all Japanese-style.

SATSUMA RAHMEN, 42 rue de la République (above av. du Maréchal-Foch), downtown Nouméa. Tel. 28-50-64.

Cuisine: JAPANESE. **Reservations:** Recommended for dinner.
$ **Prices:** Appetizers 400 CFP–1,200 CFP ($4–$12); main courses 550 CFP–1,350 CFP ($5.50–$13.50). AE, MC, V.
Open: Lunch Mon–Sat 11am–2pm; dinner Mon–Sat 7–10pm.

At its attractive, storefront quarters, across from the French high commissioner's offices, this offers a wide variety of Japanese noodle soups and sautéed dishes. The local Satsuma Rahmen, part of a chain of similar restaurants in Tokyo and Hawaii, makes its own Japanese noodles.

CHINESE, INDIAN & VIETNAMESE CUISINES

JARDIN DE CHINE, 3 rue Tabou (on route de l'Anse Vata), 3 blocks inland from Anse Vata Beach. Tel. 26-24-41.
Cuisine: CHINESE. **Reservations:** Recommended.
$ **Prices:** Appetizers 600 CFP–800 CFP ($6–$8); main courses 800 CFP–1,200 CFP ($8–$12). AE, MC.
Open: Lunch Wed–Sun 11:30am–2pm; dinner daily 6:30–11pm.

The elegant, first-rate Jardin de Chine occupies a house behind a tree-shaded lawn, just 2 blocks from the beach in Anse Vata, and offers near-gourmet selections from the traditional cuisine of several of China's provinces. Steamed whole fish or local lobsters go for about 2,800 CFP ($28).

ANNAPURNA RESTAURANT INDIEN, 138 route de l'Anse Vata, 2 blocks inland from Anse Vata Beach. Tel. 26-10-35.
Cuisine: INDIAN. **Reservations:** Not usually required.
$ **Prices:** Appetizers 450 CFP–600 CFP ($4.50–$6); main courses 1,000 CFP–1,900 CFP ($10–$19). AE, DC, MC.
Open: Lunch Mon–Sat 10am–2pm; dinner Mon–Sat 6pm–midnight.

Step down from the sidewalk to tables on the veranda or inside a pleasant dining room decorated with Indian artifacts at this establishment, then enjoy a selection of spicy northern Indian curries or tender meat or chicken from the tandoori oven.

JADE PALACE RESTAURANT, route de la Baie des Citrons, on the beach. Tel. 28-12-15.
Cuisine: CANTONESE. **Reservations:** Recommended.
$ **Prices:** Appetizers 700 CFP–950 CFP ($7–$9.50); main courses 900 CFP–1,400 CFP ($9–$14). AE, MC, V.
Open: Lunch Wed–Sun 11am–2pm; dinner Wed–Sun 6:30–10pm.

The nearest Chinese restaurant to the Baie des Citrons beach area, the dining room here has enough Far Eastern decor to set an appropriate atmosphere for its wide range of Cantonese dishes. A few, such as lobster or crab, run up to 2,800 CFP ($28).

TAN VIET, 15 rue de Sébastopol (corner of rue Barlaux), downtown Nouméa. Tel. 28-30-76.
Cuisine: VIETNAMESE. **Reservations:** Recommended at dinner.
$ **Prices:** Appetizers 400 CFP–1,000 CFP ($4–$10); main courses 700 CFP–1,000 CFP ($7–$10). AE, MC, V.
Open: Lunch Mon–Sat 10:30am–1:30pm; dinner Mon–Sat 5:30–10pm.

For reasonably priced and delicately seasoned Vietnamese dishes, try the Tan Viet. The menu includes beef, pork, and chicken dishes. The second-floor dining room is a good spot to watch the residents stroll by on the sidewalks below.

MAY GARDEN SNACK BAR, 30 rue de Sébastopol (at rue Sourcouf), downtown Nouméa. Tel. 28-45-15.
Cuisine: CANTONESE. **Reservations:** Not accepted.
$ **Prices:** Main courses 700 CFP–1,000 CFP ($7–$10). No credit cards.
Open: Mon–Sat 8:30am–1:30pm.

This popular, cafeteria-style restaurant offers quick Cantonese lunches, such as fried noodles or rice and chow mein. You don't need a word of French: Just point to what you want on the steam table and pay the amount on the check when you're finished.

SNACK BARS

FARE POINTE MANGIN, on Pointe Mangin, Anse Vata Beach beyond Club Méditerranée. Tel. 26-23-66.

Cuisine: FRENCH/SNACK BAR. **Reservations:** Not accepted.

$ Prices: Sandwiches, burgers, and hot dogs 250 CFP–450 CFP ($2.50–$4.50); appetizers 750 CFP–1,000 CFP ($7.50–$10); main courses 1,000 CFP–2,000 CFP ($10–$20). AE, V.

Open: Daily 8:30am–6pm.

For a more substantial lunch of juicy hamburgers, crisp salads, or grilled steaks, fish, lamb chops, or lobster, wander down Anse Vata Beach past the Club Med and the Hobie Cat Club to this breezy, open-air snack bar. Its big thatch roof sits right next to the sand. I often do my "beaching" near Faré Pointe Mangin; the water is warm, the sand soft, the pulchritude plentiful, and when thirst dictates, it's a short crawl to the bar.

SNACK JULIUS, promenade Roger Laroque, next to Lantana Beach Hôtel, Anse Vata Beach. Tel. 26-13-38.

Cuisine: SNACK BAR. **Reservations:** Not accepted.

$ Prices: Sandwiches and burgers 200 CFP–400 CFP ($2–$4); budget meals 500 CFP ($5); regular meals 1,100 CFP–1,600 CFP ($11–$16); pizzas 1,000 CFP–1,400 CFP ($10–$14). No credit cards.

Open: Mon–Fri 7am–10pm, Fri–Sat 7am–midnight.

The original Snack Julius has Anse Vata's best-value budget meals: either steak, chicken, or sausages with french fries and a small salad. The take-out bar is now flanked by two other related establishments: a more upscale **Julius Jr.'s** with salads (including Tahitian poisson cru) and grilled steaks and chops, and **Pizza Minute,** which has wood-fired pies. Take your pick. It's all good value.

SNACK BAMBINO VATA, 29 promenade Roger Laroque, beside Le Nouvàta Beach Hôtel, Anse Vata Beach. Tel. 26-11-77.

Cuisine: SNACK BAR. **Reservations:** Not accepted.

$ Prices: Breakfast special 800 CFP ($8); sandwiches, burgers, and hot dogs 200 CFP–450 CFP ($2–$4.50); meals 400 CFP–850 CFP ($4–$8.50). No credit cards.

Open: Daily 8am–midnight.

I am particularly fond of this establishment—primarily for its steaks and hamburgers cooked over real charcoal after being lightly tinged with garlic. It also has a wide range of sandwiches, hot dogs, and other snacks, plus Vietnamese-style meals. The cooked breakfast special includes coffee, fresh orange juice, fruit, toast, and bacon and eggs nicely garnished with onions, tomatoes, pickles, and lettuce. It's a good deal.

LE BILBOQUET, in the Palm Beach shopping arcade, promenade Roger Laroque, Anse Vata Beach. Tel. 26-46-60.

Cuisine: SNACK BAR. **Reservations:** Not accepted.

$ Prices: Salads and sandwiches 200 CFP–600 CFP ($2–$6); plats du jour 850 CFP ($8.50); children's menu 600 CFP ($6). No credit cards.

Open: Sun–Fri 6:30am–7:30pm, Sat 6:30am–9:30pm.

This smaller, open-air version of the bistro by the same name in downtown Nouméa has an ice-cream bar. Order there for salads, sandwiches, and very well prepared plats du jour for lunch. The children's menu is a smaller version of the daily specials.

TACO TACO, in Palm Beach shopping center, promenade Roger Laroque, Anse Vata Beach. Tel. 26-26-29.

Cuisine: MEXICAN. **Reservations:** Not accepted.

$ Prices: 450 CFP–950 CFP ($4.50–$9.50). No credit cards.

Open: Daily 11am–9pm.

This fast-food establishment is owned by Californian Patrick Helmy (of the *Mary D Princess*), and the tacos, burritos, and enchiladas look more like the real thing than they taste (more hot sauce, please). Nevertheless it's the only place in New

Caledonia to get Mexican food, and Patrick certainly knows how to hire beautiful people to do the serving.

PETER'S GRILL, route de la Baie des Citrons, on the beach. No phone.
Cuisine: SNACK BAR. **Reservations:** Not accepted.
$ **Prices:** Sandwiches, burgers, and hot dogs 200 CFP–500 CFP ($2–$5); grilled steak or chicken with salad 550 CFP–800 CFP ($5.50–$8). No credit cards.
Open: Daily 9am–9pm, later if busy.

Baie des Citrons' answer to the snack bars on Anse Vata Beach, this one is in a small shack on the beach near the Nouméa Ibis Hôtel. It has sandwiches, juicy burgers, hot dogs, and *steak frites* and *poulet frites* (steak or chicken with a mound of french fries), plus ice cream and milk shakes.

LA TERRASSE SNACK BAR, corner av. du Maréchal-Foch and rue de la République, downtown Nouméa. Tel. 28-37-77.
Cuisine: SNACK BAR. **Reservations:** Not accepted.
$ **Prices:** Croissants and casse-croûtes 100 CFP–250 CFP ($1–$2.50); lunch 800 CFP ($8). No credit cards.
Open: Mon–Sat 6am–5:30pm.

This is one of my favorite spots in downtown Nouméa for a morning croissant and coffee. The decor is pleasant, the service friendly, and you can point to your choice of pastry on the counter by the cash register without having to explain yourself in French. At lunch, La Terrasse serves huge plats du jour cafeteria-style and is one of Nouméa's less expensive spots for a full midday meal.

SNACK CENTRALMA, in Centralma shopping mall, rue Clemenceau between rues de l'Alma and de la République, downtown Nouméa. Tel. 28-81-82.
Cuisine: SNACK BAR. **Reservations:** Not accepted.
$ **Prices:** Breakfasts 500 CFP ($5); sandwiches, crêpes, and pastries 200 CFP–500 CFP ($2–$5). No credit cards.
Open: Mon–Fri 5:30am–6pm, Sat 5:30am–2pm.

Along with Snack Bambino Vata at the beach, this pleasant snack bar inside the Centralma mall is one of Nouméa's best places to have a cooked breakfast: Ham, eggs, toast, and coffee for just 500 CFP ($5) is good value. It's also a relaxing spot for a midday break of crêpes, the house specialty, or an afternoon choice of beers from around the world.

8. EASY EXCURSIONS

ISLE OF PINES

Lying about 42 miles southeast of Grande Terre but still within its barrier reef, the ✪ **Isle of Pines** is renowned for its towering, ship's mast–like *Araucaria columbaris* pines, its talcumlike white-sand beaches, and its fine scuba diving in both freshwater caves and over the colorful coral offshore. The overgrown remains of the old prison still stand in memory of the Paris Commune political prisoners who served there between 1871 and 1880.

GETTING THERE

Air Calédonie has an early-morning and a late-afternoon round-trip flight between Magenta Airport and the island every day. The typical day-trip costs about 18,500 CFP ($185) per person, including airfare, a tour of the island, lunch, and time for sunbathing and swimming. The day-trips are popular with Japanese tourists, and many residents of Nouméa like to fly over for a weekend away from town. In other words, book early.

You can book the Isle of Pines day-trip, lodging at one of the gîtes, and Nauticlub scuba diving through Air Calédonie (tel. 25-12-77), AMAC Tours (tel. 26-38-38), or through your travel agent at home. If you're planning to stay overnight, make your plane and lodging reservations at the same time so you'll be assured of accommodations.

GETTING AROUND

The airport sits in the north-central part of the island on a raised plateau punctuated on its south end by N'Ga Peak (865 ft.). The plateau gives way to a flat shelf along the shore, where most of the people live and the gîtes are located. Most visitors stay in the area around **Kuto,** a rocky peninsula joined to the mainland by a narrow, casuarina-studded isthmus separating two little bays with two of the world's most incredibly beautiful beaches, **Kuto Beach** and **Kanuméra Beach.**

Bus service from the airport to Kuto will cost 1,200 CFP ($12) per person round-trip. **Jean-Marie Vakie's minibus** (tel. 46-12-16) can be reserved for transportation. He charges 1,300 CFP ($13) a head for a tour of the island, less for other excursions. **Rental cars** are available at Station Kodjeue and Gîte Naitaiwatch (see "Where to Stay," below). **Scooters** can be rented from Nauticlub (tel. 46-11-22), the scuba-diving operation at Kuto (see "Scuba Diving," below). Otherwise, there is no regular public transportation on the island.

There is no bank on the Isle of Pines, so take enough cash to meet your expected expenditures. Nor are there stores that sell alcoholic beverages, film, or batteries; if you need these items, bring them with you. The post office, infirmary (with doctor and dentist on hand), and most other government offices are at **Vao,** on the island's southeast corner. The gendarmerie is on the Kuto peninsula.

Topless or nude sunbathing is not acceptable on the Isle of Pines. English is rarely spoken, so a knowledge of French will be necessary to fully enjoy anything other than sightseeing.

WHAT TO SEE & DO

A Walking Tour of Kuto

The highlight of the island is the area around Kuto and Kanumêra bays and their two great beaches. To see it on foot, start at the southeastern end of Kanuméa Beach near Gîte Naitaiwatch and walk along the beach until you come to the **tree-topped islet** sitting in the bay and joined by sand to the beach. This little semi-island is the most photographed spot on the Isle of Pines. You can walk over to it, climb up its craggy sides, and follow a set of trails around its flat top.

Keep going westward on the beach until you come to the narrow peninsula separating the two bays. Follow the dirt road to the left toward Kuto peninsula. On Kuto Beach (your right) stand ruins not from convict days but more from more recent times: The rotting two-story structure with "kanaky" grafitti is what's left of **Le Relais de Kanuméra,** a hotel built in 1957 by Henri Martinet, a French pharmacist who made the first Nouméa-to-Paris flight in 1938. The hotel operated until 1979, when Martinet tried to sell it to Club Med. The local Melanesians (or *kunies*) are strongly pro-independence, and when they objected, the hotel closed.

The island's 1,500 or so inhabitants, all but a few of them Melanesian, are still very much pro-independence, and they still will not allow a European-owned hotel to be built there (Club Med must water at the mouth at the thought of these two grand beaches side by side). The kunies' Melanesian language, which contains many English words, still has not been reduced to writing.

Take the left fork in the dirt road past the relais ruins and pass by a long **stone wall.** The French put their penal colony administrative offices on Kuto and built this fortified wall to separate themselves from the prisoners, who lived along the island's western side. The French also demanded that all kunies leave the island, but when Queen Hortense, wife of the high chief, objected, they divided it in two: Melanesians to the east, prisoners to the west. The Paris Commune prisoners, including 12 women, were allowed to live freely. They built entire villages complete with theaters and restaurants, but when freedom came in 1880, every one of them still alive went home to France. Nothing remains of their Isle of Pines endeavors. After they left, the French used the island as a regular prison until 1912. The entire island was then returned to its Melanesian owners, who had little contact with the outside world until U.S. troops arrived in 1942 to build the airstrip and a radio listening post atop N'ga Peak.

Keep going to a path to the left, which leads to the **Nauticlub** scuba-diving base (see below) and **Créations Ile des Pins** (tel. 46-12-68), where New Zealander Hilary "Cleo" Roots sells her hand-painted clothing. Her book of photographs and text, *Ile des Pins: Where Nature Dreams,* makes a nice if somewhat expensive souvenir at 4,500 CFP ($45) a copy.

Backtrack and follow the path past the beige colonial house with tin-roofed veranda. Now the island's **gendarmerie,** this was the home of the penal colony's doctor. Keep going along the path to the paved road, turn left, and follow it to the red-roofed colonial house on the right. That was the **governor's home.** The road continues to the new wharf, where a fortnightly boat arrives to take away the island's major products, sandalwood and snails (the entire place literally crawls with snails, which will end up under garlic butter in Nouméa's French restaurants).

Turn around and backtrack until you emerge from the forest at the old prison dock. The adjacent **stone ruin** that looks like a prison cell actually was a storehouse; it now houses a small historical display.

Now follow the paved road back past the relais ruins and northward along **Kuto Beach.** During World War II, this flat area was home to the several hundred U.S. troops, some of them African-Americans, who built the airstrip. The kunie women did their laundry; in return, the Americans returned the laundry bags stuffed with such items as sugar and chocolate.

You can spend the rest of your day enjoying this magnificent, unspoiled setting. Stop at the beachside **Snack Kou-Bugny** for some refreshment (this little snack bar primarily caters lunch for the day-trippers who come over from Nouméa).

Scuba Diving

Nauticlub, B.P. 18, Vao, Ile des Pins (tel. 46-11-22), based on the Kuto peninsula, takes scuba divers to exciting dive spots in the Gadji Pass on the north end of the island or into the freshwater Paradise Cave inland. A minimum of four divers is required for an outing, so book early. Prices are 6,000 CFP ($60) for one dive, 8,000 CFP ($80) for two. PADI open-water courses cost 39,000 CFP ($390).

WHERE TO STAY & DINE

Accommodations are available in gîtes. As a general rule, these small establishments have a few Melanesian-style bungalows, usually constructed of thatch, and a dining room and bar in a central building. Most are on the basic side of comfortable; you'll have to share a shower and toilet and do without mosquito netting (take your repellent). Other than Snack Kou-Bugny on Kuto Beach (see "A Walking Tour," above), which is open only to feed day-trippers their lunch, you will have to dine at one of the gîtes. Be sure to reserve a meal well in advance.

To reserve a room, call Air Calédonie Gîtes (tel. 28-65-64) in Nouméa. Air Calédonie accepts American Express, Diners Club, MasterCard, and VISA credit cards; the gîtes do not.

STATION KODJEUE, Isle of Pines. Tel. 46-11-42. 9 bungalows (all with bath), 6 rms (none with bath). **Location:** West coast on Baie de Ouameo.

$ Rates: 3,700 CFP ($37) single room; 3,800 CFP ($38) double room; 5,300 CFP ($53) single or double bungalow. No credit cards.

Owned by a former plumber from Paris, this has the most comfortable and modern accommodation on the island. Of the nine bungalows, six have private baths and kitchenettes; the other three have private baths but no cooking facilities. A dining room with good French food, bar, and grocery shop are on the premises.

GITE KUBERKA, Baie de Kuto, Isle of Pines. Tel. 46-11-18. 5 bungalows (all with bath). **Location:** Across the road from Kuto Beach.

$ Rates: 3,000 CFP ($30) single old bungalow, 3,500 CFP ($35) double old bungalow; 4,000 CFP ($40) single new bungalow, 4,500 CFP ($45) double new bungalow. No credit cards.

Located in a casuarina grove just off Kuto Beach, this establishment is the most popular with Nouméans making their weekend escapes. Three modern bungalows have kitchens; three older houses are smaller and do not have cooking facilities. The dining room serves meals.

GITE NATAIWATCH, Baie de Kunaméra, Isle of Pines. Tel. 46-11-31. 8 bungalows (4 with bath). **Location:** Southeastern end of Kunaméra Beach.

$ Rates: 4,000 CFP ($40) single; 4,600 CFP ($46) double; 750 CFP ($7.50) one person camping, 1,050 CFP ($10.50) two persons camping. No credit cards.

This has four older bungalows with kitchenettes (but shared bathrooms), four new bungalows with their own showers and toilets, and a restaurant and a bar, both of which are closed on Sunday. Don't expect luxury here, but do expect reasonable cleanliness.

LIFOU

Lifou, geographic and administrative center of the Loyalty Islands, lies 190km (114 miles) east of Grande Terre. An uplifted coral atoll, the center of the island is a flat plateau ringed at its edges by the original barrier reef, now rising more than 100 feet above the surrounding plain. The outside of the old barrier reef drops about 300 feet to a narrow seaside shelf indented by some of the South Pacific's most beautiful beaches. The limestone island is dotted with caves and sinkholes which capture its drinking water (it has no streams). With some 420 square miles of land, Lifou is larger than Tahiti.

All but about 100 of Lifou's 15,000 or so residents are Melanesians, who speak Dehu (which also is the native name for Lifou), the most widely spoken of New Caledonia's indigenous languages. The London Missionary Society set up shop at Mou on the southeast coast in 1842; along with sandalwood traders, they contributed such words as cup, fork, spoon, money, coffee, and tea to Dehu.

The missionaries found the island divided into three hereditary chiefdoms (it still is). They converted the chief of Losi, the southern district at Mu. Catholic priests arrived in 1858 and went to work on the chief of Wé, the northern division at Hnathalo. The northern chief converted, and immediately made war against the Protestants. The French government put a stop to the conflict in 1864. Today you will see Protestant and Catholic churches sitting side by side at **Qanono,** just north of **Wé,** the French administrative center midway along the east coast.

Lifou is a native preserve, and Melanesian custom remains fairly strong (but not anything like in Vanuatu and Solomon Islands). You will still see multitudes of conical-roofed thatch buildings used primarily for sleeping. The flèches on top are carved with the symbol of the local chief.

GETTING THERE

Air Calédonie has very early morning and late-afternoon flights each day from Magenta Airport to Lifou, making possible a day-trip. **La Maison de Lifou** in Nouméa (see "Information, Entry Requirements & Money," above) gives out information about the island and will arrange day-trips or accommodation. So will Air Calédonie Gîtes (tel. 28-65-64).

GETTING AROUND

The airport is at **Wanaham** on the north central plateau, about 20 minutes by bus to Wé on the east coast. The trip to the village or nearby gîtes costs 800 CFP ($8) one way.

Minibuses fan out from Wé to most points on the island during daylight. The maximum fare is 200 CFP ($2).

Car rentals are available at **Lifou-Plaisance** (tel. 45-14-44), **Gîte Luécilla** (tel.

45-12-43), and **Garage Soetikno** (tel. 45-11-42), all near Wé. Rates are about 5,000 CFP ($50) a day plus 25 CFP (25¢) a kilometer. (See "Where to Stay & Dine," below.) It's possible to hitchhike on Lifou.

The post office, gendarmerie, infirmary, pharmacy, other government offices, and a grocery store all are at Wé. The **Municipal Tourism Office** (tel. 45-14-25) in the Town Hall at Wé gives out some information about the island. Westpac Bank has an office at Wé, the only bank in the Loyalty Islands.

WHAT TO SEE & DO

There isn't much to do on Lifou except sightsee, swim, snorkel, scuba dive (at Lifou-Plaisance), and meet the local kanaks and talk pro-independence politics (you must know French, because few people on Lifou speak English). Let's see some sights.

The central village of Wé sits on picturesque Baie de Châteaubriand, and it's an easy stroll north along the beach to the nearby villages of Qanono and Luécilla. The former has its two churches; the latter has one of its own. From Wé, roads fan out north, west, and south.

To the north, Jokin is known for its cliff-top dwellings overlooking the sea. Hnathalo still is home to the ruling chief of the north; you can look but not enter his chiefly compound. To the west, the high chief lives at Drueulu on Baie du Santal (Sandal Bay). There is a nice beach and sacred cave nearby.

To the south, the road runs just far enough away from the shore to obscure sea views. However, dirt tracks at Luengöni go off to one of the most beautiful beaches I have ever seen. I could take a picnic and drink there and spend eternity. The road goes on to Mu, where the ruins of the early mission church and a monument to the Protestant missionaries sit beside a picturesque little bay. The road ends just past Xodre, where you can walk out on a razor-sharp raised reef for a nice view over the sea to Maré, another Loyalty island, in the distance.

WHERE TO STAY & DINE

As on the Isle of Pines, both accommodation and dining are in gîtes. If you're not going to dine at your own, reserve early elsewhere.

LIFOU-PLAISANCE, B.P. 63, Lifou. Tel. 45-14-44. Fax 45-13-33. 12 rms (all with bath). **Location:** Jozip, 10km (6 miles) south of Wé.
$ Rates: 5,000 CFP ($50) single; 6,000 CFP ($60) double. AE, V.

This little resort sits on a flat shelf backed by limestone grottoes; across the road a path leads down to three small beaches separated by overhangs. Clapboard bungalows hold three or four rooms each. The rooms are basically but adequately furnished, with ceiling fans and push-out, unscreened windows in the corner. Activities include scuba diving, snorkeling, tennis, and a workout in a fitness center. There is a small swimming pool beside a building with dining room and bar.

GITE LUECILLA, B.P. 95, Lifou. Tel. 45-12-43. 4 bungalows, 4 rms (all with bath). **Location:** Near beach at Luécilla village north of Wé.
$ Rates: 3,500 CFP ($35) single or double rooms; 4,500 CFP ($45) single or double bungalow; 750 CFP ($7.50) per person camping. No credit cards.

This establishment is in a coconut grove a short stroll from the lovely beach at Baie de Châteaubriand. Accommodation is in simply furnished, thatch-roofed bungalows, or in rooms in a motellike block. The bungalows have kitchenettes. A dining room was being replaced with a new restaurant when I was there.

HOTEL LES COCOTIERS, B.P. 75, Lifou. Tel. 45-11-38. 10 bungalows (all with bath). **Location:** Hnassee village, next to Wé; ½ mile to beach.
$ Rates: 4,000 CFP ($40) per bungalow. No credit cards.

Two types of basic bungalows here: Those of European construction have exposed tin roofs. Others have Lifou-style conical thatch roofs but concrete floors and small windows. They are in a yardlike setting next to a large oval building, in which there's a dining room.

CHAPTER 17

SOLOMON ISLANDS

If Guadalcanal, largest of the Solomon Islands, was 100 miles from Washington, DC, instead of in the far South Pacific, it probably would rank with Gettysburg as one of America's most important national shrines, for it was on Guadalcanal that the U.S. Marines took on the reputedly invincible Japanese Imperial Army in 1942.

The bloody battle raged for 6 months, seesawing back and forth on the island and in waters like "Iron Bottom Sound" and "the Slot" offshore. When the smoke finally cleared from the jungles and grassy plains, more than 5,000 American and 13,000 Japanese soldiers—and an uncounted number of Solomon Islanders—had been killed or wounded. Thousands more had been lost in the hundreds of planes shot down and in the nearly 60 ships dispatched to watery graves during seven major naval engagements. But the Japanese advance on Samoa, Fiji, and New Caledonia was stopped in its tracks, and the door to Tokyo was pried open.

Today the rusting or coral-encrusted wreckage of that battle is a highlight of any visit to the lovely Solomon Islands, now an independent, developing country with a busy little capital, Honiara, that didn't even exist until the great battle was won.

The Solomons still may be one of the least "touristy" areas in the South Pacific, but smiling faces wait there to show you why their home is called "The Happy Isles."

1. GETTING TO KNOW THE SOLOMONS

Locals call their country Solomon Islands, without a "the" in front. Their 900-plus islands fill the 600-mile gap between Vanuatu and Papua New Guinea. Six big islands dominate the group: **Guadalcanal, Malaita, Makira, New Georgia, Choiseul,** and **San Cristobal.** New Georgia and its neighbors lie in the **Western Province,** a region known for the splendor of **Marovo Lagoon** and **Roviana Lagoon,** two of the world's most picturesque bodies of water. **Gizo,** sleepy little capital of the Western Province, is a throwback to the South Seas of tin warehouses and trading boats.

Guadalcanal, the economic and administrative center, is the most visited island. Its tall and wild mountains—some soaring to more than 8,000 feet high—fall into

WHAT'S SPECIAL ABOUT SOLOMON ISLANDS

Monuments

- ☐ Red Beach, Bloody Ridge, Iron Bottom Sound, the Slot: places living in memory of the Battle of Guadalcanal.

Museums

- ☐ Vilu Village War Museum: It has no buildings, just well-preserved World War II junk.
- ☐ Solomon Islands National Museum: has feather money, pigs' tusks, and a club used to kill a white man.

Activities

- ☐ Scuba diving: Hundreds of wrecked planes and ships lie in crystal-clear lagoons.

Shopping

- ☐ *Nguzunguzus* and bukaware: Solomon Islanders are great carvers and basket weavers.

the sea on the south coast but give way gradually in the north to the country's only sizable flat area, the **Guadalcanal Plain.** Some 15 miles wide at places, much of the plain is covered with coconut-palm plantations and jungle, but part of it supports not trees but sharp-edged *kunai* grass. **Henderson Field,** the airstrip built on the plain by the U.S. Marines after the invasion in 1942, now serves as Honiara's international airport.

Honiara, the national capital, originally was an ammunition dump built by the Americans after the Japanese retreated in 1943. The capital was moved there after the war, since the old seat of government on **Tulagi** in the **Florida Group** had been blown to bits. Now a busy commercial and governmental center of some 23,000 residents, the town sits on a narrow shelf of land between **Point Cruz,** a small peninsula that forms the harbor, and a series of ridges that almost reach the sea. Today Honiara has many buildings of glass and concrete, but you'll pass a number of rusty Quonset huts left over from the war and still very much in use 50 years later. Honiara takes its name from *naho-ni-ara,* which in one of the local languages means "facing the east and southeast wind."

Between the airport and Honiara, the road suddenly emerges at the edge of **Iron Bottom Sound.** During the battle this usually quiet body of water was often lit up with fireworks as American and Japanese warships battled it out at night, sometimes at point-blank range. The blue-green islands straight across the Sound are the Florida Group; the eroding volcanic cone to the west is infamous **Savo Island.**

HISTORY

DATELINE

- **3000 B.C.** Melanesians settle in Solomon Islands.
- **1568** Alvaro de Mendaña discovers the islands, gives them Spanish names.
- **1595** Mendaña returns, tries un-

(continues)

In 1567 Alvaro de Mendaña set out from Peru to search for allegedly gold-rich islands some "600 leagues" west of South America. In February 1568 he discovered and named Santa Isabel, and set out to explore the other islands that lay nearby. The biggest he named for a town in Spain—Guadalcanal—and there planted a cross on a small peninsula and claimed the entire group for Spain. The peninsula he called Point Cruz. Many of the Spanish names he assigned are still in use today.

Mendaña returned 27 years later and attempted unsuccessfully to set up a colony in the Santa Cruz Islands. After he died of disease, the crew pulled up stakes and went to the Philippines. Mendaña's navigator on that last voyage, Pedro Ferdández de Quirós, tried unsuccessfully to colonize Santo in Vanuatu in 1606.

No other European visited the Solomons until HMS *Swallow* stumbled across Santa Cruz and Malaita in 1767. The *Swallow* had left England a year earlier, in company with Capt. Samuel Wallis in HMS *Dolphin*. The two ships became separated in a fog at Cape Horn. *Swallow* sailed on to find—but misplot—Pitcairn Island, future hideout of the *Bounty* mutineers, then continued west to rediscover the Solomons. Meanwhile, Wallis located more romantic prey: Tahiti.

A year later another Tahiti veteran, the French explorer Louis Antoine de Bougainville, happened across the northernmost islands. He gave his name to Bougainville, an island just over the present border with Papua New Guinea.

European whalers and traders appeared in the early 19th century. Missionaries, copra planters, and the infamous "blackbirder" slave traders soon followed. Some unscrupulous behavior created resentment, and an antiwhite backlash cost the lives of many honest traders and missionaries—some of them devoured in cannibalistic rituals. Some islanders would kill any white man who came ashore, regardless of who he was. "The Terrible Solomons" succeeded the recently colonized Fiji as the most notoriously dangerous islands in the region.

Although they were busy elsewhere in the South Pacific between 1842 and 1890, neither France nor Great Britain made a move in the Solomons until Germany colonized New Guinea. Britain followed that move in 1893 by declaring a protectorate over the eastern Solomons. Other islands were added in 1897 and 1898, and in 1899 Germany ceded the Shortland Islands, Choiseul, Santa Isabel, and Ontong Java in exchange for a free hand in Western Samoa.

Headquarters of the British Solomon Islands Protectorate (BSIP) was on Tulagi, a small, centrally located island between Guadalcanal and Malaita. Law and order soon followed, as did some of the world's largest copra plantations. The British governed loosely, building a hospital and creating a police force but not much else. The missions took care of education, and the islanders were pretty much left alone—until the Japanese arrived in 1942.

The Japanese war plan was to move into the Solomons and construct airfields from which to bomb the new American forward base on Santo in the New Hebrides. They seized Tulagi without opposition in April 1942. When U.S. reconnaissance planes spotted construction of a new airfield on the Guadalcanal Plain in July, the U.S. sped up a plan called Operation Watchtower.

In the wee hours of August 7, 1942, a huge American fleet steamed quietly around Cape Esperance on the western end of Guadalcanal, and at dawn 16,000 U.S. Marines waded ashore at Red Beach, near the Tenaru River, and quickly captured the airfield. The rest of the contingent struck at Tulagi, where the Japanese were dug in, but even there, the island was secured within days.

Everything went smoothly at Guadalcanal until after midnight on August 8, when a Japanese fleet slipped unnoticed by Savo. The ensuing Battle of Savo Island was

DATELINE

successfully to establish Spanish colony, dies on Santa Cruz.

- **1767** Capt. Philip Carteret in HMS *Swallow* rediscovers Santa Cruz and Malaita.
- **1768** Bougainville briefly explores the northern Solomons, names Bougainville for himself.
- **1840s** Whalers, sandalwood traders, planters, missionaries, and slavers arrive; some are killed by islanders, who give "The Terrible Solomons" a bad reputation.
- **1871** Bishop Patteson and two missionaries murdered on Nukapu; British man-of-war shells the village in reprisal.
- **1893** Britain declares a protectorate over central Solomons, establishes headquarters at Tulagi but essentially governs from Fiji.
- **1899** Germany cedes western Solomons to Britain.
- **1908** Author Jack London cruises the islands, catches pellagra, and withdraws by steamship to Australia; his *Snark* becomes a blackbirding boat.
- **1942** Japanese troops seize Tulagi, begin airstrip on

(continues)

one of the worst defeats ever suffered by the U.S. Navy. The body of water between Guadalcanal and Tulagi promptly earned the name Iron Bottom Sound.

The U.S. transport ships withdrew, leaving the marines on Guadalcanal with less than half their equipment and supplies. They quickly dug in, established a defense perimeter from the Tenaru River in the east to Kukum village in the west, and completed the airstrip begun by the Japanese. The marines named the new field in honor of Maj. Loften R. Henderson, one of their compatriots who was killed leading a squadron of fighter aircraft in the Battle of Midway.

For the next 2 months, during which six more major naval battles were fought in the waters nearby, the marines held off one Japanese attack after another. "Edson's Raiders" under the legendary Col. Merritt A. Edson fought off the Japanese on a grassy ridge for 2 days and nights. Edson lost seven men; the Japanese, between 600 and 700.

American navy and air forces ruled the sea and sky during the day; the Japanese, by night. Japanese bombers named "Louie the Louse" and "Washing Machine Charlie" kept the marines awake at night. "Pistol Pete" and other artillery pieces pounded away from the jungle, adding to the misery of malaria, heat, and low rations. While the harassment was going on, the Japanese sent reinforcement and resupply ships down the Slot nightly on "the Tokyo Express." Iron Bottom Sound earned another name: "Sleepless Lagoon."

In October 1941, Pres. Franklin D. Roosevelt personally ordered Guadalcanal reinforced, and help soon arrived. From then on the Allies went on the offensive instead of the defensive.

Yet the Tokyo Express continued to get through. Unbeknownst to the Americans, however, it was conducting a piecemeal evacuation. By February 5, 1943, all but a few Japanese stragglers had slipped away into the night. The great battle that had begun so quietly 6 months before drew to a close the same way.

The war in the western Solomons raged on until the war's end. In April 1943, the U.S. Army Air Corps ambushed and killed Adm. Isoroku Yamamoto, the mastermind behind the Pearl Harbor attack and then supreme commander of Japanese forces in the southwestern Pacific, as he was flying to Bougainville. On the night of August 1, a Japanese destroyer ran down and cut in two a boat that was later to become famous: PT-109. Eight of the surviving crewmen got into a raft, and with the skipper—Lt. John F. Kennedy—swimming alongside carrying a shipmate, managed to reach little Olosana Island 5 hours later. Two Solomon Islanders, working as scouts for an Australian coastwatcher, found the survivors and paddled them to safety in camouflaged canoes.

Hundreds of Solomon Islanders assisted the Americans during the war. Many of them were captured, tortured, and executed by the Japanese. They and the coastwatchers—the hundreds of traders, missionaries, and others who manned lookouts behind Japanese lines and radioed intelligence information to the Allies—were all local heroes of the war. A plaque on a monument just outside the terminal

DATELINE

Guadalcanal; U.S. Marines invade, bloody Battle of Guadalcanal begins.

- **1943** Battle of Guadalcanal ends in Allied victory; U.S. planes shoot down Japanese Admiral Yamamoto; Lt. John F. Kennedy survives PT-109 sinking near Gizo.
- **1946** Influenced by U.S. troops and matériel, "Marching Rule" movement begins on Malaita, opposes British protectorate.
- **1947–49** British arrest 2,000 Marching Rule members, but opposition continues.
- **1950** British compromise, set up appointed local government councils on Malaita.
- **1965** Government councils spread to other islands, shift to elected status.
- **1974** New constitution sets up protectoratewide legislative assembly of 24 members.
- **1978** Solomon Islands become 37th independent member of British Commonwealth of Nations.
- **1984** Relations with U.S. cool when Solomon Islands naval vessel seizes American purse seiner *Jeanette Diane*, charges it with

(continues)

DATELINE

poaching in Solomon waters.

- **1985** Strong U.S.-Solomon relations restored; Solomon Islands reject Soviet request for fishing rights.
- **1991** U.S. Congress approves $5 million to build new parliament house as memorial to Battle of Guadalcanal.
- **1992** Solomon Islands celebrate 50th anniversary of U.S. Marine invasion of Guadalcanal.

at Henderson Field reads: "We, the Marines, salute the Coastwatchers, our Solomon Island scouts, guides, and stretcher bearers. Their loyalty, dedication, and bravery was equal to all, surpassed by none. We remember you."

Even today Americans are welcomed warmly to the Solomon Islands, and many American veterans of the conflict return each year to the bloody scene of their youth.

After the fighting had ended, Guadalcanal and other outposts were turned into huge supply depots and support bases. Many Solomon Islanders for the first time saw material goods—and they saw them on a vast scale. As had happened elsewhere in Melanesia, semireligious "cargo cults" developed.

Solomon Islanders also saw American soldiers, including African Americans, living in relatively equal status to their officers; at least it seemed equal compared with the vast social, economic, and political disparity between themselves and the British. One of the cults on Malaita—the so-called Marching Rule—became a political as well as a religious movement and openly opposed the British after the war. Despite the jailing of some 2,000 Solomon Islanders between 1946 and 1949, opposition continued. The British compromised in 1950 and established local governments. These expanded until 1974, when an elected Legislative Assembly was created in Honiara and a constitution was adopted. Full internal self-government was granted in 1976, followed by independence on July 7, 1978.

GOVERNMENT, POLITICS & ECONOMY

Solomon Islands government has a Westminster-style Parliament of 39 members, which chooses a prime minister and a governor-general to serve as the queen's representative. Below Parliament are seven provincial governments, including one for Guadalcanal and one for the town of Honiara.

Politics tends to focus on personalities more than on ideology and political parties. Provincial identification is strong, especially in the resource-rich Western Province, which often sees itself threatened by more populous Guadalcanal. People in the west are closely akin to those on beleaguered Bougainville, just across the border in Papua New Guinea, and many of them have actively supported the secessionist movement there. Some Westerners would like to see their province joined with Bougainville and its rich copper mine to form an independent country of their own.

Agriculture and fishing constitute more than 60% of Solomon Islands' gross national product and almost all of their exports. Major exports are copra, palm oil, timber, cocoa, and fish (the latter caught offshore and either canned or frozen at a huge new plant and supporting town at Noro on New Georgia). Considerable exploration for minerals has taken place, but as yet no major exploitation has occurred. Tourism has not been a significant part of the economy, and government support for the development of hotels and resorts has been lukewarm.

GEOGRAPHY

The larger islands, all long and narrow, are arranged in two lines with the New Georgia Sound (the Slot of World War II fame) in between. Except for raised atolls off to the east and south, the islands are made up of rugged, jungle-clad mountains sliced by rivers that flow swiftly down to the sea, passing through coastal areas with some of the largest coconut-palm plantations in the world. In all, the country has about 16,500 square miles of dry land, making it one of the larger South Pacific island countries.

Most of the high islands are covered by dense rain forests inland and by coconut palms or thick mangrove swamps along the shore.

HONIARA

ACCOMMODATIONS:
Hibiscus Hotel 1
Honiara Hotel 3
Solomon Kitano Mendana Hotel 2
ATTRACTIONS:
Botanical Gardens 1
Chinatown 7
Guadalcanal Club 2
High Court 3
Market 6
NPF Plaza 5
Tourist Authority/Museum 4
N
0
300 m
330 y
Iron Bottom Sound
← To Cape Esperance
Point Cruz
La Pérouse Restaurant
Mbokona Bay
Tandai Highway
Mendana
Post Office
Town Ground
Coronation Gardens
Avenue
Hibiscus Avenue
Lenggakiki Ridge
Mud Alley
Ashley Street
Vaaya Ridge
Mendana Avenue
Kua Bay
To Henderson Field →
Central Hospital
Mandarin Restaurant
Library
Watts Dr.
Matiniko River
Highway
Kukum
Cape Esperance
Tambea
Vilu Village War Museum
Iron Bottom Sound
Lungga Point
Henderson Field
Red Beach
Lambi Bay
Honiara
Mt. Austen
CDC3
Vulelua Island
Aola
Marau Sound

IMPRESSIONS

I am proud—vengefully proud, if you will—of what my generation accomplished at Guadalcanal.

—JAMES A. MICHENER, 1951

Indigenous land animals consist of opossums, bats, rats, and more than 70 species of reptiles—crocodiles, snakes, turtles, lizards, skinks, frogs, and toads. Some snakes are poisonous, but they are not numerous and generally will move away from humans. Crocodiles live along the banks of some rivers and are hunted for their skins, but it's highly unlikely that you'll see one. More than 140 species of birds include many colorful parrots and the **megapode,** a flightless creature about the size of a hen which buries its relatively enormous, billiard ball–size eggs in the warm sands of thermal areas. Offshore many colorful species of coral and fish abound, but one must be wary of sharks, stone fish, and poisonous shells. Always seek advice before swimming in Solomon Islands waters, and always wear shoes when walking on the reef.

PEOPLE

The total number of friendly Solomon Islanders is approximately 300,000, of which 93% are Melanesians and 4% Polynesians. All but a few of the others are either Micronesians, Chinese, or Europeans (the latter referring to Caucasians, regardless of origin). The population growth rate exceeds 3% a year, which means that a majority of Solomon Islanders are under the age of 18.

Polynesians inhabit the smaller atolls lying to the east and south of the big islands. Thousands of Micronesians from the Gilbert Islands (now the independent country of Kiritabi) were resettled near Honiara and on Gizo in the 1950s. Chinese merchant families are found in all the main towns and occupy **Chinatown,** an area of Honiara on the banks of the **Mataniko River.**

Some 90% of the Melanesians still live the traditional—or "custom"—way of life in small villages of thatch huts surrounded by little gardens of taro, yams, and other subsistence crops. Social structure, traditions, and even languages vary from island to island and often from village to village. In the old days, members of each tribe kept to themselves except for an occasional raid on their neighbors when, on some islands, heads would be hunted and perhaps an earth oven stoked and a meal made of the victims. Ancestor worship was practiced, and next to land, pigs and wives were the most valuable possessions.

Out in the countryside of Guadalcanal and on the other islands, villagers still wear traditional garb—grass skirts and no tops for women, loincloths or sarongs for men. Christianity has made a significant impact on the old ways, however, as has the immigration of young people to the towns. The population of Honiara consists of people from throughout the islands, and some neighborhoods are dominated by peoples originally from the same island.

Just as culture and tradition vary among the Melanesians, so does their physical appearance. With the exception of those on Malaita, people in the eastern islands tend to have lighter skin, while those in the western islands are very dark. Although most Solomon Islanders have black hair, many have naturally blond or ginger-colored hair, which contrasts sharply with their dark complexions.

IMPRESSIONS

[D]uring the war I flew The Slot, and so help me it was beautiful, passionately wonderful with craggy islands, spangled lagoons and towering clouds. Now that war was gone, it is even more so.

—JAMES A. MICHENER, 1951

IMPRESSIONS

"We have everything," the people say. They don't want roads or cars or an airstrip. They have no use for telephones. They don't want electricity; they don't want television, though they have a yen for videos.
—PAUL THEROUX, 1991

LANGUAGE

English is the official language, but a form of Pidgin English is more likely to be used by members of one tribe to communicate with those of another who speak a different native language. Like the versions spoken in Vanuatu and Papua New Guinea, Solomon Islands pidgin sprang from the simplified English used by the 19th-century sandalwood and bêche-de-mer traders to communicate with the native peoples. The version used in Solomon Islands more closely resembles English than do the pidgins of Vanuatu and Papua New Guinea. The vocabulary is basically from English, while the grammar and sentence structure are Melanesian.

The most readily noticeable difference between pidgin and English is the use of prepositions. In pidgin, *bilong* denotes possession, as in *pikinni bilong mi* ("child belongs to me" or "my child"). *Long* is used for all other prepositions. Accordingly, to the untrained ear most pidgin sentences seem filled with *bilong* and *long*.

2. INFORMATION, ENTRY REQUIREMENTS & MONEY

INFORMATION & ENTRY REQUIREMENTS

The helpful staff at the **Solomon Islands Tourist Authority,** P.O. Box 321, Honiara (tel. 22442, fax 23986), distribute information about the country, including brochures and a list of hotels and current room rates. The authority's office and information desk are in an octagonal building beside the Solomon Kitano Mendana Hotel.

The authority publishes a very fine source book, *Solomon Islands,* by Ann Stevenson. It's available from the authority or from Lahood Publishers, Ltd., P.O. Box 9733, New Market, Auckland, New Zealand (tel. 09/547496).

Visitor **visas** are issued upon arrival at Honiara to British subjects or citizens of the United States, Commonwealth nations, and some European countries who possess valid passports and onward or return air tickets. Your initial visa is likely to expire within 7 days or on the departure date of your international flight, as indicated on your return ticket, whichever is earlier. Applications for advance visas may be made at any British embassy, consulate, or high commission. **Vaccinations** are not required unless a person has been in a yellow fever area within 14 days of arrival.

Customs allowances are 200 cigarettes, two bottles of alcoholic beverages, and personal belongings. Your baggage stands a very good chance of being opened and inspected upon arrival. Pornography, firearms, and illegal narcotics and drugs are

IMPRESSIONS

Heads are a medium of exchange, and white heads are extremely valuable. . . . A man needs only to be careful—and lucky—to live a long time in the Solomons . . .
—JACK LONDON, 1911

against the law and punishable by fine or imprisonment. All agricultural products must be inspected and, if necessary, fumigated, and your pets will be quarantined.

MONEY

Local **currency** is the Solomon Islands dollar—abbreviated SBD by the banks but denoted in this chapter by **SI$.** It is linked to a basket of currencies and not to any one in particular. At the time of writing, SI$1 was worth about U.S. 40¢, the exchange rate used to calculate the U.S. dollar prices in this chapter. The rate is not quoted in overseas newspapers, but your bank or travel agent may be able to give you the present rate. Solomon Islands currency is worthless outside the country except to collectors or as souvenirs. Your credit-card bills will come back in Australian dollars, then converted to your local currency.

In most cases, **bargaining** is not an accepted practice in the Solomons. In dealing with an individual handcraft dealer, however, you can ask if he or she has a "second price." Don't push the point if one isn't offered.

WHAT THINGS COST IN SOLOMON ISLANDS	U.S. $
Taxi from airport to Honiara	5.00
Bus from airport to Honiara	2.50
Double room at Solomon Kitano Mendana Hotel (expensive)	72.00
Double room at Honiara Hotel (moderate wing)	40.00
Double room at Honiara Hotel (budget wing)	28.00
Lunch for one at Hibiscus Hotel (moderate)	9.60
Lunch for one at Family Favourites (budget)	4.00
Dinner for one, without wine, at La Pérouse (expensive)	24.50
Dinner for one, without wine, at Mandarin Restaurant (moderate)	13.00
Dinner for one at Kingsley's Snack Bar (budget)	2.60
Beer	1.50
Coca-Cola	.80
Cup of coffee	.60
Roll of ASA 100 Kodacolor film, 36 exposures	8.50
Movie ticket	.80

3. WHEN TO GO — CLIMATE, HOLIDAYS & EVENTS

The southeast trade winds blow strongly from May to November, bringing relatively dry weather and making the days seem cooler than the 86°F average daily high. Even then, however, the near-equatorial sun can be brutal at midday. The islands experience a mild monsoon season from December through April, when the wind backs around to the northwest; although the breeze moderates the temperature somewhat, it also brings humidity and rainfall, often in downpours. The amount of rain varies depending on which side of the islands you are on; Honiara, for example, gets considerably less rain than the old capital at Tulagi. Things usually cool down in the evenings, but the temperature rarely drops below 72°F at sea level. Unless you're going into the high country, therefore, sweaters and jackets seldom are needed.

Holidays are New Year's Day, Easter weekend (Friday, Saturday, Sunday, and Monday), the Friday closest to June 14 (in honor of Queen Elizabeth's birthday), July 7 (Solomon Islands Independence Day), Christmas Day, and December 26 (Boxing

THE SOLOMON & U.S. DOLLARS

At this writing, SI$1 = approximately 40¢, the rate of exchange used to calculate the U.S. dollar prices given in this chapter. This rate has remained fairly stable during the past few years but may change by the time you visit. Accordingly, use the following table only as a guide.

$ SI	$ U.S.	$ SI	$ U.S.
.25	.10	15.00	6.00
.50	.20	20.00	8.00
.75	.30	25.00	10.00
1.00	.40	30.00	12.00
2.00	.80	35.00	14.00
3.00	1.20	40.00	16.00
4.00	1.60	45.00	18.00
5.00	2.00	50.00	20.00
6.00	2.40	75.00	30.00
7.00	2.80	100.00	40.00
8.00	3.20	125.00	50.00
9.00	3.60	150.00	60.00
10.00	4.00	200.00	80.00

Day). In addition, August 1 is a provincial holiday on Guadalcanal; August 15, on Malaita.

4. GETTING THERE & GETTING AROUND

GETTING THERE

The most direct routing from North America is to Fiji on a major international carrier, then on to Honiara via **Solomon Airlines** or **Air Pacific.** You can also fly to Cairns, Australia, on **Qantas Airways,** then to Honiara via Solomon Airlines. The national carrier, Solomon Airlines also connects Honiara to Port Vila, Auckland, Brisbane, and Port Moresby in Papua New Guinea. **Air Niugini** flies between Honiara and Port Moresby. See "Getting There" in Chapter 2 for more information.

All visitors arrive at **Honiara International Airport** (also still known as Henderson Field) 11km (7 miles) east of town. The small terminal building has a snack bar, a pay phone, and a currency-exchange counter. The Budget and Avis rental-car agents will meet your flight if you have reserved one of their automobiles; otherwise, take the **Red Bus** that will be waiting in front of the terminal. The one-way fare to the hotels in Honiara is SI$6 ($2.50). The bus will also pick you up at your hotel for the trip back to the airport; to reserve, call 21291. Taxi fare to town is SI$12 ($5).

An **airport departure tax** of SI$20 ($8) is levied of all passengers leaving the country. It's paid at the check-in counter in Solomon Islands currency.

Take a moment to look at three **monuments** in front of the terminal building. One is to members of the First Marine Division who were killed during the battle, one to the Marine Raiders who died, and one to the coastwatchers and Solomon Islanders who aided the U.S. forces. A rusting Japanese field gun sits by the side of the road.

GETTING AROUND

Perhaps more in than any other major South Pacific country, boats are still used for transportation among the islands and foot or canoe for transportation between villages. There are few roads, even on Guadalcanal, and those that do exist are likely to be in poor condition. Once you stray far from Honiara or the main towns or villages on the other islands, you'll have to use your wits to get around.

BY PLANE

Solomon Airlines (tel. 20031) flies Monday through Saturday between Honiara and Gizo, Munda on New Georgia Island, and Auki on Malaita, less frequently between Honiara and the other islands. Its main reservation office is on Mendana Avenue in the heart of Honiara's business district.

There are no reduced round-trip fares, and free stopovers aren't allowed; therefore, you'll have to pay a separate fare for each sector in order to island-hop. Following are one-way fares over some of its more heavily traveled routes: from Honiara to Auki, SI$69 ($27.50); to Seghe, SI$140 ($56); to Munda, SI$173 ($69); to Gizo, SI$200 ($80). Overseas visitors can save 20% if they book and pay for their domestic flights along with their international tickets.

The **baggage allowance** is 16kg (35 lb.) on domestic flights, 20kg (44 lb.) on international flights.

A plane based at Gizo connects the centers of the Western Province—Gizo, Munda, Balalai, Ringi Cove, and Seghe—to Honiara. This route is a "flightseeing" experience in itself, since the plane takes you at low altitudes right over the colorful reefs, hundreds of small islands, and ragged coastlines of the magnificent Marovo and Roviana lagoons and the Blanche Channel off New Georgia Island.

BY SHIP

Yumi Now, a ferry with cabins and airline-type seats in an air-conditioned lounge, usually leaves Honiara at 11am Sunday, stops at the Russell Islands and transits the Morovo Lagoon that night, then arrives at Gizo on Monday. It then leaves Gizo and spends Monday night at anchor in a channel off Noro on New Georgia. On Tuesday it makes stops along the New Georgia coast and goes back through the Marovo Lagoon before dark. That night it crosses open sea to the Russells, and arrives back at Honiara on Wednesday. Although the return trip requires 2 nights on board, it is much more scenic since it passes New Georgia and goes through the Roviana and Marovo lagoons during the daylight hours. One-way fares between Honiara and Gizo are SI$51 ($20.50) for economy class, SI$65 ($26) first class, and SI$90 ($36) for a cabin. Contact **Coral Seas Ltd.** (tel. 22811) on the east end of Hibiscus Avenue in Honiara.

Other ships are operated by: **Solomon Islands Navigation Services** (tel. 22404); **Markwarth Shipping Co.** (tel. 22444); **South New Georgia Corp.** (tel. 23337); the **Roman Catholic Church** (tel. 21943); the **Church of Melanesia** (tel. 22321); and the **South Seas Evangelical Church** (tel. 22800). Contact them for schedules and fares.

BY CAR

Rentals

Budget and Avis both have agencies on Guadalcanal, but rental cars are not available elsewhere. **Budget** (tel. 23953, or toll free 800/527-0700 in the U.S.) has only unlimited-kilometer rates. They start at SI$90 ($36) for tiny Suzuki sedans. Mid-size air-conditioned models cost about SI$120 ($48). Budget charges SI$30 ($12) a day for complete insurance coverage. The office is in Solomon Motors on Mendana Avenue, in the heart of town.

Avis (tel. 22821, or toll free 800/331-1212 in the U.S.) has comparable prices and two offices: One is across the highway from the airport and the other is in the Solomon Kitano Mendana Hotel in Honiara.

Gasoline is available at stations in Honiara. A liter cost SI$1.10 (45¢) when I was there recently, or about $1.70 for an American-size gallon.

Driving Rules

Your valid home driver's license will be honored. Solomon Islanders drive on the left-hand side of the road. There are no stringent drunk-driving laws in Solomon Islands, but don't press your luck. You need to be sober to watch out for the other drivers, who may or may not be intoxicated, and the usual assortment of pigs, dogs, chickens, children, and enormous potholes.

Roads

Guadalcanal has just one stoplight, but the only tricky traffic pattern is in the center of Honiara, where for 3 blocks Mendana Avenue becomes one-way to traffic heading east. Accordingly, westbound traffic coming into town from the airport is funneled over to Hibiscus Avenue, the street that runs parallel to Mendana Avenue. Be cautious, since the intersections aren't well marked and you will make the maneuvers from the left lane, not the right.

The highway from Honiara east is paved to CDC3 village well past the airport, and for about 25km (15 miles) on the west side of town. Otherwise, the roads can be very rough. Many small streams are forded rather than bridged, and they can flood during the rainy season. You may not see the fords until you are to them, so drive slowly and carefully at all times. Some bridges look like steel Erector sets and are very narrow, so wait your turn to cross.

BY TAXI

A number of rattletrap taxis patrol the streets of Honiara, but since none of them have meters, negotiate a fare before you leave for your destination. In general, you should pay about SI$2 (80¢) per kilometer or SI$20 ($8) per hour. From downtown Honiara to Chinatown should cost about SI$4 ($1.50). If your destination has a Melanesian name, you can avoid misunderstandings by writing it on a piece of paper for the driver. When traveling alone, feel free to sit in the front seat next to the driver—Solomon Islanders do.

BY BUS

Unmarked minibuses patrol the roads from 6am to 7:30pm Monday through Saturday from White River west of Honiara to Kukum east of town. The buses go through Honiara along Mendana and Hibiscus avenues. The fare is SI60¢ (25¢) a trip in town, and you should tender as close to the correct change as possible. There is less-frequent service to King George VI School, about halfway to the airport, and approximately four buses a day travel on past Henderson Field to CDC3 village. The buses are not air conditioned and can be crowded.

If you're really adventuresome, trucks bring passengers into Honiara from the outlying villages in the morning and return in the afternoon. Don't count on getting back to Honiara the same night. If you want to take a chance, you'll find the trucks congregating around the market during the day.

HONIARA

The following information is about Honiara. Villages on the other islands are quite small, and you'll have no trouble figuring out the facts of life when you get there.

American Express There is no American Express representative. See "American Express" in "Fast Facts" in Chapter 2 for information about reporting lost or stolen credit cards.

Area Code The international country code is 677.

Baby-sitters The hotels can make arrangements.

IMPRESSIONS

We found no japs, but on the topmost point of Mono we stumbled into a filthy, unpleasant village bearing one of the loveliest names I'd ever heard: Bali-ha'i. From my pocket I drew a scrap of paper, soggy with sweat, and thought: "I'll take a note of that name. It has a musical quality." Years later, Rodgers and Hammerstein were to think the same.

—James A. Michener, 1951

Bookstores The Bookstore, on Mendana Ave. near Solomon Airlines, has a few books.

Business Hours Shops are open Mon–Fri 8am–5pm, Sat 8am–noon. A few shops along Mendana Ave. and in Chinatown are open later on Sat and for limited hours on Sun and holidays. Government offices keep hours Mon–Fri 7:30am–noon and 1–4pm.

Climate See "When to Go—Climate, Holidays & Events" in this chapter.

Clothing Lightweight, casual summer clothing (especially cotton) is worn throughout the year. Men wear shorts during the day; women can, but they should be long and loose (no short shorts or swimwear in the villages or towns, please). While native women in some villages may go around with bare breasts, female visitors should cover theirs. Footwear should be worn outdoors to avoid stepping on centipedes or picking up hookworm, and always when walking on the reef.

Credit Cards The three hotels in Honiara, the Avis and Budget rental-car offices, and the Gizo Hotel accept American Express and MasterCard. Diners Club and VISA cards are not accepted. If you venture to the other islands except Gizo, take enough local currency with you.

Crime See "Safety," below.

Currency See "Information, Entry Requirements & Money," above.

Currency Exchange The Australia and New Zealand (ANZ) Bank, Westpac Bank, and the National Bank of the Solomon Islands all have offices on Mendana Ave. at the Point Cruz turnoff. Hours are Mon–Fri 8:30am–3pm.

Customs See "Information, Entry Requirements & Money," above.

Dentist Ask someone at the U.S. Embassy (see "Embassies/Consulates," below) or the U.S. Peace Corps office (tel. 21612) for a recommendation.

Doctor There are private medical clinics. Ask someone at the U.S. Embassy (see "Embassies/Consulates," below) or the U.S. Peace Corps office (tel. 21612) for a recommendation.

Documents Required See "Information, Entry Requirements & Money," above.

Driving Rules See "Getting Around," above.

Drug Laws The penalties are severe, the prison even more so.

Drugstores The Pharmacy, on Mendana Ave. in the heart of town (tel. 22911), dispenses Maloprim, an antimalarial drug, without a prescription, but you should have started a regimen at least 2 weeks prior to arrival in Honiara. Maloprim should not be taken by children or pregnant women.

Electricity Only Honiara and five other communities have regular electric power. The current is 230 volts, 50 cycles. Outlets take the angled, heavy prongs used in Australia and New Zealand. Honiara's three hotels have 110-volt outlets for shavers only.

Embassies/Consulates A very small U.S. Embassy (tel. 23890) on Mud Alley (between Mendana and Hibiscus avenues behind the Central Bank of Solomon Islands) is open Mon–Fri 8am–noon and 2–4pm. High commissions are maintained in Honiara by Great Britain (tel. 21705), Australia (tel. 23106), New Zealand (tel. 21502), and Papua New Guinea (tel. 21591). A Japanese Embassy (tel. 22466) and a consulate of the Republic of China (Taiwan) (tel. 22590) are also here.

Emergencies The emergency telephone number throughout the country is 999. The direct-access numbers in Honiara are 22999 for police, 22299 for fire, 22200 for ambulance, and 23600 for Central Hospital.

Etiquette Seek permission from the chief or other person in authority before visiting a village or using its beach. Do not insist on staying at a village if you are not invited. Shell and coral collecting is strictly forbidden and is closely monitored. See "Clothing," above.

Eyeglasses Bring a spare pair with you.

Firearms Guns are strictly forbidden.

Gambling Gambling is illegal in this strongly Christian country.

Hairdressers/Barbers Trish's Cosmetic Salon and Hair Dressing Shop (tel. 23461) is in NPF Plaza opposite the tourist authority.

Hitchhiking It's possible, but women should not do so without a male companion.

Holidays See "When to Go—Climate, Holidays & Events," above.

Hospital Central Hospital, which was built by the U.S. forces during World War II, is east of downtown. The care there is far below Western standards.

Information See "Information, Entry Requirements & Money," above.

Insects Mosquitoes—especially those that carry malaria—are the only deadly insect. Carry a good insect repellent with you, and use it from dusk to dawn (see "Health & Insurance" in Chapter 2, and "Drugstores," above). Tiny sand flies can be a nuisance at some beaches around nightfall. If you go "bush walking" or hiking, keep an eye out for centipedes, scorpions, and large black ants, all of which can inflict nasty stings; fortunately, you aren't likely to encounter them in the towns or where vegetation is kept under control.

Language See "Language," above.

Laundry The hotels have same-day service for laundry and dry cleaning. Solclean (tel. 30194) is the only professional laundry facility.

Library Honiara Public Library (tel. 23227) is on Watts Drive near the Mataniko River.

Liquor Laws Beer, wine, and spirits can be purchased at the grocery stores, but not on Sun.

Mail The General Post Office, on Mendana Ave. west of the business district, is open Mon–Fri 8am–noon. Air letters to the U.S. cost SI80¢ (30¢); postcards, SI40¢ (15¢).

Maps Maps of Honiara and Guadalcanal are in the tourist authority's free brochure, "Welcome to Honiara" (see "Information, Entry Requirements & Money," above). The Survey and Mapping Division of the Department of Lands and Surveys (tel. 21511) sells very good topographical maps of the islands. Its sales office is off Mendana Ave. behind the High Court building.

Newspapers/Magazines Two weekly newspapers are published in Honiara: the *Solomon Star* and the *Solomon Toktok*. The international editions of *Time* and *Newsweek* can be found at The Bookstore, located on Mendana Ave.

Passports See "Information, Entry Requirements & Money," above.

Pets Your pets will be quarantined.

Photographic Needs Many shops in downtown Honiara and in Chinatown carry color-print film. One-hour color-print processing (Kodak C-41 process only) is available at Solomon Fast Foto Services in the NPF Plaza shopping arcade, opposite the tourist authority office on Mendana Ave.

Police The Central Police Station (tel. 22999) is on Mendana Ave. a block west of Solomon Kitano Mendana Hotel.

Radio/TV The government-owned Solomon Islands Broadcasting Corporation operates the country's only radio station, which can be received on the AM band. Most programs are in pidgin, although the local news is read in English at 7am and 6:30pm daily and emergency bulletins are given in both pidgin and English. The country has no television station, but videotapes are popular.

Religious Services Some 95% of the population professes to be Christian, although there still are pagan areas where the spirits of ancestors are worshiped. Roman Catholic, the Melanesian church (Anglican), United church (Methodist), South Seas Evangelical, and Seventh-Day Adventists are the main denominations, although there are small numbers of Jehovah's Witnesses and members of the Baha'i Faith. The hotel staffs can provide the times and places of church services.

Rest Rooms Visitors must rely on the hotels and restaurants. The Solomon Kitano Mendana Hotel downtown has public rest rooms in its bar and dining areas.

Safety A publication issued by the Solomon Islands Tourist Authority says it best: "Streets are generally well lit and safe but like any large city there are areas where it is not advisable to be alone at night." By that, the authority means the areas in the immediate vicinity of the hotels are safe, as is the rest of the country outside Honiara, but caution is always advised late at night. Don't leave valuables in rental cars or unattended at the beach. Women should not swim alone on isolated beaches or wander off into rural villages without a male companion. Women visitors won't be knocked over the head and traded for a pig, but there is definitely separation of the sexes in some villages, and local sensibilities can easily be offended. See "Health & Insurance" and "Fast Facts" in Chapter 2 for more warnings.

Shoe Repair Don't laugh: Inmates at the Central Prison make shoes for the police. Ask someone at your hotel if they can intercede with the warden to get your repairs done.

Taxes Hotel accommodations are subject to a 10% room tax, but there are no other sales taxes. The airport departure tax is SI$20 ($8).

Telephone/Telex/Fax You'll find pay phones at the post office and in the lobby of the Solomon Kitano Mendana Hotel. Lift the handset, listen for the dial tone, deposit a 10-cent coin, and dial the local Honiara number. To get the operator, dial 000; for directory assistance, 101; to book an international call, 104.

International calls can be placed from the hotels 24 hours a day or at the Solomon Telekom (SOLTEL) office, next to the General Post Office on Mendana Ave., Mon–Fri 8am–10pm, Sat–Sun and holidays 8am–noon. Rates to North America are SI$22 ($9) for the first 3 minutes, SI$7.25 ($3) per minute thereafter. Pay with cash. SOLTEL also will send faxes and telexes.

You can dial directly into Solomon Islands from most Western nations. The country code is 677.

Time Local time is 11 hours ahead of Greenwich mean time. In other words, if it's 8am on Mon in Honiara, it's 5pm on Sun in New York and 2pm on Sun in Los Angeles (during daylight saving time, it's 4pm in New York and 1pm Los Angeles).

Tipping Tipping is actively discouraged.

Visas See "Information, Entry Requirements & Money," above.

Water All tap water should be boiled before drinking. Bottled water is not available, but rainwater is widely used for cooking and drinking. If in doubt, ask at your hotel for advice.

Weights/Measures The country has officially converted to the metric system, but most residents still are familiar with the British imperial weights and measures (and many continue to use them). For methods of conversion, see the appendix.

5. WHAT TO SEE & DO

The prime attractions of Guadalcanal are the World War II battlefields and the wreckage left from that conflict, both on the island and beneath the waters just offshore. Many "wreck divers"—scuba enthusiasts who enjoy diving to underwater wreckage—find the Solomons irresistible for this reason, and quite a few sunken planes and boats can be seen by those wielding only snorkel, mask, and fins. Jungle growth, scrap-metal dealers, and souvenir hunters have taken their toll on the onshore leftovers, but many relics are still left to be seen.

SIGHTSEEING

A day or two easily can be spent wandering around Honiara, the battlefields, and other nearby points of interest.

IMPRESSIONS

Visiting Guadalcanal is like standing on the shores of Spain and looking toward Trafalgar, like walking the fields of Gettysburg. The entire island is a monument to the courage of free men to throw back the rampaging enemy. Although I knew it well during the war, I was moved to deep spiritual excitement when I saw it again, and I feel certain any American visitor will have the same reaction. For beyond its people, beyond its governmental problems—even beyond the battle records—Guadalcanal must always have a unique place in American history.

—JAMES A. MICHENER, 1951

After moving their administrative headquarters to Honiara from Tulagi in 1945, the British used the flat shelf of land along the shore west of Point Cruz for government buildings and constructed residential areas farther west along the edge of the lagoon and on the ridges overlooking the town. The main shopping and business district is on Mendana and Hibiscus avenues near the turnoff to the wharf on Point Cruz. A few businesses on the side streets still use rusting World War II Quonset huts. Although not a well-protected harbor, Point Cruz itself was turned into a seaport during the war and remains so today.

A WALKING TOUR OF HONIARA

A stoll around Honiara should take about 1 hour. Start at the **tourist authority** office, next to the Solomon Kitano Mendana Hotel on Mendana Avenue. After you've collected maps, brochures, and booklets, walk across Mendana Avenue to the:

✪ **Solomon Islands National Museum.** Exhibits explain the natural environment of the islands, including the ecosystems of the forests and coral reefs, and various aspects of traditional life in the villages. Among the exhibits are actual feather money used to pay for brides, circular tusks still embedded in the jawbone of a pig, intricately carved canoe prows known as *nguzunguzu* (noozoo-noozoo), an *alafolo* (war club) reputedly used to kill a white man, a dugout canoe, and a model "custom" house with carved statues holding up the thatch roof. You'll quickly learn about village life and gain at least a rudimentary understanding of the wood carvings to be seen later in the handcraft shops. The museum is open from 9am to 4:30pm Monday through Friday, from 9am to noon on Saturday, and from 2 to 4:30pm on Sunday. Admission is free, but donations are requested. A handcraft shop has a small selection.

Now walk west along Mendana Avenue. The lawnlike park on your right is the:

War Memorial. A plaque on the monument commemorates the 25th anniversary of the Battle of Guadalcanal on August 7, 1967. A commemorative wreath was laid that day by Sgt. Maj. Sir Jacob Vouza, a Solomon Islander who survived severe torture at the hands of the Japanese while serving as a scout for the U.S. Marines. Keep going west to the gates of:

Government House. Once the residence of the British high commissioner, the mansion is now home to the governor-general, the locally chosen representative of the British Crown in the Solomons. It is not open to the public. Keep going west along Mendana Avenue. On your left is the central police station, the modern Central Bank building, SOLTEL's office in front of its big satellite-dish antenna, and the General Post Office. Across the side street from the post office stands the:

High Court, the round structure with office wings to each side. Although it ordinarily is used by the country's highest court, **Parliament** holds its sessions here. The U.S. government has appropriated $5 million to build Parliament a new home; it will be the American monument to those who died in the battles in the Solomons. The office buildings directly across Mendana Avenue house the **Prime Minister's Office.** Keep going west past the playing fields known as the **Town Ground** until you reach the arch-topped gate of the:

Guadalcanal Club. Once a British bastion, the "G-Club" is now a somewhat ramshackle but multiracial social club with a bar, restaurant, snooker pool tables, and a slimy swimming pool. Visitors are welcome to purchase guest memberships at the manager's office. If you're up to walking another few blocks, keep going west until, just before St. John School, a road runs inland to the:

Botanical Gardens. The lily ponds, herbarium, orchid house, and lush paths through the gardens' rain forest are attractive. Walkways along the stream running through the gardens lead to **Watapamu,** a typical Solomon Islands village of thatch houses.

Now head back to the east along Mendana Avenue to the business district—or as an alternative to retracing your steps, cut through the Town Ground and walk along Hibiscus Avenue.

You can take a break at the Solomon Kitano Mendana Hotel's pleasant harborside bar and lounge and then look for handcrafts in the business district.

Your stroll east along Mendana Avenue will take you to the bustling **Honiara market** 4 blocks east of Point Cruz; there you can see and hear the villagers briskly vending tropical fruits and vegetables. The town's only stoplight lets pedestrians cross Mendana Avenue to the market.

GUIDED TOWN TOURS

As an alternative to walking around town, you can take a 3-hour guided tour by bus that will include not only the downtown area and the museum but Vavaya Ridge, Skyline Drive (a World War II Jeep trail that commands panoramic views of the town and sound), Chinatown, and Betikama Adventist High School and wood-carving workshop several miles east of Honiara. **Tour Solomons** (tel. 21630) charges SI$40 ($16) for one person, SI$30 ($12) per person if two or more go. It's important to book as far in advance as possible.

To see the sights from a helicopter, contact Dick Grouse of **Heli Solomons Ltd.** (tel. 30033).

CHINATOWN

After the war, Honiara's Chinese community settled on the banks of the Mataniko River about a mile east of downtown in the area now known as Chinatown. They built a collection of high-porched shops along dusty streets that make this 3-block district look like a set for a Wild West movie. To get to Chinatown from downtown, go east on Mendana Avenue and turn right on the first road past the river bridge (by the National Stadium).

THE BATTLEFIELDS

The tourist authority may mark the battlefield sights prior the 50th anniversary celebrations in August 1992, but during my previous visits none were. Consequently, finding your own way to places such as Red Beach and Bloody Ridge is difficult. For this reason, a guided tour of the battlefields will be well worth the cost. **Tour Solomons** (tel. 21630) and **Guadalcanal Travel Service** (tel. 22586) charge about SI$70 ($28) if one person goes, SI$50 ($20) per person for two or more.

Most of the fighting occurred east of Honiara, and the tour takes you along what the American soldiers called "Highway 50," now known as Kukum Highway as far as Kukum, then as Prince Philip Highway. First you see **Central Hospital,** built by the American troops after the fighting was over. The rusty freighter stranded on the sand just beyond the hospital was washed up during Cyclone Namu, a hurricane which devastated the country in 1986.

Vura Road runs inland beside the big Seventh-Day Adventist (SDA) church and leads to **Mount Austen,** today a tranquil place where the crowing of roosters and the laughter of playing children drift up from the villages below. If you're driving, bear left at the fork in Vuna Road after the SDA church. The road is narrow but paved all the way to the memorial. Kunai grass covers the summit, so you can't miss the big **Solomon Islands Peace Memorial** atop Mount Austen, its four white monoliths inscribed "Rest in Peace." This simple but impressive structure was erected in 1981 by a Japanese veterans group as a memorial to all the men who died on Guadalcanal.

Mount Austen overlooks Henderson Field and in 1942 gave the Japanese a natural vantage point from which to direct their artillery barrages at the airstrip. The marines weren't able to dislodge them from this strategic perch until nearly 5 months after the Battle of Guadalcanal began. The Japanese held out on neighboring Gifu, Galloping Horse, and Sea Horse ridges for another month until, surrounded and cut off from resupply, they either starved to death or were killed in suicidal *banzai* charges.

Back on Kukum Highway and heading east, you soon pass the golf course on the left. When the war broke out there was a village here named **Kukum,** a small settlement nestled on the shore in a coconut plantation. During the conflict, the Americans built an airstrip at Kukum known as "Fighter One" and offloaded supplies over the adjacent beach. Much of the surrounding area was planted in coconut palms, most of them blown away or intentionally cleared during the fighting. The flat links of **Honiara Golf Club** now lie where the airstrip was. **King George VI School,** across the highway, is Guadalcanal's largest public high school.

The tour proceeds inland on the first road past the "Welcome to Honiara" arch to **Betikama Adventist High School,** whose students produce excellent wood carvings and objects crafted of copper. The prices are high but the quality is also consistently high. The front yard of the **Betikama Museum** is filled with warplanes, aircraft engines, guns, and other paraphernalia of the war.

Back on the main road, the next stop is about 200 yards past the Lungga River bridge, where Col. William J. Fox had his concrete **command bunker** during the Battle of Guadalcanal, thereby giving his name to every "foxhole" dug thereafter. The small, dreary bunker sits on a grassy slope opposite the first of several small concrete houses. The next dirt road to the right leads to an **underground hospital** whose entrance now looks like a cave. Inside, however, is a large room where the wounded were tended. Several Quonset huts, once covered with earth to protect them from enemy shells but now partially collapsed, may be seen in this area.

The bus now will take you past Henderson Field, where the solitary steel-frame skeleton of the original control tower still stands along the highway, and then inland, across the rolling hills of a cattle ranch, to **Bloody Ridge.** This grassy knoll is silent today except for the wind whipping the kunai grass, but it was here in September 1942 that Edson's Raiders turned back the Japanese in two of the bloodiest nights of the battle. A white triangular monument marks the spot where the raiders rallied and repulsed the last Japanese charge.

East of the airport the land becomes increasingly flat. You soon cross the one-lane bridge over **Alligator Creek**—somewhat misnamed, since it's infested with crocodiles—and another over the **Tenaru River,** the original eastern boundary of the marines' defense perimeter and site of several battles and skirmishes. The first dirt road past the Pacific Timbers sawmill east of the river leads through a lumberyard to a suburban-looking housing development and **Red Beach,** a gorgeous stretch of deep sand. In front of the houses, a rusting Japanese gun points toward the sea as if keeping a lonely vigil.

As far as the U.S. Marine Corps is concerned, you have just crossed from west to east across hallowed ground.

CAPE ESPERANCE

The main highway is paved for about 25km (15 miles) west of Honiara, then turns into crushed coral or graded surfaces for another 40km (24 miles) to Lambi Bay. It fords several streams that can flood and close the road during the rainy season. If the weather is settled and you've got a day to spend, a trip through the coconut plantations to the west end of Guadalcanal can be enjoyable. Or you can ride out with **Tour Solomons** (tel. 21630) or **Guadalcanal Travel Service** (tel. 22586). Their west Guadalcanal tours cost about SI$80 ($32) per person. They have the advantage of knowing where "Jezebel," the last Sherman tank left on the island, lies hidden in the bush.

Until you reach **Cape Esperance,** you won't see much of the sea. From there on, the views are great, both of Iron Bottom Sound and of several primitive, leaf-roofed villages along the road.

✪ **Vilu Village War Museum,** with its huge collection of World War II wreckage, makes the trip more than worthwhile. The creation of Fred Kona, a colorful and well-known Solomon Islander, the museum is an open-air affair some 25km (15 miles) west of Honiara. American warplanes—all of them thoroughly shot up but still in remarkably good condition considering the elements and the passage of half a century—sit under the palm trees. Artillery guns, armored vehicles, helmets, small arms, canteens, uniforms, and a ton of other souvenirs are on display. There are several monuments erected by various Japanese and American veterans groups. The village charges SI$3 ($1.20) per-person admission, and if Fred is around he'll personally show you through and entertain you with stories about the war and how he found all this loot. The museum is open from 8:30am to 5:30pm daily.

Tambea Village Resort (tel. 23639) sits on a beach in a little cove at Tambea, 45km (27 miles) west of Honiara, and serves lunch from 11:30am to 1:30pm daily and makes a nice place to stop before you head back to town. Meals range from SI$9 to SI$18 ($3.50 to $7). The beach is safe for swimming.

SPORTS & RECREATION

As the sailors whose ships were sunk in the Slot during the war can tell you, the waters around Solomon Islands have more than their fair share of sharks. Obviously that puts a crimp on snorkeling, but Honiara's two scuba-dive operators both take guests snorkeling not only over bright reefs but over sunken World War II ships and aircraft as well.

Canadians Rick and Jane Belmare run **Island Dive Services** (tel. 22103), out of the Solomon Kitano Mendana Hotel. They and **Dive Solomons** (tel. 23639), at the Guadalcanal Club, take **snorkelers** along on their dive trips for A$20 ($16) per person, including equipment rentals. (The dive operators list their prices in Australian dollars. At the time of writing, 1 Australian dollar—A$—was worth approximately U.S. 80¢, the exchange rate used here.)

Snorkeling only scratches the surface, so to speak, for **scuba diving** attracts enthusiasts to the Solomons from around the world. The hulks of such World War II victims as the *Kinugawa Maru* and the *Ruiniu* off Guadalcanal and the *Tao Maru* near Gizo join the carcasses of fighter planes and bombers to offer some of the best wreck diving to be found. Divers can actually sit in the cockpits of downed fighter planes, their coral-encrusted guns appearing still to be at the ready. Add colorful live corals, plentiful sea life, and crystal-clear waters, and you have a diver's paradise.

Both **Island Dive Services** and **Dive Solomons** welcome novices to try a preliminary "resort course" for A$100 ($80) per person, all equipment included. If you then catch the bug, full certification courses run A$375 ($300) if four persons participate, A$475 ($380) if there are two, and A$600 ($480) for a private course. After that, dive trips cost A$35 ($28) per person plus gear rental. Get the appropriate medical examinations before you leave home.

In Gizo (see "Gizo" in "Easy Excursions," below), Tim Luckel of **Island Dive Services** (tel. 60153) at the Gizo Hotel, and Danny Kennedy of **Adventure Sports** (tel. 60253) offer certification courses for A$350 ($280) and one-tank dives for A$35 ($28).

In addition to its regular operations, Island Dive Services also has the 121-foot-long *Bilikiki* stationed in Honiara and the 65-foot *Kirio* up in the Russell Islands. Rates are US $250 per person a day, which includes everything except your bar bill.

Except for the excellent snorkeling and diving, sporting activities on Guadalcanal are limited.

IMPRESSIONS

Mataniko is considered one of the most spectacular waterfalls in the South Pacific, which has about as many spectacular waterfalls as Europe has cathedrals.

—Jeff Greenwald, 1987

Tennis players can join the Guadalcanal Club (tel. 22212) upon payment of a temporary membership fee of SI$5 ($2) per week and use of the club's courts. Bring your own racket. The **Squash Courts** (tel. 22230), near the Honiara Hotel in Chinatown, obviously has squash courts, which must be reserved in advance. Fees are SI$5 ($2) an hour except to guests of the Honiara Hotel next door, who can play for free from 10:30 to 11:30am daily.

The **Honiara Golf Club** (tel. 30181) has a very flat nine holes at Kukum. Visitors are welcome to visit the club or to call during business hours to reserve a starting time. Greens fees are SI$5 ($2) per nine holes. Bring your own clubs.

Most Solomon Islanders travel from village to village by well-worn pathways, which means that Guadalcanal is laced with good **hiking** trails. In fact, one track runs the entire length of the rugged (and very wet) south coast. **Tour Solomons** (tel. 21630) has several bush walks; the best are to spectacular **Mataniko** and **Tenaru waterfalls.** These cost about SI$40 ($16) per person. Another day tour involving walking is to **Savo Island,** where you can see the islanders harvesting megapode eggs laid in the hot volcanic sands to hatch. Contact Tour Solomons for details. Remember that the Solomons are hot and humid, so don't head off into the bush without the proper clothing, equipment, and water to drink.

SHOPPING

Although Honiara has no duty-free shopping, there are still good buys to be found: handcrafts.

Traditionally, Solomon Islanders made few handcrafts strictly as pieces of art. Fishhooks, shell ornaments and money, woven baskets and mats—all had their utilitarian purposes. Wood carvings, for which the islanders are best known, also had their everyday uses, whether it was a bowl intricately carved to depict a fish or a war club heavily fashioned to crack skulls. The number of distinct styles reflects the great variety of cultures present in the islands. Carvings in the western Solomons were more likely to be of human forms, while the eastern Solomons carvers got their inspiration from birds, reptiles, and fish. The sculptures were deeply embedded in the culture, and the art was passed down on some islands to a few carefully chosen people.

Some islanders still carve items only for their own use, not for the "tourist trade." The most authentic items are more likely to come from the eastern Solomons, where mother-of-pearl inlay and etching are used to highlight the wood underneath. People on Santa Cruz Island make finely woven strips of feathers which they use as money.

The central Solomons, especially Guadalcanal and Malaita, are famous for their sturdily woven baskets, trays, and other items known as bukaware or **buka baskets.**

FROMMER'S FAVORITE SOLOMON ISLANDS EXPERIENCES

The Battlefields I live not far from Gettysburg, but I never get the same chills there that I do touring the plains and steep hills here. Maybe it's because I was born during the Battle of Guadalcanal.

Vilu Village War Museum In the absence of any government effort to preserve the remains of the great battle, Fred Kona took it upon himself to pull the wrecked planes, tanks, and field guns from the bush. I'm always astonished at how much he found—and how well made it all was.

Gizo Along with Neiafu in Tonga and Levuka in Fiji, this little town is a throwback to the old South Pacific. To me, strolling among the tin waterfront warehouses—with Kolombangara's cone looming across the lagoon—is like a journey in a time machine.

They are much more closely woven and stronger than those made in Tonga and other parts of the South Pacific.

The people of Malaita still produce shell money, but since it is in great demand for buying brides, you may not see any of it on the market in Guadalcanal.

Carvers in the western Solomons have adopted styles more marketable to tourists, although their work still is of very good quality. You will see many war clubs and **nguzunguzus** (*noo*zoo *noo*zoos), the mother-of-pearl-inlaid canoe prows once used to bring spiritual success to head-hunting forays. These items have been reduced in size from the original versions (the better to fit in your luggage) but still are handsomely carved.

Remember that you cannot legally bring handcrafts made of sea turtle, whale, or porpoise into the United States and most other Western countries. Bat's teeth are all right; whale's teeth are not.

Before you start spending, have a look through the Solomon Islands National Museum (see "A Walking Tour of Honiara," above) so that you'll have a firm idea of what you're looking at when you find it. The museum has a small handcraft shop. All five of Honiara's other handcraft shops carry essentially the same merchandise, and all but one are on Mendana Avenue, so there's little point in my listing them in detail. Here's where to look:

Start by examining the wares of the carvers who gather outside the entrance to the **Solomon Kitano Mendana Hotel.** You won't believe their lifelike crocodiles and birds. Then go across the street to the NPF Plaza and look in **Melanesian Handicrafts** (tel. 21195) and **Solomon Islands Arts Gallery** (tel. 23981), both in the shopping center. Now walk east on Mendana Avenue a block until you reach **King Solomon Handicrafts** (no phone) in a storefront beyond The Pharmacy. Another block east on Mendana will bring you to the second outlet of **Melanesian Handicrafts** (tel. 22189). Now that you've seen it all, go back and make your purchases.

Lastly, there's the **Betikama Adventist High School** (tel. 30223). You may already have been here on a guided tour of Honiara or the battlefields, but this is definitely worth a stop. East of Honiara about halfway to the airport, the school teaches students the art of wood carving and ornamental copper work. Although the prices are high, the craftsmanship is excellent and the selection usually large. If you're driving, go east of town and turn right on the first dirt road past the "Welcome to Honiara" archway. Proceed about 2km (1.2 miles) to the high school and follow the signs through the campus to the workshop. It's open Sunday through Friday from 8am to noon and 1 to 5pm.

EVENING ENTERTAINMENT

Honiara is one of those towns that rolls up its sidewalks at 5pm. Most residents go home for dinner with the family and perhaps a video movie, since the projector at the Lena Theatre on Mendana Avenue is likely to be broken down as often as not. A heavy night on the town is dinner at a restaurant, a function at the Point Cruz Yacht Club, or snooker pool at the Guadalcanal Club.

Visitors, however, can take advantage of **traditional dance shows** at the Solomon Kitano Mendana and Honiara hotels. The schedule may change according to the number of visitors in town, so call the hotels to make sure of the night and time.

HONIARA HOTEL, Chinatown. Tel. 21737.

Gilbertese dancing at the Honiara is a lively affair, since the dancers' families, friends, and fellow villagers often join in. Their traditional style of dancing has more in common with the graceful hand and foot movements of the Samoans than with the foot-stomping rhythms of their Melanesian neighbors.

Admission: Free. **Prices:** Drinks SI$4 ($1.50).
Times: Wed and Fri 8pm.

SOLOMON KITANO MENDANA HOTEL, Mendana Ave. Tel. 20071.

In case you didn't catch the Gilbert Islanders at the Honiara Hotel on Wednesday, they move on to the Mendana on Sunday. On Friday the Mendana switches to

Melanesian-style traditional dances, which feature war dances and costumes made of fresh leaves.

Admission: Free. **Prices:** Drinks SI$4 ($1.50).

Times: Fri 7:30pm, Sun 8pm.

6. WHERE TO STAY

Despite the limited choices in the Solomon Islands, the quality of accommodations is remarkably good and the prices are quite reasonable. There are no hostels, so low-budget backpackers will have to find church or government rest houses. The Solomons Islands Tourist Authority has lists of these and their rates.

SOLOMON KITANO MENDANA HOTEL, P.O. Box 384, Honiara. Tel. 20071. Fax 23942. Telex 66315. 95 rms. A/C TV TEL **Location:** Mendana Ave. waterfront, 2 blocks west of Point Cruz.

$ Rates: SI$160 ($64) single, SI$180 ($72) double water view; SI$150 ($60) single, SI$170 ($68) double garden view; SI$100 ($40) single, SI$120 ($48) double economy rooms. AE, MC.

Kitano, a Japanese construction company, had bought this former government hotel and was renovating it thoroughly during my recent visit. Guests relax in the comfortable tropical chairs of the hotel's breezy bar and lounge, their conversation enhanced by the view of a shady lawn and beachside swimming pool, as well as of the yachts anchored behind Point Cruz. It's a pleasing and surprisingly picturesque setting for a hotel in the middle of town.

The Mendana's rooms are in modern three-story blocks, two of them built right along the beach so that the balconies or patios of most rooms are mere steps from Iron Bottom Sound. Although they have water views, the less expensive and much smaller economy rooms are upstairs over the bar and can be noisy. A central building between the two wings houses a Japanese restaurant, a coffee shop, the lounge/bar area, a small boutique, a gift shop that carries handcrafts and books, and a tour desk and rental-car agency.

HONIARA HOTEL, P.O. Box 4, Honiara. Tel. 21737. Fax 20376. Telex 66347. 63 rms (43 with bath). TV (16 rms) TEL (43 rms) **Location:** Chinatown, 2km (1.2 miles) from downtown. Go east from Honiara, turn right on first road east of Mataniko River.

$ Rates: SI$55 ($22) single, SI$70 ($28) double economy room without A/C or bath; SI$80–SI$90 ($32–$36) single, SI$95–SI$100 ($38–$40) double room with A/C and bath; SI$135 ($54) single, SI$155 ($62) double suite. AE, MC.

The Honiara Hotel offers three grades of rooms at its location at the base of a steep hill in Chinatown. The original concrete building houses the reception area, dining room, and seven air-conditioned hotel rooms with private baths. A middle-aged concrete-and-glass structure has 20 air-conditioned rooms with private bath downstairs and 20 economy rooms without bath or air conditioning (they do have ceiling fans). The upstairs rooms share large toilet-shower rooms at the end of the building. Up on the hill—a strenuous climb by covered stairs—are 16 new well-equipped suites with gorgeous views over Honiara and Iron Bottom Sound. These new suites have TVs with in-house video programming. The suites are the most spacious accommodation in Honiara; the economy rooms are the town's best budget place to stay.

Next door to the old building, a large thatch roof covers a bar, a lounge area with rattan furniture, and a stage on which groups from one of Guadalcanal's Gilbert Islands settlements perform traditional dances on Wednesday and Friday at 8pm. There is a swimming pool beside the thatch hut. The dining room serves plain meals. Although the furniture throughout the older buildings has a 1950s look to it, the establishment is well run and clean.

HIBISCUS HOTEL, P.O. Box 268, Honiara. Tel. 21205. Fax 21771. Telex 66409. 14 rms (all with bath). A/C (4 rms) **Location:** Hibiscus Ave., behind the National Museum.

$ Rates: SI$65 ($26) single, SI$80 ($32) double without A/C; SI$75 ($30) single, SI$95 ($38) with A/C. AE, MC.

Ken Ferris's Pices Seafood Restaurant (see "Where to Dine," below) is much better than his rooms at this conveniently located, motellike little establishment surrounded by a high chain-link fence. The rooms are simply furnished. Most have ceiling fans, but four have window air-conditioning units. The Hibiscus is popular with Pacific islanders in town on business, so book early. The small bar is a popular after-work gathering spot for locals.

7. WHERE TO DINE

LA PEROUSE RESTAURANT, Mendana Ave. Tel. 23720.

Cuisine: NOUVELLE CUISINE. **Reservations:** Recommended. **Location:** Mendana Ave., west of Point Cruz. Take the first dirt path after passing the Guadalcanal Club and go to the water.

$ Prices: Appetizers SI$11–SI$16 ($4.50–$6.50); main courses SI$22–SI$35 ($9–$14), half price at lunch. AE, MC.

Open: Mon–Sat 9am–midnight (lunch noon–2pm; dinner 6:30–10pm).

You enter La Pérouse by a thatch-covered walkway leading through a tropical garden complete with footbridge across a lily pond and caged parrots. That leads to a magnificent plaited thatch roof supported by sturdy beams of coconut logs. The far side is open to Iron Bottom Sound, whose waves lapping ashore add to a very relaxed atmosphere. The tables and bent-cane chairs are widely separated in keeping with the spaciousness of the building. The food is worthy of Nouméa, being the delicious nouvelle-cuisine offerings of French chef Alain Grimma, such as nicely seasoned veal Cordon Bleu and tender local freshwater prawns served head-and-all and covered in a delightful sauce of garlic and cherry tomatoes. In between meals, you can sit and enjoy the ambience while sipping tea.

PICES SEAFOOD RESTAURANT, in the Hibiscus Hotel, Hibiscus Ave. Tel. 21205.

Cuisine: SEAFOOD. **Reservations:** Recommended for dinner Fri–Sat. **Location:** Hibiscus Ave., behind the National Museum.

$ Prices: Appetizers SI$8–SI$11 ($3–$4.50); main courses SI$22–SI$40 ($9–$16). AE, MC.

Open: Breakfast daily 7–8:30am; lunch daily noon–2pm; dinner daily 6:30–9:30pm.

This dining room sits in a low-slung air-conditioned building with floor-to-ceiling louvered windows along two sides. It is nicely appointed with cane-back chairs around square tables. The menu of about six selections varies from day to day, with whole "mud crab" served under a finger-licking, lip-tingling chili sauce the house specialty. Otherwise, look for such items as reef cod with local *nali* nuts, broiled lobster, chicken roasted in honey, or grilled rib-eye steak.

SEA KING RESTAURANT, Mendana Ave. Tel. 23621.

Cuisine: CHINESE SEAFOOD. **Reservations:** Not accepted. **Location:** Water side of Mendana Ave., center of town.

$ Prices: Main courses SI$18–SI$28 ($7–$11); whole crabs SI$50 ($20). No credit cards.

Open: Lunch Mon–Sat 11:30am–2pm; dinner Mon–Sat 6:30–10pm.

Stay away from everything in this tiny, very plain storefront eatery except the coconut and mud crabs, but try them steamed, either plain or under black-bean sauce. The coconut crabs are those strong-armed devils we ate in Vanuatu; the mud or "sand" crabs grow in local mangrove swamps, like the ones we devoured in Western Samoa. The mangrove version is much like the Maryland blue crab, except the shell is softer.

MANDARIN RESTAURANT, Chinatown. Tel. 22832.

Cuisine: CANTONESE. **Reservations:** Recommended for dinner Fri–Sat. **Location:** Chinatown, on Mataniko River.

$ Prices: Appetizers SI$4–SI$15 ($1.50–$6); main courses SI$16–SI$25 ($6.50–$10). MC.

Open: Dinner Tues–Sun 6:30–9:30pm.

This overlooks the Mataniko River and sites of the bloody fighting that waged back and forth across the winding waterway in 1942. While only jungle and mangrove stood here in those days, the ramshackle buildings of Chinatown now come to the river's edge. The Mandarin's limited menu includes Cantonese-style dishes of vegetables with beef, pork, or chicken. It is not air conditioned, but it's only open for dinner and by then the evening breezes along the river usually keep the temperature in the comfortable range.

HONG KONG PALACE, Hibiscus Ave. Tel. 23338.

Cuisine: CANTONESE. **Reservations:** Recommended for dinner Fri–Sat. **Location:** East end of Hibiscus Ave.

$ Prices: Appetizers SI$2.50–SI$8 ($1–$3); main courses SI$12–SI$40 ($5–$16). No credit cards.

Open: Lunch daily 10:30am–2pm; dinner daily 5–10pm.

This restaurant serving adequate, if not gourmet, Cantonese dishes is operated by a young couple from mainland China. It is popular with local residents. The menu includes fish and beef dishes and local lobster and prawns.

G-CLUB RESTAURANT, in the Guadalcanal Club, Mendana Ave. Tel. 22212.

Cuisine: REGIONAL. **Reservations:** Not required. **Location:** In the Guadalcanal Club, Mendana Ave. west of Point Cruz.

$ Prices (including tax): Full meals SI$13–SI$20 ($5–$8). No credit cards.

Open: Lunch daily 11:45am–1:30pm; dinner daily 6:30–9:30pm.

Formerly the dining room of the venerable "G-Club," this restaurant offers prawns in garlic plus grilled sausages, steaks, lamb, pork chops, and ham steaks with potatoes and vegetables. Nothing fancy here, just plain home-cooking.

FAMILY FAVOURITES, in the NFP Plaza, Mendana Ave. Tel. 23435.

Cuisine: REGIONAL. **Reservations:** Not accepted. **Location:** In the NFP Plaza opposite the tourist authority and Solomon Kitano Mendana Hotel.

$ Prices: Meals SI$7–SI$9 ($3–$3.50). No credit cards.

Open: Mon–Sat 9am–3pm.

For a sample of down-to-earth local food (and prices to match), find this clean place run by Rosie Maelaua. One wall sports a colorful mural of village life painted by local artist Eddie Daiding. In the kitchen, brothers Roxley and Festus whip up a selection of local favorites, beginning with taste-tempting "curry puff" pastries for morning tea and proceeding to beef curry, cheese omelets, and fried fish for lunch. If you want more traditional Melanesian fare, go in early and they will arrange to serve roast pork from an earth oven, local fish steamed in coconut cream, and "slippery cabbage," a spinachlike green.

THE FOUNTAIN CORNER, in the NFP Plaza, Mendana Ave. No phone.

Cuisine: CHINESE/PIZZA/SANDWICHES. **Reservations:** Not accepted. **Location:** In the new wing of NFP Plaza, opposite the tourist authority.

$ Prices: Sandwiches and pizza slices SI60¢–SI$2 (25¢–80¢); meals SI$6.50–SI$8 ($2.50–$3). No credit cards.

Open: Mon–Fri 8:30am–4:30pm, Sat 8:30am–1:30pm.

This plain but clean local establishment is the only place in Honiara to get pizza, albeit by the slice at lunch. Otherwise, it has toasted sandwiches and plate lunches such as chop suey and roast chicken. The banana cake goes well with morning tea.

KINGSLEY'S SNACK BAR, in Kingsley Arcade, Ashley St. Tel. 22936.

Cuisine: SNACK BAR. **Reservations:** Not accepted.
Location: Ashley St., opposite Solomon Airlines between Mendana and Hibiscus Aves.
$ Prices: Sandwiches and burgers SI$1.50–SI$4.50 (60¢–$2); meals SI$5 ($2). No credit cards.
Open: Mon–Fri 6:30am–8pm, Sat–Sun 8:30am–noon.

Honiara's answer to McDonald's, this Chinese-owned snack bar has stools upon which customers can sit and eat their sandwiches, burgers, or daily specials such as curry and rice, chicken and rice, or beef chop suey.

8. EASY EXCURSIONS

Too few visitors to the Solomons get off Guadalcanal for a look at some of the South Pacific's most fascinating and beautiful islands. A trip to Gizo and its collection of veranda-fronted, clapboard Chinese stores and rusty tin warehouses hanging over a lovely little harbor takes you back at least 40 years to a time quickly disappearing in the South Pacific. And if its residents are in the mood, a day-trip to Auki on Malaita provides a glimpse at one of the Solomons' most fascinating "custom villages."

See "Getting Around" earlier in this chapter for information about getting to these destinations.

GIZO

Centered around New Georgia Island, the **Western Province** is a maze of large and small volcanic islands surrounded by huge blue lagoons, like Marovo and Roviana, dotted with a maze of green islets cut apart by narrow waterways. Residents run among them in speedy canoes powered by large outboard motors as if they were driving cars. Diving and fishing are excellent; the scenery is marvelous.

The main centers are at **Seghe,** beside the Marovo Lagoon on the southeast end of New Georgia, where American forces built an airstrip in just 10 days in 1943; at **Munda,** on the central coast, where the Japanese had built an airstrip earlier, camouflaging their activities by suspending the tops of coconut palms over the construction project; and at the charming old town of **Gizo,** the administrative center of the province.

Most visitors eventually land at Gizo, on the centrally located, hilly island of the same name, either by the ferry *Yumi Now* or on the daily Solomon Airlines flight, which lands on skinny, aircraft carrier–like Nusatupa Island just offshore. If you fly over, you will pay SI$6 ($2.50) for the 15-minute boat ride across to one of the few remaining examples of what South Sea towns were like before World War II. Behind you looms the sloping, imposing volcanic cone of Kolombangara; not far away lies Olosana Island—sometimes called Kennedy Island—where the late president was rescued in 1943.

Except for the main street, Gizo's "roads" are best described as a series of washed-out ruts. A stroll along that main street, which curves with the bay, is a sightseeing experience in itself. Villagers gather on the waterfront on Monday, Wednesday, and Friday mornings to sell their produce. Beyond are the clapboard stores that were rebuilt after Gizo was bombed to smithereens during the war; they resemble a setting for a Hollywood Western movie. Have a long look, for they are the remnants of a South Seas era quickly disappearing.

Both **ANZ Bank** and the **National Bank of the Solomon Islands** have offices in Gizo where you can cash traveler's checks (the boat with "NBSI" on its side actually is a floating bank that makes a weekly run through the province's coastal villages). **Solomon Airlines** has an office beside the Gizo Hotel; don't forget to reconfirm your return flight as soon as possible after arrival. The **post office** and **Solomon Telekom** offices are on the waterfront opposite the market (two phones for making long-distance calls are handed over the counter to you, making privacy impossible).

WHAT TO SEE & DO

Diving on the reefs and among World War II wrecks around Gizo is the area's big attraction. As mentioned above, both American Danny Kennedy of **Adventure Sports** (tel. 60127) and Australian Tim Luckel of **Island Dive Services** (tel. 60153) have full scuba-diving operations and take guests on snorkeling trips. They will even leave you on a deserted island and pick you up when they return from diving expeditions. Their rates are in "What to See & Do," in the Honiara sections above. Adventure Sports is on the north end of town; Island Dive Services is based at the Gizo Hotel.

For **other daytime activities,** such as trips to Olosana (Kennedy) Island, gorgeous Saeragi Beach on the other side of Gizo Island, or the Gilbertese village of Titiana, see the staff at the Gizo Hotel (tel. 60199). The hotel also rents bicycles, surfboards, and Windsurfers.

Danny and Kerrie Kennedy of Adventure Sports have a small **handcraft shop** in their headquarters on the north end of town.

Evening entertainment consists entirely of whatever is going at the Gizo Hotel: a "bamboo" band (the guys play bamboo tubes by striking them with shower sandals) some nights, dancing Monday to Saturday from 9 to 10:30pm, to 1:30pm on Friday.

WHERE TO STAY

GIZO HOTEL, P.O. Box 30, Gizo, Western Province. Tel. 60199. Fax 60137. 15 rms (13 with bath). **Location:** On the waterfront, south end of town.

$ Rates: SI$25 ($10) bunk; SI$85–SI$120 ($34–$48) single or double room. AE, MC.

Australian Anthony Ferris, son of Ken Ferris of the Hibiscus Hotel in Honiara, manages a simple little establishment perfectly suited to this backwater location. Woven mats and printed drapes accent the walls and windows of the spacious rooms, six of them upstairs in the main building and nine in two wooden, motel-style facilities in the backyard. Two rooms with shared baths are devoted to dormitories. The others have their own private bathrooms with shower stall (there's even hot water). Guests take their meals under a thatch-roofed dining room to one side; behind sits another similar building housing a bar and lounge. The hotel, in fact, is the only place in Gizo to get a meal or to enjoy any evening entertainment.

PARADISE LODGE, G.P.O., Gizo, Western Province. Tel. 60021. 36 bunks, 12 rms (4 with bath). **Location:** A hilltop behind Gizo town. Guesthouse provides transport, or climb up the road inland beside Solomon Airlines, adjacent to Gizo Hotel.

$ Rates: SI$25 ($10) bunk; SI$55 ($22) single, SI$65 ($26) double room. No credit cards.

Australians Rob and Wendy Scheeres completely renovated one of the largest houses on Gizo and turned it into a guesthouse. Ground level has a dormitory and rooms with shared baths. Upstairs has four rooms with baths and their own doors opening to a whopping veranda with gorgeous views over Ferguson Passage and the nearby islands. There also are a large central lounge and communal kitchen up there.

KOBURUTAVIA LODGE, P.O. Box 50, Gizo, Western Province. Tel. 60257. Fax 60297. 9 bunks, 3 rms (none with bath). **Location:** Hilltop, next to Paradise Lodge (see above).

$ Rates: SI$35 ($14) per person, SI$65 ($26) per person with breakfast and dinner. No credit cards.

Former Parliamentarian Lawry Wickham offers accommodations at his clean, European-style house; guests can rent their own bedroom or share dormitory-style. Some scuba divers on package tours arranged by Adventure Sports stay here, so check with Danny Kennedy or wife Kerrie at their dive shop on the north end of town.

WATERFRONT LODGE, P.O. Box 21, Gizo, Western Province. Tel.

IMPRESSIONS

Now below us is one of the wonders of the Pacific, Marovo Lagoon . . . Once seen, with pillars of cloud reflected in its quiet waters, it can never be forgotten.
—JAMES A. MICHENER, 1951

60253. Fax 60297. 10 bunks in 4 rms (none with bath). **Location:** Waterfront opposite Adventure Sports, north end of town.
$ Rates: SI$35 ($14) per person. No credit cards.
This European-style house on stilts sits right on the water and is used primarily by Adventure Sports' divers. A veranda overlooks the harbor and Gizo's tin warehouses. The rooms all have fans and share two bathrooms.

Q-ISLAND LODGE, P.O. Box 131, Gizo, Western Province. Tel. 60253. Fax 60297. 2 cottages (both with bath and kitchen). **Location:** Q-Island, 1 hour by boat from Gizo.
$ Rates: SI$27 ($11) single; SI$47 ($19) double. No credit cards.
Here's the ultimate answer to the question often put to me—"Where can I get away all by myself on a deserted island?" Ellen Paia owns these two cottages with kitchen and bath on Q-Island. She will arrange to take you and your provisions out there by boat and leave you for as long as you can pay. If you rent both cottages, there will be no one except you to enjoy the palms, the beach, and the lagoon. You will, of course, have to cook your own meals.

WHERE TO DINE

Other than the Gizo Hotel, you've got two choices, both simple but clean establishments on the main street (you can't miss them) and both run by local women.

ZIPALE KAI PLACE, Main St., opposite the National Bank. No phone.
Cuisine: LOCAL. **Reservations:** Not accepted.
$ Prices: Sandwiches and plate lunches SI$1–SI$5 (40¢–$2); dinners SI$7.50–SI$18 ($3–$7). No credit cards.
Open: Breakfast and lunch Sun–Fri 7am–4pm; dinner Sun, Mon, Wed, Sat 7–9:30pm; closed for dinner Tues, Thurs, Fri.
Ellen Paia serves sandwiches and cooked lunches such as beef stew and fish-and-chips. At dinner, you can have local lobster Mornay or a seafood combination. It's all good home-cooking here.

TRESCOLS ISLAND RESTAURANT, Main St., rear of the Stationery Shop. Tel. 60231.
Cuisine: LOCAL. **Reservations:** Not accepted.
$ Prices: Sandwiches and meals SI$1.50–SI$6 (60¢–$2.50). No credit cards.
Open: Mon–Sat 7:30am–9pm.
You can get megapode bird eggs boiled and served with sweet potatoes at Barbara Unusu's restaurant (go through the Stationery Shop on the main street). Otherwise, she serves up local-style meals made with whatever vegetables and seafood she can round up.

MUNDA

Although less enchanting than Gizo, the little village of Munda lies on the edge of Roviana Lagoon and gives easy access to its myriad islands. The monstrous airstrip, only a portion of which is used today by Solomon Airlines' little planes, was deviously constructed under disguise by the Japanese until an American pilot noticed that the coconut-palm fronds hung over it were turning brown. After a bloody battle, U.S. forces captured the strip in 1943 and expanded it to handle large bombers.

Activities at Munda involve walking around the village and getting out on the lovely Roviana Lagoon. Agnes Lodge (see below) has various small boats and motorized canoes to rent and will organize excursions to offshore islands.

WHERE TO STAY

AGNES LODGE, P.O. Box 9, Munda, Western Province. Tel. 61133. 11 rms (7 with bath), 4 suites (all with bath), 3 offshore cottages. TEL (suites only). **Location:** Lagoonside by the airstrip.

$ Rates: SI$50 ($20) single or double room without bath; SI$100 ($40) single or double room with bath; SI$150 ($60) single or double suite; SI$60 ($24) single or double offshore cottage. No credit cards.

Originally built as a government rest house when the British returned after World War II, this waterside establishment has been refurbished and extended. Rooms in the older units are rather basic. A modern addition opened in 1991 has four rather comfortable suites. A large thatch pavilion provides a pleasant, lagoonside bar and restaurant. The two cottages are on Hopei Island, a 10-minute boat ride from Munda. You take your own food and get away from it all.

MALAITA

The second largest but most populous of the Solomons, mountainous Malaita—about 65 miles north of Guadalcanal—is also the most diverse from a cultural standpoint. On the other islands, the population is based mostly in villages along the shores, and Malaita has its coastal dwellers, too. But tribes also live inland on Malaita—strongly independent tribes. In ancient times they were fierce warriors. After World War II they flocked to the cargo-cultist, anti-British Marching Rule movement, and many of them continue to worship the spirits of their ancestors. There are still areas in the interior where even government officials dare not go without a local escort.

The coasts of Malaita, surrounded by magnificent lagoons, are a different story. More than 17 generations ago the lowland peoples built artificial islands out on the reef and moved there to escape the ferocious hill tribes, who had no canoes and knew nothing of seamanship. They continued to farm on Malaita, but they retreated at night or in times of danger to the safety of homes on the artificial islands offshore. This location also had—and still has—the advantage of getting them away from Malaita's hordes of malaria-bearing mosquitoes.

Although they frequently feud over who's going to get the tourist business, **Laulasi** and **Alite** villages in the Langa Langa Lagoon on Malaita's south coast usually allow tour groups to visit their artificial islands; watch the residents make shell money; examine their "spirit" houses, which contain the skulls (and hence the spirits) of their ancestors; and perhaps be entertained by traditional dancing. There are men's spirit houses and women's spirit houses, but the two sexes aren't allowed to trespass on the other's turf.

Neither Laulasi nor Alite welcomes overseas visitors who just show up, but they will receive tour groups arranged by **Tour Solomons** (tel. 21630) in Honiara. These day-trips cost about SI$500 ($200) each for two to four persons, SI$400 ($160) each if more than five go. At least two must make the trip. The price includes round-trip airfare, lunch, and the entrance fees charged by the villagers. Give Tour Solomons plenty of notice, since several days may be needed to make the arrangements.

WHERE TO STAY & DINE

If you decide to stay over on Malaita for a night, the tiny town of **Auki** at the north end of the Langa Langa Lagoon is the administrative and economic center of the island.

AUKI LODGE, P.O. Box 9, Auki, Malaita Province. Tel. 40131. 6 rms (all with bath). **Location:** In Auki township near the wharf.

$ Rates: SI$44 ($17.50) single; SI$66 ($26.50) double. No credit cards.

The only recommendable accommodations are at David Afia's clean and pleasant guesthouse on a small hill overlooking the town and the lagoon. The small rooms have private baths with showers, ceiling fans, and fully screened windows. Auki Lodge is also the only place to eat. Meals are plain home-cooking but include fresh local lobster at dinner.

APPENDIX

METRIC MEASURES

LENGTH

1 millimeter (mm)	=	.04 inches (*or* less than 1⁄16 in.)
1 centimeter (cm)	=	.39 inches (*or* just under ½ in.)
1 meter (m)	=	39 inches (*or* about 1.1 yards)
1 kilometer (km)	=	.62 miles (*or* about ⅔ of a mile)

To convert kilometers to miles, multiply the number of kilometers by 0.62. Also use to convert speeds from kilometers per hour (kmph) to miles per hour (m.p.h.).

To convert miles to kilometers, multiply the number of miles by 1.61. Also use to convert speeds from m.p.h. to kmph.

CAPACITY

1 liter (l)	=	33.92 fluid ounces	=	2.1 pints	=	1.06 quarts
	=	0.26 U.S. gallons				
1 Imperial gallon	=	1.2 U.S. gallons				

To convert liters to U.S. gallons, multiply the number of liters by 0.26.

To convert U.S. gallons to liters, multiply the number of gallons by 3.79.

To convert Imperial gallons to U.S. gallons, multiply the number of Imperial gallons by 1.2.

To convert U.S. gallons to Imperial gallons, multiply the number of U.S. gallons by 0.83.

WEIGHT

1 gram (g)	=	0.035	ounces (*or* about a paperclip's weight)			
1 kilogram (kg)	=	35.2	ounces			
	=	2.2	pounds			
1 metric ton	=	2,205	pounds	=	1.1 short ton	

To convert kilograms to pounds, multiply the number of kilograms by 2.2.

To convert pounds to kilograms, multiply the number of pounds by 0.45.

AREA

1 hectare (ha)	=	2.47 acres		
1 square kilometer (km^2)	=	247 acres	=	.39 square miles

To convert hectares to acres, multiply the number of hectares by 2.47.

To convert acres to hectares, multiply the number of acres by 0.41.

To convert square kilometers to square miles, multiply the number of square kilometers by 0.39.

To convert square miles to square kilometers, multiply the number of square miles by 2.6.

TEMPERATURE

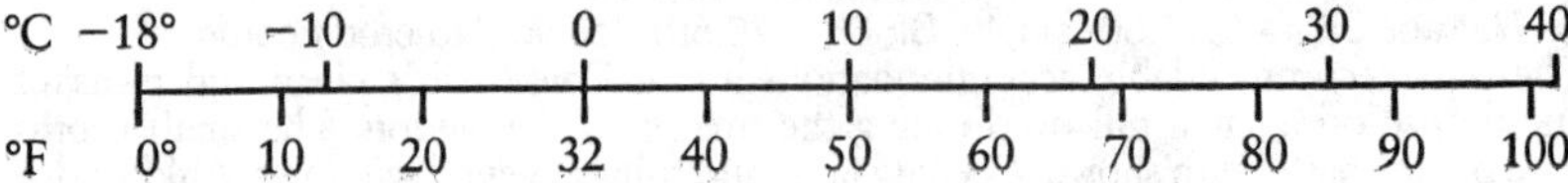

To convert degrees Celsius to degrees Fahrenheit, multiply °C by 9, divide by 5, and add 32 (example: 20°C × 9/5 + 32 = 68°F).

To convert degrees Fahrenheit to degrees Celsius, subtract 32 from °F, multiply by 5, then divide by 9 (example: 85°F − 32 × 5/9 = 29.4°C).

INDEX

GENERAL INFORMATION

DESTINATIONS

KEY TO ABBREVIATIONS: *B* = Budget; *CG* = Campground; *E* = Expensive; *GH* = Guest House; *M* = Moderately priced; *OR* = Offshore Resort; *VE* = Very Expensive; * = an Author's Favorite; $ = Super-Value Choice